AF352535

LOCALISM IN HELLENISTIC GREECE

PHOENIX

Journal of the Classical Association of Canada
Revue de la Société canadienne des études classiques
Supplementary Volume LXI
Tome supplémentaire LXI

EDITED BY SHEILA AGER
AND HANS BECK

# Localism in Hellenistic Greece

UNIVERSITY OF TORONTO PRESS
Toronto  Buffalo  London

ISBN 978-1-4875-4831-5 (cloth)     ISBN 978-1-4875-4837-7 (EPUB)
ISBN 978-1-4875-4838-4 (PDF)

---

**Library and Archives Canada Cataloguing in Publication**

Title: Localism in Hellenistic Greece / edited by Sheila Ager and Hans Beck.
Names: Ager, Sheila L., 1956– editor. | Beck, Hans, 1969– editor.
Series: Phoenix. Supplementary volume ; 61.
Description: Series statement: Phoenix. Supplementary volume ; 61 | Includes
bibliographical references and index.
Identifiers: Canadiana (print) 20230477925 | Canadiana (ebook) 2023047795X |
ISBN 9781487548315 (cloth) | ISBN 9781487548377 (EPUB) | ISBN
9781487548384 (PDF)
Subjects: LCSH: Greece – History, Local. | LCSH: Globalization – Greece – History. |
LCSH: Cultural fusion – Greece – History. | LCSH: Greece – Civilization. | LCSH:
Halicarnassus (Extinct city)
Classification: LCC DF78 .L63 2023 | DDC 938/.08–dc23

---

Cover design: John Beadle
Cover image: Cattle grazing in the Lake Kopais region in Boiotia, near the
ancient sanctuary and spring of Tilphossa. ©Hans Beck

We wish to acknowledge the land on which the University of Toronto Press
operates. This land is the traditional territory of the Wendat, the Anishnaabeg,
the Haudenosaunee, the Métis, and the Mississaugas of the Credit First Nation.

University of Toronto Press acknowledges the financial support of the Government
of Canada, the Canada Council for the Arts, and the Ontario Arts Council, an
agency of the Government of Ontario, for its publishing activities.

# CONTENTS

# PREFACE

Scholarly approaches to the Hellenistic Age – variously labelled the "Age of Experiment," the "Age of Conquest," or the "Age of Revolution" – have always been subject to socio-cultural discourses of the day. Current interest in the gripping narrative of cultural globalization lends the latest fascination to the period. The rapid growth in connectivity, propelling the dynamic fusion of societal interactions across Hellenistic Eurasia, marked a macroscopic movement that, almost naturally, attracts scholars of both ancient history and globalization. Coupled with a new wave of postcolonial studies that urge us to carefully consider the mechanics of transculturality and to rethink the governing ideas that steer conversations about cultural centre and periphery, the local-global entanglement of the Mediterranean world and the Afro-Asian landmass make the Hellenistic Age a poster child of world history.

What unites these new approaches is that they tend to conceive of mainland Greece as a cultural space typically belittled by the pervasive force of fast-expanding horizons. Appraisals of central Greece and the Peloponnese as a local backwater, depopulated and inherently at odds with their grandeur of the previous centuries, are not uncommon. At a first glance, these assessments do not appear to be far-fetched. Indeed, several ancient authorities articulated a similar concern with their contemporary state of affairs, a perception that was formulated in response to the challenges put before communities in the mainland by the dramatic changes in a world that changed so swiftly – and so dramatically – around them.

The emphasis on local decline has come under scrutiny in recent scholarship. The local or epichoric turn – another paradigm that is in close conversation with how the world is read in many places around the globe today – has brought the local horizon (back) to the agenda of scholarship. In gauging vectors of regional and global entanglement, it has become a pivotal concern, lending depth also to key concepts such notions of locality, localism, and boundedness in place. In this vein of study, the inherent quality of the local is not seen any longer in, let along reduced to, the confinement of space and meaning. Rather, the local appears as the warp and woof in the rich social fabric of self-assertion, resilience, and cultural competition. Nor is the local static, reduced to one voice. Local discourse environments, it has been argued, are dynamic and diverse, evoked by and subject to a polyphony of voices by multiple actors and agencies.

This volume delves into some of the local hubs of Hellenistic Greece, that is, the mainland region of central Greece and the Peloponnese, from Thessaly to Cape Tainaron. Exploring, in an exemplary fashion, how *polis* and *ethnos* societies positioned themselves in a swiftly expanding horizon, it examines the meaning-making force of the local. The assembled chapters disclose how local discourses were energized by local agencies (which themselves were the result of long-standing sentiments prevalent in place) and – much like an echo chamber – how these discourses related back to and resonated with the community and the place it occupied, prioritizing the local as the critical resource of social orientation. In some instances, the endeavour to unravel local discourses jaunts into regions beyond, including Asia Minor and Sicily, yet the attentive reader will quickly note that the discussion in the respective chapters all relate back in one way or another to the mainland region under scrutiny in this book.

The essays assembled in this volume were solicited from a larger crop of presentations at a workshop organized by the editors and held under the inspirational aegis of the Waterloo Institute for Hellenistic Studies (WIHS) in April 2018. The meeting was made possible through financial support from WIHS, the German Humboldt Foundation, the Social Sciences and Humanities Research Council of Canada, and the John MacNaughton Chair of Classics at McGill University, which Hans Beck held at the time. At University of Toronto Press, Suzanne Rancourt handled the acquisition and peer review process with due diligence and utmost care. Lukas Duisen and Daniel Hagen in Münster assisted with the formatting of the manuscript. To all we offer our heartfelt thanks.

Sheila Ager and Hans Beck

LOCALISM IN HELLENISTIC GREECE

*The introductory chapter explains how the local and its prioritization in communal conversations serve as a vantage point for this volume. Starting from the discussion of the creative blending of cultural traditions in the famous Salmakis inscription from Halikarnassos, Hans Beck charts how globalization has become a salient paradigm in the study of Hellenistic history. The local perspective works in close conjunction with this, as it looks at processes of negotiation, appropriation, and dissemination of diverse cultural influences in spaces with a distinctly local quality. Against hidden, implicit conceptualizations of local as tiny in size and meaning, the chapter moves on to define this quality. A physical and an imagined trait of local are identified. While the former represents the manageable, accessible realm through which individuals navigate in their everyday lives, the imagined quality extends the local experience to circles of individuals, groups, and, eventually, the community as a whole. In the context of a vibrant open-air culture, so characteristic of the Hellenistic city, such imaginations were particularly persuasive, if not compelling: similar to an echo chamber, ideas of local collectivity and rootedness in place, argues Beck, endorsed local readings of the world writ large; effectively, such auto-reference steered Greek cities, almost naturally so, to the local horizon as a source of meaning and orientation. In the concluding section, the chapter returns to Halikarnassos and explores how its inhabitants, amid complex cultural negotiations of the day, balanced the experience of cultural globalization by accentuating the distinct quality of their local and its place in the world.*

*Keywords: Halikarnassos, globalization, local modelling, cultural competition*

1

# Introduction: Localism in Hellenistic Greece

HANS BECK

The famous verse inscription from Halikarnassos, often referred to as the Salmakis inscription, offers exciting new insight into the history and culture of the Hellenistic world. Salmakis was an eponymous local water nymph. Discovered in 1995 on an ancient interior wall (in situ) of her Fountain House, the epigram documents how the people of Halikarnassos took stock with their community in the later second century BCE, and how they saw their sacred covenant with the gods, their cultural achievement, and, most importantly, their place in a world vastly connected across time and space. Comprising 60 lines of text that are arranged in two columns of equal length, the elegiac poem sets out with two queries: "What is it that brings honour (τὸ τίμιον) to Halikarnassos? I have never been told this" (lines 3–4); and "What words does she [scil. Halikarnassos] utter when she proudly boasts?" (4). Aphrodite's answer is passionate, if not poignant, bursting with confidence and self-esteem, at times effusive. And it is long. The response runs through some fifty verses (5 to 54) that touch on various rubrics of fame and distinction, before the text moves to a summary and final morale in the concluding section (55 to 60).[1]

A quick glance at the main rubrics as they surface from the surviving text (lines 31 to 42 are severely damaged) tells us what the Halikarnassians thought was noteworthy about them. The text sets out to explain why the gods favoured the city. The reason was that "a crop of earthborn men (γηγενέων … ἀνδρ[ῶν])" (5) "placed first under a hollow crest Zeus, newborn, son of Rhea" (7–8), so that he was hidden from the ill-conceived plans of his father Kronos. In return for their contribution to the creation of a new religious order (no marginal feat!), the "sons of earth" (γῆς υἵας: 11) were rewarded good things: in particular, they were given a special place, "the lovely promontory sung of as dear to the immortals by the sweet stream of Salmakis" (15–16). In the pleasant, life-giving surrounding of the well the nymph Salmakis had sex with Hermaphroditos, "our boy" (17), to turn him into a man with exceptional civilizing abilities. From her fountain, the location of which is described in detail (where "the sacred streams drip in the cave": 21–2), Salmakis wielded a civilizing force over all mankind: she "tempers the savage minds of men" (22).

The subsequent section, the largest chapter of the poem (23–40), reports, in sequential order, three foundational moments, or *ktiseis*, in the early history of the city. The first two were performed by Bellerophon, "tamer of the winged Pegasos" (23–4), and Endymion, who "led chosen men from Apis' land," that is, the Peloponnese (30). In the subsequent lines, the damaged text identifies Anthes and/or his descendants, the Antheadai, as third colonizer(s); most likely, Anthes' heroic pedigree tied the people of Halikarnassos to Troizen in the Argolid, across the Aegean. The *ktiseis* sequence is followed by the second largest section of the inscription (41–54), a catalogue of authors and learned men from Halikarnassos. Not surprisingly (and quite luckily, as the readable text commences precisely here), this sets off with Herodotus, "the prose Homer in historical enquiry" (43–4). The record that follows is formidable. In total, it distinguishes twelve epichoric authors, many of which are listed in conjunction with a literary genre. Toward its end, the list segues into a forceful outro, in which "all proofs of her fame" in the past and present amalgamate with "the unending future" (55). On land and at sea, and in conjunction "with the leaders of the Hellenes" (58), the city enjoys "an all-honorable gift in reward for her pious acts" (59), that is: the love of the gods.

The poem attests to a captivating dialectic between local and global horizons, each one implicit and nested in the other. On the one hand, Halikarnassian affairs are entangled with Hellas writ large. In particular, the sequence of foundations taps into the wider web of meaning of universal traditions such as those of Bellerophon and Endymion, youthful lover of Selena/Artemis. In so doing, the related *ktiseis* bear testimony to long-distance kinship relations: in its surviving sections, the privileged regions of Halikarnassian kinship connectivity cut across the Aegean to Athens, the Saronic region (Troizen), and, more generally, the Peloponnese.[2] In combination with its mythical charge, recollection of various points of origins located the city in the wider ethnic and cultural geography of the Hellenistic world. Focusing on this section of the poem, Renaud Gagné (2006) has disclosed the traces of a complex symbolic narrative that situates Halikarnassos not only in space but in the strands of time. The epigram's close aetiological association of each step of the foundation with ritual practices that were designed to commemorate them grounds the portrait of pride in the contemporary life of the *polis*. In this way, Gagné argues, the poem locates the city in the space of cult, inscribing the time of primordial origins in the recurrent present of ritual practice.

On the other hand, discursive prioritization of the local is omnipresent. Calling on Aphrodite as divine interlocutor (instead of Apollo or the Muses) might have appeared unexpected to some, but Aphrodite's rare epithet Schoinitis (line 1), "of the reeds," was certainly surprising. From the opening line, the topographical reference to a prominent botanical feature in the Halikarnassian coast led the audience to the epichoric horizon.[3] Thematically, this focalization of reader attention onto the local continued with the declaration of having provided the birthplace of Zeus (lines 5–14). When baby Zeus was saved from his father by men who were earthborn, the claim for autochthony further magnified the importance of place and the corresponding sense of attachment to it.[4] Salmakis herself provided a critical link to the local. Legendary traditions of Hermaphroditos' initiation into his adult life heralded the significance of the site.[5] The nymph's dwelling is presented as the primordial nucleus of Halikarnassos. From there, the poetic space of the city radiates outward into the plain and across the *chōra*, where "the boundaries of the land of Pedasa" (26) were located, which demarcates the topographical endpoint of the poem. In a nutshell, the epigram married the themes of cult and culture, both couched in a wide geographical network and presented in purposeful local continuity from primordial times to the present day. The Salmakis inscription proclaimed the privileged role of Halikarnassos in the Hellenistic world as its inhabitants saw it.

## Globalizing Hellenistic Culture

It is commonplace to conceive the Hellenistic Age, from the Age of Alexander to Rome's conquest of the Hellenistic monarchies in the eastern Mediterranean and beyond, as a connected, fast-paced world. Energized by an unprecedented movement of people and ideas, and powered by breathtaking advances in material and immaterial culture – including science, medicine, philosophy – the Hellenistic period was an age buzzing with opportunity and change. The cultural development was paralleled by new heights of migration, productivity, and trade. On land, improved infrastructures cast a tightly meshed net of administrative arteries to connect to places previously out of reach; the rise of common monetary currencies across diverse, heterogeneous territories added to the calculability of economic exchanges. At sea, technical innovation in shipbuilding and advanced nautical skills allowed interactions at an ever-faster pace, and over ever-greater distances.

Recent studies in cultural globalization, often inspired by postcolonial theory, have profoundly reshaped the conversation about connected human geographies. In the study of Hellenistic history, globalization has become a salient paradigm. For instance, scholars have demonstrated how shifting horizons of engagement created a new type of cultural hybridity. In the Mediterranean context, the sea figures both as an analytic unit and backdrop to the hybridization of culture. This has given rise to the label Mediterraneanization – an awkward term, to be sure, but the emphasis on process rather than timeless Mediterraneanism is important. Mediterraneanization thinks through the obvious, namely, that locally encoded, bounded cultures are never pristine but energized by a plethora of connections with others near and far. Material evidence casts a spotlight on those connections and their resonance in everyday practice: for instance, securing raw materials, developing crafts, trading objects, and consuming imported goods. Some of this was impacted by long-distance connectivity; however, Peregrine Horden and Nicholas Purcell have argued that the highest density of exchanges occurred and indeed clustered in significantly smaller realms. Variously labelled as micro-regions or regional network zones that were formative to the rhythm of life, the notion of Mediterraneanization signals that those regions were the actual base units of interregional, cross-cultural movements in the Mediterranean Sea. While more traditional models of Mediterranean interactions had placed the state – its urban manifestation in particular – at the heart of their reasoning (the city of Rome, Athens, Antioch, Tyre), the new focus on micro-regions de-emphasizes the formative force of these rubrics. In lieu of hardwired categories such as political organization and boundaries between urban and rural, it zooms in on both the fluidity and continuity of circumstances in realms where those categories are mostly blurred. Effectively, this has also altered the way in which fringe zones and the relations between centre and periphery are conceived of. Micro-regions were connected far and wide, and the linkage left its marks on those who experienced it. Within the region, however, microclimates, artisanal epistemologies, idiosyncrasies in the conduct of religion, and a distinct cultural output, for instance, all added to robust self-perceptions that turned the micro-region into a quantity of prime meaning to its inhabitants – a cosmos of its own.[6]

The creative tension between connected macro-realms and micro-regions that were in themselves entangled reached new heights with the early Hellenistic world, again construed in the broad terms. Recent work on the period has emphasized inclusion of the entire Mediterranean into corresponding exchanges (i.e., not only the eastern and central regions). Beyond this "boundless sea,"[7] intercultural conversations extended into the Afro-Eurasian world region, with, from a Mediterranean perspective, territories as remote as today's Mauretania, Somalia, Uzbekistan, and India; through people and places who acted as intermediaries, intermittent cultural contacts extended as far as China. Cultural theory, its advancement in the understanding of materiality and its interplay with human practice, has disclosed how people in the Hellenistic Age experienced a new type of cultural hybridity that was formative to their assessment of the world. Rather than charting exchanges in a linear, one-dimensional, and top-down fashion (so beautifully captured in the traditional term "Hellenization"), Arjun Appadurai posited to view the related networking and globalization processes not as heavy-headed developments that force themselves onto defenceless, passive micro-worlds.[8] Instead, they should be charted as "localizing processes," developments that occur "from below" (rather than top-down only). This view fully appreciates the role of smaller spatial constellations as feeders of universal networking processes. Appadurai's model warns us not to subscribe to connected master narratives that discount complex combinations of local diversity, difference, and distinction. A similar warning was issued by Tamar Hodos, who advocates for the deconstructions of global generalizations that occlude the "multicoded nature of cultural materials and beliefs."[9]

Material examples range from large to small, from "globalizing luxuries"[10] to more mundane items. For instance, the celebrated terracotta figurines from Tanagra in Boiotia are commonly considered vessels of a Greek lifestyle prevalent throughout the Hellenistic world. Surfacing from excavations in Greece in the early 1870s, at a peak time of Historical Classicism, the elegant and artistically designed statuettes quickly caught the attention of European art markets. During the Exposition universelle de 1878 in Paris their popularity fuelled a sheer Tanagra-mania. Typically 20 to 30 centimetres high, the figurines represented mostly young women and in a few cases youthful males. The female sculptures are usually dressed in sumptuous clothing, sport sophisticated hairstyles, and present striking poses. They are further accentuated with fancy accessories such as sunhats (the characteristic *tholia*), earrings, fans, or floral wreaths. Dresses are tightly wrapped around the body, with fabrics and folds billowing in motion. Before firing, the figurines were coated with a liquid white slip that enhanced the effects of subsequent tinting with watercolours, further highlighting their appearance.[11]

The purpose of the figurines is a matter of significant debate. In light of an overwhelming variety of postures, gestures, and details it might be best to account for multiple contexts in which they were used, from grave goods to talismanic objects to portraits of "ideal" femininity, either in a ritualized or a more casual, everyday setting. The number of surviving pieces is revealing. Ranging in the thousands, their production must have shaped a formidable industry at Tanagra, involving sourcing of workable clays and colorants, coroplastering (the fabrication of the models that were used for the moulds), and the artistic finish of each figure. The manufacturing process underlines the idea of mass production. Like those of the Qin Dynasty Terracotta Army, albeit in miniature, the heads were produced separately, presumably to resemble the looks of their owners (in the Chinese case this is much contested), and then attached to the prefabricated body. Based on the analysis of colour pigments, scholars were able to identify a significant range of workshops in Tanagra, operating on different scales. Their output can be traced through many find spots in the Mediterranean world, including sites as distant from mainland Greece as Etruria and Sicily, Thanaïs in the northeastern corner of the Black Sea, Babylon, and Kuwait.[12]

The material evidence of the figurines and their wide circulation in the Mediterranean and Eurasian worlds suggest an impressive degree of connectivity. Corresponding charts of dispersal and distant find spots support this picture. At the same time, they conflate a variety of data that are best kept apart. For one, the timeline during which the figurines were produced and traded (if indeed they were traded) spans over approximately four centuries, from the later fourth century BCE to the early Imperial period; Mediterranean connectivity experienced profound changes during that time. Second, the circumstances under which the Tanagran ladies arrived in their later archaeological find spots, whether in Tanaïs, Babylon, or Etruria, are obscure. By the later third century BCE, the high demand for figurines led to their production in other places, including Tarentum and Alexandria. With the establishment of secondary workshops of production that satisfied the demands of local markets, the *chaîne opératoire* from Tanagra to, say, Persia, was neither linear nor unbroken. In such a scenario, the artistic biography of the figurines attests to changing preferences in cultural consumption in the Hellenistic world in general; hence, their status as global commodities was the result of a complex mediation between local patterns in cultural consumption and tectonic shifts of global exchange. On sheer practical grounds, reusage and reproductions, due to the wearing of moulds, implied that styles were developed further, with significant local variations and hybrid designs over time. There will have been a back ripple to Tanagra, but the city's main contribution was that it energized these processes, providing local supplies – tangibly and/or through the inspiration of a new style – to markets near and far.[13]

Seleukos Nikator founded a city named Tanagra in the Persian heartland. It is not clear whether this was a new city (its name being a globalizing reference?) or if Tanagra in Persia originated from a settlement of Greeks who had been relocated to the region by the Persian king Dareios (or a combination of both). There is no way of knowing who the inhabitants of Tanagra in Persis were.[14] Further toward the northeast, the city of Ai Khanoum in Baktria was founded in the decades of either side of 300 BCE, most likely during the reign of Seleukos. No Tanagra figurines have been discovered in Ai Khanoum as of yet. However, Greek epigraphic and material evidence – small finds, pottery, as well as the urban layout and public institutions – have fuelled imaginations of Ai Khanoum as a shining outpost of Hellenism in the Far East. Indeed, the presence of substantial Greek remains in what is the most extensively excavated site in Central Asia from the Hellenistic period to date lends Ai Khanoum supreme weight in scholarly conversations about the Seleukid empire. By extension, the spacious settlement provides an ideal test scenario for conceptual debates about the governing ideas behind and dynamic processes commonly associated with denominators such as Hellenistic and Hellenism, and what they stand for as signifiers of culture.[15]

Ai Khanoum was located at the confluence of the Oxus and Kokcha Rivers, a strategic landmark where vital travel routes between Iran, India, and China intersected (the later Silk Road). The site occupied a triangular plain rising some 60 metres above the riverbed. From its urban centre, the agricultural hinterland was permeated with an elaborate system of irrigation canals that were in place in the centuries prior to the Seleukid foundation. The Pamir Mountains upstream the Oxus (modern Amu Darya) were known since the Bronze Age for their rich deposits of lapis lazuli. Hence, although no pre-Hellenistic building structures have been found in the upper city and lower town, the location was recognized, and made use of, long before the arrival of the Macedonians. Excavations by French archaeologists from the 1960s and 1970s uncovered about one-third of the settlement; the Soviet Union's invasion of Afghanistan put an end to further field research. In the upper town, the excavators unearthed the remains of a central administrative complex, a theatre and gymnasium, all built from local sun-dried mud-brick and limestone for the columns, and two temples. In the middle of this convoluted topography, a tomb or mausoleum from the earliest construction period was placed, maybe in commemoration of the city's hero-founder. By the mid-third century, the building was decorated with a Greek inscription on a stone block, written in elegiac couplets, reading:

These wise sayings of men of former times, the words of famous men, are consecrated at holy Pytho. From there Klearchos copied them carefully, to set them up, shining from afar, in the precinct of Kineas. When a child, show yourself well behaved. When a young man, self-controlled. In middle age, just. As an old man, a good counselor. At the end of your life, free from sorrow. (Austin 186)[2]

Reference to Delphi, addressed here as "holy Pytho," the sanctuary's ancient Homeric name, along with Pindaric phrases ("shining from afar"), suggests that Klearchos' copy was both faithful and well-preserved throughout his

5,000 kilometre journey. In conjunction with Ai Khanoum's theatre and gymnasium, these pieces of evidence have been greeted by scholars with considerable enthusiasm as indicative of the spread of Greek culture into Central Asia. The picture is endorsed also by the spectacular discovery of a ceremonial silver plate from the third century, depicting Kybele, the Greek goddess of nature.[16] Further finds from the excavated temple structure, including the marble pieces of a sandalled foot of a Greek cult statue, decorated with a winged thunderbolt, also fuelled the idea that religious practice in Ai Khanoum was largely governed by worship of the Greek pantheon.[17]

All the while, there is reason for caution. To begin with, it was already noted by the excavators that the Greek horizon was complemented with material evidence commonly classified as Mesopotamian, Iranian, Indian, and Baktrian. In their seminal assessment of the site, Amélie Kuhrt and Susan Sherwin-White argued that there is no way of conjecturing, let alone knowing, what the Delphic maxims from Kineas' tomb (and Greek religious practice overall) might have effected among the people of Ai Khanoum, simply because it is unknown who had lived in the city – or who was behind the rapid growth of the site in the second phase of its existence, from the mid-third to the early second century BCE: Greeks, Baktrians, Iranians, and others? The interpretative jump from material culture and religious labels to ethnicity is hazardous; evidence from other Hellenistic contexts makes this painstakingly clear.[18]

Globalization theory informs an advanced reading of conditions on the ground. Rather than seeing the blend of Greek, Mesopotamian, and Iranian material culture as indicative of an ethnic mixture heavily dominated by the Greeks, it is preferable to shift the focus to the dynamic processes of cultural entanglement that brought about this mixture. In other words, while conventional interpretations of Ai Khanoum's Hellenicity built on binary relations between colonizers and colonized, in which the Greeks ultimately prevailed over the local or indigenous populations, globalization models accentuate the negotiation, appropriation, and dissemination of multiple cultural influences among various ethnic groups. Wherever traceable, such disclosure establishes how, and why, some cultural commodities and currents became globalized – with all local alterations – while others did not.

In her analysis of Ai Khanoum, Milinda Hoo has demonstrated how this approach helps to place the local circumstances in context. In light of vast distances and countless ethnic rifts between Central Asia and the Greek homeland, it bears little promise, Hoo argues, to container-box the cultural pieces of Ai Khanoum and connect them in unilinear fashion with their point of origin in Greece (or Mesopotamia, India, and so forth, for that matter).[19] Much like the Tanagra figurines discussed earlier, expressions of Greek culture will have come to Baktria only by means of multiple cultural mediations. Once they arrived in Central Asia, they were again translated into local traditions, those of the Oxus Valley – a micro-region with long-standing cultural connections not only towards Syria and Mesopotamia in the West, but also towards India and China in the East. From a Baktrian perspective, the region was situated at the juncture of tremendous upheaval in Eurasia from the later fourth century BCE, triggered by the fall of the Persian Empire in the West and the rise of a globalized economy and new intellectual as well as religious traditions in South and East Asia. In Gandhāra, across the Hindu-Kush from Ai Khanoum, the rise of Buddhism under the reign of Ashoka has led to a traceable, vibrant amalgamation of Greek and Indian material and immaterial expressions of culture. Nothing in these conversations was pristine, neither ethnicities nor expressions in material culture. It *is* intriguing to see how Greek-style material output and corresponding urban institutions fared in this process, that is, how Hellenicity offered cultural choices that were seemingly attractive and suitable to express power, lend authority, and display social distinction. The globalizing nature of Hellenism is evidenced in its inherent quality to write itself, alongside others, into the cultural DNA of Ai Khanoum – and elsewhere in Eurasia.

It has long been noted that the quantum leap in connectivity and contact, both across Eurasia and in the microcosm of individual cities where diverse cultures met, bore heavily on the notion of Hellenicity itself, that is, how the defining principles and practices considered as foundational to "Greekness" were conceived of, by Greeks and non-Greeks alike. It is difficult to measure or quantify the global back ripple towards Aegean Greece. Also, it is worthwhile to recall that foreign influences, from the Age of the Successors, related back to Hellas not only from the eastern Mediterranean and Eurasian arenas, but from the central and western segments of the sea also; we already noted the universal scale of cultural convergence in the Hellenistic Mediterranean.

The dense web of interaction resonated with a growing sense of what is labelled in the ancient sources as a cosmopolitan attitude. Its earliest traces are associated with Diogenes the Cynic's coining of the term *kosmopolitēs* around the mid-fourth century BCE. When asked where he was from, he is famously reported to have answered, "(I am) a cosmopolitan (κοσμοπολίτης)." The saying is associated with Diogenes in a single instance and with no further context, which makes it difficult to conjecture what precisely Diogenes had in mind.[20] It was recently observed that Diogenes' point, rather than heralding the arrival of a full-fledged concept of a "citizen of the world," was mostly a "dramatic, parrhesiastic act of self-identification."[21] Hence, Diogenes was in all likelihood not proclaiming the revolutionary idea of world citizenship; there was no ideologically charged demand for the freeing from the narrow, exclusionary boundaries of *polis* citizenship behind Diogenes' claim. That said, the creative combination of the inherently siloing concept of "being a citizen" with the universal notion of κόσμος did resonate with a new horizon of cultural entanglement, if only in recognition that the context of the lived experience – in the Aegean, the Asian steppes, and everywhere else – had become visibly and mentally more diverse. Manuel Castells has identified this type of a connected mentality as a key marker in the study of network societies, that is, their adherence to a grammar of loosely structured, horizontal connections that complement or, in the most advanced stage, marginalize more conventional categories such as "top and bottom" or "centre and periphery." In a network society, Castells argues, the new benchmark is one of belonging to the network as such. Effectively, the development of a connected mindset is determined not only by a new degree of linkages and information flow, but also by the tacit consent of participants to adhere to the recalibration of time and space as dictated by the network.[22] Diogenes' neologism seems to reverberate the creative tension from ever-growing and intensifying network exchanges in his times, when prevailing attitudes and dispositions of culture were always probed, challenged, and, effectively, renegotiated, in ways and means that were in themselves malleable over time. In other words, while the place of the *polis* remained principally the same, inspiring long-standing patterns of meaning, this long duration of sentiments was exposed to swiftly shifting parameters. Hellenism, as a globalizing force, might have brought with it challenges to practical issues such as urban change, demographic development, or the rule of citizenship. But most eminently, it put the task of positioning oneself in a world of accelerated cultural change before the communities of Aegean Greece.

## Negotiating Hellenistic Localism

Hellenistic Greece, that is, geographically speaking, the Greek mainland and Peloponnese along with the Aegean island-world at its doorstep, has been considered for the longest time a world in crisis and demise. Drains in people and resources, it was argued, led to a state of desertedness, both of demographies and economies, and to the deprivation of the adventurous Hellenic spirit that had powered both. On the one hand, this view resonated with inflated admiration for the Classical Age now irrecoverably lost. W.W. Tarn's infamous phrase of the death of the political animal with Aristotle fully captures this idea.[23] Indeed, it has been argued "that the conquest of Asia and the creation of the Hellenistic kingdoms only accelerated the decline of Greece. Its fate no longer depended on the deliberations of the assemblies at Athens,

Sparta, or Thebes; the real decisions were now taken at the courts of Pella, of Antioch, or of Alexandria. Many of the ablest men left their country to take up rewarding positions in Asia or Egypt. The poor left, too, in order to find a living as mercenaries or a piece of land as colonists. The proud cities of Greece became beggars who asked for material help from the kings, for corn, for schoolmasters, or for the building of porticoes."[24] On the other hand, this verdict seems to have had several ancient authorities in its support, some of them considered crown witnesses to their times, who had diagnosed a state of omnipresent disarray. For instance, commenting on affairs in Boiotia, home to the celebrated Tanagra figurines, Polybios (20.4.1–4, trans. W.R. Paton) remarked that

the Boiotians had long been in a very depressed state, which offered a strong contrast to the former prosperity and reputation of their country. They had acquired great glory as well as great material prosperity at the time of the Battle of Leuktra (371 BCE); but by some means or another from that time forward they steadily diminished both the one and the other under the leadership of Abaiokritos (died 245); and subsequently not only diminished them, but underwent a complete change of character, and did all that was possible to wipe out their previous reputation.

Along with the wipe-out, says Polybios (20.6.1–4, trans. W.R. Paton), came political impotence:

Public affairs in Boiotia had fallen into such a state of disorder that for nearly twenty-five years justice, both civil and criminal, had ceased to be administered there, the magistrates by issuing orders, some of them for the dispatch of garrisons and others for general campaigns, always contriving to abolish legal proceedings. Certain strategies even provided pay out of the public funds for the indigent, the populace thus learning to court and invest with power those men who would help them to escape the legal consequences of their crimes and debts and even in addition to get something out of the public funds as a favor from the magistrates.

Polybios' depiction, echoed in a multitude of scholarly voices, has shown to be both formative and extremely long-lasting; in fact, attempts to reconcile some of the more obvious problems of the Polybian assessment, such as the pretentious chronology and its mismatch with the archaeological evidence, have led to an implicit endorsement of Polybios' views rather than a critical engagement with the tenor of wipe-out and demise. Only recently a more profound analysis of the cited passages has concluded that they resonate with traditional tropes and prejudices against Boiotia – a popular theme among the Hellenes since the early Classical period. Polybios' account is clearly a literary construct rather than accurate historical reflection.[25] Alex McAuley has provided further analytical depth by placing Polybios' Boiotia in the broader context of Central Greek affairs, including in Euboia and the Argolid, in the early and middle Hellenistic periods. In his study of a broad array of different rubrics of evidence, McAuley detects no signs of stagnation or sad decline but rather notes vibrant vectors of regional and local continuity.[26] The main focal point of communal action, argues McAuley, continued to be determined by a "horizon of the immediate," that is, the local environment of the city-state that was as lively as it was, at times, conflictual, and that provided the meaningful frame for all types of communal activity (political, religious, cultural, economic). In a magnified, widely connected Hellenistic world, the local outlook of the city-state had forfeited nothing of its innate value as high-powered social currency.[27]

Directness and immediacy of the communal horizon remind us of the dialectic between panhellenic or global exchanges and their grounding in local place; this dialectic, so characteristic of Greek culture, had lost nothing of its vibrant tension in the Hellenistic Age. Here, too, globalization research has helped us to rethink the interrelation between both spheres. To chart the interplay, the terms "glocal" and "glocalization" have entered the debate, which signal intricate interdependence. According to the conventional cycle of cross-fertilization between the local and the global, globalization triggers delocalization, an increasing sense of disconnect from the local. This fuels a new need of locality; beyond its casual meaning of having a location, the term denotes the long-standing patterns that emerge from the association with the local, including all expressions of local culture, knowledge production, and communal conviction, each one in relation to the local horizon that inspires them. In its most immediate variant, this need of locality inspires the sentiment of localism, that is, a mindset that prioritizes the sum of these local expressions and experiences over alternative sources of meaning from outside the community. Localism, in turn, challenges the basic tenets of globalization. "Glocal" indicates that the rotations in this cycle happen all at once and in both directions, signalling the hybridization of the ways in which existing socio-cultural practices are creatively recombined with new forms, processes, and routines.[28]

Globalization scholarship recognizes the importance of the local as a world where the strands of connectedness translate into real-life constellations, with multiple adaptations across the global-local binary. Yet, while the former part of the glocal contraction has received tremendous attention in research, conceptual debates have mostly bypassed the local.[29] The word has hidden connotations of tininess. Local insinuates confinement in place and relevance; effectively, it suggests an implicit relation to something of greater exposure. This is even clearer with the noun, when the plural "locals" is used in a patronizing sense, referring to people with a limited understanding of prevailing complexities in the world. Semantic pettiness has also been detected in the genre of local historiography, a field that developed with so much vigour in the Hellenistic world. The verdict that the writings of countless local historians resemble "images of tiny, parochial studies which might be of interest perhaps only to the equivalent of a minor local history society" fully captures this assessment.[30]

It is worthwhile at this point to turn to some of the key concepts in current conversations about localism and the local. Rather than adhering to casual semantics, an advanced understanding of local space and its prioritization in human agency requires us to surpass the inherent connotation of containment. Local, as has been pointed out, is defined by its twofold quality as a physical and an imagined realm. As a physical, geographical concept, the local is the manageable, accessible realm through which individuals navigate in their everyday lives. Such an embodied experience implies multiple groups of human agents. It expresses itself in a kaleidoscope of functional localities in which group relations are realized, for instance, as neighbourhoods, places of artisanal or agricultural productivity; hence, the distinction between the urban centre and the countryside. Religious and profane places, again associated with demarcated locations in the local's territory, were also subject to divergent strategies of communal maintenance. The local of the farmer in the countryside was not the same as that of the perfumer in the agora, or of the *kapēleion*-keeper who sold wine to the residents of their neighbourhood. What united these sublocal localities was that they fell in the same radius of quotidian interaction.[31]

Scholarly attempts to scale the local horizon differ widely, depending on the area, time, and culture under investigation, or all three. Our own experience today betrays how deceptive the local can be. For instance, in the so-called locavore movement, spawned as a result of issues of food sustainability and eco-consciousness, participants typically restrict themselves to the consumption of food that is grown within a radius of 100 miles, or 160 kilometres, a number that is neat and arbitrary at the same time.[32] Greek cities had their own scales. Survey archaeology has disclosed a tremendous florescence of activity in the countryside of many city-states from the Classical period; as we have seen, there is no reason to suggest a sudden withering of this development in the Hellenistic Age. In what can be considered an exemplary investigation in the Hellenistic countryside, Sylvian Fachard has disclosed the intricate interaction between military fortifications in the *chōra* of Eretria on Euboia and the organization of the city's agricultural productivity. While the territory of the Hellenistic city did not inevitably grow

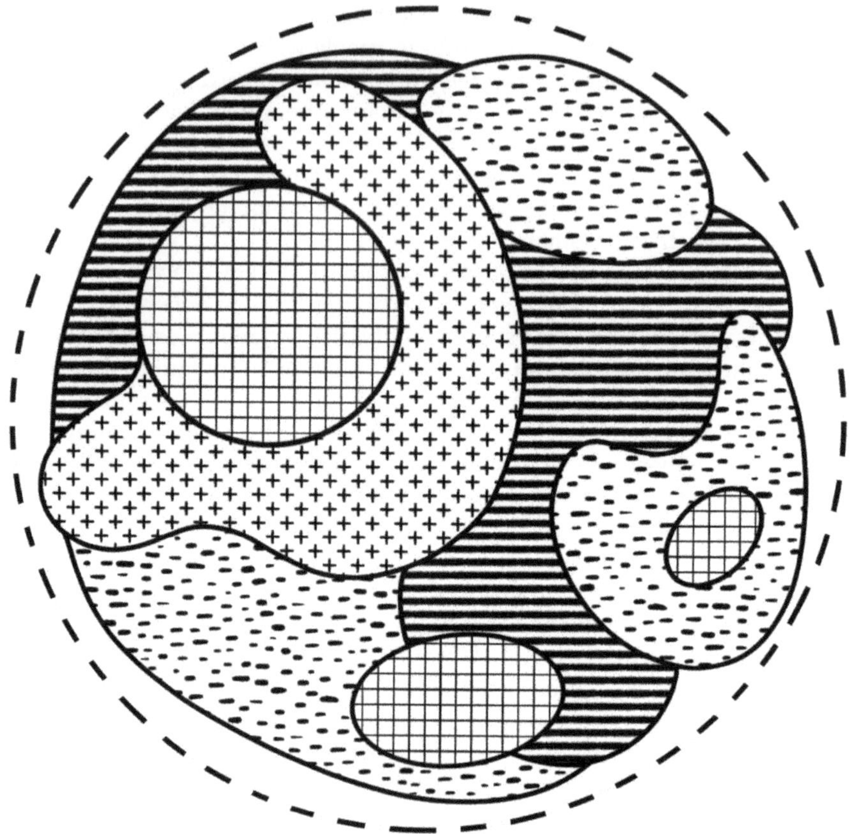

Figure 1.1. Outline of local accumulation, real and imagined. The physical local comprises irregularity, diversity, and convolution, as indicated by coded areas. The dashed circle depicts the imagined local as a unifying force.

larger, resource exploitations in the hinterland did.[33] Moreover, archaeologists detected a diverse mixing and blending between and within functional localities. Rather than assuming neat segregation, for instance between living quarters and production spaces, or between city and hinterland, we are advised to view the local world of the *polis* as a tapestry of localities that were both malleable and permeable, stitched together into a convoluted space syntax.

With the large majority of inhabitants being peasant farmers (Hans-J. Gehrke has suggested a number as high as 80 per cent),[34] the local radius was subject to the daily commute of farmers to their fields in the country-side, usually a short ride or walk from their homes in the city. John Bintliff has calculated a distance of not more than 5 to 6 kilometres, or less than a two-hour walk. If farmers lived in villages or hamlets, they would find the distance between their homes and the marketplace in the city equally manageable.[35] The question is of course complicated by huge discrepancies in the natural environment. Mobility schemes are distorted by differences between travel on flat land, steep climbs, or the crossing of rivers and runlets. Recent GPS research on the countrysides of Hermione and Methana in the southern Argolid has gauged the temporal and physical realities in both cities. The emerging picture of least-cost paths and path distances suggests that, while daily commutes of up to three hours (one-way) were generally possible, the highest density by far of farmsteads in the *chōra* fell within a 90-minute radius or ca. 5 kilometres respectively.[36]

The Bintliff Diameter translates into a *chōra* size of ca. 80 to 110 square kilometres, to which we would add the area of the city itself, another 5 to 20 square kilometres, depending on the urban environment. The resulting grand total has been found to be typical for many city-states in the Classical and Hellenistic periods.[37] What can be drawn from these numbers is that the landscape of the average Greek city was "experienceable" – that is to say, the knowledge of people about their local environment was acquirable through first-hand encounters with place, and it was communicated directly and between individuals who were, in principle, equally familiar with and knowledgeable about the quotidian horizon. This triangle of place, knowledgeability, and communication marks not only a landmark trait of the local, but also a decisive distinction between local and non-local realms.

At this point our definition of local segues into the second arena of spatial semantics, that is, the local's quality as a metaphorical or imagined place. This quality extends the local experience to an imaginary circle of individuals and, eventually, an imagined community, a notion explored in the works of Benedict Anderson. It has long been argued that the metaphorical manifestation of space is in dialogue with the physical world but also separate from it. As we have seen, physical space segregates in that it shapes multiple localities that exist in proximity to and within each other: we noted the existence of multiple functional localities in one and the same local. Social space, on the other hand, in the words of Henri Lefebvre, suggests "actual and potential assembly at a single point, or around that point. It implies, there, the possibility of accumulation."[38]

The possibility of accumulation is contextual. First, it is informed by real-life constellations, for instance, infrastructure and technology. The natural environment, too, galvanizes the idea of accumulation in that it provides a canvas for the projection of social space (e.g., a valley, plateau, island). This does not imply that the environment – its topography and geography – wields a deterministic force over society. If anything, the causal relation went in the opposite direction. As David Harvey has demonstrated, the social quality of space is not determined by geography, but is defined through human practice, that is, through an ongoing, complex, and often non-linear negotiation in the course of which space is made subject to, and appropriated by, the governing ideas of society. Identities of place, no matter how deep the conversation with place, are always the result of the human imagination.[39]

In the open-air culture of the Greek city, public discourses were, in principle, visible and audible to all. The general openness of communications in, for instance, the theatre, street, agora, and in spaces that were reserved for the conduct of religion and politics, facilitated lively and often heated conversations. With no clear-cut opposition between public, political, and profane communications, public conversations were always of a variegated nature; hence, the quest for one single discourse and one coherent public opinion misses the point. The local discourse environment of the *polis* was thus shaped by a polyphony of voices and a plurality of realms where conversations between shifting groups of speakers and audiences took place. Despite complex and nuanced differentiations within, the unifying element of the discourse was that voice and place were bracketed by the horizon of directness; the local delineated a communicative boundary. Conversations *in* the *polis* were often identical with conversations *about* the *polis*; the intricate role of citizens who were the makers, adjudicators, and keepers of history created a rather peculiar circle of self-reinforcement. This is again not to suggest that there was ever only one theme up for debate, let alone one public opinion. Rather, whatever conversation there was drew on long-term sentiments, conditions, and beliefs as they prevailed in place: for instance, images of primordial descent and ownership of the land, the social reality of economic practice, cultural distinction, communal expertise, the legacy of ancestral calamity, and so on. These sentiments predetermined the course of the conversation. And, as the debate unfolded, they rendered validity to communal assessments. This quality made the local discourse environment similar to an echo chamber: energizing the imagination of local collectivity, distinction, and resilience to broader currents, it endorsed local readings of the world writ large.[40]

Our inquiry into the local and locality reveals a lively dynamic of mutual cross-fertilization: drawing on the idea of potential accumulation in the local world of the city, this imagination was expressed in and made possible by a discourse environment that suggested precisely this, the assemblage of all-in-one place. This metaphor of local thus implied more than a firm footing from which to struggle forward. In the rapidly changing world, it made the imagined local an anchor that stabilized quotidian interpersonal relations; it became a resource that powered communal strategies of distinction and competition, and a venue where the past intersected in a meaningful way with the present, binding everyone together by their familiarity with their local world.

## Returns to Halikarnassos: Making Local Sense<br>in the Vastness of the World

In their edited volume *Belonging and Isolation in the Hellenistic World*, Sheila Ager and Riemer Faber observe that not all local communities, and within communities not all people, would have responded in the same fashion to the challenges and opportunities the shifting horizons of the Hellenistic Age bestowed upon them. Rather than charting networks of fast-paced exchange, they address the critical question of how Hellenistic globalization was perceived at the local level. For many communities, the editors posit, "the broadening horizons of the Hellenistic period would have brought with them a crisis of identity, a sense of being adrift in a world that had undergone a radical structural change" (2013: 3). Southwestern Asia Minor was one of the hotspots where identity crises such as the ones diagnosed by Ager and Faber played out. Karia and its surrounding island-world were a particularly muddled micro-region in the political and cultural mosaic of the eastern Aegean. From Philip V's campaigns in the region (202–200) and for much of the second century, the area was a notorious bone of contention between the Seleukids and Ptolemies, the Attalids, and the Antigonids, in varying constellations and with swiftly changing fortunes. Ptolemaic and Seleukid influences were curbed by Rome and Halikarnassos after it was "freed" in 192 (Liv. 37.10.16). The demise of Rhodes after 167/166 BCE, when the Romans rerouted the main traffic arteries from the eastern Mediterranean into the Aegean to Delos, reminded everyone that resistance to Rome was risky, if not futile. In 129, the establishment of the Roman province Asia led to temporary de-escalation, but the rise of Mithridates' VI kingdom of Pontus soon complicated things on the ground further. In addition to these macro-conflicts, local imperialism continued in a seamless fashion from the Classical to the Hellenistic period. From the Karian perspective, the heyday of Hekatomnid imperial ambitions in the fourth century was long gone, but Halikarnassos held on to a domain with various dependencies in the Myndian peninsula and beyond its natural borders.[41] Land rivalries were not uncommon. For instance, for about a decade after 188, the Karian settlement of Pidasa on the slopes of Mount Grion was forced into a *sympoliteia* with the Milesians, who also sent a garrison to the city, which casts a spotlight on ongoing tensions in the region.[42]

We do not know where the Salmakis inscription fits in the crowded timeline. The most likely window, the later second century, makes it clear that it was issued under the experience of volatile, at times erratic, interstate affairs. With the arrival of Rome, the general unpredictability of power relations was further complicated by deep cultural rifts in the conduct of foreign policy; put before the Roman senate, attempts to win the favours of a remote power in the pursuit of regional goals were subject to a body both alien and inscrutable to many Greek cities. Transformation and change are otherwise visible also. Epigraphy captures the onomastic imprint of migrants from Syria on the populations in the Southwestern Aegean. On Kos and Rhodes, where the body of evidence is especially rich, the influx of foreigners is also attested in the administration of local cults. On the small island of Syme, south of the Knidian peninsula, the members of the mixed ritual community labelled themselves "the *koinon* of the residents in Syme." Presumably, the cultural demography on the ground was disparate, hence the careful avoidance of the language of political entitlement in the document.[43] We should be surprised if the situation in Halikarnassos was unimpacted by migratory diversification. A notorious melting pot of Aegean and Anatolian influences (and Persian, prior to Alexander), the lived experience in second-century Halikarnassos was shaped by a cultural demography that was both diverse and heterogeneous.[44]

It is striking to see that the inscription reflects none of these shifts, neither their imperial context nor the more nuanced cultural changes from movement and migration. Curiously enough, the term "Karia" is not used at all in the surviving portions of the elegy.[45] The regional history of the Myndian peninsula is supplanted by peculiar spatial semantics. We saw already that the local topography of the poem moves from Salmakis' fountain, presented as the primordial nucleus of Halikarnassos, to the borderlands of Pedasa (lines 23–6), with no reference to the urban settlement in between. While the verses thus suggest a coherent settlement, the actual situation was more complicated. The nymph's dwelling was located in a prominent spot to the south of the Hellenistic city, on the west bank of the entry to the fortified harbour (Vitr. *De arch.* 2.8.11; Ps.-Scyl. 99). In the fifth century, the area was apparently a district of Halikarnassos with its own political administration; maybe the formerly independent community had been absorbed by its larger neighbour by means of a *sympoliteia*.[46] Note that no association of the Salmakians with the water nymph is attested at the time. With no link between settlement and Salmakis traceable prior to the inscription, it is impossible to tell how prominent the connection between the two might have been in the Classical and early Hellenistic periods, if there was an early connection at all. It has been posited that the toponym Σαλμακίς and the city-ethnic Σαλμακίτης derived from a local language in Asia Minor.[47] If correct, we might conjecture that the myth of Salmakis was indicative of the attempt to fill local sounds with Greek sense, an aetiology that evolved along the fourth-century synoikism or even later. The situation was probably not dissimilar from that in Pedasa at the opposite end of town, ca. 3.5 kilometres to the northeast of Halikarnassos. Prior to its unification under the leadership of Maussollos (reign 377 to 353 BCE), when many inhabitants were relocated to Halikarnassos, Pedasa was an independent city, famous for its sanctuary of Pedasian Athena. Unlike Salmakis, the site of Athena at Pedasa was recognized by Herodotus, although he provides no further information about Pedasa's relations with his home town.[48] For both locations, Salmakis and Pedasa, the ways in which they were integrated into the urban, cultic, and political fabric of Halikarnassos were glossed over in silence. Ignoring the details, the inscription endorses a compressed spatial ontology. It crafted a poetic space in which all Halikarnassians assembled in a unified and coherent place, surrounded and in turn sanctioned by divine borders established by Pallas Athena (lines 23 and 25–6).

Conversations with the universal were equally implicit. Kathryn Stevens (2016: 79) has posited that the document is subject to the language of euergetism, that is, the mutual assurance of loyalty and benefaction so often employed in correspondences between Hellenistic cities and their rulers. Indeed, the reciprocity of reliability and reward runs through the document. In the final line (60), it culminates in the verdict that, thanks to their "goodly deeds," the Halikarnassians laid claim "to the most honoured crowns." So fine actions were answered with corresponding thanks. Panhellenic religious motifs are omnipresent in similar fashion. The pantheon is Greek throughout, and so is the religious frame of reference into which the Halikarnassians placed themselves. In line 35, an unidentifiable "son of Phoibos" is assigned a critical role in the foundation of the city;[49] we already noted above how Delphi's religious authority radiated as far as Ai Khanoum. In recognition of the wider world, the Salmakis inscription chooses to pass in silence over domains of imperial power and the dynamics of socio-cultural change. Instead, it evokes the existence of a larger cultural commonwealth before which the city's cultic and cultural achievements are showcased, a universal *koinē* that is both timeless and foundational to the present day.

The ways in which the Halikarnassians capture their place in the world, however, their global self-positioning, as it were, followed a thoroughly local logic. The epichoric horizon is both the perspective and the scope of the inscription; the local's signature is so strong that the universal script of

Panhellenism is deliberately appropriated by and made subject to the local sphere. Two aspects stand out.

First, religion and cult. Declaring their city the birthplace of Zeus (above) documents how the audience, from the opening lines of the inscription, was drawn to the local horizon. In more widespread versions of the myth, the events surrounding Zeus' birth were couched in the wilderness of Mount Ida on Crete.[50] Pausanias, all the while, frowned over the fact "that it is impossible even for a man who puts his heart in it to enumerate all who claim that Zeus was born and reared there" (4.33.1). It seems, therefore, that the Halikarnassian version was not unique, although the bid was hitherto unknown.[51] We already observed in passing that claims to Zeus were magnified by the assertion that the toddler was protected by a band of "earthborn men" (line 5) and "sons of earth" (line 11) respectively. Note how γηγενέων is the first word in Aphrodite's response to the initial question about the fame of Halikarnassos. Reference to earthbornness and, correspondingly, Gaia, whose "innermost recesses" (Γαίης ἀμφ' ἀδύτοισιν) are mentioned in line 9, is key.[52] Already Jane Harrison (1927: 396–415) has pointed out that worship of Gaia, Mother Earth, was typically associated with ideas of centrality and boundedness in place. In some cases, for instance in Argos, Eleusis, Phlious, or on Delos, the notion of a central terrestrial location correlated with interpretations of the cosmological order and the alignment of the stars, which was believed to mirror, and effectively endorse, the image of centrality.[53] It is striking to see how other groups of people, beyond the "sons of earth," are portrayed as bringing settlers to Halikarnassos. In the lengthy section on three subsequent *ktiseis* (lines 23–40), the various groups are led to the city as if a chosen place: their arrival is depicted by means of a "centripetal movement toward the city" (Stevens 2016: 78) that assigns a sublime quality to the local. Complementing their claim for earthbornness with the influx of people who were headed for a location favoured by the divine, the Halikarnassians fostered a peculiar spatial mentality, one that presented their city as the centre in a wide, far-flung geography.[54]

Earthborn caretakers of Zeus and the descendants of sanctioned acts of migration, the Halikarnassians were deeply entangled with the religious order of Hellenistic Greece. But the vectors of primordial time and space became visible only through the kaleidoscope of local place. The local fully captured the creative merging of these developments, the generation of social meaning, and its recurrent reassertion in ritual practice. Salmakis was the key agent. Nymphs qua nymphs were bound to place; typically, they occupy a discrete environment that is easily identifiable and discernable from other sites, because of prominent topographical features.[55] We already took note of how the text elaborates on the details of Salmakis' spring, which is assigned ontological qualities: it is a "beautiful dwelling" (17) by a "sweet stream" (16). From the "lovely promontory" (15) Halikarnassos extends into the plain and across the *chōra*. The fertile expanses provided the notion of attachment with a real portfolio, a rich source of income and wealth that supplemented and secured the cultural legacy. Furthermore, the land inspired and corresponded with ideas of belonging; the physical sense of place was supported by imaginations of the divine. For instance, in their rites of procession through the countryside, to the Fountain House and/or other sites, the Halikarnassians will have paid due homage to topographical features in the countryside and associated spirits. There is no explicit testimony for this, but picturesque evidence from across the bay to the north for similar procession rituals from Miletus to Didyma suggests that the Halikarnassians, too, would have venerated places in their hinterland that spoke to the traditions of their origins.[56] We might also conjecture that hymnic evocation in prayer and song – of Salmakis, Zeus, Gaia, among others – will have highlighted this relation to place, localizing the divine in the environment. When Aphrodite was addressed to sing about her Halikarnassian protégés, the evocation invited conversations with the divine in which the presence of the goddess melted into the local horizon.

The second arena of Halikarnassos' localism builds off the first. It has to do with the universal practice of staking claims in a culturally dynamic, competitive environment. It is impossible to assert how successful the Halikarnassians were with their contention to have raised Zeus. What is more important here is the mindset behind the claim. If the southeastern quadrant of the Aegean was a major junction in the traffic of people, goods, and ideas, this was inspired also by the cultural prestige accumulated by various cities in the region. South of Halikarnassos, the island and city of Kos had launched a concerted and largely successful campaign to brand-label itself as a centre in the sciences from the early third century BCE. Koan sacred ambassadors travelled widely in the Greek world to seek recognition for the Sanctuary of Asklepios.[57] Miletus, to the north, was recognized as the esteemed (symbolic) capital of Ionia. In addition to multiple traditions of learning and political prestige, the city was the home to a flourishing school of literature in the second century BCE and renowned Crown Games in honour of Apollo: celebrated every four years, the Didymaia attracted festival embassies from various corners of the Greek world.[58] Knidos, on the tip of the Datça peninsular, while also striving for medical fame, fully capitalized on its strategic location along the trade routes towards the eastern Mediterranean. In the third century, the city received a costly gymnasium with *palaistra*, which added to its cultural prestige.[59]

In this constellation, much of Halikarnassos' localism was relational, articulated in response to the achievement of others. Maybe the elegant Fountain House and shrine of Hermaphroditos nearby (Vitr. *De arch.* 2.8.11) were erected, or jazzed up, in reaction to lavish building programs elsewhere. Inquiries in the τίμιον of the city (line 3) betray not only the quest for traits of local particularity but something that was immune to the challenge of others. Beyond the highly contested realm of religious tradition, extra traits of uniqueness were desirable. After the badly damaged section from lines 31, the text kicks in again with the forceful claim that "on Phoibos's command she sowed Herodotus, the prose Homer in historical enquiry" (Φοίβου ἐφημοσύναις Ἡρόδοτον τὸν πεζὸν ἐν ἱστορίαισιν Ὅμηρον ἤροσεν: 43–5). Herodotus is identified as a universal quantity: he is sanctioned by Phoibos Apollo and celebrated as an equal to Homer. At the same time, Herodotus was an undisputed local authority (we note in passing that many cities in Asia Minor laid claims to the birthplace of Homer) who was at the heart and soul of Halikarnassos' cultural creativity. When Samos advertised its native son Pythagoras, Miletus Thales, and Kos Hippocrates (and from the third century the famous Babylonian priest Berossos, founder of the local astrological school), the local elites of Halikarnassos prided themselves in Herodotus.

Local pride did not end with Herodotus. On the contrary, his reference introduces a much larger and also a more extensive tradition of eruditeness of which Herodotus appears only as the most illustrious protagonist. We already learned how the second largest part of the poem assembles the names of scholarly men, twelve in total (41–54). The format of the catalogue most likely reflects prevalent modes of literary self-fashioning in the second century BCE, so the application of the principle, too, was relational and in implicit competition with others.[60] Several of these are listed in conjunction with their field of expertise. Much as with Herodotus, the arrangement insinuates that they each mastered the art of their respective genre. Immediately after Herodotus, and before his relative and epic poet Panyassis (line 45), the inscription mentions Andron, a man of "famous ability" (44). According to his latest editor, Andron, author of a work on *Kinsmen*, dates to the first half of the fourth century BCE. The fragments show a particular interest in Zeus and divine genealogies; most likely his work provided the backdrop to the sequence of Halikarnassian *ktiseis* discussed earlier in the inscription.[61] Other names added to the τίμιον. A large number of poets are listed apart from the epic poet Panyassis: Kyprias, author of an *Iliaka*; Menestheus, "loved by the Muses"; Theaitetos, a source of "divine inspiration"; Dionysios, "the writer of comedy"; Zenodotos, "expert writer of tragedies"; Phanostratos, "the servant of Dionysos"; and Timokrates, "a wise poet." Between the latter two another epichoric historian is listed, a certain Nossos, "a leading chronologist in history" (ἐν ἱστορίαισι χρόνων σημάντορα: 53).[62]

By the time of the inscription, Herodotus had long obtained the status of a Greek cultural celebrity, a quantity in its own right.[63] From the local perspective, however, the Halikarnassians propagated a more complex taxonomy of fame, one in which emphasis on the individual (Herodotus) is complemented with the cultural success of their city overall. In other words: Herodotus, champion of Halikarnassos' learned culture, is appropriated to the role of one academic representative among others: together they all breathed, as it were, a local esteem through their works. In doing so, they contributed to an atmosphere that inspired "good men to succeed the good" (line 55). To the locals, then, the sum of these writers weighed heavier than the individual voices of Herodotus (and Panyassis, among others), because they were the product of a local environment that allowed and empowered learned men to flourish. The list of famous scholars can be seen both as an expression and as a mirror of this environment; it emphatically showcases how the Halikarnassians promoted their city within the Hellenistic world.

As their world rapidly grew larger, demanding new ways of communal self-positioning, the people of Halikarnassos turned to the τίμιον they found within. It is striking to see how the inscription in the Fountain House staked everything on Greek traditions, including divine genealogies, mythology, and traditions of Hellenic *paideia*. We ought to recall, however, that there is no way of knowing whether this pursuit of Greek meaning-making resonated with the entire, ethnically heterogeneous population of the city, or was confined to the local elites of the city, families like the Antheadai from the highest echelon in society.[64] Roman presence in the quadrant brought yet another voice to the cultural conversation, and it blurs the picture presented in our sources. Within two or three generations after the Salmakis inscription, authors like Vitruvius, Strabo, and Ovid picked up the local tradition. The curiosity and zeal with which they engaged with Salmakis' story and, presumably, expanded its narrative make it obvious that these authors were fascinated by the elegant Fountain House and its storied environment. In Ovid's case, this is amply attested by his lengthy exposition of Salmakis' special role among the naiads and the animated description of her sexual encounter with Hermaphroditos.[65] As Roman writers eagerly absorbed the myth, their interests were implicitly carried by the evolving idea of a Graeco-Roman cultural commonwealth, the interweaving of cultural currents at the macro-level of Mediterranean exchanges. In so doing, the Romans established their own perceptions of Hellenicity, remodelling, if not palliating, ethnic complexities in the local arena.

These caveats do not prevent us from an appreciation of Halikarnassos' localism. Local discourses are shaped not by one single voice but by a polyphony of attitudes and expressions in a plurality of realms; as we have seen, the quest for a single voice is both futile and counterintuitive to the nature of local discourse environments. Despite complex and nuanced differentiations within, the unifying element of the local discourse was that voice and place are bracketed by the horizon of immediacy and directness, the type of manageability we encountered above. In this sense, the local delineates a communicative boundary, rather than streamlining the contents of the communication as such. It was observed that the poet of the Salmakis inscription does not "give a simple recording of the local collective memory." Effectively, its value "for the reconstruction of local history" was only limited.[66] The warning is in order. Religious life in Halikarnassos itself was clearly richer and more multi-faceted and diverse than the focus on Salmakis might suggest. There is no way of subsuming the canon of religious plurality under one umbrella.[67] But the study of localism and the writing of local history are two different exercises. The quest for the governing force of the local entails more than the narration of history in a local context. It seeks to break into discourse environments that are not only confined in place but relate to it; that prioritize place, real and symbolic, as a source of inspiration and meaning; and, in turn, that receive orientation from the local horizon in changing circumstances that occur in the world writ large. The Salmakis inscription is a powerful document to speak to this type of investigation. If, in the complex cultural negotiations of the day, the Halikarnassians experienced a sense of being adrift, it seems that they sought to balance this experience by highlighting the unifying quality of their local world.

## The Force of the Local: An Afterthought

Across the bay from Halikarnassos to the south, less than 10 nautical miles away, lies the island of Kos. In *Idyll 7*, Theokritos describes how a poet named Simichidas, along with his friends on their way to a harvest festival in the country there, encountered a goatherd who was known far and wide for being the best piper. They chatted. Simichidas and the goatherd each performed a song. Then they parted ways. The poem ends with Simichidas and his party lying down

on deep couches of sweet rush and newly cut vine leaves. Many a poplar and elm murmured above our heads; trickling down from a cave of the nymphs, a sacred spring splashed nearby; on the shady branches the dusky cicadas worked hard at their song; far off in the dense brambles the tree frog kept up its crooning; linnets and finches sang; doves were cooing; and humming bees were flying around the spring. Everywhere was the smell of rich harvest, the smell of gathered fruits. Pears rolled plentiful at our feet and apple by our side … wine jars were opened that had been sealed for four years. (135–47)

Theokritos' translation of the countryside into poetic space is highly artificial, the literary trope of a *locus amoenus* that is masterfully crafted to evoke the image of a real place, rich in sensual excitement. The exercise was rooted in traditions about the epichoric horizon. Theokritos' contribution to this was that his pastoral in many ways highlighted the culminating point of Greek depictions of the local since the Archaic Age. At the same time, it marked the arrival of an all-new literary genre, that of bucolic poetry. The rise of this reappraisal of the local in the Hellenistic period was not accidental; nor was it geared towards the charms of tranquillity alone. More profoundly, contributing to conversations about the fainting force of globality, bucolic poetry resonated the challenge of rethinking and, presumably, reinvigorating the local as an essence of social significance in a world that had long surpassed the local. Whether imagined or real, local place was appreciated and, in its poetic sublimation, fetishized for its inherent quality as a commodity of sense. Much like the Halikarnassians in the Salmakis inscription, then, Theokritos' poetry gives voice to the local as a quantity that provided meaning and orientation to human agency.


## NOTES

1 *Editio princeps*: Isager 1998, reprinted in Isager and Pedersen 2004 (translation thereafter, with adaptations). Discussions since include Lloyd-Jones 1998 and 1999; Isager and Pedersen 2004; Gagné 2006; Bremmer 2009; Graf 2009; Stevens 2016: 78–9; Santini 2016 and 2017; McInerney 2021.
2 Cf. Jameson 2004; see also *GIBM* 4.891.
3 Bremmer 2009: 293. Cf. Plin. *HN* 5.104; Pomp. Mela 1.84 on the Reed Gulf near Hyla (not in Barrington).
4 See Loraux 1996/2000; Beck 2020: 51–61.
5 Bremmer 2009: 298–302. Later traditions charged the story of the sexual encounter with all sorts of stereotypes: Strabo 14.2.16; Vitr. *De arch.* 2.8.12; Mart. 14.174; Santini 2016: 20–1.
6 Horden and Purcell 2000; Morris 2005; Thonemann 2016.
7 Horden and Purcell 2019.
8 Appadurai 1996, 2002.
9 Hodos 2010: 16.

10  See http://www.bristol.ac.uk/arts/research/globalising-luxuries/ (last accessed
   27 August 2020).
11  *Tanagra: Mythe et archéologie* 2003 (Louvre Museum catalog).
12  Dillon 2012.
13  *Tanagra: Mythe et archéologie* 2003: 120–52.
14  Ptol. *Geog.* 6.4.4; cf. Hdt. 3.39, 6.20, 6.119; Diod. Sic. 17.110.4–5; Cohen 2013:
   199–200.
15  Ai Khanoum: Cohen 2013: 255–76 (with much bibliography); Kosmin 2014:
   224–5, 237–8; Mairs 2014.
16  Bernard 1969: 329; Cohen 2013: 268 (Kybele) and 264 (theatre and
   gymnasium); Kosmin 2014: 196 (irrigation) and 237 (Pindar). For confidence in
   Ai Khanoum's Greekness, see Green 1993: 70 ("a Greek city" with a "character
   essentially Hellenic") and the literature cited by Mairs 2014: 22–3, 183–4.
17  Religious structures: Cohen 2013: 264–5; Mairs 2014: 85–9; Hoo 2018:
   168–71.
18  Ai Khanoum: Sherwin-White and Kuhrt 1993: 178–80; Mairs 2014: 186–7 and
   48–52 for discussion of the epigraphically attested names of treasury employees
   in the city. Elsewhere: e.g., *OGIS* 737 from Memphis (112 BCE?), a decree of
   the "*polis* of the Idoumaioi" in honour of Dorion, a man of Egyptian descent
   and priest of the *machairophoroi* (a group of professional soldiers). The decree
   was set up in the local Apollonieion. While the labels are all Greek, none of
   the involved agents was Greek, including the deity worshipped in the shrine of
   the Apollonieion (which was sacred to Qos, a major god in the pantheon of the
   Idoumaioi): Sänger 2019: 114–20.
19  Hoo 2018.
20  Diog. Laert. 6.63 (*Life of Diogenes*); cf. Chin 2016.
21  Chin 2016: 134.
22  Castells 2004; Castells et al. 2006; see also Malkin 2011: 1–15.
23  Tarn and Griffith 1952: 79.
24  Giovannini 1993: 266.
25  See Müller 2013; note, however, the scepticism articulated earlier by Walbank
   2002.
26  McAuley 2016.
27  McAuley 2016: 339; Börm and Luraghi 2018. See also the various volumes
   in the series *Die Hellenistische Polis als Lebensform* (ed. M. Zimmermann)
   that explore the interplay between urban structures and civic identities in the
   Hellenistic city.
28  Cf. Malkin 2011; Hodos 2015, 2017.
29  See, however, Fine 2010; Whitmarsh 2010; Hodos 2010.
30  Thomas 2014a: 145; also Thomas 2014b; see Beck 2020: 165–75.
31  Beck 2020: 31–6.

32  Locavores: Filson and Adekunle 2017. Translocal scales: Herod 2008; Greiner
    and Sakdapolrak 2013; Brickell and Datta 2016.
33  Fachard 2012; see also Bintliff et al. 2017 (Thespiai).
34  Gehrke 1986: 18.
35  Bintliff 2002, 2006, with much bibliography.
36  See McHugh 2017: 99–131 (Argolid).
37  See Hansen and Nielsen 2004: 70–3, based on their inventory of 1,035 city-
    states; cf. Ober 2015: 22–32, 87.
38  Lefebvre 1974/1991: 101.
39  Harvey 1979/2006: 275; cf. Crumley et al. 2017.
40  Echo chamber and local discourse environment, cf. Beck 2020: 34–5.
41  Cf. Isager and Pedersen 2004.
42  *Milet* 1.3.149. Cf. already Hdt. 5.121 and 6.20 on Pidasa's location in-between.
43  *IG* XII 3, Suppl. 1269 + 1270 (τὸ κοινὸν τῶν ἐν Σύμαι κατοικούντων);
    Constantakopoulou 2015. Rhodes, see Zachhuber 2023; McInerney 2023. Delos,
    Dignas 2003; Steinhauer 2014. Cf. also the various contributions in Horster and
    Klöckner 2013.
44  See only *SEG* 43.713 (mid-fifth cent.) and 40.991 (from Mylasa 354/3 BCE, ll.
    15–16); *SGDI* 5727 (fourth cent.) with Blümel 1993; Santini 2016, who fleshes
    out the ethnically heterogeneous context (esp. 12–15 and 28). The cult for
    Isis and Sarapis is evidenced in Halikarnassos from the first half of the third
    century: *GIBM* 4.906 and 908.
45  Cf. Gagné 2006: 19–25; Bremmer 2009: 308.
46  See M&L 32, the so-called Lygdamis inscription (ca. 465 to 450 BCE); Flensted-
    Jensen 2004: 1132; for detailed discussion, Piñol-Villanueva 2017.
47  See C. Binder, in *DNP* s.v. Salmakis.
48  In times of crisis, the priestess of Athena grew a long beard: Hdt. 1.175; see also
    *CIG* 2660; Flensted-Jensen 2004: 1131; Ruzicka 1992: 35.
49  There is significant disagreement over who this son of Phoibos was (Maussollos?):
    Jeppsen 2004; Isager 2004: 229.
50  See Bremmer 2009: 294.
51  Isager 2004: 233–4 points to possible parallels between the inscriptions and the
    sculptural program of the Temple of Hekate at Lagina. Did the Halikarnassian
    version resonate elsewhere in Karia?
52  Cf. Bremmer 209: 295.
53  See Beck 2023 for a collection of evidence from Phlious, Argos, Eleusis, and
    Delos, among others.
54  For Magnesia on the Maeander, ca. 150 km to the north of Halikarnassos, the
    articulation of a similar worldview has been detected by Wiemer 2009: 86–94, in the
    inaugural document of the famous Crown Games for Artemis Leukophryene (late
    third cent.): *I. Magnesia* 16 = *Syll.*³ 557 = *BNJ* 482 F 2 = Rigsby 1996: 185–90, no. 66.

55  Larson 2001; Beck 2020: 69–71.

56  See the famous Law of the Molpoi, *Milet* 1.3.133 = *LSCG* 50, with Fontenrose 1988: 28–30; Herda 2006.

57  See the renowned *Asylieurkunden* collected by Herzog and Klaffenbach 1952; Rigsby 1996: 106–53, nos. 8–52. Cf. Buraselis 2000; Nelson 2002; Höghammar 2004.

58  *Syll.*³ 590; Rigsby 1996: 174–6.

59  *IK* 41 (Knidos 301); Blümel 1995: 62–3; Reger 2019.

60  Cf. Isager 2004: 232–3, on potential Alexandrian influences. The Lindian Chronicle of 99 BCE (*BNJ* 532) proceeds in similar fashion, see McInerney 2023.

61  *BNJ* 10 (ed. Toye). Zeus: F 1, 3, 17.

62  See the commentary in Isager 2004: 229–32 on this section of the text.

63  Cf. Priestley 2014.

64  Steph. Byz. s.v. *Athēnai* = A 80 Billerbeck; Isager 2004: 229.

65  *Met.* 4.302–15, 356–373; cf. Strabo 14.2.16 (where the story of migration from Greece has a sequel set in the surroundings of Halikarnassos); Vitr. *De arch.* 2.8.11–12. Ovid's exposition inspired the 1971 Genesis song "The Fountain of Salmacis."

66  Bremmer 2009: 308.

67  See, e.g., the epigraphical testimony on a variety of cults in the Hellenistic period, including Apollo (*GIBM* 4.896), Aphrodite (901), Dionysos (902, 909, 910), Demeter and Kore (903), Zeus Labraundos (904), and Isis and Sarapis (906 and 908).

## REFERENCES

Ager, S.L., and R.A. Faber (eds.). 2013. *Belonging and Isolation in the Hellenistic World*. Toronto.

Appadurai, A. 1996. *Modernity at Large: Cultural Dimensions of Globalization*. Minneapolis.

Appadurai, A. (ed.). 2002. *Globalization*. London.

Beck, H. 2020. *Localism and the Ancient Greek City-State*. Chicago.

Beck, H. 2023. "Images of Centrality: Phlious and Its Coinage in the Classical Period." In Y. Stoyas and S. Damigos (eds.), *Memory and Impression. Papers from a Conference Held in Tegea, Greece*. Athens (in press).

Bernard, P. 1969. "Quatrième campagne de fouilles à Aï Khanoum." *Comptes Rendus des Séances de l'Académie des Inscriptions et Belles-Lettres* 113.3: 313–55. https://doi.org/10.3406/crai.1969.12397.

Bintliff, J.L. 2002. "Going to the Market in Antiquity." In E. Olshausen and H. Sonnabend (eds.), *Zu Wasser und zu Land – Verkehrswege in der antiken Welt*. Stuttgart: 209–50.

Bintliff, J.L. 2006. "City-Country Relationships in the 'Normal Polis'." In R.M. Rosen and I. Sluiter (eds.), *City, Countryside, and the Spatial Organization of Value in Classical Antiquity*. Leiden: 13–32.

Bintliff, J.L., et al. 2017. *Boeotia Project, Volume II. The City of Thespiai: Survey at a Complex Urban Site*. Cambridge.

Blümel, W. 1993. "SGDI 5727 (Halikarnassos): Eine Revision." *Kadmos* 32: 1–18. https://doi.org/10.1515/kadm.1993.32.1.1.

Blümel, W. 1995. "Inschriften aus Karien I." *Epigraphica Anatolica* 25: 35–64.

Börm, H., and N. Luraghi (eds.). 2018. *The Polis in the Hellenistic World*. Stuttgart.

Bremmer, J. 2009. "Zeus' Own Country: Cult and Myth in the Pride of Halicarnassus." In U. Dill and C. Walde (eds.), *Antike Mythen: Medien, Transformationen und Konstruktionen*. Berlin and New York: 292–312.

Brickell, K., and A. Datta (eds.). 2016. *Translocal Geographies: Spaces, Places, Connections*. London.

Buraselis, K. 2000. *Kos between Hellenism and Rome: Studies on the Political, Institutional, and Social History of Kos from ca. the Middle Second Century B.C. until Late Antiquity*. Philadelphia.

Castells, M. (ed.). 2004. *The Network Society: A Cross-Cultural Perspective*. Northampton, MA.

Castells, M., et al. 2006. *Mobile Communication and Society: A Global Perspective*. Cambridge, MA.

Chin, T.T. 2016. "What Is Imperial Cosmopolitanism? Revisiting Kosmopolitēs and Mundanus." In M. Lavan, R.E. Payne, and J. Weisweiler (eds.), *Cosmopolitanism and Empire: Universal Rulers, Local Elites, and Cultural Integration in the Ancient Near East and Mediterranean*. Oxford: 129–52.

Cohen, G.M. 2013. *The Hellenistic Settlements in the East from Armenia and Mesopotamia to Bactria and India*. Berkeley.

Constantakopoulou, C. 2015. "Beyond the Polis." In C. Taylor and K. Vlassopoulos (eds.), *Communities and Networks in the Ancient Greek World*. Oxford: 214–36.

Crumley, C.L., T. Lennartsson, and A. Westin. 2017. *Issues and Concepts in Historical Ecology: The Past and Future of Landscapes and Regions*. Cambridge and New York.

Dignas, B. 2003. *Economy of the Sacred in Hellenistic and Roman Asia Minor*. Oxford.

Dillon, S. 2012. "Hellenistic Tanagra Figurines." In S.L. James and S. Dillon (eds.), *A Companion to Women in the Ancient World*. Malden, MA: 231–4.

Fachard, S. 2012. *La défense du territoire: Étude de la chôra érétrienne et de ses fortifications*. Gollion.

Filson, G.C., and B. Adekunle. 2017. *Eat Local, Taste Global: How Ethnocultural Food Reaches Our Table*. Waterloo, ON.

Fine, E.A. 2010. "The Sociology of the Local: Action and Its Publics." *Sociological Theory* 28: 355–76. https://doi.org/10.1111/j.1467-9558.2010.01380.x.

Flensted-Jensen, P. 2004. "Karia." In M.H. Hansen and T.H. Nielsen (eds.), *An Inventory of Archaic and Classical Poleis*. Oxford: 1108–38.

Fontenrose, J. 1988. *Didyma: Apollo's Oracle, Cult, and Companions*. Berkeley.

Gagné, R. 2006. "What Is the Pride of Halicarnassus?" *Classical Antiquity* 25: 1–33. https://doi.org/10.1525/ca.2006.25.1.1.

Gehrke, H.-J. 1986. *Jenseits von Athen und Sparta: Das dritte Griechenland und seine Staatenwelt*. Munich.

Giovannini, A. 1993. "Greek Cities and Greek Commonwealth." In S. Bulloch et al. (eds.), *Images and Ideologies*. Oxford: 265–86.

Graf, F. 2009. "Zeus and His *Parhedroi* in Halikarnassos: A Study on Religion and Inscriptions." In A. Martínez Fernández (ed.), *Estudios de Epigrafía Griega*. La Laguna: 333–48.

Green, P. 1993. "Introduction: New Approaches to the Hellenistic World." In P. Green (ed.), *Hellenistic History and Culture*. Berkeley: 1–12.

Greiner, C., and P. Sakdapolrak. 2013. "Translocality: Concepts, Applications, and Emerging Research Perspectives." *Geography Compass* 7: 373–84. https://doi.org/10.1111/gec3.12048.

Hansen, M.H., and T.H. Nielsen (eds.). 2004. *An Inventory of Archaic and Classical Poleis*. Oxford.

Harrison, J. 1927. *Themis: A Study of the Social Origins of Greek Religion*. 2nd ed. Cambridge.

Harvey, D. 1979/2006. "Space as a Keyword." In N. Castree and D. Gregory (eds.), *David Harvey: A Critical Reader*. Malden, MA: 270–94.

Herda, A. 2006. *Der Apollon-Delphinios-Kult in Milet und die Neujahrsprozession nach Didyma*. Mainz.

Herod, A. 2008. "Scale: The Local and The Global." In S. Holloway et al. (eds.), *Key Concepts in Geography*. 2nd ed. London: 217–35.

Herzog, R., and G. Klaffenbach (eds.). 1952. *Asylieurkunden aus Kos*. Berlin.

Hodos, T. 2010. "Local and Global Perspectives in the Study of Social and Cultural Identities." In S. Hales and T. Hodos (eds.), *Material Culture and Social Identities in the Ancient World*. Cambridge: 3–31.

Hodos, T. 2015. "Global, Local, and In Between: Connectivity and the Mediterranean." In M. Pitts and M.J. Versluys (eds.), *Globalisation and the Roman World: World History, Connectivity and Material Culture*. Cambridge: 240–53.

Hodos, T. (ed.). 2017. *The Routledge Handbook of Archaeology and Globalization*. London.

Höghammar, K. 2004. *The Hellenistic "Polis" of Kos*. Uppsala.

Hoo, M. 2018. *Ai Khanum in the Face of Eurasian Globalisation: A Trans-local Approach to a Contested Site in Hellenistic Bactria*. Kiel.

Horden, P., and N. Purcell. 2000. *The Corrupting Sea: A Study of Mediterranean History*. Oxford and Malden, MA.

Horden, P., and N. Purcell. 2019. *The Boundless Sea: Writing Mediterranean History*. Abingdon and New York.

Horster, M., and A. Klöckner. 2013. *Cities and Priests: Cult Personnel in Asia Minor and the Aegean Islands from the Hellenistic to the Imperial Period*. Boston.

Isager, S. 1998. "The Pride of Halikarnassos: Editio Princeps of an Inscription from Salmakis." *Zeitschrift für Papyrologie und Epigraphik* 123: 1–23.

Isager, S. 2004. "Halikarnassos and the Ptolemies I: Inscriptions on Public Buildings." In S. Isager and P. Pedersen (eds.), *The Salmakis Inscription and Hellenistic Halikarnassos*. Odense and Portland: 133–45.

Isager, S., and P. Pedersen (eds.). 2004. *The Salmakis Inscription and Hellenistic Halikarnassos*. Odense and Portland.

Jameson, M. 2004. "Troizen and Halikarnassos in the Hellenistic Era." In S. Isager and P. Pedersen (eds.), *The Salmakis Inscription and Hellenistic Halikarnassos*. Odense and Portland: 93–109.

Jeppsen, K. 2004. "A Propos of the List of Colonizers in the Salmakis Inscription: Was Maussollos or His Mythological Namesake Referred to in Lines 35–36?" In S. Isager and P. Pedersen (eds.), *The Salmakis Inscription and Hellenistic Halikarnassos*. Odense and Portland: 89–93.

Kosmin, P.J. 2014. *The Land of the Elephant Kings: Space, Territory, and Ideology in the Seleucid Empire*. Cambridge, MA.

Larson, J. 2001. *Greek Nymphs: Myth, Cult, Lore*. Oxford.

Lefebvre, H. 1974/1991. *The Production of Space*. Translated by D. Nicholson-Smith. Malden, MA.

Lloyd-Jones, H. 1998. "The Pride of Halicarnassus." *Zeitschrift für Papyrologie und Epigraphik* 124: 1–14.

Lloyd-Jones, H. 1999. "Corrigenda and Addenda." *Zeitschrift für Papyrologie und Epigraphik* 127: 63–5.

Loraux, N. 1996/2000. *Born of the Earth: Myth and Politics in Athens*. Ithaca.

Mairs, R. 2014. *The Hellenistic Far East: Archaeology, Language, and Identity in Greek Central Asia*. Oakland.

Malkin, I. 2011. *A Small Greek World: Networks in the Ancient Mediterranean*. Oxford.

McAuley, A. 2016. *Basking in the Shadow of Kings: Local Culture in the Hellenistic Greek Mainland*. PhD diss., McGill University.

McHugh, M. 2017. *The Ancient Greek Farmstead*. Philadelphia.

McInerney, J. 2021. "Salmakis and the Priests of Halikarnassos." *Klio* 103: 59–89. https://doi.org/10.1515/klio-2020-0309.

McInerney, J. 2023. "The Lindian Chronicle and Local Identity." In H. Beck and J. Kindt (eds.), *The Local Horizon of Ancient Greek Religion*. Cambridge: 232–61.

Morris, I. 2005. "Mediterraneanization." In I. Malkin (ed.), *Mediterranean Paradigms and Classical Antiquity*. Mediterranean Historical Review 18. London: 30–55.

Müller, C. 2013. "The Rise and Fall of the Boeotians: Polybius 20.4–7 as a Literary Topos." In B. Gibson and T. Harrison (eds.), *Polybius and His World: Essays in Memory of F.W. Walbank*. Oxford: 267–79.

Nelson, E.D. 2002. "Coan Production and the Authorship of the Presbeutikos." In P. Van der Eijk (ed.), *Hippocrates in Context*. New Castle: 209–36.

Ober, J. 2015. *The Rise and Fall of Classical Greece.* Princeton.

Piñol-Villanueva, A. 2017. "Halicarnassus – Salmakis. A Pre-Classical sympoliteia?" *Klio* 99: 26–50. https://doi.org/10. /klio-2017-0002.

Priestley, J. 2014. *Herodotus and Hellenistic Culture: Literary Studies in the Reception of the Histories.* Oxford.

Reger, G. 2019. "New Work on Knidian Amphorae: Links to the Hellenistic Economy." *Herom: Journal on Hellenistic and Roman Material Culture* 8: 1–423.

Rigsby, K.J. 1996. *Asylia: Territorial Inviolability in the Hellenistic World.* Berkeley.

Ruzicka, S. 1992. *Politics of a Persian Dynasty: The Hecatomnids in the Fourth Century B.C.* Norman, OK.

Sänger, P. 2019. *Die ptolemäische Organisationsform politeuma.* Tübingen.

Santini, M. 2016. "A Multi-Ethnic City Shapes Its Past: The 'Pride of Halikarnassos' and the Memory of Salmakis." *Annali della Scuola Normale Superiore di Pisa. Classe di Lettere e Filosofia. Serie 5. 8.1:* 3–35.

Santini, M. 2017. "Bellerophontes, Pegasos and the Foundation of Halikarnassos: Contributions to the Study of the Salmakis Inscription." *Studi Classici e Orientali* 63: 109–43.

Sherwin-White, S., and A. Kuhrt. 1993. *From Samarkhand to Sardis: A New Approach to the Seleucid Empire, Hellenistic Culture, and Society.* London.

Steinhauer, J. 2014. *Religious Associations in the Post-Classical Polis.* Stuttgart.

Stevens, K. 2016. "Empire Begins at Home: Local Elites and Imperial Ideologies in Hellenistic Greece and Babylonia." In M. Lavan, R.E. Payne, and J. Weisweiler (eds.), *Cosmopolitanism and Empire: Universal Rulers, Local Elites, and Cultural Integration in the Ancient Near East and Mediterranean.* Oxford: 65–89.

Tarn, W.W., and G.T. Griffith. 1952. *Hellenistic Civilisation.* London.

Thomas, R. 2014a. "The Greek Polis and the Tradition of Polis History: Local History, Chronicles and the Patterning of the Past." In A. Moreno and R. Thomas (eds.), *Patterns of the Past: Epitēdeumata in the Greek Tradition.* Oxford: 145–72.

Thomas, R. 2014b. "Local History, Polis History, and the Politics of Place." In G. Parmegianni (ed.), *Between Thucydides and Polybius: The Golden Age of Greek Historiography*, Washington, DC: 239–62.

Thonemann, P. 2016. *The Hellenistic World.* Cambridge.

Walbank, F.W. 2002. *Polybius, Rome, and the Hellenistic World: Essays and Reflections*. Cambridge and New York.

Whitmarsh, T. (ed.). 2010. *Local Knowledge and Microidentities in the Imperial Greek World*. Cambridge.

Wiemer, H.-U. 2009. "Neue Feste – neue Geschichtsbilder? Zur Errinerungsfunktion städtischer Feste im Hellenismus." In H. Beck and H.-U. Wiemer (eds.), *Feiern und Erinnern: Geschichtsbilder im Spiegel antiker Feste*. Berlin: 83–109.

Zachhuber, J. 2023. "Protecting the Local: Conflicting Narratives in 4th Century BCE Rhodes." In H. Beck and J. Kindt (eds.), *The Local Horizon of Ancient Greek Religion*. Cambridge: 262–89.

*This chapter guides readers to the area around Lake Kopais, a micro-region in central Greece that provided its inhabitants with distinct living conditions (see also chapter 3). The Kopais basin comprised a vibrant lacustrine ecosystem that was known for its rich variety of plants and abundance of animal species, and the buzzing economic opportunity derived from both. Inundation, however, posed a constant problem; the region often suffered from flooding, which put the health of people and communities at risk. Ruben Post explores the broad array of human-environmental interactions that played out before the canvas of fluctuating lakeshores. The most impactful ancient attempt to control the hydrology in the region – the famous Mycenaean drainage works notwithstanding – was carried out under Alexander the Great, whose engineers stabilized conditions by clearing sinkholes (katavothres) and digging drainage channels. Beyond grand interventions such as these, Post traces how the lived experience in the Kopais basin was subject to multiple cycles of time. Charting the environment, its microclimate, flora, and fauna in the opening sections of his paper, he next turns to corresponding resonances with human practice, including agriculture, pastoralism, hunting, and fishing. A key witness to these activities was Theophrastos, who, in his* Inquiry into Plants, *provides a comprehensive ecological description of the Kopais. By means of a close reading of the corresponding passages, Post extrapolates invaluable information on the interplay between local vegetations, artisanal practice, and cultural preference: the case in point is the local production of musical instruments (auloi) that were a much-appreciated commodity throughout Hellenistic Greece, and a source of social meaning at home. In the midst of a swiftly expanding world, the Kopais people thus positioned themselves through practices that deeply tied them to, and resonated with, the local horizon.*

*Keywords: Orchomenos, Theophrastos, environmental localism, hydrology, inundation,* aulos industry

# 2

## Localism and Environmental History in the Hellenistic Kopaic Basin

RUBEN POST

The first part [of this book] is devoted to a history whose passage is almost imperceptible, that of man in his relationship to the environment, a history in which all change is slow, a history of constant repetition, ever-recurring cycles. I could not neglect this almost timeless history, the story of man's contact with the inanimate, neither could I be satisfied with the traditional geographical introduction to history that often figures to little purpose at the beginning of so many books, with its descriptions of the mineral deposits, types of agriculture, and typical flora, briefly listed and never mentioned again, as if the flowers did not come back every spring, the flocks of sheep migrate every year, or the ships sail on a real sea that changes with the seasons.

(Fernand Braudel 1972, vol. 1: 20)

Sometime during his reign, Alexander the Great sent a mining engineer in his employ, Krates of Chalkis, to help mitigate the chronic flooding around Lake Kopais in western Boiotia. When he arrived, Krates set about clearing several clogged sinkholes blocking the drainage of the Kopaic basin.[1] As Strabo notes, citing a letter Krates himself wrote to Alexander, he succeeded in clearing many sinkholes but ultimately could not complete his project because "the Boiotians were quarrelling" (στασιασάντων τῶν Βοιωτῶν). This story nicely illustrates the connections between the local and the international in Hellenistic Greece. While the vast resources of the new Hellenistic monarchies could have had major impacts locally, parochial dynamics often proved resilient, and these local forces in turn influenced the formation of a new, interconnected Greek world. In this paper, I analyse the local history of the Kopaic basin in the Hellenistic period from the perspective of human-environment interactions. I wish to emphasize above all the cycles that defined the lives of the inhabitants of the shores around Lake Kopais, spanning seasons, years, and generations. The geology and environment of the Kopaic basin set it apart both from eastern Boiotia and from most other regions of the Greek world. The lake that formed within it was unique in mainland Greece for its size and, as a result, was a source of rich plant and animal resources, but also of flooding and disease. I turn first to the lake itself, which constantly fluctuated in size according to changes in winter precipitation, summer heat, and the functioning of sinkholes. I then turn to the testimony of Theophrastos, early modern travellers, and ethnographic comparison to illuminate how this fluctuating landscape affected local communities and their activities, including agriculture, foraging, fishing, and hunting. Finally, I examine the impact of the lake's ecology on the health of those who resided around it, focusing on the malaria that was rampant in this region until modern times.

## Geology, Climate, Hydrology

The Kopais region is a large, flat basin surrounded by mountains which, up until its complete drainage in the late nineteenth century, was home to an exceptionally dynamic landscape.[2] This is a classic example of a *polje* – a closed limestone basin relying exclusively on subterranean channels, called in modern Greek *katavothres*, to drain accumulated water.[3] Two large rivers feed into the basin, the Kephissos, which drains a large area to the west, including much of Mount Parnassos, and in the past skirted the south of the basin, and the Melas ("Black"), which emerges from *katavothres* in the northwest of the basin and used to run along its northern edge. Some other smaller rivers also feed into the basin from the south.[4] The *katavothres*, which were so crucial for the drainage of the basin, were primarily located along its northeastern edge.[5]

These elements were the primary components of a complex hydrogeological system that governed the dynamics of Lake Kopais.[6] From October to March, rainfall and melting snow would gradually fill the basin. Then, under normal conditions, excess water would flow out through the *katavothres*, into the smaller lakes Hylikē and Paralimnē to the northeast, and eventually out to the Euboian Gulf. Up until the basin was drained in the late nineteenth century, Lake Kopais normally occupied an area of ca. 230 square kilometres at its greatest extent. However, between April and September, when rainfall was minimal and the temperature increased, evaporation would gradually reduce the standing water in the basin and the lake would eventually turn into a swamp, or sometimes even completely dry up. During years of heavy precipitation, on the other hand, the lake could become perennial. Between the two seasonal extremes of the total desiccation of the basin and its complete inundation, the Kephissos and Melas Rivers often formed permanent channels flowing through it, while the "lake" itself was in some places a proper lake, in others more of a swamp.[7] Because the Kopaic basin reached only a maximum depth of 3–4 metres, its shoreline could change drastically with relatively small fluctuations in inflow or precipitation.[8] Further complicating matters was that over time erosion from the surrounding slopes would deposit debris in the *katavothres*, eventually blocking them and causing the lake to swell.[9] It was this problem that the engineer Krates was sent to solve.

## Plants and Foraging

All that is visible today of the formerly rich lacustrine ecosystem of the Kopaic basin are the meagre vestiges of the rivers that once fed into its lake. But while we can no longer investigate Lake Kopais, we can reconstruct much of its ecology from the invaluable information recorded by ancient authors and early modern travellers.[10] The abundance of water in the basin for much of the year allowed for the growth of a large variety of plants that were rare in much of the rest of Greece. Indeed, the lacustrine flora of the Kopais region was so lush that Plutarch, a native of Chaironeia, even compared it to that of the Nile.[11] This botanical variety attracted the attention of Theophrastos, who in his *Inquiry into Plants* provides a firsthand description of the plant life of the region;[12] this is in fact the most comprehensive ecological description of any region of the Greek world to survive from antiquity.[13] The Peripatetic makes clear that he obtained information from local informants, and often goes out of his way to note the unique local names for parts of the basin and the plants that grew in it.[14] For instance, the area between the Kephissos and the Melas Rivers was full of natural pits the locals called the "potholes" (χύτροι),[15] while the thick reed-beds that normally extended across shallow portions of the lake they called "the bundles" (κώμυσι).[16] In periods when the lake was fuller, these reed-beds could disappear, though large chunks of them might detach and form floating islands; Theophrastos notes that these often clustered around Orchomenos in particular, and that the largest were up to 500 metres in circumference and were overgrown with goat-willow trees.[17]

Theophrastos provides an abundance of detail on the ways in which the inhabitants of the Kopais region used the perilacustrine flora. The lake produced a variety of different kinds of reeds, and he notes that the slenderer variety that commonly grew on the floating islands was used by the locals for weaving, while the stouter variety that grew in "the bundles" was used to make stakes.[18] Other products thus produced would have included goods woven from rushes, such as the hundreds of sturdy mats made of that material supplied by a Thespian merchant for a construction project at Delphi in 337/336 BCE,[19] and wicks made from plantains, such as those peddled by Aristophanes' Theban merchant in the *Acharnians*.[20] Theophrastos states that the locals also harvested different parts of cat's tail grass – which could be found throughout all parts of the basin, though the finest kind grew in deeper water and on the floating islands[21] – for use as soap, baby food, or basket-weaving material.[22] He further notes that the inhabitants of the basin were known to eat the sweet fruit of the yellow water lily (called *nymphaia* by most Greeks, but *madōnais* locally) and use its leaves for various medicinal purposes.[23] Another notable botanical product of the western part of the basin, and in particular the area around Orchomenos, was perfume made from the irises, roses, white lilies, and narcissus that grew in abundance there.[24] Thus, the aquatic plants that flourished around Lake Kopais were crucial to every aspect of local life.

The most fascinating intersection between the environment, culture, and the economy of the Kopaic basin, however, is found in Theophrastos' lengthy excursus on its most famous plant product, the double-bodied wind instrument known as the *aulos*.[25] The Boiotians were famously fond of this instrument in their musical performances,[26] and the Thebans, said to have been "judged by Greece the champions of playing the *aulos*" (ἣν προεκρίθησαν ὑπὸ τῆς Ἑλλάδος νικᾶν ἐπ᾽ αὐλητικῇ),[27] produced a number of famous *aulētai*.[28] This was in large part due to the fact that Lake Kopais was the primary source in Greece of the only reed species used to produce the mouthpieces that were the most crucial determinant of an *aulos'* sound.[29] The reeds that grew in the area around Orchomenos in particular were considered the finest in the ancient world for *auloi*, and among those the most exemplary grew in a locale near the mouth of the Kephissos known as *Oxeia Kampē*, literally "sharp bend," but also in musical parlance "high-pitched modulation."[30] Thus, it is fitting that while Thebes produced the most famous *aulētai*, Pindar – himself a renowned Theban musician[31] – was careful to note that their success was only possible thanks to the "reeds that grow beside the lovely-chorused city of the Graces [Orchomenos], in the Sanctuary of Kaphisis, the faithful witnesses of dancers" (δονάκων, τοὶ παρὰ καλλιχόρῳ ναίοισι πόλει Χαρίτων, Καφισίδος ἐν τεμένει, πιστοὶ χορευτᾶν μάρτυρες).[32]

Theophrastos goes into great detail about the history of the local *aulos* industry:[33]

Τὴν δὲ τομὴν ὡραίαν εἶναι πρὸ Ἀντιγενίδου μέν, ἡνίκ᾽ ηὔλουν ἀπλάστως, ὑπ᾽ Ἀρκτοῦρον Βοηδρομιῶνος μηνός· τὸν γὰρ οὕτω τμηθέντα συχνοῖς μὲν ἔτεσιν ὕστερον γίνεσθαι χρήσιμον καὶ προκαταυλήσεως δεῖσθαι πολλῆς, συμμύειν δὲ τὸ στόμα τῶν γλωττῶν, ὃ πρὸς τὴν διακτηρίαν εἶναι χρήσιμον. ἐπεὶ δὲ εἰς τὴν πλάσιν μετέβησαν, καὶ ἡ τομὴ μετεκινήθη· τέμνουσι γὰρ δὴ νῦν τοῦ Σκιρροφοριῶνος καὶ Ἑκατομβαιῶνος ὥσπερ πρὸ τροπῶν μικρὸν ἢ ὑπὸ τροπάς. γίνεσθαι δέ φασι τρίενόν τε χρήσιμον καὶ καταυλήσεως βραχείας δεῖσθαι καὶ κατασπάσματα τὰς γλώττας ἴσχειν· τοῦτο δὲ ἀναγκαῖον τοῖς μετὰ πλάσματος αὐλοῦσι. τοῦ μὲν οὖν ζευγίτου ταύτας εἶναι τὰς ὥρας τῆς τομῆς.

Until the time of Antigenidas, before which men played the *aulos* in the simple style, they say that the proper season for cutting the reeds was the month Boedromion (September-October), about the rising of Arcturus. Although reeds when cut do not become fit for use for many years after and need a great deal of preliminary playing upon, the opening of the reed-tongues is well closed, which is a good thing for the purpose of accompaniment. But when a shift was made to the more elaborate style of playing, the time of cutting the reeds was also altered; in our own time they cut them in the months Skirrophorion (June-July) or Hekatombaion (July-August), about the solstice or a little earlier. They say that the reed becomes fit for use in only three years and only needs a little preliminary playing upon, and that the reed mouthpiece has ample vibration, which is essential for those who play in the elaborate style.

This Antigenidas was a famous Theban *aulētēs* who flourished in the first half of the fourth century BCE,[34] and the new "elaborate style" he introduced involved considerable modification of pitch or tone requiring a stronger reed than was previously used.[35] Antigenidas was not the only Boiotian to innovate in flute design, however. His fellow Theban Pronomos, who flourished earlier, in the latter half of the fifth century BCE, and became the most famous *aulētēs* of antiquity, also invented a hybrid *aulos* capable of playing multiple modes,[36] while yet another Theban, Diodoros, invented an *aulos* with many more fingerholes than had previously been the case.[37] These men designed their own instruments; however, they had to rely on the expertise of local *aulopoioi* to manufacture them.[38] *Aulos* production seems to have been something of a boutique industry, with renowned craftsmen often manufacturing instruments to order for high-powered customers.[39] While it may have taken years to produce such instruments, they could apparently have fetched a high price: the famous fourth-century BCE Theban *aulētēs* Ismenias is said to have paid 42,000 drachmas for a single *aulos* — undoubtedly an exaggeration, but a telling one.[40] Thus, the Thebans were so able to innovate in *aulos* playing because of their proximity to the Kopais region and its *aulos* industry;[41] in return, Pronomos, Antigenidas, Diodoros, and other famous musicians brought the *auloi* of Lake Kopais international renown.[42]

The production of the famed Kopaic *auloi* was affected by more than shifts in musical taste, however. Theophrastos, who notes that the reed in particular was sensitive to a lack of rainfall,[43] elaborates:[44]

Περὶ δὲ τοῦ αὐλητικοῦ τὸ μὲν φύεσθαι δι᾽ ἐννεατηρίδος, ὥσπερ τινές φασι, καὶ ταύτην εἶναι τὴν τάξιν οὐκ ἀληθές, ἀλλὰ τὸ μὲν ὅλον αὐξηθείσης γίνεται τῆς λίμνης· ὅτι δὲ τοῦτ᾽ ἐδόκει συμβαίνειν ἐν τοῖς πρότερον χρόνοις μάλιστα δι᾽ ἐννεατηρίδος, καὶ τὴν γένεσιν τοῦ καλάμου ταύτην ἐποίουν τὸ συμβεβηκὸς ὡς τάξιν λαμβάνοντες. γίνεται δὲ ὅταν ἐπομβρίας γενομένης ἐμμένῃ τὸ ὕδωρ δύ᾽ ἔτη τοὐλάχιστον, ἂν δὲ πλείω καὶ καλλίων· τούτου δὲ μάλιστα μνημονεύουσι γεγονότος τῶν ὕστερον χρόνων ὅτε συνέβη τὰ περὶ Χαιρώνειαν· πρὸ τούτων γὰρ ἔφασαν ἔτη πλείω βαθυνθῆναι τὴν λίμνην· μετὰ δὲ ταῦτα ὕστερον, ὡς ὁ λοιμὸς/ λιμός ἐγένετο σφοδρός, πλησθῆναι μὲν αὐτήν, οὐ μείναντος δὲ τοῦ ὕδατος ἀλλ᾽ ἐκλιπόντος χειμῶνος οὐ γενέσθαι τὸν κάλαμον· φασὶ γὰρ καὶ δοκεῖ βαθυνομένης τῆς λίμνης αὐξάνεσθαι τὸν κάλαμον εἰς μῆκος, μείναντα δὲ τὸν ἐπιόντα ἐνιαυτὸν ἁδρύνεσθαι· καὶ γίνεσθαι τὸν μὲν ἁδρυθέντα ζευγίτην, ᾧ δ᾽ ἂν μὴ συμπαραμείνῃ τὸ ὕδωρ βομβυκίαν.

As to the reed used for *auloi*, it is not true, as some say, that it only grows once in nine years and that this is its regular rule of growth; it grows in general whenever the lake is full. But because in former days this was supposed to happen generally once in nine years, they believed the growth of the reed corresponded, taking what was really an accident to be a regular principle. As a matter of fact, it grows whenever after a rainy season the water remains in the lake for at least two years, and it is finer if the water remains longer. This is especially remembered to have happened recently at the time of the Battle of Chaironeia (338 BCE). Before that event, they told me that the lake was for several years deep, and that afterwards, when there was a severe famine/plague,[45] it filled up; however, as the water did not remain but disappeared in winter, the reed did not grow. They say, apparently with good reason, that when the lake is deep the reed increases in height, and, persisting for the next year, matures its growth, and that the reed which thus matures is suitable for making a mouthpiece, while that produced when the water has not remained is suitable only for making the body of the *aulos*.

While such local traditions might have changed with fluctuations in the climate,[46] Repapis did in fact find that precipitation fluctuated on an average cycle of almost nine years in twentieth-century rainfall data from Haliartos, suggesting that there may have been some merit to the tradition recorded by Theophrastos.[47]

From Theophrastos' extensive commentary we can thus reconstruct a history of the Kopaic *aulos*-making industry in the Classical and Hellenistic periods. When the *katavothres* were plugged and/or there was sufficient rainfall to fill the basin for at least two years, the reeds would grow enough to produce suitable mouthpieces; in years when the lake did not remain full perennially, the reeds were harvested instead to make the bodies of the *auloi*.[48] Until the early fourth century BCE, the cutting of the reeds occurred in September-October, and they then had to be treated for many years before they would be suitable for playing. After Antigenidas introduced the elaborate style sometime in the early fourth century BCE, demand for the new type of *aulos* necessary to perform it spread throughout the Greek world, and the local industry adjusted. By the late fourth century BCE, reeds were harvested instead between June and August and only needed to be treated for three years. The long periods of time individuals would have had to wait both to harvest and to prepare these reeds would have imbued locals' lives with a long-term rhythm. Indeed, the average person might only have experienced a handful of mouthpiece reed harvests in a lifetime, and *aulopoioi* must have been acutely aware of the environmental conditions needed to produce a sufficient quantity of their highly sought-after product. As Theophrastos notes, *aulos* production flourished in the years before 338 BCE, when the lake's persistence perhaps allowed for harvests over successive years. The timing of this stretch appears to have been very convenient, as the rapid expansion of Greek colonization in the wake of Alexander's conquests no doubt produced an increase in the demand for this specialized product.[49]

Pliny noted that among *aulētai*, "reeds that had been washed by the waters of Kephissos itself were rated as immeasurably superior" (*inmensum quantum praelatis quas ipse Cephisus abluisset*).[50] As new generations of artists emerged and musical tastes shifted in the agonistic international settings in which they performed, Boiotian *aulētai* would in turn have been driven to innovate, returning once again to the *aulopoioi* of the Kopaic basin with new designs. According to Pausanias, when Epameinondas oversaw the construction of Messene in 369 BCE, he had his men work to the tunes of Pronomos (the man himself was almost certainly dead by then), played on Boiotian *auloi* in competition with those of a famous Archaic Argive *aulētēs*, Sakadas, played on corresponding instruments of Argive manufacture.[51] This distinctly local Boiotian musical tradition was thus constantly being reworked vis-à-vis other such traditions within Greece, made possible by the distinct ecology of the Kopais region and the local artisanal traditions it produced.[52]

## Flooding, Drainage, and Agriculture

It was not just the local *aulos*-makers whose relationship with Lake Kopais was dominated by its fluctuations, however; hydrological oscillations had a major impact on even basic aspects of everyday life in the basin. As Strabo writes:[53]

ἐγχωσθέντων δὲ κατὰ βάθους τῶν πόρων αὔξεσθαι τὰς λίμνας συμβαίνει μέχρι τῶν οἰκουμένων τόπων ὥστε καὶ πόλεις καταπίνεσθαι καὶ χώρας, ἀνοιχθέντων δὲ τῶν αὐτῶν ἢ ἄλλων ἀνακαλύπτεσθαι, καὶ τοὺς αὐτοὺς τόπους ποτὲ μὲν πλεῖσθαι ποτὲ δὲ πεζεύεσθαι, καὶ τὰς αὐτὰς πόλεις ποτὲ μὲν ἐπὶ τῇ λίμνῃ ποτὲ δὲ ἄπωθεν κεῖσθαι.

When the channels in the depths of the earth are stopped up, the waters of the lake expand as far as inhabited areas, so that they swallow up both cities and their territories; when the same channels or others are opened up, these cities and districts are uncovered. The same regions at one time are traversed in boats and at another on foot, and the same cities at one time are situated on the lake and at another far from it.

Dodwell echoes this, noting that in the early nineteenth century there were distinct summer and winter roads around the lake, and that travel on foot between communities in the basin was generally much quicker in summer, when the waters normally receded.[54] When the lake was full, on the other hand, it was easier simply to sail around it, as Pausanias did in his day.[55]

As Strabo mentions, inundation was a constant problem in the basin, and tales of flooding feature prominently in the local histories of the Kopaic *poleis*. Krates' drainage project of the later 330s or 320s BCE apparently exposed the remains of several communities that had been completely inundated for some time.[56] Since in mythology the Kopais region had been home at one point or another to many groups that ultimately moved southward,[57] Krates' project apparently prompted contemporary debate over their identity,[58] with some claiming that the original site of Orchomenos was uncovered, others the original settlements of Athens and Eleusis founded by the first Athenian king, Kekrops.[59] Similarly, Strabo notes that at some point prior to the late fourth century BCE, the lake had apparently risen to such an extent that the entire *polis* of Kopai (appropriately, "Oars") was threatened with submersion, only for one of the *katavothres* to open and allow the waters to recede.[60] Perversely, the relative scarcity of local springs meant that in dry years these communities were also at greater risk of drought than most:[61] a history of Orchomenos written by a certain Hellenistic author named Kallippos of Corinth asserted that the early *polis* of Aspledon on the northern shore of the basin was abandoned by its inhabitants because of a water shortage.[62] It is unsurprising, then, that some of the most important cults of the Kopaic basin – the sanctuaries of Ptoios near Akraiphia; of Trophonios at Lebadeia; and of Apollo at Telphousa, Tegyra, and Thourion – were centred on springs and hydromancy.[63]

Given its hydrological fickleness, it is no surprise that the ancient inhabitants of the Kopaic basin attempted to control its waters as much as possible. In the late Bronze Age, the inhabitants famously constructed dikes and canals that diverted water towards raised canals skirting the basin to the north and south, allowing for drainage through the largest *katavothres* situated in its northeast.[64] This both freed up much of the lakebed to be cultivated and allowed for controlled irrigation.[65] Perhaps the single most remarkable project aimed at controlling the basin's hydrology was, however, the so-called Kefalari tunnel, a nearly two-kilometre-long channel carved through the living rock that was apparently intended to serve as an artificial *katavothra*; this project, most likely begun by the Mycenaean inhabitants of the basin but never completed, consisted of vertical shafts, sunk into the mountains to the northeast of the basin, that were to be joined into a gently sloping drainage channel emptying into the Euboian Gulf near Larymna.[66]

These drainage works were abandoned ca. 1200 BCE, and would quickly have become unusable on account of the accumulation of sediment in the *katavothres*.[67] Nonetheless, traces of the works persisted, and with them the memory of this massive hydrological system.[68] Just as the remains of abandoned settlements were apparently discovered after Lake Kopais was fully drained by Krates, a reference in the third century BCE Pseudo-Aristotelian work *On Marvellous Things Heard* suggests that the unfinished remnants of the Kefalari tunnel were also rediscovered by the early Hellenistic period.[69] The entry states:[70]

Ἐν τῇ τῶν Ὀρχομενίων πόλει τῇ ἐν Βοιωτοῖς φανῆναί φασιν ἀλώπεκα, ἣν κυνὸς διώκοντος εἰσδῦναι εἴς τινα ὑπόνομον, καὶ τὸν κύνα συνεισδῦναι αὐτῇ, καὶ ὑλακτοῦντα ἦχον μέγαν ποιεῖν ὡσανεὶ εὐρυχωρίας τινὸς ὑπαρχούσης αὐτῷ· τοὺς δὲ κυνηγέτας ἔννοιαν λαβόντας δαιμονίαν, ἀναρρήξαντας τὴν εἴσδυσιν συνῶσαι καὶ αὐτούς· ἰδόντας δὲ διά τινων ὀπῶν εἰσερχόμενον ἔσω τὸ φῶς, εὐσυνόπτως τὰ λοιπὰ θεάσασθαι, καὶ ἐλθόντας ἀπαγγεῖλαι τοῖς ἄρχουσιν.

In the city of Orchomenos in Boiotia, they say that a fox was seen which, when pursued by a dog, dived into an underground passage, and that the dog dived in after it and made a loud noise by barking, as if it were in a wide-open space. The hunters, assuming some supernatural agency, broke down the entrance and forced their way in as well. Seeing that light was coming in through some openings, they had a complete view of the remains, and went and reported it to the magistrates.

The entrance to the Kefalari tunnel was located in the northeast of the basin, and not in the territory of Orchomenos in the west, but the author may have been unfamiliar with the geography of the area and simply mentioned this *polis* in order to situate the anecdote in the Kopaic basin. As for the dikes and channels whose remnants remained visible throughout antiquity, Diodorus and Pausanias relate that, according to the Thebans, both their construction and destruction could be attributed to their own hometown hero, Herakles. In their narrative, the Minyans of Orchomenos had subjugated Thebes and employed Herakles to build the works; later, however, the hero organized Theban resistance to the Minyans, sacked Orchomenos, and blocked up the *katavothres* in order to flood the basin and permanently destroy Orchomenian power.[71] It is thus appropriate that Herakles was worshipped in a temple beside the source of the Melas River.[72]

Once the drainage works were abandoned at the end of the Bronze Age, there seems to have been little effort to drain the Kopaic basin again until the late fourth century BCE, when, as was mentioned at the beginning of this chapter, Krates of Chalkis was sent by Alexander the Great for this purpose.[73] This new effort to "reclaim" agricultural land was likely driven by demographic pressure, since Boiotia had reached a population in the fourth century BCE that would not be surpassed until the nineteenth century.[74] Among the many ancient dikes and channels that have been identified in the basin is one large canal running through its centre that has been dated roughly to the Classical period and consequently associated with Krates' project.[75] Unlike the Mycenaean works, which were intended to drain most of the basin, this canal would never have allowed for total drainage in years of average or above-average rainfall, and thus seems to have been intended simply to mitigate flooding and reclaim some portions of the lakebed for agriculture.[76]

As Strabo notes, however, infighting among Boiotian *poleis* ultimately prevented the completion of Krates' project. As such, it must often have fallen to individual *poleis* and even households to manage the basin's hydrology with a patchwork of small-scale landscape modifications. A fragmentary inscription, probably of the third century BCE, listing plots of land in the territory of Orchomenos refers to a dam and several ditches,[77] while at the other end of the basin Akraiphia relied on a large dike, originally Mycenaean in date but maintained over time, to cultivate the land of what otherwise became a bay when the lake was full.[78] Such local measures operating in tandem with the large but crude central canal probably mitigated the risk of perilacustrine communities suffering flooding for much of the Hellenistic period; without a concerted effort to keep the *katavothres* clear, however, they would have gradually become blocked again and flooding would have recurred. This is exactly what happened by the early Imperial period, when, as several inscriptions attest, the rising waters of the lake again became a problem for the Kopaic *poleis*.[79]

Thus, the agriculture of the Kopaic basin, which formed the foundation of its *polis* economies, was conditioned by the duality of its environmental conditions. On the one hand, the annual inundation of the basin created exceptionally fertile soils, allowing for the cultivation of a rich variety of crops;[80] Orchomenos, for instance, prominently featured a grain or ear of wheat on its coinage,[81] and it was also known for its sweet melons (σίκυοι πέπονες).[82] On the other hand, the frequent fluctuations of the lake's shoreline always threatened cultivated land. Under normal climatic conditions in the fourth century BCE, as Theophrastos' passage on reed production quoted earlier notes, the lake normally remained perennially full only one year in nine, allowing for several years of widespread cultivation around the lake's margins before a major flooding event.[83] The fertile lakebed exposed for long stretches of time during periods of drought thus presented some compensation for the loss of the lake's rich aquatic resources.[84]

Early modern travellers note that the locals farmed right up to the edge of the water and were quick to cultivate any land that emerged from the receding lake,[85] and the situation was likely similar in antiquity – a fragment of writings from the fourth century BCE by the comedian Antiphanes has a Boiotian character mention that he "farms by the lake" (παρὰ λίμνην γεωργῶν).[86] The above-mentioned Hellenistic decree listing plots of land in the territory of Orchomenos includes prices for each,[87] suggesting that land exposed by the recession of the water was claimed and offered for lease on a short-term basis by perilacustrine *poleis*.[88] That the cultivation of such "black earth" could have been highly fruitful is indicated by Henri Belle's observation in the nineteenth century that "in two months the corn stalks grow there thick as arms; in three months tobacco gives a harvest there double in weight and superior in quality."[89] As such, it is no surprise that neighbouring communities vied for parts of the lakebed; for instance, a third-century rupestral inscription on a promontory near the lake records that the Boiotian League had to arbitrate a border dispute between Kopai and Akraiphia.[90] Such conflicts were no doubt exacerbated by the fact that the water would have drained more quickly from the territories of some *poleis* than from others.[91]

The consequence of the recession of Lake Kopais' waters was, however, that in subsequent years of heavy rainfall much agricultural land would inevitably have been lost again. If this happened around harvest time, the impact could have been disastrous, such as when, in 379 BCE, Haliartos apparently suffered "a great failure of crops and the encroachment of the lake" (τὴν μεγάλην ἀφορίαν καὶ τὴν ἐπίβασιν τῆς λίμνης);[92] when the basin remained full perennially for years on end, the flooding could also kill otherwise flood-resistant fruit trees.[93] And while, as Theophrastos notes, the lake when full acted as a heat sink, preventing freezing episodes that might have damaged or killed olive, vine, and fruit tree crops throughout Boiotia and even neighbouring Euboia,[94] when it was drained, the thick winter fogs that lingered in the basin could damage or kill these same crops.[95] As a result, the basin was not especially well suited to the cultivation of tree crops, making its plains, like those around Orchomenos, "level and treeless" (ὁμαλὸν… καὶ ἄδενδρον).[96]

## Pastoralism

As in other parts of the Greek world, pastoralism was another important element of life in the Kopaic basin. This region was set apart from much of the rest of Greece, however, in that it was capable of supporting herds of large livestock, notably cattle and horses. In addition to supplying the plentiful water necessary to raise such animals, the lake provided an abundance of hygrophilous plants that made for perfect fodder.[97] Theophrastos elaborates:

Ἐδώδιμα δ᾽ ἐστὶ τῶν ἐν τῇ λίμνῃ τάδε· ἡ μὲν σίδη καὶ αὐτὴ καὶ τὰ φύλλα τοῖς προβάτοις, ὁ δὲ βλαστὸς τοῖς ὑσίν, ὁ δὲ καρπὸς τοῖς ἀνθρώποις. τοῦ δὲ φλεὼ καὶ τῆς τύφης καὶ τοῦ βουτόμου τὸ πρὸς ταῖς ῥίζαις ἁπαλόν, ὃ μάλιστα ἐσθίει τὰ παιδία. ῥίζα δ᾽ ἐδώδιμος ἡ τοῦ φλεὼ μόνη τοῖς βοσκήμασιν.

Of the plants of the lake, the edible parts are as follows: of the water lily, both the flower and the leaves are good for sheep, the young shoots for pigs, and the fruit for people. Of cat's tail grass, galingale, and sedge, the part next to the roots is tender, and is mostly eaten by children. The root of cat's tail grass is the only part which is edible by cattle.

While abundant standing water was, as we have seen above and will see further below, often the cause of many problems for those living nearby, it was thus of great benefit to livestock; indeed, Artemidoros in his treatise on interpreting dreams declared that "swamps are beneficial to shepherds alone" (Ἕλη ποιμέσι μόνοις συμφέρει).[98] Pastoralism was consequently so prevalent in the Kopaic basin that it was imprinted on its toponymy: Theophrastos records that the lakeshore below Orchomenos was called by locals either

Hippia or Boedria, from the words *hippos*, "horse," and *bous*, "cow," respectively; a small river feeding the basin from the south was called Probatia, from *probaton*, "sheep";[99] and an imperial inscription of Hyettos in the north refers to a locale in its territory called Hippobotos ("Horse-grazed").[100]

The wealthier inhabitants of the Kopais region appear to have raised exceptionally large numbers of livestock by ancient Greek standards, as Hellenistic inscriptions discussing the granting of *epinomia*, or free pasturage rights, suggest.[101] One such inscription from Orchomenos dating to ca. 230–210 BCE records that the *polis* repaid a debt owed to a certain Euboulos, a Phokian, in part by granting him the right to graze 220 cattle or horses and a thousand sheep or goats on public pasturage for four years.[102] Another inscription from Kopai dating to the early second century BCE also refers to the repayment of debts to two women through the granting of *epinomia* for 200 head of livestock.[103] Finally, a third-century inscription from Akraiphia records the repayment of a debt to an Akraiphian citizen through the granting of *epinomia* for 50 head of livestock.[104] These documents indicate that Kopaic cities closely regulated the use of public pasturage. In the case of Orchomenos, an official known as a *nomōnas* was charged with tracking livestock grazing on public land according to their brands and collecting the requisite taxes, which must have been an important source of revenue for the perilacustrine *poleis*.[105]

The plain around Orchomenos, which Pindar calls the "seat of fine horses" (καλλίπωλον ἕδραν)[106] and the supposed epitaph on Hesiod's tomb in that city the "land of the horse-striking Minyans" (πληξίππων γῆ Μινυῶν),[107] was considered one of the best regions for raising horses in Greece south of Thessaly.[108] Orchomenos was a staunchly oligarchic *polis* in the Archaic and Classical periods, and, like other Greek aristocrats, wealthy Orchomenians considered horses to be emblematic of their power.[109] In Boiotian mythology, however, the abundance of their horses also made them a target. Pausanias records that one of the most celebrated episodes in Herakles' conflict with Orchomenos was when he stole and tied up the Minyans' chariot horses, for which he received the epithet Hippodetos ("Horse Binder");[110] Polyainos adds that Herakles specifically blocked up the *katavothres* and flooded the basin in order to render the Orchomenian cavalry useless.[111]

## Hunting and Fishing

The unusual ecology of the Kopaic basin also made it rich in wildlife,[112] and the exploitation of the lacustrine fauna played a central role in the culture and economy of local populations in the Hellenistic period. The marshy area around the lake made for ideal hunting grounds both for birds and small mammals. Among the former, quarry would have included the birds listed for sale by the Theban merchant visiting Athens in Aristophanes' *Acharnians*, including ducks, francolins, coots, sandpipers, and grebes.[113] These waterfowl were eaten as delicacies in the Greek world,[114] with the francolin particularly prized.[115] Such marsh birds would mostly have migrated to Greece in winter, making it the prime hunting season. Pliny notes that the best birding could be had when the lake was full and reeds had been able to grow for a full year or more.[116] Among the small mammals were those hunted particularly for their fur and skins, such as the foxes, moles, hedgehogs, cats, and martens also offered for sale by Aristophanes' Theban trader.[117] Larger game, like wild boar and deer, would mainly have been found in the mountains around the basin itself,[118] but Dodwell noted that when the reeds and other marsh plants of the lake were at their fullest, boar could be found rooting around the lakeshore as well.[119] It is notable that after Haliartos' territory was given by the Romans to Athens in 171 BCE, an association of Athenian hunters was established there, as a late second-century inscription attests;[120] this seems to have been a sort of hunting club, with members granted access to communally held lakefront property.[121]

The most famous animals of Lake Kopais were, however, its fish, more specifically its eels, those "asp-bodied eel goddesses of Boiotia" (αἱ τ' ἐχιδνοσώματοι Βοιωτίας ἐγχέλεις θεαί), as the fourth-century comic poet Euboulos called them.[122] According to ancient sources, Lake Kopais had a limited variety of fish, but its eels were exceptionally large and pleasant-tasting;[123] indeed, the gourmand Archestratos, writing in the mid-fourth century BCE, declared that in the entire Mediterranean only those from Rhegion in southern Italy were superior.[124] A famous late third- or early fourth-century list of prices for fish found near Akraiphia includes, after a long catalogue of imported marine species, a series of entries titled "of the lake" (λιμνήων).[125] These local fish, including pike, bream, and carp, were much cheaper than imported marine species,[126] and must have been consumed widely by the local population.[127] The notable exception is the famous eel, which ranks alongside the tuna as the most expensive species on the entire list.[128] This is undoubtedly a reflection of the demand for this delicacy outside of Boiotia, in particular at Athens. Eels were not just caught like other fish; as Aristotle describes, they were also kept by specialist "eel raisers" (ἐγχελυοτρόφοι) who maintained them in natural enclosures or special plastered tanks.[129] While such aquaculture required careful management, it would have both allowed these fish to grow to large sizes and ensured a steady supply of them; when they were ready for sale, Aristotle notes, they could then have been transported alive overland in portable tanks to regional markets.[130] Eel fishing thus must have been important in the economies of perilacustrine *poleis*, especially those of Akraiphia and Kopai, whose contiguous lakefront in the northeast of the basin was the best area for this activity.[131]

But beyond their economic value, the eels of Lake Kopais held cultural importance for the inhabitants of the basin as well. A fragment of the second-century historian Agatharchides of Knidos notes:[132]

τὰς ὑπερφυεῖς τῶν Κωπαίδων ἐγχέλεων ἱερείων τρόπον στεφανοῦντας καὶ κατευχομένους οὐλάς τ' ἐπιβάλλοντας θύειν τοῖς θεοῖς τοὺς Βοιωτούς. καὶ πρὸς τὸν ξένον τὸν διαποροῦντα τὸ τοῦ ἔθους παράδοξον καὶ πυνθανόμενον ἓν μόνον εἰδέναι φῆσαι τὸν Βοιωτὸν φάσκειν τε ὅτι δεῖ τηρεῖν τὰ προγονικὰ νόμιμα καὶ ὅτι μὴ καθήκει τοῖς ἄλλοις ὑπὲρ αὐτῶν ἀπολογίζεσθαι.

The Boiotians sacrifice to the gods the largest Kopaic eels, putting wreaths on them and sprinkling them, like sacrificial animals, with whole barley grains. To the foreigner puzzled by this odd behaviour and inquiring about it, the Boiotian says that he can think of only one thing to say, and declares that people need to maintain their ancestral customs and should feel no need to defend them to others.

This is notably the only known "ethnographic" anecdote from Agatharchides' work *On Affairs in Europe*,[133] and it is probable that this was based on the first-hand observation of the historian, who lived in Athens in the third quarter of the second century BCE.[134] As both a product and a literary trope, the Kopaic eel would have been well known to the grammarian Agatharchides and his educated kin; yet, the specific way in which the locals exploited these animals remained idiosyncratic. This nicely encapsulates the interplay between the local and the global in the Hellenistic period: Kopais and its natural products were increasingly interconnected with other regions of the broader Greek world at this time, but rather than supplanting distinctive local practices, this interaction in fact compelled the inhabitants of the basin to continue with their "ancestral customs" in the face of outside scrutiny.

## Malaria

One final aspect of life in the Kopais region is only hinted at in our ancient written evidence but must have played a large role in the lives of its inhabitants: malaria. This disease, associated in antiquity as it is today with shallow bodies of stagnant water that served as ideal breeding grounds for disease-transmitting mosquitoes,[135] was endemic in the basin up until quinine and DDT were introduced in the mid-twentieth century.[136] Symptoms of malaria include recurrent episodes of fever lasting three to six days as well as attendant side-effects, ranging from fatigue and nausea to stunted growth, renal failure, and brain damage.[137] Herakleides the Critic, a travel writer of the third century BCE, provides a list of characteristics associated with the inhabitants of Boiotian cities, and to Onchestos, on the eastern edge of the basin, he tellingly assigns fever (πυρετὸν).[138] Malaria's most insidious effects tend to be on the young, since it can induce miscarriage in pregnant women and serious health problems, such as impaired cognitive abilities or even death, in infants.[139] One of the most visible symptoms of chronic malaria is an enlargement of the spleen, especially in children, and this condition was so prevalent in the basin that in the nineteenth century its inhabitants were known as *bakaniarides* ("big-bellies").[140] In the late nineteenth century, Henri Belle paints a vivid picture of malaria's grip on the population:[141]

All around Lake Kopais fever ... decimates the population. Out of four children, three die of fever, and those who are left behind are miserable and sickly. One sees them warming their slender limbs in the sun, with their hollow eyes, leaden complexion, bloated bellies, and blue fingernails.

As with so many other aspects of the environment of the Kopaic basin, the impact of malaria in the Hellenistic period would have followed a seasonal cycle. Outbreaks would generally occur in summer and early autumn, when high temperatures would have created ideal breeding conditions for mosquitoes,[142] as the Hippocratic writers record.[143] In more recent history, the severity of malarial outbreaks generally fluctuated with precipitation levels; thus, dry spells tended to minimize the prevalence of malarial sickness in the basin.[144] Paradoxically, however, drainage projects could actually have exacerbated outbreaks, as the pooling of water in canals and ditches can create conditions even more favourable for mosquito breeding.[145] Thus, Krates' drainage efforts may not have brought much relief to local inhabitants afflicted by this disease.

Such cyclical malarial outbreaks may have prompted seasonal migration, as is attested in recent centuries for some of the villages in the Kopaic basin whose inhabitants were said to have moved away from the nearby lake every summer to avoid the disease.[146] Summer and early autumn was, however, a period of crucial economic activity, notably the harvesting, ploughing, and planting of crops, as well as the collection of reeds and other plants from the lakeshore; as such, malaria would have had a major impact on the economy of the Kopais region.[147] Indeed, early nineteenth-century studies found that in regions of Greece where malaria was endemic, on average at least half of the labourers were incapacitated for an average of six man-days during the May-June harvest;[148] following a countrywide effort to eradicate malaria in the 1940s, researchers observed increases in yield of well over 100 per cent in these regions.[149]

On a longer time scale, endemic malaria acts as a force of natural selection, favouring genetic mutations of the blood that protect against malaria, including thalassaemia and sickle-cell disease.[150] The single most effective genetic resistance to malaria known is the presence of Hemoglobin S, which causes sickle-cell disease.[151] When researchers began studying genetic variation within Greece in the 1950s and 1960s, they found very high frequencies of sickle-cell disease, thalassaemia, and Glucose-6-phosphate dehydrogenase deficiency – all relatively rare mutations[152] – among the population of the Kopaic basin.[153] In the case of Hemoglobin S, research suggests that it would only have taken about 40–50 generations, or about 1,000–1,200 years, for high rates to have emerged among a sedentary human population as a result of selective pressure.[154] Research has now established that malaria spread into Greece by the second millennium BCE,[155] and as such many of the inhabitants of the Kopais region would undoubtedly have developed such mutations already by the Hellenistic period. Unfortunately, such genetic mutations often also produce anaemia, which in turn causes chronic fatigue and other health problems; as a result, the populations of endemic regions have been found to have life expectancies about half that of populations of non-endemic regions.[156] Thus, ultimately the environment of the Kopaic basin even left an imprint on the very bodies of its inhabitants.

## Conclusion

To outsiders, the inhabitants of the Kopaic basin were Boiotians, like the residents of the Teneric basin to its east. The citizens of many of the perilacustrine *poleis*, chief among them the Orchomenians, preferred, however, to label themselves the "guardians of the ancient-born Minyans" (παλαιγόνων Μινυᾶν ἐπίσκοποι),[157] a group distinct from the *Boiōtoi* in the Catalogue of Ships.[158] Despite the remarkable resilience of the Boiotian League in the Hellenistic period, Orchomenos continued to emphasize the distinct Minyan identity of the inhabitants of the basin through a rich network of mythological associations.[159] As we have seen, these associations were inextricably linked with the unique ecology of the Kopais region.

Over time, the groups that moved through and settled in the Kopais region left their mark on its landscape, so that the basin itself became a sort of palimpsest of past activity, from the Bronze Age dikes and canals that crisscrossed its surface to the rupestral arbitration inscriptions that marked the resolution of prior border disputes. As noted at the beginning of this chapter, perhaps the most famous figure to have altered the Kopaic landscape was Alexander the Great, who encountered it both in 338 BCE, when he fought in the Battle of Chaironeia, and again in 335 BCE, when campaigning against

Thebes. The Macedonian king viewed its environment as both a problem to be solved and an opportunity to be exploited: the flooding around this time would have compromised the major route connecting northern and southern Greece, potentially hindering any military response to Greek uprisings while he campaigned in the East,[160] but it also allowed him to emulate his marsh-draining ancestors, both earlier Argead monarchs and Herakles.[161] He consequently deployed Krates of Chalkis to drain the basin.

The most vivid examples of historic events leaving a mark on the landscape of the Kopais region in the Hellenistic period come, however, not from waterworks, but from the episodes of mass violence that lent Boiotia the moniker "the dancing floor of war" (πολέμου ὀρχήστραν).[162] The basin, a crucial choke point for movement in Greece, was the site of numerous battles the memories of which were indelibly imprinted on local communities, as Giroux explores in her contribution to this volume. The most infamous was the confrontation between Macedonian and Greek forces that occurred at Chaironeia in 338 BCE. But as troops frequently traversed this region in the course of subsequent centuries, the basin continued to be a site of resistance to foreign intervention. Livy narrates how in 196 BCE, Roman soldiers on leave began to disappear while passing through this area; after T. Quinctius Flamininus sent agents to investigate the matter, they discovered that the inhabitants of the Kopaic *poleis* had made something of an industry of robbing and murdering itinerant Roman troops. He writes:[163]

plurimae caedes circa Copaidem paludem inventae; ibi ex limo eruta extractaque ex stagno cadavera saxis aut amphoris, ut pondere traherentur in profundum, adnexa; multa facinora Acraephiae et Coroneae facta inveniebantur.

Most of the murders, it was found, had been committed around the Kopaic marsh. There, bodies were dug out of the muck and drawn from the swamp, with stones or amphoras fastened to them so that the weight might drag them into the depths. Many other crimes were found to have been committed at Akraiphia and Koroneia.

Indeed, two distinctively mid-Republican Roman helmets, very rarely found elsewhere in Greece, were recovered from the Kopaic basin, one near Akraiphia.[164] In 86 BCE, a little over a century after Flamininus launched his inquiry, Sulla's forces then famously met those of Mithridates VI in battle near Chaironeia. Plutarch, a Chaironeian, writes of the area between his hometown and Orchomenos:[165]

καὶ κατέπλησαν ἀποθνήσκοντες αἵματος τὰ ἕλη καὶ νεκρῶν τὴν λίμνην, ὥστε μέχρι νῦν πολλὰ βαρβαρικὰ τόξα καὶ κράνη καὶ θωράκων σπάσματα σιδηρῶν καὶ μαχαίρας ἐμβεβαπτισμένας τοῖς τέλμασιν εὑρίσκεσθαι, σχεδὸν ἐτῶν διακοσίων ἀπὸ τῆς μάχης ἐκείνης διαγεγονότων.

The dying filled the marshes with their blood and the lake with their bodies, so that even to this day many barbarian bows, helmets, fragments of iron breastplates, and swords are found embedded in the mud, although almost two hundred years have passed since this battle.

Over time, such traces of violence were apparently exposed by the fluctuations of the shoreline. In this way, the history of Greece was literally imprinted on the shifting landscape of Kopais.

But as foreign kings and soldiers passed through and left such marks on the Kopaic basin in the Hellenistic period, its inhabitants persisted in their local traditions, regulated as they always had been by the rhythms of life around the lake. With the arrival of the rainy season in the autumn, the Kephissos and Melas Rivers and the other surrounding tributaries that fed the basin would swell and begin to fill it, with its fertile plains growing marshier until the distinct pools on the valley floor merged into a lake. In anticipation of this inundation, the perilacustrine communities would have done their best to shore up dikes and clear out canals; after sowing their crops, those nearer the shore would have watched anxiously in the hope that their arable land would not be swallowed up. In the winter, a full lake would have allowed the reeds and other vegetation for which the region was famous to grow, and the water would also have acted as a heat sink, mitigating freezing episodes. This was the prime season for fishing, especially for eels, and fowling, as migratory birds returned to the lake.[166] The locals would reach the best spots for these activities by boat, paddling around the floating islands that sometimes formed as the water rose. In this same season, smaller livestock would have been grazed among the lush vegetation of the lakeshore; perhaps, as Pliny the Younger himself once witnessed on a lake in Italy, some of these animals might occasionally have wandered onto the floating islands and drifted around the lake as well.[167] As the weather warmed and the cereal harvest approached with the coming of spring, farmers would then have hoped for limited rain to prevent the flooding that could kill their crops. If all went well they could expect a good harvest from the basin's rich soils, and if they were lucky they might even have been able to sow fast-growing spring cereals on land exposed by the lake as it began to shrink in spring or early summer, yielding a second harvest. As the rising heat lowered the water level, the vegetation around the lakeshore would also have become easier to both graze and collect. The height of the summer was marked by the reed harvest, provided the lake had been sufficiently full over the prior months. Late summer and early autumn was also, however, the worst time for malarial outbreaks, and shepherds and many other locals who did not have to remain must have withdrawn at that time from the water, if possible, to avoid infection. For those who stayed, malarial outbreaks would have been a fact of life.

Just as Braudel in the quotation that opened this chapter appealed to "a history of constant repetition, ever-recurring cycles" in his effort to write a history *of* the Mediterranean rather than simply history *in* the Mediterranean,[168] the local identity of the Kopais region cannot be understood without examining cyclical human-environment interactions in detail. But while Braudel viewed such quotidian history as the domain of the *longue durée*, largely remote from the *histoire événementielle* of the Mediterranean,[169] Appadurai's conception of globalization as a localizing process, emerging through the interplay of impulses moving both from the bottom up and the top down,[170] allows us to understand how such recurring cycles formed local identities, which, through network exchange, in turn produced the "globalizing" Hellenistic world.[171] The lived experience of the inhabitants of the Kopaic *poleis* was defined by the hydrology of the basin, which in turn determined the rhythms of the flora and fauna that populated it; but how those individuals interacted with and thought about their local environment was constantly influencing and being influenced by their connections with other local communities throughout the Greek world. As Theophrastos perceptively notes, climatic fluctuations had a major impact on the quantity and quality of reeds used to produce the *aulos* in the basin. Similarly important to the local *aulopoioi*, however, was their relationship with the famed *aulētai* of neighbouring Thebes; many of these performers were musical innovators, and their novel designs for *auloi* influenced musical trends internationally, in turn driving demand for such instruments produced in the Kopaic basin. The successive generations of musicians who turned to the Kopaic *aulopoioi* to produce redesigned instruments thus set trends internationally and prompted changes in local craft traditions. Similarly, in the passage of Agatharchides of Knidos quoted above, the historian notes that the Boiotians declared the sacrifice of the largest eels fished from Lake Kopais to be one of their "ancestral customs" (τὰ προγονικὰ νόμιμα), a uniquely local practice. And yet, the value, both economic and cultural, of these animals was elevated by their international fame. Agatharchides, the Knidian who had worked in the library of Alexandria most of his life, was undoubtedly interested in these fish because of their literary prominence, above all in Attic comedy. But when he investigated this familiar element of the Kopaic environment further, he found the way in which the locals handled them to be entirely alien. It is hard to think of a more perfect example of what it meant to preserve local identity in the Hellenistic world.

## NOTES

1 Strabo 9.2.18.
2 On the modern efforts to drain completely the Kopaic basin, see Idol 2018.
3 Grove and Rackham 2001: 323–4.
4 Argoud 1987: 31; Rackham 1983: 315.
5 Philippson and Kirsten 1952: 476.
6 For a good overview of this system, see Farinetti 2008: 115–21, 127.
7 Rackham 1983: 337.
8 Farinetti 2008: Fig. 1.
9 Farinetti 2008: 121.
10 Rackham 1983: 329.
11 Plut. *Sull.* 20.3.
12 Theophrastos indicates that he personally recorded his description at *Hist. pl.* 4.12.2.
13 Rackham 1983: 329.
14 Theophr. *Hist. pl.* 4.10.1.
15 Theophr. *Hist. pl.* 4.11.8
16 Theophr. *Hist. pl.* 4.11.1.
17 Theophr. *Hist. pl.* 4.10.2, 13.4. Rackham 1983: 314.
18 Theophr. *Hist. pl.* 4.11.1.
19 *CID* II 56, ll. 10–14. Cf. Hdt. 1.179.1–2, Thuc. 2.76.1.
20 Ar. *Ach.* 874.
21 Theophr. *Hist. pl.* 4.10.6.
22 Theophr. *Hist. pl.* 4.10.4, 7.
23 Theophr. *Hist. pl.* 9.13.1. Cf. Dioskorides 3.148. The fruit of this plant was still sold as food in the vicinity of Lake Kopais in the nineteenth century (Rackham 1983: 338). For medical practice and healing cults in the vicinity of Chaironeia, see Giroux in this volume.
24 Paus. 9.41.7. Iris perfume: Theophr. *Hist. pl.* 9.7.3, 9.9.2. Rose perfume: Theophr. *Hist. pl.* 6.8.2. White lily perfume: Theophr. *Hist. pl.* 3.13.6, 3.18.11. Narcissus perfume: Paus. 9.41.7. For perfume making in general, see Reger 2005. Cf. Beck 2020: 81.
25 Bélis and Péché 1996: 12–18.
26 Ath. 4.184d–e.
27 Dio Chrys. *Or.* 7.120–1.
28 Demand 1978: 86–9; Roesch 1989; Landels 1998: 182–4; Wilson 2010: 188–91.

29  Theophr. *Hist. pl.* 4.11.8–9.

30  Plin. *HN* 16.66.172; Plut. *Sull.* 20.4. Wilson 2010: 189.

31  Roesch 1989: 207; Wilson 2010: 190–1.

32  Pind. *Pyth.* 12.25–7. Cf. Pind. F 70.

33  Theophr. *Hist. pl.* 4.11.4–5.

34  Roesch 1989: 209–10; West 1992: 367; Anderson 1994: 126–34; Bélis and Péché 1996: 17.

35  Landels 1998: 29.

36  Paus. 9.12.5–6. Roesch 1989: 208–9; Wilson 2010.

37  Pollux 4.80. Roesch 1989: 207; cf. Mathiesen 1999: 183, n. 54.

38  Bélis 1998.

39  Bélis 1998: 781–4.

40  Luc. *Adv. Indoctum* 5. Bélis 1998: 780–1.

41  Cf. Demand 1978: 87.

42  An Attic red-figure vase of ca. 400 BCE depicting Pronomos playing his *aulos* amid a theatrical troupe found in Puglia (the appropriately named "Pronomos Vase") suggests that he was a major international celebrity of his day (Wilson 2007: 142, n. 6). Cf. *IG* II² 8883, a funerary epigram from Phaleron for another Theban *aulētēs*, Potamon, whom "Greece awarded first prize in the art of playing the *auloi*" (Ἑλλὰς μὲν πρωτεῖα τέχνης αὐλῶν ἀπένειμεν).

43  Theophr. *Hist. pl.* 4.10.7.

44  Theophr. *Hist. pl.* 4.11.2–3.

45  The manuscript tradition differs on whether this word should be read as λοιμός or λιμός (Amigues 1988: xliii–xliv).

46  Wheler in the seventeenth century records a similar local belief, that neighbouring Lake Hylikē would dry up completely "every thirtieth or one and thirtieth Year" (Wheler 1682: 469).

47  Repapis 1989.

48  Cf. Mathiesen 1999: 182–3.

49  Cf. Roesch 1989: 204–5.

50  Plin. *HN* 16.66.172.

51  Paus. 4.27.7. For the significance of this episode, see Wilson 2010: 194–6; Gartland 2016b: 86–8.

52  Cf. Beck 2020: 96–7, 103–6.

53  Strabo 9.2.16.

54  Dodwell 1819, vol. 1: 235.

55  Paus. 9.24.1. Rackham 1983: 337.

56  Cf. Hope Simpson and Hagel 2006: 204–5.

57  Kowalzig 2007: 358–9.

58  Strabo 9.2.18.

59  For the valences of these differing identifications, see Kowalzig 2007: 388–9.

60  Strabo 9.2.18.

61  Corvisier 1985: 14.

62  Kallippos of Corinth (*BNJ* 385) F 2.

63  Schachter 1967; Kowalzig 2007: 375–6.

64  For the basic mechanics, see Argoud 1987: 32–3; Farinetti 2008: 123.

65  Lauffer 1986: 131–47; Knauss 1995; Hope Simpson and Hagel 2006: 187–209.

66  Argoud 1987: 33–4; Knauss 1990: 113–24, 243–79; Knauss 1995; Chatelain
    2001: 93–7. Hope Simpson and Hagel's doubts about assigning this project to
    the late Bronze Age (Hope Simpson and Hagel 2006: 204) based on the fact
    that no ancient canal leading to its entrance is visible can be countered by the
    explanation that no such canal would have been constructed before the project
    was finished in order to prevent the shaft flooding prematurely.

67  Knauss 1984: 182; Chatelain 2001: 96, n. 51.

68  Knauss 1984: 233.

69  Haussoullier 1894. For the date of this work, see Flashar and Klein 1972: 39–50.

70  Arist. *[Mir. ausc.]* 99.838b4–12.

71  Diod. Sic. 4.10.2–5, 18.7; Paus. 9.38.7–8; Polyaenus *Strat.* 1.3.5. Cf. Eur. *Heracl.*
    48, 220. On the Theban myths related to the Minyans, see Giroux forthcoming.

72  Paus. 9.38.6.

73  Strabo 9.2.18. While Mackil suggests that this was an initiative of the Boiotian
    League (2013: 306), it seems far more likely that Alexander initiated this effort,
    as Strabo suggests (Gartland 2016a: 157–9).

74  Farinetti 2008: 123. Even assuming a conservative estimate of ca. 150,000 for
    Boiotia's population in this period (Bintliff and Snodgrass 1985: 141–3; Hansen
    2006: 84–7; Hansen 2008: 271–3), according to the proportional divisions of
    the early 4th-century BCE Boiotian League the Kopaic basin would have been
    home to some 55,000 individuals (*Hell. Oxy.* 19.3–4), a greater population than
    attested for the entirety of Boiotia in both the sixteenth and nineteenth century
    (Hansen 2006: 87–8). Incidentally, a major motivation for draining the basin
    in the nineteenth century was the need to produce more wheat domestically in
    Greece (Idol 2018: 77).

75  Knauss 1990: 113–24, 252–65.

76  Knauss 1984: 53, 153–4, 225, 233–6. While Strabo describes Krates as a
    μεταλλευτής, a miner, Diogenes Laertios designates him a ταφρωρύχος, literally
    a "ditch-digger" but clearly a more specialized engineer (Diog. Laert. 4.23),
    and Stephanos of Byzantion (s.v. *Athēnai*) states that he "dug a ditch through"
    (διετάφρευσεν) Kopais. Unlike Chatelain (2001: 96, n. 52), I do not see any
    conflict between these different terms, and it is not hard to imagine that an
    engineer with expertise in mining could have been hired to carry out work on
    both above-ground drainage works and the clearance of underground drainage
    channels.

77 *IG* VII 3170, 5. Roesch 1965: 185–6.

78 Cf. *IG* VII 2712, 33–7. Fossey 1988: 275; Kalcyk 1988.

79 *IG* VII 2712; Paus. 9.38.6. Argoud 1987: 35–6; Fossey 1990; Farinetti 2008: 125. This also occurred in more recent centuries after Ottoman authorities failed to maintain drainage works (Thiersch 1833, vol. 2: 17; Gardikas 2018: 159).

80 Strabo 9.2.16. Cf. Rackham 1983: 297; Idol 2018: 77, 83. Theophrastos notes that the soils around "the bundles," the thick reed-beds near the shore, were the most fertile in the basin (Theophr. *Hist. pl.* 4.11.1).

81 *BCD Boiotia*, 44–9, nos. 183–219; Farinetti 2008: 133–4.

82 Arist. *[Pr]*. 20.32 (926a5–7).

83 Cf. Dodwell's comment that "in the winter [the lake] is divided into several large pools, while intermediate portions of land are adorned with villages and cultivation" (1819, vol. 1: 235).

84 Lytle 2010: 280–1. Cf. Gartland 2016a: 157–8.

85 Wheler 1682: 330; Dodwell 1819, vol. 1: 235.

86 Antiphanes F 131 (ed. Edmonds).

87 *IG* VII 3170, 8, 13, 17.

88 Roesch 1965: 59–60; Chandezon 2003: 45, n. 19. Cf. Idol 2018: 83–4.

89 Belle 1881: 138–9.

90 *IG* VII 2792, and cf. also a similar boundary stone delimiting the border of the two cities of the sixth century BCE (*SEG* 30.440). Roesch 1965: 64; Argoud 1987: 35. Cf. Sartre 1979; Daverio Rocchi 1988: 120–2.

91 Gartland 2016: 158. Cf. Farinetti 2008: Fig. 2, 117.

92 Plut. *Mor.* 578a. Cf. Farinetti 2008: 121, 125, 128, 129; Farinetti 2011: 146–7.

93 Theophr. *Caus. pl.* 5.14.9, and cf. *Hist. pl.* 3.1.2.

94 Theophr. *Caus. pl.* 5.12.3.

95 Cf. Theophr. *Caus. pl.* 5.14.3. Farinetti 2008: 122. The inhabitants of the basin noted the same problem after the total drainage of the lake in the late nineteenth century (Philippson and Kirsten 1952: 473).

96 Plut. *Sull.* 20.4.

97 Cf. Dodwell 1819, vol. 1: 213.

98 Artem. 2.28.

99 Theophr. *Hist. pl.* 4.11.8–9.

100 *SEG* 32.459, 24. Roesch 1982: 158. The name Boiotia itself is also a compound including the Greek word *bous* (Michell 1940: 61).

101 Chandezon 2003: 44–5.

102 *IG* VII 3171, 38–40.

103 *SEG* 22.432, 16–18.

104 *SEG* 3.356.

105 *IG* VII 3171, 41–8. Roesch 1965: 212–13; Migeotte 1994: 6–7; Chandezon 2003: 43–4.

106  Pind. *Ol.* 14.2.

107  Paus. 9.38.4.

108  Theophr. *Hist. pl.* 4.11.8–9; Plut. *Sull.* 20.3–4.

109  Farinetti 2003: 6.

110  Paus. 9.26.1.

111  Polyaenus *Strat.* 1.3.5.

112  Rackham 1983: 315, 337.

113  Ar. *Ach.* 875–6, 878–90. Aristophanes again makes reference in *Peace* to the "geese, ducks, pigeons, and larks of Boiotia" (Βοιωτῶν... χῆνας νήττας φάττας τροχίλους) (Ar. *Pax* 1003–4).

114  Jackdaw: Antiphanes F 302 (ed. Edmonds). Grebe: Ar. *Av.* 304; Dionysios *Ornithiaka* 2.12, 3.24. Coot: Ar. *Av.* 565.

115  Ar. *Av.* 249, 761; Ar. F 448; Phoenikides F 2 (ed. Edmonds). As marsh birds, many francolins could be also found at Marathon (Suda s.v. *Attagas*), but apparently not in sufficient numbers to meet the demand of the Athenian market (Dalby 2003: 150).

116  Plin. *HN* 16.66.169.

117  The reference to the sale of moles and hedgehogs seems perplexing, but both animals were in fact hunted for their skins in antiquity: Pliny notes that the skins of the former, which thrived around Orchomenos (cf. Arist. *Hist. An.* 8.28), were used to make luxurious bedcovers (Plin. *HN* 8.83), while the skins of the latter were used like combs to card wool (Plin. *HN* 8.56).

118  Paus. 9.23.7. Ulrichs 1840: 232.

119  Dodwell 1819, vol. 1: 213.

120  *SEG* 32.457.

121  Roesch 1982: 171.

122  Euboulos F 37 (ed. Edmonds). Cf. Ar. *Lys.* 36, 702; *Vesp.* 510–11; *Pax* 1005.

123  Matron F 1 (ed. Olson-Sens); Agatharchides of Knidos (*BNJ* 86) F 5; Paus. 9.24.2. Cf. Dodwell 1819, vol. 1: 237. The only other region of the Greek world whose eels could compete in size with those of Kopais was the Strymon River, in northern Greece (Antiphanes F 105 (ed. Edmonds)).

124  Archestratos F 10 (ed. Olson-Sens).

125  *SEG* 60.495B, 20–37.

126  Vatin 1971: 108–9; Mylona 2008: 104, table 9.1.

127  Cf. Idol 2018: 86. For possible osteological evidence of freshwater fish consumption in Classical and Hellenistic Thebes, see Vika, Aravantinos, and Richards 2009; Vika 2011.

128  *SEG* 60.495, 31–2.

129  Arist. *Hist. An.* 7.592a2–5, 13–20. Given Theophrastos' intimate knowledge of the ecology of Boiotia and the fame of its eels, Aristotle's description almost certainly derives from autopsy.

130  Marzano 2013: 200–3.
131  Frazer 1898, vol. 5: 132–3.
132  Agatharchides of Knidos (*BNJ* 86) F 5.
133  Agatharchides of Knidos (*BNJ* 86) F 5, Commentary.
134  Burstein 1989: 16–17.
135  Corvisier 1985: 15–19; Corvisier 1994: 314; Sallares 2002: 45–6; Craik 2017: 157–8. See note 45 above for a discussion about a possible reference to a malarial outbreak when the lake was exceptionally full.
136  Gardikas 2018: 86–97.
137  Morgan-Foster 2010: 45; Craik 2017: 155.
138  Herakleides Kritikos (*BNJ* 369A) F 1.25.
139  Retief and Cilliers 2004: 129; Morgan-Foster 2010: 44–5.
140  Gardikas 2018: 89–90, 92–3, 95.
141  Belle 1881: 136.
142  Gardikas 2018: 89.
143  Hippoc. *Epid.* 1.6–7, 24 26; *Aph.* 3.21–2; *Aer.* 10. Corvisier 1985: 15–19; Retief and Cilliers 2004: 128–31; Craik 2017: 160–1.
144  Gardikas 2018: 91.
145  Gardikas 2018: 94–6; Idol 2018: 86.
146  Gardikas 2018: 88–9; cf. Morgan-Foster 2010: 46–7.
147  Morgan-Foster 2010: 45–6.
148  Morgan-Foster 2010: 46.
149  Livadas and Athanassatos 1963: 181, 183–4. Cf. Gardikas 2018: 96.
150  Sallares 1991: 279.
151  King et al. 2002: 54.
152  Sallares et al. 2004: 324.
153  Choremis et al. 1951; Choremis, Zannos-Mariolea, and Kattamis 1962; Stamatoyannopoulos and Fessas 1964; Stamatoyannopoulos et al. 1966.
154  Weatherall 1995; Vogel and Motulsky 1997: 525; Sallares et al. 2004: 322–3, n. 54.
155  Morgan-Foster 2010.
156  Morgan-Foster 2010: 45.
157  Pind. *Ol.* 14.4.
158  Hom. *Il.* 2.511–16. Kowalzig 2007: 365.
159  Strabo 9.2.3; Paus. 9.24–41. Kowalzig 2007: 358–71; Gartland 2016a: 155–7; Giroux forthcoming. For the varied identities of Classical Boiotia, see generally Kowalzig 2007: 328–91.
160  Theophr. *Hist. pl.* 4.11.2–3. On the impact of flooding on nearby roads in the 19th century, see Dodwell 1819, vol. 1: 235.
161  Gartland 2016a: 157–9.
162  Plut. *Mor.* 193e.
163  Livy 33.29.6.

164  Kalligas 1985: 161.

165  Plut. *Sull.* 21.4. See also Giroux in this volume.

166  About 1855: 104.

167  Plin. *Ep.* 93.

168  Cf. Horden and Purcell 2000: 2–3.

169  Braudel 1980: 25–54.

170  Appadurai 1996: 178–200.

171  Beck 2020: 7.

## REFERENCES

About, E. 1855. *Greece and the Greeks of the Present Day*. Edinburgh.

Amigues, S. 1988. *Recherches sur les plantes. Tome I: Livres I-II*. Paris.

Anderson, W.D. 1994. *Music and Musicians in Ancient Greece*. Ithaca, NY.

Appadurai, A. 1996. *Modernity at Large: Cultural Dimensions of Globalization*. Minneapolis.

Argoud, G. 1987. "Eau et agriculture en Grèce." In Pierre Louis, J. Métral, and F. Métral (eds.), *L'homme et l'eau en Méditerranée et au Proche-Orient. Volume IV. L'eau dans l'agriculture*. Lyon: 25–43.

Beck, H. 2020. *Localism and the Ancient Greek City-State*. Chicago.

Bélis, A. 1998. "Les fabricants d'auloi en Grèce: L'exemple de Délos." *Topoi* 8.2: 777–90.

Bélis, A., and V. Péché. 1996. "'Du bon usage du roseau': Commentaires sur la fabrication des anches et des tuyaux dans l'antiquité gréco-romaine." In J. Coget (ed.), *L'Homme, le végétal et la musique (Livre A)*. Saint-Jouin-de-Milly: 10–29.

Belle, H. 1881. *Trois Années en Grèce*. Paris.

Bintliff, J., and A. Snodgrass. 1985. "The Boiotia Survey, a Preliminary Report: The First Four Years." *Journal of Field Archaeology* 12: 123–61. https://doi .org/10.2307/530288.

Braudel, F. 1972. *The Mediterranean and the Mediterranean World in the Age of Philip II*. London.

Braudel, F. 1980. "History and the Social Sciences: The *Longue Durée*." In *On History*. Chicago: 25–54.

Burstein, S.M. 1989. *Agatharchides of Cnidus: On the Erythraean Sea*. London.

Chandezon, C. 2003. *L'élevage en Grèce (fin Ve–fin Ier s. a.C.): L'apport des sources épigraphiques*. Bordeaux.

Chatelain, Thierry. 2001. "Assèchement et bonification des terres dans l'antiquité Grecque: L'exemple du lac de Ptéchai à Éretrie: Aspects terminologiques et techniques." In P. Briant (ed.), *Irrigation et drainage dans l'antiquité, Qanāts et canalisations souterraines en Iran, en Égypte et en Grèce, Séminaire tenu au Collège de France sous la direction de Pierre Briant*. Paris: 81–108.

Choremis, C., et al. 1951. "Sickle-Cell Anæmia in Greece." *The Lancet* 257.6665: 1147–9. https://doi.org/10.1001/archpedi.1929.01930070115014.

Choremis, C., L. Zannos-Mariolea, and M.D.C. Kattamis. 1962. "Frequency of Glucose-6-Phosphate Dehydrogenase Deficiency in Certain Highly Malarious Areas of Greece." *The Lancet* 279.7219: 17–18. https://doi.org/10.1016/S0140 -6736(62)92640-5. Medline:13879181.

Classical Numismatic Group. 2006. *Triton IX: The BCD Collection of the Coinage of Boiotia*. Lancaster, PA.

Corvisier, J.-N. 1985. *Santé et société en Grèce ancienne*. Paris.

Corvisier, J.-N. 1994. "Eau, paludisme et démographie en Grèce péninsulaire." In R. Ginouvès (ed.), *L'eau, la santé et la maladie dans le monde grec*. Athens and Paris: 297–319.

Craik, E. 2017. "Malaria and the Environment of Greece." In O.D. Cordovana (ed.), *Pollution and the Environment in Ancient Life and Thought*. Stuttgart: 153–62.

Dalby, A. 2003. *Food in the Ancient World, from A to Z*. London and New York.

Daverio Rocchi, G. 1988. *Frontiera e confini nella Grecia antica*. Rome.

Demand, N.H. 1978. *Thebes in the Fifth Century: Heracles Resurgent*. London, Boston, Melbourne and Henley.

Dodwell, E. 1819. *A Classical and Topographical Tour through Greece, during the Years 1801, 1805, and 1806*. 2 vols. London.

Farinetti, E. 2003. "Boeotian Orchomenos: A Progressive Creation of a Polis Identity." In H. Hokwerda (ed.), *Constructions of Greek Past: Identity and Historical Consciousness from Antiquity to the Present*. Groningen: 1–10.

Farinetti, E. 2008. "Fluctuating Landscapes: The Case of the Copais Basin in Ancient Boeotia." *Annuario della Scuola Archeologica di Atene e delle Missioni Italiane in Oriente* 86: 115–38.

Farinetti, E. 2011. *Boeotian Landscapes: A GIS-Based Study for the Reconstruction and Interpretation of the Archaeological Datasets of Ancient Boeotia*. Oxford.

Flashar, H. 1972. *Aristotelis Opuscula II: Mirabilia*. Berlin.

Flashar, H., and U. Klein. 1972. *Mirabilia*. Berlin.

Fossey, J.M. 1988. *Topography and Population of Ancient Boiotia*. Chicago.

Fossey, J.M. 1990. "The Copaïc Basin in the 2nd Century A.D." *Papers in Boiotian Topography and History*: 215–19.

Frazer, J.G. 1898. *Pausanias's Description of Greece*. 6 vols. London and New York.

Gardikas, K. 2018. *Landscapes of Disease: Malaria in Modern Greece*. Budapest and New York.

Gartland, S.D. 2016a. "A New Boiotia? Exiles, Landscapes, and Kings." In S.D. Gartland (ed.), *Boiotia in the Fourth Century B.C.* Philadelphia: 147–64.

Gartland, S.D. 2016b. "Enchanting History: Pausanias in Fourth-Century Boiotia."
In S.D. Gartland (ed.), *Boiotia in the Fourth Century B.C.* Philadelphia: 80–98.

Giroux, C. Forthcoming. "Mythologizing Conflict: Memory and the Minyae."
*Ancient History Bulletin.* Supplemental volume.

Grove, A.T., and O. Rackham. 2001. *The Nature of Mediterranean Europe: An
Ecological History.* New Haven, CT, and London.

Hansen, M.H. (ed.). 2006. *The Shotgun Method: The Demography of the Ancient
Greek City-State Culture.* Columbia, MI.

Hansen, M.H. 2008. "An Update on the Shotgun Method." *Greek, Roman, and
Byzantine Studies* 48: 259–86.

Haussoullier, B. 1894. "Le dessèchement du lac Copaïs par les anciens et ps. Aristote,
Περὶ Θαυμασίων Ἀκουσμάτων, XCIX (103)." *Revue de philologie, de littérature et
d'histoire anciennes* 18.1: 99–100.

Hope Simpson, R., and D.K. Hagel. 2006. *Mycenaean Fortifications, Highways,
Dams and Canals.* Sälvedalen.

Horden, P., and N. Purcell. *The Corrupting Sea: A Study of Mediterranean History.*
Malden, MA: 2000.

Idol, D. 2018. "The 'Peaceful Conquest' of Lake Kopaïs: Modern Water
Management and Environment in Greece." *Journal of Modern Greek Studies*
36.1: 71  95. https://doi.org/10.1353/mgs.2018.0002.

Kalcyk, H. 1988. "Der Damm von Akraiphia. Landsicherung Und Landgewinnung
in Der Bucht von Akraiphia Am Kopaissee in Böotien, Griechenland." *Boreas* 11:
5–14.

Kalligas, P.G. 1985. "Ρωμαϊκά Κράνη Στην Ελλάδα." Αρχαιολογικά Ανάλεκτα Εξ
Αθηνών 18, nos. 1–2: 161–4.

King, R.A., A.G. Motulsky and J.I. Rotter. 2002. *The Genetic Basis of Common
Diseases.* Oxford.

Knauss, J. 1984. "Systemanalyse der antiken Wasserbauten." In J. Knauss, B.
Heinrich and H. Kalcyk (eds.), *Die Wasserbauten der Minyer in der Kopais, die
älteste Flußregulierung Europas.* Munich: 167–242.

Knauss, J. 1990. *Wasserbau und Geschichte: Minyische Epoche – Bayerische Zeit
(vier Jahrhunderte, ein Jahrzehnt).* Munich.

Knauss, J. 1995. "Technical and Historical Aspects of the Unfinished Ancient
Drainage Tunnel at the Outmost Northeast Corner of the Kopais-Basin." In
A.X. Christopoulou (ed.), Β' Διεθνές Συνέδριο Βοιωτικών Μελετών, Athens:
83–95.

Kowalzig, B. 2007. *Singing for the Gods: Performances of Myth and Ritual in
Archaic and Classical Greece.* Oxford.

Landels, J. 1998. *Music in Ancient Greece and Rome.* London and New York.

Lauffer, S. 1986. *Kopais: Untersuchungen zur historischen Landeskunde
Mittelgriechenlands.* Frankfurt am Main.

Livadas, G., and D. Athanassatos. 1963. "The Economic Benefits of Malaria Eradication in Greece." *Rivista Di Malariologia* 42, nos. 4–6: 177–87. Medline:14118423.

Lytle, E. 2010. "Fish Lists in the Wilderness: The Social and Economic History of a Boiotian Price Decree." *Hesperia* 79: 253–303.

Mackil, E. 2013. *Creating a Common Polity: Religion, Economy, and Politics in the Making of the Greek Koinon*. Berkeley, CA.

Marzano, A. 2013. *Harvesting the Sea: The Exploitation of Marine Resources in the Roman Mediterranean*. Oxford.

Mathiesen, T.J. 1999. *Apollo's Lyre: Greek Music and Music Theory in Antiquity and the Middle Ages*. Lincoln and London.

Michell, H. 1940. *The Economics of Ancient Greece*. Cambridge.

Migeotte, L. 1984. *L'emprunt public dans les cités Grecques: Recueil des documents et analyse critique*. Québec and Paris.

Migeotte, L. 1994. "Ressources financières des cités béotiennes." In J.M. Fossey (ed.), *Boeotia Antiqua IV: Proceedings of the 7th International Congress on Boiotian Antiquities, Boiotian (and Other) Epigraphy*. Amsterdam: 3–15.

Morgan-Foster, A.H. 2010. *Climate, Environment and Malaria during the Prehistory of Mainland Greece*. PhD diss., University of Birmingham.

Mylona, D. 2008. *Fish-Eating in Greece from the Fifth Century B.C. to the Seventeenth Century A.D.: A Story of Impoverished Fishermen or Luxurious Fish Banquets?* Oxford.

Philippson, A., and A. Kirsten. 1952. *Die griechischen Landschaften: Eine Landeskunde. Band I, Der Nordosten der griechischen Halbinsel. Teil 3, Attika und Megaris*. Frankfurt am Main.

Rackham, O. 1983. "Observations on the Historical Ecology of Boeotia." *Annual of the British School at Athens* 78: 291–351. https://doi.org/10.1017/S0068245400019742.

Reger, G. 2005. "The Manufacture and Distribution of Perfume." In Z.H. Archibald, J.K. Davies, and V. Gabrielsen (eds.), *Making, Moving and Managing: The New World of Ancient Economies, 323–31 BC*. Oxford: 253–97.

Repapis, C.C. 1989. "A Quasi-Nine-Year Oscillation of the Water Level in Lake Copais (Greece) Cited by Theophrastus (4th Century B.C.) and Pliny (1st Century A.D.)." *Climatic Change* 14: 81–7. https://doi.org/10.1007/BF00140176.

Retief, F., and L. Cilliers. 2004. "Malaria in Graeco-Roman Times." *Acta Classica* 47: 127–37.

Roesch, P. 1965. *Thespies et la fédération béotienne*. Paris.

Roesch, P. 1982. *Études béotiennes*. Paris.

Roesch, P. 1989. "L'aulos et les aulètes en Béotie." In H. Beister and J. Buckler (eds.), *Boiotika: Vorträge vom 5: Internationalen Böotien-Kolloquium zu Ehren von Professor Dr. Siegfried Lauffer*. Munich: 203–14.

Sallares, R. 1991. *The Ecology of the Ancient Greek World*. Ithaca, NY.

Sallares, R. 2002. *Malaria and Rome: A History of Malaria in Ancient Italy*. Oxford.

Sallares, R., A. Bouwman, and C. Anderung. 2004. "The Spread of Malaria to Southern Europe in Antiquity: New Approaches to Old Problems." *Medical History* 48: 311–28. https://doi.org/10.1017/s0025727300007651. Medline:16021928.

Sartre, M. 1979. "Aspects économiques et religieux de la frontière dans les cités grecques." *Ktèma* 4: 213–24.

Schachter, A. 1967. "A Boeotian Cult Type." *Bulletin of the Institute of Classical Studies* 14: 1–16. https://doi.org/10.1111/j.2041-5370.1967.tb00040.x.

Stamatoyannopoulos, G., and Ph. Fessas. 1964. "Thalassaemia, Glucose-6-Phosphate Dehydrogenase Deficiency, Sickling, and Malarial Endemicity in Greece: A Study of Five Areas." *British Medical Journal* 5387.1: 875–9. https://doi.org/10.1136/bmj.1.5387.875. Medline:14102772.

Stamatoyannopoulos, G., A. Panayotopoulos, and A.G. Motulsky. 1966. "The Distribution of Glucose-6-Phosphate Dehydrogenase Deficiency in Greece." *American Journal of Human Genetics* 18.3: 296–308. https://doi.org/10.1111/j.1445-5994.2007.01618.x. Medline:18290815.

Thiersch, Frédéric. 1833. *De l'état actuel de la Grèce et des moyens d'arriver à sa restauration*. 2 vols. Leipzig.

Ulrichs, H.N. 1840. *Reisen und Forschungen in Griechenland*. Bremen.

Vatin, C. 1971. "Le tarif des poissons d'Akraiphia." In F. Salviat and C. Vatin (eds.), *Inscriptions de Grèce Centrale*. Paris: 95–109.

Vika, E. 2011. "Diachronic Dietary Reconstructions in Ancient Thebes, Greece: Results from Stable Isotope Analyses." *Journal of Archaeological Science* 38: 1157–63. https://doi.org/10.1016/j.jas.2010.12.019.

Vika, E., V. Aravantinos, and M.P. Richards. 2009. "Aristophanes and Stable Isotopes: A Taste for Freshwater Fish in Classical Thebes (Greece)?" *Antiquity* 83: 1076–83. https://doi.org/10.1017/S0003598X00099361.

Vogel, F., and A.G. Motulsky. 1997. *Human Genetics: Problems and Approaches*. Berlin.

Weatherall, D.J., et al. 1995. "The Hemoglobinopathies." In C.R. Scriver et al. (eds.), *The Metabolic and Molecular Basis of Inherited Disease*. New York: 3: 3417–84.

West, M.L. 1992. *Ancient Greek Music*. Oxford.

Wheler, G. 1682. *A Journey into Greece*. London.

Wilson, P. 2007. "Pronomos and Potamon: Two Pipers and Two Epigrams." *Journal of Hellenic Studies* 127: 141–9. https://doi.org/10.1017/S0075426900001671.

Wilson, P. 2010. "The Man and the Music (and the Choregos?)." In L. Burn, O. Taplin, and R. Wyles (eds.), *The Pronomos Vase and Its Context*. Oxford: 181–212.

*Following the chapter on the Kopais basin (chapter 2), Chandra Giroux further zooms in on the local horizon of this micro-region. Her focus is on Chaironeia, a small town in the lower Kephissos Valley. How did the inhabitants view their local world and what was the everyday Chaironeian experience? Giroux's voicing of local narratives begins with a discussion of the intriguing constellation in which the Chaironeians found themselves. Some of the defining military encounters in antiquity were fought in their countryside. The settlement thus was a place, real and imagined, where parochial perspectives intersected with power shifts in the world writ large. Giroux traces how the erection of battle monuments lent a certain mediating quality to the localscape. Conversations between these monuments resonated with the inhabitants and an ever-increasing number of visitors alike, although in rather different ways. While the former adapted global events such as Alexander's presence in the battle of 338 BCE to their local discourse, Greek and Roman travellers were eager to embrace the genius loci of battle sites that had altered the world. Beyond the seismic shifts of war, on a more nuanced scale, Chaironeia occupied a transitory zone between local, regional, and transregional realms that all left their marks on local attitudes; prevailing discourses on the ground were not confined to war. In the second section of the paper, Giroux turns to archaeohistorical and epigraphical evidence that sheds light on more personalized encounters with the local horizon. Her analysis shows how discourses about disease and healing as well as the manumission of slaves wielded impact on and, in turn, reverberated with quotidian experiences, providing the city and countryside of Chaironeia with distinctly local traits.*

*Keywords: victory monuments, intersignification, healing cults, Plutarch, manumission records, dark tourism*

3

# Healing a Battlefield: The Local World of Hellenistic Chaironeia

CHANDRA GIROUX

The local world of Chaironeia is undoubtedly one of conflicts, with battles on its soil stretching from the Hellenistic era, all the way until the Greek War of Independence.[1] As such, Chaironeia largely becomes defined by these confrontations, particularly the famous Battle of Chaironeia of 338 BCE, marking Philip II's victory over the Hellenic alliance, and the Battle of Chaironeia in 86 BCE, won by Sulla during the First Mithridatic War. That Chaironeia is largely synonymous with battles is unsurprising, as relatively little is known about the *polis* or its history.[2] Furthermore, the shifting frontiers and growing connectivity of the Greek world after Alexander, through the Roman Republic and into the Roman Empire, tend to overshadow the local world of Chaironeia's inhabitants. As Andrew Erskine points out, "the Hellenistic period is defined and bounded by political events," but he also rightly states that it "is as much a cultural phenomenon as a political one."[3] With this in mind, in this chapter I ask if it is possible to reconstruct a local discourse for Hellenistic Chaironeia, one that lives in this time of expansion, recognizes the conflicts and its history, and simultaneously steers us away from these conflicts. In other words, what is Chaironeia beyond its battles?

To begin voicing these local narratives of Chaironeia, it is important to consider what Hans Beck has termed the local discourse environment.[4] This local discourse was entrenched in ideas of "self" and "other," which instilled a sense of belonging.[5] The associated script was defined by two separate areas: the physical and the imagined space. The physical space is subject to human mobility, a "manageable, accessible realm" of the everyday lives of its inhabitants (approximately a five or six kilometre radius, or a two-hour walk),[6] defined by infrastructure, modes of communication, and the natural environment. There is also the imagined realm, where relationships, sacred rituals, and modes of defining oneself become a source of connected knowledge and meaning.[7] In order to supply meaning, however, the local must extend to a broader context as a means for comparison. In this way, the regional sphere becomes a necessary component to any discussion of the local, as it provides interactions that help to shape this inside-outside perspective. As the lens continues to span outward and as more "others" are encountered, in the global arena for instance, the stronger that local definition becomes.

This chapter endeavours to give meaning to the local elements of Chaironeia. It will build on the scholarship of Boiotia and its local worlds by investigating Chaironeia's unique aspects in the Hellenistic period. It will ask two main questions: (1) what did it mean to be Chaironeian during the Hellenistic period? and (2) how did the people of Chaironeia experience their local environment, both physical and imagined? These questions will continually overlap through a consideration of how the local becomes entangled with the regional and global spheres,[8] and how, in light of this expanding world, the local is prioritized to provide orientation for its inhabitants.

This chapter begins with a brief investigation of Chaironeia and its history to provide context for the discussion. This is followed by an overview of Chaironeia's archaeological sites and their importance as *lieux de mémoire*. If one focuses particularly on the battle monuments, one can see how these key markers in Chaironeia's landscape play an essential role in its local narratives. Here, I suggest that these narratives inspire an image of Chaironeia that is focused on its battles, creating a sort of "battlescape." The following section shifts the perspective by analysing examples of local narratives found in the literature in order to understand how this projection of Chaironeia as a site of conflict shaped a distinct identity. However, Chaironeia cannot be reduced simply to a place of conflict. People like Plutarch[9] spent their lives there; it was their everyday local horizon and thus must have had meaning beyond the momentary clash of arms that occurred on their home's soil. With this in mind, the chapter moves on to exploring other aspects of Hellenistic Chaironeia, looking at its agricultural output and religious life. The final section considers the manumission records of Chaironeia as evidence of a practice that helped define the local world. Throughout, there are many instances where the local, regional, and global come into contact, overlap, interact, and express themselves in Chaironeia's local context. Most importantly, these narratives bring to life aspects of what it meant to be Chaironeian in the Hellenistic Age by showing that Chaironeia, while largely being defined by its battles, also had a life and an identity beyond these conflicts.

## Chaironeia

In the *Inventory of Archaic and Classical Poleis*, Chaironeia is classified as type A, as it is referred to as a *polis* in ancient sources.[10] It occupies a space of about 55 square kilometres, and is the westernmost town of Boiotia, bordering Phokis.[11] Chaironeia itself has three streams and is located in the Kephissos Valley, a plain that stretches about three kilometres east to west and occupies the space between its southern mountain range and river.[12] Unfortunately, Chaironeia is one of the least well known Boiotian *poleis* and has very little in terms of excavations, since the modern village lies atop the ancient foundations.[13] As a result, any knowledge of Chaironeia tends to rely on the ancient sources. For example, Plutarch says (*Cim.* 1.1) that, according to legend, Chaironeia was the first city that the Boiotians founded as they migrated from Thessaly. This comes as no surprise as this movement of peoples from Thessaly into Boiotia to settle in Chaironeia reflects the natural geography of the area.[14] Evidence confirms an early settlement, with a prehistoric mound known as Magoúla Baloménou and from pot sherds in the area that show occupation from the Neolithic times until the Roman Empire.[15]

In the Classical era, both Thucydides (4.76.3) and Hellanikos (*FGrH* 4 F 81) describe Chaironeia as being syntelically dependent on Orchomenos – a *polis* 13 kilometres east of Chaironeia – and was therefore obligated to provide military and financial aid to it. Later, it became an independent member of the Boiotian League, although it is not known when its status shifted from an Orchomenian dependency to an independent *polis*.[16] Chaironeia continued to exist into the Roman period until it was destroyed by an earthquake in 551 CE.[17]

Upon further inspection, it is possible to see that throughout this time much of Chaironeia's history and culture was largely determined by its geography. Despite its unassuming nature, Chaironeia was very well positioned on an arterial road running between northern and southern Greece, which placed it in close proximity to an important route that crossed Boiotia, making Chaironeia easily accessible from all directions.[18] These routes would become even more important in the Hellenistic era, as the geographic reach of Greek *poleis* expanded with the foundations of new *poleis*, larger populations, improved urban development, and more elaborate inner-city contacts and relations.[19] If one also considers Chaironeia's position on an outcrop of Mount Parnassos, linking it not only with Boiotia, but also with eastern Phokis (and thus with Delphi),[20] Chaironeia was well situated.

Yet these advantages also made its plain tactically advantageous for defending southern Greece. Its position in a small plain by a narrow pass that controlled access from Phokis to Boiotia meant that Chaironeia became a sort of contact zone,[21] embroiled in either tension or cooperation at the micro-regional level (Eastern Phokis and Orchomenos),[22] the macro-regional level (Boiotia),[23] and in the greater Hellenic world (Athens, Sparta, Thessaly),[24] as different groups competed for influence over territory. Interestingly, the competition of the Phokians and Boiotians for control of the fertile Kephissos Valley occurred not only as armed conflict, but also in myth and the imagined realm.[25] The fighting and shifting alliances meant that, at times, Phokis was at war with Boiotia and, at other times, it was a friend of Boiotia, and even at one point was incorporated into Boiotia.[26] As McInerney explains, "In many of these borderlands the border was 'soft' and only became apparent as one travelled from one community to the next, as, for example, when one walked from Phokian Panopeus to the next town east, Chaironeia, which lay in Boiotia. These fuzzy boundaries and the configuration of territory as zones of competing affiliation were vital for the formation of regional identities."[27] The regional boundary between Phokis and Boiotia was therefore not clear-cut. This is most obvious in the location of two Phokian *poleis*, Panopeus and Daulis, which were actually on the Boiotian side of the pass.[28] Chaironeia's location nearby as a part of the narrow pass that led out of Phokis and into Boiotia likely meant that the Chaironeians had some sort of relationship with these nearby Phokian towns (e.g., Panopeus, Daulis, Kalapodi), even if only in trade.[29] As such, Chaironeia's identity of place was – unsurprisingly – relational.[30]

Boiotia, the "dancing floor of Ares" (Plu. *Marc.* 21), frequently consisted of micro-regions, which often caused internal division of the Boiotian *ethnos*.[31] In the Hellenistic period, however, the macro-region of Boiotia had once again come together to provide a sense of stability during a time of expansion and change,[32] though this alliance still saw some regional divide.[33] It is feasible to suggest that these shifting alliances and the soft boundary with Phokis affected the local world of Chaironeia, not only in terms of the battles they provoked, but also in the political leanings of the *polis* and the formation of its identity.[34] The frequent alliance with Orchomenos, for example, implies that the local Chaironeians had an affinity with the Orchomenians and shared their alliances (Thessaly and Athens) as well as their rivalries (Thebes) during the Hellenistic period. Chaironeia's location in a fertile valley and near the pass that leads from Phokis into Boiotia also meant that Chaironeia was embroiled in disputes over this fuzzy boundary area. It seems, then, that even in its regional world, Chaironeia was surrounding by conflict.[35]

## Archaeological Sites and *Lieux de mémoire*

There have been no extensive archaeological investigations in Chaironeia.[36] Most of the material evidence, therefore, comes from accidental finds and rescue excavations.[37] But there are some visible archaeological sites worthy of note. First, the only public architecture discovered thus far is a small rock-cut theatre of the fifth or fourth century BCE, found on the northern slope of the acropolis and identified by an inscription.[38] The most looming site, however, is the acropolis and its surrounding walls. These walls were constructed in four phases, the third of which was during the Hellenistic era, echoing other defensive projects in Boiotia during this time.[39] This points to regional influence in this *polis*: the Boiotian *koinon* chose to include the relatively small *polis* of Chaironeia in its defensive measures. This is unsurprising, given its key defensive position in central Greece by the pass that connects Phokis and Boiotia, its location in the contested space of the fertile Kephissos Valley,[40] as well as Chaironeia's placement on an arterial road. Nevertheless, the involvement of Chaironeia in these defensive acts should be recognized as a sign of cooperation and negotiation in their regional sphere. This also recalls the micro-region of Chaironeia, that of eastern Phokis and western Boiotia, and indicates that during the Hellenistic period at least, Chaironeia seems to have identified with the Boiotians. These fortifications thus become a local symbol of regional affinity, one of defence against other *koina*, such as the nearby Phokians. In other words, the defensive structures show that, in some capacity, to be Chaironeian in the Hellenistic Age was to be part of a Boiotian military defence strategy, one that guarded central Greece from its northern and western neighbours.

This defensive role was also immediately present in the landscape, in the only other obvious visual sites from the ancient period, namely, its *lieux de mémoire* that commemorate the Battle of Chaironeia in 338: the Lion of Chaironeia, marking the burial place of the Theban Sacred Band close to the acropolis, and the Macedonian tomb, located in the plain outside of the *polis*. The Macedonian tomb, excavated in 1902, contained evidence of a collective burial followed by an elaborate funeral and monumentalization.[41] Pausanias states (9.40.7–9) that the Macedonians did not have the tradition of erecting victory trophies, hinting that this is why none exist in the plain. However, John Ma suggests that the tomb still functioned as a symbolic trophy, placed aggressively in the local landscape as a reminder of Macedonian triumph.[42] The effect of this *lieux de mémoire* is immediately apparent in the archaeology of the site, as the absence of sherds around the mound implies that it was no longer fertilized and cultivated.[43] The alteration of Chaironeian activities in the area from agricultural to commemorative suggests that the local inhabitants of Chaironeia respected this monument and its place in their local landscape, creating an emotional space of communal memory: an intersection of a physical and imagined space. The change in activity also indicates that the Chaironeians likely interpreted this monument, or perhaps this battle, as one of importance to their local identity. In this way, the local and events in the local sphere become symbolically prioritized during a time of change in the Greek world. Perhaps it can cautiously be stated that this space of communal memory was one of pride for the local Chaironeians, not necessarily in the political change it represented, but perhaps in the sheer fact that it happened *here*. It happened *on our soil*.

Similarly, the burial of the Thebans is found below the monumental Lion of Chaironeia. Compared to the Macedonians, the Thebans were hastily buried, and the monument itself was not erected until later in the Hellenistic period.[44] However, its dominant position along the arterial road at the focal point of the plain,[45] and facing the tomb of the Macedonians, indicates the continued importance and presence of the memory of this battle for the Greeks, in what Ma terms a kind of "intermonumental meditation."[46] As such, the lion becomes a memorial that reflects the Macedonian tumulus, not only in the sense that it was built afterwards, but also in that it reminds the viewer of the conflict; as it looks towards the Macedonian tomb and over the plain, its silent contemplation is a loud reverberation for the viewer of the conflict that took place in its environs. Perhaps the Lion of Chaironeia can also be understood as a defiant response to the Macedonian intrusion in the Greek landscape. Its very nature draws the eye of the viewer away from both the Macedonian tomb and other, smaller, sites and monuments. By doing so, it almost defines the local landscape, in the same way that today the lion and Chaironeia have become synonymous. But it also suggests a mourning for the loss of Greek lives in the plain, the lion watching, or even scrutinizing, the nearby Macedonians who lie at rest.

In whatever way the symbolism of the lion is interpreted, its presence in the *polis* is an important aspect of the investigation of Chaironeia's local world, its interconnections with its micro- and macro-regional affiliations, and its global identity. In this monument the three spheres converge into one: it represents the global through the commemoration of the battle; its very construction by Thebes displays a regional interference in the local landscape; and, finally, the local context comes into play through the use of local marble and the placement of the lion at a prominent intersection in the *polis*.[47] The use of local building materials anchored the *chōra* of Chaironeia to the *polis* proper, announcing the local bond to their land,[48] while simultaneously cementing their position in the historical narrative.

All three spheres are entangled and derive meaning through each other. Chaironeia in the Hellenistic era thus became an important site for the commemoration of battle, one in which the Chaironeians were apparently actively involved.

But the memorialization of conflict did not end there: there is also evidence of trophies set up by Sulla after the Battle of Chaironeia in 86 BCE. The dedications have been investigated extensively by modern scholars and thus will only be briefly visited here.[49] Not only does Pausanias remark on them (9.40.7), but Plutarch, who is eerily quiet on the Lion of Chaironeia, and tells us very few details of his hometown, also references the trophies (*Sul.* 19.5–6).[50] When combined with Plutarch's testimony, one of the inscriptions, *SEG* 41.448, contains some interesting hints concerning the intersection of local contexts, regional influence, and global events. The trophy gives the names of two men from Chaironeia, Homoloïchos and Anaxidamos (the local element). According to Plutarch (*Sulla* 19.5–6), these are the men who excelled at the Battle of Chaironeia under Sulla (the global element), and he says that this monument is a commemoration of their heroic deeds in the battle.[51] The inscription itself, crudely executed, is in the Boiotian dialect (the regional element).[52] Once again the local, regional, and global come together in one monument, the meaning of which would be read differently by each viewer. Local pride is evident in the erection of the trophy and through the actions of Homoloïchos and Anaxidamos.[53] An outsider might see this differently. Regional *poleis* who had originally sided against Rome, for instance, may look upon this with contempt. But a Roman might be satisfied (if he could read the Boiotian script and understood the context), knowing that the Chaironeians helped Rome achieve a victory. Artistic literacy aside, this inscription offers a glimpse of what seemed to be important to this local world (or at least to two of its men): setting up a trophy, with all its symbolic might,[54] to declare to the passerby that two men from Chaironeia (and thus, in a way, the town itself) aided Sulla in his great victory.

It seems, then, that to be Chaironeian in the Hellenistic era was not only about defensive measures for Boiotia but also involved engaging with, symbolically commenting on, and remembering the battles of the plain, and thus their bloody past.[55] This remembrance necessarily focused on the local landscape and its monuments. The shift in activities around these places and the mention of the monuments by Plutarch indicate a source of local pride that brought meaning to the lives of the inhabitants of Chaironeia during times of change, either through the boast that it happened on their soil (338 BCE), or that they themselves brought victory and supported the new regime (86 BCE).

## Chaironeia as a "Battlescape"

Considering the focus on its battles and the place of pride these were given by the locals, it is possible in the Hellenistic era, running into the Roman Empire, that Chaironeia and its plain can be cautiously recognized as a sort of memorial park, an ancient example that is similar to, albeit on a much lesser scale, modern battlefields such as Vimy Ridge, Dunkirk, or Gallipoli. In its narrowest definition, tourism as a commercialized entity for mass consumption is a modern phenomenon.[56] However, if the term is broadened to describe not just the mass movement of peoples to view a location but, rather, individual travel, it can be placed within a form of ancient tourism.[57] This is even more conceivable in the observation of an increase in travel as an elite cultural activity in the Hellenistic period, which may have been the result of Alexander the Great's conquests. Ada Cohen speculates that Alexander "showed the world to be traversable in ways it had never been before and initiated *'l'âge de la curiosité.'*"[58] At the very least, if travel was not possible for everyone, evidence of travel writing indicates that there was a potential audience of "armchair travellers."[59]

But why travel? What drove the interest of these Hellenistic Greek elites to venture to certain locations and record their experiences for these "armchair" enthusiasts? As Stumpf explains, "Not until the Hellenistic era, with its mix of Greek and native and its impulses towards canonization, do Greeks become openly nostalgic for their past. *Tourism was a byproduct of an international age.* It became imperative to establish what was and was not Greek, what was memorable, what should be consigned to oblivion, and what was *axios theas* – worth seeing."[60] Thus, the expanding world of the Hellenistic Age, which enabled travel and tourism, simultaneously brought about the prioritization of the local to bring meaning and orientation to Chaironeia and to the Greek world. It is in this context that I wish to place the battlefield of Chaironeia.

Visiting battlefields was of interest to ancient travellers.[61] However, as explained by John Gatewood and Catherine Cameron, "Many battlefields, if stripped of casualties and the detritus of war, are physically unremarkable and need to be transformed from neutral terrains into culturally meaningful landscapes. The transformation is done by the placement of physical artifacts such as monuments, statues, and gelded war machines, as well as the use of verbal text."[62] It is therefore possible to imagine that visitors to Chaironeia experienced the battlefield through its monuments so that it became a place of multiple meanings, similar to how Brad West defines Gallipoli as a plain of dialogical memorialization.[63] Like Ma's "intermonumental meditation" mentioned above,[64] the Lion of Chaironeia, the tumulus of the Macedonians, and the trophies of Sulla share in this space and in a conversation about nations and war that ultimately deemphasizes the individual warrior and promotes power.[65] Moreover, the symbolic nature of battlefield trophies evolved in the Hellenistic period from one associated with the hoplite phalanx and ritual, to a marker of military prowess, therefore issuing reminders of power, rulers, and military capabilities.[66] Lauren Kinnee argues that this transformation in meaning was the result of a shift in battle tactics, a consequence of Alexander's conquests and the victory of the Macedonians at Chaironeia in 338 BCE, that made the hoplite phalanx outdated.[67] The shift in meaning of these battlefield markers is thus a direct result of the growing global lens of the Greek world, one that encouraged symbols of power. And it all began in Chaironeia.

Modern touring of battlefields has been described as a form of "Dark Tourism," or thanatourism.[68] This form of tourism, whether conscious or subconscious, involves travelling to visit sites that have some symbolic representations of death and/or the remembrance of the dead, like a battlefield.[69] However, it is also important to note that research into dark tourism and its draw for visitors on modern battlefields has not been able to define a distinct group of people who list their primary motivation for visiting a battlefield as a desire for encountering the dead.[70] This complicates our understanding of the audience for this kind of tourism, as well as the reception of battlefields as possible sites of dark tourism. Furthermore, the concept itself is anachronistic, and thus its application to the ancient world is one that must be approached cautiously. Therefore, before investigating Chaironeia's battlescape as a possible place of thanatourism, I will briefly explore the prospect of the notion of dark tourism and the macabre in the ancient world.

From Roman gladiatorial combats to executions, death served as an attraction in the ancient world.[71] However, as mentioned above, dark tourism is not always about death; rather, it can also represent visiting a site as a place of remembrance of the dead. Remembrance, in this case, can also focus on history, genealogy, and ancestry.[72] This provides an important distinction that allows for the idea of dark tourism in ancient society. First, the emergence in the Hellenistic era of epigrams as a literary form and writers who specialized in their composition is a clear indication that the remembrance of the dead in this visual medium was important in the Greek world at this time.[73] What it does not do, however, is suggest significant numbers of travellers visiting and remembering the dead.

It is possible, however, to catch a glimpse of purposeful travel to visit the dead in the actions of Alexander the Great. Plutarch tells us that Alexander stopped his campaign to pay tribute in Troy to Athena and the heroes. In particular, he sought out the tomb of Achilles. There, he anointed the tomb with oil, held a contest, and proclaimed Achilles happy for having both a good friend in life and a herald to his fame in death (*Alex.* 15.4).[74] Another example, is found in the macro-regional world of Chaironeia, that is, Boiotia. Here, the Battle of Plataiai was commemorated through panhellenic travel for a ritual celebration to remember the dead.[75] Plataiai becomes an important *lieux de mémoire* for the Greek world, a place of nostalgia and constructed memory that focuses on the dead of the Persian Wars and their remembrance.[76] Both of these examples have all the requirements of dark tourism: travel to a place, the remembrance of the dead, and symbolism (the symbolic actions of Alexander for the spirit of Achilles and inscriptions/ritual celebration at Plataiai). Examples of dark tourism in the ancient world can thus be found.

Another form of dark tourism is also found in the writings of Plutarch. Interest in the macabre is found in Plutarch's *Life of Sulla* (21.4), where he recounts the after-effects of one of Sulla's battles waged outside of Orchomenos, near Chaironeia. Plutarch describes the abandoned armour and weapons buried in the mud that are still visible in his day. This place of remembrance was thus turned into a sort of deathscape, imbued with particular meaning centred on the effects of fighting.[77] Plutarch may have taken his guests, in the same way that he takes his reader (the "armchair tourists"),[78] to these nearby sites to witness the past like modern tourists to battlefield memorials. Tourists seldom visit sites alone and usually inquire with the locals, making the locals "reputational entrepreneurs."[79] Plutarch thus acts as a reputational entrepreneur for his visitors, in the same way that he does for his modern readers.

Unfortunately, despite the seemingly synonymous nature of Chaironeia with battles, there is no evidence for ancient visitors attending to local Chaironeian heroes or to the tombs on Chaironeia's battlefield (though the change in activity around the Macedonian tumulus should be considered). However, we do have evidence of Chaironeia as a battlescape yet again in the writings of one of its locals, Plutarch. Plutarch's tales and quick asides about his home bring to light how a native of Chaironeia may have interpreted some of these spaces. Although Plutarch was living under the Roman Empire and not in the Hellenistic Age, he nonetheless, as we saw above, becomes an important source for how Hellenistic events were remembered by Chaironeians. His writings give an indication of the local narratives and meanings that grew out of these constructed places of remembrance. Plutarch therefore acts as a guide to Chaironeia and its environs for his reader, albeit a reluctant one.[80] In what follows, I will briefly present three distinct instances where Plutarch provides a testimony of how Hellenistic battles and conflicts infiltrated the local Chaironeian imagination and their local discourse environment.

In the first example, Plutarch mentions that his great-grandfather used to tell a tale of Chaironeians carrying corn on their back for Antony's troops, spurred on by men with whips (*Ant.* 68.4–5). This is firsthand evidence of an ancient family sharing wartime stories about their local world. The link to the famous conflict between Antony and Octavian, although not a battle itself, would be obvious, and thus we can tentatively place it within the boundaries of Jay Winter's argument that local remembrance of past battles often constitutes families remembering a series of myths.[81] In this example, Plutarch's family is the one remembering what is either real or a myth to emphasize a negative quality of Antony. The motivation behind this is not immediately clear;[82] nevertheless it gives us evidence of how a Chaironeian family recollected an effect of a conflict, one that touched upon their family and fellow *politai*. In this memory, the local discourse environment is moulded by Plutarch to create one where global players and events are active in the local world, one that prioritizes the (real or imagined?) narrative of victimization of the local sphere.

In the second tale, Plutarch speaks of an ancient oak which still stood in his day and was called "Alexander's oak," for local tradition held that Alexander the Great pitched his tent below it before the battle of 338 BCE (*Alex.* 9.2). Like the Antony episode, the historicity of the narrative is not what concerns us. Instead, it should be recognized that a local tradition about a marker in the landscape lent that spatial area meaning. According to Plutarch, the Chaironeians revered this oak, which helped define the landscape through a connection to the past. Again, as with the Antony story, this connects Chaironeia to larger global events, giving the *polis* a place of importance by claiming the memory of men like Antony and Alexander, and providing the local inhabitants with fuel to bring to light stories that formed part of their imagined local world. Furthermore, both tales focus on conflict, once again giving importance to the battlescape of Chaironeia in relation to times of global change.

In the last example, Plutarch describes a bathhouse in Chaironeia. This bathhouse was visited by the ghost of Damon, a Chaironeian active at the time of Sulla, who slayed some Romans and was in turn killed by his fellow townsmen. Plutarch tells us that because "for a long while thereafter certain phantoms appeared in the place, and groans were heard there, as our Fathers tell us, the door of the vapour-bath was walled up, and to this present time the neighbours think it the source of alarming sights and sounds" (*Cim.* 1.6; Loeb translation). Although this is not directly a tale about a battle, it is one that derives from conflict and formed part of the local discourse environment at least until Plutarch's time. It was also a story played out between local (Damon and the Chaironeian officials), regional (Orchomenos),[83] and global (Lucullus and the Roman officials) actors. This again grants a level of importance to Chaironeia, as it becomes the location of events that brought about a visit of Lucullus, who had to solve the regional (and global) issues. It also moves the local narratives of the *polis* beyond the battles that were fought there and into the Roman political arena. Not only that, but it seems to have done so successfully, as the story was still being played out in the imagination of the locals of the Roman Imperial era, who were still reminded of this part of their history and, in many ways, were haunted by it.

In these three short descriptions by Plutarch, we witness how global events were reimagined through local Chaironeians as part of the local script. A war story told by one local family, an oak in the Chaironeian landscape, and a bathhouse are all seemingly banal things, that is, until Plutarch tells us their stories: tales that give meaning to these spaces. These anecdotes related by Plutarch help show the parts of Chaironeia that were not only physical spaces but were also imagined spaces. Furthermore, they were incorporated into the local discourse environment that ensured that Chaironeia became entangled with the larger Roman story. It is thus not only the *lieux de mémoire* of Chaironeia, but also Plutarch and local narratives that mould this *polis* into a battlescape,[84] a landscape that held reminders of past conflicts that continued to hold meaning for the viewer.

Finally, the oak of Alexander may also be cautiously interpreted within the realm of battlefield tourism. The oak recalled the actions of Alexander the Great before a momentous battle in the area and was still remarked upon by locals hundreds of years after the event (at least according to Plutarch). While there is no indication in the ancient sources that the oak served as a metaphorical tomb for those who died, or for Alexander himself, its location near the battlefield and its association with this important conflict are signals of the connection of this tree to Alexander and the battle, and thus the possibility that it was a part of battlefield tourism in Chaironeia. The link between the tree, battles, and death are hinted at in Plutarch's placement of the tree in his narrative (*Alex.* 9.2): the Chaironeian sandwiched the mention of the tree between Alexander's participation in the battle and the tomb of the Macedonians. Not only that, but Plutarch says that the tree and the sepulchre are geographically close to each other. In this way, Plutarch (willingly or not) incorporated the tree into the memorial landscape of the battle of 338 BCE. The symbolic nature of this tree thus transported the visitor to a time of remembrance, not only for those who died at the battle, but also for the great deeds of a man now dead. As such, the oak may have served in this place of remembrance.

Another witness, Pausanias, also focused his representation of Chaironeia on the battles fought in its plain.[85] With the exception of his discussions of the origin of the name of Chaironeia (9.40.5), the staff worshipped in Chaironeia (9.40.11–12), and the distilling of unguents from local flowers (9.41.7), Pausanias reserved his conversation of Chaironeia for its battle monuments. The first mention he makes of a marker in the landscape is that of the trophies of Sulla (9.40.7). Then, in this same passage, he includes a discussion of Philip and why he did not erect a trophy in Chaironeia. This is followed by his description of the approach to Chaironeia, where the visitor finds the lion (9.40.10). Pausanias remarks that nothing was inscribed on the monument, and conjectures that this is because the courage of the Thebans was not reflected in their terrible fate.

Like Plutarch, Pausanias focused on Chaironeia as the site of battles and commemorations. He does not mention any buildings, monuments, trophies, or the like, unless they are in relation to battles. Our guide thus seems to confirm the suspicion that Chaironeia aroused interest from its Roman Age visitors mainly in relation to the Hellenistic conflicts that occurred on its soil and thus in some kind of battlefield tourism. Evidently, these conflicts were still an active agent in local conversations in Chaironeia in the Roman period, reflecting the importance of these earlier battles to the locals. The continued (or perhaps continual) remembrance and emphasis on them also supports the idea of a communal memory that grew around the battles, one that was so strong that it was evident to outsiders like Pausanias. The power of these memories and these narratives also make it likely that these tales had been told for a long time, at least back to the Hellenistic period when these events occurred.[86] The battlefield of Chaironeia became an "imagined local anchor" for the inhabitants,[87] one that fed the narrative of their local world, united the citizens, and spoke to outsiders about the importance of the past to the present. It firmly set Chaironeia on the map of Hellenic politics through a strong link to battle narratives.[88] Visitors to Chaironeia, therefore, were engaged in a sort of dark tourism, whether they wanted to or not, simply because local discourses were subject to the omnipresent notion of a battlescape.

## Other Archaeological Evidence

But, Chaironeia was not simply a place of battles, and other incidental finds point to a local life in the Hellenistic period that did not centre on conflict. This includes burials, though these are few in number.[89] However, one interesting piece is a grave *stēlē* from ca. 400 BCE made of Thespian limestone with strong island influences.[90] Either a local Chaironeian purchased this *stēlē* from abroad, or a foreigner to Chaironeia was buried there. In either case, the local context of Chaironeia once again mixes with the regional through the use of Thespian limestone, but also with a broader, sub-global island influence in its design. More regional networks and trade are found in terracotta figurines and protomes discovered in Chaironeia.[91] Clearly, Chaironeia was somehow connected to a growing Greek world and the evidence of the *stēlē*, the figurines, and the protomes complicates the picture of this relatively small *polis*. Although it cannot be clearly reconstructed, Chaironeia was certainly more than its battles.

Chaironeia also had many sanctuaries. The list is rather extensive: two sanctuaries to Artemis,[92] one to Apollo,[93] one to the Mother of the Gods, one to Leukothea and the Muses, one to Asklepios,[94] one for a sceptre known as *dory*,[95] one to the Egyptian gods, and lastly, possible worship spaces for Dionysos and Herakles.[96] Unfortunately, no sanctuaries have been excavated, but it is apparent, through the mere presence of these sacred spaces, that Chaironeia was actively engaged in many cults and practised its own sacred rites.[97] More importantly for the discussion of the local discourse environment, Elizabeth A. Meyer points out that these deities possessed healing properties, which she suggests may be in relation to the soothing and healing properties of the plants in Chaironeia's territory.[98]

To begin unravelling why these sanctuaries focused on healing, we turn to the agricultural properties of Chaironeia. A GIS-based study by Emeri Farinetti on Boiotian landscapes shows that Chaironeia was an agriculturally rich area.[99] Unfortunately, no surveys have been conducted on the *chōra*,[100] so the literary evidence must be relied upon. Plutarch provides some possible hints. Plutarch's local friend Soklaros was an expert on conifers,[101] suggesting experience in their cultivation. Plutarch also mentions, in his *Life of Antony* (68.4–5), that his great grandfather Nikarchos, with other Chaironeians, had to supply corn for Antony's troops, thus providing evidence for grain cultivation in the region. This is strengthened by a second-century BCE inscription from Chaironeia that discusses the local price of wheat.[102] Finally, Plutarch also touches on pastoral activities in the *polis* with the mention of his father's excellent horses.[103] These casual mentions therefore provide three possible agricultural industries for this small *polis*, something that hints of the life of Chaironeia beyond its battles.

What cannot be gathered from these hints, however, is why Chaironeia's religious life centred on healing. Instead, this is elucidated by Pausanias' description of Chaironeia's agricultural industry, something that is not found in any other account: that is, Chaironeia's healing plants (9.41.7):

Here in Chaironeia they distil unguents from flowers, namely, the lily, the rose, the narcissus and the iris. These prove to be cures for the pains of men. The unguent from the rose, if it be smeared on wooden images, prevents their decaying. The iris grows in marshes, is in size as large as a lily, but is not white in color, and smells less sweet.

(Loeb translation)

We can imagine Pausanias walking towards Chaironeia, the air sweetly perfumed with the scent of flowers being cultivated and prepared for this flourishing healing industry.[104] It obviously struck him, as his description of Chaironeia is rather short, but it nonetheless concludes with this proportionally lengthy depiction of its flower production. We can therefore assume that the healing and perfume industry in Chaironeia, complemented by local shrines to healing deities, was thriving at the time that he wrote this.

The focus on a healing industry in Chaironeia will not come as a surprise. Chaironeia was located on Lake Kopais, which, as Ruben Post points out in this volume, formed a unique ecological micro-region in Boiotia. However, while Post notes that the sanctuaries around the lake were centred on water, Chaironeia's healing sanctuaries are likely related to his second observation of the area: disease. Chaironeia's focus on healing deities is thus possibly related to the prevalence of malaria and the subsequent need of the inhabitants for medicine. In this way, the situation in Chaironeia agrees with Post's final point that the historical episodes "punctuated" local lives, but it was the ecology of the area that defined it.

It would not be unreasonable, therefore, to search for this healing industry at a time before Pausanias and the Roman era. For example, Victoria Sabetai suggests that the female protomes of Chaironeia from the Archaic period followed a pattern of the trade routes for perfumes, rather than religious routes.[105] It is thus possible that the unguent and perfume industry in Chaironeia was one that carried on from at least the Archaic period into the Roman Empire, becoming a fixed staple of local identity, for economic development depends on both "a region's historically embedded resources" and the identity it projects to internal and external audiences.[106] In Chaironeia, this local identity moved beyond battle narratives to one focused on healing, as seen in the small finds of the area, as well as the powerful description of outsiders, like Pausanias.

This provides an interesting contrast to the previous conclusion that being Chaironeian in the Hellenistic era meant being part of a narrative of combat. Not only were the locals engaged in defensive acts and remembering conflict and bloodshed, but through their best-known agricultural endeavours and their local religious cults, they were also involved in healing and preservation. Local identity and the local discourse environment were therefore complex not only in terms of their local, regional, and global mingling, but also in their oppositions.

## Manumission Records

Identifying aspects of Chaironeia's Hellenistic identity is further complicated when looking at its manumission records.[107] Boiotia is particularly rich in manumission records, with over 170 inscriptions found in seven different *poleis*. However, more than 70 per cent of those found come from Chaironeia,[108] all of which belong to the Hellenistic period.[109] In general, the inscriptions are brief because of a law from the *polis* that regulated how a slave was to be manumitted.[110] This law dictated the language of the inscription as well as the nature of the manumission, thus allowing for only small discrepancies in the epigraphic record. Laurence Darmezin originally argued that because of their formulaic nature, they are rarely exploitable.[111] More recent scholarship, however, has revealed that it is possible to draw further conclusions from these inscriptions. For example, the use of the local Chaironeian archon for dating the inscriptions, as opposed to the Boiotian one (such as in *IG* VII 3378),[112] should be considered in combination with the unique manumission law from Chaironeia on many of these inscriptions.[113] From this, it can be posited that there was a desire to create a local practice that differed from other *poleis* in Boiotia and Greece, or, at the very least, one that made it evidently Chaironeian. If this is too strong a hypothesis, it can still be asserted that the practice was different in its epigraphic and symbolic nature from other *poleis* in the macro-region of Boiotia. One of the difficulties with this, however, is the very nature of ancient remains.[114] It is possible that the inscriptions from Chaironeia are extant as a result of the accident of survival, leaving us with an incomplete record and thus prohibiting serious comparison with the manumission practices of other Boiotian *poleis*.

Keeping in mind this methodological difficulty, these inscriptions still speak to the local discourse of Chaironeia. First, differences in gender roles in these inscriptions are evident, where women, unlike men, had to be assisted by a close male relative in order to manumit a slave. While this is a common practice in Boiotia, it is not in the rest of Greece.[115] Thus we have a Greek practice of manumitting a slave, modified at the regional level in Boiotia to include male assistance for women,[116] and again altered in the local sphere through the Chaironeian law and the local context of the manumission. Furthermore, studies on the prosopography of these records indicate that the manumitters from Chaironeia are very much tied together as members of powerful local families.[117] This suggests that elite members of Chaironeia in the Hellenistic period were actively engaged in manumitting slaves, perhaps as a result of concern for the health of their religious centres. Whatever their motivation in manumitting slaves, this activity stretches across these elite families, forming a part of what was likely a familiar practice in the area, and thus a part of the local narrative.

Chaironeian elites are not the only ones to manumit slaves in this *polis*. For instance, there is evidence of a Phantantean (*IG* VII 3376),[118] a man from Lebadeia (*IG* VII 3360), an Orchomenian (*IG* VII 3372), and a manumitter from Phokian Daulis (*IG* VII 3333).[119] Regional connections through marriage are also seen in inscriptions like that of Karais, a woman whose husband is identified as being from Lebadeia.[120] It can thus be tentatively suggested that these inscriptions from outsiders demonstrate that Chaironeia may have had some sort of religious pull, drawing citizens of various Boiotian *poleis* to this relatively small town in order to dedicate slaves to these local sanctuaries.[121] Even if this is not the case, and these dedications are the exception rather than the rule, the practice still seems to be familiar to some Boiotian outsiders, who chose to manumit their slaves in Chaironeia, following local Chaironeian practices. And so, while it is difficult to reconstruct the local narrative around these manumissions, or to comment on how they may have been unique, it can nonetheless be safely argued that they were part of Chaironeia's local discourse.

These manumission records also grant an opportunity to observe changes over time. Where once Asklepios was a popular deity in Chaironeia, the cult of the Egyptian gods seems to have usurped some of his popularity for the manumission of slaves.[122] The Egyptian gods were the object of worship in Boiotia from the third century BCE to the third century CE, because they likely provided a sense of community during the Roman Empire.[123] It seems, then, that Chaironeia was also engaging with this regional religious trend.[124] This may explain the manumissions made by outsiders, who were familiar with the Egyptian gods, but it does not preclude that the manumissions made in Chaironeia were unique. As mentioned above, they contain the local archon, the local law, and are done in a local context, a context chosen by locals and outsiders alike. As such, they remain part of the local discourse environment as witnesses to a practice that was seemingly popular and perhaps unique to this local sphere.

Furthermore, we can also detect changes in language when the texts transition from the Boiotian dialect into *koinē*.[125] Here, Chaironeia follows the rest of the Greek world by changing their epigraphic habit into one that was more clearly understood by non-Boiotians. This has symbolic power, perhaps suggesting that more travellers were coming through and that the manumitters wanted their texts to be understood by them. It may also signify a more connected *polis*, one that was changing in its language and was engaging more with neighbours from further afield. As Hans Beck explains, "Networks are prone to trigger a shift in the mindsets of those who engage in them. They disregard the juxtaposition of near and far."[126] We cannot know if the change in dialect was an active choice or a passive change with time (one that disregarded near and far), but either way, these later *koine* inscriptions point to an alteration of the local epigraphic habit to one that was more universal in the Greek world and thus shows a more connected Chaironeia in the Hellenistic period.

This brief survey of the manumission records of Chaironeia repeats a trend seen throughout this chapter: the regional and global intermixing and being reinterpreted in a local sphere. The manumissions are local because they are from Chaironeia, follow Chaironeian laws, and are dedicated to sanctuaries in Chaironeia. They are regional through evidence of marriage ties, dialect, and outside manumitters. Finally, they have a global horizon not only through the global nature of the gods, but also through the eventual success of *koinē*, whose propagation was only possible in a more connected Greek world.[127] Hellenistic Chaironeia, then, was not just about battles, bloodshed, and commemoration, it was also about healing (plants and gods), connectivity (in Boiotia and beyond), and the liberation of slaves.

## Conclusion

More research on Chaironeia and its local environs is needed. The above examples, while possibly relating to all classes of the population of Chaironeia, likely reflect mainly (or only) the elites, since they had more of an ability to physically move and figuratively manoeuvre, and thus to connect with these other networks. Until more work is done on the *chōra*, or large-scale excavations are carried out, it is unlikely that we will be able to speak extensively on these other members of Chaironeia in the Hellenistic period. In this regard, Christel Müller cautions us that "the idea that poleis were linked together in different types of networks does not mean that every member of every community was permanently connected with the rest of the Greek world."[128] But from what we have seen, some in Chaironeia obviously were.

To be an elite Chaironeian in the Hellenistic period was not only about being engaged in the "manageable, accessible realm," but also about being a player in the activities and symbolic language of an increasingly connected world. They partook in defensive measures, in creations of *lieux de mémoire*, in agricultural endeavours, in healing practices, and in religious rites, seen most obviously in the manumission of slaves. Chaironeia clearly fostered an identity of place that was more than the battles that usually define it. It was shaped both by its physical spaces (e.g., its theatre, acropolis, and sanctuaries) and by its imagined spaces, mainly those surrounding the memories of the battles of Chaironeia, creating a local battlescape. This helped to form a rich local discourse that brought meaning to these spaces for locals and visitors: one in which the local, regional, and global connections interplayed and were reinterpreted in this local space, showing a more complex picture than one of a simple *polis* with a good battleground.

## NOTES

1 The "battles of Chaironeia" include those in 338 BCE (Philip vs Hellenic Alliance); 245 BCE (Aitolian League vs Boiotian League); 146 BCE (Roman general Matellus defeats 1,000 Arkadians); 86 BCE (Sulla vs Mithridates); 1311 (Catalans vs Franks); 1823, 1825 (Greek War of Independence). It is possible that more ancient battles were fought in the vicinity of the *polis*, which may help to explain some of the defensive walls on the acropolis (see page 73). However, without more archaeological investigations, we can only speculate that conflict near or in Chaironeia spurred this defensive endeavour.
2 Meyer 2008: 71. For more on Chaironeia, see Giroux 2021 with corresponding bibliography.
3 Erskine 2005: 2–3.
4 Beck 2018: 16; Beck 2020: 4, 34. See this volume, page 18.
5 Beck 2020: 2. It was also "shaped by a polyphony of voices and a plurality of realms where conversations between shifting groups of speakers and audiences took place. Despite complex and nuanced differentiations within, the unifying element of the discourse was that voice and place were bracketed by the horizon of directness; the local delineated a communicative boundary" (Beck 2020: 34).
6 Beck 2018: 23; Beck 2020: 3–4, 30–2.
7 Beck 2018: 24–5; Beck 2020: 33–4.
8 The term "global" is one that is fraught with division and difficulties, especially when discussing the ancient world. While the ancient world is not "global" in the modern geographic sense of the idea, I use the term here to convey a larger world beyond that of the regional sphere. For Chaironeia, this would be anything beyond the Greek world, such as the range of Alexander's conquests, or later, one that encapsulated the larger Roman Empire. In this sense, "global" is also a useful term, as it captures ancient concerns that were associated with a growing world of interconnections, networks, and cultures. These questions and concerns in many ways reflect modern anxieties of what can be truly referred to as a "global world." As such, I follow Inglis and Robertson 2004, 2005; Clarke 2005; Hingley 2005; Sweetman 2007; Seland 2008; Pelling 2010; Müller 2016; Hodos 2017; Witcher 2017; and Beck 2018. For a cohesive argument against the use of "global" and "globalization" in the ancient world, see Naerebout 2006–7.

9 It must be noted that Plutarch lived under the Roman Empire and not in Hellenistic Chaironeia. However, as the most famous representative of this polis, not to mention the unique opportunities afforded by his writings to understand a local context (or at least a man from this local context), he provides an *exemplum* of the kind of men that *may* have lived in Hellenistic Chaironeia: elite, connected, educated. For more on Plutarch and his local world, see Giroux 2021. For more on the local inhabitants of Hellenistic Chaironeia and their practices, see pages 109–23.

10 Hansen and Nielsen 2004: 81.

11 Hansen and Nielsen 2004: 81–2.

12 Ma 2008: 72. See also, Funke 2006. Chaironeia's streams are known as the Molos, Haimon, and Morios (Pritchett 1958: 307–9).

13 Farinetti 2011:101; Fossey and Gauvin 1990: 249; Ma 1994: 67.

14 For more on the geography of the area and how it lends itself to history to create the micro-region of eastern Phokis and western Boitoia, see Giroux 2021: 48–55.

15 Fossey (1973–4: 18) suggests that Magoúla Baloménou should be identified as Arne. For evidence of occupation: Pritchett 1958: 309; Buck 1979: 5; Funke 2006. Archaeology in Chaironeia: Dawkins 1907: 286 (Neolithic remains); Dilke 1950 (theatre); Pritchett 1958 (topography); Fossey and Gauvin 1990: 250 (Roman era remains); Germani 2015, 2018 (theatre); Sabetai 2015 (female protomes); Charami 2016 (third-century CE villa).

16 Hansen and Nielsen 2004: 82; Hammond 2000: 83–6; Funke 2006. See also *Hell. Oxy.* 19.3.394–6. The first epigraphical reference to Chaironeia as a polis is from a second-century BCE proxeny decree, *IG* VII 3287 (Hansen 1996: 81; Hansen and Nielsen 2004: 82). A Hellenistic inscription (*IG* VII 2724c.6) also mentions Chaironeia as a member of the Boiotian League. Diodorus (16.39.8) speaks of Chaironeia as a member of the Second Boiotian Federation. For the durability of the institution of the boiotarch, see Fossey 1991: 97–109.

17 Procop. *Goth.* 4.25.16f (Funke 2006).

18 Farinetti 2011: 103; Jones 1971: 4; Ma 2008: 73; Titchener 2014: 485.

19 Billows 2005: 196.

20 Jones 1971: 3–4. Delphi is located approximately 80 km from Chaironeia. Since Chaironeia lies on an arterial road, it is not inconceivable that travellers would pass through the polis on their way to and from Delphi. Further, a local Chaironeian, Plutarch, was a priest at Delphi (700e; 792f). Although Plutarch lived during the Roman period, and is thus not necessarily representative of the influence of Hellenistic Chaironeian elites, his position in Delphi nonetheless provides a potential example of

the relationship between the two *poleis* that likely grew from Chaironeia's geographic location.

21  Although McInerney (2015: 204, 207) uses this term in reference to Phokis, Chaironeia's proximity to Phokis (for example, Parapotamioi is only 7 km away from Chaironeia: Fossey 1986: 70–1) and its location at the pass makes it another suitable candidate for a "contact zone." This makes Chaironeia similar to Beck's (2020: 14–16) example of Phlious, who was subject to the power politics that surrounded it, transforming some of their local world into one defined by relational attributes.

22  As mentioned above (page 71), Chaironeia was subject to Orchomenos until the end of the fifth century BCE, after which it became independent. We can thus identify Chaironeia as a likely participant in the alliances and conflicts of Orchomenos during these times (e.g., Orchomenos' friendly relations with Thessaly meant that they did not help the Phokians when Thessaly invaded Phokis and may also have been the cause of the Thessalians invading Boiotia; Buck 1972: 94–7, 100). Micro-regional conflict is largely seen between Boiotians (usually Thebes vs Orchomenos [see, e.g., Bakhuizen 1994: 323; Hammond 2000: 88–92; Mackil 2013: 87–8; Beck and Ganter 2015: 149]) or between Boiotians (usually Thebes) and Phokis for control of territory (Buck 1972: 94–7; Buckler 1985; Fossey 1986: 98; Hammond 2000: 90; McInerney 2011, 2015: 215–17; Mackil 2013: 82–5; Schachter 2016: 122; Beck 2020: 63–4). For Phokis and its relationship with Philip, see Larsen 1965. For recent work on the region of Phokis that grants insight into its role in this micro-region, see McInerney 1999 (see esp. pp. 55–6 on the routes in Phokis and their relationship to conflict in the area); McInerney 2011 (Delphi and its relationship with Phokis) and 2015 (Phokis as a regional entity); Sporn 2018, 2019 (archaeology in the area, wealth, and fortifications); Sporn and Laufer 2019 (Kephissos Valley and Tithorea).

23  Boiotia and internal war: Bakhuizen 1994: 323; Vottero 1998: 105–7; Hammond 2000: 88–92; Buckler and Beck 2008: 13–14; Mackil 2013: 87–8; Beck and Ganter 2015: 149. Cooperation as a means of stability, however, is key to the Hellenistic Boiotian world, and is a good example of how a region can become insular in times of change and expansion. One form of regional collaboration is the pan-Boiotian elite soldiers, made up of men from across Boiotia, which existed even after the Boiotian confederacy was dissolved in 171 BCE (Schachter 2016: 193–215). Interestingly, Beck (2014: 26–7) demonstrates that the *Boiōtoi* as a distinct group grew from an origin in warfare and that they were already recognized in inscriptions by the end of the sixth century BCE (cf. Hammond 2000: 81). The history and continuity of this affiliation with warfare thus marks it as one of the most important factors for this *ethnos*. For more on the inscription on the Athenian Acropolis that mentions

the *Boiōtoi* and their loss to the Athenians, see Bakhuizen 1986: 67. For economic cooperation and regional coinage, see Hammond 2000: 81–2, 87–91; Larson 2007: 106–9; Meidani 2008: 157; Mackil 2013: 28; Beck and Ganter 2015: 138; and Schachter 2016: 48–9. For a critical and sceptical response to the use of coinage as being indicative of regional cooperation, see Mackil 2013: 26.

24 For example, Boiotian infighting over Plataiai's decision to join Athens led to arbitration by the Corinthians and fighting with Athens: Buck 1972: 94 and Hammond 2000: 80–1 (citing Hdt. 6.108). See Buck (1972: 99–101) for more on Boiotian-Athenian conflict and its implications for the Boiotian League, or Pantelidis' (2017) examination of the Boiotian dialect and its relationship to political borders (with a focus on Attika). Buck (1972: 94) argues that the Thessalian invasion of Boiotia may have led to the formation of the Boiotian League, thus providing another example of how Boiotia came together as a region during a time of change and expansion. For more on Boiotia and their involvement in conflicts across the Greek world in the Hellenistic period, see Mackil 2013: 91–143.

25 McInerney 2015: 205, citing Paus. 9.17.4 and the stealing of soil from the tombs of Amphion and Zethos for dedications at Phokos and Antiope: "In this way, ritual and myth together supplied a way of conceptualizing competing territorial claims" (McInerney 2015: 205). Interestingly, like Chaironeia, the Phokians have an eponymous hero, Phokos, who is also associated with Thessaly (McInerney 2015: 204). For more on Boiotia and its localized heroic figures and their relation to war, see Buck 1979 (Boiotian heroes) and Schachter 2016: 32 (Kadmos). For Boiotian ethnogenesis and its relationship to regional cults and mythology, see Buckler and Beck 2008: 13–14. Beck (2020: 64) argues, "In the course of time, some petty border disputes that had originated from local grievances there quickly evolved into full-blown warfare on a regional or a Panhellenic scale." He then gives the Sacred Wars and the Corinthian Wars as examples (2020: 221, n. 49; cf. Beck 2020: 198–205).

26 Hammond 2000: 90; Rzepka 2010: 117. For micro-regional politics, Beck (2020: 39) notes that "archaeologists have traced a lively entanglement in micro-regions united by distinct natural features and favourable lines of translocal communication – for instance, in the Kephissos Valley from Phokis into Boiotia."

27 McInerney 2015: 201. For more on micro-regions that move beyond the boundaries of *koina* in the ancient Greek world, see McInerney 2011 and Pantelidis 2017. For more on the pass and Chaironeia's relation to it, see Hammond 1938: 187.

28 McInerney 1999: 55.

29 McInerney (2011) points to dedications at Kalapodi in both the Boiotian and Thessalian dialects and suggests that this is indicative of Kalapodi's central

position in this network. It is thus likely that Chaironeia also participated in this network and in dedications to the sanctuary, given its proximity and participation in this micro-region. Beck (2020: 129) points to Kalapodi as an example of an "intermediary space," one that was translocal, regional, and federal all at the same time. As such, these cult centres become nodes of interaction in regional spaces (Beck 2020: 129–30).

30 Similar to Beck's (2020: 14, cf. 12–18) description of Phlious.

31 Beck and Ganter 2015: 146. See Mackil 2013: 83–4 for the effect of Phokian attacks on the internal cohesion of Boiotia.

32 Though this new alliance did not have Thebes in control and saw more rights given to individual *poleis* than in previous manifestations: Buck 1985: 295; Buckler and Beck 2008; Mackil 2013: 2, 91, 113; Beck and Ganter 2015: 150–1. This follows a pattern throughout Greece for the Hellenistic period, where almost half of mainland Greece was under some kind of regional alliance (Mackil 2013: 1). For Phokis' regional alliance, see McInerney 2015: 219.

33 This can be seen, for example, in the war of Perseus against Rome (Fossey 1979: 582). For a discussion on the possibility of Boiotia as a "client" of Rome, see Edlund 1977.

34 E.g., through the invasion of Thessaly into their territory.

35 It is also important to consider that the battles that occurred in or nearby Chaironeia were not one-off events that were quickly forgotten; reminders in the landscape ensured that their effects lingered in the communal memory of the *polis*. As Susan Alcock explains: "All aspects of human activity – settlement patterns, boundaries, ritual sites, roads, monuments, burial places – together with their intersection with the natural world, are bound up in the concept, which also highlights emotional ties to particular places and the memories invested within them" (Alcock et al. 2005: 354–5). When looking at a landscape, there is an opportunity to assess changing local conditions over time (355), or, in this investigation of Hellenistic Chaironeia, to glimpse at a local context during a particular time.

36 See above, 71.

37 Farinetti 2011: 101.

38 *IG* VII 3409; Dilke 1950: 35–7; Hansen and Nielsen 2004: 82; Germani 2018; Giroux 2021: 70–4.

39 For the phases of the walls, see Hammond 1938: 2, n. 1, and Fossey 1988: 376–8. For Boiotian defensive measures in the fourth century, see Fossey and Gauvin 1990: 116–18 and Beck 2020: 65–8.

40 By securing Chaironeia, the regional world thus laid claim over the land and its *chōra* (Beck 2020: 67).

41 Ma 2008: 77.

42 Ma 2008: 78.

43 We know that it was fertilized before this, as sherds were found in deposits
   in the tomb (Ma 2008: 78). As Mayo explains (1988: 63), "There are social
   expectations about personal behavior in a sacred place. Social sanctions must
   exist that keep a place sacred by allowing it to be ritualized temporarily or
   that assume it will remain sacred even when people are absent." Clearly, social
   sanctions ensured that the space around the mound in the plain of Chaironeia
   remained sacred by removing any agricultural activities around it.
44 Ma 2008: 77, 84.
45 Ma 2008: 83–4.
46 Ma 2008: 85. As Mayo argues (1988: 69), "War memorials, whether sacred or
   not, subtly permeate lives more than is realized." This lends weight to Ma's
   idea of the monuments communicating over the plain of Chaironeia, perhaps
   in a subconscious way for both locals and visitors.
47 Local marble and placement: Ma 2008: 81. For more on Charioneia and
   movement through the *polis*, see Giroux 2021: 67–97.
48 The anchorage of a *polis*, both literally and metaphorically, through the
   use of local building materials is suggested by Beck (2020: 128) in relation
   to dedications at Olympia. Here, I propose that it is also possible to view
   the selection of local Chaironeian marble in a similar light. Two potential
   problems arise: (1) this is a Theban tomb, somewhat divorcing the idea of a
   local connection, and; (2) the use of marble was also likely a practical decision
   based on the proximity of the quarry, which would remove any transportation
   costs. Nevertheless, the local Chaironeians surely aided in the acquiring of and
   shaping of the marble, and lived with the visual reminder in their landscape
   daily. In this way, the local tie is once again strengthened and functions as a
   reminder of the connection to their land as well as pride in their role in the
   events of that day.
49 See, e.g., Camp 1992; Mackay 2000; Assenmaker 2013; Kalliontzis 2014. For a
   discussion on the commemoration of battles in Boiotia, see Kalliontzis 2014,
   esp. 343–67. The differences between Greek and Roman trophies are discussed
   by Kinnee 2018: 67–9.
50 For the importance of this mention in relation to Plutarch and autopsy in his
   works, see Buckler 1992. For Plutarch's silences on Chaironeia, including that
   of the Lion of Chaironeia, see Giroux 2022.
51 Although the inscription itself does not mention Sulla or the exploits of
   Homoloïchos and Anaxidamos, Plutarch outright says that the trophy is
   in commemoration of this event and that these two men were the heroes
   of the day (ἐπισημαῖνον Ὁμολόϊχον καὶ Ἀναξίδαμον ἀριστεῖς). We may
   infer, therefore, that in local memory and local discourse, this trophy
   represented an important contribution of Chaironeia and its citizens to
   this moment in time.

52  Mackay 2000: 171. For more on the Boiotian dialect see Vottero 1998, 2001; Pantelidis 2017.

53  Plutarch, at least, seems to have pride in the aid the Chaironeians gave to Sulla: *Sulla* 16.8–19.6.

54  Like the symbolic weight of the Lion of Chaironeia, discussed above. For more on war memorials and their symbolic power, see Mayo 1988.

55  For the tendency of the Greeks in the Hellenistic period to turn to the past, see Kalliontzis 2014: 343 and Stevens 2016: 67.

56  Büttner (2006) explains that the term "tourism," despite appearances in the English language in the nineteenth century, narrowed its definition to an educational and/or pleasure trip after the end of World War II.

57  Stumpf (2013) describes different kinds of tourism in antiquity. For tourism in antiquity as related to religious experience, see Casson 1974: 234 and Romero 2013: 149. For tourism of famous deeds (legendary or historical) or the tombs of heroes (e.g., Pindar's tomb [Paus. 9.23.2] or Alexander's tomb [Strabo 17.794]), see Stumpf 2013. For tourism as fully developed by Roman antiquity, see Büttner 2006 and Stumpf 2013. A view of ancient tourism from the eye of the tourist is available in Lomine 2005 (see especially page 77 for her discussion on Strabo's distrust of the talking statue of Memnon at Thebes). This is a great example of the idea of the "tourist gaze," coined by John Urry in 1990 (updated in 2011). Urry's basic argument is that "the concept of the gaze highlights that looking is a learned ability and that the pure and innocent eye is a myth" (2011: 1). We must, therefore, also consider the role that the tourist plays in the interpretation of a site. The tourist gaze is also discussed by MacCannell 2001, who argues for multiple gazes.

58  Cohen 2001: 97. Evidence of travellers is given by Stumpf (2013): "The itineraries of Cicero, Apollonius of Tyana, Aemilius Paullus, Hadrian, and others can be reconstructed. The draw of some attractions is suggested by the international origins of competitors at games, literary testimonia such as Plutarch's Delphic dialogues, and graffiti left behind by travelers to the Egyptian Valley of the Kings." This also fits nicely with Erskine's (2005: 2–3) contention that the Hellenistic period is not just a politically active era, but also a culturally relevant one (see page 69). As Chaniotis (2009: 253) points out, "The travels and the performances of epic, tragic and choral poets in the Hellenistic period ... are part of a more general phenomenon: the mobility of culture, the mobility of texts, images and performances." The importance of this cultural experience is further highlighted by the profession of the tour guide, for which we have evidence in the early Roman Empire (Lucian *Amores* 8, Plut. *Mor.* 395a; Lomine 2005: 82–3; Romero 2013: 151), but which, I believe, likely evolved from the Hellenistic and Roman Republican interests in these sites.

59 Stumpf (2013) points to excerpts of Polemon, Diodorus, Heliodorus, and papyri in Egypt. An interesting study on Pausanias, perhaps our most famous travel writer of antiquity, is given by Cohen (2001), who argues that while Pausanias was writing during the Roman Empire, his views are reflective of Hellenistic attitudes. Note that Casson (1974: 95–6) describes Herodotus as the first travel writer. The use of guidebooks as mainly a preparatory reading is discussed by Lomine (2005: 82). Note that Chaniotis (2009: 253–4) cautions that the transmission of "memory" in the Hellenistic period was mainly oral, but also points to the importance of written narratives, itinerant historians, diplomats, poets, singers, pilgrims, and mercenaries to the transmission of "memory" in the Hellenistic Greek world.

60 Stumpf 2013, italics are my own. A modern example that explains feelings of nostalgia linked to a location is found in an essay by Hilaire Belloc, when he says, "Time does not remain, but space does, and though we cannot seize the Past physically we can stand physically upon the site, and we can have (if I may so express myself) a physical communion with the Past by occupying that very spot which the past greatness of man or of event has occupied" (1948: 230). Two cases of the globalized world leading to an interest in the local is found in Chaniotis 2009: 259–60 (citing *SEG* 28.534 and *IG* XI 4, 697). These two examples also demonstrate the interest of both the elites and the audience during the Hellenistic period for historical works. See Chaniotis 2009 for more examples of this historical interest.

61 Chaniotis 2005: 237; Baldwin and Sharpley 2009: 186. Note, however, that in the Hellenistic world, it is likely that visitors' interest in the site was both historical and religious (Chaniotis 2005: 145). For travels specifically to battlefields, Casson gives the examples of trips to Marathon, where tourists were shown the mound of the Athenians (1974: 235–6; cf. Chaniotis 2009: 258), and the tour Aemilius Paullus took after his victory at Pydna, which included not only sites dedicated to gods, but also those of historical significance (1974: 230; cf. Romero 2013: 151 [citing Livy 45.27–8 and Plutarch *Aem.* 28]). Baldwin and Sharpley (2009: 186) provide two other examples, namely, that of Alexander the Great visiting the Tomb of Achilles, and the presence of Simonides' epigram in Thermopylae. Similarly, Chaniotis (2005: 51–3; 2009: 258) discusses the honorary inscriptions to ephebes in the Hellenistic period (e.g., *IG* II² 1006), which indicate visitation to war monuments and participation in rituals that enabled the transmission of cultural memory to Athenian youths. Chaniotis (2009: 258–9) finds a pattern in which a preference is given to wars against barbarians or, "for victories that legitimised claims," but also discusses the importance of near contemporary history and heroic deeds in battle to the collective memory of local worlds (2009: 262, 265). See also the articles on landscapes of war and

the interest that authors took in their recreation in Reitz-Joosse, Makins, and Mackie (2021).

62  Gatewood and Cameron 2004: 193. See Carman and Carman (2020: 217, 225–6) for an interesting discussion of how a visitor to the battlefield projects the present onto the past in order to make the chaotic nature of war comprehensible. In this way, they argue, the battlefield is more a thing of the imagination than reality. Chaironeia's battlefields, then, would be part of the physical (monuments) and imagined local script.

63  West 2010. See the discussion on the possible multiple interpretations of the trophy of Homoloïchos and Anaxidamos in the previous section, page 75. For the multiple meanings of war trophies in the Greek world, see Kinnee 2018, esp. pp. 1–3.

64  See page 74.

65  Inspiration for this idea comes from West (2010: 212), who argues that the tombs set up in Gallipoli de-emphasize the individual and promote the national. See also Mackie 2021. A similar view is expressed by Hölscher (2006: 30–2), who focuses on the political power of the trophy. Other symbolic uses of the trophy include to mark territorial ownership (Kinnee 2018: 29, 37 [citing Thuc. 8.24.1]), to declare victory (Kinnee 2018: 36–7), as a symbol of *aretē* and achievement (Kinnee 2018: 25, 38), as a religious dedication (Kinnee 2018: 25), and as a transmitter of cultural memory (Chaniotis 2005: 234, 240). Kinnee (2018: 39) cautions the reader that the trophy as a symbol of the military achievements of one individual is a Roman trend, though examples, such as the trophy of Agesilaus as described by Xenophon (*Ages.* 6.2), do exist. For more on micro-regional politics and landscape archaeology as claims to space, see Beck 2020: 64–5.

66  Carman and Carman 2005: 43; Kinnee 2018: 57.

67  Kinnee 2018: 3, 24–5, 40, 49, 57.

68  Eade and Katić (2017: 1–12) explore the relationship between tourism and dark tourism. Cf. Iles 2006; Baldwin and Sharpley 2009; Light 2017; Seaton 2018.

69  For this definition of dark tourism, I follow Seaton (2018: 13). Seaton explains that remembrance can come through written and oral texts (such as Greek and Roman epic poetry), social networks, and monuments (20), but that it must be place specific (21).

70  Seaton (2018: 9–10) explains that they list history, national pride, and pilgrimage as their factors for visiting.

71  Lennon 2010: 216. Sharpley (2009: 5, 9) reminds the reader that dark tourism as a historic phenomenon is contentious, but that the draw to death has occurred for as long as people have travelled: "In other words, it has always been an identifiable form of tourism" (Sharpley 2009: 9). Since we know that elites were travelling in the Hellenistic world, it is thus possible that they

would travel and be drawn to these historic sites that are also associated with war and death.

72  Walter 2009: 47–8. An interesting Boiotian example of the political instrumentalization of a festival to commemorate a victory, the Basileia at Lebadeia, is provided by Ganter (2013: 94–6) and Schachter (2016: 117). They argue that the festival was primarily inaugurated as a reminder of the Theban leadership of the region. In the Hellenistic period; however, this festival was reimagined as an inclusive Boiotian festival, not one that purely celebrated Theban hegemony. As such, Ganter (2013: 96) contends, what was meant as an advertisement for one *polis'* leadership managed to bring cohesion to Boiotia through myth and a common past.

73  Gutzwiller 1998: 2–4; Seaton 2018: 21.

74  Similarly, we find Hesiod's, Iolaos', and Pindar's tombs in Thebes described by Pausanias (9.38.4, 9.23.1–2), who thus likely visited them. The tomb of Alexander the Great has often been described as an ancient tourist attraction; however, Erskine (2002: 165) cautions that this may be overstated. Cf. Mackie 2021: 235.

75  Chaniotis 2005: 234; 2009: 268.

76  As argued by Kalliontzis 2014. In this article, Kalliontzis shows that the commemoration of war dead in Boiotia did not find a uniform expression. Instead, "each city chose its own way" (367).

77  See Eade and Katić (2017: 1–12, esp. 4) for more on deathscapes. See also Minchin (2021), who explores Homeric descriptions of battlefields to build a "cognitive collage" for the audience. Plutarch, in these descriptions, employs a similar method to bring the experience of the battle to his readers.

78  See page 76.

79  West 2010: 218. Cf. Iles 2006: 167.

80  Plutarch as reluctant to discuss his home and regional environment: Hirsch-Luipold 2014: 165. Plutarch as providing incidental information on Chaironeia: Jones 1971: 3; Buckler 1992: 4801.

81  Winter 2014: 36.

82  I have argued elsewhere that this tale helps to emphasize a continuity of loyalty to Rome – one where the locals were antagonized by Antony and thus "freed" when he lost to Octavian (see Giroux 2021, 2022).

83  See *Cim.* 2.1, for the attempt of Orchomenos to have Chaironeia prosecuted for the slaying of the Roman soldiers.

84  Plutarch frequently refers to Chaironeia in relation to battles: e.g., *De fort. Rom.* 318d (Sulla trophy); *Sull.* 16.8, 17.5–6, 18.1 (local Chaironeians helping Sulla); *Thes.* 27.6 (Amazons buried near Chaironeia); *Ages.* 17.2 (encamps near Chaironeia and has a vision); *Dem.*19.2 (description of local topography and

a local river name in relation to a battle fought there); *Lys.* 29.3 (his burial on the road leading from Delphi to Chaironeia). Cf. Giroux 2021.

85 Pausanias, like Plutarch, is of course in the Roman period rather than the Hellenistic. It is nevertheless important to include him in this discussion because of his comparatively lengthy account of Chaironeia and because his interest in the *polis* seems to be similar to that of Plutarch: to remember the battles that were fought there, mainly those of the Hellenistic period. It is also likely that Pausanias' information was gathered from the locals of the town, and thus his testimony probably contains evidence of the local memory of these events and thus speaks to the local discourse environment of Chaironeia that continued to his time.

86 For Pausanias as having Hellenistic rather than Roman attitudes, see Cohen 2001.

87 I borrow this term from Beck 2020: 35.

88 For more on "big" politics through the local lens, see Beck 2020: 161–206.

89 Fossey 1988: 379; Fossey and Gauvin 1990: 250. A more complete discussion of the small finds and epigraphic landscape of Chaironeia is found in Giroux 2021: 98–123.

90 In the Museum of Chaironeia (*MX* 849). Cf. Giroux 2021: 98–100.

91 Alexandropoulou 2015, esp. 351; Sabetai 2015, esp. 151 and 160; Giroux 2021: 100–3. Although these are Classical examples, it can be assumed that such trade connections and regional influences continued into the Hellenistic era, as this period likely saw an increase in connectivity (see pages 69, 71).

92 Schachter 1981: 98.

93 Schachter 1981: 43.

94 Schachter 1981: 107–10; Gallet de Santerre 1952: 224.

95 Leake 1967/1835: 115; Schachter 1981: 199. See also Pausanias 9.40.11–12.

96 Gallet de Santerre 1952: 224; Schachter 1981: 173–4, 200; Fossey 1988: 383; Meyer 2008: 71–2; Fossey and Darmezin 2014: 191–2; Giroux 2021: 82–91. Cf. Plutarch *Cim.* 2, *Dem.* 19; *Quaest. Rom.* 16; *Sull.* 17.

97 For example, Plutarch explains one such ritual (*Quaest. Rom.* 16), saying, "The Grecians say the maid was of an Aetolian family and was called Antiphera. Therefore, with us also in Chaeronea the sexton, standing before the temple of Leukothea (Matuta) holding a wand in his hand, makes proclamation that no man-servant nor maid-servant, neither man nor woman Aetolian, should enter in" (Loeb translation). This seems to be an established ritual in Plutarch's time, as evidenced most clearly by his explanation of its origins. We can therefore assume that this rite, or something similar, was being performed during the Hellenistic Age, providing at least one example of local religious life.

98 Meyer 2008: 72 citing Pausanias 9.41.7. For more information on the plant life of Lake Kopais, see Theophr. *Hist. pl.* 4.10–12. See also: Fossey and Gauvin 1990: 265; Farinetti 2011: 51; Beck 2020: 85; Post in this volume.

99  Farinetti 2011: 54.

100  Farinetti 2011: 102.

101  640b. Cf. Farinetti 2011: 103.

102  Lytle 2010: 284.

103  641f–642a. Cf. Post (this volume) for the region of Lake Kopais and animal husbandry.

104  Beck (2020: 81) gives the example of the wildflowers of Orchomenos and Chaironeia as part of the sense-experience of the local world, here, a smellscape (Cf. Beck 2020: 78–81 for the psychological and physiological experience of smell). For more on Orchomenos' flowers, see Post in this volume.

105  Sabetai 2015: 154.

106  Romanelli and Khessina 2005: 355. Similarly, Beck (2018: 30–1) explains, "Seeing artisanal expertise as representative of communal values, norms, and habits, scholars have argued that cultural output reverberates a sense of belonging, a sense that was again magnified through repetition over time." Cf. Giroux 2021: 88–91.

107  For the importance of epigraphy and what it can reveal about a city, see Ma 2013.

108  Based on 125 inscriptions found in Chaironeia of the 172 found in Boiotia. The other *poleis* where manumission records have been found are recorded by Darmezin (1985: 325): Orchomenos, Koroneia, Lebadeia, Thespiai, and Thisbe.

109  Grenet 2014: 395. See Giroux 2021: 115–23.

110  For the uniqueness of this law: Fossey 1991: 123; Grenet 2014: 426; Schachter 2016: 296. Evidence of the law can be found, e.g., in *IG* VII 3307 and *IG* VII 3376.

111  Darmezin 1985: 326.

112  Meyer 2008: 73. Grenet (2014: 400) points out that all but five of the inscriptions from Chaironeia are dated by the local archon. From these archons, Grenet (2014: 401) concludes that the corpus covers approximately 90 years.

113  Fossey 1991: 123. Zelnick-Abramovitz (2009: 307) argues, based on *IG* VII 3314, that these inscriptions were a manumission performed by the Assembly or Council, hence the local law attached to it.

114  For some factors relating to the presence or absence of inscriptions in Boiotia, see Kalliontzis 2007: 511–12.

115  Fossey 1991: 134; Fossey and Darmezin 2014: 158. For woman engaging more in male practices in the Hellenistic period, with a focus on euergetism, see Howe 2013.

116  We see other regional variations, such as the use of the word φίλοι (see, e.g., *IG* VII 3329, 3357, 3365, 3385, 3387) for those accompanying the female manumitter, not attested outside of Boiotia (Fossey and Darmezin 2014: 159). Notably, almost as many manumissions are made by women as by men (Fossey and Darmezin 2014: 158).

117 Fossey 1991: 132; Meyer 2008: 68–72; Grenet 2014: 412; Schachter 2016: 293. It is important to keep in mind the concept of homophily – "the tendency for like people to connect with each other" (Reger 2013: 144–5) – which helps to explain the clustering of groups. In the case of ancient Chaironeia, and in these manumissions in particular, this clustering is visible in the form of local elites, powerful families who controlled considerable resources (Meyer 2008: 78).

118 Fossey 1991: 123; Meyer 2008: 56, 61; Fossey and Darmezin 2014: 169–70.

119 Fossey and Darmezin 2014: 170.

120 Meyer 2008: 63.

121 This is not to say that other Boiotian *poleis* did not have a similar draw, but without the requisite evidence, we cannot say for sure.

122 Meyer 2008: 82. The cult quickly became entrenched in the upper classes of Chaironeia, as evidenced not only through the many manumission records, but also through generations of worshippers. See, e.g., *IG* VIII 3380, where three generations of worshippers are mentioned in one inscription (Schachter 2016: 293).

123 Roesch 1989: 621; Schachter 2007: 364. Chaironeia is one of the sites that provides the most evidence for the worship of the Egyptian gods, through the numerous manumission decrees that have survived (Schachter 2007: 364, 368).

124 Along with the construction projects mentioned above (page 73), Chaironeia was also engaged in other regional trends, such as changes to the shape of its theatre, perhaps a need related to the prominence of musical performance in Boiotian society (Germani 2015; Germani 2018: 98–105).

125 Schachter 2016: 306. Schachter (2016: 307) comments on the futility of trying to date these texts and the importance of recognizing that the transition was not smooth, with dialect and *koinē* coexisting over an extended period. For more on the transition to *koinē* Greek, see Vottero 1998; Meyer 2008: 73–5; Knoepfler 2014; Müller 2016.

126 Beck 2018: 20. For more on Chaironeia and its epigraphic habit in the Hellenistic period, with a focus on military catalogues and proxeny decrees as demonstrable of a not-so-isolated *polis*, see Kalliontzis 2007.

127 Müller 2016.

128 Müller 2016.

## REFERENCES

Alcock, S.E., J.E. Gates, and J.E. Rempel. 2005. "Reading the Landscape: Survey Archaeology and the Hellenistic *Oikoumene*." In A. Erskine (ed.), *A Companion to the Hellenistic World*. Malden, MA: 354–72.

Alexandropoulou, A. 2015. "Terracotta Figurines from Cemeteries of Chaironeia in North Boeotia." In A. Muller (ed.), *Figurines de terre cuite en Méditerranée grecque et romaine*. Villeneuve d'Ascq: 349–56.

Assenmaker, P. 2013. "Les trophées syllaniens de Chéronée." *Latomus* 72 : 946–55.

Bakhuizen, S.C. 1986. "The Ethnos of the Boeotians." In H. Beister and J. Buckler (eds.), *Boiotika*. Munich: 65–72.

Bakhuizen, S.C. 1994. "Thebes and Boeotia in the Fourth Century." *Phoenix* 48: 307–30. https://doi.org/10.2307/1192571.

Baldwin, F., and R. Sharpley. 2009. "Battlefield Tourism: Bringing Organised Violence Back to Life." In R. Sharpley and P.R. Stone (eds.), *The Darker Side of Travel: The Theory and Practice of Dark Tourism*. Bristol: 186–206.

Beck, H. 2014. "Ethnic Identity and Integration in Boeotia: The Evidence of the Inscriptions (6th and 5th centuries BC)." In N. Papazarkadas (ed.), *The Epigraphy and History of Boeotia: New Finds, New Prospects*. Leiden: 19–44.

Beck, H. 2018. "'If I am from Megara': Introduction to the Local Discourse Environment of an Ancient Greek City-State." *Teiresias Supplements Online* 1: 15–45.

Beck, H. 2020. *Localism in the Ancient Greek City-State*. Chicago and London.

Beck, H., and A. Ganter. 2015. "Boiotia and the Boiotian Leagues." In H. Beck and P. Funke (eds.), *Federalism in Greek Antiquity*. Cambridge: 132–57.

Belloc, H. 1948. "The Absence of the Past." In J. Bingham (ed.), *Hilaire Belloc: Selected Essays*. London: 230–4.

Billows, R. 2005. "Cities." In A. Erskine (ed.), *A Companion to the Hellenistic World*. Malden, MA: 196–215.

Buck, R.J. 1972. "The Formation of the Boeotian League." *Classical Philology* 67: 94–101. https://doi.org/10.1086/365837.

Buck, R.J. 1979. *A History of Boeotia*. Edmonton.

Buck, R.J. 1985. "Boiotia and Political Theory in the Fifth and Fourth Centuries." *La Béotie Antique: Lyon-Saint-Etienne 16–20 mai 1983*: 291–5. https://doi.org/10.2307/283608.

Buckler, J. 1985. "Thebes, Delphoi, and the Outbreak of the Third Sacred War." In *La Béotie Antique: Lyon-Saint-Etienne 16–20 mai 1983*. Paris: 237–46.

Buckler, J. 1992 "Plutarch and Autopsy." *Aufstieg und Niedergang der römischen Welt* 2: 4788–830. https://doi.org/10.1515/9783110854725-023.

Buckler, J., and H. Beck. 2008. *Central Greece and the Politics of Power in the Fourth Century BC*. Cambridge.

Büttner, N. 2006. "Tourism." In H. Cancik and H. Schneider (eds.), *Brill's New Pauly*. Consulted online 20 July 2020. https://doi.org/10.1163/15749347 _bnp_e15304820.

Camp, J., et. al. 1992. "A Trophy from the Battle of Chaironeia of 86 B.C." *American Journal of Archaeology* 96: 443–55. https://doi.org/10.2307/506067.

Carman, J., and P. Carman. 2005. "Ancient Bloody Meadows: Classical Battlefields in Greece." *Journal of Conflict Archaeology* 1: 19–44. https://doi.org/10.1163/157407705774928917.

Carman, J., and P. Carman. 2020. *Battlefields from Event to Heritage*. Oxford and New York.

Casson, L. 1974. *Travel in the Ancient World*. Toronto.

Chaniotis, A. 2005. *War in the Hellenistic World: A Social and Cultural History*. Oxford.

Chaniotis, A. 2009. "Travelling Memories in the Hellenistic World." In R. Hunter and I. Rutherford (eds.), *Wandering Poets in Ancient Greek Culture: Travel, Locality and Pan Hellenism*. Cambridge: 249–69.

Charami, A. 2016. "The Excavation of a Roman Building in Chaeronea." In M. Germani (ed.), *Tra Oriente ed Occidente: Miscellanea di studi sul mondo antico*. Frosinone: 21–35.

Clarke, K. 2005. "Parochial Tales in a Global Empire: Creating and Recreating the World of the Itinerant Historian." In L. Troiani and G. Zecchini (eds.), *La cultura storica nei primi due secoli dell'impero romano*. Rome: 111–28.

Cohen, A. 2001. "Art, Myth, and Travel in the Hellenistic World." In S.E. Alcock, J.F. Cherry, and J. Elsner (eds.), *Pausanias: Travel and Memory in Roman Greece*. New York : 93–126.

Darmezin, L. 1985. "Quelques problèmes relatifs à l'affranchissement en Béotie." *La Béotie Antique: Lyon-Saint-Etienne 16–20 mai 1983*: 325–31.

Dawkins, R.M. 1907. "Archaeology in Greece (1906–1907)." *Journal of Hellenic Studies* 27: 284–99. https://doi.org/10.2307/624446.

Dilke, O.A.W. 1950. "Details and Chronology of Greek Theatre Caveas." *Annual of the British School at Athens* 45: 20–62.

Eade, J., and M. Katić (eds). 2017. *Military Pilgrimage and Battlefield Tourism: Commemorating the Dead*. London.

Edlund, I.E.M. 1977. "Invisible Bonds: Clients and Patrons through the Eyes of Polybios." *Klio* 59: 129–36. https://doi.org/10.1524/klio.1977.59.12.129.

Erskine, A. 2002. "Life after Death: Alexandria and the Body of Alexander." *Greece & Rome* 49: 163–79.

Erskine, A. (ed.). 2005. *A Companion to the Hellenistic World*. Malden, MA.

Farinetti, E. 2011. *Boeotian Landscapes: A GIS-Based Study for the Reconstruction and Interpretation of the Archaeological Datasets of Ancient Boeotia*. Oxford.

Fossey, J.M. 1973–4. "The End of the Bronze Age in the South West Copaïc." *Euphrosyne* 6: 7–21.

Fossey, J.M. 1979. "The Cities of the Kopaïs in the Roman Period." *Aufstieg und Niedergang der römischen Welt*. Berlin: 549–91.

Fossey, J.M. 1986. *The Ancient Topography of Eastern Phokis*. Amsterdam.

Fossey, J.M. 1988. *Topography and Population of Ancient Boiotia*. Chicago.

Fossey, J.M. 1991. *Epigraphica Boeotica I: Studies in Boiotian Inscriptions.* Amsterdam.

Fossey, J.M., and L. Darmezin. 2014. "A Dedication and More Manumissions from Khaironeia." In J.M. Fossey, *Epigraphica Boeotica II: Further in Boiotian Inscriptions.* Amsterdam: 140–92.

Fossey, J.M., and G. Gauvin 1990. "Les fortifications de l'acropole de Chéronée." In J.M. Fossey, *Papers in Boiotian Topography and History.* Amsterdam.

Funke, P. 2006. "Chaeronea," In H. Cancik and H. Schneider (eds.), *Brill's New Pauly.* English edition by Christine F. Salazar. Consulted online 25 February 2019. https://doi.org/10.1163/1574-9347_bnp_e231070.

Gallet de Santerre, H. 1952. "Chronique des fouilles et découvertes archéologiques en Grèce en 1951: Première Partie. Tableau d'ensemble de l'activité archéologique en Grèce: Eubée, Béotie, Phocide, Locride, Étolie: Chéronée." *Bulletin de Correspondance Hellénique* 76: 201–88.

Ganter, A. 2013. "A Two-Sided Story of Integration: The Cultic Dimension of Boiotian Ethnogenesis." In P. Funke and M. Haake (eds.), *Greek Federal States and Their Sanctuaries.* Stuttgart: 85–105.

Gatewood, J.B., and C.M. Cameron. 2004. "Battlefield Pilgrims at Gettysburg National Military Park (1)." *Ethnology* 43: 193–216.

Germani, M. 2015. "Boiotian Theatres: An Overview of the Regional Architecture." In R. Frederiksen, E.R. Gebhard, and A. Sokolicek (eds.), *The Architecture of the Ancient Greek Theatre.* Athens: 351–64.

Germani, M. 2018. "The Theatre of Chaeronea and Rectilinear Koila." *Hypothekai: Journal on the History of Ancient Pedagogical Culture* 2: 97–105. https://doi.org/10.32880/2587-7127-2018-2-2-97-105.

Giroux, C. 2021. *Plutarch's Chaironeia: The Local Horizon of World Empire.* PhD diss., McGill University.

Giroux, C. 2022. "Silence of the Lions: Exploring Plutarch's Omissions on Chaironeia." In J. Beneker, C. Cooper, N. Humble, and F. Titchener (eds.), *Plutarch's Unexpected Silences.* Leiden: 188–209.

Grenet, C. 2014. "Manumission in Hellenistic Boeotia: New Considerations on the Chronology of the Inscriptions." In N. Papazarkadas (ed.), *The Epigraphy and History of Boeotia: New Finds, New Prospects.* Leiden: 395–442.

Gutzwiller, K.J. 1998. *Poetic Garlands: Hellenistic Epigrams in Context.* Berkeley.

Hammond, N.G.L. 1938. "The Two Battles of Chaeronea (338 B.C. and 86 B.C.)." *Klio* 31: 186–218. https://doi.org/10.1524/klio.1938.31.jg.186.

Hammond, N.G.L. 2000. "Political Developments in Boeotia." *Classical Quarterly* 50: 80–93. https://doi.org/10.1093/cq/50.1.80.

Hansen, M.H. 1996. "An Inventory of Boiotian Poleis in the Archaic and Classical period." In M.H. Hansen (ed.), *Introduction to an Inventory of Poleis = Acts of the Copenhagen Polis Centre 3.* Copenhagen: 73–116.

Hansen, M.H., and T.H. Nielsen (eds.). 2004. *An Inventory of Archaic and Classical Poleis*. Oxford and New York.

Hingley, R. 2005. *Globalizing Roman Culture: Unity, Diversity and Empire*. Routledge.

Hirsch-Luipold, R. 2014. "Religion and Myth." In M. Beck (ed.), *A Companion to Plutarch*. Chichester, West Sussex: 163–76.

Hodos, T. (ed). 2017. *The Routledge History of Archaeology and Globalization*. London and New York.

Hölscher, T. 2006. "The Transformation of Victory into Power: From Event to Structure." In S. Dillon and K. Welch (eds.), *Representations of War in Ancient Rome*. New York: 27–48.

Howe, T. 2013. "Shepherding the Polis: Gender, Reputation and State Finance in Hellenistic Boiotia." *Zeitschrift für Papyrologie und Epigraphik* 186: 152–6.

Iles, J. 2006. "Recalling the Ghosts of War: Performing Tourism on the Battlefields of the Western Front." *Text and Performance Quarterly* 26: 162–80. https://doi.org/10.1080/10462930500519374.

Inglis, D., and R. Robertson. 2004. "Beyond the Gates of the Polis: Reconfiguring Sociology's Ancient Inheritance." *Journal of Classical Sociology* 4: 165–89. https://doi.org/10.1177/1468795X04043932.

Inglis, D., and R. Robertson. 2005. "The Ecumenical Analytic: 'Globalization,' Reflexivity, and the Revolution in Greek Historiography." *European Journal of Social Theory* 8: 99–122. https://doi.org/10.1177/1368431005051759.

Jones, C.P. 1971. *Plutarch and Rome*. Oxford.

Kalliontzis, Y. 2007. "Décrets de proxénie et catalogues militaires de Chéronée trouvés lors des fouilles de la basilique paléochrétienne d'Haghia Paraskévi." *Bulletin de Correspondance Hellénique* 131: 475–514.

Kalliontzis, Y. 2014. "Digging in Storerooms for Inscriptions." In N. Papazarkadas (ed.), *The Epigraphy and History of Boeotia: New Finds, New Prospects*. Leiden: 333–72.

Kinnee, L. 2018. *The Greek and Roman Trophy: From Battlefield Marker to Icon of Power*. London.

Knoepfler, D. 2014. "ΕΧΘΟΝΔΕΤΑΣΒΟΙΩΤΙΑΣ: The Expansion of the Boeotian Koinon towards Central Euboia in the Early Third Century BC." In N. Papazarkadas (ed.), *The Epigraphy and History of Boeotia: New Finds, New Prospects*: 68–94.

Larsen, J.A.O. 1965. "Phocis in the Social War of 220–217 B.C." *Phoenix* 19: 116–28. https://doi.org/10.2307/1087018.

Larson, S. 2007. *Tales of Epic Ancestry: Boiotian Collective Identity in the Late Archaic and Early Classical Periods*. Stuttgart.

Leake, W.M. 1967/1835. *Travels in Northern Greece*. Volume 2. Hakkert.

Lennon, J. 2010. "Dark Tourism and Sites of Crime." In D. Botterill and T. Jones (eds.), *Tourism and Crime: Key Themes*. Oxford: 215–28.

Light, D. 2017. "Progress in Dark Tourism and Thanatourism Research: An Uneasy Relationship with Heritage Tourism." *Tourism Management* 61: 275–301. https://doi.org/10.1016/j.tourman.2017.01.011.

Lomine, L. 2005. "Tourism in Augustan Society (44BC–AD 69)." In J.K. Walton (ed.), *Histories of Tourism: Representation, Identity, and Conflict*. Clevedon and Buffalo: 69–87.

Lytle, E. 2010. "Fish Lists in the Wilderness: The Social and Economic History of a Boiotian Price Decree." *Journal of the American School of Classical Studies at Athens* 79: 253–303.

Ma, J. 1994. "Black Hunter Variations." *Proceedings of the Cambridge Philological Society* 40: 49–80.

Ma, J. 2008. "Chaironeia 338: Topographies of Commemoration." *Journal of Hellenic Studies* 128: 72–91. https://doi.org/10.1017/S0075426900000069.

Ma, J. 2013. "Grandes et petites cités au miroir de l'épigraphie classique et hellénistique." *Topoi* 18: 67–86.

MacCannell, D. 2001. "Tourist Agency." *Tourist Studies* 1: 23–37.

Mackay, C.S. 2000. "Sulla and the Monuments: Studies in His Public Persona." *Historia* 49: 161–210.

Mackie, C.J. 2021. "War in a Landscape: The Dardanelles from Homer to Gallipoli." In B. Reitz-Joosse, M.W. Makins, and C.J. Mackie (eds.), *Landscapes of War in Greek and Roman Literature*. London: 229–40.

Mackil, E. 2013. *Creating a Common Polity*. Berkeley and London.

Makins, M.W. 2021. "Introduction." In B. Reitz-Joosse, M.W. Makins, and C.J. Mackie (eds.), *Landscapes of War in Greek and Roman Literature*. London: 1–22.

Mayo, J.M. 1988. "War Memorials as Political Memory." *Geographical Review* 78: 62–75. https://doi.org/10.2307/214306.

McInerney, J. 1999. *The Folds of Parnassos: Land and Ethnicity in Ancient Phokis*. Austin.

McInerney, J. 2011. "Delphi and Phokis: A Network Theory Approach." *Pallas* [Online]. Accessed 23 July 2020. https://doi.org/10.4000/pallas.1948.

McInerney, J. 2015. "Phokis." In H. Beck and P. Funke (eds.), *Federalism in Greek Antiquity*. Cambridge: 199–221.

Meidani, K. 2008. "Les relations entre les cités béotiennes à l'époque achaïques." *Kentron* 24: 151–64. https://doi.org/10.4000/kentron.1659.

Meyer, E.A. 2008. "A New Inscription from Chaironeia and the Chronology of Slave Dedication." *Tekmeria* 9: 53–89. https://doi.org/10.12681/tekmeria.215.

Minchin, E. 2021. "Homer's Landscape of War: Spatial Mental Model and Cognitive Collage." In B. Reitz-Joosse, M.W. Makins, and C.J. Mackie (eds.), *Landscapes of War in Greek and Roman Literature*. London: 23–37.

Müller, C. 2016. "Globalization, Transnationalism, and the Local in Ancient Greece." *Oxford Handbooks Online*. http://www.oxfordhandbooks.com/view/10.1093/oxfordhb/9780199935390.001.0001/oxfodhb-9780199935390-e-42.

Naerebout, F. 2006–7. "Global Romans? Is Globalization a Concept That Is Going to Help Us Understand the Roman Empire?" *Talanta* 38–9: 149–70.

Pantelidis, N. 2017. "Boeotia and Its Neighbors: A Central Helladic Dialect Continuum?" In G. Giannakis, E. Crespo, and P. Filos (eds.), *Studies in Ancient Greek Dialects: From Central Greece to the Black Sea*. Berlin and Boston: 167–87.

Pelling, C. 2010. "Plutarch's 'Tale of Two Cities': Do the 'Parallel Lives' Combine as Global Histories?" In N.M. Humble (ed.), *Plutarch's Lives: Parallelism and Purpose*. Swansea: 217–36.

Pritchett, W.K. 1958. "Observations on Chaironeia." *American Journal of Archaeology* 62: 307–11. https://doi.org/10.2307/501959.

Reger, G. 2013. "Networks in the Hellenistic Economy." In S. Ager and R. Faber (eds.), *Belonging and Isolation in the Hellenistic World*, Toronto: 143–54.

Reitz-Joosse, B., M.W. Makins, and C.J. Mackie (eds.). 2021. *Landscapes of War in Greek and Roman Literature*. London.

Roesch, P. 1989. "Les Cultes Égyptiennes en Béotie." In L. Criscuolo and G. Geraci (eds.), *Egitto e storia antica dall'Ellenismo all'età Araba*. Bologna: 621–9.

Romanelli, E., and O.M. Khessina. 2005. "Regional Industrial Identity: Cluster Configurations and Economic Development." *Organization Science* 16: 344–58. https://doi.org/10.1287/orsc.1050.0131.

Romero, F.G. 2013. "Sports Tourism in Ancient Greece." *Journal of Tourism History* 5: 146–60. https://doi.org/10.1080/1755182X.2013.828784.

Rzepka, J. 2010. "Plutarch on the Theban Uprising of 379 B.C. and the Boiotarchoi of the Boeotian Confederacy under the Principate." *Historia* 59: 115–18.

Sabetai, V. 2015. "Female Protomes from Chaeroneia (Boeotia)." In A. Muller (ed.), *Figurines de terre cuite en Méditerranée grecque et romaine*. Villeneuve d'Ascq: 149–63.

Schachter, A. 1981. *Cults of Boeotia. Volume 1: Acheloos to Hera*. London.

Schachter, A. 2007. "Egyptian Cults and Local Elites in Boiotia." In L. Bricault, M.J. Versluys, and P.G.O. Meyboom (eds.), *Nile into Tiber: Egypt in the Roman World: Proceedings of the IIIrd International Conference of Isis Studies, Faculty of Archaeology, Leiden University, May 11–14, 2005*. Leiden: 364–91.

Schachter, A. 2016. *Boiotia in Antiquity*. Cambridge.

Seaton, T. 2018. "Encountering Engineered and Orchestrated Remembrance: A Situational Model of Dark Tourism and Its History." In P.R. Stone et al. (eds.), *The Palgrave Handbook of Dark Tourism Studies*. London: 9–31.

Seland, E. 2008. "The Indian Ocean and the Globalisation of the Ancient World." *Ancient West and East* 7: 67–79. https://doi.org/10.2143/AWE.7.0.2033253.

Sharpley, R. 2009. "Shedding Light on Dark Tourism: An Introduction." In R. Sharpley and P.R. Stone (eds.), *The Darker Side of Travel: The Theory and Practice of Dark Tourism*. Bristol: 3–22.

Sporn, K. 2018. "Ancient Phokis: Perspectives on the Study of Its Settlements, Fortifications, and Sanctuaries." *Australian Archaeological Institute at Athens Bulletin* 14: 18–25.

Sporn, K. 2019. "Das fruchtbare Kephissostal: Wie sich die antike Landschaft Phokis verändert." *Archäologie Weltweit* 1: 61–4.

Sporn, K., and E. Laufer. 2019. "Tithorea, Griechenland. Topographische Untersuchungen im Stadtgebiet. Die Arbeiten der Jahre 2016 und 2017." *E-Forschungsberichte des Deutschen Archäologischen Instituts* 99–105. https://doi.org/10.34780/561a-d792.

Stevens, K. 2016. "Empire Begins at Home," In M. Lavan, R.E. Payne, and J. Weisweiler (eds.), *Cosmopolitanism and Empire: Universal Rulers, Local Elites, and Cultural Integration in the Ancient Near East and Mediterranean*. Oxford: 65–88.

Stumpf, J.A. 2013. "Tourism." In R.S. Bagnall et al. (eds.), *The Encyclopedia of Ancient History*. Malden, MA: 6787–9.

Sweetman, R.J. 2007. "Roman Knossos: The Nature of a Globalized City." *American Journal of Archaeology* 111: 61–81. https://doi.org/10.3764/aja.111.1.61.

Titchener, F.B. 2014. "Fate and Fortune." In M. Beck (ed.), *A Companion to Plutarch*. Chichester: 479–87.

Urry, J., and J. Larsen. 2011. *The Tourist Gaze 3.0*. Los Angeles and London.

Vottero, G. 1998. *Le dialecte béotien I*. Nancy and Paris.

Vottero, G. 2001. *Le dialecte béotien II*. Nancy and Paris.

Walter, T. 2009. "Dark Tourism: Mediating between the Dead and the Living." In R. Sharpley and P.R. Stone (eds.), *The Darker Side of Travel: The Theory and Practice of Dark Tourism*. Bristol: 39–55.

West, B. 2010. "Dialogical Memorialization, International Travel and the Public Sphere: A Cultural Sociology of Commemoration and Tourism at the First World War Gallipoli Battlefields." *Tourist Studies* 10: 209–25. https://doi.org/10.1177/1468797611407756.

Winter, J. 2014. "Sites of Memory, Sites of Mourning." *Oklahoma Humanities*. Accessed 23 April 2018: 35–38. http://www.okhumanities.org/Websites/ohc/images/Sites_of_Memory,_Sites_of_Mourning.pf.

Witcher, R. 2017. "The Global Roman Countryside: Connectivity and Community." In T. de Haas and G. Tol (eds.), *The Economic Integration of Roman Italy: Rural Communities in a Globalising World*. Boston: 28–50.

Zelnick-Abramovitz, R. 2009. "Freed Slaves, Their Status and State Control in Ancient Greece." *European Review of History* 16: 303–18. https://doi.org/10.1080/13507480902916779.

*Among the most prominent tools of the Hellenistic polis to extend its radius of engagement was the institution of guest-friendship. Grants of* proxenia *connected city-states across remote distances. Recent research has identified proxenic ties as critical markers of Mediterranean-wide Greek networks and, correspondingly, as instrumental to the widening of worldviews that has long been seen as characteristic of the Hellenistic world. This chapter offers a fresh reappraisal. Alex McAuley turns to an area in central Greece that has produced rich epigraphic evidence for the* proxenia: *Chalkis, Oropos, and the various Boiotian cities in the vicinity. Despite the division lines between them, demarcated by the Euripos channel as well as the political borders of their respective federal states, McAuley's study highlights the idea of interaction. At the political level, he traces this interaction in frequent grants of* proxenia *to citizens in neighbouring cities, a practice that was hardly fuelled by the desire of making long-distant networking connections. What were the ramifications of the high volume of local* proxenia *grants across the micro-region of the Euboian Gulf, for awarding cities and recipients alike? A close reading of the literary evidence at hand reveals that the term and concept of* proxenia *reverberated more than ambassadorial functions. Instead, it resonated strong and lasting, often intergenerational, ties between communities, subsumed under the rubrics of privilege and status a guest-friend enjoyed in the granting* polis. *McAuley demonstrates that* proxenoi *made practical use of the rights awarded to them. Discussion of a decree from Thespiai suggests that* proxenoi *moved to their granting city to reside there permanently and enjoy civic rights, including taxation, intermarriage, and land-owning privileges (see also chapter 11). Effectively, such go-between individuals helped to forge lasting ties between their communities. Returning to the micro-region of the Euboian Gulf, the final section of the chapter reveals the vibrancy with which cities made use of local* proxenia *grants. On the one hand, this was a mind- and meaningful measure to overcome separation, while on the other, emanating from the awarding city and governing quotidian affairs within, it recognized and indeed reinforced the inherent quality of the local as prime point of reference for all.*

*Keywords: proxeny, federalism, Chalkis, Oropos, Boiotia, civic culture*

# 4

# The Other Side of the Stone: Local *Proxenia* in the Hellenistic Euboian Gulf

ALEX McAULEY

In around 230 BCE, during the archonship of Kallikles and the priesthood of Olympiachos, at the instigation of Damaretos a man named Zopyros, son of Dionysios, was given the honour of being made a *proxenos* (guest-friend) and *euergetēs* (benefactor) of the city of Oropos by its *boulē* and *dēmos*.[1] The following lines of the inscription are immediately familiar to anyone who has worked with the hundreds of such proxenic decrees that the Hellenistic period has produced. They list the various privileges given to him and his ancestors which are the perks of his status awarded in return for beneficial acts towards the community: *enktēsis, isoteleia, asylia, asphaleia*, and all the other benefits accorded to the city's *proxenoi*.[2] By all accounts this is typical of the myriad civic decrees that collectively attest to the web of exchange and communication which bound Hellenistic civic communities across the broadened Greek world of the period.

But there are two rather curious features of this decree that can all too easily escape our notice and prompt further reflection. The first is that Zopyros, son of Dionysios, was a citizen of Chalkis, a town which, relatively speaking, is just around the corner from Oropos. The two communities are separated by about 30 kilometres as the crow flies, which would equate to roughly half a day's journey by land and less by sea.[3] Given that *proxenia* is typically viewed as an institution connecting two communities far distant from one another, why would Oropos bother giving the status of *proxenos* and the honours associated with it to a man who was from a neighbouring *polis*? How does *proxenia* play out on a very local level such as this? The second feature is that at the time of this decree Oropos and Chaklis were members of two different *koina*, so the question then naturally arises as to how such local civic decrees and the interaction they facilitate function at the border between two different federal structures. These are the questions to which we shall return throughout this chapter as we seek to examine the local side of *proxenia* in this corner of the Hellenistic world. In order to do so we shall begin by reconsidering "the local" as an analytical category in the Hellenistic period, and then examine some of our basic assumptions regarding *proxenia*, before returning to our Euboian case study. Through this micro-regional focus, I hope to show that there is another side of the stone, as it were, when it comes to understanding *proxenia*, one that is more local, immediate, and practical than we may have thought.

### Finding the Hellenistic Local in the Euboian Gulf

"The local" as a concept is not one that is traditionally associated with the Hellenistic period. The period was long viewed as a cosmopolitan age, defined more by "international" exchange through the vastly broadened Greek world carved out by Alexander and his successors than the smaller-scale civic preoccupations of the Classical period. Indeed the implication to be drawn from the work of several recent scholars is that the antiquated ties of kinship and ethnicity which bound Classical civic communities were self-consciously superseded in favour of a trans-local sense of Greekness rooted in the more malleable criteria of culture and education.[4] This shift from ethnicity to culture manifests itself not only in the alleged transition from *polis* to *cosmopolis* in the Hellenistic world, but also provides the base for the pluralistic "new style Hellenism" which Tim Whitmarsh argues united the cultural world of the Roman Empire by creating a sort of "imperial ecumenism," to borrow from Daniel Richter's summation.[5] Labelled as something of a post-national globalized space *avant la lettre*, the Hellenistic world has primarily been characterized as one of long-distance exchange among different cultures who were suddenly part of this urban network. Fluid notions of language, culture, and self-representation are thus held to have succeeded the prior emphasis on autochthony, familial descent, and shared ethnicity that bound Classical *poleis* communities.[6] From the late Classical to the early Hellenistic period, the traditional narrative goes, Greek parochialism gave way to Greek cosmopolitanism.[7] The translocal, in other words, lies at the heart of what we think is "Hellenistic."

There are some consequences to this translocal perspective that are particularly relevant to this volume. The first is the implicit idea that the perceived decline of the traditional *polis* community and the rise of vast Hellenistic empires somehow meant the death of "the local." Allegations of a stagnant, exhausted Greek mainland depopulated by waves of emigration, and cities deprived of the autonomy that had allegedly been their Classical hallmark, imply that the local was no longer prominent.[8] The *polis* ceded its place to the Hellenistic *oikoumenē*; *ta patria* were replaced by the broader and more generic cultural *koinon*. In many regions of the Greek mainland the local *polis* was also superseded by the various federations, and thus the local civic community gave way to the regional *koinon*.[9] It is precisely this dominance of the regional over the local that traditionally lay at the heart of federal studies since the days of Jakob Larsen and Victor Ehrenberg, which were largely guided by the assumption that member *poleis* implicitly ceded their local autonomy to federal institutions.[10] In recent years, however, this presupposition has been questioned by studies which demonstrate the bottom-up impact of member communities on these federal states, as well as the enduring role of ethnic and communal ties in and across federations.[11] Hans Beck's 2020 monograph has highlighted the local with all of its polyvalence as an indispensable analytical category of Greek civic communities of the Classical period and into the fourth century, and it is clear in this volume and beyond that there is a great deal of insight to be gained from applying this paradigm beyond the fourth century.[12] Although such thinking may not have been traditionally in vogue in Hellenistic scholarship, the local world of these civic communities certainly did not come to an abrupt end with the campaigns of Philip II or the empires of Alexander's successors.[13]

The region of the Greek mainland on either side of the Euboian Gulf provides a fascinating case study, one that further complicates matters as it compels us to examine a local world between regions that are held to have characterized the Hellenistic Greek mainland and the federations into which they were organized.[14] This maritime micro-region straddling the Boiotian and Euboian Leagues also leads us to reconsider the basic geography of each *koinon* as we realize that communities on either side of the Euboian Gulf would have had much more frequent and easier interaction with each other than with members of their respective federal states.[15] In Euboia this is particularly pronounced: Eretria, for instance, is today a gruelling two-hour drive away from the next major member city of the Euboian League to the south, Karystos, which itself is even farther away from the two other members of the Euboian *tetrapolis*, Chalkis and Histiaia. Even by sea the journey would take between a day and a day and a half, depending on conditions.[16] In the same vein, Boiotia was a decidedly large place in which a port city like Anthedon was several days' journey from Thespiai, a fellow member city of the League in the foothills of Mount Helikon, and even farther away from Thisbe or Koroneia.[17]

If, however, we consider the Euboian Gulf from a micro-regional perspective by making it the centre rather than periphery of our consideration, it quickly becomes clear that for cities such Chalkis, Histiaia, Eretria, and Oropos, their closest neighbours were not necessarily their fellow *koinon* member-states, but rather communities on the opposite coast that were in an entirely different federation. In spite of this political separation, geographical proximity was nevertheless paramount and must have given rise to a high degree of maritime interaction among them.[18] The communities on the Euboian coast in particular would have been just as (if not more) preoccupied by their maritime horizons as they were by their terrestrial neighbours.[19] The proxenic decree honouring Oropos encountered at the outset of this chapter attests to precisely this kind of local interaction between Oropos and Chalkis, and it is only one among dozens of similar proxenic decrees linking communities in this micro-region. This flurry of proxenic activity among communities on either side of the gulf is only the tip of the iceberg: as we shall discuss in further detail below, the institution of *proxenia*, by its very nature, indicates both a prior relationship between the individual honoured and the community, while presupposing that this interaction will continue in the future. Proxenic decrees such as this provide an instantaneous snapshot, as it were, of much broader patterns of interaction and exchange between communities in micro-regions such as this.

## Rethinking (Local) *Proxenia*

Just as the local environment of the Euboian Gulf causes us to reconsider some of our preconceived notions of the Hellenistic Greek mainland, so too does it prompt a reappraisal of some basic assumptions regarding the institution of *proxenia* more generally. *Proxenia* in the Hellenistic world is almost automatically considered an outward-looking institution acting as a key relay for the social networks that bound the Greek world – and that have been of such interest to recent scholars. *Proxenia* bears connotations of external relations, interstate diplomacy, and the general assumption that it links two communities otherwise separated by great distances. Judging by the map of Eretria's proxenic decrees provided by Denis Knoepfler in 2001, at first glance this community was no exception to this trend.[20] The sheer reach of the comparatively humble *polis* of Eretria in the Hellenistic period is striking: *proxenoi* of the city hail from such far-flung locales as Italy, Alexandria, the Ionian Coast of Asia Minor, the northern Aegean, and Macedon.[21] There is, however, another side to this, as tracing long-range interactions as these can obscure the smaller scope of the many of the city's proxenic decrees which involved communities much closer to home. Such local proxenic decrees have generally received less attention both in Euboia and elsewhere. On a broader level the sheer scale of *proxenia* throughout the Hellenistic world is striking, as is the quantity of inscriptions that have been compiled into Oxford's immensely useful *Proxeny Networks of the Ancient World*.[22]

The scholarship on *proxenia* is vast, and with the rise of network theory as an analytical perspective, first in sociology and more recently in ancient history, the institution has enjoyed a resurgence in popularity, thanks in no small part to Mack's 2015 monograph *Proxeny and Polis*. The subtitle of the monograph – *Institutional Networks in the Ancient Greek World* – places it firmly in the footsteps of Malkin's 2011 network study *The Small Greek World*.[23] Both scholars examine *proxenia* as an outward-looking institution which expands the geographical horizons of a given community, and Mack in particular is interested in the external implications of *proxenia*, that is, what having a *proxenos* in a foreign community entails for the city which granted the status.[24] To Mack especially this creation of a network lies at the core of the institution: he defines a *proxenos* as an "intermediary figure who could be expected to help visitors from the granting city."[25] The services expected of a *proxenos* at home "collectively amounted to an intermediary role, allowing individuals from one city access to the institutions and networks of their *proxenos'* polis."[26] Underlying this perspective, though, is an assumption that several other scholars before have made: *proxenia*, according to Mack, "conveyed the basic assumption that the *proxenos* was and would continue to be active in his own *polis*," and goes on to write "there is, however, no evidence that proxeny was regularly granted to individuals expected to permanently reside at the granting *polis*."[27] He concludes that "Proxenoi, for the most part, lived and indeed died where they were expected to, in political contexts external to the granting *polis*."[28] While the monograph offered many fascinating insights into the institution of *proxenia*, particularly in the case of communities far apart from one another, I would emphasize that the very local privileges granted to *proxenoi* – *asylia* (inviolability), *ateleia* or *isoteleia* (tax exemptions), *enktēsis* (the right to hold property), and *eisodos* (the right to approach civic institutions) – were not just symbolic gestures that would not regularly be employed.[29] They may well be generous honorifics of little utility to far-flung *proxenoi*, but in the context of local cross-federal interactions such as those in the Euboian Gulf, these privileges would have been immensely valuable to the individual receiving them – such as Zopyros, son of Dionysios.

I argue that in this corner of the Greek world between Euboia and Boiotia there is substantial evidence for a local aspect of *proxenia*, which had much more direct ramifications for the granting city. Here *proxenia* was not necessarily a distant diplomatic measure but rather a practical way of regulating the legal status of outsiders within a given community in a manner that is loosely akin to "landed immigrant' status in contemporary society. In this particular micro-regional context, *proxenia* is a critical tool that facilitates federations and allows member states the flexibility to operate autonomously outside the purview of federal structures. Local, small-scale *proxenia* such as this would have implied at least partial residence or fluidity between the two communities. To develop the point, two comments about *proxenia* in general must be made before turning to the specific environment of the Euboian Gulf.

The first is that beyond the Athenian context, *proxenos* is a fairly vague term that simply means guest-friend of the city. At first glance this may seem to be a minor philological nuance, but the notion that *proxenoi* do not regularly live in the community that honoured them is a fifth-century, generally Athenian, notion. The definition of *proxenoi* as "persons representing the interests of a foreign state in their own community" is derived almost exclusively from literary – not epigraphic – attestations in predominantly Athenian literary sources. Aeschines, for instance, mentions twice (2.141 and 143) that Demosthenes was a *proxenos* of Thebes and, as summarized by Trevett, "he had been appointed to by the Thebans as a form of honorary consul to look after the interests of their citizens at Athens."[30] Prior to Demosthenes, *proxenoi* of Athens had such a pivotal role to play in the promotion of Athenian interests among the city's fifth-century allies that they were given the same protection abroad as the city's own citizens.[31] The Attic orator Andokides describes the Athenian Miltiades son of Kimon as "πρόξενον ὄντα Λακεδαιμονίων," and it is telling that this has been translated as "being Sparta's representative at Athens" rather than the more precise "being a *proxenos* of the Spartans."[32] In Plato's *Laws*, the Spartan Megillos provides a definition of *proxenia* that captures this consular role while also bringing to the fore the (oft-overlooked) hereditary nature of the status:

O Stranger of Athens, you are not, perhaps, aware that our family is, in fact, a "proxenus" of your State. It is probably true of all children that, when once they have been told that they are "proxeni" of a certain State, they conceive an affection for that State even from infancy, and each of them regards it as a second mother-land, next after his own country. That is precisely the feeling I now experience."[33] (trans. R.G. Bury, 1967–8)

There are various other attestations of similar *proxenoi* residing in their home community that can be found in Thucydides, Isocrates, and Aeschines, but to classify all *proxenoi* under this ambassadorial rubric glosses over the ambiguity of the term in other contexts.[34] In Herodotus, Alexander of Macedon is identified as "πρόξεινός ... καὶ εὐεργέτης" of Athens, and on account of this acts an intermediary between Mardonios and the Athenians.[35] A few sections later, in the Athenian reply, *proxenos* and *philos* are essentially synonymous.[36] Earlier, while describing the prerogatives of Spartan kings, Herodotus mentions that they have the right to name *proxenoi* who are charged with entertaining and attending to foreign guests.[37] The same understanding of *proxenos* as a public host or someone charged with looking after foreigners also appears thrice in Euripides and once in Aristophanes.[38] Xenophon uses the term *proxenos* in non-Greek contexts to mean a more generic "friend" or "advocate" of a given ruler or polity to another community.[39] Elsewhere he identifies (5.4.2) another non-Greek intermediary or envoy as *proxenos* between the people of Trapezous and the Mossynoikoi – whom he later describes as the "most barbarian people," whose customs were at the farthest possible remove from the Greeks, thereby further highlighting the ambiguity in the term *proxenos* and extending it beyond the Hellenic civic context.[40] Other definitions of the word included in the *LSJ*'s entry for "πρόξενος" include "patrons or representatives of guilds," "witnesses to a will," and "patron, protector," particularly among tragedians.[41] The abstract noun, *proxenia*, thus becomes shorthand for the various privileges of associated with the status. The point that I wish to make with these philological comments is not to discard the prominent ambassadorial role of many Classical-era *proxenoi*, but rather to bring to light the fact that there are less formalized, more diverse uses of the term that can relate to everything from traditional *xenia* and *philia* to the intergenerational ties between communities mentioned by Plato. Denis Knoepfler's comments aptly summarize the diversity and regional variation of *proxenia*:

Si, en effet, l'institution de la proxénie peut à juste titre être regardée comme panhéllenique dans ses traits essentiels, il est non moins certain qu'elle n'a pas connu partout le même développement: d'un état ou du moins d'une région à l'autre, son histoire (date d'apparition et de disparition), son contenu (nombre et étendue des privilèges associés au statut du proxène), son usage même ont pu varier assez considérablement.[42]

The second comment to make is that, despite prevailing assumptions, *proxenoi* could and indeed did reside either permanently or semi-permanently in the community which honoured them with the status. Take, for instance, the "Sostratos Decree" from Thespiai in Boiotia, dated to roughly 250–240 BCE.[43] In this inscription, a certain Sostratos the Athenian is made a *proxenos* of Thespiai and given all the honours accorded to him and the city's other *proxenoi*. Interestingly, though, Sostratos is given these honours for having admirably taught military skills to the young boys and adolescents of Thespiai in the past, and by all accounts he will continue to do so, granted the annual salary provided to him by the city, which is also recorded in this inscription.[44] Clearly this particular *proxenos* will be residing in the city for the indefinite future, and it does not seem to me coincidental that the first privilege after *proxenia* awarded to him and his descendants in this decree is the right to acquire land and houses in Thespiai, followed by the right to be taxed as a citizen. The fact that he is identified as an Athenian and thus hails from outside the Boiotian *koinon* further demonstrates that such privileges can be conferred on outsiders without any apparent hindrance. Other patterns from the aftermath of the Hellenistic period also help to clarify this picture. In her 1993 study of Roman Greece, *Graecia Capta*, Alcock notes that early in the Roman occupation of Greece, a "supra-civic landowning class began to be formed at the elite level, as wealthy families held office (for example as *proxenos*) in other cities."[45] These networks developed in part through *proxenia* that "allowed and encouraged individuals from one city to purchase or receive land in other communities," and Alcock then goes on to cite a variety of examples of this from throughout the mainland. While such large-scale landowning by elite families is in and of itself exceptional, this is a trend, she notes, for which the documentary evidence argues consistently.[46] Given the explicit right to purchase and hold land granted by the usual proxenic formulae, it would seem that this elite system is predicated on the actual use of the privileges conferred by *proxenia*. This trend of elites using patronage networks and benefaction to gain *proxenia* – and thus the right to purchase land in a city of which they were not a citizen – is also highly visible in the Peloponnese, and Rizakis goes so far as to argue for the Hellenistic origin of this later imperial trend.[47] With regard to the north of the mainland, Daverio-Rocchi has likewise argued for a similar practical utility of *proxenia* in Lokris; thus, this practice is by no means confined to one specific region.[48]

Finally, the specific right of *proxenoi* to buy and hold both houses in the city and land in the countryside, *enktēsis*, has a long history in the Greek world, and the exhaustive 1966 study by Jan Pecirka demonstrated that this privilege was given in three main contexts in Attica:[49] first, to deities whose sanctuaries would acquire and hold the land in perpetuity; second, to exiles who were allowed to buy and hold property for a limited amount of time; and third, to resident foreigners in the city who had rendered some kind of service to Athens and whose ancestors would also enjoy the privilege, thereby ensuring the hereditary transmission of whatever they bought or acquired.[50] In light of these various observations the general picture of *proxenia* has certainly broadened its strict ambassadorial confines: *proxenia* can be local, it can be practical, and it can be employed in the immediate vicinity of a city or community. *Proxenoi* certainly did live in locales far removed from the city which accorded them the status, but this was not always necessarily the case and they could also be from communities much closer to where they received the honour. In the same vein, while in long-distance cases many of the privileges accorded to *proxenoi* would be honorific, *proxenoi* nevertheless could and indeed did own houses and land in the granting community, and they would certainly be able to transmit these acquisitions to their children, who also inherited the status and the practical rights that came with it.[51] The aforementioned Sostratos of Thespiai was an exceptionally clear example of this, but in the vast web of Hellenistic *proxenia* he cannot have been the only individual to have resided semi-permanently in the city which honoured him. When the hands of cities would otherwise have been tied by the exclusive rights of citizens at home and the constraints of federal foreign policy stipulations, in the realm of *proxenia* at least they were able to establish lasting connections with whomever they wanted.

## Local *Proxenia* in Practice: The Euboian Gulf

With these additional, more general, observations on *proxenia* we can now return to the micro-region of the Euboian Gulf, and the decree making Zopyros, son of Dionysios, a *proxenos* of Oropos can be read in a much different light. Given that his native city of Chalkis and his host city of Oropos are, as mentioned, separated by only ca. 30 kilometres there seems to me no reason to think that he would not have taken advantage of the very precise privileges that were granted to him and his descendants. Unlike some of the more distant proxenic connections, it is certainly plausible in this case that he would have spent some of the year in Oropos or at least maintained property there. The reference to the other *proxenoi* and *euergetai* of the city in the last lines of the inscription perhaps implies a resident community of *proxenoi* in the city as well. An examination of the broader epigraphic *corpus* further suggests that this might be the case. Zopyros is by no means the only Chalkidian to be involved with nearby Oropos. To my knowledge there are 11 cases from the third and second centuries of Chalkidians being made *proxenoi* of Oropos, and it seems to be little coincidence that the in the vast majority of these decrees (9 out of 11) *enktēsis* is the first privilege to be listed.[52] All except one similarly include *isoteleia*, which would of course have been a valuable concession for any Chalkidian doing business in or with Oropos.[53] Again I see no reason why these Chalkidian *proxenoi* of Oropos would not have taken advantage of their financial and legal privileges in the city, thereby reinforcing the possibility of a not insignificant number of Chalkidians holding property on the other side of the Euboian Gulf. Given that the status was hereditary, this body of inscriptions provides only a snapshot of the first generation of new *proxenoi*, and thereby obscures prior and subsequent recipients of *proxenia*.[54]

There is also a noteworthy number of other Euboians who are also *proxenoi* of Oropos, thus it seems that these links were cultivated across the region rather than exclusively between Chalkis and the Boiotian coast. A relatively robust set of *proxenoi* from Karystos are attested by six decrees similarly dating to the middle of the third century.[55] In the case of these Karysteians as well, *enktēsis* is always listed as the first privilege awarded by these decrees, and again this was not necessarily a hollow honour. Karystos is approximately 80 kilometres from Oropos and the journey sailing north along the Euboian Gulf would have taken less than a day.[56] A noteworthy feature of this particular group of inscriptions is the fact that three of the honorandi – Stibandros, Alexinos, and Kallias – are all identified by the patronymic Θεώρου.[57] This, along with the close chronological span and formulary consistency of the *corpus*, makes it likely that here we are dealing with three sons of Theoros of Karystos, who are all made *proxenoi* of Oropos. The grant of *proxenia* to subsequent generations would have further expanded the links between Boiotian Oropos and this Euboian family from Karystos. This also raises the possibility, albeit speculative, that there is a familial dynamic at work with some of these ties between the two communities.

This naturally raises the question of what precisely are these ties that are being formalized between the two communities, and why is there so much proxenic activity between Oropos and the communities on the other side of the Euboian Gulf. Perhaps there is an ethnic component at work here. According to the Boiotian historian Nikokrates, Oropos was originally a colony of Eretria, and its dialect likewise seems to hint at the Euboian origins of the city.[58] These old links, however, were severed when Oropos fell to the Athenians in ca. 507/506, and the city subsequently vacillated between being ruled by the Boiotian League or by Eretria for much of the fourth century.[59] According to Diodorus, it only became a full-fledged member of the Boiotian League in 312–304; thus it would not necessarily have been fully integrated within the *koinon* at the time these grants of *proxenia* were made.[60] Perhaps, then, these proxenic links between Oropos and Euboia are indicative of older ethnic and communal ties being formalized through a third-century mechanism. Or perhaps these ties are economic. For much of the fifth century Oropos produced a large surplus of grain which was exported to Attica, so the citizens of Chalkis and Eretria who were honoured as *proxenoi* of the city were perhaps somehow instrumental in cultivating trade links between these communities.[61] In this particular case we are able to posit some further details regarding the specific goods traded. Chalkis, and to a lesser extent Eretria, had always been major centres of metal production, especially bronze; thus it seems likely that they were exporting bronze to Oropos and importing its grain.[62] Individuals like Zopyros, son of Dionysios, were perhaps the brokers of this economic exchange. There is also a possible cultic dimension to this as well. By the end of the fourth century Oropos had only recently regained full control of the Amphiareion, located 2.2 kilometres outside the city itself.[63] The eponymous priest of the Amphiareion enjoys pride of place in these proxenic decrees, coming first after the federal archon, and it may well be the case that these Euboian individuals played some part in the third-century activity at the sanctuary attested epigraphically. These possibilities, of course, are not mutually exclusive; nor can they be proven to satisfaction, though speculation does not diminish the concrete attestation of third-century interactions among these communities. All of them, however, would have been able to transcend the federal border that separated communities on either side of this region of the Euboian Gulf.

Such a local proxenic network was not exclusive to the Euboian Gulf south of Chalkis between Euboia and Boiotia. A similar local pattern is at work farther north, along the coast of the island, that sheds further light on the potential practical ties being forged by local *proxenia*. Histiaia/Oreos on the northern tip of the island granted *proxenia* to a number of individuals from communities in its local orbit: Echinos, Larisa Kremaste, Herakleia Trachinia, and Kytinion.[64] These, however, are only partially preserved on a long list of *proxenoi*, dated to 264 BCE, which does not outline the individual privileges accorded to each. With the near-universal inclusion of *enktēsis* in Hellenistic proxenic decrees, however, I see no reason to suspect that these *proxenoi* would not have been given the right to hold property in Histiaia. Whether or not these proxenic links all cross federal boundaries is unclear, given the scant documentation for the region, but there are some suggestions that these cities – especially Echinos – would have been members of the Hellenistic Thessalian League.[65] Why would a city like Histiaia be motivated to grant *proxenia* and its associated privileges to individuals from communities on the other side of the gulf? Again, perhaps we can find the answer in the vagaries of the local economy, and again perhaps this is related to the importation of grain. As we learn from a well-known inscription from Histiaia from ca. 230 BCE honouring Athenodoros, son of Peisagoras from Rhodes, towards the end of the third century, the city was actively trying to encourage grain importation. In this situation the community was sure to reward publicly individuals who had been influential in securing a well-priced grain supply for the city after its usual imports from the Black Sea had been blocked.[66]

Due to the agricultural fertility of the opposite side of the gulf, in Thessaly, these neighbouring communities would be likely candidates for grain exporters to Histiaia. Indeed, the *chorā* of Echinos is described by Polybios as *gē pamphoros* (9.41.11), and in the 370s even Thebes had sought to import a substantial amount of grain from this part of Thessaly as well.[67] To reiterate the point made above, by working through the mechanism of *proxenia* a city such as Histiaia could negotiate something like trade agreements with individuals from other communities and not run afoul of federal mechanisms in the process. In return, the wine for which Histiaia was famous, and the ore that was prevalent in the region, could be exported in exchange for these grain imports.[68] Such trade would have been greatly facilitated by the practical privileges granted to the city's *proxenoi*, who themselves would have received added incentive to ensure it continued in the future. The city of Histiaia/Oreos, incidentally, provides us with an anecdote that brings to light the potential, at least, for corruption when it comes to *proxenia*. Demosthenes (18.18) levels an accusation against Aeschines that he and his fellow ambassadors to Oreos abandoned their duties as Athenians and instead sought proxenies for themselves by bribing the city's inhabitants. The question that arises is rather rhetorical but nevertheless telling: why would Aeschines and his fellow ambassadors have allegedly bribed Oreos for a status whose benefits were purely symbolic? There must have been the prospect of a solid return on their investment for such an attempt at bribery. At any rate, by reputable or disreputable means Aeschines must have been successful in securing the status, as he himself mentions that he was a *proxenos* of Oropos.[69]

Finally, as we turn to the case of Eretria we can see how the city's conferral of proxeny to neighbouring communities outside the federation proceeds in step with the economic organization of its territory. As mentioned previously, while there are some far-flung *proxenoi* of Eretria, there are also cases of the city's *proxenoi* hailing from communities that are closer to home: Tanagra, Athens, Karystos, Lamia, and Herakleia Trachinia.[70] The possibility thus presents itself that here in Eretria we are seeing the same kind of regional exchange dynamic that we just discussed in Histaia and Oropos. There is a common thread that runs through all Eretrian proxenic decrees regardless of the distance to the *proxenos'* home community: all of the decrees list *ateleia* and *enktēsis* as the first specific privileges given to the recipient. Therefore, freedom from taxation and the right to hold property are the most prominent benefits of this newly accorded status. In isolation, this creation of a local proxenic web around the Euboian Gulf, by Eretria, is in keeping with the general patterns we have seen elsewhere in the region, but what is striking in the Eretrian context is how this regional network is being created at the same time as the Euboian economy is being reoriented towards the export of olives and grapes grown in its newly fortified countryside. Karl Reber has identified several large houses with olive and grape presses in the centre of the city, while Sylvain Fachard's study of the territory of Eretria describes how in the third century the city's *chōra* was protected and organized in such a way that boosted the city's economy productivity.[71] The intriguing possibility presents itself that in these decrees we catch an epigraphic glimpse of the formalization of Eretria's export economy as it has been attested archaeologically. The dispersal of the local proxenic decrees along the Euboian Gulf hints that Eretria was casting a wide net for the export of its olive and grape products, perhaps in return for grain imports, as we have seen elsewhere. To indulge in purely idle speculation, perhaps the large houses and storehouses identified by Karl Reber on the south slope of the acropolis in the northern part of the city have something to do with this burgeoning export economy, and perhaps some of these structures were the product of the local privileges given to Myrmidon of Lamia and the other *proxenoi* of the city.[72] Regardless, here, as elsewhere in this region, we see the local scale on which these proxenic networks operate as a means of linking communities on either side of the gulf and facilitating exchange – be it ethnic, cultic, or economic.

## Conclusions

Now that we have examined this corner of the Greek mainland in some detail, what general conclusions about localism in the Hellenistic world can we derive from this local side of *proxenia*? The first observation that comes to mind is that there is a relationship between the proliferation of proxenic decrees during the third and second centuries and the prominence of federal leagues. To me it seems to be beyond mere coincidence that the institution of *proxenia* flourishes at the same time as Hellenistic federalism, and it is tempting – though ultimately impossible to prove with any certainty – that the expansion of *proxenia* either proceeds along with or is a response to the development of various Greek *koina*. Mack's graph of the number of communities attested inscribing proxeny decrees per 50-year period is telling in this regard: the figure begins to rise steady sharply from 340 to 300 BCE and hits its peak after sustained highs in 199–150 BCE, only to decline over the second half of the second century and into the first.[73] This trend seems to coincide with the formation and consolidation of Hellenistic *koina* over the course of the third century before they were eclipsed by the expansion of Roman power and later dissolved after 146 BCE.[74]

The fate of federalism and *proxenia* in the Hellenistic mainland thus seem to be intrinsically linked. The possibility then presents itself that the popularity of *proxenia* was a side-effect of or a reaction to the creation of federal structures. As much as Hellenistic *koina* unified their member states on a regional basis, they also created an institutional barrier between communities on either side of federal borders, as we have seen in the Euboian Gulf. Communities that were otherwise separated by federal barriers thus seem to have found other means of formalizing the persistent local ties among themselves. In the process, cities such as Chalkis and Oropos looked away from the state and towards the level of the individual in the recognition and formalization of these connections.[75] The institution of *proxenia*, particularly in the local context, thus allows member states a level of flexibility and autonomy that might not otherwise have been possible in their federal system.

Local *proxenia* of the sort that we have seen in the Euboian Gulf is something of a clever mechanism in the federal milieu: it allows a non-citizen of a given community to interact with it almost as if they were citizen; indeed the *proxenos* enjoys nearly all the rights of citizenship except the right to vote and serve as a magistrate. *Proxenia* can thus involve a non-citizen almost fully in the economic and political life of a given community without eroding the exclusive bedrock of citizenship. In other words, it facilitates access to the city without compromising the civic community itself. There are some vital implications to this observation. Federalism has often been viewed, at least partially, as an institutional response to the growing power of the Hellenistic kings – a response that required, in many ways, that some aspects of local autonomy be surrendered in return for collective security. But we see in these local proxenic networks in the Euboian Gulf that localism was not sacrificed on the altar of federalism, and that communities could, and indeed did, establish meaningful, practical relationships between and through federal boundaries. Federalism and access to the peer-polity network that bound Greek-style civic communities across the Hellenistic world were thus not mutually exclusive, and just as cities from different imperial configurations clearly interact with one another as equals, so too do cities from different federal structures.

Perhaps the most consequential observation to be derived from our review of local *proxenia* proceeds from the nature of *proxenia* itself. It is tempting to look at the massive increase in epigraphic attestation of the institution during the third and second centuries and see in this attestation a sudden and unprecedented wave of interaction among Greek cities. But this conclusion implicitly characterizes such interaction as a Hellenistic phenomenon and *proxenia* as a one-off snapshot of momentary intercommunal ties. As Mack has described, however, *proxenia* is both a backward- and forward-looking institution: on the one hand it recognizes and formalizes the past interaction of an individual with a given community; on the other hand, it presupposes that that interaction will has significance for the future by ensuring that this relationship between the individual and the community becomes hereditary and transmissible.[76] This increase in proxenic activity thus does not represent the sudden creation of new intercommunal ties, but rather the formalization of much older ties through a contemporary third- and second-century mechanism. In this wave of Hellenistic *proxenia* we see at once the shadow of much older intercommunal ties and the foretaste of their perpetuation.

In the same vein, the sort of small-scale *proxenia* we have seen in the Euboian Gulf adds further nuance to our understanding of localism in the Hellenistic milieu. The immediate temptation is to simply consider "local" as synonymous with "geographic," "regional," "ethnic," or "federal," yet the two sides of the Euboian Gulf that we have explored above remind us that localism is a complicated beast, one that does not align with the usual divides through which we make sense of Greek society. The Boiotian League was as integral to the local world of Oropos as the Euboian League was to the local world of Chalkis, but at the same time these two cities were also very much part of a shared local world, bound by ties of shared history, ethnic traditions, and economic exchange. These local ties did not suddenly become any less meaningful or prominent amid the expanded cultural and geographic horizons of the Hellenistic period, and this ought to be borne in mind with respect to the Greek mainland. The conquests of Seleukos in Baktria, or the building projects of the Ptolemies in Alexandria, did not suddenly erase or annul the local ties that bound Chalkis and Oropos, or any number of Greek communities. Yes, the Greek world was unquestionably larger in the Hellenistic period, but it was still ultimately composed of individuals like Zopyros, son of Dionysios, living in his local world that spanned both sides of the Euboian Gulf.

NOTES

1 The inscription itself is *I. Oropos* 110 = *IG* VII 388, dated to ca. 230 BCE. I would like to thank the organizers of this fascinating conference and the editors of this volume for their guidance and insight. It is not my intention here to cite the entire scholarly history of *proxenia*, given that Mack 2015 has recently done a commendable job of precisely this task. In this chapter I limit myself to citing only scholarship directly related to these lines of discussion. Several resources could not be accessed due to the restrictions related to the COVID-19 pandemic.

2 *I. Oropos* 110 ll. 6–8: πρόξε[ν]ον εἶναι καὶ εὐεργέτη[ν τῆς πόλεως] / Ὠρ]ωπίων καὶ αὐτὸν καὶ ἐκγόνους καὶ εἶναι αὐτοῖς γῆς καὶ οἰκίας ἔγκτησιν κ[αὶ ἰσοτέλειαν καὶ ἀσυλί]-/ αν κ]αὶ ἀσφάλειαν καὶ πο[λέμ]ου καὶ ἰρήνης καὶ κατὰ γῆν καὶ κατὰ θάλατταν [καὶ] τἆλλα πάντα / ὑπάρ[χειν] αὐτ[ῶι.

3 Throughout this chapter all distances are rough figures, determined using Google Maps. Journey times and travel methods have been calculated using the Stanford ORBIS project. Although the project is relevant to the Roman imperial context, given that means of travel between these communities would not have changed substantially between the third century and imperial period it suffices to provide an approximation.

4 Richter 2011: 6–9 for a thorough overview of the relevant scholarly voices, on which I have based this discussion.

5 Richter 2011: 8, from which all quotations are taken.

6 According to Richter 2011's line of argument, the notion among Greek intellectuals in the Roman Imperial context that the Mediterranean was a "a unified, homogeneous whole composed of a diversity of parts" emerged in the late Classical Athenian context (4). Richter describes this cultural ecumenism as a critical response to "parochial, local, and ultimately ethnic modes of political thought" (16) among fourth-century Athenian thinkers, which was then adopted by Imperial-period commentators. It is noteworthy that the terms "parochial," "local" and "ethnic" take on a quasi-pejorative hue.

7 Bevan 1902: 1.14 declares that as a result of Alexander's conquests "the vessel [of Greek culture] is broken and the long-secreted elixir poured out for the nations"; in this metaphor of course Bevan was following previous Hellenistic historians, stretching back to Droysen.

8 A notion most explicitly elaborated by Giovannini 1993, especially page 266, in which he claims that "the proud cities of Greece became beggars who asked for material help from the kings, for corn, for schoolmasters, or for the building of porticoes." Giovannini was following in the footsteps of Glotz's claim that Chaironeia marks the end of the Greek city (1928: 448) and Tarn's assertion that Greeks as a "political animal, a fraction of the *polis* or self-governing city-state, had ended with Aristotle" (1952: 79).

9 For the history of federal scholarship in the Greek context see Beck and Funke 2015.

10 To Ehrenberg, as discussed by Beck and Funke (2015: 7), "the true federal state" was predicated on the "transfer of the Polis constitution to the league" (Ehrenberg 1960: 126, quoted in Beck and Funke 2015: 7.

11 For an overview of this see again Beck and Funke 2015: 8–13.

12 Beck 2020, especially chapters 1 and 6, for an overview of the "local" as an analytical category.

13 As Mack (2015: 124) discusses, that older analytical *proxenia* and the rights entailed were viewed as being incompatible with citizenship; hence the proliferation of *proxenia* inevitably weakens the institution of citizenship itself.

14 On the Boiotian League see most recently the overview of Beck and Ganter 2015; and on the Euboian League see Knoepfler 2015.

15 In this sense this chapter is firmly ensconced in the micro-ecology approach of Horden and Purcell 2000, especially chapter 5 on connectivity.

16 Again a figure estimated using the Stanford ORBIS Project.

17 Interestingly, the centre of the Boiotian League itself can also be understood as another micro-region, this time composed of communities situated around the Lake Kopais basin.

18 The prominence of sea-lanes and the maritime coast in sight of land has been highlighted by Horden and Purcell (2000: 123–6) as one of the characteristics of the Mediterranean basin itself. The Euboian Gulf provides an ideal example of this, given how relatively narrow it is, further increasing what they (following Febvre and Braudel) characterize as the connectivity of micro-regions.

19 Indeed Horden and Purcell (2000: 348) describe Chalkis and Euboia more generally as a significant milieu of redistribution, in this case of metal, since the Archaic period, and the cities of Euboia have a maritime outward-looking perspective since the Archaic period.

20 The map itself is Knoepfler 2001, fig. 102.

21 Knoepfler 2001: 429, fig. 102.

22 The *Proxeny Networks of the Ancient World* is a database created by William Mack during his DPhil studies at Oxford, and includes thousands of literary and epigraphic attestations. For a discussion of the evidence for *proxenia* see in particular this superb overview on the website: http://proxenies.csad.ox.ac.uk /evidence.

23 Mack 2015 and Malkin 2011. On the network of relationships among *poleis* in the Hellenistic period see also Ma 2003.

24 Malkin (2011: 85–6) discussed a proxenic decree linking Naukratis with Lindos on Rhodes as an example of networking among island communities. Again, the geographic span of this particular instance of *proxenia* is striking.

25 Mack 2015: 23.

26 Mack 2015: 49.

27 Mack 2015: 49 and 56.

28 Mack 2015: 57.

29 Mack (2015: 122–33) provides a concise overview of the privileges of *proxenoi* and discusses how they could be employed in certain contexts. In this chapter I do not mean to disagree with or revise his observations, but instead consider these rights in the specific micro-regional context of the Euboian Gulf.

30 See Trevett 1999 for a discussion of the relationship between Demosthenes and Thebes, which in no small measure revolves around his status as *proxenos*.

31 Meiggs 1949 provides a short but fascinating discussion of the legal protection guaranteed to Athenian *proxenoi* resident in allied cities. The murder of *proxenos* of Athens was treated as the murder of Athenian citizen, and Athenian magistrates were quick to protect their external representatives.

32 Andoc. 3.3. The entire passage itself is noteworthy and highlights the ambassadorial role of these *proxenoi*, as Miltiades had been ostracized from Athens but then was recalled so that he could be sent to Sparta to request an armistice agreement on behalf of Athens: καὶ Μιλτιάδην τὸν Κίμωνος ὠστρακισμένον καὶ ὄντα ἐν Χερρονήσῳ κατεδεξάμεθα δι' αὐτὸ τοῦτο, πρόξενον ὄντα Λακεδαιμονίων, ὅπως πέμψαιμεν εἰς Λακεδαίμονα προκηρυκευσόμενον περὶ σπονδῶν. The translation quoted above is by K. J. Maidment, 1968.

33 Plat, *Leg.* 1.642b: ὦ ξένε Ἀθηναῖε, οὐκ οἶσθ' ἴσως ὅτι τυγχάνει ἡμῶν ἡ ἑστία τῆς πόλεως οὖσα ὑμῶν πρόξενος. ἴσως μὲν οὖν καὶ πᾶσιν τοῖς παισίν, ἐπειδὰν ἀκούσωσιν ὅτι τινός εἰσιν πόλεως πρόξενοι, ταύτῃ τις εὔνοια ἐκ νέων εὐθὺς ἐνδύεται ἕκαστον ἡμῶν τῶν προξένων τῇ πόλει, ὡς δευτέρᾳ οὔσῃ πατρίδι μετὰ τὴν αὑτοῦ πόλιν: καὶ δὴ καὶ ἐμοὶ νῦν ταὐτὸν τοῦτο ἐγγέγονεν.

34 Isocrates 15.166 recounts that Pindar was made *proxenos* of Athens and given a present of 10,000 drachmas. Aeschines 3.138 identifies Thrason of Erchis as a *proxenos* of Thebes. Later in the speech he interestingly identifies Arthmios of Zeleia as another *proxenos* of Athens, one who transported Median gold into Greece. Thucydides mentions *proxenoi* as ambassadors or representatives at 2.29.1, 2.85.5, 3.2.3, 3.52.5, 3.70.1, 4.78.1, 5.59.4, 5.76.3, 8.92.8.

35 Hdt. 8.136.

36 Hdt 8.143: οὐ γάρ σε βουλόμεθα οὐδὲν ἄχαρι πρὸς Ἀθηναίων παθεῖν ἐόντα πρόξεινόν τε καὶ φίλον.

37 Hdt 6.57: καὶ προξείνους ἀποδεικνύναι τούτοισι προσκεῖσθαι τοὺς ἂν ἐθέλωσι τῶν ἀστῶν.

38 Eur. *Andr.* 1103; Eur. *Ion* 551, 1039; and Ar. *Av.* 1021 – in which the Inspector asks the pithy question "Where are the *proxenoi*?" (ποῦ πρόξενοι;).

39 Xen. *Anab.* 5.6.3–11 uses the term *proxenos* and *philos* interchangeably in describing the relationship between Hekatonymos of Sinope and Korylas, Satrap of the Paphlagonians. In 5.6.3 he is identified as a *philos* of the Paphlagonians, while later in 5.6.11 he identifies him as a *proxenos* but mentions that this is out of *philia* for Korylas.

40 Xen. *Anab.* 5.4.34 – τούτους ἔλεγον οἱ στρατευσάμενοι βαρβαρωτάτους.

41 See *LSJ* s.v. πρόξενος, available via the Perseus Project. For πρόξενος, meaning patron or protector, see Aesch. *Supp.* 420; Ar. *Thesm.* 602; and Soph. *El.* 1451.

42 Knoepfler 2001: 21.

43 *I. Thesp.* 29, *SEG* 32.496, dated ca. 240 BCE. The relevant lines of the inscription are:

Φαείνω ἄρχοντος, ἔδοξε τοι δάμοι
πρόξενον εἶμεν τας πόλιος Θεισ-
πιείων Σώστρατον Βατράχω Ἀθανηον
κὴ αὐτὸν κὴ ἐκγόνως κὴ εἶμεν αὐ-
[τ]οις γας κὴ ϝοικίας ἔππασιν κὴ ϝι-
[σο]τέλειαν κὴ ἀσφάλιαν κὴ ἀσουλί-
[αν] κὴ πολέμω κὴ ἰράνας ἰώσας κὴ κα-
8 τὰ γαν κὴ κατὰ θάλατταν κὴ τάλλα
πάντα καθάπερ κὴ τοις ἄλλοις προ-
ξένοις·

44 *I. Thesp.* 29, ll. 1–8, for the proxenic honours. On this inscription and its Megarian context see McAuley 2018.

45 Alcock 1993: 78.

46 Alcock 1993: 78, and further discussion on 79.

47 Rizakis 2007, especially 7–10.

48 Daverio-Rocchi 2019.

49 Pecirka 1966: 148. See also Mack's overview of *enktēsis* at Mack 2015: 122–7.

50 See Kamen 2013: 55–8 for an overview of Pecirka's understanding of *enktēsis* and the subsequent comments of Henry (*non vidi*).

51 Mack (2015: 124) emphasizes this point when he argues against the *opinio veterior* that *proxenoi* could only have made effective use of their privileges by migrating permanently to the community which gave them status. Instead, Mack continues (125–7) to clearly outline events such as religious and civic festivals at which *proxenoi* would have been prominently present, thanks to the privilege of *prohedria*. In the same vein, he makes the astute observation that *enktēsis* would only have fulfilled its function if indeed it was taken up. He cites several examples in which precise restrictions are placed on the grant of *enktēsis*, which further suggests its practical utility.

52 These inscriptions are *I. Oropos* 40, 57, 89, 110, 112, 121, 127, 154, 216, 217, and 258. *Enktēsis* is the first privilege listed after *proxenia* and *euergesia* in all except *I. Oropos* 216 and 217, which both interestingly are dated to the middle of the second century. It thus seems that the mid-third-century trend is to list *enktēsis* as the first privilege granted.

53 *I. Oropos* 258 is the only one of these decrees which does not mention *isoteleia*, though the inscription is badly mutilated and only lines 2–4 have survived mostly intact.

54 Indeed, all of these inscriptions, except *I. Oropos* 258, conclude with the "all else given to *proxenoi*" formula, further suggesting a sizeable community of *proxenoi* in the city.

55  These inscriptions are *I. Oropos* 60, 122, 124, 150, 157, and 189.

56  Given that the ORBIS project is a Roman Imperial–era tool, it does not contain either Oropos or Karystos as travelling points; however, the nearest equivalent journey between Geraistos and Chalkis (131 km) is estimated to take 1.1 days by sea. Karystos and Oropos, however, are only approximately 80 km apart as the crow flies, so this would then have been less than a day – roughly 16 hours by my (admittedly rough) calculations.

57  Kallias, son of Theoros, is mentioned in *I. Oropos* 122, while Stibandros and Alexinos are listed in *I. Oropos* 189. All have been dated to the third century BCE.

58  Nikokrates *FGrH* 376 F 1. As discussed by (M.H.) Hansen (2004: 448), the dialectical idiosyncrasy of Oropos points to its origins being neither Athenian nor Boiotian.

59  Hansen 2004: 448–9.

60  Diod. Sic. 19.78.3, discussed by Hansen (2004: 449, with full references).

61  Given that Chalkis and Eretria are both located in the Lelantine Plain, which is its own terrestrial micro-region of an alluvial plain surrounded by limestone and serpentine hills, it follows logically that these two communities would have closer relations with each other and communities on the other side of the gulf than in the vastly different other regions of Euboia. For a map of this see Horden and Purcell 2000: 226, map 14.

62  As discussed by Horden and Purcell (2000: 348–9), and in the case of Chalkis this involvement in the broader metal trade in the Mediterranean dates to the seventh century BCE. For the full bibliography on Euboian, especially Chalkidian, metal production see also Horden and Purcell 2000: 609.

63  The Great Amphiareia were instituted by Athens in 329/328 and must have been taken over by the city, and to some extent the Boiotian League, after it joined in 312–304.

64  These are preserved in *IG* XII 9, 1187.

65  On the Thessalian League see Bouchon and Helly 2015. See also *IACP* 429 for a discussion of the territory of Echinos (Decourt et al. 2004: 710).

66  *SEG* 49.973, *Syll.* 493, Bresson 2015: 385–8.

67  Xen. *Hell.* 5.4.56.

68  On the long history of imports and exports between Euboia and the Aegean see Leone 2012. The prevalence of the nymph Histiaia wearing a wine wreath on the silver and bronze coinage of the city in the fourth century further attests to the prominence of its wine trade.

69  Aeschin. 2.18.

70  Following the decree numbers in Knoepfler 2001: Tanagra (XVIII / *IG* XII 9, 203); Athens (11 / *SEG* 51.1113); Lamia (16 / *SEG* 51.1117); Karystos (XII / *IG* XII 9, 211); Herakleia Trachinia (14 / *SEG* 51.1116). See Knoepfler 2001 ad loc.

for a discussion of the specific restoration and context of each decree, which are so robust in each context that his points need not be repeated here.

71  Reber 2007: 286–8 for the presence of these new economic facilities within the wall of the city. While he places this in the context of a general and unspecified "economic crisis that troubled the Greek world" (288), Fachard's reconstruction of the period and its economy is much more plausible. See Fachard 2012: 263–87 on the organization of the countryside as well as the construction of defence and storage facilities for the city's agricultural produce for protection from military and meteorological threats. Fachard notes previously (111–23) that Eretria does not hit the peak of its agricultural productivity until the third and second century.

72  Reber 2007: 281–6. See also Reber 2002.

73  This graph is reproduced online at http://proxenies.csad.ox.ac.uk/evidence.

74  Mack 2015: 233, 253, in the chapter aptly entitled "The Disappearance of Proxeny and the Domination of Rome."

75  This was certainly not unique to Euboia: Mackil (2013: 271) captured this perfectly in her discussion of a decree in which Orchomenos borrowed money from Eubolos of Phokian Elateia, which "attests once again the need for economic mobility and the advantages derived from breaking down the economic barriers created by political boundaries."

76  Mack 2015: 28–38 for a detailed discussion of the expectations surrounding the status.

## REFERENCES

Alcock, S.E. 1993. *Graecia Capta*. Cambridge.

Beck, H. 2020. *Localism and the Ancient Greek City State*. Chicago.

Beck, H., and P. Funke. 2015. "An Introduction to Federalism in Greek Antiquity." In H. Beck and P. Funke (eds.), *Federalism in Greek Antiquity*. Cambridge: 1–29.

Beck, H., and A. Ganter. 2015. "Boiotia and the Boiotian League." In H. Beck and P. Funke (eds.), *Federalism in Greek Antiquity*. Cambridge: 132–57.

Bevan, E.H. 1902. *The House of Seleucus*. 2 volumes. London.

Bouchon. R., and B. Helly. 2015. "The Thessalian League." In H. Beck and P. Funke (eds.), *Federalism in Greek Antiquity*. Cambridge: 231–49.

Bresson, A. 2015. *The Making of the Ancient Greek Economy*. Trans. S. Rendall. Oxford.

Daverio-Rocchi, G. 2019. "Lokrian Federal and Local Proxenies in Interstate Relations: A Case Study." In H. Beck, K. Buraselis, and A. McAuley (eds.), *Ethnos and Koinon. Heidelberger althistorische Beiträge und epigraphische Studien* 61. Stuttgart: 29–44.

Decourt J.-C., et al. 2004. "Thessalia and Adjacent Regions." In M.H. Hansen and T.H. Nielsen (eds.), *An Inventory of Archaic and Classic al Poleis*. Oxford: 678–731.

Ehrenberg, V. 1960. *The Greek State*. London.

Fachard, S. 2012. *La défense du territoire: Étude de la "chôra" érétrienne et de ses fortifications*. Athens.

Giovannini, A. 1993. "Greek Cities and Greek Commonwealth." In S. Bulloch et al. (eds.), *Images and I deologies*. Oxford: 265–86.

Glotz, G. 1928. *La cité grecque*. Paris.

Hansen, M.H. 2004. "Boiotia." In M.H. Hansen and T.H. Nielsen (eds.), *An Inventory of Archaic and Classical Poleis*. Oxford: 431–61.

Horden, P., and N. Purcell. 2000. *The Corrupting Sea: A Study of Mediterranean History*. Oxford.

Kamen, D. 2013. *Status in Classical Athens*. Princeton.

Knoepfler, D. 2001. *Décrets érétriens de proxénie et de citoyenneté*. Lausanne.

Knoepfler, D. 2015. "The Euboian League – An 'Irregular' Koinon?" In H. Beck and P. Funke (eds.), *Federalism in Greek Antiquity*. Cambridge: 158–78.

Leone, B. 2012. "A Trade Route between Euboea and the Northern Aegean." In *Zagora in Context: Settlements and Intercommunal Links in the Geometric Period (900–700 BC)*. Proceedings of the conference held by the Australian Archaeological Institute at Athens and the Archaeological Society at Athens, 20–22 May. Athens: 229–41.

Ma, J. 2003. "Peer Polity Interaction in the Hellenistic Age." *Past & Present* 180: 9–39.

Mack, W. 2015. *Proxeny and Polis: Institutional Networks in the Ancient Greek World*. Oxford.

Mackil, E. 2013. *Creating a Common Polity*. Berkeley.

Malkin, I. 2011. *A Small Greek World: Networks in the Ancient Mediterranean*. Oxford.

McAuley, A. 2018. "From the Cradle: Reconstructing the Ephebeia in Hellenistic Megara." In P.J. Smith and H. Beck (eds.), *Megarian Moments: The Local World of an Ancient Greek City-State. TSO* 1: 217–36.

Meiggs, R. 1949. "A Note on Athenian Imperialism." *Classical Review* 63.1: 9–12. https://doi.org/10.1515/9780748631247-014. Retrieved 18 June 2021 from http://www.jstor.org/stable/706127.

Pecirka, J. 1966. *The Formula for the Grant of Enktesis in Attic Inscriptions*. Prague.

Reber, K. 2002. "Die Südgrenze des Territoriums von Eretria." *Antike Kunst* 45: 40–54.

Reber, K. 2007. "Living and Housing in Classical and Hellenistic Eretria." *British School at Athens Studies* 15: 281–8.

Richter, D. 2011. *Cosmopolis: Imagining Community in Late Classical Athens and the Early Roman Empire*. Oxford.

Rizakis, A.D. 2007. "Supra-civic Landowning and Supra-civic Euergetic Activities of Urban Elites in the Imperial Peloponnese." In *Being Peloponnesian: Cohesion and Diversity through Time*. Nottingham: 1–16.

Tarn, W.W., and G.T. Griffith. 1952. *Hellenistic Civilisation*. 3rd ed. London.

Trevett, J. 1999. "Demosthenes and Thebes." *Historia* 48.2: 184–202. Retrieved 18 June 2021 from http://www.jstor.org/stable/4436539.

*This chapter continues where the preceding chapter on the granting of local civic privileges left off. Regulations regarding housing and property as well as intermarriage are at the heart and soul of the local's social texture. Pertaining to the outline of the* oikos, *the foundational unit of Greek communities, matrimonial laws in particular had the capacity to reconfigure and also rescale local society. We have seen in chapter 4 that the award of* proxenia *usually included the right to perform epigamy and exogamy, that is, to conclude legal matrimonial unions with individuals from outside the community, and that* proxenoi *made active use of this opportunity. In a world of fast-paced change, with increased mobility and migration, and a multitude of new foundations of cities, did Hellenistic* polis *societies steer clear from the traditional practice of endogamic marriage? Sara Saba discusses the curious case of the sympolity between Latmos and Pidasa in Asia Minor, by which it was stipulated that the citizens of the newly established union intermarried across their former communal boundaries. Considered a deliberate act of social engineering, the regulation is debated also for its nature as exception or endorsement of prevailing practices. Saba's analysis of the epigraphic record points to the former; similar to a document from Arkadia that governed the union between Orchomenos and Euaimon, the sympolitic charter of Latmos and Pidasa does not void the idea that civic endogamy remained common practice in the Hellenistic period. The chapter draws far-reaching and indeed fascinating conclusions from this: calling for a more nuanced discourse on the interplay between marriage practices and the lived local experience, Saba highlights the quality of local practice as a compass to navigate the tides of societal challenge in epochal change.*

*Keywords: sympolity, intermarriage, housing, Latmos, Pidasa, social engineering*

# 5

# Notes on Matrimonial Strategies in Civic Contexts

SARA SABA

At the end of the fourth century BCE, two communities in the region of Karia, Latmos and Pidasa produced a document detailing the process of their unification, a document that was subsequently inscribed on stone and put on display. In 1997 W. Blümel published the inscription recording this document that was discovered on spolia found on an island of the Bafa Lake, most likely brought from the city of Herakleia, as M. Wörrle has suggested.[1] The text has drawn the attention of many noted scholars ever since.[2] The stone is broken on the top and the bottom part, leaving us with the central section of the *stēlē* and an incomplete, yet very informative, text. The readable document does not give a name to the unification process it envisions for the two communities, although it is safe to infer it was *sympoliteia*. The inscription instead provides its readers with otherwise rare pieces of information on the policies that communities adopted while reshaping their own structures, such as policies on housing, matrimonial strategies, debt control, and other topics. In the present essay, this epigraphic document shall become a guide for offering a few considerations on one theme in particular, namely how matrimonial strategies were adjusted to fit into the policies promoted by different players, for example, merging communities, while defining new, local contexts. New communities multiplied in the Hellenistic period, but these were not always brand-new towns; communities frequently came together to create new civic units. In this chapter I examine how families were formed under these new circumstances and how states adapted local practices to new realities.

## *Poleis* and Policies: Marriage and the Local Community

In the ancient Greek world marriage was essentially a local matter. The citizens of a *polis* preferred to marry within the community: to use the technical terminology, endogamy (marrying within the community) was preferred to exogamy (marrying outside the community). When we try to place the institution of marriage in the context of issues of mobility, colonization, foundations and refoundations, and therefore networks and interconnectivity that so deeply shaped the Hellenistic period, we must ask if and how matrimonial strategies changed and how they fit in the new order that was being created. In particular, the question is whether we can detect changes in these strategies in the context of the creation of new, enlarged communities.

A recurring query in my past investigations concerns the practical implementation of rules deriving from new city policies. Here, I continue on that theme, and in particular, I look at whether, with the foundation of new communities, a new attitude towards matrimonial strategies emerged in the institutions or/and at a societal level. A change in attitude from the top towards matrimonial strategies could affect any society because administrators could try to influence the way families were created and thus shape civil society. How did matrimonial strategies at an institutional level influence and inform the sense of belonging to a new community? How did these shape local communities and their histories? These are by no means straightforward and simple queries, as they not only involve many complex themes – from colonization to citizenship rights – but also ask difficult questions of our limited evidence. The scant epigraphic sources we possess, which I will discuss in this essay, indeed seem to clothe the issue of marriage with an aura of localism and traditionalism: communities in general, including new communities, appear to have subscribed faithfully to the preference for matrimonial unions within their own boundaries. But the new communities were "artificial": their citizenry was either made up of or had been enlarged by newcomers, and their boundaries (physical and mental) had expanded in some form. The tension between the need to include newcomers and the desire to stay true to local customs and rules must have influenced how new, in particular merging, communities thought about the institution of marriage. The evidence shows that while allowing for the creation of families outside traditional social boundaries, communities tried to keep up the appearance that they were using the old brand of traditional, local (endogamic) practice. New members of a community were asked to conform to local practices, but, at the same time, we have the unique example of a clause in the Latmos-Pidasa inscription promoting forced intermarriage between groups in the context of *sympoliteia*. Yet, it is necessary to keep in mind that this case represents only an apparent contradiction, and therefore exception, to the traditional practice of endogamy, as the goal was to create a more cohesive community through forced intermarriage. The tension lies in how communities tried to retain local practices and at the same time reconcile those with interventions, such as a *sympoliteia* process, which had a strong impact on a *polis'* society.

## Creating Family Ties: The Epigraphic Evidence

Greek cities appear to have practised civic endogamy through to the Hellenistic period.[3] One can safely draw this conclusion by studying the epigraphic evidence and the few existing literary sources that reflect upon marriage as an institution within a community. For example, Aristotle stresses that civic endogamy is what "citizens do,"[4] even if this practice was not sufficient to create a community. With civic endogamy as an axiom among Classicists in mind, I turn my attention to historical circumstances that must have tested this rule in local communities and especially in newly founded Hellenistic communities. As I have noted earlier, the evidence we possess is slim and consists of a few Hellenistic inscriptions that never focus on the regulation of matrimonial rules and strategies; rather these are refoundation acts or grants of citizenship, or deal with other themes. The topic of marriage emerges usually incidentally: the surviving clauses meant to regulate this aspect of civic life are mostly devoted to defining additional criteria for citizenship eligibility and therefore institutional aspects and participation in *polis* life, sometimes by conceding the grant of *epigamia*.[5] In particular, I intend to review the cases of communities that have been assigned the status of "exception" in regard to their matrimonial practice: the point I hope to make is that no exception to the standard practice of civic endogamy actually exists, apart from perhaps the case of Latmos and Pidasa.[6] This case, however, has a specific, highly localized context that makes it a remarkable exception.

## Exogamy or Endogamy? The Epigraphic Evidence

Neither Latmos nor Pidasa was a "new" community in the fourth century. But new communities could grow out of old ones, for example by following the implementation of institutional and political tools, such as *sympoliteia*. This term does not appear in the inscription, but as I have noted at the beginning, the unification process between Latmos and Pidasa described in the text can be safely defined in terms of sympolity.[7]

The first lines of the text are missing, thus depriving us of a clear legal definition of the nature of the document and, probably, of a few more potentially valuable details on this institutional attempt to unite the two communities.[8] The surviving text starts by listing procedural provisions probably tied to a (now lost) extension of citizenship rights to the lawful members of the community that had to move in, namely the citizens of Pidasa. The text does this by mixing the administrative, social, and religious ingredients that make up the texture of society of a Greek *polis* (lines 2–13). After that, financial matters – in terms of public debt – are treated (lines 13–19). The text moves then to other practical issues, namely the topic of housing and marriage, which related to the daily life of the new *polis* both in the short and long term. Housing has a prominent place, since the text deals first with temporary housing for newcomers and then (lines 19–20), a few lines later, addresses the clearly difficult topic of arrangements for permanent housing (lines 27–8).[9] Framed within the lines devoted to housing arrangements is a reference to the rarely spoken of topic of an official matrimonial strategy (lines 21–5).[10] The scholars who have studied this document have pointed out repeatedly that one historical figure, that is, Asander, must have been heavily involved in the unification process of Latmos and Pidasa.[11] Proof of this would be the creation of a tribe for the new community that was to be named after him, Asandris, and that was to include both Latmians and Pidaseans among its members (lines 4–6). The *communis opinio*, which I accept and mostly follow here, asserts that Asander promoted this sympolity, and probably brokered the agreement, but the end of his tenure marked also the end of the unification process. Whether this sympolity was brought to completion, and how far its provisions were implemented, need not concern us here. A remark on this point seems relevant, however. If we look closely at this act of sympolity, it is impossible not to consider the difficulty of the actions prescribed and the steps required to bring them to completion. If the events in which Asander had been involved truly abruptly ended his tenure in Karia and, with it, the unification process that the inscription from Latmos and Pidasa describes, this text would be the memory of an unfulfilled "constitutional" promise. But two communities were involved and, as Mack stresses in his 2013 article,[12] I assume that it took some time to untangle the ties the administrators of the cities had at least started establishing by following the decisions inscribed on stone. While I believe that Asander was the driving force, I cannot imagine that the cities were completely unwilling parties to this unification process. This is a historical question we cannot answer, and instead here I would like to think about whether our evidence for the creation of communities reflects actual concerns for the foundation process only or attempts to move beyond the act of the foundation itself to envision the structure of an entirely new community. Did those in charge of the creation of communities think beyond the act of foundation of a new *polis*? If yes, how did they do this? What was of immediate and what was of long-term concern? The agreement of Pidasa-Latmos and other surviving texts may help us in trying to answer these questions.

This exercise of asking what it took to actually found a community has been done many times before. Hellenistic inscriptions are a good, if the only, guide we have, but they can only provide a "checklist" of how those who were in charge of foundations went about their task. Antigonos' letters to Lebedos and Teos are illuminating in that they stress the numerous issues to be taken into account and were presented to the king to decide or help arbitrate.[13] Other surviving documents tend to describe the formation process of a new community in a "negative" way; namely, these texts react to issues that the founding-initiative triggered.[14] Be that as it may, in a new foundation the surviving documents seem to assign high priority to the definition of a body of laws and to the settling of financial and (outstanding) judicial matters (debts, but also taxes and liturgies), along with the concession of citizenship. These texts often replicate the standard precepts on the repartition of the (new) citizens in the different subdivisions of a city. In brief, the recurring themes in various foundation documents are the following: citizenship (with practical issues attached), laws, finances. While those appear to be the immediate concerns, at times we find clauses devoted to two additional themes: housing and marriage, namely other long-term issues or, better, practical concerns affecting the lives of the citizens of a new community in a very tangible way.

In 2007, I demonstrated how provisions for temporary and permanent housing can be found in several *sympoliteia* projects and tried to draw conclusions on the intention of the involved communities.[15] Marriage appears to have been an additional preoccupation for some communities, and it certainly figures as such in the Latmos-Pidasa agreement. This text indeed contains a most extraordinary clause on the topic of marriage:

[ὅ]πως δ' ἂν καὶ ἐπιγαμίας ποιῶνται πρὸς ἀλλήλους, μὴ ἐξέστω Λάτμιον Λατμίωι διδόναι
θυγατέρα μηδὲ λαμβάνειν μηδὲ Πιδασέ(α) Πιδ[α]-
24 σεῖ, ἀλλὰ διδόναι καὶ λαμβάνειν Λάτμιομ μὲ[ν]
Πιδασεῖ, Πιδασέα δὲ Λατμίωι ἐφ' ἔτη ἕξ· (§ 8)[16]

Riet van Bremen discusses these lines and comments, very fittingly, that they describe a project of social engineering.[17] In this document, the legislator imposes on the citizenry of the new foundation an internal form of exogamy by prescribing that Latmians and Pidaseans intermarry for six years. These were supposed to be members of the same new community, which means that this provision, technically, upheld the principle of civic endogamy, but, to the citizens of the community coming as they were from two different *poleis*, it must have felt like exogamy. The goal was clear: force the families of the two communities to unite in order to create, at both a political and a social level, one community.[18]

Scholarship has looked at this agreement in context and stressed that this attempt to sympolity must have been fairly short-lived because around 180 BCE Pidasa entered in sympolity with another town, namely Miletus, as *Milet* I.3.149 testifies. In this text, too, appears a short reference to the theme of marriage. This reference is usually explained away as the result of the conflicting matrimonial practices between Miletus and Pidasa. The text (lines 10–12) affirms:

εἶναι Πιδασεῖς Μιλησίων πο/λίτας καὶ τέκνα καὶ γυναῖκας, ὅσαι ἂν ὦσιν φύσει
Πιδασίδες ἢ πόλεως Ἑλλη/νίδος πολίτιδες …

Scholars, notably relying on the work by Verilhac and Vial, suggest that these lines signal that Pidasa and Miletus had diverging matrimonial practices: Pidasa must have practised exogamy, as the explicit and differentiated reference to Pidasean and Greek brides should attest, while Miletus practised endogamy.[19] The discrepancy in marriage policies would therefore be the reason behind the insertion of this clause in the agreement: Miletus was willing to tolerate the inclusion of Greek wives in its community, even if they were not Pidaseans, but not of non-Greek ones. In the past I have accepted this interpretation, but another way to understand the implications of these lines is possible. In fact, all the text says is that women legally married and living in Pidasa could receive Milesian citizenship, granted they were Pidaseans or, most importantly, Greek. Does this truly mean that Pidasa had practised exogamy as a rule? And even if that were the case, what would that mean? If we accept the reading of the exogamy practices for Pidasa, we must also consider that this inscription would be our only piece of evidence for this conclusion. The inscription containing the agreement between Pidasa and Latmos, published in 1997 and unknown to Verilhac and Vial when they published their work (1998), does not confirm that Pidasa practised exogamy, for example. On the contrary, the latter document seems to imply that action was necessary to break the practice of endogamy in both cities involved, Pidasa and Latmos.

If we hypothesize for a moment that Pidasa did not practise civic exogamy routinely, but, eventually, of necessity, then we also should and could read differently the clause included in *Milet* I.3.149 concerning the inclusion of Pidasean and Greek wives in Miletus' citizenry. I believe that another possible explanation for this clause can indeed be found by looking further in the work by Verilhac and Vial. These two scholars note that in the third and second centuries BCE Miletus offered the option of acquiring Milesian citizenship to a number of residents, among whom we count women and children.[20] Verilhac and Vial point out, too, that the number of children known to have been granted citizenship every year was not very high – but our sample is also very small – and think these children might have come from mixed marriages. Their situation was adjusted through ad hoc legislation, that is, the children of unions between two people who were not (both) citizens could acquire Milesian citizenship. Thus, Verilhac and Vial note that Miletus, while practising civic endogamy, also had mixed marriages, and these were numerous enough to require legislative interventions. If we pursue this further, while the clause of *Milet* I.3.149 could mean that Pidasa routinely practised exogamy (unconfirmed), and the agreement was thus trying to adjust its situation to the new sympolitic reality, it could also indicate that Miletus moved to extend its legislation on mixed marriages to Pidasa and its inhabitants. This does not mean that Pidasa practised exogamy routinely or that Miletus did, but only that Greek mixed marriages were, in a certain measure, common, and increasingly accepted and needed to be accounted for in the newly shaped citizen body of Miletus.

The other possible attested local exception to the practice of endogamy, according to the seminal work by Verilhac and Vial, comes from two old communities that were also to become a new one through sympoly.[21] The small Achaian town of Euaimon was to be united with Orchomenos in the middle of the fourth century BCE as *IPark* 15 testifies. This inscription (lines 41–3) asserts:

… ὅτις ξένας / γεγάμηκε, τὸς παῖδας [κ/α]ὶ τὰς γυναῖκας Ἐ[ρ]/χομινίας ἦναι …

Most scholars have interpreted these lines as referring to Euaimon only, but already in 1976 Hannik assigned to this clause a broader meaning.[22] She indeed thought that the clause did not necessarily refer exclusively to Euaimon and suggested that it could be extended in its meaning, and that this was a general provision applicable to both Euaimon and Orchomenos. The sentence reads: "… whoever has married a foreigner, both the children and the women are to be Orchomenians." But if "Orchomenian" was the new citizen qualification for foreigners entering the community, perhaps this "label" extended to every legal member of the new community: therefore, it would be immaterial to whom the foreign woman had been married to; whether to a man from Euaimon or one originating from Orchomenos, they were all Orchomenians. While we do not find clauses on forced intermarriage, local authorities clearly anticipated mixed marriages and moved to regulate the status of those couples. Most likely, such marriages were already a reality, probably in Euaimon more than in the bigger

Orchomenos, and this was only a seal to their legitimacy. If this were the case, I think that what we need is a more nuanced discourse on the use of exogamy and/or endogamy since local realities were clearly more complicated than a clear-cut rule would imply.

The cases that scholarship routinely considers exceptions may be looked at from a different angle. The evidence indicates that no city practised civic exogamy routinely, even less as a rule; instead, civic endogamy was the common or, most likely, preferred practice. Yet there are many indications that mixed marriages took place and must have increased in number with time, and would become even more numerous in the context of new foundations. The tension between preferred matrimonial practices and actual societal and political situations was probably solved through ad hoc legislation to help people retain their citizen status and therefore their rights.

## Exogamy or Endogamy: Conclusions

I must return briefly to the case of Latmos and Pidasa: the clause devoted to intermarriage from this text seems to be the one openly acknowledged exception we have to the regular and preferred practice of endogamy in Greek *poleis*. According to the text, Latmians and Pidaseans were supposed to suspend their allegedly rooted and preferred practice of endogamy, which makes the remarks by Riet van Bremen on the character of social engineering of this plan even more appealing. To my knowledge, this indeed is the only actual epigraphic piece of evidence we have showing an attempt to force intermarriage between communities. But it was policy for six years, in pursuance, I believe, of the goal to mix families and make them part of one community. After six years perhaps, exogamy would have felt like endogamy. Even in the creation of new communities the attempt to keep or start or even restart the practice of civic endogamy can be seen at work. In the case of Latmos and Pidasa, a time-limited prescription of forced intermarriage (exogamy) between members of two communities coming together appears directed to promote a form of endogamy.

In a world where endogamy seems to have been the norm, exogamy appears to have a very particular role: in the one case that has survived, we see how de facto exogamy but pseudo-endogamy was forced so that, from it, a bigger community would result. In the few other cases where thought was given to the issue of marriage, this was done to rectify a possible problem that may have had to do more with citizenship than with matrimonial practices. The real issue must have been citizenship, at an institutional level, while more specific concerns with social structures are reflected (only) in the unique provision of the Latmos-Pidasa agreement.[23]

In the Hellenistic period, many colonies were founded and people of different provenance must have lived in these new communities. We know that when bigger groups came from the same area, for example the Cretans in Myous, from settled communities, their members were not ready to mix with others.[24] This may have been the case also in new communities, but when one had become a "citizen" of a new city, even an objectively mixed-marriage was, technically, endogamy. It is possible that a tendency to "civic" endogamy existed in new cities and probably prevailed over "technical" endogamy.

Communities (old ones, and, as far as we know, new ones too) tried to retain or to build their particularism by legitimizing the "other"; in one case we have seen that authorities tried to accomplish this even by touching upon the realm of the family. Intermarriage among different groups that ended up under one denomination must have been difficult to promote, especially if the union was part of a larger political plan triggered by a third party, as we see in the case of Latmos and Pidasa. Even in a world that was supposed to be expanding, marriage was a local affair in the sense that civic groups seemed to prefer to intermarry and new ties were difficult to forge. The question that I pose here, namely which approach to marriage new communities used with individuals coming from different places, is a fascinating one since it looks at how local dimensions and a local practice actually reacted to external impulses or provisions. While unevenly applied stress on society could break resistance, the *polis* appears to have been able to rethink and adapt its local practices without truly modifying them. While epochal changes brought about the necessity to rethink political and societal issues as a whole, the latter were slower to change and *poleis* looked at their own local, traditional models to adapt them to new realities as and when needed. In this regard, the Latmos-Pidasa inscription is again an exceptional document as it could be seen as a regulation for micromanaging a sympolity. One more observation is in order: as exceptional as the provision on forced intermarriage is, failure to implement did not incur penalties. Whether one can draw conclusions from this is an open question, but it could be interpreted as an indirect admission of the difficulty of implementing the prescription listed in the document. An oath seals the document, and this certainly was a powerful way to end the agreement, but the question of control and implementation of decisions remains. Top-down decisions that were to shape anew a given society are hard to envision in general, but especially so in a world like the *polis*, where the sense of identity and attachment to certain forms of political structures and, even more, to social local practices seems to have been extremely strong. Again, we can turn to the illuminating work by Verilhac and Vial and their conclusion that endogamy was the widely preferred practice within the *polis*: no imposition from the top can break long-established practices, and social changes were clearly slow to come about. Mixed marriages must have become more and more common in the Greek world, but as ad hoc legislation to which epigraphic evidence testifies, top-down decisions did not to shape matrimonial practices to the extent that long-term changes determined by events or actual on-the-ground-situations did.

## NOTES

1  Wörrle 2003a: 124.
2  The inscription was discovered on the site of Herakleia under Mount Latmos, in the area of its Athena sanctuary, not too long before its publication in Blümel 1997, with *addenda* in 1998, A more recent edition of the text and commentary is in Bencivenni 2003, no. 6 and Wörrle 2003a, with a new edition of the text and its translation, and 2003b. Mack (2013, esp. 95–100) presents his considerations on the documents as well as the attitude that the signing communities of this and other *sympoliteia* agreements displayed.
3  Verilhac and Vial (1998) have devoted an entire chapter to this theme, namely chapter 2, in their seminal work on the topic of Greek marriage.
4  Arist. *Pol.* III 1280 b36.
5  On the question of *epigamia*, see Saba 2011 with additional bibliography.
6  In their work Verilhac and Vial (1998, esp. 72–3) stress that the alleged exceptions to the practice of endogamy, which I discuss in what follows, are represented by small rural towns. The assumption is that these communities had to resort to exogamy mainly because of demographics. This is a logical conclusion, as Gauthier (1999: 333–4) suggests in his review of Verilhac and Vial's 1998 volume. I do not intend to dispute this assumption; instead, here I ask how strong the impact of a local and traditional approach to marriage was in shaping new communities, and how the analysis of these alleged exceptions can contribute to this query.
7  See Bencivenni 2003: 157.
8  On the legal nature of the text, and possible consequences for its interpretation, see Mack 2013: 95–100.
9  On housing, see also Saba 2007.
10  Lines 25–6 are devoted to the question of offices that would have to be filled jointly by Latmians and Pidaseans.
11  Wörrle 2003b, esp. 1362–3 on Asander.
12  Mack 2013: 95–100.

13  For the text, see Welles *RC* 3. A new edition with commentary and more recent bibliography is in Bencivenni 2003, no. 7. See also the considerations in Mack 2013: 100–4. Mack reflects on the willingness of communities to enter into a sympolity and does so with a keen eye and interesting observations. This is, however, a thorny issue that we can hardly settle on the basis of the official documents that we possess.

14  I am mainly thinking of the case of Arsinoe-Nagidos, on which see again Bencivenni 2003, no. 10, and also Saba 2020: 25–7.

15  See Saba 2007.

16  Text by Bencivenni 2003: 152. My translation follows: "So that they intermarry with each other, it has been decreed that it is prohibited to a Latmian to give a daughter [as a wife] to a Latmian or to take [one as a wife] and to a Pidasean a Pidasean; instead for six years a Latmian should give or take [as a wife the daughter? of a] Pidasean, and a Pidasian (should (give or) take [as a wife the daughter? of a]) Latmian."

17  See van Bremen 2003: 313–30.

18  On this see also Saba 2011: 397–8. This inscription and this clause in particular have been the object of consideration by LaBuff 2010. I cannot claim to share his interpretation, as I noted in Saba 2012: 160 n. 4, or his methodology, LaBuff 2010, esp. 121, but he is right in interrogating the effectiveness of a measure so drastically limited in time. This indeed is an open question.

19  Verilhac and Vial 1998: 72–3. Again, it is necessary to read this in context since these scholars stress the different nature of the communities of Miletus and Pidasa. It is undeniable that size and location of a community must have played a role in matrimonial practices. My question is whether we should talk about exogamy as an exception, thus upgrading a practice born out of necessity, to the status of a rule. Again, I believe we need to be more nuanced in our discourse. On the agreement between Miletus and Pidasa see the considerations in Gauthier 2001: 117–27.

20  Verilhac and Vial 1998: 63–5.

21  Verilhac and Vial 1998: 72.

22  See Hannick 1976: 142.

23  As the most common lists of topics addressed by merging communities in epigraphic documents show (see *supra*), other matters were relevant to new foundations, i.e., merging, and also to matrimonial strategies. For example, the issue of property rights was certainly one point to be considered, as marrying also meant merging fortunes. This aspect deserves more attention as it opens a new range of motivations for both promoting and discouraging exogamy.

24  See *Milet* I.3.34–99; on the lot of these mercenaries, see now Baker 2013: 268–92. For an analysis of the social aspects, see Petropoulou 1985, appendix 6 and pp. 128–31.

## REFERENCES


Baker, P. 2013. "Mère-patrie et patrie d'adoption à l'époque hellénistique: Réflexions à partir du cas des mercenaires crétois de Milet." In S. Ager (ed.), *Belonging and Isolation in the Hellenistic World*. Toronto: 268–92.

Bencivenni, A. 2003. *Progetti di riforme costituzionali nelle epigrafi greche dei secoli IV–II a.C.* Bologna.

Blümel, W. 1997. "Vertrag zwischen Latmos und Pidasa." *Epigraphica Anatolica* 29: 135–42.

Blümel, W. 1998. "Addendum zu dem Vertrag zwischen Latmos und Pidasa: φρατόριον." *Epigraphica Anatolica* 30: 185.

Gauthier, P. 1999. "Compte rendu A.-M. VÉRILHAC et Cl. VIAL, Le mariage grec du VIe siècle av. J.-C à l'époque d'Auguste (BCH Suppl. 32), Athènes-Paris (1998), 412 p. et 5 pi." *Topoi* 9.1: 331–45.

Gauthier, P. 2001. "Les Pidaséens entrent en sympolitie avec les Milésiens: La procédure et les modalités institutionnelles." In A. Bresson and R. Descat, *Les cités d'Asie Mineure occidentale au IIe siècle a.C.* Bordeaux: 117–27.

Hannick, J.-M. 1976. "Droit de cité et mariages mixtes." *L'Antiquité classique*: 133–48.

LaBuff, J. 2010. "The Union of Latmos and Pidasa Reconsidered." *Epigraphica Anatolica*: 115–24.

Mack, W. 2013. "Communal Interests and Polis Identity under Negotiation: Documents Depicting Sympolities between Cities Great and Small." *Topoi* 18: 87–116. https://doi.org/10.3406/topoi.2013.2461.

Petropoulou, A. 1985. *Beiträge zur Wirtschafts- und Gesellschaftsgeschichte Kretas in hellenistischer Zeit*. Frankfurt.

Saba, S. 2007. "Temporary and Permanent Housing for New Citizens." *Epigraphica Anatolica*: 125–34.

Saba, S. 2011. "Hellenistic Greek Cities and Families." In B. Rawson (ed.), *A Companion to Families in the Greek and Roman Worlds*. Malden, MA: 395–407.

Saba, S. 2012. "Nagidos, Arsinoe and *Isopoliteia*." *Dike* 15: 159–70.

Saba, S. 2020. *Isopoliteia in Hellenistic Times*. Leiden and Boston.

van Bremen, R. 2003. "Family Structures." In A. Erskine (ed.), *A Companion to the Hellenistic World*. Oxford: 313–30.

Verilhac, A.-M., and Cl. Vial. 1998. *Le mariage grec du VIe siècle av. J.-C à l'époque d'Auguste (Bulletin de Correspondance HelléniqueSuppl. 32)*. Athens and Paris.

Wörrle, M. 2003a. "Inschriften von Herakleia am Latmos III: Der Synoikismos der Latmioi mit den Pidaseis." *Chiron* 33: 121–43. https://doi.org/10.34780/o49a-b9cu.

Wörrle, M. 2003b. "Pidasa du Grion et Héraclée du Latmos: deux cités sans avenir." *Comptes Rendus des Séances de l'Académie des Inscriptions et Belles-Lettres*: 1361–79.

*Rome's victory over the Antigonid kingdom triggered different local responses among the cities and leagues of mainland Greece. In Larisa, situated on the banks of the Peneios River in Thessaly, it inspired the establishment of a freedom festival that echoed Titus Quinctius Flamininus' declaration of Greek freedom from 197 BCE. Scholars typically place the festival for Zeus Eleutherios in the context of global transformation and its translation into the regional arena of the rejuvenated Thessalian League. Denver Graninger pays due attention to these spatial vectors. His main focus, however, is directed at the local horizon of the festival: its place in societal interactions in Larisa, in particular its twofold role as a feeder and a platform for the prioritization of local meaning. The chapter begins with observations on the Larisan matrix of space and place. The main agents to tie the people to their land, Graninger argues, were the local founding hero Akrisios and an eponymous nymph. We encounter here once again the inherent quality of nymphs to foster connections to the local (chapter 1). Tracing the salient nature of Larisa outside the framework of the Thessalian League, the article next turns to a curious compression of local and non-local realms, a creative mixing and blending that energized local and regional conversations. Most prominently, the compression condensed in the notion of Pelasgians, a notorious people from the time before the arrival of the Hellenes. Stigmatized as uncivilized rogues by others, the Larisans positively identified with the Pelasgians, who were assigned a real presence in the built environment of the city and in corresponding discourses. Over time, they also shaped the way in which local champions were recorded in the victory lists of the Eleutheria. Resonating with other media, Graninger concludes, such a designation deeply imprinted on quotidian discourses on the ground, drawing the people of Larisa to their city and community as prime sources of meaning and orientation.*

*Keywords: Thessalian League, Pelasgians, nymphs, epinician poetry, festivals, athletic competition*

# 6

# Local Horizons for the Thessalian Eleutheria

DENVER GRANINGER

## Introduction

Following the defeat of Philip V at Kynoskephalai in 197, T. Quinctius Flamininus, the victorious consul, began a program of liberation and reorganization of territories formerly under Antigonid control. In Thessaly, a rejuvenated Thessalian League appeared and commemorated these revolutionary events with a new festival, the Eleutheria, in honour of Zeus Eleutherios, probably already in the late 190s, held in the league's capital city, Larisa.[1] The festival participates in a wider Hellenistic vogue of "freedom festivals," as described by A. Chaniotis, that celebrated military victory over perceived outsiders, followed by the (constructed) beginning of a new, more prosperous era.[2] While some elements of the festival program in broad outline can be suggested by comparison with other, better known festivals of this type, insight into its agonistic component is offered by a series of fragmentary, second- and first-century victor lists from Larisa.[3] No list survives in complete form, but we may piece together a reasonable program of the melic, gymnic, and equestrian contests; it is virtually certain that there were dramatic contests as well, but these are less well known.[4] Some elements of the program are normative within the festival culture *koinē* of the Hellenistic period, while others are distinctive and appear to represent regional agonistic traditions, if not to brand the "Thessalianness" of the festival: e.g., contests for dismounting a horse (or chariot) with a lit torch (*aphippolampas*) and bull-hunting (*taurothēria*).[5] The profile of competitors is likewise distinctive: approximately half of the attested victors (ca. 25 in number) hailed from non-Thessalian locations throughout the central and eastern Mediterranean world; the other half are Thessalian (ca. 25 in number, among which Larisans are especially numerous, ca. 18), who, while active throughout the program, are dominant in both the equestrian contests and those drawing on regional agonistic tradition. Indeed, only Thessalian victors are attested in those two categories of contest, and no ordinary Thessalians at that – many are also attested as holding high office in the Thessalian League at some point in their careers.[6]

Recent scholarship has tended to privilege regional – what was or could be construed broadly as "Thessalian" – and global – what was or could be construed broadly as "Hellenic," "panhellenic," or "eastern Mediterranean" horizons of the Eleutheria.[7] Yet, as the preceding sketch of the festival has suggested, we might equally consider the festival's local horizon: Larisan victors are, after all, especially prominent in the evidence: Larisa offered the primary cult and competition venues for the festival; and, in the final analysis, Larisa was a, if not the, dominant city in later Hellenistic Thessaly beginning with the Flamininan refoundation of the Thessalian League. This essay offers an initial exploration of the Eleutheria within its local, Larisan setting, while bearing in mind throughout Beck's invitation and advisement to such study: "the quest for the local [is] a kaleidoscopic endeavor rather than one that aims for coherence."[8]

A key problematic of the essay and of any study of localism, frankly, centres on the relationship between local and non-local, understood as regional or global, although I am not especially interested in policing an imagined limit between the two, in either a theoretical or applied setting.[9] Larisa possessed a local discourse environment that was spatially and symbolically rooted; it offered a way for the community to engage with and understand themselves as participating in, regional and global environments, but to do so in their own language and system of reference.[10] At another level, however, every localism is unique and particular and the story that I tell below emphasizes how the boundaries of the local seem to extend well beyond the boundaries of the *polis*, and as a result what is local and Larisan can be made to appear in certain circumstances as regional and Thessalian, or even global and Greek.[11]

I begin with some broad reflections on characteristic spatial and symbolic constituents of localism in Larisa, with attention to the natural and built environment as well as Akrisios, the city's founding hero, and Larisa, the eponymous nymph. I then consider two case studies where the local is less easy to isolate and the sources are instead suggestive of a compression of local and non-local frames of reference. First, I will consider a selection of agonistic and other commemorative monuments from Thessaly, with an emphasis on Larisa, that represents the honorand's activities as significant simultaneously within local and non-local settings. Second, I turn to expressions of what I call "Pelasgianism," that is, an advertisement of Pelasgian influence, in Thessaly, again with an emphasis on Larisa, that reveals complex local attitudes towards a wider, Hellenic phenomenon – the positing of an earlier, pre-Greek population in Greek lands, whose customs differed substantially from those of contemporary inhabitants. In the concluding section of the paper, I return to the Eleutheria and attempt to situate it within this complex, Larisan localism.

## Local Larisa: Space and Symbol

As Beck writes, "the twofold meaning of the local speaks to a particular ontology of place, one that amalgamates physical and imagined realms, marries relational and contextual approaches, and combines nature and society. It turns space into place."[12] In what follows, I aim to offer a first encounter with the local in ancient Larisa. While space and symbol are not completely discrete categories, as one often merges with the other, they offer a helpful organizational schema.

We begin with the Peneios, on the banks of which the *astu* of Larisa took root. With headwaters high in the Pindos Mountains and nourished by tributaries from throughout Thessaly, the Peneios was a powerful river, more akin to the great waterways of Epirus, Macedonia, and Thrace than those of the southern Greek mainland and Aegean Islands. It did not fail to impress outsiders. Xerxes could boast, for example, that the Thessalians' medism, orchestrated by the Aleuadai of Larisa, was understandable because by controlling the river, he held the fortunes of Thessaly in the palm of his hand: he could simply dam up the Tempe, flood the region's wondrous farmland, and return Thessaly to a diluvian state, as it had been before Poseidon's intervention.[13] The river must have been a blessing and a curse for Larisa. Strabo explains the absence of much of inland Thessaly in Homer to the fact that the area was miserable at the time and not amenable to large-scale human settlement due to the regular flooding of the Peneios.[14] By the later Classical period, matters seem more in hand. Theophrastos describes an ambitious program of draining marshlands in Larisa's *chōra*, a process that must have brought additional land under cultivation, but at a cost: a colder, less humid climate in which olives no longer grew and grapevines could freeze.[15] Anthropogenic climate change has a significant impact on local economy and society. The constant companions of the Peneios are the great plains of Thessaly. These form a second important spatial axis for Larisa, particularly that segment of the eastern plain known as the Dotion plain.[16]

The built environment of Larisa developed in relation to both river and plain. Several millennia of continued human occupation have unfortunately rendered scattershot our view of the city's settlement history and architectural development. The city's Early Iron Age material record, while difficult to parse, does not seem especially predictive of the power and influence later visibly exercised by the city at the turn of the sixth century: the city appears to have been a "late bloomer" (but this picture could change quickly with new excavation).[17] Helly has provocatively suggested that Larisa in the early Archaic period had been a boundary market that eventually outgrew the communities that it served. Such a scenario seems to explain the results of a nearest neighbour analysis survey of eastern Thessaly and helps to make sense of both Larisa's apparent late rise to prominence and its engagement with and borrowing from neighbours, resulting in a marked heterogeneity in material culture:[18] it is the amalgamation of distinct, non-local and regional materials and styles that characterize the city.[19]

The acropolis was home to Athena Polias and perhaps founding hero Akrisios, whom I discuss further below.[20] Aristotle famously described the two agoras characteristic of Thessalian cities – one "free," one banausic – and one assumes that Larisa, too, would have fit the mould.[21] Gerogiannis has recently argued for a massive reorganization of the *astu* on an orthogonal plan under Macedonian leadership, a plan that delineated precisely between public and private spheres of activity.[22]

The city took its name from a nymph, Larisa.[23] Souidas, a historian from Thessaly active in the Hellenistic period and author of a *Thettalika* in at least two books, describes the nymph falling into the Peneios while playing with a ball.[24] Nymph becomes heroine in this telling: Larisa's hybrid qualities as nymph and heroine are not unparalleled;[25] Larsen has attractively associated these scant details of her mythology with another, better attested figure, Ino.[26] She is often represented on Larisan coinage throughout the Classical period and then, strikingly, there are revivals under the reorganized Thessalian League, Roman Republic, and Roman Empire.[27] A ball is a common attribute,[28] but she is also depicted at or near a fountain, or with a water-carrying vessel, which suggests that she must have been associated with principal fountain(s) in the city.[29]

The Phokaian sculptor Telephanes, whose work was ranked beside Myron and Polykleitos, is known to have lived in Thessaly probably in the early fifth century, where he produced celebrated works, among which was a statue of Larisa.[30] Telephanes would move on to Persepolis after his Thessalian phase, where his influence has been sought in a range of sculptures in Greek style.[31] Pliny may attribute Telephanes' undeserved lack of reputation to his choice of patrons, Thessalian and Persian, but we are authorized to imagine the impact of his work in shaping the local discourse in Larisa, where his statue of Larisa was probably prominently displayed; Larisa is a plausible, although by no means necessary, context for his other well-known works as well (e.g., sculptures of the pentathlete Spintharos and of Apollo). Older stereotypes about a culturally isolated or backward Thessaly are thankfully beginning to wane: support for a figure like Telephanes is in keeping with a wider, regional pattern of elite investment that saw Simonides, Bakchylides, and Pindar employed by Thessalian patrons.[32]

Nymphs, like heroes, are eminently local recipients of cult. They are imma-nent in the physical landscape of communities, where they can be called on for assistance. Like heroes, nymphs are genealogically pliable, capable of con-necting the local to the regional and the global. While there are elements to the mythology of Larisa that are Argive or at least place the heroine in the orbit of Argos, she seems to have been a much more prominent figure in Thessaly, where she is represented frequently and over a long period of time on coinages minted in the city; to date, no Argive representation of the figure is known.[33]

Akrisios, well known in handbooks of Greek mythology as king of Argos, father of Danae, and grandfather of Perseus, has strong connections to Larisa.[34] Some sources relate that he was accidentally killed by Perseus in Larisa and buried there. The manner of death and location of burial are both of interest: one variant claims that during funeral games that the local king of Larisa, Teutamides, was holding for his deceased father, Perseus was com-peting in the pentathlon and accidentally struck Akrisios in the foot with a discus;[35] a not incompatible variant claims that Perseus was publicly display-ing his skill in throwing the discus, which is presented in this tradition as his invention, when Akrisios was accidentally struck and killed by a throw.[36] Nor was this some rococo suite of local tales: they were the subject, for example, of Sophokles' *Larisaioi*.[37] After death, Akrisios was buried at Larisa. Sources vary about the precise location: either in a heroon somewhere outside the walls of the city[38] or, more intriguingly, on the acropolis of Larisa in proxim-ity to a precinct of Athena, one of the city's tutelary divinities.[39] The tradi-tion of burial on the acropolis conforms with another trace in the ancient mythography: that Akrisios was in fact the founder of Larisa.[40] Cult is not otherwise attested or implied, but there are no good grounds to suppose that it did not exist.[41] Some sources even associate Akrisios with the Delphic Amphictyony, either as founder or early organizer; such a point may also have not gone without notice, given the prominence of Thessalian *ethnē* in the Amphictyony.[42]

Pushing into the Hellenistic period, we have evidence of the continued evolution of local discourses in Larisa. The city emerged quickly after the Second Macedonian War as a privileged centre of the reorganized Thessalian League. The city probably enjoyed such a status in the third century as well, when some form of regional Thessalian polity also seems to have been active, with Larisa prominent within it.[43] But it is important to stress that Larisa was culturally and politically salient outside of the institutional framework of the Thessalian League and one must parse carefully, when possible, the spatial and symbolic boundaries between Larisa as an independent city and Larisa as capital of the Thessalian League.[44] The experience of other *koina* suggests as well that Larisa's capital status is more likely to have benefited the city, or at least some of its elites, than not.[45] Compare, for example, the dominance that other federal capitals could exercise in shaping policy as well as decentralizing strategies to limit the concentration of such influence, like rotating the location of assembly meetings, deployed by some *koina*.[46]

Consider, too, the issue of dialect. Larisa qua *polis* continued to publish decrees in local dialect into the first century BCE. The Thessalian League, however, seems to have published in *koinē* in the post-196 BCE era; a third-century decree of the Thessalians is not in *koinē* but in a local Thessalian dialect.[47] Such a distinction is unlikely to have passed unnoticed, either among the Larisans themselves or others visiting the city. One may compare the famous exchange between Philip V and Larisa in 217 and 214, where the Macedonian king cajoled a recalcitrant city into enrolling new citizens: the dossier of royal letters and city decrees is preserved – Philip writes in *koinē*, the Larisans in their traditional dialect.[48] And when Rome begins to actively navigate Thessalian politics beginning with Flamininus, they do not translate and publish documents in local dialect, but in *koinē*.[49] Consider as well venues for the publication of such documents so inscribed. Within Larisa, the Sanctuary of Apollo Kerdoios was the prime venue for display of city decrees (and in the third century, for decrees of the Thessalians, too), while *koinon* documents could be seen in the Sanctuary of Zeus Eleutherios. Such a distinction was not merely a question of visibility but communicated important priorities of Larisa qua *polis* and qua member and head of the Thessalian *koinon*.

## Local and Non-local Compression

The preceding section has offered a series of sketches of some constituent elements of Larisan localism, with emphasis on the natural and built environment together with the heroic and divine figures who were imagined to haunt them. Even on this partial, if, I would posit, representative basis, we have seen how regularly Larisan localism is drawn into a non-local frame of reference. Whether we are considering the Peneios River and Thessalian plains, which are critical to understanding not just Larisa but other Thessalian localities, or the nymph Larisa and king Akrisios, where Argive (and other) notes are sounded, it seems as if it is impossible to fully isolate and disentangle the local from this larger matrix. I turn in this section to consider the phenomenon more fully. Much of the evidence is commemorative and agonistic in character and so will facilitate comparison with localism in later Hellenistic Larisa, particularly as it intersects with the Eleutheria. Archaic lyric, especially epinician, offers a useful point of departure. Pindar, Bakchylides, and Simonides each composed poetry for Thessalians and participated in the self-representation and self-understanding of these Thessalian elites.[50] Recent historicist scholarship on epinician stresses the importance of the local to this poetry: while there are certainly epinician strategies that seem typical of the genre, these were adapted specifically to diverse local honorands, audiences, and performance settings.[51]

I begin with Pindar, Pythian 10, his earliest epinician, probably composed in 498 in honour of Hippokleas "of Thessaly," who won the boys' diaulos at Delphi. In an opening priamel, Thessaly is positively contrasted with Lakedaimon – Ὀλβία Λακεδαίμων / μάκαιρα Θεσσαλία (lines 1–2) – and thus a regional frame of reference is made initially prominent. There follow in rapid succession references to: Delphi, where Hippokleas won his victory; Pelinna, the honorand's home city; and the Aleuadai, a well-known Larisan family exercised on occasion dynastic power within the region and appears, if not explicitly as "commissioners" of the poem, then in an adjacent role. These three communities are all eager to see Hippokleas receive due praise (lines 3–6). Further local and regional reference follows in the second half of the epinician. The poem appears to refer to the mechanism of its own performance: "when the Ephyraians pour forth my sweet voice beside the Peneios" (trans. Race, lines 55–6: Ἐφυραίων / ὄπ' ἀμφὶ Πηνειὸν γλυκεῖαν προχεόντων ἐμάν). A scholiast on these lines mentions that the city of Krannon in Thessaly had previously been called Ephyra. The poem closes with extended praise of the Aleuad commissioners of the poem – Thorax, for his hospitality, and his brothers, "because they uphold and exalt the state of the Thessalians; with good men rests the governance of cities as a cherished inheritance" (trans. Race, lines 69–72: ὅτι / ὑψοῦ φέροντι νόμον Θεσσαλῶν / αὔξοντες· ἐν δ' ἀγαθοῖσι κεῖται / πατρώιαι κεδναὶ πολίων κυβερνάσιες). The poem underscores the complexities of Thessalian localism in the early fifth century. Representatives of the Aleuadai, based in Larisa, commission an epinician to honour a Pythian victor, Hippokleas, from another city, Pelinna; the epinician is to be performed apparently by a chorus from a third city, Krannon. These geographical linkages are nicely framed by reference to Thessaly and Thessalians at the beginning and close of the epinician.

A similar progression is visible in the fragmentary Bakchylides 14B, which celebrated Aristotle of Larisa, perhaps for his accession to a prominent civic office rather than for athletic success.[52] The text begins with an invocation of Hestia, who is qualified first by her relationship with a family or clan, that of the Agathoklids, who enjoy her divine patronage (lines 1–3: Ἑστία χρυσόθρον', εὐ/δόξων Ἀγαθοκλεαδᾶν ἆτε ἀφνε[ῶν] / ἀνδρῶν μέγαν ὄλβον ἀέξεις). This material relationship is next located in space: Hestia is seated among roads on the banks of the Peneios in Thessaly (lines 4–6: ἡμένα μέσαις ἀγυιαῖς / Πηνειὸν ἀμφ' εὐώδεα Θεσσαλία[ς] / μηλοτρόφου ἐν γυάλοις), from which place the honorand Aristoteles departed to compete in the Pythian games in Delphi, where he won victories, as apparently had other members of his family (lines 7–9: Κεῖθεν καὶ Ἀριστοτέλης Κίρ/ραν πρὸς εὐθαλέα μολών / δὶς στεφανώσατο). It is in connection with these victories that Larisa is first explicitly mentioned, and we are authorized to see the cult of Hestia and seat of Agathoklids as indeed located there.[53]

Monumental epigrams commissioned by Thessalians reiterate this tendency to combine local and non-local frames of reference for an honorand's activities, similar to what has been observed in Pindar and Bakchylides. A funerary monument honouring Theotimos, son of Menyllos, from Atrax, offers an associative logic whereby his participation in battle with the "best of the Hellenes" at Tanagra (457 BCE) is recast as a moment where he "fashions … a crown for Thessaly" and does not "shame the glory of his city," Atrax.[54] Compare a late Classical epitaph for Menon, son of Pothon, presumably from Pherai, where the entire city grieves his death. Hellas herself had hoped Menon would adorn Thessaly with crowns: κρύπτει μὲν χθὼν ἥδε Μένωνα Πόθωνος ὃν | Ἑλλας / ἤλπισε κοσμήσειν Θεσσαλίαν στεφ[ά]|νοις.[55]

Such blending of local and non-local frames of reference can also be ascertained in the Daochos monument, a later fourth-century family representation that commemorates the exceptional achievements of a prominent Pharsalan family in war, politics, and sport.[56] The monument was erected in a prominent location within the Sanctuary of Apollo at Delphi, above the temple terrace, and this global setting offers tantalizing interpretive possibilities. Aston, for example, has drawn attention to the monument's spatial and symbolic position within the topography of the sanctuary; she offers a compelling reading of the Aiakid associations of its placement and the monument's concomitant claim that Daochos and family are part of a supraregional northern Greek cultural milieu that is distinct from the generalized "panhellenism" that is so often associated with the site.[57] Her close reading of the monument's epigrams reveals, however, their complex, competitive engagement with a canon of Thessalian literary self-representation on how best to rule, one that would include Pindar's *Pythian* 10.[58]

A Pharsalan localism peaks through occasionally, although it is less textured than either the regional or supra-regional discourses sketched above. The epigram for Hagias son of Aknonios begins: πρῶτος Ὀλύμπια παγκράτιον, Φαρσάλιε, νικᾷς, / Ἁγία Ἀκνονίου, γῆς ἀπὸ Θεσσαλίας ("You, Pharsalan, Hagias son of Aknonios, are the first from the land of Thessaly to win the *pankration* at the Olympia"). The epigram's direct address to the honorand with the ethnic adjective "Pharsalan" may be construed as a local touch, but it provides at the same time the banal, however poetically expressed, information that could be expected in a global setting like Delphi: name, father's name, ethnic.[59] A more profound expression of localism can be glimpsed, however, in a companion monument set up in Pharsalos that appears to have preceded the monument at Delphi. A base for a bronze statue of Hagias, son of Aknonios, signed by Lysippos of Sikyon seems to have been inscribed with an epigram at least eight lines in length, the last four of which are quoted nearly verbatim on the base of Hagias' statue at Delphi.[60] The Pharsalan inscription is fragmentary and too little is preserved of the first four lines to indicate how local elements may have been figured there, although Pharsalos may be described as Hagias' *patris* (line 4). The priority of the Pharsalan monument to the Delphian seems assured by Lysippos' signed bronze, which most probably offered the prototype for the extant marble statues of the Daochos monument, clearly Lysippan in style, at Delphi.[61] Such a commission in Pharsalos must have impacted the local discourse environment there, even if we are not well-positioned to know precisely how. While Aston is quite right to question the particularly Thessalian associations of the position of the Daochos monument at Delphi,[62] the existence of an earlier, partially parallel, and no doubt extremely prominent monument at Pharsalos opens the possibility that, despite the understated presence of local elements in the Daochos epigrams, there is actually a quite dramatic expression of localism here, albeit one that was mostly accessible, as perhaps all localisms are, to an in-group: the Pharsalans themselves.

The hippic poems of the third-century poet Poseidippos can be seen to stand in relation to earlier epinician and epigram on Thessaly, with respect to genre and, specifically, to the compression of local and regional perspectives in the case of Thessalian victors: "Posidippus' epigrams for Thessalian victories are conspicuously for Thessalian victories; no mention is made of the native city of the victor, although the herald who announced the victory will have proclaimed the victor by his or her city."[63] One may wonder whether the shifting designations for Thessalians in catalogues of third-century *olympionikai* reflect how the herald would in fact have announced victories; if so, then there may have been considerable variability even on this point: of the four Thessalian victors mentioned there, one appears with a city ethnic, two appear with a regional ethnic *Thessalos* rather than a city ethnic, and a third seems to have been designated by a combination of regional and city ethnics.[64] An additional noteworthy feature of Poseidippos that finds confirmation in epinician and other sources is a continuing interest in the traditional, elite families of Thessaly.[65]

Our survey has brought us to the threshold of the Flamininan reorganization of Thessaly. The key implication of these findings for our understanding of the Eleutheria is that there was a lengthy tradition, visible already in the later Archaic period, in Larisa and elsewhere in Thessaly, of compression of local and non-local, particularly regional, frames of reference, especially in agonistic and commemorative settings. While possible causes are manifold, I find Mili's recent discussion of Thessalian elite networks to be particularly helpful. In it, she stresses how traditional narrative models of Archaic and Classical Greek history poorly suit Thessaly and that, rather than assuming political weakness or instability (or exaggerating their opposites – strength and stability) due to perceived violation of (or conformity with) these models, we should read again the sources and to try to understand Thessaly on its own terms. An alternative understanding that emerges is that of a densely networked regional elite, whose core, often competitive, relationships could be adapted to a dizzying range of forms of political organization; this elite maintained a sense of Thessaly as an *ethnos* throughout.[66] Elite relationships construct the region in a very concrete manner; there follows naturally the compression of local and regional visible in the high elite sources discussed above.[67] In any case, such tradition can only have facilitated the legibility of the Eleutheria at the local level and offers powerful insight into Larisan localism in the later Hellenistic period.[68]

### "Larisa, Mother of Our Kindred the Pelasgians"[69]

If this discussion of commemorative and agonistic poetry and related literary sources has suggested a certain direction to this compression, from the local to the non-local, it would be worth pursuing a second series of case studies where an opposite progression may be on display. My subject here are those notorious Pelasgians whom many Greek communities regarded as the original inhabitants of Greek lands. Several recent, formidable studies have helped to reorient scholarship away from reductive attempts to discern the actual identity and movements of Pelasgians as a people, and towards more nuanced questions about how Greek communities used the Pelasgians to construct past narratives in order to explain present circumstances and, broadly, to reflect on what it meant to be Greek.[70] But in Thessaly in general and in Larisa in particular, the Pelasgians seem to have been more than simply "good to think with." While Fowler was surely correct to write in his trenchant study of Pelasgians that "no one would shake your hand in agora or forum and say: 'I am a Pelasgian,'" one must admit that Pelasgians are imagined with real presence and personality in Larisa.[71]

The role of Pelasgos in local genealogies is distinctive. In some accounts, Pelasgos is tied into the lineage of Thessalos, the eponym of the Thessalians, as grandfather; in others, crucially, the nymph Larisa was herself the mother of Pelasgos.[72] The Pelasgians in Thessaly thus appear as ancestors. Vestiges of the relationship were everywhere. For example, the principal administrative structure of Thessaly was divided into four parts, or tetrads, one of which was named Pelasgiotis and included the city of Larisa:[73] Dionysios of Halikarnassos records a broader Pelasgian imprint on other aspects of the division.[74] An intriguing epitaph for a Thessalian adolescent who died abroad in Delphi in the early Imperial period suggests that one's tetrad of birth or residence was at that late date not just a stale administrative convenience; it continued to play an influential role in shaping and advertising the identity of individual Thessalians:

Χρῆστος
Πρώτου Θεσσα-
λὸς Λαρεισαῖος
Πελασγιώτης
ἐτῶν ιη᾽
Ἥρως
χρηστὲ χαῖρε

Christos, son of Protos, Thessalian, Larisan, Pelasgiotid, 18 years (old). Best hero, farewell.[75]

We would appear to be outside of the realm of basic public administration here.

Local historians of Thessaly suggest that active interest in and recollection of earlier names of people and places in the region, including the region itself, continued down into the Hellenistic period;[76] these often had Pelasgian associations and are suggestive of a more thoroughgoing interest in the relationship of their Hellenistic present to a range of potential pasts.[77] For example, Staphylos of Naukratis treated in his *Thessalika* the genealogy and mobility of Pelasgos, who was Argive by origin, but later moved to Thessaly and became the eponym of Thessaly, known then as Pelasgia.[78] In his poem in at least 16 books, *Thettalika*, Rhianos of Crete points to a different progression of names: "Once the ancients called it Pyrrhaie / from Pyrrhe, the ancient bride of Deukalion; later they called it Haimonie from Haimon, whom Pelasgos / begot as the best son; and in turn Haimon begot Thessalos, / and from this one the people changed the name to Thessalia."[79] While Hollis observes that such interest in change of name was a *topos* in Hellenistic prose and poetry, the development of such *topoi* was no mere antiquarian development in scholarly culture, but a response to a real interest on the part of the audience in knowing these earlier stages in their collective history, remnants of which no doubt lurked everywhere precisely in the form of names.[80] And, if Rhianos' *Messēniaka* are any guide, it is certain that there was much more of local and regional importance in his *Thessalika* than just changing place names.[81] Interest in the *Messēniaka* has progressed in tandem with the development of scholarship on intentional history in the ancient Greek world:[82] Luraghi helpfully reorients discussion away from content and towards function, observing that "Rhianus show[s] that the Messenian Wars were a crucial element of the Messenian past as perceived by the Messenians themselves."[83] The *Thettalika* potentially played an analogous role in Thessaly.[84]

This Pelasgian presence was not limited to current and past names of places. In one conspicuous case, a direct continuity of cult practice between Pelasgos and the Hellenistic present could be asserted. Baton of Sinope, a historian with wide-ranging interests who was active in the second half of the third century or first half of the second, composed a work entitled "On Thessaly and Haimonia."[85] A lengthy fragment from the work survives, in which an aetiology of the Thessalian Peloria in honour of Zeus Pelorios is offered. The festival appears as a classic festival of inversion, in which social hierarchies were suspended or overturned for a period of time in commemoration of several events: the drainage of the plain of Thessaly through the Tempe via the Peneios River; the exposure of the region's vast and fertile plains; and, perhaps most significantly, the communication of news of these events to Pelasgos, then king of the Pelasgians, by Peloros, who seems to have occupied a lower status rank. Baton claimed that the festival was celebrated by the Thessalians "still even now" as their greatest festival (καὶ τὸ σύνολον ἔτι καὶ νῦν Θεσσαλοὺς μεγίστην ἑορτὴν ἄγοντας προσαγορεύειν Πελώρια).[86] Emphasis falls on continuities between this deep, Pelasgian past and the Thessalian present: "the world of the Thessalians appears to be unchanged and autochthonous."[87]

Finally, it would be useful to return to the local epigraphic record in Larisa in the Hellenistic period. Earlier scholarship on Pelasgians has often concentrated not just on high literary, Archaic and Classical sources – to the exclusion of much of interest at the local level – but on literary sources, tout court. There is good reason for this in that explicitly Pelasgian themes are absent in Greek epigraphy, with the exception of Larisa. A curious third-century funeral monument appears to commemorate a Larisan state burial for a non-citizen.[88] The text is worth citing in full:

Ἡρίλλος Ἡροδώρου
Καλχηδόνιος ·

*vacat*

τὸν ξεῖνον ἁ Λάρισα τᾶι Πελασγίδι
κάλυψε βώλωι καὶ ποταγορήσατο ·
τὸν Ἡροδώρου προφρόνως ἐδεξάμαν
Ἡρίλλον, ἦ γὰρ οἶδα τὰν Καλχαδόνα
εὔξεινον οὖσαν, ἇς πάτρας ἀείδετο,
αὐτόν τε πά[ν]τα πρὸς χάριν τετραμμένον ·

*vacat*

Ἑρμῆι Χθονίωι

Herillos, son of Herodoros, Kalchedonian. Larisa covered the foreigner with the Pelasgian clod and made an address: "I gladly received Herillos, son of Herodoros. For indeed I know that Kalchedon is friendly to foreigners and that he in every respect committed to the delight of the fatherland of which he sang." To Hermes Chthonios.[89]

Herillos, son of Herodoros, a Chalkedonian poet, apparently died while travelling abroad in Larisa. The city seems to have awarded him public burial in recognition of both Kalchedon's habitual kindness to strangers and, by extension, Herillos' skill in singing about these admirable qualities of his home city.

There is little in the text that does not command study, but I will limit myself to consideration of the Pelasgian clod with which the city buried Herillos. The adjective seems to be a hoary synonym for "Thessalian" or, more likely, "Larisan." Since the publishing authority appears to be the city of Larisa itself, we confront a particularly clear designation of physical earth in Larisa's *chōra* as "Pelasgian." One may be tempted as well to see a learned and subversive allusion to one of the other Larisas, that in Aiolis in Asia Minor, which receives the epithet "well-clodded" and is populated by tribes of Pelasgians at *Iliad* 2.840–1.[90] A note of competition with Larisa Kremaste may as well be suggested: that Larisa, located in Achaia Phthtiotis, which region was perioikic to Thessaly, was also called Pelasgia Larisa.[91]

A second monument from Hellenistic Larisa, again largely overlooked in scholarship, offers valuable additional perspective on the visibility and tangibility of Pelasgian themes in a local setting. This inscribed statue base, tentatively dated to the first century on the basis of palaeography, reads: οὐδενὸς ἐκ θνα[τοῦ], Μελία, Ζανὸς δ' ἐλόχευσα | χάρμα Πελασγιάδαις Αἵμονα γεινάμενα ("From no mortal but from Zeus did I, Melia, conceive and give birth to Haimon, who was a joy to the Pelasgiadai").[92] This base apparently held a statue of Melia, whose name is suggestive of an (ash-tree?) nymph. While Strabo and Rhianos relate a tradition that Haimon was son of Pelasgos and father of Thessalos,[93] a different genealogy is offered here, with Melia, otherwise unknown, and Zeus, imagined as parents of Haimon. Questions abound. If Pelasgos has been written out of the immediate lineage of Haimon in Larisa, what were the implications for the Pelasgiadai? And who are these Pelasgiadai to be understood as? The Thessalians as an *ethnos* or the inhabitants of a comparatively narrower territory around Larisa or even a still narrowed family or phratry in Larisa? How one answers such questions would have some bearing on whom the dedicator of the monument might have been: the Thessalian League, Larisa, or some smaller sub-*polis* entity. Our inability to answer such questions should not detract from the evidence for a continuing interest in Pelasgian topics offered by this monument. The dimensions of the base are suggestive of public display, and if Melia merited such treatment, possibly so too did Zeus, Haimon, Thessalos, and even Pelasgos himself.[94]

## Localizing the Eleutheria

I attempt now in the final section of this paper to situate the Eleutheria within this local discourse environment or, for lack of a better expression, to localize the festival. The move to localize is authorized, I submit, by a recent debate between Chaniotis and Wiemer on the nature of commemorative festivals in the Hellenistic world. In a series of invaluable studies, Chaniotis has developed an interpretive framework for understanding new or newly reorganized religious festivals in the Hellenistic era. He pushes back against the idea that Hellenistic festivals were programmatically different from their Archaic and Classical forebears, noting instead changed emphases: "greater weight of political content, the tighter connection to the self-representation of the *polis*, the special importance of the procession, the attempt to attract many foreign visitors, and ... the increased importance of musical, thymelic, and athletic contests."[95] There can be cumulative consequences to these shifts in emphasis, however, and Hellenistic festivals were consequently increasingly and deliberately made to serve purposes and achieve ends beyond simply honouring the gods: central concerns now included diplomacy, *polis* marketing, and civic cohesion.[96] While such features had often been secondary or collateral outcomes of earlier

Greek festivals, now they seem to become the primary purpose; increasing secularization follows accordingly.[97]

Several contributions to the important 2009 volume *Feiern und Erinnern: Geschichtsbilder im Spiegel antiker Feste,* edited by Beck and Wiemer, sketch alternative approaches to some of the materials that Chaniotis collected and studied. In a lucid and wide-ranging introduction, the editors are critical of Chaniotis' adoption of a "declinist" model of the Hellenistic city and his strict demarcation of religious and historical festivals.[98] Wiemer suggests that the long-lasting celebrations of "thanksgiving days" associated events of the recent past with something older, more traditional, and more essential to the life of the community.[99] In sum, Wiemer invites us to privilege the local setting of these individual festivals and to read them within the context of their respective local discourse environments.[100]

What is at stake for the Eleutheria? From the synchronic, global perspective of Chaniotis, the Eleutheria is a significant case of the wider Hellenistic phenomenon of "freedom festivals" that commemorate recent, transformative political events that resulted in the military deliverance of the celebrating community from existential danger posed by an opponent constructed as cultural "other,"[101] that is, the defeat of the Antigonids by Flamininus and Rome during the Second Macedonian War and the subsequent liberation and reorganization of Thessaly as a *koinon*. The template here is global and tends to make the Eleutheria exemplary of a wider Hellenistic pattern: what is important about the festival is that it illustrates that these larger processes were taking place in Larisa and the Thessalian *koinon,* too. A local reading along the lines of Wiemer would privilege the local setting of the festival, seek out what elements in that environment were activated by this new festival, and ask how the discursive environment shaped and was shaped by these events: durative, meaningful historical commemoration does not occur on a tabula rasa. The Eleutheria become as a result not a typical Hellenistic phenomenon, but a unique expression of Larisa and the Thessalian League.[102]

Returning to Larisa, Thessaly, and the Eleutheria, then, we may appreciate the complications entailed by the entanglement of local, regional, and global frames of reference as a feature, not a bug, of the study of any Hellenistic local discourse environment. But we must nevertheless ask: How might the Eleutheria have resonated locally in Larisa and/or how might Larisan localism resonate within the Eleutheria? I offer by way of conclusion an abbreviated discussion of three possibilities:

1) As founding hero, Akrisios is among the most conventional components of Larisan localism. Travel, contact with outsiders, competition,

and spectacle are essential elements of his story, all of which resonate strongly with the Hellenistic Eleutheria.[103] Although no further details of Akrisios' cult are known, his physical presence in the suburban or urban space of the city make it likely that festival attendees would have encountered him at some point during the Eleutheria, possibly on arrival or departure if his temenos was outside the city, or when moving between cult and competition locations within the city if he was buried on the acropolis. The so-called First Theatre of Larisa, which is likely to have served as the principal venue for dramatic and melic events during the second and much of the first centuries BCE, was cut into the acropolis of Larisa; hence spectators would have been in close physical proximity to Akrisios by default.

2) Even those most Thessalian events of the Eleutheria may have been previously deployed in attempts at local self-definition. Larisan coinage of the Classical period has been interpreted as displaying two of these spectacular contests: the *taurothēria* and the *aphippodromos*. Such representations form the basis for the hypothesis that the Eleutheria contests draw on an older agonistic tradition.[104] The history of these coin types may also suggest that the type of local/non-local entanglement discussed in the preceding section was a factor here, too. The types are common on Larisan coins, but are also present in smaller number on other contemporary local coinages of Thessaly. It has been hypothesized that Larisa in fact headed a "coinage union" at the time and that these types were adopted to distinguish member cities from one another. The so-called *taurokathapsia* occurs on Larisan obols and hemiobols in the second quarter of the fifth century BCE; while the type is shared by a number of other important Thessalian cities, Larisa appears to be the centre of gravity of the network.[105] Again, a confusion of local and regional layers of discourse appears. Member cities of this "coinage union" use local ethnics to designate the minting authority, but the iconography is shared among the varied mints.

3) Finally, I note a slight shift in epigraphic habit in later Hellenistic Larisa: Larisan victors in the Eleutheria organized by the Thessalian League began to be identified with a distinctive, complex ethnic – " Thessalian from Larisa Pelasgis"[106] – as opposed to simpler designations previously used – "Larisan"[107] or "Thessalian from Larisa."[108] This new ethnic is attested only in Eleutheria victor lists and in no other category of document. The earliest preserved uses occur in the first half of the first century BCE, while the latest known uses of either simpler ethnic date to the middle of the second century BCE. Such a shift must most immediately reflect a shift in the sense of audience for these documents

on the part of the issuing authority, the Thessalian League.[109] As a genre, the victor list offers a terrific opportunity to grasp the entanglement of local and non-local, especially in the case of contests that had a supra-local catchment area. In the case of the Eleutheria, we can fairly think of a Thessalian (regional) and then eastern Mediterranean/panhellenic (global) event, with respect to both contestants and spectators. While the regular, day-to-day audience for such documents is quite likely to have been local, especially in the time between penteteric celebrations of the Eleutheria, these victor lists anticipate a global reception.

Framing the change in terms of epigraphic habit encourages us to consider audience, which in turn nudges us to consider the catchment area of the festival, both for athletes and spectators. We do not possess *theōrodokoi* lists or festival invitations for the Eleutheria, unfortunately, and so cannot write confidently about catchment attendance. Certainly, a Larisan and perhaps more broadly eastern Thessalian attendance catchment is plausible, given the location of the festival; since the *koinon* was the organizing body, it is equally likely that delegations from member cities, whether or not they were styled as *theōroi*, also participated. Beyond that, it becomes harder to reconstruct a picture, but there are some hints. Already in the 180s, for example, the Delphian Amphictyony could request that the honours decreed by it for a Larisan, who had served as a *hieromnēmōn* of the Thessaloi to the Amphictyony and travelled to Rome to negotiate on behalf of Amphictyonic interests, be announced at the Eleutheria; a fragmentary decree in honour of his brother likely contained similar provisions. In related fashion, ... the Thessalian League announced honours for non-Thessalians at the Eleutheria, again from an early date, which may hint at the presence of representatives from the honorand's *polis*; such displays had an impact on attendees from other communities, too, in the later Hellenistic economy of interstate status: the Thessalians demonstrate that they know how to reward benefactors, which could help to attract new benefactors.

A widening catchment area seems a likely proximate cause for the use of a new expanded ethnic for Larisan victors. For a global audience, the new ethnic may indeed have helped to disambiguate Larisa from Larisa Kremaste among other Larisas now networked in part by the Eleutheria. In the local worlds of Larisa, however, such a designation must have resonated strongly amid the Pelasgian names and Pelasgian monuments so visible in the area, inspiring all who could claim membership in the city to connect with a sense of shared Pelasgian ancestry through the Eleutheria and its Larisan victors.[110]

## NOTES

1  *BE* 2013, no. 224, based on *CID* 4.106 and a plausible emendation of *IG* IX 2, 508, presented ad loc. All dates BCE unless otherwise noted.

2  Chaniotis 1991; Chaniotis 1995; Chaniotis 2005: 227–33.

3  See Graninger 2011, Epigraphic Appendix, nos. 1–7.

4  Graninger 2011, Epigraphic Appendix, no. 8. For a revised text, see *BE* 2011.

5  A third such competition is attested: *aphippodromos,* or the dismounting of a horse or chariot and running alongside of it. For this "Thessalian triad" of contests, see Graninger 2011: 78–85.

6  Graninger 2011: 82–4.

7  Regional: see, e.g., Bouchon and Helly 2015; "Hellenic," etc.: see, e.g., Chaniotis 1995.

8  Beck 2018: 16.

9  For local, regional, and global as terms of analysis, see Beck 2018, passim, and especially at p. 23 on the distinction between local and regional systems of exchange: "in their experience of the local and the regional, individuals turn to strategies of exchange that are categorically different. One strategy is governed by directness, auto-referentiality, and complicity; the other by intermediary contact, cyclical exchanges, and a hybrid of inside/outside perspectives."

10  For local discourse environment, see Beck 2018, passim, but clearly at p. 31: local discourse environment "was a dynamic engine that powered strategies of distinction and competition, and most eminently, a vibrant stage for the dialectic interplay between the local, the regional, and the global."

11  See now Beck 2020 which, on the basis of meticulous study of a range of diverse local discourse environments across the central Greek world, is able to tease out some larger patterns in how localism works.

12  Beck 2018: 25.

13  Hdt. 7.128–30. For Poseidon's role in draining Thessaly through the Tempe, see, e.g., schol. Pind. *Pyth.* 4.138a; Mili 2015: 237–8.

14  Strabo 9.5.10.

15  Theophr. *Caus. pl.* 5.14.2–3. See Hughes 2014: 221. The course of the river was irregular and shifting, particularly as it flowed north and east from Larisa towards the Tempe (Strabo 9.5.2: Peneios often overflows; Strabo 9.5.19: Larisans use embankments to control course of Peneios, to keep it from overflowing and washing away arable soil).

16  For the Dotion plain, see Helly 1987, a rich study.

17  For the Late Bronze Age–Early Iron Age archaeology of Larisa, see Morgan 2003: 89–91.

18  Helly 1984: 214–16. For Helly, such features can be attributed to the economic role of the settlement in the region and may in fact reflect the early status

of Larisa as a border/frontier market that served a range of neighbouring communities.

19 Recent scholarship has drawn attention to a broader pattern of interaction with outsiders, which is typical of Thessaly: see, e.g., Mili 2015: 296–9, and passim; Aston 2016. Even in this setting, local and regional merge.

20 Mili 2015: 104–11.

21 Arist. *Pol.* 1331a24–36.

22 Gerogiannis 2018.

23 Hellanikos *BNJ* 4 F 91. For an incisive recent discussion of nymphs in myth and cult across the Greek world with reference to fundamental earlier scholarship, see Sourvinou-Inwood 2005: 103–5.

24 *BNJ* 602 F2. Souidas is described by Strabo (7.7.12 (Radt), with Kramer's plausible emendation) as pandering to Thessalian tastes for fantastic stories: Σουίδας μὲν τοῖς Θετταλοῖς μυθώδεις λόγους προσχαριζόμενος… For *to mythōdes* as a concern of local historiography, see Thomas 2019: 74–99. Further details about Souidas' biography: Jacoby ad *FGrH* 602. For ball-playing as a sport accessible to women in Greek antiquity, see O'Sullivan 2012: 19–20; literary (mythic) representations are often erotically charged.

25 Sourvinou-Inwood 2005.

26 Larson 2001: 165. Ino's divine alter-ego, Leukothea, is a common recipient of cult in Thessaly, including Larisa; see Graninger 2011: 103, with n. 59.

27 Liampi 1992: 213–17. The appearance of Larisa on league issues may suggest that this local nymph had broader regional visibility and appeal.

28 Liampi argues that this is a distinctively local type (Liampi 1992: 215). The coinage of Trikka also apparently shows that city's eponymous nymph playing ball, apparently under the influence of Larisa (Liampi 1997).

29 Liampi 1992.

30 Plin. *NH* 34.68.

31 Telephanes in Persepolis: Kawami 1986; Linder 2015. Langlotz 1951 argued that the influence of Telephanes' Larisa is visible in some fragments of Greek style sculpture recovered from Persepolis, above all the "Persepolis Penelope." Liampi 1992: 216 is sceptical. Cf. Palagia 2008, which offers a wider view of the monument from the perspective of marble source.

32 See, e.g., Stamatopoulou 2007.

33 Liampi 1992.

34 For Akrisios, see, among others, Moreau 1988.

35 Apollod. 2.4.4.

36 Paus. 2.16.2. Cf. schol. ad Ap. Rh. 4.1091, where Perseus recognized Akrisios in Larisa and convinced his grandfather to return with him to Argos. As they are about to leave, they encounter a contest of *neoi* taking place in the city; the specification of age category may situate us immediately in a more routinized

agonistic setting, not bound to the specific occasion of a funeral game, and is in any case broadly evocative of gymnasium culture.

37  Soph. F 373–81 Radt².

38  Pherekydes *FGrH* 3 F10 (*BNJ* 3 F 10) = schol. ad Ap. Rh. 4.1091: Perseus and the Larisans buried Akrisios in front of the city and the locals (οἱ ἐπιχώριοι) made a heroon there.

39  Antiochos *FGrH* 29 F2 (*BNJ* 29 F2); Antiochos-Pherekydes *FGrH* 333 F1 (*BNJ* 333 F1) = Clem. Alex. *Protrep.* 3.45: "In the temple of Athena in Larisa on the acropolis, there is a tomb of Akrisios, and at Athens on the acropolis (sc. in the temple of Athens there is a tomb) of Kekrops." There is considerable controversy about the identities of Antiochos and Antiochos-Pherekydes, which I do not enter into here. I regard the mention of Larisa as a reference to Thessalian (Pelasgiotid) Larisa and not Larisa, one of the two acropoleis of Argos. For further discussion of these conflicting traditions about the burial site of Akrisios, see Mili 2015: 193–5.

40  Schol. ad Ap. Rh. 1.39–40.

41  One might adduce as a loose comparandum, as does Antiochos, the constellation of cults centred in the Erechtheion on the Athenian acropolis.

42  Founder: schol. ad Eur. *Or.* 1087; Organizer: Strabo 9.3.7; Liban. *Orat.* 3.472 (Reiske).

43  Malay and Ricl 2009. While the decree purports to represent a decision of the Thessalians undertaken at Olympos during the Olympia festival in honour of Thessalos, the document is dated by the priest of Zeus Olympios and, in addition, five *tagoi* in Larisa; copies of the decree are moreover to be erected within the Olympeion, at Itonos (probably the Sanctuary of Athena Itonia near Philia), and, significantly, in Larisa in the Sanctuary of Apollo Kerdoios, which sanctuary is otherwise known as a venue for the display of *polis* documents.

44  The impact of *koinon*-membership on *polis* institutions is of continuing research interest. See, e.g., Freitag 2015 on the apparent negligible impact of membership in the Boiotian League on Megarian institutions. On the problem of "capital cities," see, e.g., Roy 2007: 291–2, which has helpful observations on the status of Megalopolis within the Arkadian League, especially on architecture. *Koinon* architecture is likely to be indistinguishable from *polis* architecture in strict archaeological perspective, and when additional evidence allows for the attribution of such a function, it is unlikely, on purely practical grounds, that such buildings would have been restricted to *koinon* activities. Cf. Mackil 2013, passim.

45  Of the 78 known *stratēgoi* of the league in the second and first centuries BCE, 35 are Larisan: Kramolisch 1978: 24. The wider region of Pelasigiotis is likewise overrepresented in the sample compared to other tetrads: 22 non-Larisan Pelasgiotis, 8 Hesitiaiotis, 2 Thessaliotis, 0 Phthiotis. Despite the vastness of

territories administered by the league, elites from Larisa and environs are disproportionately represented.

46 Beck and Funke 2015: 15.

47 Malay and Ricl 2009.

48 *IG* IX 2, 517.

49 See, e.g., Sherk 1969: 208–9.

50 See the rich discussion in Stamatopoulou 2007.

51 See, e.g., Morgan 2015 on Pindar and Sicily, the papers collected at Fearn 2011 on Pindar and Aegina, and Stenger 2004 on Bakchylides.

52 The fragment has posed interpretive challenges. I follow Maehler and others in seeing the fragment as celebrating the accession of Aristotle to prominent office in Larisa; there are strong parallels for the inclusion of such poems within corpora of epinicians in Pindar and for the prominence of Hestia therein, who is otherwise not at home in an agonistic setting (Maehler 1982, vol. 2: 302–3, comparing Pindar, *Nem.* 11). What is preserved of Bacchyl. 14, for Kleoptolemos of Thessaly, victor in a chariot race at the Petraia, is heavily gnomic and seems less immediately helpful for understanding local discourse environment: for useful discussion in a regional setting, see Stenger 2004: 305–10.

53 Fearn has suggested that there is an aggressive claiming of a cult that, in a normative Greek *polis*, would effectively serve the entirety of that community by an especially powerful clique within an oligarchic city like Larisa (Fearn 2009, passim; see esp. 35, where it is revealed that there is "no strict division between 'political' or 'public' on the one hand and 'personal' or 'private' o nthe other … in Larisa, aristocratic festivity shuts out broader society"). Mili is sceptical and hypothesizes that the specific Hestia mentioned here is not a formal civic cult but a cult organized by a local association in which the Agathoklids played a central role (Mili 2015: 131–5).

54 *I. Atrax* 160 (*CEG* 2.637).

55 *CEG* 2.643; cf. Lorenz 2019: 116–18 for full bibliography.

56 *CEG* 2.795.

57 Aston 2012: 49–53.

58 Aston 2012: 53–8.

59 In a similar vein, the epigram of Daochos I opens Δάοχος Ἀγία εἰμί, πατρὶς Φάρσαλος ("I am Daochos, son of Hagias, my fatherland is Pharsalos"). The epigram of Daochos II further, if tentatively, develops this general association of family and *polis* identity by asserting that this dedication to Apollo honoured his family and fatherland (γένος καὶ πατρίδα τιμῶν).

60 *I. Thess. Enip.* 57, with Decourt's essential commentary.

61 The coincidence of the texts of the epigrams and the styles of the statues begs an additional, unanswerable question: Might Hagias' statue at Pharsalos been part of a larger group, like the Daochos monument at Delphi?

62  Aston 2012: 49–53.

63  Dickie 2008: 37, and passim. For lucid discussion of the implications of such a strategy of elite self-representation, see Scharff 2016.

64  *P.Oxy.* XVII 2082 (*BNJ* 257a); cf. Christesen 2007: 334–6, 520 n. 4. The victors are: 1) Pandion of Thessaly, no city ethnic mentioned, victorious in the *kelēs* in 296 (Moretti 1957: 134, no. 523); 2) Karteros of Thessaly, victorious in the four-horse chariot ca. 268 (Moretti 1957: 136, no. 546: 3–4). Two other Thessalian victors are also mentioned at *P.Oxy.* XVII 2082, although little has been preserved of their names: one, M[——] from Krannon, was victorious in the *kelēs* (Moretti 1957: 136, no. 547); the other, [——] of Thessaly, won the *synōris* competition (Moretti 1957: 136, no. 548).

65  For Poseidippos' reference to the Skopadai, see AB 83; cf. Theoc. *Id.* 16. Euphorion of Chalkis wrote a work on the Aleuadai (F 62–4 (Cusset) (= F 177–9 Van Groningen)), in which he is known to have discussed Simonides' fateful sojourn among the Skopadai. An Ephoros "the Younger," whose floruit is uncertain (but may be later imperial), is described in the Suda as also having written a work on the Aleuadai, but corruption has been suspected in the passage and interpretation remains difficult. See Suda E 3952, s.v. Ἔφορος (= *FGrH* 212; *BNJ* 212; Bleckmann and Gross 2016: 101–5 (*KFHist* A 4)). Cf. Janiszewski 2006: 188–90, 329–31; Hartmann 2008: 909–10. Such interests ought not be marginalized as "learned" or "Alexandrian": "It is one thing to suppose that Alexandrian poets in cosmopolitan Alexandria were using what they took to be obscure items from little known cities, but for those cities and communities themselves, these histories were about their own land and people, with audiences in the place itself" (Thomas 2019: 393).

66  Mili 2019: 281, and passim. Cf. Beck 2016: 96; Beck observes how *koina* can accommodate a membership of organizational diversity – conditions which seem to describe Thessaly quite well – by fostering a sense of shared identity: "unification … was facilitated not only through political skill but through the lively sense of togetherness and, hence, the willingness to unite on the grounds of ethnic belonging."

67  The lapidary formulation of Mili 2019: 280, which, while applied to a different setting (formal political institutions, diplomatic relationships with non-Thessalians), seems to capture a necessary implication of these conditions: "… whenever we see the Thessalians, they are never the same."

68  The absence of Thessalian *polis*-based local histories in Jacoby may echo this phenomenon; local historians of Thessaly, whether themselves Thessalian or not, seem to have preferred to write *Thettalika*. See also Aston 2017, who points to similar issues in the interpretation of the sources for the Lapith and Centaur myths characteristic of the region: "Establishing where local ends and interregional or Panhellenic begins is also both impossible and unnecessary …

we cannot – and should not – hope to maintain a clear distinction between the purely local and the purely external" (105).

69 Soph. F 379 Radt: Λάρισα μήτηρ προσγόνων Πελασγίδων. I quote here the somewhat free translation of Lloyd-Jones.

70 Fowler 2003; Sourvinou-Inwood 2003; McInerney 2014.

71 Fowler 2003: 2.

72 Schol. Ap. Rh. 1.580. No source is named for the datum, but a local historian is likely. The genealogies of Pelasgos are, in general, complex and seem to reflect the attempts of both historians and mythographers to rationalize variant traditions and the utility of such a figure.

73 Hellanikos of Lesbos, author of a *Thettalika*, was already aware of the division of Thessaly into four units, or tetrads: Pelasgiotis, Thessaliotis, Phthiotis, Hestiaiotis (*FGrH* 601 a F1 (= *BNJ* 601 a F1); cf. Gschnitzer 1954; Helly 1995: 170–5). The Aristotelian constitution of the Thessalians attributed the territorial reform to Aleuas the Red, Arist. F 497 (Rose). Four Thessalian polemarchs, one for each tetrad, swear a treaty oath in Athens in 353/2 (*IG* II² 175). Grain production quotas were imposed by Rome on each tetrad in the mid-second century (*SEG* 34.558). Strabo offers a detailed description of the geographic extent of each of the tetrads in the Augustan era (Strabo 9.5.3).

74 Dion. Hal. *Ant. Rom.* 1.17.3–18.3.

75 *CIG* 1723; *SGDI* II, p. 931, n. 1; Daux 1944: 121–2, no. 33, who is hesitant about the date: "I^er siècle ap. J.-C.? ou II^e?" Christos and Protos are otherwise unknown (*LGPN* 3B s.v. Χρῆστος 1; Πρῶτος 7). The triple *ethnikon* for an 18-year-old is quite striking. Boeckh supposed that the third term, Πελασγιώτης, was used to distinguish the famous Larisa from other Larisas in Thessaly, above all Larisa Kremaste. For "other" Larisas in the Mediterranean, see, e.g., Strabo 9.5.19, which describes three in Thessaly (Larisa in Pelasgiotis, Larisa Kremaste, and a third, poorly attested and otherwise dubious, Larisa on Ossa). The observation has merit. Even within Thessaly there was risk of misunderstanding and confusion, and a concomitant desire to specify precisely which Larisa was meant. The recourse here is to the name of the tetrad and, formally speaking, it is Christos, not Larisa, who is identified as "Pelasgiotid."

76 Local historians from outside of Thessaly also took an interest in the Pelasgian stages of Thessalian history. See, e.g., Anonymous, *De Chio* (*FGrH* 395 F 2 (*BNJ* 395 F 2)): oikists of Chios were Pelasgians from Thessaly.

77 For "Pelasgian Argos" and the possible continued currency in the Hellenistic period, see Rigsby 2004, which restores the term in a Koan document concerning *theōroi* for the *Asklepieia*. Cf. *IG* XII 4, 1, 207, with Halloff's more conservative text and commentary.

78 *FGrH* 269 F 10 (*BNJ* 269 F 10). Little is known of his biography: a floruit by or before the middle of the second century is certain and the titles of a number

of other works of local history are preserved, including studies of Arkadians, Aiolians, and Athens. See further Jacoby ad *FGrH* 269 and Pitcher ad *BNJ* 269.

79 *FGrH* 265 F 30a (*BNJ* 265 F 30a) = schol. Ap. Rhod. *Argon.* 3.1090b. Tantalizing details of Rhianos' biography are preserved: most probably from Lebena, port of Gortyn. Rhianos was a former slave and *palaistrophylax* turned prolific scholar and poet, working probably in the second half of the third century. His oeuvre included a critical edition of the *Iliad* and *Odyssey*, erotic epigrams, and a series of epic poems on mythical and regional topics. For discussion of key details, see *BNJ* 265 (Bertelli) – preferable to Jacoby ad *FGrH* 265 – and Rigsby 1986: 350–5 (*SEG* 36.500). Meineke 1843: 186, followed by Powell 1925: 13, ad n. 24, hypothesized that these were the opening lines of the epic, while Jacoby ad *FGrH* 265 F 30a ascribed them to the "Archaeology" of this work.

80 Hollis 1992: 278–9.

81 Pausanias 4 is heavily indebted to Rhianos, especially his coverage of Aristomenes in the so-called Second Messenian War, whose role in the epic the periegete likens to that of Homer's Achilles (Paus. 4.6.3). Luraghi 2008: 87 suggests that Apollonius' Jason may be a more fit comparison. Discussion of contents of *Messēniaka*: Ogden 2004: 155–75, 198–9, and passim.

82 E.g., Foxhall et al. 2010.

83 Luraghi 2008: 88. Cf. *BNJ* 265 (Bertelli): "little historical value in technical sense [*sic*], but of high symbolic meaning."

84 For we would have very little idea indeed about the contents of the *Messēniaka* on the basis of the citations in Stephanus Byzantinus alone: it is the use of the work by Pausanias that offers an opportunity to imagine narrative and themes and their relation to a Messenian audience. Cf. Cameron 1995: 298: "More significant are the links [of regional epic] to city enkomion. For the regional epic is surely a more systematic version of the prize poems that 'made worthy mention' of the gods, myths, temples and ancestors of the cities hosting the great festivals … They are also linked to the great outpouring of regional historical writing all over the early Hellenistic world."

85 *FGrH* 268 F 5 (= *BNJ* 268 F 5).

86 Observing the complete absence of any other literary or epigraphic evidence for such a festival, Jacoby hypothesized that the festival was a complete invention of Baton's. Christesen is agnostic in the *BNJ*. The scepticism is excessive.

87 Mili 2015: 241. The word "appears" is critical in Mili's formulation, for we know that the world of the Thessalians was changing, dramatically so, during the late third and early second centuries when Baton was active, and so we must reckon with the possibility that the assertion or reassertion of autochthonous and direct, unmediated descent from the Pelasgos is a response to shifts in the rules governing critical status distinctions, for there are indications of a wider social realignment within the region, including the apparent end of the institution of

the *penestai*, a curious Helot-like population that furnished dependent labour,
who do not seem to be mentioned again after about 200, and the inauguration
of the Thessalian series of manumission inscriptions, which begin in the early
second century. For extensive discussion of the *penestai*, see Ducat 1994: 104–13;
cf. Decourt 1990; Helly 1995: 186, 302–11. For possible enrolment of *penestai*
as citizens in a range of Thessalian cities in the later third century, see *I. Thess.
Enip.* 50, with earlier bibliography (Pharsalos); Decourt and Tziaphalias 2001: 144
(Krannon); Garcia Ramon et al. 2007: 98 (Mopsion). Thessalian manumissions:
Zelnick-Abramovitz 2013. Such evidence may suggest a profound renegotiation
of political and economic status within the region, conducted at Roman behest
and by, one must often assume, the Thessalian elites privileged by the settlement.

88  *Editio princeps*: Tziafalias 1993: 258–9, no. 64 (ΑΕΜΛ 93/22); cf. *SEG* 47.735;
*BE* 2000, no. 52. See now Santin's recent excellent study: Santin 2018. For
the localization of the findspot as Gyrton, a finding that may have significant
implications for the extent of the territory of Larisa at this date, see *BE* 1999, no. 302.

89  The mention of Hermes Chthonios is common in the funerary epigraphy of
Thessaly, especially Pelasgiotis, and southern Macedonia in the Hellenistic
era. For a wide-angle study, see Avagianou 2002; see also *SEG* 52.546, which
summarizes: "in Thessalian popular religion the dedication of funerary *stēlai*
to Hermes Chthonios reflects the heroization of the dead and his identification
with Hermes Chthonios." Cf. Mili 2015: 274–5; Mili is sceptical of Avagianou's
hypothesis that Hermes Chthonios is to be associated with Dionysian-Orphic
mystery cult. If we are indeed correct in understanding the monument as
commemorating a public burial, then the presence of Hermes Chthonios here
would be unique; Avagianou 2002: 70 is emphatic in the assertion that the
mention and/or representation of Hermes Chthionios on funerary *stēlai* is
limited entirely to private monuments. The city of Larisa would thus seem
here to allow an outsider to participate in this typical, popular, Thessalian and
Macedonian eschatology. One might press the monument and see Larisa as
laying a no less emphatic, local claim to this eschatology which enjoyed a much
broader purchase in the northern Greek world.

90  Thessalian Larisa is somewhat famously not mentioned in Homer, at least the
versions accessible to modern scholars via the Alexandrians (see, e.g., Strabo
9.5.10: Homer has so little to say about inland Thessaly because there was so little
to say about it due to settlements made wretched by flooding). How might this
absence, in so fundamental a panhellenic text, have shaped Larisan conversations
about Larisa and its participation in a broader Thessalian context – for there is no
shortage of other Thessalian places, and associated heroes, mentioned in Homer,
and one might assume the sting of omission to linger in Larisa – and the Hellenic
world? Compare the important role of Homer in the development of Megarian
local discourse environment: Thomas 2019: 161–9; cf. Tober 2018.

91  Strabo 9.5.13.

92  *IG* IX 2, 582.

93  Strabo 9.5.23; *FGrH* 265 F 30a (*BNJ* 265 F 30a) = schol. Ap. Rhod. *Argon.* 3.1090b.

94  For a regional cult of Thessalos associated with that of Zeus Olympios, see Parker 2011; Mili 2015: 248–51.

95  Chaniotis 1995: 162.

96  Chaniotis 1995: 162.

97  Chaniotis 1995: 163.

98  Beck and Wiemer 2009: 27. There is partial overlap here with a separate critique of Chaniotis developed at Chankowski 2005: 190–2, and passim: Chankowski is critical of: 1) Chaniotis' rigid distinction between religious and political festivals, for the two do not differ so much in content as in origin; 2) Chaniotis' synchronic emphasis and traditional periodization, in which the Hellenistic period runs from Alexander to Actium as a single, undifferentiated chronological unit; Chankowski sees merit in distinguishing between an early (to ca. 200 BCE) and later (post-200 BCE) Hellenistic period; and 3) Chankowski would shift emphasis from the festivals themselves to the epigraphic habit representing them; that the habit is changing is certain, but the picture concerning the events themselves is less clear.

99  Wiemer 2009. Nor was this tendency limited to the Hellenistic period; it can be traced into earlier periods of Greek history. For the example of the Persian Wars, see, e.g., Beck 2009: 60–1, who acknowledges the role of the Persian Wars in structuring Greek historical memory in the fifth and fourth centuries. This shared foundation of Greek historical understanding did not, however, crowd out local perspectives that emphasized the specific role played by individual *poleis* in those events. See Yates 2019.

100  And, in a similar vein, Chankowski 2005: 190–2 encourages us to be sensitive to change over time within the Hellenistic period, where Chaniotis' synchronic approach tends to flatten out such developments. Chaniotis would respond in 2013, noting that, while "oversimplified and at times inaccurate versions of my views have been criticized," he was grateful for these interventions which offered "the opportunity to clarify, but not change my views" (Chaniotis 2013: 24–5, 34–5, 40 n. 31).

101  Chaniotis 2005: 227–33.

102  The provocative suggestion of Bouchon and Helly 2013 points in a local direction, namely, that the cult of Zeus Eleutherios was grafted onto an earlier cult of Zeus Olympios, whose cult is now known to have been of wider regional significance in the third century BCE (Malay and Ricl 2009) and who may have possessed a sanctuary in Larisa (Helly 1970).

103 Soph. *Larisaioi* F 378 Radt: πολὺν δ᾽ ἀγῶνα πάγξενον κηρύσσεται ("And he caused to be proclaimed a great contest, where all would be entertained" [trans. Lloyd-Jones]). The line may be attributed to a messenger or secondary character reporting the speech of Teutamides, who here organizes the festival at which Akrisios will later be killed by Perseus. Similar sentiments doubtless animated the foundation of the Eleutheria and its presumed subsequent announcements through theoric networks.

104 See, e.g., Stamatopoulou 2007.

105 Liampi 1996.

106 E.g., *IG* IX 2, 528, dated ca. 90–70.

107 *IG* IX 2, 526, dated ca. 196–150.

108 *IG* IX 2, 525, dated to the late 190s or 180s.

109 For the concept of "epigraphic habit," the contribution of MacMullen 1982 remains fundamental. Some recent adaptations and applications: Chaniotis 2004; Meyer 2013; Lloris 2014; Graninger 2018.

110 This paper has benefited enormously from discussion with the participants in the Waterloo conference, especially the co-editors of this volume, the UCR Ancient and Medieval Studies Group, and the SWANCies – Denise Demetriou, Jeremy LaBuff, John Lee, and Matt Simonton. Many thanks to all. The errors that remain are my own.


## REFERENCES

Aston, E. 2012. "Thessaly and Macedon at Delphi." *Electrum* 19: 41–60. https://doi.org/10.4467/20843909EL.12.002.0743.

Aston, E. 2016. "Welcome Visitors: Religious Inclusivity in a Pharsalian Cave-Cult." In Ἀρχαιολογικό Ἔργο Θεσσαλίας και Στέρεας Ἑλλάδας 4, 2012. Volos: 223–7.

Aston, E. 2017. "Centaurs and Lapiths in the Landscape of Thessaly." In G. Hawes (ed.), *Myths on the Map: The Storied Landscapes of Ancient Greece*. Oxford: 83–105.

Avagianou, A.A. 2002. "Ἑρμῆι Χθονίωι: Θρησκεία Καὶ Ἄνθρωπος Στη Θεσσαλία." In A.A. Avagianou (ed.), Λατρεῖες στην 'περιφέρεια' του αρχαίου ελληνικού κόσμου. Athens: 65–111.

Beck, H. 2009. "Ephebie – Ritual – Geschichte: Polisfest und historische Erinnerung im Klassischen Griechenland." In H. Beck and H.-U. Wiemer (eds.), *Feiern und Erinnern. Geschichtsbilder im Spiegel antiker Feste*. Berlin: 55–82.

Beck, H. 2016. "Between Demarcation and Integration: The Context of Foreign Policy in Ancient Greece." In G. Hellman, A. Fahrmeir, and M. Vec (eds.), *The Transformation of Foreign Policy: Drawing and Managing Boundaries from Antiquity to the Present*. Oxford: 75–104.

Beck, H. 2018. "'If I Am from Megara': Introduction to the Local Discourse Environment of an Ancient Greek City-State." In H. Beck and P. Smith (eds.), *Megarian Moments: The Local World of an Ancient Greek City-State*. Montreal: 15–45.

Beck, H. 2020. *Localism and the Ancient Greek City-State*. Chicago.

Beck, H., and P. Funke. 2015. "An Introduction to Federalism in Greek Antiquity." In H. Beck and P. Funke (eds.), *Federalism in Greek Antiquity*. Cambridge: 1–29.

Beck, H., and H.-U. Wiemer. 2009. "Feiern und Erinnern – Eine Einleitung." In H. Beck and H.-U. Wiemer (eds.), *Feiern und Erinnern: Geschichtsbilder im Spiegel antiker Feste*. Berlin: 9–54.

Bleckmann, B., and J. Gross. 2016. *Historiker der Reichskrise des 3: Jahrhunderts I.* Paderborn.

Bouchon, R., and B. Helly. 2013. "Construire et Reconstruire L'état Fédéral Thessalien: Nouveaux Documents, Nouvelles Perspectives." In P. Funke and M. Haake (eds.), *Greek Federal States and Their Sanctuaries*. Stuttgart: 205–26.

Bouchon, R., and B. Helly. 2015. "The Thessalian League." In H. Beck and P. Funke (eds.), *Federalism in Greek Antiquity*: 231–49.

Cameron, A. 1995. *Callimachus and His Critics*. Princeton.

Chaniotis, A. 1991. "Gedenktage der Griechen: Ihre Bedeutung für das Geschichtsbewusstsein griechischer Poleis." In J. Assmann (ed.), *Das Fest und das Heilige: Religiöse Kontrapunkte zur Alltagswelt*. Gütersloh: 123–45.

Chaniotis, A. 1995. "Sich selbst feiern? Städtische Feste des Hellenismus im Spannungsfeld von Religion und Politik." In P. Zanker and M. Wörrle (eds.), *Stadtbild und Bürgerbild im Hellenismus*. Munich: 147–72.

Chaniotis, A. 2004. "From Communal Spirit to Individuality: The Epigraphic Habit in Hellenistic and Roman Crete." In *Creta Romana e Protobizantina: Atti del Congresso Internazionale, Iraklion, 23–30 Settembre 2000*. Padua: 75–87.

Chaniotis, A. 2005. *War in the Hellenistic World*. Malden, MA.

Chaniotis, A. 2013. "Processions in Hellenistic Cities. Contemporary Discourses and Ritual Dynamics." In R. Alston, O.M. Van Nijf, and C.G. Williamson (eds.), *Cults, Creeds and Identities in the Greek Cit y after the Classical Age*. Leuven: 21–47.

Chankowski, A.S. 2005. "Processions et cérémonies d'accueil: Une image de la cité de la basse époque hellénistique?" In *Cityonneté et participation à la basse époque hellénistique, Actes de la table ronde des 22 e 23 mai, Paris, Bnf*. Genève: 185–6.

Christesen, Paul. 2007. *Olympic Victor Lists and Ancient Greek History*. Cambridge.

Daux, G. 1944. "Inscriptions de Delphes." *Bulletin de Correspondance Hellénique* 68–9: 94–128.

Decourt, J.-C. 1990. "Décret de Pharsale pour une politographie." *Zeitschrift für Papyrologie und Epigraphik* 81: 163–84.

Decourt, J.-C., and A. Tziaphalias. 2001. "Une liste civique à Crannon: La stèle die des Ménandridai." *Zeitschrift für Papyrologie und Epigraphik* 137: 139–52.

Dickie, M. 2008. "The Ἱππικά of Posidippus." In D. Cairns and S. Cairns (eds.), *Papers of the Langford Latin Seminar* 13: 13–54.

Ducat, J. 1994. "Les Pénestes de Thessalie." Paris.

Fearn, D. 2009. "Oligarchic Hestia: Bacchylides 14b and Pindar, Nemean 11." *Journal of Hellenic Studies* 129: 23–38. https://doi.org/10.1017/S0075426900002937.

Fearn, D. (ed). 2011. *Aegina: Contexts for Choral Lyric Poetry. Myth, History, and Identity in the Fifth Century BC*. Oxford.

Fowler, R. 2003. "Pelasgians." In E. Csapo and M.C. Miller (eds.), *Poetry, Theory, Praxis. The Social Life of Myth, Word and Image in Ancient Greece*. Oxford: 2–18.

Foxhall, L., H.-J. Gehrke, and N. Luraghi (eds.). 2010. *Intentional History: Spinning Time in Ancient Greece*. Stuttgart.

Freitag, K. 2015. "Poleis in Koina: Zu den Auswirkungen von bundesstaatlichen Organisationsformen auf Strukturen in griechischen Poleis der hellenistischen Zeit unter besonderer Berücksichtigung der Polis Megara." In A. Matthaei and M. Zimmermann (eds.), *Urbane Strukturen und bürgerliche Identität im Hellenismus*. Heidelberg: 56–67.

García Ramón, J.L., B. Helly, and A. Tziaphalias. 2007. "Inscriptions inédites de Mopsion: Décrets et dédicaces en dialecte thessalien." In M. Hatzopoulos (ed.), *Φωνῆς Χαρακτήρ Εθνικός: Actes du Ve Congrès international de dialectologie grecque (Athènes 28–30 septembre 2006)*. Athens: 63–103.

Gerogiannis, G.M. 2018. "Larisa: L'immagine di una città scomparsa, memorie dal sottosuolo." In M. Livadiotti, R. Belli Pasqua, and L.M. Caliò (eds.), *Theatroeideis: L'immagine della città, la città delle immagini. Atti del Convegno internazionale, Bari, 15–19 giugno 2016, vol. 1, L'immagine della città greca ed ellenistica*. Rome: 161–76.

Graninger, D. 2011. *Cult and Koinon in Hellenistic Thessaly*. Leiden and Boston.

Graninger, D. 2018. "New Contexts for the Seuthopolis Inscription (IGBulg 3.2 1731)." *Klio* 100: 178–94. https://doi.org/10.1515/klio-2018-0006.

Gschnitzer, F. 1954. "Namen und Wesen der thessalischen Tetraden." *Hermes* 82: 451–64.

Hartmann, U. 2008. "Die Geschichtsschreibung." In K.-P. Johne (ed.), *Die Zeit der Soldatenkaiser: Krise und Transformation des Römischen Reiches im 3. Jahrhundert n. Chr. (235–284)*. Berlin: 893–924.

Helly, B. 1970. "À Larisa: Bouleversements et remise en ordre de sanctuaires." *Mnemosyne* 23: 250–96.

Helly, B. 1984. "Le territoire de Larisa: Ses limites, son extension, son organisation." *Ktèma* 9: 213–34.

Helly, B. 1987. "Le 'Dotion Pedion,' Lakéreia et les origines de Larisa." *Journal des Savants* (1987: 3-4): 127–58.

Helly, B. 1995. *L'état thessalien: Aleuas le Roux, les tétrades et les tagoi*. Lyon.

Hollis, A.S. 1992. "Hellenistic Colouring in Virgil's Aeneid." *Harvard Studies in Classical Philology* 94: 269–85. https://doi.org/10.2307/311432.

Hughes, J.D. 2014. *Environmental Problems of the Greeks and Romans: Ecology in the Ancient Mediterranean*. Baltimore.

Janiszewski, P. 2006. *The Missing Link: Greek Pagan Historiography in the Second Half of the Third Century and in the Fourth Century AD*. Warsaw.

Kawami, T.S. 1986. "Greek Art and Persian Taste: Some Animal Sculptures from Persepolis." *American Journal of Archaeology* 90: 259–67. https://doi.org/10.2307/505686.

Kramolisch, H. 1978. *Die Strategen des thessalischen Bundes vom Jahr 196 v. Chr. bis zum Ausgang der römischen Republik*. Bonn.

Langlotz, E. 1951. "Die Larisa des Telephanes." *Museum Helveticum* 8: 157–70.

Larson, J. 2001. *Greek Nymphs: Myth, Cult, Lore*. Oxford.

Liampi, K. 1992. "Larisa." In *Lexicon Iconographicum Mythologiae Classicae (LIMC) VI, 1*, Zurich and Dusseldorf: 213–16.

Liampi, K. 1996. "Das Corpus der Obolen und Hemiobolen des Thessalischen Bundes und die politische Geschichte Thessaliens im 2. Viertel des 5. Jahrhunderts v. Chr." In W. Leschhorn, A.V.B. Miron, and A. Miron (eds.), *Hellas und der Griechische Osten: Studien zur Geschichte und Numismatik der griechischen Welt. Festschrift für Peter Robert Franke zum 70. Geburtstag*. Saarbrücken: 99–126.

Liampi, K. 1997. "Trikka." In *Lexicon Iconographicum Mythologiae Classicae (LIMC) VIII, 1. Part 1*. Zurich and Dusseldorf: 53–5.

Linder, M. 2015. "Forgotten Masterpieces of Art: Reflections of External and Internal Policy in Fifth Century Greece." *Athens Journal of History* 1: 51–64. https://doi.org/10.30958/ajhis.1-1-4.

Lloris, F.B. 2014. "The Epigraphic Habit' in the Roman World." In C. Bruun and J. Edmondson (eds.), *The Oxford Handbook of Roman Epigraphy*. Oxford: 131–48.

Lorenz, B. 2019. *Griechische Grabgedichte Thessaliens: Beispiele für poetische Kleinkunst der Antike*. Heidelberg.

Luraghi, N. 2008. *The Ancient Messenians: Constructions of Ethnicity and Memory*. Cambridge.

Mackil, E. 2013. *Creating a Common Polity: Religion, Economy, and Politics in the Making of the Greek Koinon*. Berkeley.

MacMullen, R. 1982. "The 'Epigraphic Habit in the Roman Empire." *American Journal of Philology* 103: 233–46. https://doi.org/10.2307/294470.

Maehler, H. 1982. *Die Lieder des Bakchylides*. Leiden.

Malay, H., and M. Ricl. 2009. "Two New Hellenistic Decrees from Aigai in Aiolis." *Epigraphica Anatolica* 42: 48–55.

McInerney, J. 2014. "Pelasgians and Leleges: Using the Past to Understand the Present." In J. Ker and C. Pieper (eds.), *Valuing the Past in the Greco-Roman World: Proceedings from the Penn-Leiden Colloquia on Ancient Values VII*. Leiden and Boston: 25–55.

Meineke, A. 1843. *Analecta Alexandrina*. Berlin.

Meyer, Elizabeth A. 2013. "Inscriptions as Honors and the Athenian Epigraphic Habit." *Historia* 62: 453–505. https://doi.org/10.25162/historia-2013-0021.

Mili, M. 2015. *Religion and Society in Ancient Thessaly*. Oxford.

Mili, M. 2019. "Ἄπιστα τὰ τῶν Θετταλῶν: The Dubious Thessalian State." In H. Beck, K. Buraselis, and A. McAuley (eds.), *Ethnos and Koinon: Studies in Ancient Greek Ethnicity and Federalism*. Stuttgart: 271–83.

Moreau, A. 1988. "Le Discobole Meurtrier." *Pallas* 34: 1–18.

Moretti, L. 1957. *Olympionikai, I Vincitori Negli Antichi Agoni Olimpici*. Rome.

Morgan, C. 2003. *Early Greek States beyond the Polis*. London.

Morgan, K. 2015. *Pindar and the Construction of Syracusan Monarchy in the Fifth Century B.C*. Oxford.

Ogden, D. 2004. *Aristomenes of Messene: Legends of Sparta's Nemesis*. Swansea.

O'Sullivan, Lara. 2012. "Playing Ball in Greek Antiquity." *Greece & Rome* 59: 17–33.

Palagia, O. 2008. "The Marble of the Penelope from Persepolis and Its Historical Implications." In S.M.R. Darbandi and A. Zournatzi (eds.), *1st International Conference. Ancient Greece and Ancient Iran: Cross-Cultural Encounters, Athens, 11–13 November 2006*. Athens: 223–37.

Parker, R. 2011. "The Thessalian Olympia." *Zeitschrift für Papyrologie und Epigraphik* 177: 111–18.

Powell, J.U. 1925. *Collectanea Alexandrina*. Oxford.

Rigsby, K.J. 1986. "Notes sur la Crète hellénistique." *Revue des Études Grecques* 99: 350–60.

Rigsby, K.J. 2004. "'Theoroi' for the Koan Asklepieia." In K. Höghammar (ed.), *The Hellenistic 'Polis' of Kos: State, Economy and Culture: Proceedings of an International Seminar Organized by the Department of Archaeology and Ancient History, Uppsala University, 11–13 May, 2000*. Uppsala: 9–14.

Roy, J. 2007. "The Urban Layout of Megalopolis in Its Civic and Confederate Context." In R. Westgate, N. Fisher, and J. Whitley (eds.), *Building Communities: House, Settlement, and Society in the Aegean and Beyond*. Exeter: 289–95.

Santin, E. 2018. "Poeti e conferenzieri stranieri in Tessaglia in età ellenistica: L'epigramma funerario per Herillos figlio di Herodoros di Kalchedon." In F. Camia, L. Del Monaco, and M. Nocita (eds.), *Munus Laetitiae: Studi miscellanei offerti a Maria Letizia Lazzarini*. Volume 2. Rome: 223–49.

Scharff, S. 2016. "Das Pferd Aithon, die Skopaden und die Πατρὶς Θεσσαλία. Zur Selbstdarstellung hippischer Sieger aus Thessalien im Hellenismus." In C. Mann, S. Remijsen, and S. Scharff (eds.), *Athletics in the Hellenistic World*. Stuttgart: 209–29.

Sherk, R.K. 1969. *Roman Documents from the Greek East: Senatus Consulta and Epistulae to the Age of Augustus*. Baltimore.

Sourvinou-Inwood, C. 2003. "Herodotus (and Others) on Pelasgians: Some Perceptions of Ethnicity." In P. Derow and R. Parker (eds.), *Herodotus and His World: Essays from a Conference in Memory of George Forrest*. Oxford: 103–44.

Sourvinou-Inwood, C. 2005. *Hylas, the Nymphs, Dionysos and Others: Myth, Ritual, Ethnicity*. Martin P. Nilsson Lecture on Greek Religion, delivered 1997 at the Swedish Institute at Athens. Stockholm.

Stamatopoulou, M. 2007. "Thessalian Aristocracy and Society in the Age of Epinikian." In S. Hornblower and C. Morgan (eds.), *Pindar's Poetry, Patrons, and Festivals from Archaic Greece to the Roman Empire*. Oxford: 309–41.

Stenger, J. 2004. *Poetische Argumentation: Die Funktion der Gnomik in den Epinikien des Bakchylides*. Berlin and New York.

Thomas, R. 2019. *Polis Histories, Collective Memories and the Greek World*. Cambridge.

Tober, D. 2018. "Megarians' Tears: Localism and Dislocation in the Megarika." In H. Beck and P. Smith (eds.), *Megarian Moments: The Local World of an Ancient Greek City-State*. Montreal: 183–207.

Tziafalias, A. 1993. "Περισυλλογή – Παράδοση Αρχαίων." *ArchDelt* 48 B1: 253–60.

Wiemer, H.-U. 2009. "Neue Feste – Neue Geschichtsbilder? Zur Erinnerungsfunktion städtischer Feste im Hellenismus." In H. Beck and H.-U. Wiemer (eds.), *Feiern und Erinnern: Geschichtsbilder im Spiegel antiker Feste*. Berlin: 83–108.

Yates, D. 2019. *States of Memory: The Polis, Panhellenism, and the Persian War*. Oxford.

Zelnick-Abramovitz, R. 2013. *Taxing Freedom in Thessalian Manumission Inscriptions*. Leiden and Boston.

*Reference to the Thessalian League in the preceding chapter invites a more in-depth, nuanced discussion on the interplay between local prioritization and federal integration, between localism and federalism. The case in point in chapters 7 and 8 is the Aitolian League. Anti-Aitolian sentiments in the literary sources notwithstanding – the region was stigmatized for the ruthless character of its people – the political success of the Aitolians is beyond questioning. Ancient authors and modern scholars amply comment on the carefully crafted* koinon *that allowed for the malleable, creative integration of new members. The Aitolian League might thus claim a paradigmatic role in debates about local-federal interactions in Hellenistic Greece. Joseph Scholten unravels the Aitolian paradox, that is, the inherent opposition of active engagement in the Mediterranean-wide networks of exchange and ostentatious preference for an Aitolian way of life. Turning to Polybios and the famous allegations levelled by him against the Aitolians, Scholten discusses prominent examples of ethnic stereotyping, notably the bad habit of "extracting plunder from plunder." According to Scholten, there was more to this than the etic eye. In quest for an emic perspective, the chapter takes readers to Thermon, the central node in sentiments of Aitolian belonging. Scholten vividly discloses the symbolic meaning the place had to the* ethnos, *especially its capital role as stage where important religious and civic rituals were performed. Moreover, Thermon was critical for the display of wealth and its demonstrative (re-)distribution by rich individuals to the less so. Economic transactions such as these had a deeper meaning than references to lavishness and self-aggrandizement, prominently voiced by Polybios, suggest. The concluding section shows how Thermon embodied the qualities of an imagined local, casting a cultural shadow onto the Aitolians that was both indicative of and instrumental to their federal ventures.*

*Keywords: Polybios, Philip V, Thermon, citizenship, euergetism, civic rituals, ethnic stereotyping*

# 7

## The Problematic Localism of
## the Hellenistic Aitolians

JOSEPH B. SCHOLTEN

The focus of this collection – the power of place and the local in the construction of systems of meaning and behaviour – implicitly raises the question of scale: How far can a specific place cast its cultural shadow? The Aitolian *koinon* of the Hellenistic era offers an interesting case study.

The behaviour of the Hellenistic Aitolians leaves a distinct impression of bipolarity. On the one hand, the Aitolians are among the great historical actors of the period, creators of arguably one of the most successful regional states (*koina*) known from the ancient Greek world, one that managed to transcend old boundaries of family and place to create a polity that, for most of the third century, knit together ever-larger portions of central Greece into a state capable of balancing the power of the kings of Macedonia. In all this, the Aitolians seem fully immersed in the main currents of the global Mediterraneanized culture of the Hellenistic Age, utilizing all its tools of interstate diplomacy, embracing and patronizing the full panoply of cultural expressions and outlets.

And yet these same Aitolians also exhibited behaviours that their peers present as idiosyncratic and highly objectionable, suggesting that the Aitolians had seen the Hellenistic world, and nevertheless chosen the local in deliberate response to global challenges to quotidian meaning and orientation in their lives. Most notably, Aitolians had a conspicuously extravagant, self-promoting lifestyle whose maintenance led them to grant to the individual licence when outside Aitolia to raid as often as trade.

Modern scholars have tried to address this seeming Aitolian paradox through denigration, denial, or some combination of the two. Some, for example, see the ancient accounts of the Aitolians as tendentious, and their portrait of them as a gross caricature. Others see the Aitolians as a culturally frozen people, locked in the past by their geographic isolation from the mainstream of Greek culture. The prism of localism offers, perhaps, a clearer lens through which to understand the Hellenistic Aitolians. Rather than an "either-or," the notion of localism, understood as a prioritization of the local horizon over other sources of meaning, allows us a "both-and" option in understanding Aitolians' seemingly contradictory behaviours.

Aitolians' individual and collective embrace of the global Mediterranean culture of the Hellenistic Age is well known.[1] Aitolians commissioned great public buildings, such as the three massive stoas at Thermon,[2] and a plethora of sculptural works of high quality and expense at Thermon, Delphi, Olympia, et cetera, to honour their friends or their own.[3] To pay for these works, and other expenses, the *koinon* developed a coinage with the conventional mix of bronze, silver, and gold issues that also served to propagate Aitolian imagery and prestige.[4] Aitolians celebrated their own age-old autumn festival – the Thermika – with due magnificence, but also inaugurated at Delphi a new panhellenic cultural celebration and competition, the Sotēria which they ultimately made penteteric to rival the Olympics.[5] The *koinon* was an active participant in the Hellenistic Mediterannean diplomatic network, issuing grants of proxenia and (iso)politeia,[6] sending and receiving diplomatic missions in accordance with the era's highly developed conventions.[7] This latter included adherence to the Hellenistic penchant for creative diplomatic genealogies, such as the appeal to Xanthos in Lykia by an Aitolian delegation (discussed elsewhere in this collection by Peter Funke), based on a mythic ancestry shared with the Ptolemies.[8]

Then, there are those "other Aitolians," the ones described by their contemporary, Polybios (4.3.1), as "slaves to their innate love of self-display, that caused them to live an avaricious, feral existence ... preying on their neighbours rather than living within their own means."[9] Aitolians, according to Polybios (18.4.8), considered everything potential booty, and had a custom that allowed individual Aitolians to "extract plunder from plunder" (τὸν νόμον ... τὸν διδόντα τὴν ἐξουσίαν... ἄγειν λάφυρον ἀπὸ λαφύρου). That is, they had licence to plunder not only enemies with whom the Aitolians were at war, but any party to any conflict at any time, even if the parties were friends and allies of the Aitolians (18.5.1–3).[10] In interstate politics, Aitolian leaders assumed their opponents practised bribery, which they did, as well (18.34.7).[11]

Polybios' well-known antipathy for the Aitolians sometimes leads modern scholars to question whether Aitolian behaviour was in fact unusual.[12] But Polybios is not the only ancient source that levels such accusations against Aitolians – quite the contrary; we can trace a fairly continuous through-line of complaints back from Polybios through the third and fourth centuries and as far as Thucydides and his fifth-century Athenian contemporaries.[13]

Scholars acknowledge this longer narrative, but note as well that Polybios and the other sources that complain of the Aitolians are normally doing so against the background of interstate conflict with them. Thucydides' report (3.94.5), for example, that the largest subgroup within the Aitolian *ethnos*, the Eurytanes, spoke a language that was barely intelligible and ate raw meat; Euripides' description of the great Aitolian mythic hero, Meleagros, as "half-barbarian" in appearance; and Aristophanes' depiction of Kleon's thieving as "Aitolian hands" (*Eq. 79*) all occur against the background of a failed Athenian incursion into eastern Aitolia in 427, which was turned back with significant loss.[14] And early third-century comparisons of Aitolians to a greedy Oidipodean sphinx – found in an ithyphallic hymn chanted by Athenians to their saviour god, Demetrios Poliorketes – likewise occur in the context of conflict: Demetrios' unsuccessful attempt to expel the Aitolians from Delphi.[15]

Yet a variety of epigraphic testimonia from the Hellenistic era seem to indicate that the literary tradition with respect to the Aitolians is more than a tendentious *topos*. Among these are a set of documents (*StV* III 508=*IG* IX 1², 1, 169A + 169B; *IG* XII 5, 526, 532) that are often cited as examples of Aitolian "normalcy." Originating from the island of Kea, these inscription(s) record a multi-actor negotiation involving "the Aitolians," their *synhedroi*, and an Aitolian member community, the *polis* of Naupaktos. The Keians had sent a delegation to the Naupaktians, and then to the Aitolian *synhedroi* (*IG* XII 5, 532, *StV* III 508 III) to renew their existing friendship (*philia/philotamia*). The *synhedroi* of the Aitolians and the Naupaktians assure the Kean delegation of their continuing goodwill towards the *poleis* of Kea, and the Naupaktians extend their citizenship (*politeia*), including *enktēsis* both of land and property (*oikia*) and all other things that Naupktians partake of, to the Keans. A decree of the Aitolians, which leads the inscription, promises to safeguard the existing Aitolian friendship towards the Keans "as the Keians are Aitolians."

This interaction forcefully demonstrates the functional structure of the Aitolian *koinon* during the Hellenistic period: a triangulation between the respective authorities of an Aitolian local community – the Naupaktians – the Aitolian *synhedrion*, and "the Aitolians" writ large. In this instance, we have a strong index of the prerogatives of an Aitolian member community, in that the Naupaktians seem to have the ability to extend their citizenship to a non-Aitolian community, thereby rendering the recipient community "Aitolian." That is, membership in the *koinon* seems to "flow up" from membership in a local community.[16]

But this same set of documents also underscores the validity of the complaints in the literary tradition. If we return again to the decree of the Aitolians that leads the Kean dossier, we find that the privileges that becoming

Aitolians confer on the Keans consist mainly in protection from plundering by Aitolians, and also protection from prosecution, even by the Delphic Anthelic Amphictyony, for plundering. This protection, which is also articulated in other grants of Aitolian *politeia*, seems to have been the main desideratum of suitors such as the Keans. As if to underscore Polybios, another inscription, this one from Delphi and dating from the early third century (*IG* IX I[2], 1, 171), seems to grant immunity to all Aitolians for any judgments against them for pillage, even by the Amphictyony, except in cases of pilfering sacred property. And the decree is retroactive.

A less apologetic explanation for the Aitolians, found both in ancient sources and in modern scholarship, reflects a broad cultural condescension. In this line of approach, the physical isolation of the core Aitolian lands – ruggedly mountainous in general and cut off from the main arteries of Hellenic commerce and cultural evolution – left Aitolians in a state of arrested development, frozen in the Archaic past – or, to use the common epithet, backward.[17] Recent advances in our understanding of the Greek northwest in the Classical and Hellenistic eras have revealed a regional cultural *koinē* – but one in which Aitolian communities do not seem fully to have participated.[18] Yet, as noted above and widely, Aitolians of the Hellenistic era, at least, were fully connected to the broader Mediterranean *koinē* of their day.

The poster children for Aitolian misbehaviour in the extant portions of Polybios' *History* are the pair Skopas and Dorimachos, whose promotion of semi-sanctioned Aitolian plundering in the western Peloponnese in the aftermath of the death of Antigonos III Doson sparked the so-called Social War of 220–217, in Polybios' telling (4.3.1–5). Dorimachos is introduced here as the son of an Aitolian leader – Nikostratos – notorious for having violated a major Hellenic festival (the Panboiotia). Yet all of these miscreants hail from the settlement of Trichonion, located on the homonymous lake that itself drains into the Acheloos River basin to the west, as the Acheloos itself made its way south to the Gulf of Corinth. That is, Trichononion was in no way physically isolated by its environment. In fact, it could itself stand in (along with its neighbour to the north, Agrinion) as representative of a major shift in the settlement pattern of Aitolia that arose in late Classical period: the appearance of significant conurbations, with substantial local agricultural hinterlands.[19] Even eastern Aitolia, regarded by Thucydides as beyond the pale of his world, saw the development of a major urban centre – Kallion/Kallipolis – at a confluence to its major waterway, the river Daphnos/Mornos.[20] Alongside these new settlements, the Aitolian *koinon* also embraced coastal sites such as Pleuron, Kalydon, and Naupaktos, and their direct access to major Hellenic trade arteries. Isolation, therefore, does not adequately explain Aitolians' continued adherence to behaviours that, by the standards of many of their contemporaries, seemed backward.

The Aitolians' preferences could well be, however, an example of the capacity of traditions of meaning tied to place to influence behaviour even at a regional level. Polybios points us in this direction. His report on the Aitolian custom of "extracting plunder from plunder" includes a claim that Philip V and the other Greeks had repeatedly begged the Aitolians to give up this custom. According to Polybios, the Aitolian response was that they would sooner "remove Aitolia from Aitolia" (Polyb. 18.4.8).[21] It is hard to imagine a clearer statement of the connection between place and its occupants' system of thought and behaviour.

The obvious rejoinder is, of course, that "Aitolia" covers far too broad a geographic area to serve as the place – the locus – from which all of the various manifestations of local-based culture derive. If, however, community is defined by adherence to and performance of shared rituals – be they cultic, political, social, or other – then a locus of "Aitolianness" is clear: Thermon, on the high plateau overlooking the eastern end of Lake Trichonis.

There, as noted above, around the time of the fall equinox, a great market fair and festal gathering occured. The archaeological record suggests continuous cultic activity in the immediate area of the later precinct of Apollo since at least the early Iron Age. And that activity appears to have had a strongly local flavour that persisted even as the sanctuary and its festival progressively drew an audience from an ever-wider swath of the Mediterranean world. The renewed examination of Thermon since the 1980s under the direction of I.A. Papapostolou has confirmed the importance of its main temple building (Temple C/Temple of Apollo) as a landmark in the development of Greek sacred architecture. But the decorative elements of that early building are now understood to reflect a tradition specific to a region of northwest Greece that correlates well with Thucydides' presentation of the region as possessing a distinct cultural unity.[22] And the program of decoration – the mythologic characters and scenes depicted – are highly specific to Themon's location. Moreover, and tellingly for our concerns here, the architectural form and the decorative scheme of this temple seem to have persisted across the Classical and Hellenistic eras. The building seems to have undergone repair multiple times during these centuries yet, even as the sanctuary around it experienced a series of ever more grandiose enhancements beginning in the late fifth and early fourth centuries – including the construction of a monumental facade for the great spring, the formalization of an oblong "agora" by the construction of two of the massive stoas (east and west) capped off by a *bouleutērion* at the south, and the enclosure of the adjacent space via another stoa (south) and a major, fortified temenos wall – the temple and its decoration retained their original form. Only after the sack of sanctuary by the Macedonian twice in the final decades of the second century (218: 207) did the Aitolians modify the basic design of their central shrine, equipping the final version of the temple with a peristyle. Yet even then, they kept the original decorative program, reusing damaged pieces that had been repaired and restored according to the initial Archaic style and techniques.[23]

Thermon was clearly a place of deep symbolic meaning to its community: it was there that they gathered year after year at the autumn equinox to celebrate and renew what it meant to be Aitolian. The site itself suggests the amalgam of external and local that defined that identity and thought system in the Hellenistic era.

One can imagine processions of the Thermika wending along a "sacred way" from the main gate at the southwest corner of the enclosed temenos, east along the face of the south stoa to the *bouleutērion*, then turning north into the agora and proceeding to the main temple. If Polybios is to be believed, such a route by 218 would have taken participants past nearly two thousand statues, and even greater quantities of military gear dedicated to the gods in celebration of Aitolian victories – all attesting to the power and prestige that the Aitolian community had achieved.

These were works of the highest artistry, both in their execution and in the poetic captions on their bases.[24] Among them were a standing male representing an eponymous hero – "Aitolos" – and a female warrior seated atop a pile of enemy weaponry – "Aitolia" deified. Both statues appear on coins issued by "the Aitolians";[25] both signal an ongoing accretion to the meaning of Aitolianness expressed at Thermon. "Aitolos" seems to have been a development of the fifth and fourth centuries,[26] "Aitolia" of the third. For the weapons upon which she sits are clearly Celtic, and a visual cue to the great achievement of the Hellenistic Aitolians: the repulse of the Gallic invasion of central Greece and the assault on Delphi in 279.[27]

The Aitolians' decoration of the panhellenic sanctuary to their east with memorials to their *aristeia* – in part to justify retroactively their seizure of control over the region surrounding Delphi in the late fourth or early third century – has long been recognized.[28] But they clearly also wove that narrative into the tapestry of meaning that was Thermon: the repulse of the Gauls – and, by extension, the protection of central Greece – became part of what made them Aitolians.[29] Indeed, Polybios indicates that the functional purpose of the great third-century stoas at Thermon was as display space for 15,000 panoplies (Polyb. 5.8.9). This role mirrors that of the West Stoa at Delphi, and the massive number of such trophies at Thermon suggests that some (most?) of them might likewise have been taken from the Gauls.[30]

Yet the culmination of our procession reflected the Aitolians' abiding, deep attachment to their local past: a building unaltered in form and decoration since time immemorial, and that decorative scheme featuring a set of stories and characters with highly local valence (Meleagros and the Kalydonian boar hunt; Aedon and Chelidon). What ceremonies and rituals took place at and around this central building are, unfortunately, obscure. For the present argument, however, it is interesting to note that the ongoing decorative scheme is not obviously tied to the ultimate resident of the *naos*, Apollo. Rather, the female subjects and chthonic associations dominate, yet another indication that at the core of the locus that was the centre of Aitolianness what mattered most were traditions and ways of constructing meaning that were rooted in the deep past.[31]

The archaeology of Thermon suggests, therefore, that, in creating new expressions of their identity, Hellenistic Aitolians remained deeply attached to long-held modes of meaning attached to that place.[32] A similar adherence to tradition amid change, and focused on Thermon as a site of expression, may underlie Aitolians' refusal to give up their age-old practice of "taking plunder from plunder."

In describing the annual autumnal gathering at Thermon, Polybios (5.8) notes a third aspect, beyond the fair and the festival: a convening of the Aitolian assembly, to consider weighty matters such as war and peace, and to elect their annual magistrates, especially their governor-general (*stratēgos*). This practice aligns perfectly with the pattern that modern scholars have identified in other Greek polities, especially regional *koina*, where the cultic, the economic, and the political come together at one location to form three legs of communal identification.[33] A variety of evidence, including Polybios' writings, suggest that the fall Thermika assembly functioned as a primary institution, that is, that all eligible adult males present sat and voted as a body.

Other sources, however, suggest that among the Aitolians a core group of a few thousand aristocrats steered the state.[34] Moreover, when we look at the demotics of those Aitolians who held the highest office in the Aitolian *koinon* – the *stratēgeia* – a striking geographic pattern emerges. Of the one hundred or so known Aitolian *stratēgoi*, nearly a third come from a single community: Trichonion. If we add to them those *stratēgoi* who hail from other communities in the Lake Trichonis basin, the percentage rises to nearly half.[35] On a certain level, there should be no surprise in this. Trichonion is the closest to Thermon of the communities who boast *stratēgoi*, and so most easily able to get its residents to the Thermika to sit in the electoral assembly. Close-in demes are similarly dominant in the political process in Athens, as were close-in tribes in Rome. In both of those cases, however, a recurring phenomenon was the linkage of political struggles and control over common gathering spaces, especially sacred sites. Did Trichonion's prime position near Thermon give its leaders some sort of cachet by virtue of proximity to the locus of Aitolian identity and meaning? Is it pure coincidence that many of the known practitioners or defenders of the Aitolian tradition of freebooting hail from Trichonis or other settlements close to Thermon?[36]

Polybios may illustrate the mechanism by which the few led the many, with Thermon again as its locus. In describing Philip V's sack of Thermon in summer 218, and noting the coincidence there of the great fair, religious festival, and the Aitolians' annual legislative and electoral assembly, Polybios also pointedly notes that individual Aitolians maintained homes near the temenos and in surrounding settlements, and that these were the most luxurious in Aitolia. Further, their owners only occupied these dwellings during the Thermon festival and kept them chock full of luxury goods with which to entertain and impress other visitors.[37] The location at a sanctuary of repositories for luxury goods is certainly a practice known at Delphi, Olympia, and other sites. At those sanctuaries, however, the repositories are associated with communities, not individuals. Why this accumulation of static individual wealth at Thermon?

For Polybios, there are a couple of explanations. Thermon's remoteness assured its security, making the sanctuary a sort of Aitolian acropolis (Polyb. 5.8.6). Aitolians could store their wealth here and not worry about it. And flashing their wealth at the Thermon festival was, to Polybios, a matter of pure, inbred Aitolian posturing (*alazoneia*). Yet for Polybios, Aitolian *alazoneia* is 24/7, 365. If Aitolians were habitual showboaters, why would they leave their bling far away, at a site they visited only once a year?

Perhaps the Aitolians' personal treasure houses at Thermon had a practical function rooted in age-old custom specific to this location. Wealthy Aitolians' conspicuous consumption at the Thermika may have been functional: an annual ritual of wealth distribution connected to the selection of community leaders, and one that also allowed individuals and groups to influence the general assembly of the Aitolians.

The earliest literary account of Aitolians' predilection for plundering – Thucydides' *Archaeology* – explicitly makes this connection between wealth distribution and leadership in the community.[38] Moreover, Thucydides just as clearly links this politico-economic nexus to the practice of predation. And he identifies this cultural nexus as an age-old one that already in his day was a local hallmark.

Polybios' focus is on the behaviour of wealthy Aitolians at the Thermon festival. But they can only represent a distinct minority among those gathered. Emily Mackil's recent general study of the origins of Greek *koina* emphasizes the importance of economic forces in promoting regional identity, in particular the insufficiency of many Greek communities in basic commodities and the development of trading systems for the exchange of complementary resources. In the case of the Aitolians, she mines to great effect the thorough survey work done in the 1980s by the Dutch Aetolia Studies Project, which itself utilized records and reminiscences of premodern conditions to produce a provisional model of the Aitolian regional economy. What emerges is a series of intersecting networks connecting communities around five main hubs and moving the surplus of largely pastoral products of the mountainous interior towards markets in the lowlands and coast regions, whence resources of various types unavailable in the interior could be obtained.[39] The key node in this web of exchange networks is Thermon. But was more being exchanged there at the Thermika than basic commodities?[40]

The reaction of the Aitolians to Philip's sacks of the sanctuary in 218 and 207 may suggest so. Philip's initial foray took place in late summer. Soon afterward, according to Polybios (5.28.1–3), a delegation from Rhodes and Chios came to Philip to try to end the Social War. Philip, in turn, sent them to the Aitolians. Unlike in previous years, Aitolians were receptive and now eager to make peace. Philip's looting of Aitolian pleasure palaces certainly disrupted wealthy Aitolians' ability to engage in their customary display at the Thermika of 218. But why would that necessarily steer them towards peace? Did the delegation in fact address an Aitolian assembly sitting amid the ruin of not just their collective sanctuary but of a larger web of local economic and political traditions and practices?

Perhaps so – but only to a degree. A fragment from Polybios (13.1–2) reports that, in the years immediately following the second sack of Thermon, Dorimachos and Skopas were appointed by the Aitolians to be *nomographoi*. The *nomoi* that they were tasked to rewrite, according to Polybios, concerned debt. Aitolians – and particularly Dorimachos and Skopas – found themselves suddenly in unsustainable debt, both because of continuous wars, but also because of their extravagant lifestyles. In response, Skopas and Dorimachos seem to have proposed some sort of cancellation of debts, but their proposal was strenuously and successfully opposed by one Alexander. As a result, Skopas' candidacy to serve once again as *stratēgos* of the Aitolian *koinon* failed, and he led a mass exodus of several thousand Aitolians into the service of the Ptolemies.[41]

If we tease this report apart, further evidence may lurk between the lines for a local explanation of the Aitolians' cultural tradition of extravagant display of wealth, and hence their enduring propensity for plundering.

The debate over a change in Aitolian *nomoi* must have played out before the Aitolian assembly at the Thermika.[42] It is striking that Alexander could win his point against two leaders from a nearby community (Trichonion) which must have been well represented in that gathering, leaders who in the immediately preceding year had demonstrated their clout in the Aitolian assembly by being chosen as the *nomographoi*.[43] Polybios does not further identify Skopas and Dorimachos' antagonist, Alexander, beyond his name. Scholars have generally identified him as Alexandros Isios, who was active in Aitolian affairs in the early second century.[44] If that identification actually applies, his success against the proposed change in the *nomoi* is doubly surprising. In a later passage, Polybios reports that Alexandros was the wealthiest man in Greece, with an estate of 200 talents.[45] Perhaps he held many of these debts, which would suggest why he opposed their cancellation. It would not explain, however, how he was able to persuade the Aitolian assembly, presumably dominated by the indebted, to reject Skopas and Dorimachos' reforms. Did Alexander and his supporters offer their fellow Aitolians more than the rhetoric that Polybios attributes to him?

Perhaps the extravagant display at the Thermika noted (and censured) by Polybios does not reflect simple self-aggrandizement, but rather a long local tradition of wealth redistribution at this festival by prosperous Aitolians to those less so, in return for support at the assembly and elections. The euergetic deployment of wealth in return for political support is a common phenomenon among Greek communities, and especially in the Hellenistic world. Perhaps Aitolians pursued the practice in a direct form at the Thermika, with the politically ambitious expected to deploy wealth for the larger community, by subsiding buildings, ceremonies, or celebrations, brokering or underwriting the exchange of goods between Aitolia's more remote and more accessible communities.

If this was how the game of politics was played among Aitolians, the increased prosperity of the Hellenistic era could well have raised the stakes significantly. In the early third century, a leader from a prosperous but inland community such as Trichonion, Charixenos, could afford to pay for one of the great stoas at Thermon.[46] Later Trichonians, such as Dorimachos and Skopas, may have needed to borrow to keep up, especially after the two wars with Philip had gutted their community and shut down their access to plunder. Alexander's Isus, on the other hand, seems to have been just north and east of Naupaktos, and thus close to the Corinthian Gulf coast.[47] That would seem to offer easier access to broader and greater sources of wealth than Trichonion, and so aid his accumulation of a vast fortune. If Naupaktos was another important node in the regional trade network, it is worth noting that one product in which it trafficked was enslaved persons. Clearly, Naupaktians did not disdain to profit from plundering.[48] Among the earliest documents we have from the coastal region is a fifth century BCE agreement between the west Lokrian communities of Chaleion and Oianthea (*IG* IX 1², 3, 717) to eliminate raiding between the two settlements.

It is also worth noting that the incident at the centre of this paper – the argument between the Aitolian delegation (including Alexander?) and Philip V during the abortive peace negotiation with the Roman Flamininus – takes place nearly a decade *after* the second Aitolian war with Philip and Philip's second sack of Thermon. Whatever the nature of the new laws that Skopas and Dorimachos had proposed in the interim, they do not seem to have involved the Aitolian custom at issue at Nikaia in 198. Skopas' subsequent behaviour in Alexandria indicates that his departure from Aitolia did not reflect any change of view, but was simply a move to replenish his debt-depleted coffers – presumably to allow him to return to his homeland and its traditional ways.[49]

In 198, then, one particular Aitolian prioritization of the local persisted: Aitolians would still sooner "take Aitolia from Aitolia" than give up their custom of "taking plunder from plunder." Philip may have destroyed the physical memorials at Thermon of the Aitolians' collective past, and appropriated the fruits accumulated there of Aitolians' traditional labours. He may even have disrupted a broader web of local meaning and practice that had grown up around that space. But he had not eradicated it. The Aitolians rebuilt their age-old temple in the age-old style (albeit with a decorative colonnade). And evidently equally local modes of thinking and behaving continued to prevail among them, in defiance of the globalized Mediterranean world in which they also lived.

## NOTES

1  See Scholten 2013: 99–104.

2  Recently re-examined, with significant new discoveries, by I.A. Papapostolou; see Thermos – 2018, *Archaeology in Greece Online*, report 6896, created 11 August 2019, viewed 31 January 2021, https://chronique.efa.gr/?kroute=report&id=6896.

3  Polybios (5.9.2) comments on the quality and expense of dedications at Thermon (πολυτελῆ ταῖς κατασκευαῖς καὶ πολλῆς ἐπιμελείας ἔνια τετευχότα καὶ δαπάνης) and notes (5.9.3) that there were nearly 2,000 such statues there in 218 when the Macedonians first sacked the sanctuary. See below, at note 24.

4  On the coinage of the Aitolian *koinon*, see Tsangari 2007.

5  Polybios (5.8.5) calls the Thermika a "most notable market fair and festal gathering" (...ἀγοράς τε καὶ πανηγύρεις ἐπιφανεστάτας). On the Sotēria see Champion 1995.

6  W. Mack's online database of known proxeny decrees (*Proxeny Networks of the Ancient World*: http://proxenies.csad.ox.ac.uk/places/home) includes 234 from Thermon.

7  For Aitolian diplomacy in general, see now Funke 2015: 103–4: Antonetti and Cavalli: 2012.

8  See Bousquet 1988.

9  Αἰτωλοὶ πάλαι μὲν δυσχερῶς ἔφερον τὴν εἰρήνην καὶ τὰς ἀπὸ τῶν ἰδίων ὑπαρχόντων δαπάνας, ὡς ἂν εἰθισμένοι μὲν ζῆν ἀπὸ τῶν πέλας, δεόμενοι δὲ πολλῆς χορηγίας διὰ τὴν ἔμφυτον ἀλαζονείαν, ᾗ δουλεύοντες ἀεὶ πλεονεκτικὸν καὶ θηριώδη ζῶσι βίον, οὐδὲν οἰκεῖον, πάντα δ᾽ ἡγούμενοι πολέμια.

10  τοῖς Αἰτωλοῖς ἔθος ὑπάρχει μὴ μόνον πρὸς οὓς ἂν αὐτοὶ πολεμῶσι, τούτους αὐτοὺς ἄγειν καὶ τὴν τούτων χώραν, [2] ἀλλὰ κἂν ἕτεροί τινες πολεμῶσι πρὸς ἀλλήλους, ὄντες Αἰτωλῶν φίλοι καὶ σύμμαχοι, μηδὲν ἧττον ἐξεῖναι τοῖς Αἰτωλοῖς ἄνευ κοινοῦ δόγματος καὶ παραβοηθεῖν ἀμφοτέροις τοῖς πολεμοῦσι καὶ τὴν χώραν ἄγειν τὴν ἀμφοτέρων, [3] ὥστε παρὰ μὲν τοῖς Αἰτωλοῖς μήτε φιλίας ὅρους ὑπάρχειν μήτ᾽ ἔχθρας, ἀλλὰ πᾶσι τοῖς ἀμφισβητοῦσι περί τινος ἑτοίμους ἐχθροὺς εἶναι τούτους καὶ πολεμίους. "The Aetolian custom was this. They not only plundered those with whom they were at war, and harried their country; but, if certain other nations were at war with each other, even though both were friends and allies of the Aetolians, none the less the Aetolians might, without a formal decree of the people, take part with both combatants and plunder the territory of both. The result was that in the eyes of the Aetolians there were no defined limits of friendship or enmity, but they were ready to be the enemies and assailers of all who had a dispute on anything" (trans. Evelyn S. Shuckburgh, *The Histories of Polybius*, 1889, reprint 1962).

11  ἤδη γὰρ κατὰ τὴν Ἑλλάδα τῆς δωροδοκίας ἐπιπολαζούσης καὶ τοῦ μηδένα μηδὲν δωρεὰν πράττειν, καὶ τοῦ χαρακτῆρος τούτου νομιστευομένου παρὰ τοῖς Αἰτωλοῖς, οὐκ ἐδύναντο πιστεύειν διότι χωρὶς δώρων ἡ τηλικαύτη μεταβολὴ γέγονε ... "For as corruption, and the habit of never doing anything without a bribe, had long been a common feature in Greek politics, and as this was the acknowledged characteristic of the Aetolians, they could not believe that Flamininus could so change in his relations with Philip without a bribe" (trans. Shuckburgh).

12  The most vigorous defence of the Aitolians is found in Grainger 1999. More nuanced is Champion 2004, esp. 129–37, 140–3; see also Champion 2007.

13  Note as well the inscription from autumn, 367 (Rhodes and Osborne no. 35) in which the Aitolian *koinon* is first clearly attested. In it, Athenians complain to the Aitolian state about a breach of the Eleusinian truce, which the *koinon* had

accepted, when residents of an Aitolian town – Trichonis (!) – kidnapped the sacred envoys, in violation of "the common law of the Greeks" (ll. 14–15).

14 Thuc. 3.94.5: (the Eurytanes) …ὅπερ μέγιστον μέρος ἐστὶ τῶν Αἰτωλῶν, ἀγνωστότατοι δὲ γλῶσσαν καὶ ὠμοφάγοι εἰσίν, ὡς λέγονται. Eur. *Phoen.* 134: ὡς ἀλλόχρως ὅπλοισι, μειξοβάρβαρος. Ar. *Eq.* 79: τὼ χεῖρ' ἐν Αἰτωλοῖς, ὁ νοῦς δ' ἐν Κλωπιδῶν. See Antonetti 1990: 69–110.

15 The ithyphallic hymn: Athen. 6.253b-f 9=*FGrH* 75 F2, F13:

τὴν δ' οὐχὶ Θηβῶν, ἀλλ' ὅλης τῆς Ἑλλάδος

Σφίγγα περικρατοῦσαν,

Αἰτωλὸς ὅστις ἐπὶ πέτρας καθήμενος,

ὥσπερ ἡ παλαιά,

τὰ σώμαθ' ἡμῶν πάντ' ἀναρπάσας φέρει,

κοὐκ ἔχω μάχεσθαι:

Αἰτωλικὸν γὰρ ἁρπάσαι τὰ τῶν πέλας, νῦν δὲ καὶ τὰ πόρρω:

μάλιστα μὲν δὴ σχόλασον αὐτός: εἰ δὲ μή,

Οἰδίπουν τιν' εὑρέ,

τὴν Σφίγγα ταύτην ὅστις ἢ κατακρημνιεῖ

ἢ σποδὸν ποιήσει.

"And crush for us yourself, for you've the power,

This odious Sphinx;

Which now destroys not Thebes alone, but Greece –

The whole of Greece –

I mean th' Aetolian, who, like her of old,

Sits on a rock,

And tears and crushes all our wretched bodies.

Nor can we him resist.

For all th' Aetolians plunder all their neighbours;

And now they stretch afar

Their lion hands; but crush them, mighty lord,

Or send some Œdipus

Who shall this Sphinx hurl down from off his precipice,

Or starve him justly."

(trans. C.D. Yonge, *Athenaeus. The Deipnosophists*, 1854)

For historical interpretation: Lefèvre 1998 in connection with a Delphic inscription recording the peace settlement between Demetrios and the Aitolians.

16 On the implications of these decrees for the internal structure and functioning of the Aitolian *koinon*, see Funke 2015: 103.

17 E.g., Thuc. 1.5.3: καὶ μέχρι τοῦδε πολλὰ τῆς Ἑλλάδος τῷ παλαιῷ τρόπῳ νέμεται περί τε Λοκροὺς τοὺς Ὀζόλας καὶ Αἰτωλοὺς καὶ Ἀκαρνᾶνας καὶ τὴν ταύτῃ ἤπειρον. "And even at the present day many parts of Hellas still follow the old

fashion, the Ozolian Locrians, for instance, the Aetolians, the Acarnanians, and that region of the continent" (trans. R. Crawley, *Thucydides: The Peloponnesian War*, 1910).

18  The cultural *koinē* of the Greek northwest: Antonetti 2010: 301–26.

19  For the rise of conurbated settlements in late Classical Aitolia, see Funke 1997; 2015: 100.

20  Kallipolis/Kallion: Rousset 2006.

21  πολλάκις γὰρ κἀμοῦ καὶ τῶν ἄλλων Ἑλλήνων διαπρεσβευομένων πρὸς ὑμᾶς, ἵνα τὸν νόμον ἄρητε τὸν διδόντα τὴν ἐξουσίαν ὑμῖν ἄγειν λάφυρον ἀπὸ λαφύρου, πρότερον ἔφατε τὴν Αἰτωλίαν ἐκ τῆς Αἰτωλίας ἀρεῖν ἢ τοῦτον τὸν νόμον. "For though both I and the other Greeks sent envoy after envoy to you desiring that you would repeal the law which allows you the privilege of taking 'spoil from spoil,' you replied that rather than abolish this law you would remove Aetolia from Aetolia" (trans. Shuckburgh).

22  Quoted above, at note 17.

23  For a convenient overview of the results of I.A. Papapostolou's excavations at Thermon, see his online summary at https://www.archetai.gr/ s.v. Θέρμος.

24  Polyb. 5.9.2–4; on the high quality of praise verse that accompanied some of these statues, see Cavalli 2010: 409–28. See also the verse inscriptions on the base of the statue of the eponymous hero Aitolos, quoted by Strabo (10.3.2).

25  See *ANS* 1944.100.19481.rev; *ANS* 1964.149.1.rev.

26  According to Strabo (10.3.2), the eponymous hero "Aitolos," as well as his statue at Thermon, was known already to Ephoros. On the development of this mythic tradition, see Funke 2015: 90–2. See also Rzepka 2013.

27  For the "Aitolos," "Aitolia" statues on Aitolian coins, see Tsangari 2007.

28  See Champion 1996.

29  For this self-referential, local meaning of the Gallic victory monuments at both Delphi and Thermon, see Mackil 2012: 212–14; Koehn 2007: 75–109. The broader scope is evident in the reverse of the Aitolians' issue of silver tetradrachms in the 230s, where a Macedonian shield is prominently inserted in the pile of Gallic spolia on which Aitolia sits: see *ANS* 1944.100.19483.rev.

30  Knoepfler 2007.

31  On these cultic and ceremonial implications of the decorative scheme and conservatism of the main temple at Thermon, see Antonetti 1990: 151–210.

32  Funke 2012 (elaborated in Funke 2013) emphasizes the continuing centrality of Thermon to Aitolians even as the territorial expansion of the *koinon* brought more and more neighbouring regional cult centres (e.g., Delphi) within its "sacred landscape."

33  For the larger phenomenon, see Mackil 2012. On the Aitolian *koinon* in particular, see Funke 2012, Funke 2013.

34  Funke 2015: 108–14.

35  This calculation is based upon the list of Aitolian *stratēgoi* compiled by G. Klaffenbach, *IG* IX 1², 1, 49–52; reproduced in Grainger 2000, table 5.

36  Phainea who opposed Philip V at the conference at Nikaia in 198, was from Arsinoe, just beyond Trichonion: *IG* IX 1², 1, 30 i.15.

37  Polyb. 5.8.4-5: τὰς οἰκίας τὰς ἐν αὐτῷ τῷ Θέρμῳ… οὔσας πλήρεις οὐ μόνον σίτου καὶ τῆς τοιαύτης χορηγίας, ἀλλὰ καὶ κατασκευῆς διαφερούσης τῶν παρ' Αἰτωλῶν. [5] καθ' ἕκαστον γὰρ ἔτος ἀγοράς τε καὶ πανηγύρεις ἐπιφανεστάτας, ἔτι δὲ καὶ τὰς τῶν ἀρχαιρεσίων καταστάσεις ἐν τούτῳ τῷ τόπῳ συντελούντων, ἕκαστοι πρὸς τὰς ὑποδοχὰς καὶ τὰς εἰς ταῦτα παρασκευὰς τὰ πολυτελέστατα τῶν ἐν τοῖς βίοις ὑπαρχόντων εἰς τοῦτον ἀπετίθεντο τὸν τόπον. "… the dwelling-houses in Thermus itself, which were full, not only of corn and such like provisions, but of all the most valuable property which the Aetolians possessed. For as the annual fair and most famous games, as well as the elections, were held there, everybody kept their most costly possessions in store at Thermus, to enable them to entertain their friends, and to celebrate the festivals with proper magnificence" (trans. Shuckburgh).

38  Thuc. 1.5.1: οἱ γὰρ Ἕλληνες τὸ πάλαι καὶ τῶν βαρβάρων οἵ τε ἐν τῇ ἠπείρῳ παραθαλάσσιοι καὶ ὅσοι νήσους εἶχον, ἐπειδὴ ἤρξαντο μᾶλλον περαιοῦσθαι ναυσὶν ἐπ' ἀλλήλους, ἐτράποντο πρὸς λῃστείαν, **ἡγουμένων ἀνδρῶν οὐ τῶν ἀδυνατωτάτων κέρδους τοῦ σφετέρου αὐτῶν ἕνεκα καὶ τοῖς ἀσθενέσι τροφῆς** (my emphasis). "For in early times the Hellenes and the barbarians of the coast and islands, as communication by sea became more common, were tempted to turn pirates, **under the conduct of their most powerful men; the motives being to serve their own cupidity and to support the needy**" (trans. R. Crawley).

39  Mackil 2012, map 6–7.

40  Mackil 2012: 276–82.

41  Polyb. 13.2: ὅτι Σκόπας Αἰτωλῶν ἀποτυχὼν τῆς ἀρχῆς, ἧς χάριν ἐτόλμα γράφειν τοὺς νόμους, μετέωρος ἦν εἰς τὴν Ἀλεξάνδρειαν. On this passage, see F. Walbank 1982: 413–15, correcting Paton's mistranslation of this passage to say that Skopas had to resign as *stratēgos* and flee into exile in Alexandria. Grainger 1999: 345 seems to rely on Paton's translation.

42  Matters of Aitolian *nomos*, and also electoral politics, played out before the annual assembly at the Thermika: Funke 2015: 108–11.

43  Note again the vastly disproportionate number of Trichonians chosen to high Aitolian office, especially the *stratēgeia*: above, n. 35.

44  See Walbank 1982: 413–14.

45  21.26.9 συνέβαινε δὲ τὸν μὲν Ἀλέξανδρον πλουσιώτατον εἶναι πάντων τῶν Ἑλλήνων… 21.26.14: πλειόνων ἢ διακοσίων ταλάντων ἔχων οὐσίαν… Polybios' assessment of Alexandros varied depending upon the use he made of his great wealth: Eckstein 1995: 23–4, 71, 74, 245.

46  *IG* IX 1², 1, 54.

47  Polyb. 18.3.1; see Walbank 1982: 554.

48  Note that Plautus' *Captivi*, adapted from a Greek comedy about the plight of war slaves, was set in Naupaktos. The volume of this trafficking of humans at Naupaktos – and the profits Naupaktians may have garnered – may be reflected in the number of manumission decrees found in sanctuaries at or near Naupaktos (see *IG* IX 1², 3, 612–43). For the Corinthian Gulf economic system, see in general Freitag 2000.

49  Polyb. 13.2: ὅτι Σκόπας Αἰτωλῶν στρατηγὸς ἀποτυχὼν τῆς ἀρχῆς, ἧς χάριν ἐτόλμα γράφειν τοὺς νόμους, μετέωρος ἦν εἰς τὴν Ἀλεξάνδρειαν, ταῖς ἐκεῖθεν ἐλπίσι πεπεισμένος ἀναπληρώσειν τὰ λείποντα τοῦ βίου καὶ τὴν τῆς ψυχῆς πρὸς τὸ πλεῖον ἐπιθυμίαν. "Skopas the strategos of the Aitolians, having failed to obtain the office, for the sake of which he had had the boldness to draw up these laws, Scopas turned his hopes to Alexandria, in the expectation of finding means there of restoring his broken fortunes, and satisfying to a fuller extent his grasping spirit" (trans. Shuckburgh).

## REFERENCES

Antonetti, C. 1990. *Les Étoliens: Image et religion*. Centre de Recherches d'Histoire Ancienne, vol. 92. Paris.

Antonetti, C. 2010. "I diversi aspetti di una 'koine' socio-culturale nella Grecia nord-occidentale di epoca ellenistica." In C. Antonetti (ed.), *Lo spazio ionico e le comunità della Grecia nord-occidentale: Territorio, società, istituzioni: Atti del Convegno Internazionale Venezia, 7–9 gennaio 2010*. Pisa: 301–26.

Antonetti, C., and E. Cavalli. 2012. "Il fondo epigrafico Petsas presso l'Università Ca' Foscari Venezia: Iscrizioni di Termo (Etolia)." *Zeitschrift für Papyrologie und Epigraphik* 180: 173–201.

Beck, H., and P. Funke (eds.). 2015. *Federalism in Greek Antiquity*. Cambridge.

Bousquet, J. 1988. "La stèle des Kyténiens à Xanthos de Lycie." *Revue des Études Grecques* 101: 12–53.

Cavalli, E. 2010. "Ὡς ἀγαθῶν οὐκ ἀπόλωλε ἀρετά: Storia e gloria nell'età dei Diadochi." In C. Antonetti (ed.), *Lo spazio ionico e le comunità della Grecia nord-occidentale: Territorio, società, istituzioni: Atti del Convegno Internazionale Venezia, 7–9 gennaio 2010*. Pisa: 409–28.

Champion, C. 1995. "The Soteria at Delphi: Aetolian Propaganda in the Epigraphical Record." *American Journal of Philology* 116: 213–20. https://doi.org/10.2307/295441.

Champion, C. 1996. "Polybius, Aetolia and the Gallic Attack on Delphi (279 B.C.)." *Historia* 45: 315–28.

Champion, C. 2004. *Cultural Politics in Polybius's "Histories."* Berkeley.

Champion, C. 2007. "Polybius and Aetolia: A Historiographical Approach." In J. Marincola (ed.), *A Companion to Greek and Roman Historiography*. Malden, MA: 356–62.

Eckstein, A.M. 1995. *Moral Vision in the Histories of Polybius*. Berkeley.

Freitag, K. 2000. *Der Golf von Korinth*. Munich.

Funke, P. 1997. "Polisgenese und Urbanisierung in Aitolien im 5. and 4. Jh. v. Chr." In M.H. Hansen (ed.), *The Polis as an Urban Centre and as a Political Community: Symposium, August 29–31, 1996*. Copenhagen: 145–88.

Funke, P. 2012. "Kultstätten und Nachtzentren: Zu den politischen Funktionen überregionaler Heiligtümer in antiken Bundesstaaten." In R. Rollinger, G. Schwinghammer, B. Truschnegg, and K. Schnegg (eds.), *Altertum und Gegenwart: 125 Jahre Alte Geschichte in Innsbruck*. Innsbruck: 53–71.

Funke, P. 2013. "*Thermika* und *Panaitolika*: Alte und neue Zentren im Aitolischen Bund." In P. Funke and M. Haake (eds.), *Greek Federal States and Their Sanctuaries*. Stuttgart: 49–64.

Funke, P. 2015. "Aitolia and the Aitolian League." In H. Beck and P. Funke (eds.), *Federalism in Greek Antiquity*. Cambridge: 86–117.

Grainger, J. 1999. *The League of the Aetolians*. Leiden.

Grainger, J. 2000. *Aetolian Prosopographical Studies*. Leiden.

Knoepfler, D. 2007. "De Delphes à Thermos: Un témoignage épigraphique méconnu sur le trophée galate des Étoliens dans leur capitale (le traité étolo-béotien)." *Comptes Rendus des Séances de l'Académie des Inscriptions et Belles-Lettres* 3: 1215–53.

Koehn, C. 2007. *Krieg – Diplomatie – Ideologie: Zur Außenpolitik hellenistischer Mittelstaaten*. Stuttgart.

Lefèvre, F. 1995. "La chronologie du III" siècle à Delp hes, d'après les actes amphictioniques (280–200)." *Bulletin de Correspondance Hellénique* 119: 161–206.

Lefèvre, F. 1998. "Traité de paix entre Démétrios Poliorcète et la confédération étolienne (fin 289?)." *Bulletin de Correspondance Hellénique* 122: 109–41.

Mack, W. *Proxeny Networks of the Ancient World*. http://proxenies.csad.ox.ac.uk /places/home.

Mackil, E.M. 2012. *Creating a Common Polity: Religion, Economy, and Politics in the Making of the Greek Koinon*. Berkeley.

Papapostolou, I.A. 2012. *Early Thermos: New Excavations, 1992–2003*. Athens.

Renfrew, C., and J.F. Cherry (eds.). 1986. *Peer Polity Interaction and Socio-Political Change*. Cambridge.

Rousset, D. 2006. "Les inscriptions de Kallipolis d'Étolie." *Bulletin de Correspondance Hellénique* 130: 381–434.

Rzepka, J. 2013. "Monstrous Aetolians and Aetolian Monsters – A Politics of Ethnography?" In E. Almagor and J. Skinner (eds.), *Ancient Ethnography: New Approaches*. London: 117–30.

Scholten, J.B. 2000. *The Politics of Plunder: Aitolians and Their Koinon in the Early Hellenistic Era, 279–217 B.C.* Berkeley.
Scholten, J.B. 2013. "The Importance of Being Aitolian." In S.L. Ager and R.A. Faber (eds.), *Belonging and Isolation in the Hellenistic World.* Toronto: 96–110.
Tsangari, D. 2007. *Corpus des monnaies d'or, d'argent et de bronze de la confédération étolienne.* Athens.
Walbank, F.W. 1982. *A Historical Commentary on Polybius.* Vol. 2. Oxford.

*We have seen in the previous chapter how the Aitolians were poster children to ancient authors for ruthlessness and misbehaviour, susceptive to a particular custom of plunder that defied views of Hellenistic advancement in politics and culture. All the while, they were, arguably, the creators of one of the most successful federal states in Greek history. Linking up with the examination of local place in a federal environment, clustered around the discussion of Thermon near Lake Trichonis (chapter 7), this chapter further explores the interplay between federalism and localism. Peter Funke begins his study with observations on the steep career of the federal paradigm from the early Hellenistic period. The shifting parameters of this federalization set the stage for a new type of localism. Shaping new spatial arenas of in-betweenness, for instance by means of administrative districts and territorial units, Greek ethnē crafted functional realms between the central government and its local members. These intermediary arenas, variously labelled* telē *or* merē *in the sources, potentially wielded sentiments of attachment to a local of their own. In support of this hypothesis, Funke revisits the evidence for the existence of districts in the Aitolian League. The few attested cases all point to the territorial fringes of the* koinon *rather than the Aitolian heartland. Funke identifies the* telē *as remnants of formerly independent federations absorbed into the league; their survival allowed new members to connect to epichoric traditions and at the same time orient themselves in the grand structure of Aitolia. The examination of Aitolian local bronze coinages further supports this reading. In sum, Funke's chapter reveals a federal policy that is geared towards the anchoring of new members in their old local and regional traditions while participating in a league that swiftly expanded beyond the geographical horizon of both.*

*Keywords: Aitolia, federalism, districts, political administration, coinage, local scaling*

8

# Aligning the Dots: Local Self-Assertion in a Politically Expanding World

PETER FUNKE

Localism in the Hellenistic world: for a long time this appeared to be a contradiction in itself. In a culturally and politically expanding world with completely new, almost global perspectives, localism seemed to have little place in the Greek *polis* world. Recently, however, this view has fundamentally changed and has almost completely turned itself around. Whereas in the past there was talk of the decline of the *poleis* and the loss of autonomy of the small political communities, today the opportunities and possibilities of local self-assertion in a politically expanding world are more strongly emphasized.[1] Now speaking of a crisis in the Greek *polis* world seems inadequate, if we look at this heyday of local historiography, where every city, however insignificant, had its "wandering poets," who sang of its own heroic past.[2]

However, I do not question the radical change in the *polis* world in Hellenistic times. A world of individual states had become a world of federal states. The political map of Greece had changed fundamentally over the course of the third and the first half of the second century BCE. The federal states known as *ethnē* or *koina* had changed the character of ancient Greece.[3] However, it was precisely this structural change that opened up completely new ways for the *poleis* to maintain an independent political position. As member states embedded in federal structures, they had to delegate parts of their state sovereignty to a central power, but a system of checks and balances between the member states and the central power constituted by these member states ensured a sufficiently large political scope of action for the individual member states. Frank W. Walbank rightly claims that

in a world of monarchies the federal states ... exemplify the continuing ability of the Greeks to respond to a new political challenge with new solutions. One is bound to ask whether, given another century without Rome, federalism might not have developed fresh and fruitful aspects … Federalism offered the possibility of transcending the limitations of size and relative weakness of the separate city-state.[4]

The federalization of the Greek world of states therefore certainly benefited the position of the member states and promoted in this way a new localism, which became a phenomenon (not only) of Hellenistic Greece. In recent research, the varying institutional, cultic, and cultural manifestations of this localism at the level of the individual members of the federal states have been widely described and discussed.[5] I would therefore like to draw attention to another specific form of localism, which is also inextricably linked to federalization. The question is, to what extent did intermediate levels of localism exist within the principally bipolar structures of federal states, which may have preserved or even generated their own localism? Furthermore, were there spatially defined intermediate areas between the member states and the central authorities of federal states in which a special localism as an expression of an own sense of identity existed or could develop? I would like to explore these questions using the example of the Aitolian League. Despite our comparatively poor knowledge of its internal structure (e.g., in comparison to the Boiotian League), the scarce sources we have do indicate a more complex structure within the Aitolian League, with respect to my aforementioned questions, compared to other federal states.

In many federal states, the division into administrative districts formed a possible intermediate level, which provided the financial and military resources for the respective league. These districts were usually units of equal size, to which the individual member states were assigned according to size and geographical distribution.[6] A well-attested example is the *merē* of the Boiotian League.[7] Whether the Aitolian League was also divided into administrative districts in a similar form is still disputed today. The treaty of alliance between the Aitolian League and Acarnanian League from the 60s of the third century BCE is the only source that seems to indicate such a division of the Aitolian League.[8] The dating form of this inscription mentions a number of magistrates of both alliance partners. On the Aitolian side, in addition to the three highest offices (*stratēgos, hipparchos, grammateus*), there are seven so-called *epilektarchontes* and seven *tamiai*. All of the mentioned magistrates are called federal officials (*archontes en Aitolia*).[9] Scholars have repeatedly regarded the mention of the college of the seven *epilektarchontes* as an indication of the existence of seven respective, equally structured, districts into which the Aitolian League had been divided. Accordingly, the Aitolian League was said to have been organized similarly to most of the other federal states with a comparable administrative internal structure.[10]

Such an assumption cannot be ruled out, even if the evidence is extremely weak and the conclusions are based primarily on comparisons with other states. A division of the Aitolian League into standardized districts is quite conceivable. However, an organizational unit designed in such a way on an intermediate level between the member states and the central power does not help in answering the question at hand: was there room for a particular type of localism in the federal league? A strictly proportional division would hardly have been suitable to create a sufficiently intense feeling of together-ness on which a localism could have been based. Still, I have dealt with the problem of district division in detail, because it is repeatedly associated with another subdivision of the Aitolian League.

This subdivision, too, is only mentioned in very few inscriptions. What is meant here is the existence of so-called *telē*. These *telē* were districts that were regionally limited according to their respective geographical name affix and quite obviously formed a special intermediate level within the federal structures of the Aitolian League. Currently, the only certain proof provided by the sources is limited to those parts of Acarnania, which were integrated in the Aitolian League (*telos Stratikon* / district of the region around Stra-tos), and to Lokris (*telos Lokrikon* / district of Lokris).[11] Up until now, these *telē* have usually been regarded as further evidence for a general district division of the entire Aitolian League according to a strictly geographical principle of division. Thomas Corsten has been particularly emphatic in advocating this thesis, equating the *telē* with the seven districts, which he has derived from the dating form of the Aitolian-Acarnanian treaty of alli-ance.[12] However, such an equation is based on hypothetical conclusions that lack sufficient evidence.[13]

It seems to me appropriate to consider the phenomenon of the *telē* apart from the question of a general district division of the Aitolian League. There are noteworthy indications that the introduction of these *telē* was connected with the integration of formerly non-Aitolian tribes and *koina* into the Aito-lian League and remained limited to their territories.[14] These *telē* were possibly a particular institutional feature that could be of importance for our question about specific spheres of localism within the Aitolian federation – beyond the individual member states, but below the federal level. I would therefore like to begin by presenting the few direct and indirect primary sources and attempt to describe the function of these *telē* within the internal structures of the Aitolian League to see if there are aspects of a localism to be made explicit.

First of all, there are four manumission inscriptions – two from Delphi and two from Naupaktos – in which the *boularchos* of a *telos* is mentioned in the dating form. Only one of the two Delphic inscriptions also mentions a precise denomination of the *telos*: *to Lokrikon telos*.[15] In the second Delphic inscription, the reference to the *telos* is missing; due to the similarity of the name, however, it must be the same *boularchos* of the *Lokrikon telos*.[16] In both inscriptions from Naupaktos, a *telos* is named whose geographical denomination is no longer preserved. Because of their finding place (Lokrian Naupaktos), *"tou Lokrikou"* has been supplemented.[17] However, this addition is by no means mandatory. Other supplements, such as the naming of a hitherto unknown *telos*, are quite conceivable.[18] Another *telos* is recorded in an inscription from Thermos. It is an arbitral award from the *telos Stratikon*, which settles a territorial dispute of formerly Acarnanian cities then belonging to the Aitolian League.[19]

These few inscriptions are the only direct evidence for the existence of *telē* in the Aitolian League. Nevertheless, they allow for a first rough characterization. The mention of an eponymous *boularchos tou teleos* shows that there was a *boulē* (council) at the level of each *telē*, which should be distinguished from the *boulē* of the federation, the *synhedrion*, and the *boulai* of the member states.[20] There have been attempts to interpret the office of a *boularchos tou teleos* as a federal one and to connect the *boulai* of the *telē* in some way with the league council.[21] However, the arguments put forth are unconvincing. They misjudge the function of the *synhedrion* as a league council in which the individual member states were represented in proportion to their size. In contrast, the *boulai* of the *telē* must have been an institution on their own, with their own decision-making competences. What kind of competences these were is hard to specify due to the scarce sources. The arbitration award of the *telos Stratikon* handed down in the above-mentioned inscription from Thermos shows that the *telē* – among other things – could at least exercise judicial functions. I am therefore convinced that the *telē* were an independent level of political action within the Aitolian League, which cannot simply be equated with a general, uniform district division, even if the geographical denomination of the *telē* suggests some kind of regional attribution. If this assumption is correct, however, the question of membership in these *telē* arises. Who and what accounted for belonging to a *telos*?

As I mentioned before there is currently no evidence for the existence of *telē* in the Aitolian heartland. We only know about two *telē*, the *telos Stratikon* and the *telos Lokrikon*. They refer to regions in western and central Greece, which were successively integrated into the federal state in the course of the expansion of the Aitolian League from the end of the fourth century BCE onwards.[22] While the *telos Stratikon* included eastern parts of Acarnania, with the so-called *Stratikē* with its *polis* Stratos in the centre, the *telos Lokrikon* certainly included western Lokris and possibly temporarily eastern Lokris as well.

Admittedly, this is only a conditionally reliable finding. Still, based on it I would like to propose an alternative to the common interpretations of the *telē*: The regional references expressed in the denomination of the *telē* suggest that with the establishment of the *telē* for the non-Aitolian member states of the Aitolian League (and only for them) a separate platform for some political interactions within the league was created. In this way, the *telē* enabled these member states – to a limited extent – to maintain a certain part of their original ethnic cohesion and, above all, of their original shared political identity. Before I continue to flesh out the thesis itself, I would like to take a closer look at some further sources – apart from the already mentioned ones – which can at least indirectly underpin my considerations.

First of all, an inscription from Xanthos published in 1988 should be mentioned here.[23] It contains a dossier of documents relating to a delegation sent in 206/205 BCE by the *polis* Kytenion – situated in the Doris in central Greece – to Xanthos in Lykia. The embassy from the *polis* Kytenion, at that time part of the Aitolian League, approached Xanthos to gather money for the rebuilding of their city's fortifications, which had been first destroyed by an earthquake and again shortly after (about 228 BCE) by Antigonos Doson. The envoys presented to the Xanthians not only a letter from their hometown, which confirmed their orders and contained a detailed description of the Kytenians' request, but also an authorizing decree from the Aitolian federal assembly and a corresponding letter from the league's highest magistrates and the league council. Of particular interest here is the answer that the Xanthians gave to the Kytenians in which they emphasized their goodwill towards both the "*koinon* of the Dorians" and the *polis* of the Kytenians.[24] Furthermore, it is astonishing that the authorizing decree from the Aitolian federal assembly was addressed to not only the Kytenians but all of the Dorians.[25] And the Kytenians in their letter, too, named themselves "the Dorians of the Metropolis who dwell in the *polis* Kytenion";[26] additionally, the Xanthians in their reply spoke of "envoys from the Aitolian League, Dorians of the Metropolis from Kytenion."[27]

The emphasis on the Dorian *syngeneia* surely was a central argument in the Kytenians' request. That is why the shared Dorian descent of the Dorians of the Metropolis and the Xanthians was especially stressed in all documents.[28] Still, it remains to be considered whether the differentiation made in the inscription dossier between the *polis* of the Kytenians, the *koinon* of the Dorians, and the other Aitolians could not be an indication of the existence of a *telos Dorikon*, whose members were at the same time independent member states of the Aitolian League. The documents carried by the delegation leave no doubt that the crucial decision for their mission was made both on the federal level and on the level of the member state Kytenion. This complies with how all matters of foreign policy in federal states were dealt with, that is, a mutual negotiation process between member states and central power. It does not exclude, however, the possibility that, in addition to this bipolar internal structure, there existed other institutionalized levels of (also political) action that offered certain groups of member states space for cooperation beyond their own *polis* boundaries, but within the Aitolian League.[29]

I leave it at this vague description for the moment and turn to another aspect, which might be helpful in characterizing the *telē*. For this purpose, I would like to draw attention to the Aitolian coinage.[30] The Aitolian League minted gold, silver, and bronze coins.[31] The minting of gold and silver coins was the exclusive responsibility of the league, according to the attached coin legends "ΑΙΤΩΛΩΝ." Among the bronze coinage, however, there is also a coin type that has the same emblems on its reverse as the Aitolian federal coinage, but instead of the inscription "ΑΙΤΩΛΩΝ" it displays the name of a *polis* or a tribal state (*ethnos*) as the indication of origin.[32] While the depictions on the obverses on both the local and the federal coinages vary, the reverses are completely identical, with the exception of the indication of origin, and display the emblems characteristic of Aitolian coinage: a spearhead and the lower jaw of the Kalydonian boar.[33] So far, these local bronze coinages of Aitolian type can be traced especially for the central Greek *ethnē* of the Ainianes and Oitaians as well as for the Phocian *polis* Tithorea, the Western Lokrian *poleis* Amphissa and Oiantheia, and the Eastern Lokrian *polis* Thronion.[34]

For a long time, these local coinages were dated to the late phase of the Aitolian League in the first half of the second century BCE, when the Aitolians had to accept a first major weakening of their league after the end of the Second Macedonian War and the Antiochos War. The local bronze coinages were interpreted as a sign of a strengthened autonomy of the member states integrated into the federation in the course of the late fourth and third century BCE. Because of the Roman-Aitolian peace treaty (189 BCE),[35] these member states would have been given latitude for political action before finally leaving the Aitolian League after the end of the Third Macedonian War (168 BCE).[36] In the 1980s, Olivier Picard cast doubt on this dating and thus also on the historical interpretation for the first time, and advocated a redating of the local bronze coinage already to the third century BCE.[37] Picard's dating approach was emphatically confirmed in the 1990s by the research of Katharina Liampi, who was able to prove that the Aitolian bronze coinages – both the federal and the local issues – already began in the early third century BCE, that is, at a time when the places where the local bronze coinages were minted were successively integrated into the Aitolian League.[38] This new chronological approach has made the previous historical interpretations of the local Aitolian bronze coinage obsolete.

A solution to the question of the local bronze coinages must therefore be sought within the institutional and legal framework of the federal structures of the Aitolian League. One should start from the observation that the local Aitolian bronze coinage is limited to those member states that were newly incorporated into the Aitolian League in the course of its expansion in the late fourth and third centuries BCE. There thus seems to be a close temporal and causal connection between the emergence of local bronze coinage and the territorial expansion of the Aitolian League. This, in turn, results in a remarkable coincidence with a structural element of the Aitolian League, which – at least according to the current state of the sources – appears to have applied to the same member states to which the local bronze coinage can also be linked. The obvious identity between the area of origin of the local bronze coinage and the area of distribution of the *telē* makes a direct causal connection between the two seem at least very plausible. I therefore assume that the right to mint local bronze coins was one of the privileges granted by the Aitolians to the newly admitted, originally non-Aitolian members of the league. I would even like to go one step further and argue that this right could have been enshrined on the *telē* level. Since we know of local bronze coinage of the *ethnē* of the Ainianes and Oitaians, as well as of some Phocian and Lokrian *poleis*, it can be assumed that a *telos* could potentially delegate this right of coinage to member states of the Aitolian League belonging to the respective *telos*.

I admit that these conclusions are full of preconditions and must remain hypothetical in many respects.[39] Nevertheless, I would like to substantiate my theses on the local bronze coinage in a little more detail by bringing them into closer connection with my previous remarks on the *telē*. The starting point for my considerations was a few barely connected set pieces that could be obtained from epigraphic and numismatic sources. They are isolated puzzle pieces that can be put together to form only a very fragmentary picture. Nevertheless, this picture can open up new perspectives on the internal structure of the Aitolian League, which are also relevant to the question of localism in the Hellenistic period.

At the beginning, I already referred to the process of fundamental political change in northwestern and central Greece that began in the fifth and fourth centuries BCE.[40] An ongoing dissolution of the traditional tribal structures took place in these regions formerly shaped by tribal states. This disintegration correlated with a growing political self-confidence of the constituents of the various collapsing tribal communities. One could indeed speak in this context of a "politicization" of the individual tribal subdivisions. These subdivisions had turned into independent *poleis* and then reintegrated into a new state – organized according to federal principles. When over the course of the third century BCE the Aitolians' federal territories spread out over nearly all of central Greece, all the tribal communities in this region, most of which were federally organized in their own right at that time, were incorporated in the Aitolian League by integrating their individual subunits as autonomous member states.

Their affiliation to one of the *koina* of the Lokrians, Phokians, Dorians, Oitaians, et al. was no longer politically relevant, but membership in the Aitolian League was. Legally, the citizens of these member states had become Aitolians, as also becomes clear from the citizens' indication of origin "Αἰτωλὸς ἐκ [+ name of the home *polis*]."[41] The Phokian from Amphissa, the Lokrian from Naupaktos, and the Dorian from Kytenion had become Aitolians from Amphissa, Naupaktos, and Kytenion. Nevertheless, the identity of the old and originally independent *koina* was obviously not completely lost. This is not only supported by the fact that these (after 168 BCE) re-established *koina* were able to politically function again remarkably quickly, despite being integrated into the Aitolian Confederation for a very long time.[42] Likewise, the aforementioned inscription dossier from Xanthos and the local bronze coinages have shown that a feeling of compatriotic and political togetherness remained alive at the level of these *koina* even in "Aitolian times." And here is also where the *telē* come into play again. Their geographical denominations quite obviously refer to the territories of these *koina*. Apparently, the *telē* corresponded to the *koina* of the Lokrians, Dorians, Phokians, and so on, which merged into the Aitolian League.

It was a primarily political, and not merely a geographical, ethnic, or administrative, aspect that determined the establishment of *telē* within the Aitolian federal structure. The *telē* served to preserve a collective political identity of the *koina* after they had been split into numerous, politically independent member states of the Aitolian League. The members of the formerly independent *koina* were thus granted – as an effect of joining the Aitolian League – at least a certain substitute for their dissolved tribal or federal organizations. Thus, the loss of institutional structures could be at least partially compensated, that had contributed decisively to securing a sense of belonging within the (former) *koina*. Since the numismatic and epigraphic evidence for activities at the level of the *telē* date back to the third century BCE, it may be assumed that the *telē* were already introduced at the beginning of the Aitolian expansion into central Greece in order to grant the *koina*, who were politically absorbed into the Aitolian League, their own level of political action after all. This may have further increased the attractiveness of the Aitolian League.

If the observations presented here are correct, then the *telē* were a unique structural element, which – as far as I can see – cannot be proven in any other ancient federal state. With the establishment of the *telē*, the Aitolian Confederation provided a certain circle of its member states with an institutionalized platform for political interactions at an intermediate level between the individual member states and the central power of the confederation. This intermediate level was a very special locus of a local or, more precisely, a regional identity, where corresponding forms of localism could develop. The local bronze coinage is only one paradigmatic example of this. It is to be hoped that more indicators can be identified in the future.

## NOTES

1 Beck 2020 (with further literature).
2 Hunter and Rutherford 2009; see also Funke 2015; Antonetti 2019.
3 Beck and Funke 2015; Funke 2018.
4 Walbank 1981: 157–8.
5 Beck and Funke 2015 (with further literature).
6 Corsten 1999.
7 Hell. Oxy. 19.3–4 (Cambers); cf. Corsten 1999: 27–31; Beck and Ganter 2015: 141–3.
8 *IG* IX 1², 1, 3A = *Staatsverträge* III.480.
9 *IG* IX 1², 1, 3A, 15–22: ἐπὶ ἀρχόντων ἐμ μὲν Αἰτωλίαι στραταγέοντος Πολυκρίτου Καλλιέος τὸ δεύτερον, ἱππαρχέοντος Φίλωνος Πλευρωνίου, γραμματεύοντος Νεοπτολέμου Ναυπακτίου, ἐπιλεκταρχεόντων Λαμέδωνος Καλυδωνίου, Ἀριστάρχου Ἐρταίου, Λέωνος Καφρέος, Καλλία Καλλιέος, Τιμολόχου Ποτειδανιέος, Παμφαΐδα Φυσκέος, Σίμου Φυταιέος, ταμιευόντων Κυδρίωνος Λυσιμαχέος, Δωριμάχου Τριχονίου, Ἀρίστωνος Δαιᾶνος, Ἀριστέα Ἱστωρίου, Ἀγήσωνος Δεξιέος, Τιμάνδρου Ἐριναῖος(!), Ἀγρίου Σωσθενέος, ἐν δὲ Ἀκαρνανίαι. Cf. also *IG* IX 1², 1, 180.
10 Corsten 1999: 133–59.
11 See below for the sources.
12 Corsten 1999, esp. 140–8.
13 Cf., e.g., Rzepka 2006: 40–2; Mackil 2013, esp. 499; Lasagni 2019, esp. 149–52.
14 Even if no final certainty can be achieved in this question, it remains to be stated that until today there are no explicit sources for the existence of *telē* within the Aitolian heartland. All attempts to attribute the origin of the *telē* to the ancient tribal structures of the Aitolian heartland described in Thuc.

3.94.4–5 (cf., e.g., Sordi 1953: 442–5) remain hypothetical. On the Aitolian *telē*, see most recently in detail Rzepka 2006: 33–45; Lasagni 2012, esp. 190–9; Mackil 2013, esp. 380–4; Lasagni 2019: 147–59 (with further literature).

15  *GDI* II 2070, 1–2: βουλαρχέοντος τοῦ Λοκρικοῦ τέλεος Δαμοτέλεος Φυσκέος.

16  *GDI* II 2139, 1–2: ἄρχοντος Ξένωνος τοῦ Ἀτεισίδα μηνὸς Ποιτροπί[ου], βουλαρχέοντος Δαμοτέλεος Φυσκέος.

17  *IG* IX 1², 3, 618, 1–3: [βουλαρ]χέοντος τ[οῦ Λοκρικοῦ τ]έλεος Λ.[.....νος Ἀγρ]ινιέος; *IG* IX 1², 3, 625A, 1–2: βουλ[α]ρχέοντος [τοῦ Λοκρικοῦ] τέλεος [Λ .....]νος Ἀγλινιέος {Ἀγρινιέος}.

18  Corsten 1999:149–55. Already Lerat 1952 1:38–41 and 2:82 had cast doubt on the supplement, since the – albeit uncertain – reading of the boularchos' *ethnikon* "Agrinieus" would presuppose an overly large extension of the *Lokrikon telos*. Corsten assumes the existence of a separate *telos*, whose name is still unknown and which extended from Naupaktos to Agrinion. For him, the geographical layout of the *telos* is an indicator of the uniform, strictly proportional district division of the Aitolian League. He sees the geographical extension of the *telos* as an indicator of the uniform, strictly proportional district division of the Aitolian League. In view of the unsolved problem of a secure interpretation of the *ethnikon "Agrinieus*," however, such a conclusion is decidedly too far-reaching; cf. also Rzepka 2006: 44; Lasagni 2012: 197–9; Lasagni 2019, esp. 163–4.

19  *IG* IX 1², 1, 3B, 11–12: στραταγέοντος Χαριξένου τὸ τέταρτον. κρῖμα γαϊκὸν Στρατικοῦ τέλεος; Mackil 2013: 381; Scholten 2000: 90–1.

20  See the fundamental study in Lasagni 2012; Lasagni 2019, esp. 159–64.

21  E.g., Bauer 1907: 53; cf. also the commentary of G. Klaffenbach on *IG* IX 1², 1, 618.

22  Dittenberger (1897: 183) interpreted the *telē* as "a temporary experiment" in the period after the Roman-Aitolian peace treaty of 189 BCE, and, for the same reasons already, Mommsen (1866: 39–40, note 75) as "eine ganz singuläre Lokrerbehörde [a very singular Lokrian authority]" as a result of a "anbefohlenen Selbständigkeit [decreed independence]." Oldfather 1926: 1239 and Scheu 1960 also argued in the same direction, although in the meantime from IG IX 1², 1, 3B, 1 the 30s of the third century BCE had emerged as the *terminus ante quem* for the establishment of the district system; cf. already Busolt and Swoboda 1926: 1513. On the expansion of the Aitolian League cf. Flacelière 1937; Lefèvre 1998; Grainger 1995; Grainger 1999; Scholten 2000; Sánchez 2001; Tsangari 2007: 22–36; Mackil 2013: 91–128, 359–61; Rzepka 2019.

23  *SEG* 38.1476; Bousquet 1988.

24  *SEG* 38.1476A, 35–7: τὴν εὔν[οιαν] ἣν ἔχομεν πρός τε τὸ κοινὸν τῶν Δωριέων καὶ τὴν Κ[υτε]νίων πόλιν.

25  *SEG* 38.1476B, 73–4: Ἔδοξε τοῖς Αἰτωλοῖς πρεσβείας δόμεν τοῖς Δωριέοις.

26 *SEG* 38.1476D, 88–9: Δωρ[ι]έων τῶν ἀπὸ Ματροπόλιος οἱ πόλιν Κυτένιον οἰκέοντες.

27 *SEG* 38.1476A, 7–11: ἐπειδὴ ἀπὸ τοῦ κοινοῦ τῶν Αἰτωλῶν παραγεγόνασιν πρεσβευταὶ Δωριεῖς ἀπὸ Μητροπόλιος ἐκ Κυτενίου Λαμπρίας, Αἴνετος, Φηγεύς, ψήφισμά τε παρ' Αἰτωλῶν φέροντες καὶ ἐπιστολὴν παρὰ Δωριέων.

28 Curty 1995, no. 75; Jones 1999: 139–43.

29 Cf. also Lasagni 2019: 154–9, who, however, remains sceptical about the assumption of a *telos Dorikon*.

30 Cf. for the following Funke 2016.

31 Tsangari 2007 (with further references); Antonetti 2019.

32 A compilation of the finds of these local coinages, which for a long time have received little attention, is provided by Liampi 1998; cf. also Caramessini-Oeconomides 1970; Kravartogiannos 1978; Kravartogiannos 1981; Kravartogiannos 1985; Kravartogiannos 1994a; Kravartogiannos 1994b; Liampi 1996; Tsangari 2007: 249–55; Mackil 2013: 252–4.

33 On the significance of these emblems typical of the Aitolian League see Jördens and Becht-Jördens 1994; Tsangari 2007: 202–3; Killen 2017, esp. 117–22, 157–62; Antonetti 2019, esp. 158–61.

34 Apollonia: *BMC* VII (Thessaly to Aitolia): 200, nos 1–2. It is possible that this site is the *castellum* Apollonia mentioned only in Liv. 28.8.9 as being located near the Aitolian Potidania. Whereas Liampi 1998, esp. 84–6, assigns this Apollonia to the Aitolian heartland, an affiliation to western Lokris does not seem to be excluded. The coin type with the indication of origin ΠΟ..(Δ?)/ AN is attributed to the Aitolian city of Potidania by Liampi 1996; Liampi 1998; Antonetti 2019: 160–1. As attractive as this attribution may seem, the supplement of the only very fragmentary coin legend remains uncertain, also since in view of the still growing abundance of non-localizable *ethnika* and toponyms, especially in central Greece, due to new epigraphic finds, another supplement cannot be ruled out. The regional attribution of these two coin types is of decisive importance for the question of whether central Aitolian cities also had the right to mint their own bronze coins. While Liampi 1996 and Liampi 1998 affirm the question, I do not consider such a far-reaching conclusion to be sufficiently sustainable at present in view of the indissoluble uncertainties presented. In the following, I will therefore exclude this problem and focus my remarks on the bronze coinages that can be located with certainty. For this reason, another coin type is not considered, which also has an "Aitolian" reverse – but without an indication of origin – and whose mint is assumed to be the Sicilian city of Panormos: *BMC* II (Sicily) 128, 18; cf. Liampi 1998.

35 *Staatsverträge* IV, no. 631.

36 This thesis, already put forward in the older coin corpora of the nineteenth and the first half of the twentieth centuries, was then helped to a breakthrough by Scheu 1960 in a fundamental study of the Aitolian coinage system. As late

as the 1990s, Kravartogiannos 1994a; Kravartogiannos 1994b; and Funke 1997: 158–9 also adopted this dating.

37  Picard 1984.

38  Based on a thorough and comprehensive numismatic analysis of all relevant datable coin hoards and archaeological findings, Katharina Liampi was able to convincingly demonstrate that the Aitolian bronze coinages did not begin only after the end of the Aitolian gold and silver coinages in the second century BCE, but almost simultaneously in the early third century BCE – at the latest after the victory over the Galatians in 279 BCE. There is even some evidence to suggest that the series of the bronze coinages had already run out in the course of the late third century or early second century BCE; see Liampi 1998.

39  The same applies to other attempts at explanation. For example, Caspari (1917: 170) assumed that "these places [i.e., places of the origin of the local bronze coinage] should be regarded as tributaries rather than as regular members of the League"; De Laix (1973: 67, n. 149) also interprets the bronze coinage "may be issues of allied states." However, there can be no question of such a distinction between "regular" and "tributary" members within the Aitolian League; cf. Funke 2016: 105–6.

40  See also Mackil 2014; Funke 2018, esp. 112–14.

41  E.g., *SEG* 29.380, 6: Αἰτωλὸς ἐγ Ναυπάκτου.

42  On the history of these *koina* in the second and first century BCE cf. Martin 1975; Rousset 2015.

## REFERENCES


Antonetti, C. 2019. "Spearhead and Boar Jawbone – An Invitation to Hunt in Aitolia: 'Foreign Policy' within the Aitolian League." In H. Beck, K. Buraselis, and A. McAuley (eds.), *Ethnos und Koinon: Studies in Ancient Greek Ethnicity and Federalism*. Stuttgart: 149–65.

Bauer, E. 1907. *Untersuchungen zur Geographie und Geschichte der nordwestlichen Landschaften Griechenlands nach den delphischen Inschriften*. Halle.

Beck, H. 2020. *Localism and the Ancient Greek City-State*. Chicago.

Beck, H., K. Buraselis, and A. McAuley (eds.). 2019. *Ethnos und Koinon: Studies in Ancient Greek Ethnicity and Federalism*. Stuttgart.

Beck, H., and P. Funke (eds.). 2015. *Federalism in Greek Antiquity*. Cambridge.

Beck, H., and A. Ganter. 2015. "Boiotia and the Boiotian Leagues." In H. Beck and P. Funke (eds.), *Federalism in Greek Antiquity*. Cambridge: 132–57.

Bousquet, J. 1988. "La stèle des Kyténiens au Létôon de Xanthos." *Revue des Études Grecques* 101: 12–53.

Busolt, G., and H. Swoboda. 1926. *Griechische Staatskunde*, vol. 2. Munich.

Caramessini-Oeconomides, M. 1970. "Ἀνέκδοτον χαλκοῦν νόμισμα Τιθορέας." Ἀρχαιολογικά Ἀνάλεκτα εξ Ἀθηνῶν. 3: 98–9.

Caspari, M.O.B. 1917. "A Survey of Greek Federal Coinage." *Journal of Hellenic Studies* 37: 168–83. https://doi.org/10.2307/625474.

Corsten, T. 1999. *Vom Stamm zum Bund: Gründung und territoriale Organisation griechischer Bundesstaaten*. Munich.

Curty, O. 1995. *Les parentés légendaires entre cités grecques: Catalogue raisonné des inscriptions contenant le terme syngeneia et analyse critique*. Geneva.

De Laix, R. 1973. "The Silver Coinage of the Aetolian League." *California Studies in Classical Antiquity* 6: 47–75. https://doi.org/10.2307/25010647.

Dittenberger, W. 1897. "Die delphische Amphiktyonie im Jahre 178 v.Chr." *Hermes* 32: 161–90.

Flacelière, R. 1937. *Les Aitoliens à Delphes: Contributions à l'histoire de la Grèce centrale au IIIe siècle a. J.-C.* Paris.

Funke, P. 1997. "Polisgenese und Urbanisierung in Aitolien im 5. und 4. Jh. v. Chr." In M.H. Hansen (ed.), *The Polis as an Urban Centre and as a Political Community*. Copenhagen: 145–88 [= Funke 2019: 93–130].

Funke, P. 2015. "Einige Überlegungen zur Genese der antiken griechischen Lokalgeschichtsschreibung." *Geographia Antiqua* 23–4: 179–85.

Funke, P. 2016. "Bundesstaatliche Kompetenz oder Kompetenz der Gliedstaaten? Einige Überlegungen zu den Bronzeprägungen des Aitolischen Bundes." In H. Nieswandt and H. Schwarzer (eds.), *"Man kann es sich nicht prächtig genug vorstellen!": Festschrift für Dieter Salzmann zum 65. Geburtstag*. Marsberg: 103–11 [= Funke 2019: 145–52].

Funke, P. 2018. "*Poleis* and *Koina*: Reshaping the World of the Greek States in Hellenistic Times." In H. Börm and N. Luraghi (eds.), *The Polis in the Hellenistic World*. Stuttgart: 109–29.

Funke, P. 2019. *Die Heimat des Acheloos: Nordwestgriechische Studien. Ausgewählte Schriften zu Geschichte, Landeskunde und Epigraphik*. Göttingen.

Grainger, J.D. 1995. "The Expansion of the Aitolian League." *Mnemosyne* 48: 313–43.

Grainger, J.D. 1999. *The League of the Aitolians*. Leiden.

Hunter, R., and I. Rutherford (eds.). 2009. *Wandering Poets in Ancient Greek Culture: Travel, Locality and Pan-Hellenism*. Cambridge.

Jones, C.P. 1999. *Kinship Diplomacy in the Ancient World*. Cambridge, MA.

Jördens, A., and G. Becht-Jördens. 1994. "Ein Eberunterkiefer als 'Staatssymbol' des aitolischen Bundes: Politische Identitätssuche im Mythos nach dem Ende der spartanischen Hegemonie." *Klio* 76: 172–84. https://doi.org/10.1524/klio .1994.76.76.172.

Killen, S. 2017. *Parasema: Offizielle Symbole griechischer Poleis und Bundesstaaten*. Wiesbaden.

Kravartogiannos, D. 1978. "Τὰ νομίσματα τῆς Ἀμφίσσης." Τετραμήνα 16/17: 1238–43.

Kravartogiannos, D. 1981. "Κατάλογος νομισματικῶν εὑρημάτων Καλλιπόλεως ἀνασκαφῆς." Τετραμήνα 19/20: 1309–40.

Kravartogiannos, D. 1985. "Χαλκᾶ νομίσματα τῶν Αἰτωλῶν εὑρήματος Ἀμφίσσης." Τετραμήνα 28/29: 1979–88.

Kravartogiannos, D. 1994a. "Οἱ 'αὐτόνομης' κοπές τῶν πόλεων τῆς Αἰτωλικῆς Συμπολιτείας." Τετραμήνα 53: 3947–55.

Kravartogiannos, D. 1994b. "Εὕρημα Ἀμφίσσης του Β' αι. π.Χ. χιλίων περίπου νομισμάτων." Φωκικά Χρονικά: 74–80.

Lasagni, C. 2012. "I boularchoi in Etolia." *Historiká* 2: 171–204. https://doi.org /10.13135/2039-4985/336.

Lasagni, C. 2019. *Le realtà locali nel mondo Greco: Ricerche su poleis ed ethne della Grecia occidentale.* Alessandria.

Lefèvre, F. 1998. *L'Amphictionie pyléo-delphique: Histoire et institutions.* Paris.

Lerat, L. 1952. *Les Locriens de l'ouest.* Vols. 1–2. Paris.

Liampi, K. 1996. "Η νομισματική παραγωγή της Ποτιδανίας, πόλεως των Αποδωτῶν." In ΧΑΡΑΚΤΗΡ: Αφιέρωμα στην Μάντω Οικονομίδου. Athens: 157–64.

Liampi, K. 1998. "On the Chronology of the Bronze Coinages of the Aetolian League and Its Members (Spearhead and Jawbone Types)." Αρχαιογνωσία 9 [1995/6]: 83–109.

Mackil, E. 2013. *Creating a Common Polity: Religion, Economy, and Politics in the Making of the Greek Koinon.* Berkeley.

Mackil, E. 2014. "Ethnos and Koinon." In J. McInerny (ed.), *A Companion to Ethnicity in the Ancient Mediterranean.* Malden, MA: 270–84.

Martin, D.G. 1975. "Greek Leagues in the Later Second and First Centuries B.C. 2 vols. PhD diss., Princeton University.

Mommsen, A. 1866. "Delphische Archonten nach der Zeit geordnet. Nebst zwei Tabellen." *Philologus* 24: 1–48.

Oldfather, W.A. 1926. "Lokris." *RE* 13.1: 1135–1288.

Picard, O. 1984. "Monnaies." *Bulletin de Correspondance Hellénique Supplement* 9 (*L'Antre Corycien II*): 91–101.

Rousset, D. 2015. "Microfederalism in Central Greece: the Dorians and Oitaians." In H. Beck and P. Funke (eds.), *Federalism in Greek Antiquity.* Cambridge: 222–30.

Rzepka, J. 2006. *The Rights of Cities within the Aitolian Confederacy.* Valencia.

Rzepka, J. 2019. "Federal Imperialism: Aitolian Expansion between Protectorate, Merger and Partition." In Beck, Buraselis, and McAuley 2019: 167–74.

Sánchez, P. 2001. *L'Amphictionie des Pyles et de Delphes: Recherches sur son rôle historique, des origines au II. siècle de notre ère.* Stuttgart.

Scheu, F. 1960. "Coinage Systems of Aetolia." *Numismatic Chronicle* 20: 37–52.

Scholten, J. 2000. *The Politics of Plunder: Aitolians and Their Koinon in the Early Hellenistic Era, 279–217 B.C.* London.
Sordi, M. 1953. "Le origini del koinon etolico." *Acme* 6: 419–45 [= Scritti di Storia Greca, Milan 2002: 31–55].
Tsangari, D.I. 2007. *Corpus des monnaies d'or, d'argent et de bronze de la confédération étolienne.* Athens.
Walbank, F.W. 1981. *The Hellenistic World.* Brighton.

*With this chapter the geographic scope of the volume shifts from central Greece to the Peloponnese. It has long been noted that Sparta, although merely a regional wrangler for most of the Hellenistic period, continued to foster images of exceptional civic value – and to bolster corresponding claims for leadership. Elena Franchi takes readers to the reign of Kleomenes III (r. 235–222 BCE, cf. also chapter 10), his campaigns in the Argolid, and in particular those led against Argos, Sparta's long-time arch-rival in the Peloponnese. The Kleomenic War typically has a regional or panhellenic ring to it, depending on whether its narration is couched in ongoing quarrels with the Achaian League or in Sparta's unwillingness to yield to the rule of Macedon. Franchi's take, however, is that of the local perspective. She explores how events on the battlefield were inspired by and, in turn, translated back into a distinct local discourse environment in Sparta. Examining historical traditions as well as a diverse body of evidence, including coinage, epigraphy, and popular Spartan sayings (apophthegmata), Franchi identifies three major themes that impacted exchanges and agencies on the ground: enmity with Argos, the Spartan education and its believed supreme value, and the myth of Herakles. Kleomenes' actions in war, which culminated in the temporary but nonetheless unprecedented feat to take into possession a wide range of members of the Achaian League, were supplemented by a local discourse that paid due attention to these themes. Their prioritization in local conversations and voicing in various public media explains the longevity of Spartan worldviews in the Hellenistic Age. Moreover, this chapter offers an exemplary case study on the local paradigm and its capacity to further our understanding of localist self-fashioning in times of shifting power configurations in the world writ large.*

*Keywords: Kleomenes III, Thyreatis, Achaian League, Argos, Spartan education, Herakles*

# 9

# The Local Voice of Enmity: Kleomenes III, Sparta, and Argos*

ELENA FRANCHI

## Local Discourses on Global Issues: A Hellenistic King in Local Garb

While investigating the fortune of Kleomenes III (r. 235–222 BCE), I was struck by the fact that in early eighteenth-century England a tragedy by John Dryden entitled *Kleomenes the Spartan Hero* (1692) was banned. The ban was due to the drama's alleged Jacobite tendencies and to the fact that, at that time, sensitivity about exiled monarchs plotting their return to power was understandably high: King James had recently been deposed by a union of Parliamentarians who were troubled by his Catholicism and close ties with France (the so-called Glorious Revolution of 1688).[1] This ban implies that Dryden's audience perceived the analogy between the English king and Kleomenes III as natural, and thus dangerous. Indeed, in Dryden's drama, Kleomenes III was depicted as a monarch in every respect, and as one who ruled quite alone. This may seem obvious for Hellenistic times, yet it sounds odd in the Spartan context, where there has always been a diarchy. However, the drama refers to an aspect of this king and more generally of Hellenistic Spartan kings that is basically accurate: they acted as Hellenistic monarchs,[2] going more "global" than local. In fact, Spartan kings "universalized" their diarchy by transforming it into a monarchy (thus evoking the universal notion of Hellenistic monarchy).

The aim of this paper is to look for local issues in a global(ized) context. I do not intend to challenge the traditional view that Hellenistic Spartan kings acted as Hellenistic monarchs. Rather, to investigate how their global acts were translated into a local, Spartan discourse, which in turn acquired a new orientation from it. Kleomenes III's attitude towards Argos and, more generally, his actions against the Achaian League provide a good example in this regard.

## Global and Local on Spartan Coins:
## A Spartan Hero Following in the Footsteps of Herakles

Before analysing the specific case of Kleomenes III's attitude to Argos, it is useful to focus on a relevant (as explained below) and already well-studied case in which the interplay between global and local – that is, between universal trends and their translation into highly localized environments – was already evident in Hellenistic Sparta: Hellenistic Spartan coins. They demonstrate how Spartan Hellenistic kings, especially Areios, Kleomenes, and Nabis, not only adopted "the very same legitimacy-building behaviour practices employed by nascent Hellenistic monarchs,"[3] thus going global, but did so in the context of Spartan local traditions, striking a balance between global tendencies and local attitudes. The silver tetradrachms struck by Kleomenes[4] provide a fitting example (Grunauer-von Hoerschelmann t. 2, 3rd group, esp. no. 1): on the obverse, they show a diademed head looking to the right: the king. His youthful and idealizing physiognomy and the royal diadem (which had not been worn by Spartan kings in Classical times) are visual features associated with the ideology of Hellenistic monarchy[5] to the point that these coins are considered "imitations of Seleucid coins."[6] Kleomenes was the first Lakedaimonian king to place his own portrait on his coins, although he refrained from naming himself in the legend.

Yet the reverse of the same coins tells a different story. It shows the cult statue of a goddess wearing a Corinthian helmet, with a bow in her left hand and an arrow in her raised right hand, an animal-skin cape draped over her shoulders, and a stag at her left side. These are all attributes of Artemis (even if not exclusively);[7] the statue is flanked by the letters L-A, the abbreviated ethnic of the Lakedaimonian state. Susanne Grunauer-von Hoerschelmann links the representation of Artemis on this and other tetradrachms struck in Kleomenes' time with the cult of Artemis Orthia, worshipped at Sparta since Archaic times.[8]

The bronze coins minted by Kleomenes are another interesting case of translating a universal, and in this sense global, discourse, into a local discourse, with various mutual adaptations and reinterpretations. The head of a youthful Herakles in a lion-skin cap is struck on the obverse of several bronze coins minted 223–222 BCE; on the reverse side, there is a club flanked by the stars of the *dioskouroi*.[9] As Olga Palagia has noted, these are both symbols of Spartan royalty: the *dioskouroi* highlighted the traditional side of Spartan royalty, that is, diarchy, whereas Herakles symbolized the more

Hellenistic, "globalized" side, that is, monarchy.[10] Some scholars have suggested that the persistent appearance of Heraklean imagery on the coins of Hellenistic Lakedaimon is best interpreted as a conscious emulation of Alexander the Great, who also claimed Herakles as an ancestor, and thus maybe also as opposition to the Antigonids.[11] Other scholars have pointed out that the fact that Herakles was a hero of the Stoic philosophers may have suited Kleomenes III, who according to Plutarch was a pupil of the Stoic philosopher Sphairos.[12] Still others emphasize, instead, that Herakles was, together with Kyros, an ideal ruler according to the Cynic philosophers.[13] This, too, could have appealed to Kleomenes, since both Polybios and Plutarch, whose source is perhaps the third-century historian Phylarchos (*BNJ* 81), portrayed the Spartan king as a Cynic hero.[14] Admittedly, it is not possible to infer more about Kleomenes' spiritual preferences or about Stoic or Cynic connections with the Spartan revolution. Palagia has rightly shifted focus to the domestic context of Kleomenes' struggle with the other royal house of Sparta, which also claimed Heraklean ancestry:[15] this domestic, local meaning of Herakles mingled with a Hellenistic, global meaning, legitimized by its association with Alexander the Great, who himself deployed Heraklean imagery very effectively.[16] And that is not all. Some pieces of evidence suggest that there is a second local-domestic meaning, which possibly developed in Hellenistic Sparta. Indeed, if we follow Plutarch (and his source Phylarchos?), Herakles has special relevance with reference to Kleomenes. First, we read that the Spartan king was perceived by Aratos and other visitors to his court as the only descendant of Herakles (*Cleom.* 13.2), and that Aratos "would not consent that the man who was a descendant of Herakles and king of Sparta, and was seeking to bring back its ancient polity, now like a decadent melody, to that restrained and Dorian law and life which Lycurgus had instituted, should be entitled leader of Sikyon and Tritaia"[17] (*Cleom.*16.4): according to Plutarch (and Phylarchos?), Aratos perceived Kleomenes to be dangerous because of his ambition to extend his power over other Peloponnesian countries,[18] and this ambition was somehow linked with Kleomenes' desire to follow in the footsteps of Herakles.[19] Second, Plutarch also says that Tyrtaios was a good poet, who was able "to inflame the souls of young men" (*Cleom.* 2.3). We know that according to Tyrtaios (F 11.1–2 West), the Spartans are "the progeny of unconquered Herakles." In Tyrtaios' lines, the call to the Spartans leads to a description of the virtues for good order and military discipline in an army fighting for its fatherland. Even more interestingly, in the *Eunomia*, Tyrtaios states that "Cronus' son himself, Zeus the husband of fair-crowned Hera, had given this city to the children of Heracles" (Tyrt. F 2.12–14 West), and this, according to John Boardman, resonates with the way in which Herakles is represented in Lakonian art: as a warrior hero.[20] These sources seem to suggest that in Hellenistic Sparta, Herakles and his descendants are directly connected to the conquests of Sparta in the Peloponnese too. We encounter here a theme in Sparta's local discourse environment:[21] focused on Herakles, this theme played an ongoing, decisive role in local conversations, allowing the Spartans to align with their community through (also) Hellenistic themes of universal concern, reflecting agendas and traditions from a glorious past. Herakles' universal significance was by then well established, had been energized by the coins, and endorsed a local reading of Herakles and of Sparta's attitude towards its neighbours. Indeed, it is tempting to establish a connection between Herakles' local Spartan significance and Kleomenes III's campaign in the Peloponnese. In order to explore whether this connection is justified, we must shift our focus to the campaigns against Argos, for reasons that will soon be made clear.

## The Argive Side of the Kleomenic War

During the so-called Kleomenic War, Argos and the Argolid were often troubled by battles, meetings, and ravages. A quick glance at the attested moments of confrontation makes this clear:

| | | |
|---|---|---|
| 228 BCE | Aristomachos, tyrant of Argos, abdicates and joins the League.[22] | Polyb. 2.44 |
| 228 BCE | Kleomenes overruns the territory of Argolid and offers battle but Aratos forces Aristomachos to retire.[23] | Polyb. 2.47.4; Plut. *Cleom.* 4;[24] *Arat.* 35.7 |
| 225 BCE (early spring?) | Failed meeting between Kleomenes and Aratos in Argos or its surroundings.[25] | Plut. *Cleom.*17; *Arat.* 39 |
| 225 BCE (July) | Kleomenes gets possession of Kaphyai, Pellene, Pheneos, Argos, Phlious, Kleonai, Epidauros, Hermione, Troizen, and Corinth, while he personally commands a siege of Sikyon.[26] | Polyb. 2.52; Plut. *Cleom.* 17–19; *Arat.* 39 |
| 224 BCE | Aratos makes peace with the royal family of Macedonia.[27] | Polyb. 2.52 |
| (before May)[28] 224 BCE | The Achaians give Aristotle of Argos assistance when he heads an uprising against the Kleomenic faction; under the command of Timoxenos the Strategos, they surprise and seize Argos.[29] | Polyb. 2.53; Plut. *Cleom.* 20 |

| 224 BCE | Kleomenes draws back, attacks Argos; the Achaians offer gallant resistance.[30] | Polyb. 2.53; Plut. *Cleom.* 21; *Arat.* 44 |
| --- | --- | --- |
| 224 BCE | Kleomenes marches back to Sparta by way of Mantineia. | Polyb. 2.53 |
| 224 BCE | Antigonos enters Argos. | Polyb. 2.54 |
| 223 BCE | Antigonos ejects the garrisons from the posts that have been fortified by Kleomenes in the territories of Aigys and Belmina, and, putting those strongholds in the hands of the people of Megalopolis, goes to Aigion to attend the meeting of the Achaian league.[31] | Polyb. 2.54 |
| 223 BCE | Antigonos recovers Tegea. | Polyb. 2.54 |
| 223 BCE | Antigonos marches into Lakonia and harasses Kleomenes with skirmishes. | Polyb. 2.54 |
| 223 BCE | Antigonos captures Orchomenos, Mantineia, Heraia, Telphousa.[32] | Polyb. 2.54; Plut. *Cleom.* 44.1 |
| (autumn)[33] 223 BCE | Kleomenes captures Megalopolis and leads his soldiers "forth to Sellasia, as though he would ravage the territory of Argos, but from there he descended into the territory of Megalopolis" (*Cleom.* 23).[34] | Polyb. 2.55; Plut. *Cleom.* 23 |
| 223 or already 224 BCE | Aristomachos the Argive is killed by Antigonos and the League.[35] | Polyb. 2.59 |
| February–March 222 BCE[36] | Kleomenes collects his army and leads them into the Argive territory; here, he devastates the country | Polyb. 2.64; Plut. *Cleom.* 25[37] |
| | A little later, hearing that Antigonos had advanced to Tegea with the intent of invading Lakonia from that city, Kleomenes ravages the Argive plain again. Antigonos goes back to Argos, Kleomenes offers sacrifices to Hera, and then leads his army off to Phlious. | Plut. *Cleom.* 26 |

According to Plutarch's third-century sources, the Spartan armies were often engaged in Argos or in the Argolid.[38] Yet, even more interesting is what happened in July 225 (17.3–18.1): Kleomenes led his army to Argos while the Achaians were celebrating the Nemean games, thus terrifying the Argives, who therefore accepted a garrison, and agreed to become allies of the Lakedaimonians and made Kleomenes the chief in command: "This greatly increased the reputation and power of Kleomenes. For the ancient kings of Sparta, in spite of numerous efforts, were not able to secure the abiding allegiance of Argos" (18.1).[39] What is the background for this statement?

## The Old Enmity between Sparta and Argos

The background is the long enmity between Sparta and Argos over the eastern seaboard beyond the crest of the Parnon, that is, the region called Kynouria (or Thyreatis, the northern part of Kynouria).[40] I have reconstructed the main struggles between them according to ancient sources:

1. a battle under Echestratos (Paus. 3.2.2);
2. a battle under Prytanis (Paus. 3.7.2);
3. a battle under Labotas (Paus. 3.2.2);
4. a battle under Charillos (Paus. 3.7.3);
5. a battle under Nikandros (Paus. 3.7.4);
6. a battle under Alkamenes (Paus. 3.2.7);
7. a battle under Theopompos (Paus. 3.7.5);[41]
8. a battle at Hysiai (Paus. 2.24.7: 669 BCE? but the numeral of the date on the manuscript is corrupted);[42]
9. the Battle of the Champions, in the middle of the sixth century (Hdt. 1.81–3);
10. the Battle of Sepeia, at the end of the sixth century or at the beginning of the fifth century (Hdt. 6.75.81);[43]
11. Sparta and Argos also decided to address the ways in which it was or was not permitted to fight for Thyrea in the eve of the Battle of Mantineia in 418 (Thuc. 5.40–1);
12. Philip II ruled on the matter (Polyb. 9.28.7; Paus. 2.20.1);
13. an arbitration was still necessary in 163 (Polyb. 31.1.6–7).

The chronology of these early battles is evidently affected by mechanisms of reduplication and back-projection to the Archaic period of Classical and Hellenistic battles fought in Thyrea, which were admittedly numerous; some battles could even have been invented. The point here is that, according to a later source, Sparta and Argos fought several battles, which Sparta won in almost all cases, but no Spartan king was ever able to seize the city, as

Kleomenes III did. This must have had an impact on a local level, in Spartan imagery, on Spartan minds.

## "Thyrea, o Zeus, belongs to the Lakedaimonians": Thyrea and Hellenistic Audiences

It is tempting to suggest that Plutarch, and/or his source, put Kleomenes III's campaigning against Argos, which had regional and even global significance (cf. the involvement of the Aitolians, Ptolemy, and Antigonos) as he was well aware, into a local perspective. There can be no doubt about the fact that, according to ancient sources, the regional struggle between Argos and Sparta over Kynouria had a local impact in Sparta, an impact which persisted from the Archaic to the Roman period. As will be shown below, the ancients believed that the Spartans celebrated those who fell in these battles during their festivals; they are supposed to have changed their hairstyles after a victory in one of these battles (the Battle of the Champions), and to have regarded their Argive enemies as trainers of their youth. The traditional enmity between Argos and Sparta is also a leitmotif in Hellenistic literature.

Our first point relates to the so-called Doric epigrams. As is well known, new poetic trends developed in the third century BCE, inspiring a return to Dorism. Sparta and her victories are the main topics of epigrams by Dioskorides, Nikandros, Damagetos, and Chairemon, as well as by the author of an epigram traditionally attributed to Simonides.[44] These epigrams all have anti-Macedonian and pro-Spartan undertones, and most of them refer to the so-called Battle of the 300 Champions (only the most relevant lines are quoted below):

Chairemon (*Anth. Pal.* 7.721.1–2): "We from Sparta engaged the Argives equal in number and in arms, Thyrea being the prize of the spear." (adapted by A. Smith from Loeb 1917)
Pseudo-Simonides (*Anth. Pal.* 7.431.1–6): "We the three hundred, O Spartan fatherland, fighting for Thyrea with as many Argives, never turning our necks, died there where we first planted our feet. The shield, covered with the brave blood of Othryadas, proclaims 'Thyrea, O Zeus, belongs to the Lacedemonians.'" (adapted by A. Smith from Loeb 1917)
Dioskorides (*Anth. Pal.* 7.430): "Who hung the newly-stripped arms on this oak? By whom is the Dorian shield inscribed? For this land of Thyrea is soaked with the blood of champions and we are the only two left of the Argives. Seek out every fallen corpse, let any left alive illuminate Sparta in spurious glory. Nay! stay your steps, for here on the shield, the victory of the Spartans is announced by the clots

of Othryadas' blood, and he who wrought this still gasps hard by.
O Zeus, our ancestor, look with loathing on those tokens of a victory
that was not won."
Damagetos (*Anth. Pal.* 7.432): "O Spartans, the tomb holds your martial
Gyllis who fell for Thyrea. He killed three Argives, and exclaimed, 'Let
me die having wrought a deed worthy of Sparta.'" (adapted by A. Smith
from Loeb 1917)

The regional conflicts between Argos and Sparta, and their local impacts, are
constantly emphasized in these epigrams, which in Hellenistic times fostered
the memory of an Archaic battle and enmity. This enmity was also often
recalled in the *apophthegmata lakōnika*, the so-called sayings of the Spartans. They are anonymous and were collected by Plutarch, who also quoted
them in some of his other writings. Tigerstedt has convincingly argued that
these collections date back to the Hellenistic period, most probably to the
third century;[45] indeed, they strongly resonate with other Lakonian writings
of the same period. Several of these sayings precisely refer to the enmity
between Sparta and Argos:

- "In answer to the Argives, who were disputing with the Spartans in
  regard to the boundaries of their land and said that they had the better
  of the case, he drew his sword and said, 'He who is master of this talks
  best about boundaries of land.'" (226C [Lysander])
- "The Argives, after the battle of the three hundred, were again overcome, with all their forces, in a set battle, and the allies urged Polydoros
  not to let slip the opportunity, but to make a descent upon the enemy's
  wall and capture their city; for this, they said, would be very easy, since
  the men had been destroyed and the women only were left. He said
  in answer to them, 'To my mind it is not honourable, when fighting
  on even terms, to conquer our opponents, but, after having fought to
  settle the boundaries of the country, to desire to capture the city I do
  not regard as just; for I came to recapture territory and not to capture a
  city.'" (231E [Polydoros])
- "When someone said, 'Why have you not killed off the people of Argos
  who wage war against you so often?' he said, 'Oh, we would not kill
  them off, for we want to have some trainers for our young men.'" (224B
  [Kleomenes, son of Anassandridas])

This is what Hellenistic audiences were familiar with. The last saying is particularly interesting because it also hints at a link between the wars between
Argos and Sparta and the education of the Spartan youth, a point which will

be addressed again below. In any case, all the cited sayings, as well as other sayings,[46] repeatedly underline the relevance of this enmity.

One may object that the evidence cited so far is representative of an etic point of view, , that is, an external rather than an internal, Spartan, emic point of view, and thus implies strategies of stereotyping and othering:[47] neither Chairemon nor Dioskorides are Lakonian, and Philippe-Ernest Legrand's arguments for Damagetos' Spartan origins are not decisive.[48] Yet, we have also evidence of the emic relevance of this enmity: Sosibios, who was, in fact, a native Lakonian scholar most probably living in the third or the second century BCE, "the first home-grown antiquary and local historian."[49] According to him (*FGrH* 595 F 5 ap. Ath.15.678b), the leaders of the choruses staged during the festival, which also involved the *Gymnopaidiai*, wore crowns, called *thyreatikoi*, in commemoration of the victory at Thyrea. In Hellenistic Sparta, choruses still sang songs for the fallen in the battles opposing Spartans and Argives.[50] At least once a year, then, Spartans were reminded of their bitter enemies, the Argives, and these memories were magnified through sound, building a specific local soundscape.[51] As Sheila Ager has stressed, emotions played a significant role in structuring polities, and "continuing Spartan attachment to territories that were long lost to it was evenly matched by the enduring memories of neighbours who had suffered in the centuries of Spartan supremacy."[52] It is difficult to imagine that, in turn, local and emotional Spartan memories about the old enmity between Argos and Sparta had no influence on Hellenistic Sparta's politics. In fact, it seems very likely that they form part of another prominent theme in local conversations, focused on the enmity between Sparta and Argos. This theme endorsed a very local meaning of Kleomenes' campaigns against Argos, which, in reality, had mostly regional and global meaning.

It is in this context, then, that Plutarch's statement "For the ancient kings of Sparta, in spite of numerous efforts, were not able to secure the abiding allegiance of Argos" acquires its full meaning: it is fuelled by the local theme focused on the enmity between Argos and Sparta. This leads us to further explore the connection between this theme and Kleomenes III's attitude towards Argos.

## A Spartan King, Kleomenes III, the New Herakles, Finally Conquers Argos

It is well known that for *The Life of Kleomenes*, Plutarch mainly relied on three third-century sources: the *Memories*, by Aratos and Phylarchos; and Polybios, writing in the following century.[53] Aratos is famously the leader of the Achaian League. He wrote a work known as *Hypomnēmata*,[54] which is no longer extant but provided an important source for Polybios' work and for Plutarch's *Life of Aratos* and *Life* of *Kleomenes*. Scholars specializing in Aratos, Polybios and Plutarch extensively explored his pro-Achaian, anti-Kleomenean arguments.[55] By contrast, Phylarchos, a third-century historian whose origin is uncertain,[56] was quite dazzled by the Spartan mirage.[57] He is also our main source for third-century Spartan history. While his works are unfortunately lost, they were often cited by Polybios and Plutarch, especially in his *Life of Kleomenes*. Polybios dismissed Phylarchos as untrustworthy (2.56.1–2),[58] yet uses him when his main source, Aratos, is not helpful; as for Plutarch, he states that Phylarchos is trustworthy only where he does not contradict Aratos. What is certain is that Phylarchos' account is anti-Achaian and pro-Spartan, and dramatizing: the passage in which Polybios deplores Phylarchos "tragic" narrative is well known.[59] My point here, however, is that Phylarchos' account is not only dramatic, but also localizing.[60]

Indeed, Plutarch's statement about Kleomenes' seizure of Argos ("For the ancient kings of Sparta, in spite of numerous efforts, were not able to secure the abiding allegiance of Argos": see above, p. 222) is found in chapter 18. There are various reasons to believe that this chapter depended almost entirely on Phylarchos. Note the striking differences from Polybios' account of these same events, several references to Spartan public discourse, and the chapter's clearly pro-Kleomenean flavour.[61] Chapter 26 is even more interesting in this regard. It describes a second invasion of the Argolid and depends for the most part on Phylarchos, as a comparison with F 57 on a special kind of sword, the ῥομφαία, reveals.[62]

Some scholars have suggested that the second invasion of the Argolid described in chapter 26 – when Kleomenes learning that Antigonos had come to Tegea with the intent of invading Lakonia from that city, ravages the Argive plain again (see above, p. 221) – is a sort of reduplication of the first invasion of the Argolid, described in chapter 25, when Kleomenes led his army into the Argive territory and devastated the country (see above, p. 221). Plutarch would have used Aratos as a source in chapter 25, and Phylarchos in the following chapter, without noticing that he has described the same invasion twice.[63] One has to admit that Polybios (2.64) describes only one invasion, that some details of the two described by Plutarch are the same, and that wonderful details are described in both texts. There is no doubt that the narration of the second invasion has a romanticized flavour, as two very curious episodes show.

The first episode concerns the already cited behaviour of Kleomenes' soldiers in the Argive plain (26.1): they ravaged the plain and destroyed the grain, "not cutting this down, as usual, with sickles and knives, but beating it down with great pieces of wood fashioned like spear-shafts. These his soldiers plied as if in sport, while passing by, and with no effort at all they would crush and ruin all the crop." In commenting on this passage, Phylarchos' tendency to stress the folkloristic aspects of this campaign are usually singled out. However, there is more. The expression which is usually translated as "as if in sport" is ἐπὶ παιδιᾷ in Greek. In other passages, it means "in jest," especially when used together with ἐπὶ γέλωτι; but the translators are right in considering "in jest" to be inappropriate here. However, even if "as if in sport" is the best possible translation, it is not completely accurate either. Indeed, it is worth noticing that, together with the adjectives μαχητικὸς and ἐριστικὸς, παιδιὰ means "competitive amusements," as for instance, ball games called σφαιρίσεις (Arist. *Rhet.* 1370b–71a),[64] and that the root 'παῖς' of the word παιδιᾷ used to describe the action of Kleomenes III's soldiers is very frequent in Hellenistic terms for cohorts of youth undergoing Spartan education: προπαίδες, πρατοπαμπαίδες and ἀτροπαμπαίδες cited by several inscriptions are the Spartan teenagers going through contests, mock battles, and games in order to become Spartiates.[65] The background of our ἐπὶ παιδιᾷ is an interplay of sport, play, and education which is typical of Sparta: it is very local, and provides a third theme foundational to the local discourse environment in Sparta, focused on education. This is not to imply that there was in reality a connection between Kleomenes' behaviour and the Spartan education, that is, between Kleomenes regional policy and a local practice, but rather that they were represented as being connected. Yet, we have to admit that putting representations of Artemis (maybe Orthia) on his silver tetradachms suggests a link between the Spartan education and Kleomenes' aspirations, which was also perceived at a local level and maybe promoted in Spartan public discourse.

This makes even more sense if we think of other passages (especially, 18.2–3) in which Phylarchos draws a close connection between Kleomenes' reform of the Spartan education and his military success in conquering the Peloponnese.[66] In chapter 18, after having stated that Kleomenes III was the first Spartan king who managed to seize Argos, Plutarch, and most probably Phylarchos, stressed that this depended on his reforms: "they had as yet barely resumed their native customs and re-entered the track of their famous discipline, when, as if before the very eyes of Lycurgus and with his cooperation, they gave abundant proof of their valour and obedience to authority, by recovering the leadership of Hellas for Sparta and making all Peloponnesus their own again." This resonates with the already mentioned saying attributed to Kleomenes, son of Anassandridas (224B: see above, p. 224), and thus with our local theme focused on the enmity between Argos and Sparta. He is the same Kleomenes who defeated the Argives in Sepeia at the beginning of the fifth century, managed to enter Argos but not to seize it,[67] and then went to the temple of Hera to sacrifice. Here, however – our source is Herodotus – the priest forbade him, saying that it was not holy for a stranger to sacrifice there. The story is well known: Kleomenes I ordered the helots to carry the priest away from the altar and whip him, and then performed the sacrifice. And it was this sacrifice that prevented him from seizing Argos: indeed, he tells the Spartans, who ask why he did not conquer the city after having defeated the Argives, that

when he was taking omens in Hera's temple a flame of fire had shone forth from the breast of the image, and so he learned the truth of the matter, that he would not take Argos. If the flame had come out of the head of the image, he would have taken the city from head to foot utterly; but its coming from the breast signified that he had done as much as the god willed to happen. (Hdt. 6.82; to compare with Plut. *Cleom.* 26.2–3 [Phylarchos])

Is it a mere coincidence that, according to Phylarchos, Kleomenes III is said to have seized Argos, but then, after having lost it, tried to conquer the city again and sent heralds to the king demanding the keys to Hera's temple, that he might offer sacrifice to the goddess before he went away? And that he sacrificed to the goddess under the walls of the temple because it was closed?[68]

It seems that Phylarchos refashioned Kleomenes' deeds in the Argive plain by mixing various elements and themes, and also by drawing inspiration from the deeds performed against Argos by Kleomenes I. Indeed, Kleomenes III's campaigning against Argos in the context of opposition to the Achaian League and the Macedonians is put on an equal footing with Kleomenes I's fifth-century campaign against Argos in his attempt to conquer the Peloponnese, a conquest whose meaning went well beyond the conflict for Thyrea but which ended up being considered in the same local theme as Thyrea. I am not suggesting that Kleomenes III's role in the Peloponnese does not have mostly global meaning in terms of relations between the Achaian League, the Macedonians and the Aitolians. Instead, I am arguing that this global meaning was translated into a local one by drawing on a local theme focused on the enmity between Argos and Sparta. The latter was a regional affair, which always had a strictly local meaning, as Sosibios' passage about Spartan choruses singing for the fallen in Thyrea testifies. A regional war having a global meaning was thus translated in order to give it *glocal* relevance, both global and local.[69] Moreover, the global and the local interweave: Sparta's enmity against Argos in the context of the Kleomenic war was perceived in the context of this traditional enmity having local relevance, which, in turn, conferred renewed vigour: Argos was finally conquered! Phylarchos himself provides evidence for a connection between this glocalizing discourse in Kleomenes' campaign in Argolid and the local theme focused on the enmity between Argos and Sparta, since he represents what may simply have been a shift of allegiance by Argos (*Arat.* 9.4) as a conquest (*Cleom.* 18.1).[70]

This glocalizing discourse on Kleomenes' campaign in Argolid also seems to be connected to Plutarch's statement about Kleomenes behaving like a new Herakles, and thus with the discourse on Herakles. I already mentioned that Kleomenes struck Herakles on the coins and that Phylarchos considered him to be a new Herakles. We also noted that Phylarchos related Kleomenes' ambition to extend his power to other Peloponnesian countries to Kleomenes' intention to follow in the footsteps of Herakles.[71] Furthermore, it is well known that in Hellenistic and Roman times, old quarrels over disputed regions in the Peloponnese were solved by bringing into play the alleged division by the Herakleidai, the descendants of Herakles: according to Tacitus (*Ann.* 4.43.1-3=Ager no. 50), during a hearing given to embassies from the Lakedaimonians and Messenians on the question of the temple of Diana in the Marshes, the Messenians alleged that in the ancient division of the Peloponnese among the Herakleidai, the Dentheliatis (where the temple stood) had fallen to their king.[72] And in an inscription dating back to a period after 163, and referring to an arbitration between the Achaian League and Sparta over Sparta's dispute with Megalopolis (*Syll.* 665=Ager 1996, no. 137), the peoples of Aigytis and Skiritis claim to have been Arkadians since the return of the Herakleidai. Indeed, according to the myth of the Return of the Herakleidai, in the third generation after the unsuccessful invasion by Hyllos, son of Herakles, the Herakleidai Temenos, Aristodemos, and Kresphontes managed to return to the Peloponnese: the Argolid was assigned to Temenos, Messenia to Kresphontes, and Lakonia to Aristodemos' sons, Eurysthenes and Prokles, ancestors of Agiad and of the Europontid lines.[73] That this myth was also used with reference to the enmity between Argos and Sparta seems very likely, since it was recalled before Mantineia in 418,[74] and since the Spartan king's genealogies stress descendance from Herakles by concealing his descent from the Argive Perseus.[75] What's more, according to Pausanias (2.20.1), Philip II handed the Thyreatis over to the Argives, thus forcing the Spartans to respect the *originally* established boundaries (ἐπὶ τοῖς καθεστηκόσιν ἐξ ἀρχῆς ὅροις τῆς χώρας), most likely those defined by the tripartition.[76] In this respect, Marcel Piérart and Nino Luraghi recall a work by Aristotle significantly entitled *The Claims of the Greek Cities* and a passage from the *Life of Aristotle* (*Vita Aristotelis Marciana* 28–32 Gigon) which claims that Philip used this work to resolve border disputes between Greeks in the Peloponnese. One is tempted to think that the tripartition, which became increasingly important in Peloponnesian politics, especially from the fourth century BCE onwards, was the regulating principle in Philip's intervention.[77]

So, if Sparta's enemies in the Peloponnese (and maybe Sparta itself) often called upon the alleged ancient division of the Peloponnese among the Herakleidai, it is easy to imagine that those on the Spartan side, Sparta's admirers and, perhaps, even the Spartans themselves, kept on stressing that the Spartan kings' lineage went back to Herakles and not to one of the Herakleidai, thus also going beyond (and further developing) the well-known domestic perspective in which Heraklid genealogy was used to separate them from the common Spartiates. This would legitimate Sparta's ambitions for the whole Peloponnese – and not only the part assigned to Eurysthenes and Prokles. It is as if the Herakleidai would have returned to the Peloponnese again to definitively defeat the other descendants of the Herakleidai and thus recover their power over all the lands once conquered by the descendants of Herakles.[78] Indeed, before being Dorian, Herakles was an Achaian hero. This was never a problem for Spartan kings, who could claim to be either Dorian or Achaian, depending on which aspect of their background they wished to emphasize. I'm wondering if our Kleomenes is hinting at both the Dorian and the Achaian Herakles, thus expressing his ambition for the whole Peloponnese, including Achaia. That would justify Aratos' fears and his resulting manipulations, as noted above (Plut. *Cleom.*16.4). But maybe this is too daring.

The following remarks, developed in the preceding paragraphs, build instead on more solid foundations: as stressed above,[79] evidence allows us to trace local conversations centred on Herakles, its domestic function and its meaning against Sparta's neighbours. It is a glocalizing discourse which certainly spread (and was even fuelled) outside Sparta, as Phylarchos and the *Life of Kleomenes* (13.2) show, but whose origin is local (cf. our bronze coins) and therefore gives voice to a local regime of truth. Other pieces of evidence discussed above point to a further theme in Sparta's local discourse environment focused on the enmity between Argos and Sparta. This is a glocalizing discourse, too, which spread (and was even fuelled) outside Sparta, as the analysed epigrams, *apophthegmata*, and Phylarchos show, but whose origin is local (Sosibios' passage). Finally, we have a theme which connects the enmity between Argos and Sparta with the Spartan education and its reforms (see above: *apophthegmata* and, again, Phylarchos) and has a local basis too (the inscriptions, and maybe the silver tetradachms with Artemis [Orthia?]). By drawing on these locally prevalent themes, Phylarchos refashioned Kleomenes III's deeds in the Peloponnese, glocalizing them through their connection with Herakles, the old enmity with Argos, and the Spartan education. Furthermore, he was also inspired by Kleomenes I's deeds against Argos, that in turn form part of the theme of enmity between Argos and Sparta. And there is more. These localizing features having a local basis penetrated Peloponnesian public discourse, as the debate about Kleomenes' contending the Achaians' league leadership prove:[80]

For Aratus … in the first place tried to force the Achaians aside and hinder their purpose; but when they paid no heed to him in their consternation at the daring spirit of Cleomenes, but actually saw justice in the demands of the Lacedaemonians, who were seeking to restore the Peloponnesus to its ancient status, [3] Aratus took a step which would have been unmeet for any Greek to take, but was most shameful for him and most unworthy of his career as soldier and statesman. For he invited Antigonus into Greece and filled the Peloponnesus with Macedonians, whom he himself had driven out of Peloponnesus when, as a young man, he delivered Acrocorinthus from their power … [4] … but he would not consent that the man who was a descendant of Heracles and king of Sparta, and was seeking to bring its ancient polity, now like a decadent moody, back again to that restrained and Dorian law and life which Lycurgus had instituted, should be entitled leader of Sicyon and Tritaea. (*Cleom.* 16.1–4)

We have already commented on the last sentence of this paragraph. The context of this sentence is even more interesting. It allows us to connect and interpret the three themes of the local discourse environment in Sparta that we have examined so far in the light of the Macedonian factor. Aratos invites Antigonos to Greece to avoid delivering the Peloponnese into the hands of the king of Sparta, who is guilty of being Dorian but descended from an Achaian hero (Herakles). The passage exemplifies the circularity between local and global that we have repeatedly noted in this essay. On the one hand, the king of Sparta behaves like a Hellenistic monarch. On the other hand, his deeds are interpreted in a strictly local key, both by himself and by his enemies, who once again underline the global relevance of such deeds: bringing Antigonos to the Peloponnese, and giving the local voice of enmity a global echo.

## NOTES

* I would like to express my gratitude to Hans Beck and the referees for the observations that have allowed me to improve a first draft of this article; any remaining mistakes are to be attributed to the author. All translations are from Loeb Classical Library Editions unless otherwise noted.
1 Cf. Africa 1961: 38; Bywaters 1991: 93–4; Schille 2004: 3; West 2018: 170–1.
2 On the autocratization of the Spartan diarchy: Millender 2009; Gehrke 2013: 78, n. 29; Luraghi 2013b: 17, 21; Walthall 2013 ("charismatic monarchy").

3 Walthall 2013: 130.

4 It is now widely acknowledged that the portraits struck on these coins are
of Kleomenes. Ferdinand Bompois (1870) tried to identify them as portraits
of Doson who, according to Plutarch (*Cleom.* 30), stayed in Sparta for three
days; it is, however, unlikely that in only three days Antigonos, whose portrait
appears on no coins whatsoever (see Merker 1960), would have minted coins,
without his name inscribed on them: Grunauer-von Hoerschelmann 1978: 9. On
the other hand, Kleomenes' money sources are well documented: Polyb. 2.51.2;
62.1; Plut. *Cleom.* 1; 6.1.

5 Münzkabinett, Staatliche Museen zu Berlin, 18200217, with comment by
Walthall 2013: 144–5. See also Grunauer-von Hoerschelmann 1978: 7–16 (with
previous bibliography); Mørkholm 1991: 149, n. 505.

6 Seltman 1933: 256; Rostovtzeff 1941: 1356 (with n. 51).

7 Artemis is often armed (Paus. 4.13.1; Marinatos 2000: 110–29; Zink Kaasgaard
Fab 2009: 137 (in the temple of Orthia); Léger 2017: 118; 125; 170); uses a bow
(Hom. *Il.* 21.479–92; see Bruns 1929: 29, 37, 42–51; and, more recently and
with previous bibliography, Marinatos 2000: 97; Zink Kaasgaard Fab 2009: 145;
Poulsen 2009: 407; 414; Léger 2017: 118; 125; 170); and wears an animal-skin
cape (Alcm. F 51 Garzya; on the *aigis*, see Zink Kaasgaard Fab 2009: 135 (in the
temple of Orthia); Léger 2017: 118; 125; 170).

8 Indeed, we have evidence proving that the Temple of Artemis Orthia (Orthia
became an epithet of Artemis in the fifth century at the latest: Zink Kaasgaard
Falb 2009: 145 commenting on an inscription: *AM* 49 1924: 15–16), which was
built at the beginning of the seventh century BCE in a natural basin between
Limnai and the west bank of the Eurotas River, was rebuilt in a period after the
first half of the third century BCE, i.e., in Kleomenes' times: Dawkins 1929:
32–3, and, more recently, Zink Kaasgaard Falb 2009: 127–32 with previous
bibliography. Grunauer-von Hoerschelmann notes that on Kleomenes' coins
Artemis' dress is bound with a plant, perhaps a *lygos* (most probably *agnus
castus*), and therefore reminds us of Pausanias' description of the alleged oldest
image of Artemis in Lakonia: an aniconic xoanon which bears both the words
Ortheia and Lygodesma, and is bound with *lygos* (3.16.7; on Lygodesma see Des
Bouvrie 2009: 155 discussing previous bibliography). Maybe these arguments
are not strong enough, yet one has to admit that what Pausanias describes in
the following chapters (3.16.9–11) – that is the ritual flogging of the teenagers
known as the *diamastigōsis* – is strictly linked to Artemis Orthia's cult, and
constitutes an important step of the Spartan education (see, however, the recent
remarks of Spawforth in Cartledge and Spawforth 1989: 207; Kennell 1995: 111;
and Powell 2018b: 21 on the possible evolution of this ritual), which in turn,
according to Plutarch, was reorganized by Kleomenes, supported by Sphairos of
Borysthenes (cf. Plut. *Cleom.* 2.2; 11.2; see below, n. 12).

9 Grunauer-von Hoerschelmann 1978: pl. 4, group VI.

10 2006: 208. Cf. with Plut. *Cleom.* 11.4, where *monarchia* is stressed, with comment by Marasco (1981: 453), who also emphasizes (461) how Spartan kings are often described as Herakles: see Plut. *Lyc.* 30.2. Cf. also Karwiese 1980 (association Lysander-Herakles) and, recently, Pagkalos 2015 with previous bibliography.

11 In fact, among Kleomenes' contemporaries, only his ally Ptolemy III Euergetes claimed to be descendant of Herakles; see, however, Theoc. *Id.* 17.26; *OGIS* 54; Huttner 1997, 124–9: the Antigonids will assume a Heraklean persona under Philip V (221–179 BCE; see *AP* 6.114; 115; 116 with comment by Edson (1934), who in turn aimed to reconnect with both Philip II and Alexander by claiming descendance from Herakles (Isoc. *Phil.* 76, 109–10; 111–16; 132 with comment by Gabba 1957: 52); this could imply that later sources (excepting Phylarchos and Aratos) stressed Kleomenes' descendance from Herakles in opposition to the Macedonians: Edson 1934; Gabba 1957: 51–2; Marasco 1981 I: 462; Huttner 1997: 166–74.

12 Plut. *Cleom.* 11.2; Ollier 1943: 76–123; Gabba 1957: 48, 52 (Gabba, however, is cautious and notes that Sphairos could have been writing at a later date); Shimron 1972: 33; Palagia 2006: 208; and, more generally, Flower 2002: 198, Michalopoulos 2016: 19, 33, 154–6 with previous bibliography, and Figueira 2016: 18, 20, 22, 26, 38. On Kleomenes III and stoic philosophy, see Erskine 1990: 123–49 and Figueira 2016: 41 (denying this connection); on Herakles as a stoic sage, see Sen. *Const.* 2.1; Herakl. All. 33.1. Sphairos is cited twice in the *Life of Kleomenes*: 2.2 (where Sphairos is said to have been in Sparta when Kleomenes was young) and 11.4 (here Plutarch says that Sphairos participated in organizing Kleomenes' reforms) and once in the *Life of Lycurgus* (5.12).

13 Diog. Laert. 6.2: Africa 1961: 17–19.

14 Polyb. 5.39.6; Plut. *Cleom.* 1.3 (Phylarchos: Gabba 1957, 35; Marasco ad l.); 13.2 (Phylarchos: Marasco ad l.); see also Athen. 4.142C–F with Hoistad 1948: 22–49; 103–49; Africa 1959; 1960: 266; 1961: 17–20. On Phylarchos more generally, see below, pp. 226–9.

15 Palagia 2006: 208. On this domestic function of the Heraklid descendance of the Spartan kings, see esp. Tyrt. F 2 West[2] with comment in Van Wees 1999: 2 and Luraghi 2008: 51–2 n. 18 (with further sources).

16 Stafford 2012: chap. 5 (with further lit. at p. 268). See also above, n. 12.

17 Cf. also 31.2 (εἰ γὰρ οὐκ αἰσχρόν ἐστι δουλεύειν τοῖς ἀπὸ Φιλίππου καὶ Ἀλεξάνδρου τοὺς ἀφ᾽ Ἡρακλέους; "For if it is not shameful that the descendants of Herakles should be in subjection to the successors of Philip and Alexander"; *Arat.* 38.5 (in *BNJ* 231 [Aratos] F 4a, but the detail of Kleomenes descending from Herakles depends on Phylarchos: see Schulz 1886, ad l. [non vidi]; Porter 1979: xviii; Landucci 2017: ad l.): εἰ δὲ Κλεομένης ἦν – λεγέσθω γὰρ οὕτως-

παράνομος καὶ τυραννικός, ἀλλ' Ἡρακλεῖδαι πατέρες αὐτῷ καὶ Σπάρτη πατρίς;
"And if Cleomenes was, as must be granted, lawless and arbitrary, still, the
Heracleidae were his ancestors, and Sparta was his native land." (In this regard,
it is interesting to note along with Hans Beck that the source for the extant
details in *BNJ* 231 F 4b, that is, *Cleom*. 16.3–5, is Aratos, who cannot accept
Kleomenes' rule over the Peloponnese exactly because he is a descendant
of Herakles, and thus not an Achaian, at least according to the later Dorian
interpretation: see Burkert 1982: 79, 97.) Cf. *ultra* Polyb.5.39; Plut. *Cleom*. 1.3,
with comments by Orsi in Manfredini, Orsi, and Antelami 2000: 234–5 and
Kralli 2017: 243.

18  On this ambition, see Shipley 2017; 2018, esp. 31–7, 68 (commenting on Polyb.
9.29.10) with previous bibliography; Ager 2019, esp. 179–80.

19  One might wonder if Aratos, in this case, intentionally repressed Herakles'
Achaian identity (see below, p. 230), precisely because it would legitimize his
ambitions in the territories controlled by the Achaian League. No Dorian king,
even if descended from Herakles, could aspire to Sikyon and Trytaia, precisely
because of being Dorian (and not Achaian – even if Herakles was an Achaian
hero). Hence, the intentional silence of Aratos. More on that below, p. 230.

20  On Herakles in Lakonian art, see Boardman 1992 commenting on Pipili 1987,
no. 1: dressed in full armour; no. 2: as a warrior with a shield and spear; no. 24
and 25 with a corselet (cf. Paus. 3.15.3: at Sparta, there was a statue of *Herakles
hoplismenos*). He was never shown wearing a helmet, and this would explain
why he is not portrayed with a helmet on coins. See also Stafford 2012: 139–41
with previous bibliography.

21  On the local discourse environment, see Beck 2018, esp. 31, and in this volume: chapter 1.

22  Shimron 1972: 36. On Aristomachos see Walbank ad l., and, more recently,
Kralli 2017: 235 and Shipley 2018: 113–15.

23  Michalopoulos 2016: 25; Stewart 2018: 393.

24  This passage probably relies on Phylarchos (as the whole of chapter 4: only
the statement about Kleomenes' *tolma* relies on Aratos or Polybios). See also
Shimron 1972: 30; Porter 1979: lxvii; Marasco ad l.

25  See Oliva 1968: 181; Porter 1979: lxxxvii; and, more recently, Kralli 2017: 239
with previous bibliography.

26  Oliva 1968: 181; Shimron 1972: 35; Porter 1979: lxxxi; Michalopoulos 2016: 44;
Kralli 2017: 230–1; 240–5; Stewart 2018: 394.

27  Gabba 1957: 13.

28  Ferrabino 1921: 268; Porter 1979: lxxix n. 45; Walbank 1933: 172; 1957: 254.

29  Oliva 1968: 182–3; Porter 1979: lxxvii; lxxxiii; McCaslin 1985–6: 93; Kralli 2017:
233.

30  *Cleom*. 21 depends on Phylarchos (see Marasco ad l.), who stresses the loss of
Argos by Kleomenes to emphasize his courage.

31  Porter 1979: lxxxv; Michalopoulos 2016: 43; Kralli 2017: 245–7; Shipley 2018: 69; Stewart 2018: 394.

32  Shipley 2018: 69.

33  Walbank ad l.

34  Kralli 2017: 245–8.

35  Gabba 1957: 10; Africa 1961: 30; McCaslin 1985–6: 93–8; Eckstein 2013: 322.

36  Walbank ad l.

37  Here Plutarch depends on Polybios (cited at 25.4); cf. with Polyb. 2.64.2: see Marasco ad l.

38  Tomlinson 1972: 158–60; Cartledge in Cartledge and Spawforth 1989: 49–56; Michalopoulos 2016: 43–5; 50–3; Shipley 2018: 69.

39  See Oliva 1968: 181; Porter 1979: lxxi, lxxviii-ix. According to Marasco (ad l.), the main source for chapter 17 is Aratos, who is cited at par. 4, but par. 1 on the conditions for entering Argos are from Phylarchos. Phylarchos is also the source for the following chapter (18.1–4), which can be compared with *Arat.* 39.4, where it is said the Argives came over to Kleomenes: this should lead us to wonder if this was simply a voluntary shift of allegiance (Kralli 2017: 232) which was represented as conquest by Phylarchos (see below, p. 229).

40  Shipley 2004: 571.

41  For the the chronological problems of these battles (or, rather, of the kings under whom they were to be fought), see Beloch 1912: 191; Carlier 1984: 316–24; Calame 1987; Musti in Musti-Torelli 1991: 171f; Nafissi 1991: index; Vannicelli 1993: 43–5; Meier 1998: 96; Richer 1998: chap. 7; De Vido 2001: 209–27; Meier 2006; Welwei 2006; Christesen 2007: app. 13 (pp. 55–7); Pirenne-Delforge 2008: 47–54.

42  See, recently, Trundle 2017: 145–4; Franchi 2018: n. 7.

43  On the chronology of this battle see, recently, Bultrighini 2016: 109–14; Franchi forthcoming, chap. 4.

44  Damagetos and Dioskorides are active in the second half of the third century (Cusset 2022; Prioux 2022, both with bibliography and discussion); Nikandros (*Anth. Pal.* 7.526) is most likely the grandfather of the homonymous author of the *Thēriaka* and is usually believed to have been active in the third century (Gow and Schofield 1953: 4; see also Argentieri 2007: 153; Fantuzzi 2007: 493–5). The dating of Chairemon is uncertain (Hellenistic Age? See Gow and Page 1965: 220). *Anth. Pal.* 7.431 is among the epigrams attributed by the ancients to Simonides, whose attribution is, however, uncertain (see Bravi 2006: 89; Bing and Bruss 2007: 129).

45  1974: 16–30.

46  223A–C; 223F; 229C; 231E; 233B–C. Cf. ultra Plut. *Ages*. 31.8.

47  Beck 2018: 16 with further bibliography.

48  1901: 187–9 (*contra* Gow and Page 1965: 224): Legrand notes that the heroes praised in his epigrams were all from countries allied with the Aitolians; since

Eleians and Spartans are given particularly emphasis, he must have been from Elis or Lakonia. On Chairemon, see Gow and Page 1965: 220; Degani 2009a; on Dioskorides: Gow and Page 1965: 235–6; Degani 2009b.

49  Cartledge 2002: 46; Figueira 2016: 18, 48–82. This does not imply that before Sosibios local memories were not recorded and elaborated: Tober 2010.

50  See Richer 2012: 389–410; Franchi 2018 with bibliography.

51  On the role of sound giving voice to the local, see Beck in this volume, chapter 1.

52  Ager 2019: 182, citing further bibliography on emotional memories and emotional decision-making.

53  Plutarch cites Phylarchos four times, with three mentions in the *Life of Kleomenes*: *Ages.* 9.3; *Cleom.* 5.3; 28.2; 30.3 (*FGrH* 81 F 32b; 51; 59; 60): Aratos four times, three times in the *Life of Kleomenes*: *Ages.* 10.4; *Cleom.* 16.4; 17.4; 19.6; Polybios twice in the *Life of Kleomenes*: 25.5 and 27.11. He also uses Aristotle, esp. with regard to information about Spartan life. See Gabba 1957: 3 with previous bibliography; Porter 1979, esp. xvi; Marasco 1981: 24–5, 33, 36.

54  Aratos *BNJ* 231 T 3 (Polyb. 2.40.4) with comment by Beck; and Walbank ad Polyb. 2.40.4.

55  Aratos *BNJ* 231 T 1 with comment by Beck, and by Marasco 2011: 105, with footnotes and further bibliography.

56  Landucci *BNJ* 81 ad T 1 with discussion and bibliography: Sikyon, Athens, or Naukratis.

57  Africa 1961, esp. 3; Flower 2002: 194 with n. 17 and Landucci 2018; *BNJ* 81, both with sources and bibliography.

58  Gabba 1957: 2, 5–13; Africa 1961: 2; Marasco 1981: 27; McCaslin 1985–6; Schepens 2005: 157; Eckstein 2013; Beck and Landucci (*BNJ*) both with discussions and further bibliography; Kurpios 2020: 594–5.

59  Ollier 1933: 540; Kroymann 1956: 477–82; Gabba 1957: 7, 37, 227–8; Africa 1960; 1961: chap. 4; David 1981: 145; Vanhaegendoren 2010. This does not imply that Phylarchos is unreliable: Walbank ad l.; Africa 1961, esp. 3; Shimron 1966: 456; Eckstein 2013; Marincola 2013; Thornton 2013, esp. 362–72; Landucci ad F 52.

60  Much more than Aratos' account (who localizes too, but in a different way: see below). "Localizing" is here understood as an action with a disposition to the local (cf. Beck, chapter 1).

61  See Oliva 1968: 181.

62  See Beck *BNJ* 233 F 2. In the first paragraph of the chapter, Plutarch states that Kleomenes' soldiers use the ῥομφαία (see Hesych. s.v.), which, in Plutarch, means a "hardened iron battle axe." The word is not attested in the Archaic, Classical, or early Hellenistic ages; its dissemination began in the third century BCE, with the first Greek translation of the Old Testament, the so-called Septuagint and with the very same Phylarchos, reported as a source by

the Scholiast Maximus Confessor (on Pseudo-Dionysios the Areopagite ed. B. Corderio, *Opera*, 2 p. 156 ed. Antv. 1634), ἡ γὰρ ῥομφαία βαρβαρικόν ἐστιν ὅπλον, ὡς ἱστορεῖ Φύλαρχος, In fact, the ῥομφαία is a barbaric weapon, as is recounted by Phylarchos. See Landucci (ad *BNJ* 81 F 57) with further sources and bibliography.

63  Klatt 1877: 85; Goltz 1888: 41–2; Walbank ad l.

64  That not only rhetorical exercise is implied is shown by the following sentences, citing ἀστραγαλίσεις, σφαιρίσεις, κυβείαι, πεττείαι, and ἐσπουδασμέναι δὲ παιδιαί.

65  Cf. *AO* 2, 20, 31, 33, 35, 87, 88. Spawforth in Cartledge and Spawforth 1989: 203; Kennell 1995: 31; 2006: 113 (with further inscriptions); Ducat 2006: 74. All this makes even more sense if Casevitz is right in considering that παιδεύω, whose route is παῖς as well, maintains a close connection to παίζω, which is also a derivate of παῖς and means "to play": Casevitz 2018: 54 with sources and bibliography (see, however, the remarks in Chantraine 2009, s.v. παῖς).

66  On this connection see Gabba 1957: 38; Shimron 1966: 452, 455–6; 1972: 29–37; Marasco, ad l. emphasizes how this connection also resonates with Plato's statement about military victories being a consequence of a good education (*Leg.* 1.641b).

67  That (at the latest) in Hellenistic times Sepeia was put on a par with Thyrea is also shown by our *apophthegma* 231 F.

68  I could go further and mention Polybios' statement (2.56) that "Phylarchus being eager to stir the hearts of his readers to pity, and to enlist their sympathies by his story, talks of women embracing, tearing their hair, and exposing their breasts" (compare with *Arat.*45.6–9: women were enslaved), a statement which reminds me of the Argive women tearing their cheeks (ἀμφιδρυφῆς) mentioned in the epicene oracle and the related episode mentioned above after the Battle of Sepeia in which Hera stopped Kleomenes I from seizing Argos through the fire coming from her breast: ἀμφιδρυφὸς (Hom. *Il.* 11.393–4 cum scolio; see Ebeling *Lex. Hom.* I 105; *LfrE* I 675) in the epicene oracle, which in my opinion refers to Hera's breast, is comparable to περιπλοκὰς in Polybios. It is certainly true that, in the two lines above, Polybios mentions Phylarchos' description of the seizure of Mantineia and the bad treatment of Arkadian cities (and not of Argos) by the Achaians. But this does not imply that the statement refers (only) to the Arkadian cities (cf. 2.56, after this statement: "And this he does again and again throughout his whole history, by way of bringing the terrible scene vividly before his readers"). And note that, even if it did, the fact that Phylarchos uses the image of the woman defeating the man and the image of Hera stopping Kleomenes with reference to a non-Argive context confirms my general argument that he localizes the Achaian war by drawing on former regional conflicts in which Sparta was involved.

69 On glocalism: Robertson (1995), who introduced the concept; Khondker 2004; Roudometof 2016 with a further bibliography. For the application of the concept to Ancient Greek history: Malkin 2011: 14–15; Gehrke 2015; Beck 2020. On the intertwining of localism and regionalism see Beck 2020, esp. 32–3; on the relevance of the local in the Hellenistic world see Malkin 2011; Ager and Faber 2013.

70 Above, n. 40. This makes even more sense if Phylarchos made use of Sphairos, as some scholars suggest: Ollier 1943: 106; Schütrumpf 1987: 475; Flower 2002: 194 with discussion (*contra*, Figueira 2016: 28).

71 Plutarch, too, strongly emphasizes this: in the *synkrisis* (2.4) he claims that Kleomenes' military success in the Peloponnese was due to a good education, is πάλιν ὑφ᾽ Ἡρακλείδαις: see Marasco ad l.

72 Pagkalos 2017: 247 with previous bibliography.

73 Apollod. 2.8. See Luraghi 2008: 48–67 for an analysis of the various competing memories in these complex traditions.

74 Thuc. 5.69 with comment by Vannicelli 2004: 289, and, more recently, Weber-Pallez 2021: 334–5.

75 Hdt. 7.204 and 8.131.2; cf. also Hdt. 6.52–3 and Paus. 2.18.7 with comment by Vannicelli 2004: 289.

76 The statement of Pausanias reminds us of two passages by Polybios (9.28.7 and 9.33.11) in which it is reported that Philip II would have resolved some territorial disputes in the Peloponnese to the disadvantage of Sparta. See Luraghi 2014: 138–9.

77 Piérart 2001: 32–7; Luraghi 2014: 140–5, both with references and literature. Cf. also Weber-Pallez (2021: 322), who makes the case that the tripartition was already an argument in Classical times, as Herodotus' passage on the Battle of the Champions shows (1.81).

78 It is now well known (Luraghi 2008: 46–61; Stafford 2012: 137–42, both with previous bibliography) that the return of the Herakleidai was heavily refashioned by fourth-century Messenians but conceived in early fifth-century Argos. In fact, Kleomenes' claim to be a descendant of Herakles seems a sort of countermyth intended to go beyond the division of the Peloponnese.

79 See above, pp. 218–20.

80 Cf. *Arat.* 38.5: see above, par. 2 (esp. n. 17) and n. 49.


## REFERENCES

Africa, T.W. 1959. "Stoics, Cynics, and the Spartan Revolution." *International Review of Social History* 4: 46–69.

Africa, T.W. 1960. "Phylarchus and the Gods: The Religious Views of a Hellenistic Historian." *Phoenix* 14.4: 222–7. https://doi.org/10.2307/1085863.

Africa, T.W. 1961. *Phylarchus and the Spartan Revolution*. Berkeley.

Ager, S. 1996. *Interstate Arbitrations in the Greek World, 337–90 B.C.* Berkeley.

Ager, S. 2019. "The Limits of Ethnicity: Sparta and the Achaian League." In H. Beck, K. Buraselis, and A. McAuley (eds.), *Ethnos and Koinon: Studies in Ancient Greek Ethnicity and Federalism*. Stuttgart: 175–92.

Ager, S., and R. Faber (eds.). 2013. *Belonging and Isolation in the Hellenistic World*. Toronto.

Argentieri, L. 2007. "Meleager and Philip as Epigram Collectors." In Bing and Bruss, 2007: 147–64. https://doi.org/10.1163/9789047419402_009.

Beck, H. 2018. "'If I am from Megara': Introduction to the Local Discourse Environment of an Ancient Greek City-State." In H. Beck and P.J.H.- Smith (eds.), *Megarian Moments: The Local World of an Ancient Greek City-State. Teiresias Supplements Online* 1: 15–45.

Beck, H. 2020. *Localism and the Ancient Greek City-State*. Chicago.

Beloch, K.J. 1912. *Griechische Geschichte*. Vol. 2. Berlin and Leipzig.

Bing, P., and J.S. Bruss. 2007. *Brill's Companion to Hellenistic Epigram*. Leiden and Boston.

Boardman, J. 1992. "For You Are the Progeny of Unconquered Herakles." In J.M. Sanders (ed.), *Philolakon: Lakonian Studies in Honour of Hector Catling*. London: 25–9.

Bompois, F. 1870. *Étude historique et critique des portraits attribués a Cléomène III, roi de Lacédémone: Restitution de ces portraits a Antigone II, Doson, roi de Macédoine*. Paris.

Bravi, L. 2006. *Gli epigrammi di Simonide e le vie della tradizione*. Rome.

Bruns, G. 1929. *Die Jägerin Artemis*. PhD diss., University of Munich.

Bultrighini, U. 2016. *Il re è pazzo, il re è solo: Cleomene I re di Sparta*. Lanciano.

Burkert, W. 1982. *Structure and History in Greek Mythology and Ritual*. Berkeley.

Bywaters, D. 1991. *Dryden in Revolutionary England*. Berkeley.

Calame, C. 1987. "Le récit généalogique spartiate: La réprésentation mythologique d'une organisation spatiale." *Quaderni di Storia* 13: 43–91.

Carlier, P. 1984. *La royauté en Grèce avant Alexandre*. Strasbourg.

Cartledge, P. 2002. *Sparta and Lakonia: A Regional History, 1300–362 BC*. 2nd ed. London.

Cartledge, P., and A. Spawforth. 1989. *Hellenistic and Roman Sparta: A Tale of Two Cities*. London.

Casevitz, M. 2018. "Les noms du jeu et du jouet en grec." *Kentron* 34: 51–60.

Chantraine, P. 2009. *Dictionnaire étymologique de la langue grecque*. 3rd ed. Paris.

Christesen, P. 2007. *Olympic Victor Lists and Ancient Greek History*. Cambridge and New York.

Cusset, C. 2022. "Damagète." In C. Urlacher-Becht and D. Meyer, *Dictionnaire de l'épigramme littéraire dans l'antiquité grecque et romaine*, vol. 1. Tournhout: 391–2.

David, E. 1981. *Sparta between Empire and Revolution, 404–243 BC*. Salem.

Dawkins, R.M. 1929. "The History of the Sanctuary." In R.M. Dawkins (ed.), *The Sanctuary of Artemis Orthia*. London: 1–51.

Degani, E. 2009a. "Chaeremon." *Brill's New Pauly*.

Degani, E. 2009b. "Dioscorides." *Brill's New Pauly*.

Des Bouvrie, S. 2009. "Artemis Ortheia – A Goddess of Nature or a Goddess of Culture?" In Fischer Hansen and Poulsen 2009: 153–90.

De Vido, S. 2001. "Genealogie di re spartani nelle *Storie* erodotee." *Quaderni di Storia* 53: 209–27.

Ducat, J. 2006. *Spartan Education: Youth and Society in the Classical Period*. London.

Eckstein, A.M. 2013. "Polybius, Phylarchus, and Historiographical Criticism." *Classical Philology* 108.4: 314–38. https://doi.org/10.1086/671786.

Edson, C.E. 1934. "The Antigonids, Heracles and Beroea." *Harvard Studies in Classical Philology* 45: 213–46. https://doi.org/10.2307/310636.

Erskine, A. 1990. *The Hellenistic Stoa: Political Thought and Action*. Ithaca, NY.

Fantuzzi, M. 2007. "Epigram and the Theater." In Bing and Bruss 2007: 477–96.

Ferrabino, A. 1921. *Arato di Sicione e l'idea federale*. Florence.

Figueira, T. 2016. "Politeia and Lakonika in Spartan Historiography." In T. Figueira (ed.), *Myth, Text, and History at Sparta*. New York: 7–104.

Flower, M. 2002. "The Invention of Tradition in Classical and Hellenistic Sparta." In S. Hodkinson and A. Powell (eds.), *Sparta: Beyond the Mirage*. London: 191–217.

Franchi, E. 2018. "Commemorating the War Dead in Ancient Sparta: The Gymnopaidiai and the Battle of Hysiai." In V. Brouma and K. Heydon (eds.), *Conflict in the Peloponnese: Social, Military and Intellectual*. Nottingham: 24–39.

Franchi, E. Forthcoming. *Sparta e Argo: I conflitti nel Peloponneso orientale*.

Gabba, E. 1957. *Studi su Filarco: Le biografie plutarchee di Agide e di Cleomene*. Pavia.

Gehrke, H.-J. 2013. "The Victorious King: Reflections on the Hellenistic Monarchy." In Luraghi 2013a: 73–98.

Gehrke, H.-J. 2015. "Methodologische Überlegungen zu aktuellen Tendenzen in der Alten Geschichte: Kulturelle Austauschprozesse und historische Narratologie." *Gymnasium* 122: 211–32.

Goltz, C.F.G. 1888. *Quibus fontibus Plutarchus in vitis Arati, Agidis, Cleomenis enarrandis usus sit*. PhD diss., Universität Insterburg.

Gow, A.S.F., and D.L. Page. 1965. *Hellenistic Epigrams*, vol. 2. Cambridge.

Gow, A.S.F., and A.F. Schofield. 1953. *Nicander: The Poems and Poetical Fragments*. Cambridge.

Grunauer-von Hoerschelmann, S. 1978. *Die Münzprägung der Lakedaimonier*. Berlin.

Hoïstad, R. 1948. *Cynic Hero and Cynic King*. PhD diss., Uppsala University.

Huttner, U. 1997. *Die politische Rolle der Heraklesgestalt im griechischen Herrschertum*. Stuttgart.

Karwiese, S. 1980. "Lysander as Herakliskos Drakonopignon: Heracles the Snake-Strangler." *Numismatic Chronicle* 20: 1–7.

Kennell, N.M. 1995. *The Gymnasium of Virtue: Education and Culture in Ancient Sparta*. London.

Kennell, N.M. 2006. *Ephebeia: A Register of Greek Cities with Citizen Training Systems in the Hellenistic and Roman Periods*. Hildesheim.

Khondker, H.H. 2004. "Glocalization as Globalization: Evolution of a Sociological Concept." *Bangladesh e-journal of Sociology* 1.2: 1–9.

Klatt, M. 1877. *Forschungen zur Geschichte des Achäischen Bundes*. Vol. 1. Berlin.

Kralli, J. 2017. *The Hellenistic Peloponnese: Interstate Relations*. Swansea.

Kroymann, J. 1956. "Phylarchos." *RE*. Supplementband 8: 471–89.

Kurpios, M. 2020. "Reconstructing the Transmission of Phylarchus' Histories: Fr.53 and Polybius' Habit in Quoting." *Greek, Roman and Byzantine Studies* 60.4: 594–620.

Landucci, F. 2017. "Phylarchos." *BNJ* 81.

Landucci, F. 2018. "I Testimonia di Filarco, storico del III sec. a. C.: riflessioni preliminari." In I.M. Intrieri (ed.), *Koinonia: Studi di Storia antica offerti a Giovanna De Sensi Sestito*. Rome: 557–69.

Léger, R.M. 2017. *Artemis and Her Cult*. Oxford.

Legrand, P.-E. 1901. "Sur quelques épigrammes du IIIe siècle." *Revue des Études Anciennes* 3: 185–95.

Luraghi, N. 2008. *The Ancient Messenians: Constructions of Ethnicity and Memory*. Cambridge.

Luraghi, N. (ed.). 2013a. *The Splendors and Miseries of Ruling Alone*. Stuttgart.

Luraghi, N. 2013b. "Ruling Alone: Monarchy in Greek Politics and Thought." In Luraghi 2013a: 11–24.

Luraghi, N. 2014. "Ephorus in Context." In G. Parmeggiani (ed.), *Between Thucydides and Polybius: The Golden Age of Greek Historiography*. Washington, DC: 133–51.

Malkin, I. 2011. *A Small Greek World: Networks in the Ancient Mediterranean*. Oxford.

Manfredini, M., D.P. Orsi, and V. Antelami (eds.). 2000. *Plutarco: Le Vite di Arato e Artaserse*. Milan. 4th ed.

Marasco, G. 1981. *Commento alle biografie plutarchee di Agide e di Cleomene*. Rome.

Marasco, G. 2011. "The Hellenistic Age: Autobiography and Political Struggles." In G. Marasco (ed.), *Autobiographies and Memoirs in Antiquity: A Brill Companion*. Leiden: 87–120.

Marinatos, N. 2000. *The Goddess and the Warrior*. London and New York.

Marincola, J. 2013. "Polybius, Phylarchus, and 'Tragic History': A Reconsideration." In B. Gibson and T. Harrison (eds.), *Polybius and His World: Essays in Memory of F.W. Walbank*. Oxford: 73–90.

McCaslin, D.E. 1985–6. "Polybius, Phylarchus, and the Mantineian Tragedy of 223 B.C." Αρχαιογνωσία 4.1–2: 77–101.

Meier, M. 1998. *Aristokraten und Damoden*. Stuttgart.

Meier, M. 2006. "Theopompus. Nicander." *Brill's New Pauly*.

Merker, I.L. 1960. "The Silver Coinage of Antigonos Gonatas and Antigonos Doson." *American Numismatic Society Museum Notes* 9: 39–52.

Michalopoulos, M. 2016. *In the Name of Lykourgos: The Rise and Fall of the Spartan Revolution Movement, 243–146 B.C.* Barnsley.

Millender, E. 2009. "The Spartan Dyarchy: A Comparative Approach." In S. Hodkinson (ed.), *Sparta: Comparative Approaches*. Swansea: 1–67.

Mørkholm, O. 1991. *Early Hellenistic Coinages: From the Accession of Alexander to the Peace of Apamea (336–188 B.C.)*. Cambridge.

Musti, D., and M. Torelli. 1991. *Pausania: Guida della Grecia*, vol. 3, *La Laconia*. Milan.

Nafissi, M. 1991. *La nascita del kosmos*. Perugia.

Oliva, P. 1968. "Die Auslandpolitik Kleomenes III." *Acta* antiqua Academiae Scientiarum Hungaricae 16: 179–85.

Ollier, F. 1933. *Le mirage spartiate: Étude sur l'idéalisation de Sparte dans l'antiquité grecque de l'origine jusqu'aux Cyniques*. Vol. 1. Paris.

Ollier, F. 1943. *Le mirage spartiate: Étude sur l'idéalisation de Sparte dans l'antiquité grecque du début de l'ecole cynique jusqu'à la fin de la cité*. Vol. 2. Paris.

Pagkalos, M. 2015. "The Coinage of King Areus Revisited: Uses of the Past in Spartan Coins." *Graeco-Latina Brunensia* 20.2: 145–59.

Pagkalos, M. 2017. "Legitimising the Present through the Past: Some Observations on the Use of the Past in Territorial Disputes." *Graeco-Latina Brunensia* 22.2: 241–53. https://doi.org/10.5817/GLB2017-2-14.

Palagia, O. 2006. "Art and Royalty in Sparta in the 3rd Century BCE." *Hesperia* 75: 205–17.

Piérart, M. 2001. "Argos, Philippe II et la Cynourie (Thyréatide): Les frontières du partage des Héraclides." In R. Frei-Stolba and K. Gex (eds.), *Recherches récentes sur le monde hellénistique: Acte du colloque en l'honneur de Pierre Ducrey*. Bern: 27–43.

Pipili, M. 1987. *Laconian Iconography of the Sixth Century B.C.* Oxford.

Pirenne-Delforge, V. 2008. *Retour à la source: Pausanias et la religion grecque*. Liège.

Porter, W.H. 1979. *Plutarch's Life of Aratus*. New York.

Poulsen, B. 2009. "The Sanctuaries of the Goddess of the Hunt." In Fischer Hansen and Poulsen 2009: 401–25.

Powell, A. (ed). 2018a. *A Companion to Sparta*. Vol. 1. Chichester.

Powell, A. 2018b. Sparta. Reconstructing History from Secrecy, Lies and Myth. In A. Powell 2018a: 3–28.

Prioux, É. 2022. "Dioscoride." In C. Urlacher-Becht and D. Meyer (eds.), *Dictionnaire de l'épigramme littéraire dans l'antiquité grecque et romaine*, vol. 1. Tournhout : 454–7.

Richer, N. 1998. *Les éphores:. Études sur l'histoire et sur l'image de Sparte (VIIIe–IIIe siècle avant Jésus-Christ)*. Paris.

Richer, N. 2012. *La religion des Spartiates: Croyances et cultes dans l'Antiquité*. Paris.

Robertson, R. 1995. "Glocalization: Time-Space and Homogeneity-Heterogeneity." In M. Featherstone, S. Lash and R. Robertson (eds.), *Global Modernities: Theory, Culture, and Society*. London: 25–44.

Rostovtzeff, M. 1941. *The Social and Economic History of the Hellenistic World*. Vol. 3. Oxford.

Roudometof, V. 2016. *Glocalization: A Critical Introduction*. London.

Schepens, G. 2005. "Polybius on Phylarchus' 'Tragic' Historiography." In G. Schepens and J. Bollansée (eds.), *The Shadow of Polybius: Intertextuality as a Research Tool in Greek Historiography*. Leuven: 141–64.

Schille, C.B.K. 2004. "Last Stands and Pratfalls: The Unevenness of Dryden's Final Tragedy, 'Cleomenes.'" *Restoration: Studies in English Literary Culture, 1660–1700* 28.2: 31–47.

Schulz, F.F. 1886. *Quibus ex fontibus fluxerint Agidis, Cleomenis, Arati vitæ plutarcheæ*. Berlin.

Schütrumpf, E. 1987. "The Rhetra of Epitadeus: A Platonists's Fiction." *Greek, Roman and Byzantine Studies* 28: 441–57.

Seltman, C. 1933. *Greek Coins*. London.

Shimron, B. 1966. "Some Remarks on Phylarchus and Cleomenes III." *Rivista di Filologia e di Istruzione Classica* 94: 452–9.

Shimron, B. 1972. *Late Sparta: The Spartan Revolution, 243–146 B.C*. Buffalo.

Shipley, G.D. 2004. "Lakedaimon." In M.H. Hansen and T.H. Nielsen (eds.), *An Inventory of Archaic and Classical Poleis*. Oxford: 569–98.

Shipley, G.D. 2017. "Agis IV, Kleomenes III, and Spartan Landscapes." *Historia* 66.3: 281–97. https://doi.org/10.25162/historia-2017-0014.

Shipley, G.D. 2018. *The Early Hellenistic Peloponnese: Politics, Economies, and Networks, 338–197 BC*. Cambridge.

Stafford, E. 2012. *Herakles*. London.

Stewart, D. 2018. "From Leuktra to Nabis, 371–192." In Powell 2018a: 374–402.

Thornton, J. 2013. "Tragedia e retorica nella polemica sulla presa di Mantinea (Polibio II, 56–58)." In M. Mari and J. Thornton (eds.), *Parole in movimento: Linguaggio politico e lessico storiografico nel mondo ellenistico*. Pisa and Rome: 353–74.

Tigerstedt, N. 1974. *The Legend of Sparta in Classical Antiquity*. Vol. 2. Stockholm.

Tober, D. 2010. "Politeiai and Spartan Local History." *Historia* 59.4: 412–31.

Tomlinson, R. 1972. *Argos and the Argolid: From the End of the Bronze Age to the Roman Occupation*. London.

Trundle, M. 2017. "Spartan Responses to Defeat: From a Mythical Hysiae to a Very Real Sellasia." In J. Clark and B. Turner (eds.), *Brill's Companion to Military Defeat in Ancient Mediterranean Society*. Leiden: 144–61.

Vanhaegendoren, K. 2010. "Outils de dramatisation chez Phylarque." *Jeux et enjeux de la mise en forme de l'histoire: Recherches sur le genre historique en Grèce et à Rome*. Besançon: 421–38.

Vannicelli, P. 1993. *Erodoto e la storia dell'Alto e del Medio Arcaismo (Sparta-Tessaglia-Cirene)*. Rome.

Vannicelli, P. 2004. "Eraclidi e Perseidi: Aspetti del conflitto tra Sparta e Argo nel V sec. a.C." In P. Bernardini (ed.), *La città di Argo: Mito, storia, tradizioni poetiche*. Rome: 280–94.

Van Wees, H. 1999. "Tyrtaeus' Eunomia: Nothing to Do with the Great Rhetra." In S. Hodkinson and A. Powell (eds.), *Sparta: New Perspectives*. London: 1–41.

Walbank, F.M. 1933. *Aratos of Sicyon*. Oxford.

Walbank, F.M. 1957. *A Historical Commentary on Polybios*. Vol. 1. Oxford.

Walthall, A.D. 2013. "Becoming Kings: Spartan Basileia in the Hellenistic Period." In Luraghi 2013a: 129–63.

Weber-Pallez, C. 2021. "Argos, l'Empire romain et les historiens aujourd'hui: Déconstruire les représentations, reconstruire l'histoire argienne." *Revue des Études Greques* 134.2: 317–60.

Welwei, W. 2006. "Prytanis; Charillos; Labotas." *Brill's New Pauly*.

West, J. 2018. *Dryden and Enthusiasm: Literature, Religion, and Politics in Restoration England*. Oxford.

Zink Kaasgaard Falb, D. 2009. "Das Artemis Orthia-Heiligtum in Sparta im 7. und 6. Jh. v.Chr." In Fischer Hansen and Poulsen 2009: 127–53.

*As we have seen in chapter 9, the reign of Kleomenes III of Sparta produced some of the most conspicuous expressions of localism in the history of Hellenistic Greece. Sebastian Scharff adds another piece to the jigsaw. Building on the general notion that localism is a relational force, formulated and voiced in juxtaposition to the local of others, he floats the concept of competitive localism: the term signals not only the role of athletics as a feeder of local sentiments, but accentuates the local ways of doing sports as well as the traces the competition leaves in the political arena. The chapter first identifies the idiosyncratic features of Sparta's agonistic culture, among them the discouragement of boxing and a certain fondness for female and team competitions. Local commemoration practices reverberated the different outlook of athletics. Scharff's discussion of Spartan Hellenistic victor epigrams suggests a strong emphasis on* polis *ideologies, couched in a constellation that segued freely from politics to athletics and back; it appears, indeed, that athletic competitions were subject to the desire to boast about the local way of life first and foremost. Evidently, the force of Sparta's athletic jingoism was so compelling that it transpired in neighbouring Messenia also. The study of evidence from there demonstrates that the theme of victory in athletic competition played a crucial role in the building of a Messenian identity of place. A curious episode from 226 BCE, which Scharff examines in conclusion to this chapter, vividly reminds readers of King Kleomenes' deliberate and somewhat bizarre attempts to translate Spartan claims for military power into the language of locally enshrined athletics.*

*Keywords: competitive localism, athletics and agonistic culture, victory epigrams, Sparta, Messenia, Olympia*

# 10

# "Sparta is my country": Competitive Localism in Hellenistic Sparta*

SEBASTIAN SCHARFF

## Competitive Localism

When Pausanias visited the Peloponnese in the second century AD, he also came to the small perioikic town of Akriai at the southern shore of Lakonia. According to his description, one of the main touristic attractions of the settlement consisted of a victory monument honouring the five-time Olympic champion Nikokles.[1] Nikokles, who is also known from no less than four agonistic inscriptions, had won all his victories in running events at the beginning of the first century BCE.[2] It is proof of the vitality of Peloponnesian athletics in the Hellenistic period that a settlement like Akriai was able to produce one of the most successful runners of its time.[3] The mere existence of Nikokles' monument some 300 years after his victories were achieved may also show that athletics had become a part of the way this polity presented itself to others: Nikokles' μνῆμα was an icon that everyone saw when they came to Akriai.

Such pride in the achievements of local athletes was not unknown in nearby Sparta as well. Yet it took a rather specific shape and form there. The aim of this essay is to analyse in detail how the Hellenistic Spartans crafted typically local narratives of athletic success, that is, narratives that both related to the local horizon and brought a particular type of meaning to it. For this purpose, I will first examine how exactly Sparta's own "agonistic culture"[4] differed from that of other Greek *poleis* at the time. I will then explore how Spartan athletes of this period presented their victories to their fellow citizens, arguing that a competitive localism played a decisive role in this self-presentation. Finally, I will investigate what impact Sparta's agonistic culture had on other polities in the city's immediate Peloponnesian neighbourhood.

A key term of this chapter is "competitive localism." In what follows it will become clear that the term is not simply used here because the chapter's focus is on athletic competition and because Hellenistic Sparta disposed of a plethora of local characteristics in the field of athletics. There is more to it than that. "Competitive localism" also refers to the fact that local ways of doing sport mattered so much to people (in Sparta and in other Peloponnesian cities) that they were referenced in political discourses as distinctive features of their polity's character.[5] Such a competitive localism sometimes included a relational dimension in the sense that it was designed to set one's community apart from others.[6]

## Sparta's Idiosyncratic Agonistic Culture

Much work has been done on Spartan athletics of the Archaic and Classical periods.[7] In contrast, the agonistic life of Hellenistic Sparta has not attracted much scholarly attention so far.[8] The reason for this imbalance lies in the fact that it was the earlier periods that saw the city's biggest Olympic successes. Sparta's athletes of these epochs had an amazing track record and were, for instance, extraordinarily successful in gymnic disciplines between 720 and 580 BCE.[9] What is more, horse owners from the city dominated the most prestigious discipline of all, the Olympic four-horse chariot race, and managed to win seven out of eight races between 448 and 420 BCE.[10] There has been much debate on the reasons for why both chains of victories in Olympia set in and ended.[11] One aspect, however, is especially striking with regard to the argument of this chapter: in spite of all these Olympic victories of Spartan athletes, there was no single Spartan success in any boxing or *pankration* event in the Archaic and Classical periods, be it at Olympia or at any other contest in the entire Greek world.[12]

In the Hellenistic Age, the evidence, or more precisely the lack of evidence, for these disciplines did not change at all. Among the 25 known Hellenistic Spartan athletes, there is no single victor attested in any *pankration* or boxing event, not only in Olympia, but throughout the widened agonistic landscape of the period.[13] It is no earlier than in the Roman Imperial period that we find the first Spartan victor in a *pankration* contest.[14] A Spartan boxing champion is never attested throughout antiquity.[15]

Interestingly enough, even the ancients themselves wondered about this surprising absence in the Spartan track record; and so a tradition was established in which the Spartans were prohibited by Lycurgus to participate in these disciplines on the grounds that the result was determined by one contestant signalling his submission.[16] Therefore, an athletic defeat in these disciplines may have cast a shadow of cowardice on the entire *polis*.[17] In this regard, *pankration* and boxing clearly differed from wrestling, which was about bringing the opponent down to the floor thrice. It is true that the association of the tradition with the name of Lycurgus makes it suspicious at first glance. However, it is not easy to find a reason for Sparta's apparent lack of success in these disciplines other than a prohibition ordered by the *polis*. In my opinion, Stephen Hodkinson is right when he observes that "the prohibitionist tradition does at least go back… to the revolutionary period of the late third century,"[18] that is, the period of the Spartan "reforming kings" Agis IV (244–241 BCE), Kleomenes III (235–222 BCE), and Nabis (207–192 BCE).[19] All three of them, despite differences in their concrete political agenda, propagated a back to Lycurgan customs attitude to sell their social reforms to a "deeply traditionalistic society."[20]

Especially the reign of Kleomenes constituted what can be understood as a perfect context for the establishment of such a tradition. According to his biographer Plutarch, Kleomenes put an emphasis of his public self-presentation on "the austere, Dorian mode of Lycurgan practices and habits"[21] and thus became "a kind of public model of self-discipline."[22] Antony Spawforth called the spirit behind that habit "the reinvention of 'Lycurgan' Sparta for statist ends."[23] With regard to localism, however, one might rather say that in referring to what was believed to be their own Lycurgan past, the Spartans became increasingly auto-referential.[24]

Yet, apart from the Spartan discouragement of boxing and *pankration* as a general policy of the *polis*, there were at least three other local peculiarities in Spartan athletics. First, the Spartans entertained a certain fondness for team competition, probably in the form of ball games, which were not very popular with other Greeks to say the least.[25] Such contests are attested in literary sources from Xenophon to Pausanias and also in several imperial inscriptions.[26] These sources show that teams called *sphaireis* competed at popular inner-Spartan contests on a regular basis. It is not so easy to detect what kind of game they were actually playing, but most scholars agree that the contests were "a hybrid of North American football, rugby, and a sort of netless volleyball," as Nigel Kennell has put it.[27] In any case, the connection between Sparta and ball games was considered so strong that ball games have at times even been interpreted as a Spartan invention in antiquity.[28]

Another element of Sparta's idiosyncratic agonistic culture is reflected in the amount of female athletic competition. Although we should not assume that there was any form of mixed competition, girls' athletics seem to have been "conducted side by side with the boys in full public view,"[29] as shown by the lines Theokritos puts into the mouths of a group of Spartan girls:

ἄμμες δ᾽ αἱ πᾶσαι συνομάλικες, αἷς δρόμος ωὑτός
χρισαμέναις ἀνδριστὶ παρ᾽ Εὐρώταο λοετροῖς...

We, as all her age mates, who run the same racecourse and oil ourselves down like men alongside the bathing pools of the Eurotas.[30]

Such athletic activities of women may not come as a surprise in a city that produced the first female Olympic victor of all times, the Spartan princess Kyniska,[31] who stated in her famous victor epigram that she was "the only woman in all Greece who won this crown."[32] The tradition of Kyniska was followed by some victorious female horse owners from the city: first, a certain Euryleonis won an Olympic victory with a carriage and pair at some point in the fourth century BCE;[33] second, a woman named Olympio was successful at the Panathenaic four-horse chariot race of the year 170/69 BCE and was announced as a Spartan victor.[34] Although these are only two examples, they are telling evidence since the majority of cases of successful female horse owners stems from the new parts of the Hellenistic world, especially from Egypt.[35] In mainland Greece, however, the agonistic activity of women still remained rather unusual. That Hellenistic Sparta was an exception in this regard is also indicated by Pausanias, who explicitly states that the successors of Kyniska as female Olympic champions were "especially women of Lacedaemon."[36]

A third element of Sparta's agonistic culture is visible in "a veritable circuit of local games held at various locations in Sparta itself, Laconia and Eastern Messenia,"[37] as shown by a long victor inscription proudly published on the acropolis of the city by the Spartan aristocrat Damonon in the middle of the fifth century BCE.[38] What is striking here is that although a lot of contests existed on Spartan territory, none of them had a catchment area that exceeded the local level before the Augustan Age.[39] This is clearly demonstrated by the fact that there was no regular participation of foreign athletes in any Spartan game before this period.[40]

In sum, Sparta clearly had a characteristic agonistic culture. The idiosyncrasies of this agonistic culture are deeply rooted in the Archaic and Classical periods and survived during the Hellenistic Age. This is not self-explanatory, since in the Imperial period there is a change induced by the fact that now Spartan pankratiasts, too, were attested, and by the observation that foreign *agōnistai* competed at "no fewer than three agonistic festivals of international status."[41]

To put it in a nutshell, although Hellenistic Sparta was a society in transition, its own agonistic culture remained more or less unaffected by this change. The reason for this continuity in the face of change must be seen in the "deeply traditionalistic society"[42] that was Hellenistic Sparta; even pushing a reform agenda was only possible by hiding behind the slogan of "back to Lycurgan customs."

### Agonistic Success on Behalf of the *Polis*: Competitive Localism in the Self-Presentation of Hellenistic Victors from Sparta

Let us now turn to the question of how agonistic victories were remembered in Sparta. Did Sparta's local agonistic culture also resonate with the way in which victories were commemorated?

It must be emphasized right from the beginning that the Spartan way of remembering athletic success was an internal part of the city's agonistic culture as well. There is, for instance, no single *epinikion* on a Spartan victor in the works of Pindar and Bakchylides.[43] What is more, there was "a marked degree of official control over privileges for Olympic victors and the forms of their victory celebration."[44] For instance, no statues for equestrian victors who were successful outside the Spartan *polis* territory are attested in Sparta.[45] Given the impressive track record of Spartan horse owners in the fifth century BCE, this cannot be a total coincidence. Other privileges for successful athletes which were common in other Greek cities seem to have been restricted to a minimum as well.[46] This does not mean, however, that the city took no interest in the victories of its athletes. To the contrary, the *polis* positively regulated the way in which victorious athletes and horse owners were allowed to commemorate their successes. Without doubt, overt public display of wealth was frowned upon in Sparta. As a consequence, the agonistic climate of Archaic and Classical Sparta was dominated by a certain modesty with regard to the self-presentation of individual athletes. This modesty, however, was a result of a general policy of the Spartan state.

But let us return now to the Hellenistic evidence. What role did Sparta's agonistic culture play for the self-presentation of agonistic victors? Did the athletes, by means of their agonistic self-presentation, foster a distinct local identity? In order to answer these questions, we have to analyse in detail the surviving examples of Hellenistic victor epigrams from the city.

The remaining evidence consists of three epigrams two of which are comparatively (and in one case even brand-) new. A recently published epigram from Olympia deals with a prominent Spartan runner of the late fourth century BCE.[47] It reads as follows:

τῶι Λακεδαιμονίωι σταδιαδρόμωι ν ο[ὗ]τος ἐοικὼς
    ἔστα ἀεθλοφόρωι ἀν[δ]ρὶ καὶ εὐδοκίμωι,
τῶι Δεινοσθένεος Δεινοσθένει, ὃς τὰ Λυκούργου
    ἄχρι γεροντείας πάντα ἐτέλεσσε φατά
εὖ γὰρ Ὀλυμπικὰ μέτρα διακριβοῦν ἐκέλευε
    Σπάρτας εὐθυνόμου πρὸς νεάταν ἀγοράν.

Resembling the Lacedaemonian stadion runner Deinosthenes, son of Deinosthenes, a victor and renowned, who accomplished every Lycurgan precept even into old age this (statue) stands (here); for he had Olympic measurements made in a good manner up to the furthest agora of lawful Sparta.[48]

The victor mentioned in this poem is the Spartan athlete Deinosthenes, son of Deinosthenes, who won the Olympic *stadion* race in 316 BCE.[49] Deinosthenes had already been known from two other sources before the epigram was published: a passage in Pausanias and an Olympic prose inscription.[50] Both texts are rather cryptic, but have in common that they refer not only to Deinosthenes' Olympic victory, but also to the distance between Olympia and Sparta.[51] Thus it comes as no surprise that distances (Ὀλυμπικὰ μέτρα) play an important role in the newly found epigram as well. This particular feature does not appear in other victor inscriptions and can only be explained by the fact that Deinosthenes took pride in his participation in the path measurement between the city and the sanctuary.[52] It is important to note right from the start that Deinosthenes is connected with an achievement beyond the field of athletics in this poem.

Although the text of the epigram is not fragmentary, it is nevertheless hard to interpret. According to its editor, Klaus Hallof, the poem praises an anonymous οὗτος, mentioned in line 1, who was responsible for the path measurement between Sparta and Olympia.[53] It is not the place here to go too much into the linguistic details of the epigram, but it must be stated that I take οὗτος as referring to an unspecified masculine noun like ἀνδριάς. In consequence, I do not distinguish two different persons (οὗτος and Deinosthenes) but identify only one individual (Deinosthenes, son of Deinosthenes) honoured in the poem. Thus, I can see no compelling reason why this poem, an epigram published in Olympia and fulfilling all the necessary characteristics of a victor epigram, should not originally have been composed in honour of an Olympic victor.[54]

If we understand the poem as a victor epigram honouring Deinosthenes, two other aspects stand out: first, Deinosthenes had a high social status and is praised not only for being a successful and famous *stadion* runner, but also for his conduct of life in general and for his adherence to the Lycurgan customs – maybe even for his political career.[55] Second, the city of Sparta plays a highly important role in the epigram. It is mentioned twice. The second word of the entire poem is Λακεδαιμονίωι – and it even receives an own epithet: whereas Deinosthenes is characterized as εὐδόκιμος, his hometown becomes εὐθύνομος.[56] What is more, with the mythical lawgiver Lycurgus a key figure of the city's imagined past, of its "intentional history,"[57] is evoked together with an important political institution like the *gerousia* and a main place of the city like the agora.[58] All of this is done in a Lakonic dialect.[59] To put it in a nutshell, one might even argue that, after Deinosthenes, Sparta becomes the second central character of the epigram. No doubt, the poem fostered an identity of place by means of agonistic self-representation.

The second epigram on a Hellenistic victor from Sparta came down to us in the *Hippika* of Poseidippos.[60] It reads:

ἅρ[ματι νικῶσαι ταὶ] τέσσαρες εἵλομε⟨ς⟩ ἁ[μέ]ς
   ἵππqι θή[λειαι] πὰρ Διὸς ἀνιόχου,
Πισᾶτ[αι στέφα]ν[ο]ν τὸν Ὀλυ⟨μ⟩πικὸν ἄλλον ἐπ᾽ ἄλλωι
   [.].. ι. ..[. .].[. . .] τqῦ Λακεδαιμονίου.

We four mares carried off the victory in a chariot that was driven in the presence of Zeus charioteer, Pisans, we won one Olympic crown after another for (?) ... the Lakedaemonean.[61]

Taking on the perspective of the victorious horses, the Olympic victories of a Spartan chariot are praised in first person plural. At times, doricisms like εἵλομε⟨c⟩ ἁ[μέ]ς, πὰρ and ἀνιόχου are used.[62] The fact that our successful horse owner was a multiple victor is indicated by line 3 of the poem, where it is explicitly stated that the mares "won one Olympic crown after another" (στέφα]ν[ο]ν τὸν Ὀλυ⟨μ⟩πικὸν ἄλλον ἐπ᾽ ἄλλωι).[63] Specifically, we are dealing with a two-time victor here, since there is no space for more than two victories in a row in what remains from the respective Olympic victor list.[64]

The epigram includes a strong reference to the *polis* which is emphatically referred to by the last word of the poem: Λακεδαιμονίου. Admittedly, the last line of the epigram is fragmentary at best and the proposed reading of the *editio minor* [Δ]ίωι Λυσι[μ]ά[χου] has the disadvantage that the *ethnikon*

Λακεδαιμονίου would somewhat strangely refer to the father of the successful athlete and not to the victor himself. In any case, we may identify a certain patriotism in the ending of the poem as well as in its doricisms, which in
my opinion do not primarily "insinuate that the horses of a Lacedaimonian
speak Doric," as Martin Hose assumed,[65] but are simply used to lend a local
colour to the epigram.

Even more than such a local colour – namely a blatant patriotism – is
expressed in a poem written in honour of a successful Spartan boy wrestler,
which is to be found in the *Anthologia Graeca*. The epigram dates to the
second half of the third century BCE and came down to us under the name
of the poet Damagetos.[66] It reads as follows:

Οὔτ' ἀπὸ Μεσσάνας οὔτ' Ἀργόθεν εἰμὶ παλαιστάς·
    Σπάρτα μοι Σπάρτα κυδιάνειρα πατρίς.
κεῖνοι τεχνάεντες· ἐγώ γε μέν, ὡς ἐπέοικε
    τοῖς Λακεδαιμονίων παισί, βίᾳ κρατέω.

I am no wrestler from Messene or from Argos;
Sparta, Sparta famous for her men, is my country.
Those others are skilled in the art, but I, as becomes
the boys of Lacedaemon, prevail by strength.[67]

It is striking that the name of the victor is never even mentioned in
the entire poem, whereas Sparta or the city's inhabitants are referred
to thrice in four verses. No doubt, there is a distinct patriotic tendency
to the epigram. The *polis* clearly takes centre stage, whereas the athlete
remains almost totally invisible. We do not even hear about the place
of his victory. It is true that the personal data of the athlete may have
been added in a prose inscription,[68] a procedure we know very well from
other victor monuments.[69] Yet, we cannot be sure if this epigram was
published as an inscription. In any case, the message of the epigram itself
is unmistakably clear: it is about the fame of the *polis*. In the words of
the second line of the poem: Σπάρτα μοι Σπάρτα κυδιάνειρα πατρίς. The
anaphora (Σπάρτα μοι Σπάρτα) emphasizes the glory of the city, a *kydos*
which is linked to the *polis*, not to the personal *aretē* of the victor. It
is the entire city that is κυδιάνειρα.[70] Thus, a keyword of the agonistic discourse (*kydos*) is connected with the whole city.[71] As in the two
other epigrams that I have already discussed, doricisms like Μεσσάνας,
παλαιστάς, and τεχνάεντες give the poem a local colour. It is important
to note that for Poseidippos and Damagetos the doricisms represented a

deliberate choice, since both poets did not use them in all their surviving victor epigrams.[72]

All this puts a strong emphasis on Spartan *polis* ideology. This ideology, however, has a foreign dimension to it as well, and so the most patriotic line of the epigram – the line already quoted twice – is embedded into a competitive constellation, which is clearly transferred from the political arena to the agonistic sphere. For there can be no doubt that line 1 ("I am no wrestler from Messene or from Argos") refers to two of Sparta's "three main Peloponnesian enemies."[73] It is exactly the Messenians and Argives that any Spartan audience would easily believe to use conniving tricks instead of plain force in a wrestling match (or in any other battle, that is). We know from other sources as well that it was a typically Spartan approach to wrestling that the stronger competitor – and not the one who knew more wrestling holds – was supposed to win.[74] From a Spartan point of view, winning by a superior technique actually came close to cheating.

In other *poleis* a completely different approach could prevail. This can be easily demonstrated by a short look into the way the Olympic wrestling champion of the year 388 BCE, a certain Aristodamos from Elis,[75] characterized his victory. According to his victor epigram, the success was achieved "not by the massive appearance of the body (πλάτεϊ σώματος), but by a (superior) technique (τέχνᾳ)."[76]

So we may conclude that in the case of the anonymous boy wrestler from Sparta an element of the agonistic culture of the city even became part of the self-presentation of the victor. It is one of the idiosyncrasies of the city's agonistic culture that is particularly highlighted in the epigram. The poem is a very good example of how agonistic poetry was put to heavily state-directed use at Sparta. What is particularly striking here is the way the competitive constellation created by the poem works. When comparable epigrams mention the origin of other competitors, these competitors stem from regions or *poleis* which are especially famous for the discipline in which the victory was won. A successful horse owner from Pergamon, for instance, stated that the other competitors came from Thessaly, Kyrene, or Argos,[77] which were all very well known for their successful horses.[78] Such a comparison clearly serves to enhance the value of the victory, since it was won against strong competitors. In our case, however, the comparison works differently: Messene and Argos were not, first of all, famous for their successful wrestlers. Argos, for instance, was known for its good runners and horses;[79] combat sports, in contrast, played a minor role in the city's track record. So in the case of our epigram it seems as if the competitive localism has more to do with politics than with athletics.

## Conversations between Local Discourses:
## The Self-Presentation of Messenian Victors as a
## Counterpart to Athletic Self-Fashioning in Sparta

Since the foundation of Messene on Mount Ithome in 369 BCE, athletics had played a decisive role in the process of "*polis* building," a process which has been described in detail in a groundbreaking study by Nino Luraghi.[80] Messenian athletes had an impressive track record right from the start: already one year after the foundation of the city, a certain Damiskos won the stadium race for boys at Olympia.[81] The victory constituted some kind of athletic miracle, since the athlete is reported to have defeated his significantly older competitors as a twelve-year-old.[82] Undoubtedly an Olympic victory represented an ideal platform for the display of a new political entity and the *polis* of Messene demonstrated this ambition very clearly.[83] The display seems to have had its intended effect, and at least Pausanias as our source of information describes Damiskos' victory as a political comeback of the city.[84]

Throughout the Hellenistic period, the successes of Messenian victors contributed to foster the city's identity. We can trace this process of how athletics helped transform the Messenian ethnic group into a polity very well now because the excavations at Messene conducted by Petros Themelis brought to light "a plethora of new evidence,"[85] including 13 new victor inscriptions.[86] In these inscriptions, the *polis* loomed large, since most of them were set up by the *damos* and not by the victors themselves. In other words, the *polis* took over.[87]

All in all, the new evidence that includes five formerly unknown Olympic victors from the city suggests that the victories of Messenian athletes could keep up with the successes of their Spartan peers:[88] during the Hellenistic period, the number of Olympic victories of Messenian athletes now equals the number of known Spartan successes (nine Spartan *olympionikai* face nine from Messene).[89] Some of these Messenian successes seem to have been triggered by new athletic venues in Messene, which were built in the third century BCE.[90] The new athletic facilities, which included a *stadion* and a *gymnasion*, may have been part of a strategy of the Messenian *polis* to increase agonistic success by enlarging the athletic venues of the city.

But how did all of this affect the way Messenian champions presented their successes to their fellow citizens and to the Hellenic public in general? All in all, four Hellenistic victor epigrams for Messenian athletes have survived.[91] The most striking example is represented by a victor epigram on a successful Messenian pentathlete, reading:

[Ἄν ἀρετὰν ἀνέφην]ε Λέων ὁ Λεωνίδα υἱὸς,
   [ἀνίκα τὰν νίκ]αν ἄρατο Πυθιάδα
[ἀνδρῶν πεντά]θλων, ὅθεν ἐστεφάνωσε παλαιὰν
   [πρᾶτος Μ]εσσάναν, αὐτόνομον πατρίδα.

His virtue has attested Leon, Leonidas' son, when he won a Pythian victory over the
men in pentathlon. From there, he brought as the first (of the Messenians) a crown
to ancient Messana, his autonomous hometown.[92]

The poem was set up in Delphi and belongs, according to its lettering, to
the second half of the third century BCE.[93] Some of its features, including
the name of the victor and the identity of his hometown, have been subject
to much debate.[94] The most remarkable element of the epigram, however, is
not constituted by the "personal data" of the victor, but by the ending of the
poem, where we clearly find an emphasis on political autonomy. Messene
is not only called "ancient" (παλαιὰν),[95] but is also proudly characterized as
*autonomos patris*[96] by the very last words of the epigram. This lends the
poem a patriotic flavour.[97] Since the publication of Joachim Ebert's seminal
work, the emphasis on autonomy or political liberty has been interpreted as a
reference to the upcoming incorporation of Messene into the Achaian League
in 191 BCE.[98] Recent studies, however, have pointed out that we should not
understand 191 BCE as too strict a *terminus ante quem*. For Zinon Papakonstantinou, for instance, "Leon's monument in Delphi was dedicated shortly
after 190 but commemorated a victory before that date."[99]
   But could we really be so sure that the emphasis on Messenian autonomy
had to be directed against the Achaians? If we bear in mind the Spartan
victor epigram written by Damagetos, with its clear anti-Messenian tendency, the Spartans may very well have been the addressee of this Messenian
emphasis on autonomy, especially since both epigrams belong to the same
chronological framework, a time when there were armed conflicts, including
repeated incursions into Messenian *polis* territory by the Spartans.[100] Since
the city's foundation, Messene's mere existence was strongly connected to
her hatred of Sparta – and it was the autonomy from Sparta which became
a main motif of political discourse in Messene.[101] So, it seems at least more
likely to link the Messenian insistence on political autonomy to a current
conflict with the city's main political enemy than to the prospect of a future
incorporation into a federal state that was far less threatening to the city's
existence.
   Whoever the addressee, it is evident that (again) a political constellation
is transferred from the political arena to the agonistic sphere: a keyword of
the Messenian political discourse is used to characterize the city in a context

where this information is technically not necessary. Leon's strong feeling that his hometown should be independent must be primarily understood as a current reference to Messenian foreign (and maybe also domestic) politics. Thus, the poem for Leon seems to belong to the same political discourse as the Spartan Damagetos epigram. Yet, we should also bear in mind that *autonomia* and *eleutheria* generally figured as keywords in Greek *polis* ideology, especially in the Hellenistic period.[102] So, although we cannot be completely sure how to exactly interpret Leon's striving for autonomy, a clear political message was sent here.

But autonomy only figures as one of two aspects which characterize Messene in the poem. Although the first aspect of political independence is certainly strongly emphasized through its position at the end of the epigram, the second aspect which concerns the old age of the city (παλαιὰν [...] Μεσσάναν)[103] likewise deserves our attention. Like the insistence on autonomy, the old age of a city constituted a standard motif of Greek *polis* ideology. With regard to Messene, though, this is a tough task. The only way to justify such a claim of old age would be to argue that the liberation of Messene in 370 BCE was actually not a foundation, but a refoundation, or "grande rentrée,"[104] as Nino Luraghi has characterized the "Theban-Messenian point of view"[105] on it. So the reference to "ancient Messana"[106] in the poem should be interpreted as being part of the new polity's attempt at "playing down its own novelty."[107]

This strategy had a clear element of compensation given that the Messenians understandably "suffered under chronic deprivation of tradition."[108] In any case, by emphasizing that his hometown was an old city, Leon applied a strategy entirely familiar to the Greek world.

How much the agonistic sphere had become part of the politics of the day in the southern Peloponnese can be best observed in a passage which came down to us in Plutarch's *Life of Kleomenes*. The episode refers to a Spartan campaign into Megapolitan *polis*-territory in the year 226 BCE. It reads as follows:

τέλος δὲ τοὺς περὶ τὸν Διόνυσον τεχνίτας ἐκ Μεσσήνης διαπορευομένους λαβών, καὶ πηξάμενος θέατρον ἐν τῇ πολεμίᾳ, καὶ προθεὶς ἀπὸ τετταράκοντα μνῶν ἀγῶνα, μίαν ἡμέραν ἐθεᾶτο καθήμενος, οὐ δεόμενος θέας, ἀλλ᾿ οἷον ἐντρυφῶν τοῖς πολεμίοις καὶ περιουσίαν τινὰ τοῦ κρατεῖν πολὺ τῷ καταφρονεῖν ἐπιδεικνύμενος.

The climax of the expedition, however, came after he [i.e. Kleomenes] had captured some members of the Guild of Dionysos on the road from Messene. He had a theatre built, right there in enemy territory, put on a contest with forty mnas as the prize, and spent all of one day just sitting and watching. The point, of course, was not the show: it was a way of mocking his enemies and taunting them with a display designed to make it perfectly clear that he had power to spare.[109]

Clearly, the protagonists of the "show" were performers (*technitai*), not athletes. Yet, there is an emphasis on the competitive character of the performance, which is not only called an *agōn* but included a victory prize consisting of a considerable amount of money.[110] Kleomenes offered the prize to demonstrate that he was able to organize a contest on campaign from close to scratch;[111] he also disposed of the leisure time to do so. He even had a temporary theatre built, supposedly a wooden construction. Watching for "all of one day" (μίαν ἡμέραν) a musical performance was just the kind of leisure activity that was suited to "mock his enemies." It was precisely the absence of military activity which was designed here to indicate that the king had nothing to fear by his Megapolitan adversaries. His control of affairs was complete and he was even so powerful that he could afford an entire day of leisure in enemy country. The passage appears to be a perfect example of what Angelos Chaniotis has called "theatricality beyond the theatre."[112] This is all the more true since Plutarch highlights the fact that Kleomenes' behaviour was not about "the show," but about "mocking his enemies." In other words, we have a clear case of symbolical communication.

The political situation of the year 226 BCE actually forced Kleomenes to make a powerful political and military statement, not only towards his hostile neighbours, but also towards his more powerful enemies, Aratos and the Achaians, who are explicitly mentioned by Plutarch at the beginning of the passage as the addressees of Kleomenes' campaign.[113]

The essence of all this is that Kleomenes marks an important point in one of his military campaigns by organizing an agonistic competition.[114] To create an actual stage for this display of power, the Spartan king has his theatre built. The metaphor of the stage materializes in the temporary construction of the theatre that turns into a political arena as a competitive showground.

## Competitive Localism Mattered – a Conclusion

Hellenistic Sparta constitutes a textbook example for the significance of the local horizon in the field of athletics. Sparta had long developed an idiosyncratic agonistic culture, characteristic of the non-participation of citizens in boxing and *pankration* contests abroad, a fondness for ball games and female competition, the organization of strictly local, that is, locally confined games, and a very clear understanding of the way a wrestling victory should be achieved and promoted. Some of these elements became part of the self-presentation of Spartan athletes, who strongly emphasized Lacedaemonian *polis* ideology in their victor epigrams. In the case of the Damagetos epigram, this ideology was framed in pronounced dichotomous opposition to other polities (i.e., Messene, Argos). Hence it was relational in the sense that it was deliberately designed to set the Spartans apart from others, but it also included a competitive dimension: doing athletics the Spartan way was presented as being superior to other Greek practices of sport. This way local identity was fostered by means of athletic self-presentation.

As in other city-states of the Hellenistic world, local elements became part not only of the self-portrayal of athletes but also of the branding of a city.[115] As we have seen, competitive constellations were transferred time and again from the political arena to the agonistic sphere in Sparta as well as in Messene. Victor epigrams from both cities formed part of a political discourse whose pillars were likewise represented by Spartan *polis* ideology and the notion of Messenian autonomy. In other words, competitive localism mattered in the field of Peloponnesian athletics.

## NOTES

* This chapter condenses ideas I developed during the work on my habilitation treatise (Scharff forthcoming). In addition to the conference in Waterloo, ON, parts of the paper have been presented to audiences in Mannheim, Olympia, Heidelberg, Regensburg, and Bielefeld. My thanks go to all participants for their constructive comments and the lively discussions. If not stated otherwise, translations are my own.

1 Paus. 3.22.4–5: προελθόντι που σταδίους ἐπὶ θαλάσσης πόλις ἐστὶν Ἀκρίαι… Ἀκριᾶται δὲ καὶ ἄνδρα ποτὲ Ὀλυμπιονίκην παρέσχοντο Νικοκλέα, Ὀλυμπιάσι δύο ἀνελόμενον δρόμου νίκας πέντε· πεποίηται δὲ καὶ μνῆμα τῷ Νικοκλεῖ τοῦ τε γυμνασίου μεταξὺ καὶ τοῦ τείχους τοῦ πρὸς τῷ λιμένι. "And some thirty stades farther is Akriai, a city on the coast … The people of Akriai once produced an Olympian victor, Nikokles, who at two Olympian festivals carried off five prizes for running. There has been raised to him a monument between the gymnasium and the wall by the harbor" (trans. W.H.S. Jones and H.A. Ormerod). *IG* V 1, 1108 (Akriai, first[?] century BCE: οἱ Ἀκριᾶτ]αι Ṇικọḳλέ[α] | [πεντάκις ὀ]λ[υ]μπι[ο]νί[καν]. "The people of Akriai [honour] Nikokles, the five-time Olympic champion") may be the remaining inscription of this monument; but note that it is in a very fragmentary state.

2 Moretti (1957, nos. 655–7 and 660–1) dates Nikokles' Olympic successes to the years 100 (*diaulos, hoplitēs,* and *dolichos*) and 96 (*diaulos,* and *hoplitēs* or *dolichos*). In addition to *IG* V 1, 1108, Nikokles, whose father's name was Nikatas, also appears in three victor lists of the Amphiaraia Rhomaia of Oropos

(*I. Oropos* 525, ll. 15–20; 49–50) and of the Eleutheria of Larisa (*IG* IX 2, 529, 14–15 [Graninger 2011, no. 5], and Arvanitopoulos 1911, no. 27, l. 4–5 [Graninger 2011, no. 4]).

3  On Akriai, Shipley 2004: 574.

4  Hodkinson 1999: 147.

5  On the concept of localism in general as it is applied in this chapter, see more elaborately Beck 2020, esp. 1–42, and Beck this volume.

6  On relational localism, cf. the case of Phlious as analysed in Beck 2020: 14.

7  Cf., e.g., Hönle 1972: 29–44, 120–59; Nafissi 1991: 153–72; Hodkinson 1999; Hodkinson 2000: 307–33, Mann 2001: 121–63; Palagia 2009; Christesen 2012; Cordano 2013; Nafissi 2013; Nobili 2013 (2016); Christesen 2014; Christesen 2019.

8  Even for the Roman Imperial period, the state of research is considerably more advanced thanks to Spawforth 2002: 176–89, 232–3.

9  See Moretti 1957, nos. 17–18, 21–2, 24, 30, 32, 34–5, 37, 40–7, 50, 55, 57, 59, 61–68, 70, 72–7, 75–6, 78, 80, 82–6, 91. The accuracy of the early Olympic victor lists is certainly up for debate (Christesen 2007), but assuming that the Spartans dominated most of the gymnic disciplines in the seventh and at the beginning of the sixth century BCE seems to be quite safe. The reason for the Spartan success has rightly been seen in the fact that the city had established a state-run education including physical training very early on (Mann 2001: 121–39, 143–54; for a different view Hodkinson 1999: 163–4). In the course of the sixth century BCE, however, an athletic specialization with regard to nutrition, physical training, and professional coaching set in in most of the Greek *poleis*. Yet the Spartans did not take part in this process of athletic specialization because specialized physical training remained rather frowned upon in their city.

10  Moretti 1957, nos. 305, 311, 315, 324, 327, 332, 339; see Mann 2001: 139–42.

11  Mann (2001: 121–63) has argued with good reason that both periods of Spartan dominance in Olympia were not interconnected and set in and ended for different reasons. For other views, see, e.g., Nafissi 1991: 153–72, esp. 165, and Hodkinson 2000: 307–33.

12  The only source attesting for a Spartan boxing champion is dubious, to say the least (*pace* Crowther 1990).

13  For the 25 sporting victors from Hellenistic Sparta, consult the Mannheim database on Hellenistic athletes: http://mafas.geschichte.uni-mannheim. de/athletes/ (accessed 18 September 2019). The 10 known Spartan Olympic champions of the period include the four successful *stadion* runners Deinosthenes, son of Deinosthenes (316 BCE, Moretti 1957, no. 478), Alkidas (244 BCE, Moretti 1957, no. 566), Nikodamos (104 BCE, Moretti 1957, no. 653), and Andreas (64 BCE, Moretti 1957, no. 702). Thus, there was one victorious *stadion* runner in each century. Since we have a complete list of the victors

in the Olympic *stadion* run, this result is not coincidental. No doubt, the Olympic victories of Hellenistic Spartan athletes are more evenly distributed than those of their Archaic and Classical predecessors. Yet, there also seems to be a certain cluster of Olympic victories in gymnic disciplines at the end of the fourth/ beginning of the third century BCE. In addition to Deinosthenes, whose victory may very well have been the first Spartan Olympic success in a gymnic discipline after an interval of more than 150 years, Seleidas, son of Alexandridas, won the Olympic wrestling competition, possibly in 308 BCE (Moretti 1957, no. 487; he was also successful at the *Lykaia* in the same discipline [*IG* V 2, 549, 31–2; cf. Bradford 1977: 371]). Another Spartan wrestler, Amphiares, won his Olympic crown in 296 BCE (Moretti 1957, no. 515; cf. Bradford 1977: 31; firmly dated via *P.Oxy*. XVII 2082). Finally, the Olympic victory of a certain Eubalkes (*IG* V 1 649; cf. Bradford 1977: 158) is tentatively put to the year 300 BCE by Moretti 1957, no. 510. So the four victories of Deinosthenes, Seleidas, Eubalkes, and Amphiares may actually reflect a revival of Spartan athletics in the early Hellenistic period. The Olympic victory of a certain Euryades is tentatively dated to the year 248 BCE by Moretti 1957, no. 565. The only known Olympic victor in a horse race from the city is the anonymous Spartan horse owner of Posidipp. *ep*. 75, where two Olympic victories in the four-horse chariot race are referred to; they date between 280 and 240 BCE (see below).

14  *IG* V 1, 669, 3–4 (Sparta, Roman Imperial period); see also *IG* V 1, 658, 14 (Sparta, before the reign of Nerva), and 670 (Sparta, probably Imperial period).

15  See note 12.

16  Plut. *Lyc*. 19.9; *Mor*. 189e, 228d; Philostr. *Gym*. 9.58; Sen. *Ben*. 5.3.1. See Hodkinson 1999: 157–60.

17  Mann 2001: 123.

18  Hodkinson 1999: 158. Finley and Pleket 1976: 70–1 go back as far as the sixth century BCE.

19  On the rule of Agis IV, Kleomenes III and Nabis, see, for instance, Shimron 1972, Cartledge 2002: 38–79, Walthall 2013, Michalopoulos 2016, and Shipley 2017.

20  Cartledge 2002: 42.

21  Plut. *Cleom*. 16.4: τὸν σώφρονα καὶ Δώριον ἐκεῖνον τοῦ Λυκούργου νόμον καὶ βίον (trans. R. Waterfield).

22  Plut. *Cleom*. 13.1: ὥσπερ παράδειγμα σωφροσύνης (trans. R. Waterfield).

23  Spawforth 2002: 176.

24  As a new victor epigram from Sparta (Hallof 2019) now clearly shows, such an attitude also played a role in the agonistic discourse (see below).

25  On team competition in Sparta, Hodkinson 1999: 148–50.

26  For the inscriptions, see Tod 1903–4. The literary sources are Xen. *Lac*. 9.5, Ath. 1.14e, and Lucian. *Anach*. 38; cf. Kennell 1995: 110–11.

27 Kennell 1995: 60–1, cf. Ollier 1933: 49; Golden 1998: 9. For a different opinion, see Poliakoff 1987: 73, and 173, n. 7, who interprets the event as boxing contests. The rules of the event may be explained in Poll. 9.104.

28 Ath. 1.14e, Lucian. *Anach*. 38, and Poll. 9.107.

29 Hodkinson 1999: 151.

30 Theoc. *Id*. 18.22–3 (trans. S. Hodkinson); cf. Hodkinson 1999: 150–2.

31 Moretti 1957, no. 373 (396 BCE), and 381 (392 BCE). Of course, this was in an equestrian event, but Sparta's female agonistic culture seems to have been idiosyncratic with regard to horse races as well as track and field athletics.

32 Kyniska's famous victor epigram has survived twice as a fragmentary stone inscription (*IvO* 160) and in an epigram collection (*Anth. Pal.* 13.16); see Ebert 1972, no. 33. The two last lines of the poem read: μόν[αν] δ᾽ ἐμέ φαμι γυναικῶν Ἑλλάδος ἐκ πάσας τό[ν]|δε λαβεῖν στέφανον "I declare that I am the only one of the women of all Hellas to have won this crown." Xen. *Ages*. 9.6, and Plut. *Ages*. 20, 1, reveal that Kyniska's brother Agesilaos convinced her to participate in order to demonstrate that an Olympic victory was not such a big deal, but simply a question of wealth. Mann (2001: 161–2) is not happy with this explanation of Agesilaos' motives and convincingly argues against them. For Kyniska's reasons, see also Cartledge 1987: 150; Hodkinson 1989: 99; Hodkinson 2000: 327–8; Pomeroy 2002: 19–24, Kyle 2003; Hodkinson 2004: 111–12; Kyle 2007: 141–5; Millender 2009: 18–26; Nobili 2013 (2016): 74–81; Fornis 2014: 316; and Paradiso 2015. One can see why Christesen (2019: 189, n. 246) has recently called scholarship on Kyniska "something of an industry unto itself."

33 Paus. 3.17.6. Euryleonis' victory is tentatively (and without further explanation) dated to the year 368 BCE by Moretti 1957, no. 418. We only know for certain that Euryleonis succeeded after Kyniska's victory in 392 BCE and that Pausanias saw her statue on the acropolis of Sparta. So, the assumption that she won her victory in the Hellenistic period is not unlikely (Christesen 2019: 81 and App. 2, #36; *pace* Cordano 2013: 199–200).

34 Tracy and Habicht 1991, col. I, l. 34. The high social prestige of Olympio's family is indicated by the fact that her brother Pedestratos was honoured with the proxeny by the people of Gortyn between the years 181 and 168 BCE (*I. Cret*. IV 208 A). He was also serving Ptolemy VI Philometor (Tracy and Habicht 1991: 214; van Bremen 2007: 362).

35 Angeli Bernardini 1995; Van Bremen 2007: 368–72. For a comprehensive list of successful female horse owners of the period, see now Scharff forthcoming: 264, n. 1680.

36 Paus. 3.8.1: Κυνίσκας δὲ ὕστερον γυναιξὶ καὶ ἄλλαις καὶ μάλιστα ταῖς ἐκ Λακεδαίμονος γεγόνασιν Ὀλυμπικαὶ νῖκαι (…). "After Cynisca other women, especially women of Lacedaemon, have won Olympic victories, (…)" (trans. W.H.S. Jones and H.A. Ormerod).

37 Hodkinson 1999: 152.

38 *IG* V 1, 213 (= *IAG* 16). On this inscription, Nafissi 2013 (cf. also Canali de Rossi 2016: 27–9); on its date Kiderlen 2010. Christesen 2019 gives a new reading of the text interpreting the phrase ἐνῃεβόhαις *hίπποις* (which is quoted eight times in the inscription) as referring to the *kalpē*, a contest for mares in which the rider dismounted and ran alongside his horse in the final part of the race.

39 In the Augustan period, however, the picture changed. Augustus even entrusted the Spartans "with the supervision" (Spawforth 2002: 99) of the Aktia in the early twenties of the first century BCE, a time that saw an immense increase in importance of these games, including their elevation to the status of the games of the *periodos* right after 31 BCE when Octavian had defeated Antony and Kleopatra at Actium. On the Aktian Games, Lämmer 1986–7; Pavlogiannis and Albanidis 2007; and Wacker 2018.

40 Spawforth 2002: 184 also provides a useful catalogue of all attested foreign competitors at Sparta (232–233). Note that there also were competitions with an explicitly local character in Sparta like the *mastigōsis*, whose victor was called *bōmonikes*, a title which has been attested since the fourth century BCE already (Nafissi forthcoming).

41 Spawforth 2002: 176.

42 Cartledge 2002: 42.

43 Although there may be a fragmentary epinician by Ibykos and one by Simonides, the evidence is far from indisputable (Nielsen 2018a: 424–5). The fragmentary ode of Ibykos is interpreted as an *epinikion* in Barron 1984, the fragment of Simonides in Nobili 2013 (2016): 67–73.

44 Hodkinson 1999: 176.

45 Hodkinson 2000: 303–3; cf. Palagia 2009 ; Christesen 2019: 80–5. As Nobili 2013 (2016): 64 puts it, "erecting a victory statue was no easy thing in Sparta."

46 Hodkinson 1999: 167–70.

47 The epigraph was found by Hans Taeuber in the so-called House of the Spoils, west of the Leonidaion, already in 1987. However, it was no earlier than in 2012 when Sebastian Prignitz and Hans Taeuber produced a new squeeze and photographs that the entire epigram became decipherable (Hallof 2019: 179).

48 Hallof 2019. I am deeply indebted to Klaus Hallof for sharing this new evidence with me prior to its publication.

49 Moretti 1957, no. 478; cf. note 13.

50 Cf. Paus. 6.16.8; *IvO* 171.

51 Paus. 6.16.8: Λακεδαιμονίῳ δὲ Δεινοσθένει σταδίου τε ἐγένετο ἐν ἀνδράσιν Ὀλυμπικὴ νίκη καὶ στήλην ἐν τῇ Ἄλτει παρὰ τὸν ἀνδριάντα ἀνέθηκεν ὁ Δεινοσθένης· ὁδοῦ δὲ τῆς ἐς Λακεδαίμονα ἐξ Ὀλυμπίας ἐπὶ ἑτέραν στήλην τὴν ἐν Λακεδαίμονι μέτρα φησὶν εἶναι σταδίους ἑξήκοντα καὶ ἑξακοσίους. "Deinosthenes the Lacedaemonian won an Olympic victory in the men's foot-

race, and he dedicated in the Altis a slab by the side of his statue. The inscription declares that the distance from Olympia to another slab at Lacedaemon is six hundred and sixty furlongs" (trans. according to W.H.S. Jones and H.A. Ormerod). *IvO* 171, ll. 7–14: ἀπὸ τᾶσδε τᾶς στά|λας ἐλ Λακεδα|ίμονα ἑξακάτι|οι τριάκοντα, ἀπ|ὸ τᾶς δὲ ποτ τὰ|ν πράταν στά|λαν τριάκον|τα. "From this *stēlē* to Lacedaemon (it is) 630 (stadia), from this to the first *stēlē* (it is) 30 (stadia)."

52 As a runner, although a sprinter, Deinosthenes may have been a *bēmatistēs* or *hēmerodromos* himself (Hallof 2019: 177–8). Yet if, as I will argue below, the entire epigram refers to Deinosthenes it is clear that he had a high social status. It might be more probable, then, that he initiated rather than conducted the path measurement.

53 Hallof (2019: 181–2) argues that the content of line 1, if referring to a statue (ἀνδριάς) of Deinosthenes, could have been expressed more easily, which is certainly true. But a quick glance at the collection of Ebert 1972 tells us that this also applies to a large number of other victor epigrams. Hallof's second argument refers to the fact that Deinosthenes only won a single victory at Olympia, so that it is unlikely, according to Hallof, that he would have received a second statue. However, the new epigram does not focus on athletic success alone, but is better understood as being one of those agonistic inscriptions that commemorate life achievements. Thus, the reason for a second monument must not necessarily be seen in a second athletic victory.

54 For a similar view, see Tentori Montalto 2022.

55 As Hallof (2019: 182–3) convincingly argues, the term ἄχρι γεροντείας (line 4) also evokes a very concrete meaning: the honorand had probably entered the Spartan council of elders, the *gerousia*.

56 Hallof 2019, l. 6.

57 Gehrke 2001; cf. also Gehrke 2014 and the volume Foxhall, Gehrke, and Luraghi 2010.

58 Lycurgus: Hallof 2019, l. 3; *gerousia*: l. 4; agora: l. 6. Although the agora is characterized more closely as νεάταν, it is not clear which of the two known Spartan marketplaces is meant (Hallof 2019: 184).

59 Note e.g. l. 1: σταδιαδρόμωι; cf. Hallof 2019: 181.

60 On the *Hippika* that came down to us as part of an epigram collection, see the commentaries of Dickie 2008 and Hose 2015. The papyrus survived as part of a mummy wrapping in Egypt. On the *New Poseidippos*, see, e.g., the volumes of Acosta-Hughes; Kosmetatou and Baumbach 2004; and Gutzwiller 2005. I am currently preparing a historical commentary on the *Hippika* that focuses on its agonistic elements.

61 Posidipp. *ep.* 75 (trans. E. Kosmetatou).

62 On the use of doricisms in Poseidippos, Sens 2004.

63 Posidipp. *ep.* 75, l. 3 (trans. E. Kosmetatou).

64  For securely (and possibly) dated Olympic victories in the four-horse chariot between the years 280 and 240 BCE, which mark the artistic prime of Poseidippos, see Remijsen 2009: 253.

65  Hose 2015: 295.

66  On Damagetos, see Gow and Page 1965: 223–4, and Harder 2019, esp. 384. Since some of Damagetos' poems reproduce the conflict lines of the Social War, his artistic prime includes at least the years 220–217 BCE (Degani 1997). So, he may have been born in about 250 BCE (Argentieri 2007: 147). On the cultural context of Damagetos' writing, see Franchi, this volume.

67  *Anth. Plan.* 16.1 (trans. W.R. Paton).

68  Additional prose inscriptions to victor epigrams can be found, e.g., in Ebert 1972, nos. 25, 32, 37, 40, 47, 51, 53, 64, 76, 81. In Ebert 1972, no. 53 (ca. 300 BCE), the name of the victor Herogeiton is not mentioned in the epigram, but only in the prose inscription. Yet the epigram on this runner from Magnesia on the Maeander does not exhibit a patriotic tendency as does the epigram on the anonymous boy wrestler from Sparta.

69  It is also true that the epigrams now found in the sixteenth book of the *Anthologia Graeca* were compiled by the Byzantine monk Maximos Planudes, who is known to have omitted lines and whole epigrams when they appeared frivolous to him or when he simply did not fully understand them (Beckby 1965: 80; on the manuscript tradition of the *Greek Anthology*, Cameron 1993 and Beta 2019). Therefore, it is a fair assumption that Planudes may have interfered with the original version of the epigram. Yet this, though not utterly impossible, is not necessarily the case. Admittedly, the fact that we have a first-person narrator here whom we cannot identify is striking. But would it be too bold to assume that we have, above all, an epigram on Sparta's agonistic culture here? A stone epigram from Athens (*IG* II² 3138) of the late fourth century BCE, for instance, has a similar patriotic tendency and omits the name of the victor (on this epigram, Scharff forthcoming: 115–17). On the phenomenon of "Hellenistic epigrammatic 'brachylogy,'" Köhnken 2007: 301.

70  A similar phrase in Ebert 1972, no. 75, l. 6 (Rhodes, end of the second century BCE); cf. Scharff forthcoming: 82–5.

71  On *kydos* as a keyword in the agonistic discourse, Kurke 1991 and Kurke 1993.

72  Since the author of the epigram on Deinosthenes (Hallof 2019) is unknown, we cannot say whether or not he used doricisms in all his epigrams.

73  Cartledge 2002: 11.

74  Plut. *Mor.* 233c, for instance, says that the Spartans deliberatively refrained from appointing wrestling coaches "so that their *philotimia* would not be directed to *technē*, but to *aretē*"; see also Plut. *Mor.* 236e; cf. Finley and Pleket 1976: 70–1; Mann 2001: 130–2.

75  Moretti 1957, no. 383.

76 Ebert 1972, no. 34, l. 2. The entire epigram runs as follows:

> Πύθια δίς, Νεμέᾳ δίς, Ὀλύμπια ἐστεφανώθην
> οὐ πλάτεϊ νικῶν σώματος ἀλλὰ τέχνᾳ
> Ἀριστόδαμος Θράσυος Ἀλεῖος πάλαν.

> Twice at the Pythia, twice in Nemea, and (once) in Olympia was I crowned; I
> have won in wrestling not by the massive appearance of my body, but by my
> (superior) technique, me, Aristodamos, son of Thrasys, from Elis.

> Ebert 1972: 114 comments that "in den einzelnen Landschaften ganz
> unterschiedliche Vorstellungen über athletische Vollkommenheit herrschten."
> Another victorious wrestler proudly referring to his technique was Athenopolis,
> son of Pythotimos, from Priene (Ebert 1972, no. 73, A, l. 4 [Priene, midst of the
> second century BCE]).

77 Ebert 1972, no. 59 (= *IvP* I 10; *IAG* 37; Merkelbach–Stauber, *SGO* 06/02/21), l. 1–3:

> [Πο]λλὰ μὲν ἐγ Λ[ι]βύης ἦλθ᾽ ἅρματα, πολλὰ δ᾽ ἀπ᾽ Ἄργευς,
>    [πο]λλὰ δὲ π[ι]είρης ἦλθ᾽ ἀπὸ Θεσσαλίης,
> [ο]ἷσιν ἐνηριθ[μ]εῖτο καὶ Ἀττάλου.

> Several chariots had come from Libya, several from Argos, several from
> fertile Thessaly, among them also Attalos' chariot.

> Attalos' victory in the Olympic four-horse chariot race for colts was won
> in 276 BCE (Moretti 1957, no. 538). For this epigram, cf. Kertész 1998; Decker
> 2012: 93; Petermandl 2013: 137–8; and Kertész 2013: 820–1.

78 A similar constellation can be found, for instance, in Posidipp. *ep.* 74, ll. 1–2
where again a Thessalian competitor in a horse race is mentioned. For this
epigram, see Bingen 2002; Bing 2003; and Hose 2015: 291–4.

79 Both aspects can be found in Ebert 1972, no. 15, a victor epigram for the
famous Argive athlete Dandis, Olympic champion of the years 476 and 472
BCE (Moretti 1957, no. 210, 222): Dandis was a very successful runner, and in
his victor epigram, Argos is presented as ἱππόβοτος (l. 2), which is already a
Homeric characterization of the city (*Il.* 2.287). On Argos as a city of runners
and horses, Scharff forthcoming: 161–2.

80 Luraghi 2008 identified "the transformation of an ethnic group into a polity" (291)
as the most striking phenomenon of the history of the Messenian identity in the
Hellenistic period. On the role of athletics in this process, see Scharff forthcoming.

81 In addition to Damiskos (Moretti 1957, no. 417; 368 BCE), other fourth-century
Olympic victors from Messene include Damaretos (Moretti 1957, no. 448;
in the boys' boxing of 344? BCE), Telestas (Moretti 1957, no. 453; boxing of
340? BCE), and Sophios (Moretti 1957, no. 496; boys' *stadion* of 304? BCE); cf.
Themelis 2011: 141; Kralli 2017: 406, 411.

82  Paus. 6.2.10. There was no middle age class between boys and men (*ageneioi*) at Olympia, so a twelve-year-old actually had to beat other youngsters who were five or even six years older (cf. Finley and Pleket 1976: 35).

83  Kralli 2017: 411.

84  Paus. 6.2.10–11: παρὰ δὲ Μεσσήνιος Δαμίσκος, ὃς δύο γεγονὼς ἔτη καὶ δέκα ἐνίκησεν ἐν Ὀλυμπίᾳ. θαῦμα δὲ εἴπερ ἄλλο τι καὶ τόδε ἐποιησάμην· Μεσσηνίους γὰρ ἐκ Πελοποννήσου φεύγοντας ἐπέλιπεν ἡ περὶ τὸν ἀγῶνα τύχη τὸν Ὀλυμπικόν. ὅτι γὰρ μὴ Λεοντίσκος καὶ Σύμμαχος τῶν ἐπὶ πορθμῷ Μεσσηνίων, ἄλλος γε οὐδεὶς Μεσσήνιος οὔτε Σικελιώτης οὔτ᾽ ἐκ Ναυπάκτου δῆλός ἐστιν Ὀλυμπίασιν ἀνῃρημένος νίκην· εἶναι δὲ οἱ Σικελιῶται καὶ τούτους τῶν ἀρχαίων Ζαγκλαίων καὶ οὐ Μεσσηνίους φασί. συγκατῆλθε μέντοι Μεσσηνίοις ἐς Πελοπόννησον καὶ ἡ περὶ τὸν ἀγῶνα τύχη τὸν Ὀλυμπικόν· ἐνιαυτῷ γὰρ ὕστερον τοῦ οἰκισμοῦ τοῦ Μεσσήνης ἀγόντων Ὀλύμπια Ἠλείων ἐνίκα στάδιον παῖδας ὁ Δαμίσκος οὗτος, καί οἱ καὶ πενταθλήσαντι ὕστερον ἐγένοντο ἐν Νεμέᾳ τε νῖκαι καὶ Ἰσθμοῖ. "Beside this is the Messenian Damiscus, who won an Olympic victory at the age of twelve. I was exceedingly surprised to learn that while the Messenians were in exile from the Peloponnesus, their luck at the Olympic Games failed. For with the exception of Leontiscus and Symmachus, who came from Messene on the Strait, we know of no Messenian, either from Sicily or from Naupactus, who won a victory at Olympia. Even these two are said by the Sicilians to have been not Messenians but of old Zanclean blood. However, when the Messenians came back to the Peloponnesus their luck in the Olympic Games came with them. For at the festival celebrated by the Eleans in the year after the settlement of Messene, the foot-race for boys was won by this Damiscus, who afterwards won in the pentathlum both at Nemea and at the Isthmus" (trans. W.H.S. Jones and H.A. Ormerod). See on this episode more elaborately, Scharff forthcoming.

85  Papakonstantinou 2018: 64; see also Makres 2021.

86  *SEG* 23.212; 228; 45.310; 46.410; 422; 51.478; 52.400; 54.464; 465; 56.478; 59.411; 416; 417; Makres 2021; no. 1, 3–5. On the agonistic output of the excavations, Themelis 1992, 1995 (1996), 1995 (1998), 2009, 2011.

87  See on this aspect more elaborately, Scharff forthcoming.

88  The new *olympionikai* are the wrestler Antisthenes son of Polystratos (*SEG* 23.228: third/ second century), Polykles son of Lysandros (*SEG* 52.400: ca 200), [Eu?]peithes son of Da[…] (*SEG* 54.464: second/first century), the boxer Kleonymos son of Perphation (*SEG* 56.478: first century) and two anonymous wrestlers who succeeded once (Makres 2021, no. 1: ca. 200 BCE) and twice at Olympia (*SEG* 59. 411: Augustan period).

89  In addition to the "new" victors listed in note 88, Messenian Olympic champions of the Hellenistic Age include Telestas (in 340? BCE according

to Moretti 1957, no. 453), the famous politician Gorgos (in 232? BCE [Moretti 1957, no. 573]), Hagesidamos (in 220 BCE [Moretti 1957, no. 580]; according to Ebert 1982: 201 [cf. Moretti 1992: 120–1], Hagesidamos even won the Olympic *pankration* thrice [228–220 BCE]), and Theodoros (in 48 and 44 BCE [Moretti 1957, nos. 713, 716]). On Gorgos' high social standing, see Pol. 7.10 ("second to none of the Messenians in wealth and birth" [οὐδενὸς ἦν δεύτερος Μεσσηνίων πλούτῳ καὶ γένει]; cf. Finley and Pleket 1976: 45). On the social identity of Messenian victors in general, see Scharff forthcoming.

90 For the new athletic facilities, see Müth 2007: 89–128; Themelis 2009; 2013: 130–41; 145–52; for the *stadion* also Themelis 1992.

91 In addition to the two Messenian epigrams already known to Ebert 1972 (no. 51 [second half of the fourth century BCE] and 71 [see below]), newly discovered evidence includes Posidipp. *ep.* 86 (ca. 280–240 BCE) and *SEG* 45.310 (fourth century BCE).

92 Ebert 1972, no. 71 (cf. Bousquet 1959 = *SEG* 18.195).

93 Bousquet 1959: 186; on a slightly later date and 191 BCE as a *terminus ante quem* of the epigram, Ebert 1972: 211–13.

94 In the discussion on the name of the victor (for Leon son of Leonidas: Bousquet 1959: 185; for Nikomachos son of Leonidas: Moretti 1964: 320 and *BE* 1965, no. 197 [Jeanne and Louis Robert]), Ebert (1972: 212) brought forward the strong linguistic argument that the name Nikomachos, which must have stood at the beginning of line two, would clearly be prone to misinterpretation. The identity of the hometown of the victor, which Bousquet (1959: 188) had originally identified as Sicilian Messana (a view he later rejected [*SEG* 22.484]), has not been sincerely questioned, since Moretti (1964: 320–7) pointed our attention to *IG* II² 2314, col. II, 58–9, where the victorious pentathlete Nikomachos, son of Leonidas, is listed as an Ἀχαιὸς ἀπὸ Μεσσήνη<ς>. Although it seems more likely to assume with Ebert loc. cit. that he actually was a relative (maybe a brother) of our *pythionikēs*, it still remains a decisive argument in support of the assumption that Leon originated from Peloponnesian Messene. A different view expressed by Prag (2007: 95) is not convincing, since it ignores important parts of the debate.

95 Ebert 1972, no. 71, l. 3.

96 Ebert 1972, no. 71, l. 4.

97 Ebert 1972: 213: "patriotische Nuance bei der Angabe der Heimat."

98 Ebert 1972: 214: "Man darf wohl aus diesem αὐτόνομον einen trotzig stolzen Ton und etwas von dem Widerstandswillen der Messenier gegen den Anschluß an den Achäischen Bund heraushören."

99 Papakonstantinou 2018: 66; cf. Remijsen and Scharff 2015.

100  In the last quarter of the third century BCE, the Spartans invaded Messene's territory under Lycurgus in 218 BCE, together with the Aitolians in 217 BCE, and again under Nabis after 205 BCE (Roebuck 1941: 69–70, 79–91; Grandjean 2003: 76–83; Luraghi 2008: 258–61).

101  Luraghi 2008: 336: "opposition to Sparta remained the main charter of the Messenian identity." The motif of Messenian autonomy is also detectable elsewhere: αὐτόνομος is, for example, a keyword in the famous Epameinondas epigram which Paus. 9.15.6 (l. 4) saw in Thebes, a poem in which the Theban general is praised for being Messene's founder (l. 2) among other things. For the epigram and its context, see Luraghi 2008: 219–21.

102  For an instructive example from third-century Thyrreion, see the dedicatory epigram Haake and Kolonas and Scharff 2007, where in l. 2 the "never-aging liberty" (ἀγηρά[v]τωι […] ἐλευθερίαι) of the city is praised.

103  Ebert 1972, no. 71, l. 3–4.

104  Luraghi 2008: 219.

105  Ibid.

106  Ebert 1972, no. 71, l. 3–4.

107  Luraghi 2008: 217.

108  Luraghi 2008: 271; cf. id. 280: "desperately poor traditions."

109  Plut. *Cleom.* 12.2 (trans. R. Waterfield).

110  For 40 mnas, you could have bought at least 13 slaves at the time.

111  On "campaign *agōnes*" as a new category of contests in addition to "competitions at recurrent religious festivals" (Nielsen 2018b: 22), *gymnasion agōnes*, and funeral contests, Mann 2020a.

112  Chaniotis 1997.

113  Plut. *Cleom.* 12.1.

114  By this, he does not necessarily imitate Alexander, who used the organization of one-time competitions quite regularly in order to mark important stages of his military expeditions (Mann 2020b), but he acts in a very similar way.

115  Similar examples include, for instance, cities like Thebes and Sidon (Scharff forthcoming).


## REFERENCES


Acosta-Hughes, B., E. Kosmetatou, and M. Baumbach (eds.). 2004. *Labored in Papyrus Leaves: Perspectives on an Epigram Collection Attributed to Posidippus (P.Mil.Vogl. VIII 309)*. Cambridge, MA.

Angeli Bernardini, P. 1995. "Donna e spettacolo nel mondo ellenisitco." In R. Raffaelli (ed.), *Vicende e figure femminili in Grecia e a Roma: Atti del convegno Pesaro 28–30 aprile 1994*. Ancona: 185–97.

Argentieri, L. 2007. "Meleager and Philip as Epigram Collectors." In P. Bing and J.S. Bruss (eds.), *Brill's Companion to Hellenistic Epigram: Down to Philip*. Leiden and Boston, MA: 147–64.

Arvanitopoulos, A.S. 1911. "Inscriptions inédites de Thessalie." *Revue Philologique* 35: 123–39, 282–305.

Barron, J.P. 1984. "Ibycus: Gorgias and Other Poems." *Bulletin of the Institute of Classical Studies* 31: 13–24.

Beck, H. 2020. *Localism and the Ancient Greek City-State*. Chicago.

Beckby, H. 1965. *Anthologia Graeca, I: Buch I–VI*. 2nd ed. Munich.

Beta, S. 2019. *Moi, un manuscrit: Autobiographie de l'Anthologie palatine*. Paris.

Bing, P. 2003. "Posidippus and the Admiral: Kallikrates of Samos in the Milan Epigrams." *Greek, Roman and Byzantine Studies* 43: 243–66.

Bingen, J. 2002. "La victoire pythique de Callicrates de Samos (Posidippe, P.Mil. Vogl. VIII 309, XI.33–XII.7)." *Chronique d'Egypte* 77: 185–90.

Bousquet, J. 1959. "Inscriptions de Delphes." *Bulletin de Correspondance Hellénique* 83: 146–92.

Bradford, A.S. 1977. *A Prosopography of Lacedaemonians from the Death of Alexander the Great, 323B.C., to the Sack of Sparta by Alaric, A.D. 396*. Munich.

Cameron, A. 1993. *The Greek Anthology from Meleager to Planudes*. Oxford.

Canali De Rossi, F. 2016. *Hippiká: Corse di cavalli e di carri in Grecia, Etruria e Roma* Vol. 2, *Le corse al galoppo montato nell'antica Grecia*. Hildesheim.

Cartledge, P. 1987. *Agesilaos and the Crisis of Sparta*. Baltimore.

Cartledge, P. 2002. "Hellenistic Sparta." In *Hellenistic and Roman Sparta: A Tale of Two Cities*. 2nd ed. London and New York: 1–90, 234–51.

Chaniotis, A. 1997. "Theatricality beyond the Theatre: Staging Public Life in the Hellenistic World." In B. Le Guen (ed.), *De la scène aux gradins: Théâtre et représentations dramatiques après Alexandre le Grand dans les cités hellénistiques*. Toulouse: 219–59.

Christesen, P. 2007. *Olympic Victor Lists and Ancient Greek History*. Cambridge.

Christesen, P. 2012. "Athletics and Social Order in Sparta in the Classical Period." *Classical Antiquity* 31: 193–255. https://doi.org/10.1525/CA.2012.31.2.193.

Christesen, P. 2014. "Sport and Society in Sparta." In P. Christesen and D.G. Kyle (eds.), *Sport and Spectacle in Greek and Roman Antiquity*. Malden, MA, and Oxford: 146–58.

Christesen, P. 2019. *A New Reading of the Damonon Stele*. Newcastle Upon Tyne.

Cordano, F. 2013. "Sparta e le Olimpiadi in età classica." In F. Berlinzani (ed.), *La cultura a Sparta in età classica*. Trento: 195–202.

Crowther, N.B. 1990. "A Spartan Olympic Boxing Champion." *L'Antiquité Classique* 59: 198–202.

Decker, W. 2012. *Sport in der griechischen Antike. Vom minoischen Wettkampf bis zu den Olympischen Spielen*. 2nd ed. Hildesheim.

Degani, E. 1997. s.v. "Damagetos, Epigrammdichter." *DNP* 3: 288.

Dickie, M.W. 2008. "The Ἱππικά of Posidippus." In F. Cairns (ed.), *Papers of the Langford Latin Seminar, XII: Greek and Roman Poetry, Greek and Roman Historiography*. Cambridge: 19–51.

Ebert, J. 1972. *Griechische Epigramme auf Sieger an gymnischen und hippischen Agonen*. Berlin.

Ebert, J. 1982. "Zur Stiftungsurkunde der Λευκοφρυηνά in Magnesia am Mäander." *Philologus* 126: 198–216.

Finley, M. I., and H.W. Pleket. 1976. *The Olympic Games: The First Thousand Years*. London.

Fornis, C. 2014. "Cynisca l'Eurypontide: Genre, autorité et richesse dans la Sparte impériale du début du IVe siècle avant notre ère." *Mètis* 12: 311–24.

Foxhall, L., H.-J. Gehrke, and N. Luraghi. (eds.). 2010. *Intentional History: Spinning Time in Ancient Greece*. Stuttgart.

Gehrke, H.-J. 2001. "Myth, History, and Collective Identity: Uses of the Past in Ancient Greece and Beyond." In N. Luraghi (ed.), *The Historian's Craft in the Age of Herodotus*. Oxford: 286–313.

Gehrke, H.-J. 2014. *Geschichte als Element antiker Kultur: Die Griechen und ihre Geschichte(n)*. Berlin and Boston.

Golden, M. 1998. *Sport and Society in Ancient Greece*. Cambridge.

Gow, A.S.F., and D.L. Page 1965. *The Greek Anthology: Hellenistic Epigrams*. Vol. 2. Cambridge.

Grandjean, C. 2003. *Les Messéniens de 370/369 au 1er siècle de notre ère: Monnayages et histoire*. Athens.

Graninger, D. 2011. *Cult and Koinon in Hellenistic Thessaly*. Boston and Leiden.

Gutzwiller, K.J. (ed.). 2005. *The New Posidippus: A Hellenistic Poetry Book*. Oxford.

Haake, M., L. Kolonas, and S. Scharff. 2007. "Fragmente einer metrischen Strategenweihung an Aphrodite Stratagis aus dem hellenistischen Thyrreion." *Chiron* 37: 113–22.

Hallof, K. 2019. "Alte und neue Inschriften aus Olympia II. 5: Epigramm über den Olympiasieger Deinosthenes aus Sparta." *Chiron* 49: 173–86. https://doi.org/10.1515/9783110611236-008.

Harder, A. 2019. "Taking Position: Later Hellenistic Epigrammatists." In C. Henriksén (ed.), *A Companion to Ancient Epigram*. Hoboken, NJ: 371–87.

Hodkinson, S. 1989. "Inheritance, Marriage and Demography: Perspectives upon the Success and Decline of Sparta." In A. Powell (ed.), *Classical Sparta: Techniques behind Her Success*. Norman, OK: 79–121.

Hodkinson, S. 1999. "An Agonistic Culture? Athletic Competition in Archaic and Classical Spartan Society." In S. Hodkinson and A. Powell (eds.), *Sparta: New Perspectives*. London: 147–87.

Hodkinson, S. 2000. *Property and Wealth in Classical Sparta*. Swansea.

Hodkinson, S. 2004. "Female Property Ownership and Empowerment in Classical and Hellenistic Sparta." In T. Figueira (ed.), *Spartan Society*. Swansea: 103–36.

Hönle, A. 1972. *Olympia in der Politik der griechischen Staatenwelt: Von 776 bis zum Ende des 5. Jahrhunderts*. Bebenhausen.

Hose, M. 2015. "Hippika (71–88)." In B. Seidensticker, A. Stähli, and A. Wessels (eds.), *Der Neue Poseidipp. Text – Übersetzung – Kommentar*. Darmstadt: 283–318.

Kennell, N.M. 1995. *The Gymnasium of Virtue: Education and Culture in Ancient Sparta*. Chapel Hill, NC.

Kertész, I. 1998. "Some Notes on Inscription IvP. no. 10–12." *Acta archaeologica Academiae Scientiarum Hungaricae* 38: 191–4.

Kertész, I. 2013. "The Role of Hellenistic Pergamon in the Ancient and Modern Olympic Movement." In P. Mauritsch and C. Ulf (eds.), *Kultur(en) – Formen des Alltäglichen in der Antike: Festschrift für Ingomar Weiler zum 75. Geburtstag, II*. Graz: 817–27.

Kiderlen, M. 2010. "Zur Datierung der Damonon-Inschrift *IG* V 1, 213." In M. Kiderlen and P. Themelis (eds.), *Das Poseidonheiligtum bei Akovitika in Messenien*. Wiesbaden: 144–5.

Köhnken, A. 2007. "Epinician Epigram." In P. Bing and J.S. Blas (eds.), *Brill's Companion to Hellenistic Epigram*. Boston and Leiden: 295–312.

Kralli, I. 2017. *The Hellenistic Peloponnese. Interstate Relations: A Narrative and Analytic History, 371–146 BC*. Swansea.

Kurke, L. 1991. *The Traffic in Praise: Pindar and the Poetics of Social Economy*. Ithaca, NY.

Kurke, L. 1993. "The Economy of Kudos." In C. Dougherty and L. Kurke (eds.), *Cultural Poetics in Archaic Greece: Cult, Performance, Politics*. Cambridge: 131–63.

Kyle, D.G. 2003. "The Only Woman in All Greece: Kyniska, Agesilaos, Alcibiades and Olympia." *Journal of Sport History* 30: 183–203.

Kyle, D.G. 2007. "Fabulous Females and Ancient Olympia." In G.P. Schaus and S.R. Wenn (eds.), *Onward to the Olympics: Historical Perspectives on the Olympic Games*. Waterloo, ON: 131–52.

Lämmer, M. 1986–7. "Die Aktischen Spiele von Nikopolis." *Stadion* 12–13: 27–38.

Luraghi, N. 2008. *The Ancient Messenians: Constructions of Ethnicity and Memory*. Cambridge.

Makres, A. 2021. "Victorious Athletes of Ancient Messene: Old and New Epigraphic Evidence." In E. Mackil and N. Papazarkadas (eds.), *Greek Epigraphy and Religion: Papers in Memory of Sara B. Aleshire from the Second North American Congress of Greek and Latin Epigraphy*. Boston, MA, and Leiden: 167–203.

Mann, C. 2001. *Athlet und Polis im archaischen und frühklassischen Griechenland*. Göttingen.

Mann, C. 2020a. "Campaign Agones: Towards a Classification of Greek Athletic Competitions." *Classica et Mediaevalia* 68: 99–117. https://doi.org/10.7146/classicaetmediaevalia.v68i0.113922.

Mann, C. 2020b. "Alexander and Athletics or How (Not) to Use a Traditional Field of Monarchic Legitimation." In K. Trampedach and A. Meeus (eds.), *The Legitimation of Conquest: Monarchical Representation and the Art of Government in the Empire of Alexander the Great*. Stuttgart: 61–75.

Michalopoulos, M. 2016. *In the Name of Lykourgos: The Rise and Fall of the Spartan Revolutionary Movement (243–146 BC)*. Barnsley.

Millender, E. 2009. "The Spartan Dyarchy: A Comparative Perspective." In S. Hodkinson (ed.), *Sparta. Comparative Approaches*. Swansea: 1–67.

Moretti, L. 1957. *Olympionikai, i vincitori negli antichi agoni olimpici*. Rome.

Moretti, L. 1964. "Epigraphica: 1. Un pentatleta Messeno; 2. Il lapidario di Axel Munthe." *Rivisita di Filologia e di Istruzione Classica* 92: 320–31.

Moretti, L. 1992. "Nuovo supplemento al catalogo degli Olympionikai." In W.D.E. Coulson and H. Kyrieleis (eds.), *Proceedings of an International Symposium on the Olympic Games, 5–9 September 1988*. Athens: 119–28. (= ibid. 1987. "Nuovo supplemento al catalogo degli Olympionikai." *MGR* 12: 67–91).

Müth, S. 2007. *Eigene Wege: Topographie und Stadtplan von Messene in spätklassisch-hellenistischer Zeit*. Rahden.

Nafissi, M. 1991. *La nascita del kosmos: Studi sulla storia e la società di Sparta*. Naples.

Nafissi, M. 2013. "L'iscrizione di Damonon (IG V 1, 213 = Moretti, IAG 16), gli Hekatombaia (Strabo 8,4,11) e il sistema festivo della Laconia d'epoca classica." In F. Berlinzani (ed.), *La cultura a Sparta in età classica*. Trento: 105–74.

Nafissi, M. Forthcoming. "Gli agoni per Orthia e l'educazione dei giovani spartani." In S. Scharff (ed.), *Beyond the Big Four: Local Games in Ancient Greek Athletic Culture*. Münster.

Nielsen, T.H. 2018a. "Athletics in Late-Archaic and Classical Arkadia." In K. Tausend (ed.), *Arkadien im Altertum: Geschichte und Kultur einer antiken Gebirgslandschaft. Beiträge des Internationalen Symposiums in Graz, Österreich, 11. bis 13. Februar 2016*. Graz: 407–40.

Nielsen, T.H. 2018b. *Two Studies in the History of Ancient Greek Athletics*. Copenhagen.

Nobili, C. 2013 (2016). "Celebrating Spartan Victories in Classical Sparta: Epinician Odes and Epigrams." *Nikephoros* 26: 63–98.

Ollier, F. 1933. *Le mirage spartiate: Étude sur l'idéalisation de Sparte dans l'antiquité grecque de l'origine jusqu'aux Cyniques*. Paris.

Palagia, O. 2009. "Spartan Self-Presentation in the Panhellenic Sanctuaries of Delphi and Olympia in the Classical Period." In N. Kaltsas (ed.), *Athens – Sparta. Contributions to the Research on the History and Archaeology of the Two City-states*. New York: 32–40.

Papakonstantinou, Z. 2018. "Athletics, Memory and Community in Hellenistic and Roman Messene." In S. Bell and P. Ripat (eds.), *Sport and Social Identity in Classical Antiquity: Papers in Honour of Mark Golden*. London: 64–78.

Paradiso, A. 2015. "L'exercice du pouvoir royal: Agésilas, Cynisca et les exploits olympiques." *Ktèma* 40: 233–41.

Pavlogiannis, O., and E. Albanidis. 2007. "Τα Άκτια της Νικόπολης. Νέες προσεγγίσεις." In K. Zachos (ed.), Νικόπολις Β. Πρακτικά του Δευτέρου Διεθνούς για τη Νικόπολη (11–15 September 2002). Preveza: 57–76.

Petermandl, W. 2013. *Olympischer Pferdesport im Altertum: Die schriftlichen Quellen*. Kassel.

Poliakoff, M.B. 1987. *Combat Sports in the Ancient World: Competition, Violence, and Culture*. New Haven et al.

Pomeroy, S. 2002. *Spartan Women*. Oxford.

Prag, J.R.W. 2007. "Auxilia and Gymnasia: A Sicilian Model of Roman Imperialism." *Journal of Roman Studies* 97: 68–100. https://doi.org/10.3815/000000007784016061.

Remijsen, S. 2009. "Challenged by Egyptians: Greek Sports in the Third Century BC." In Z. Papakonstantinou (ed.), *Sport in the Cultures of the Ancient World*. London and New York: 98–123.

Remijsen, S., and S. Scharff. 2015. "The Expression of Identities in Hellenistic Victor Epigrams." In T.F. Scanlon (ed.), *Classics@-Online Journal, Issue 13: Greek Poetry and Sport*. http://chs.harvard.edu/CHS/article/display/6059.

Roebuck, C.A. 1941. *A History of Messenia from 369 to 146 BC*. Chicago.

Scharff, S. Forthcoming. *Hellenistic Athletes: Agonistic Cultures and Self-presentation*. Cambridge.

Sens, A. 2004. "Doricisms in the New and Old Posidippus." In B. Acosta-Hughes, E. Kosmetatou, and M. Baumbach (eds.), *Labored in Papyrus Leaves: Perspectives on an Epigram Collection Attributed to Posidippus (P.Mil.Vogl. VIII 309)*. Cambridge, MA: 65–83.

Shimron, B. 1972. *Late Sparta: The Spartan Revolution 243–146 B.C.* New York.

Shipley, G.J. 2004. "Lakedaimon." In M. Hansen and T.H. Nielsen (eds.), *An Inventory of Archaic and Classical Poleis: An Investigation Conducted by the Copenhagen Polis Centre for the Danish National Research Foundation*. Oxford: 569–98.

Shipley, G.J. 2017. "Agis IV, Kleomenes III, and Spartan Landscapes." *Historia* 66: 281–97.

Spawforth, A.J.S. 2002. "Roman Sparta." In *Hellenistic and Roman Sparta. A Tale of Two Cities*. 2nd ed. London and New York: 91–233, 251–67.

Tentori Montalto, M. 2022. "Die Statuen von Olympia und die Triumphalrückkehr der Athleten in die Heimat: Neue Überlegungen zum Epigramm des Deinosthenes." *Journal of Epigraphic Studies* 5: 9–28.

Themelis, P. 1992. "Το Στάδιο της Μεσσήνης." In W.D.E. Coulson and H. Kyrieleis (eds.), *Proceedings of an International Symposium on the Olympic Games, 5–9 September 1988*. Athens: 87–91.

Themelis, P. 1995 (1996). "Μεσσήνη." *Ergon* 42: 27–36.

Themelis, P. 1995 (1998). "Ἀνασκαφὴ Μεσσήνης (Πίν. 13–42)." *PAAH* 150: 55–86.

Themelis, P. 2009. "Das Stadion und das Gymnasion von Messene." *Nikephoros* 22: 59–77.

Themelis, P. 2011. "Μεσσήνιοι αθλητές." In A. Delivorrias, G. Despinis, and A. Zarkadas (eds.), ΕΠΑΙΝΟΣ *Luigi Beschi*. Athens: 141–9.

Themelis, P. 2013. "The Doryphoros of Messene." In V. Franciosi and P. Themelis (eds.), *Pompei/Messene: Il "Doriforo" e il suo contesto*. Rome: 126–209.

Tod, M.N. 1903–4. "Teams of Ball-Players at Sparta." *Annual of the British School at Athens* 10: 63–77. https://doi.org/10.1017/S0068245400002070.

Tracy, S., and C. Habicht. 1991. "New and Old Panathenaic Victor Lists." *Hesperia* 60: 187–236. https://doi.org/10.2307/148087.

Van Bremen, R. 2007. "The Entire House Is Full of Crowns: Hellenistic Agōnes and the Commemoration of Victory." In S. Hornblower and C. Morgan (eds.), *Pindar's Poetry, Patrons and Festivals: From Archaic Greece to the Roman Empire*. Oxford: 345–75.

Wacker, C. 2018. "Die Spiele von Aktion – vom ethnischen Kultfest zum panhellenischen Megaevent." In J. Court and A. Müller (eds.), *Jahrbuch 2017 der Deutschen Gesellschaft für Geschichte der Sportwissenschaft e.V.* Berlin: 9–34.

Walthall, D.A. 2013. "Becoming Kings: Spartan Basileia in the Hellenistic Period." In N. Luraghi (ed.), *The Splendors and Miseries of Ruling Alone. Encounters with Monarchy from Archaic Greece to the Hellenistic Mediterranean*. Stuttgart: 129–63.

*Public discourses in the local arena are characterized by the immediate presence of multiple stakeholders. When it comes to politics, the polyphony of voices is particularly pronounced: the notion of political rivalries between competing groupings, sometimes merging into local violence and turmoil, was foundational to the Greek city both in the Classical and the Hellenistic periods. This chapter casts a spotlight on the local as a prime place of political agency, despite the tight entanglement of the local horizon with regional and transregional realms of conduct, and the impact they wielded on the Hellenistic city. Tracing the history of two prominent politicians – or "tyrants" – in third-century BCE Megalopolis, James Roy skilfully makes the voices of their opponents and supporters heard, both in their hometown and beyond, in emic and in etic expressions alike. Such an attempt is, by default, faced with various analytical challenges, including the ones emanating from references in the sources to Aristodamos and Lydiadas as tyrants, which Roy discusses first. Both men enjoyed broad support in Megalopolis, which was also their main theatre of action; neither of them while tyrant seems to have advanced political agendas beyond the local horizon. Roy reveals structural similarities between the protagonists, yet he also detects profound differences, beyond both men's ultimate fate: Aristodamos was assassinated by his internal enemies, while Lydiadas at some point resigned his tyranny to seek high office in the Achaian League. Polybios, proud citizen of Megalopolis and rich in local knowledge, has curiously little to say about these men, likely because of his aversion to the practice of one-man rule. The little that can be extracted from his* Histories, *however, suggests that there was a local current of memory in Megalopolis that was distinctly hostile to Lydiadas and his family. The examination of archaeological and epigraphical evidence, on the other hand, shows that the family fostered, successfully so, a favourable memory of its tyrant. We can only conjecture about the fierce competition on the ground. More importantly, Roy's chapter urges us to conceptual caution when tracing the local voice in grand histories in the style of Polybios.*

*Keywords: tyrants, local rivalry, local memory, Achaian League, Peloponnesian affairs, Polybios*

# 11

# Shaping and Reshaping Local Memories in Megalopolis: The Case of the Tyrants Aristodamos and Lydiadas

JAMES ROY

Within the Greek city-state memory of its past was highly important, but that past could be shaped and reshaped to suit the interests of different groupings within the local world of the city and to play out against the wider Greek world. In some cases, we have sufficient evidence to trace the interplay of local interests, one such being the two tyrants who controlled Megalopolis in Arkadia in the third century BCE. For them we have evidence from inscriptions found at Megalopolis, and from the writers Polybios, Plutarch, and Pausanias: each of these presents a different viewpoint on Megalopolis. This range of evidence offers both emic and etic views, a particularly promising combination, and not only from the time of the two tyrants but also from generations and even centuries later. The inscriptions show how the family of Lydiadas wanted to be seen in their own city, while Polybios, proud to be a citizen of Megalopolis, was writing for a very wide public and was concerned about how his home city would be seen in the Greek-speaking world. Plutarch had no personal connection with Megalopolis, and so, even if he shared information used by Polybios from the memoirs of Aratos, he could write more freely about the city. Pausanias equally had no direct attachment to Megalopolis, but he visited the city in the second century CE and clearly discussed its past with leading citizens, as he did elsewhere: consequently, he presents Aristodamos and Lydiadas as they were remembered at Megalopolis in his day.[1] The present chapter thus seeks to contribute to this volume's overall concern with localism by investigating a lively local discourse at Megalopolis about the organization of rule: while local political activity at Megalopolis was deeply entangled with regional and wider Greek politics, the different perspectives of the sources on the two tyrants allow us to delve into a local discourse that has hitherto been mute.

Aristodamos and later, after a short interval, Lydiadas each controlled Megalopolis for 10 or more years.[2] Aristodamos was born at Phigaleia, a *polis* in southwestern Arkadia, but was adopted by Tritaios, a leading citizen of Megalopolis (Paus. 8.27.11), while Lydiadas was born into an important Megalopolitan family (Plut. *Arat.* 30.1, Paus. 8.27.12). There is no evidence to show how either man came to power. Aristodamos' tyranny began in the mid-260s and that of Lydiadas ended in 235. The two tyrannies thus fell within a period of about 30 years in the mid-third century, a very troubled period in the Peloponnese. The Antigonid dynasty in Macedon took an active interest in the Peloponnese, and so too did the Aitolian League as its power grew. From the middle of the century the Achaian League developed, often hostile to the Aitolians and their Peloponnesian allies and also to the Antigonids, though the Achaians formed a lasting alliance with Macedon shortly after the death of Lydiadas. Sparta, though less powerful than in the fifth and fourth centuries, still played a significant role, and was constantly at odds with Megalopolis, its northern neighbour. Megalopolis thus had to face a range of threats, defending as best it could its own local interests in frequently changing military and diplomatic circumstances. It is easy to see that there would be local support in Megalopolis for a leader who could provide a measure of security.

The problem was that, while Aristodamos and Lydiadas as tyrants enjoyed support in Megalopolis, both they and Megalopolis could be criticized by anyone who – like Polybios[3] – disapproved of tyranny. However, the meaning of the term "tyrant" (*tyrannos*) as applied to men like Aristodamos and Lydiadas has recently been the subject of discussion. Paschidis (2008: 217–18) raised questions, and Shipley (2018: 97–126) has carried the analysis further, writing about the third-century Peloponnese:

A man whom others call *tyrannos* seems generally to have been more of a governor or "superintendent" (to invoke Demetrios of Phaleron's title of *epimelētēs*), drawn from the local citizenry and very likely possessing hereditary wealth, who sought to preserve stability, security, and the interests of the political elite (or their part of it), not impose a new order. Some may have been military commanders with additional civil responsibilities, or men appointed to a special magistracy under oligarchic or democratic procedure. (122)

The observation that tyrants could offer a stable regime that enjoyed local support is a good one, and could certainly be applied to both Aristodamos and Lydiadas; neither behaved like the obviously tyrannical Aristotimos, who controlled Elis for a few months in 272 with extreme cruelty.[4] Moreover Paschidis (2008: 218, n. 1) has shown, using epigraphic evidence, that under the tyrants in third-century Argos normal constitutional organs of *polis* government continued to function. For Megalopolis, Lauter-Bufe and Lauter (2011: 154–7) have argued that, since excavations show that third-century Megalopolis possessed the buildings needed for democratic organs like council and assembly, democratic government will have continued under the tyrants ("Diese Tyrannis war offensichtlich in demokratische Regeln eingebettet"): but the existence of such buildings does not prove that they were always used for democratic purposes.

Even if both Aristodamos and Lydiadas gave Megalopolis stability for a time, the evidence suggests that their rule was seen as unconstitutional; Aristodamos was assassinated, and his assassins were apparently able to return eventually to Megalopolis without arousing any criticism, while Lydiadas had to resign his tyranny in order to take Megalopolis into the Achaian League. In 195 Aristainos, then Achaian *stratēgos*, urged Nabis of Sparta to abdicate, naming tyrants of neighbouring cities who had laid down their power and then lived "not only a safe but also an honoured old age among their citizens." Livy, here following Polybios, says that Aristainos named these tyrants; he does not give the names, but the list would certainly include Lydiadas.[5] Aristainos' speech suggests that the tyrants were not constitutionally appointed (and further evidence could be cited). Neither Paschidis nor Shipley refers to an interesting observation by Mossé, who, in writing about Hellenistic tyranny, drew attention to the "bon tyran," seen especially in Asia Minor but also in Greece. The phrase is intended not to justify tyranny, but to point to the "good tyrant" who enjoyed the support of a significant number of citizens, including notables, and could ensure some local stability in difficult times.[6] Mossé in fact cited as an example of the "good tyrant" Aristodamos of Megalopolis. Mossé's approach, presenting tyrants as tyrants but recognizing that some governed competently, at least for a time, and enjoyed support from fellow citizens, seems safer than supposing that so-called tyrants in fact held constitutional office.[7]

It was for a time widely believed that Antigonos Gonatas promoted tyranny in the Peloponnese, using the tyrants as allies, but doubts about this belief have gained ground recently. Paschidis (2008: 217–18) raised questions, and so too did Kralli (2017: 127–8), noting in particular that it is difficult to assess the policy of Antigonos Gonatas towards Megalopolis. Then, after detailed analysis, Shipley (2018: 120–6) concluded, with good arguments, that there is no evidence that Gonatas systematically pursued such a policy. It follows that there is no reason to suppose that Gonatas supported any particular tyranny unless there is clear evidence. While Megalopolis seems to have been generally friendly to Macedon from the time of Philip II onwards, there is no evidence that the two Megalopolitan tyrannies were significantly affected by Antigonos Gonatas. The main theatre for the tyrants' political activity was local politics at Megalopolis.

Another point that needs to be clarified is the question of whether there was an Arkadian federation in the third century, that is, another level of political activity above the *polis*. Stavrianopoulou (2002: 133–4), while acknowledging that current scholarly opinion is against the existence of a third-century Arkadian confederacy, considered the possibility that there might have been one. However, evidence that has come to light since the publication of Stavrianopoulou's work makes a third-century Arkadian federation extremely unlikely. An Argive inscription referring to an Arkadian *koinon* and also to Kleonai as a *kōmē* of Argos had been used as argument for the survival of an Arkadian *koinon* into the early third century, on the assumption that Argos did not absorb Kleonai until then; but Kritsas has now shown that Kleonai was incorporated into Argos before ca. 350.[8] If we therefore dismiss the possibility of Arkadian federal politics in the time of the tyrants, then the focus of their political activity remains local, at Megalopolis, expanded only after Lydiadas resigned his tyranny to include the federal politics of the Achaian League.

The first tyrant at Megalopolis, Aristodamos (or Aristodemos to some non-Arkadians), held power at least from the later 260s until he was assassinated around the middle of the century,[9] but seems to have attracted little attention outside Megalopolis. The assassins were among those Megalopolitans, obviously opposed to Aristodamos, who chose to go into exile rather than remain in Megalopolis under his tyranny;[10] they organized the assassination from exile. Both Polybios (10.22.2) and Plutarch (*Phil.* 1) mention the assassination of Aristodamos simply as one episode in the colourful careers of his assassins, who eventually became tutors of Philopoimen (more on them below). Elsewhere, when discussing the liberation of Sikyon, Plutarch (*Arat.* 5.1, 7.4, 7.6) refers several times to one of Philopoimen's tutors (whom he calls Ekdelos) as an important comrade of Aratos, without mentioning the other tutor, and with no reference at all to Aristodamos. Plutarch (*Agis* 3) also mentions, in a purely Spartan context, that Aristodamos defeated a Spartan army that attacked Megalopolis. No inscriptions relevant to Aristodamos have been found.[11] Most of what we know about Aristodamos comes from Pausanias and is embedded in his account of Megalopolis. He reports (8.30.7, 32.4, 35.5) the victory over the Spartans, and that from the booty Aristodamos erected public buildings at Megalopolis: a stoa called Myropolis, a temple of Artemis Agrotera,[12] and a sanctuary of Artemis Skiaditis.

Despite the assassination, Aristodamos' supporters gave him a very honourable burial; his tomb near the city was marked by a prominent mound of earth beside the road to Mainalos (Paus. 8.36.5). At Megalopolis he was remembered as "the Good" (*Chrēstos*) (8.27.11, 36.5). Pausanias is clearly reporting what he learned at Megalopolis, where there was a strong and very favourable local memory of Aristodamos; his report makes no secret of the fact that Aristodamos was a tyrant (8.27.11, 30.7, 35.5, 36.5), but never mentions that he was assassinated.

Since the two men who organized the assassination of Aristodamos in 251 will reappear, some detail on them is needed. Like other Megalopolitans, they fled the tyranny and went into exile. They also helped Aratos to overthrow the tyrant Nikokles at Sikyon;[13] acted as legislators at Kyrene, setting up what Plutarch (*Phil.* 1.3) considered a good and effective constitution; and reappeared later at Megalopolis as tutors of Philopoimen.[14] The exact form of their names is uncertain. Polybios (who as a Megalopolitan should have been well informed) has (10.22.2) Ekdemos and Demophanes: Plutarch (*Phil.* 1.2–3) has Ekdemos and Megalophanes, but elsewhere (*Arat.* 5.1, 7.4, 7.6) Ekdelos (mentioned alone): Pausanias (8.49.2) calls them Ekdelos and Megalophanes (in an encomium of Philopoimen, without mention of Aristodamos).

Megalopolis' second tyrant, Lydiadas, was much more widely known. He took control of the city around 245,[15] and resigned his tyranny ca. 235,[16] taking Megalopolis into the Achaian League, in which he held the highest office (*stratēgos*) three times.[17] He died in a battle near Megalopolis in 227. He was a major figure in Peloponnesian politics, and appears in Plutarch's lives of his contemporaries Aratos and Kleomenes, but the local Megalopolitan evidence about him is especially interesting. The Megalopolitan Polybios says remarkably little about him, but there is very striking epigraphic evidence about the tyrant and his family in Megalopolis. Then Pausanias shows how the local memory of Lydiadas had evolved over roughly four centuries.

Lydiadas' wider fame is shown – rather oddly – in Pausanias' account (8.10.5–10, 8.27.14) of a battle at Mantineia in which the Spartan king Agis IV was defeated and killed by the Mantineians and their allies. The account is deeply flawed, since Agis was killed at Sparta (Plut. *Agis* 16–21) and the combination of allies supporting Mantineia is thoroughly implausible.[18] However the list of allies is clearly intended to impress, and it includes a Megalopolitan force commanded by Lydiadas and Leokydes. Leokydes was distinguished because his ancestor Arkesilaos saw the very aged sacred doe of the goddess Despoina wearing a collar that said it was a fawn when Agapenor set out for Troy (Paus. 8.10.10), and Lydiadas is clearly also seen as a figure who enhances the account of the battle.[19]

According to Polybios (4.77.10), Lydiadas gave Alipheira, a small town strategically placed in the borderland between Megalopolis and Triphylia, to the Eleians in return for (unspecified) personal services. Nothing else is recorded as happening at Megalopolis during Lydiadas' tyranny, and equally we know nothing of the internal politics of Megalopolis during the following years until the death of Lydiadas in 227. Nonetheless Lydiadas appears to have been able to play a leading part in Achaian politics without being challenged at home in Megalopolis. However, there were certainly others in Megalopolis with powerful connections, strong personalities, and strong views. The two Megalopolitans who had organized the assassination of Aristodamos returned to the city and acted as tutors of the young Philopoimen, later a leading figure in Megalopolis and in Achaian affairs. Philopoimen, born probably in 252, was well beyond childhood when the two took over his education,[20] and so they may well have returned to Megalopolis after Lydiadas had ended his tyranny. Polybios (10.22.4–5) does not suggest that on their return they showed any hostility to tyranny, or to an ex-tyrant: he speaks rather of their teaching Philopoimen endurance and courage in hunting and in war, simplicity and restraint in dress and in lifestyle. A few months after Lydiadas' death two other Megalopolitans, Nikophanes and Kerkidas, went on a very important embassy to Antigonos Doson, the king of Macedon. While Megalopolis was generally friendly towards Macedon, Kerkidas may also have had family connections to Macedon from the time of Philip II if he was a descendant of the Kerkidas mentioned by Demosthenes. In any case these two were linked by ancestral ties of guest-friendship (*xenia*) to the family of Aratos, the leading Achaian politician.[21] Megalopolitans like Nikophanes and Kerkidas clearly had political influence.

There was also a Megalopolitan poet named Kerkidas, who may well have been a different person from the politician of that name.[22] He wrote forcefully about the social injustice that he saw in contemporary society. According to Plutarch (*Cleom.* 17.3) social tension was widespread in the Peloponnese in the time of Kleomenes III, and it became evident at Megalopolis during the rebuilding of the city after its destruction by Kleomenes in 223, when a dispute arose between the wealthy landowners and the other citizens, severe enough for Aratos to intervene to calm matters (Polyb. 5.93.1–10). Polybios says that the dispute was due to the difficult circumstances that followed the destruction, and also to disagreement about the work of Prytanis, who was sent by Antigonos Doson to draw up laws. There is no direct proof of social tension already in Megalopolis in the lifetime of Lydiadas, but he may well have faced local political problems. That we do not hear of his being troubled by them may be due to his political skill, or to our inadequate evidence, or to both.

Plutarch reports both strengths and weaknesses in Lydiadas, whom he mentions in several texts. The clearest judgment is given in a chapter of the *Life of Aratos* that is devoted to Lydiadas and his relations with Aratos (Plut. *Arat.* 30.1–5). Plutarch mentions Lydiadas' tyranny, and says that when he gave it up, he freed himself from hatred, fear, guards, and spearmen (*Arat.* 30.2): here Plutarch presents Lydiadas as a typical tyrant ruling by force, though it is hard to tell whether he is drawing on good information about the nature of Lydiadas' regime or simply applying to Lydiadas' conventional rhetorical tropes about tyrants. In his *Life of Kleomenes* (6.4) Plutarch says more briefly that Lydiadas resigned the tyranny, restored freedom to the citizens, and took Megalopolis into the Achaian League. Elsewhere Plutarch says (*Moralia* 552B = *De sera numinis vindicta* 6) that on resigning the tyranny Lydiadas restored the laws to the citizens, again depicting an unconstitutional regime, although without mentioning anything resembling "hatred, fear, guards, and spearmen."[23] At any rate Plutarch makes clear that Lydiadas had ruled as a tyrant. He goes on (*Arat.* 30.4–5) to speak of Lydiadas' successes in the Achaian League and the support that he enjoyed there, but also of increasing rivalry with Aratos. When Plutarch compares Lydiadas with Aratos he writes of an assumed, artificial character pitted against the true, unadulterated virtue of Aratos, and says that, since Lydiadas had once been a tyrant, he was never free from suspicion.[24] Overall Plutarch's portrayal of Lydiadas is not hostile, but recognizes flaws. I will consider Plutarch's treatment of Lydiadas' death below.

The view taken of Lydiadas by his fellow Megalopolitan Polybios is very different. He simply says as little as possible about Lydiadas, and in fact mentions him only three times, always briefly, although Lydiadas' life and career fell entirely within the period covered by the books of Polybios that survive complete. These references (paraphrased) are as follows:

— Polyb. 2.44.5: While Demetrios of Macedon was still alive Lydiadas had foreseen what would happen (i.e., Aratos' attempt to end tyrannies in the Peloponnese) and had, with much wisdom and good sense, voluntarily laid down his tyranny and joined the national league (*ethnikē sympoliteia*).
— Polyb. 2.51.3: The Achaians were defeated by Kleomenes near Mount Lykaion, and again at Ladokeia in Megalopolis "when Lydiadas also fell," and at Hekatombaion in the territory of Dyme.
— Polyb. 4.77.10: Alipheira from the beginning belonged to Arkadia and Megalopolis. During his tyranny Lydiadas gave it to the Eleians in exchange for certain private services (*idias praxeis*).

Given Polybios' obvious pride in his home city of Megalopolis and in the Achaian League, it is remarkable that he chose to say so little about a Megalopolitan who played a leading role in Achaian politics. It seems in fact that he made a positive choice to write as little as possible about Lydiadas, either as tyrant or as Achaian politician. Even when Polybios recognizes that Lydiadas showed wisdom and good sense in giving up his tyranny, he says virtually nothing about Lydiadas' rule as tyrant. The report of Lydiadas' death could not be briefer, and gives no details at all. Finally, the third passage, about Alipheira, does not explain why Lydiadas gave the town to the Eleians but suggests obscurely that the grant was made for personal interests of Lydiadas rather than for the good of Megalopolis, which lost a fortified town of strategic importance.[25] Given all that Polybios could have said about Lydiadas, his choice not to write about him is evidence of strong disapproval, although such reasoning, based on absence of comment, takes us only so far. Polybios was often ready to express strong disapproval vigorously, but in the case of Lydiadas that would have been damaging for Megalopolis' reputation among Greeks, and so Polybios preferred to say next to nothing about Lydiadas. In other words, Polybios shows by his reticence that one local current of memory of Lydiadas was distinctly hostile.[26]

A very different view of Lydiadas and his family is presented by the various inscriptions concerning them, all but one discovered since the 1980s. The one inscription that has long been known is a statue base, set up at Lykosoura near Megalopolis, showing that Kaphyai, in eastern Arkadia, honoured Lydiadas, son of Eudamos (*IG* V 2, 534). (Though a *polis* in its own right, Lykosoura formed a small enclave in western Megalopolitan territory, essentially dependent on Megalopolis: Roy 2010: 60.) It is generally accepted – surely rightly – that Lydiadas and Eudamos are the ex-tyrant and his father, and this text was until recently the only attestation of Lydiadas' father. Since Kaphyai became Achaian in 228[27] and Lydiadas died in 227, and nothing in the inscription suggests that the honours were posthumous, this inscription can be dated to 228–227. The Graeco-German excavations at Megalopolis in the late twentieth century uncovered remains of a large *exedra* with lavish honours voted by Megalopolis for Eudamos and Lydiadas (Stavrianopoulou 2002): it will be discussed later in detail. In 1986 Taeuber published an inscription that he had found at Megalopolis, recording honours decreed by Megalopolis for Aristopamon, son of Lydiadas, and identified Aristopamon, previously unattested, as the son of the ex-tyrant. Taeuber suggested circumstances in which the decree might have been passed, but noted that the inscription was in any case no later than the end of the third century. Then the Graeco-German excavations also produced a statue base recording honours voted by Megalopolis for

Lydiadas, son of Aristopamon (published as *SEG* 48.524 and dated ca. 170). There was thus a second attestation of Aristopamon, while this younger Lydiadas was already known as an ambassador of the Achaian League to Rome in 180, together with Kallikrates of Leontion and Aratos of Sikyon (Polyb. 24.8.8). The epigraphic record, taken together with the literary references to the tyrant Lydiadas and to his grandson, thus shows that the family was active and powerful at Megalopolis over at least four generations, from Eudamos, the tyrant's father, to the second Lydiadas. That in itself shows that the later members of the family had the opportunity to preserve a favourable local memory of the tyrant, publicly stated and very different from the reticence of their fellow citizen Polybios. How they did it is revealed above all by the *exedra* and the inscriptions on it.

The Graeco-German excavations uncovered in the agora a rough-and-ready post-classical building erected from material taken from classical buildings ("Spolienbau").[28] Some of the material came from an *exedra* that presumably stood in the agora, since there would have been no reason to transport material from elsewhere to build the Spolienbau. The *exedra* had been circular or semi-circular, and measured roughly eight metres in width: on it there had been at least six statues, larger than life-size, and from it inscriptions were also found honouring Lydiadas and his father, Eudamos.[29] The lettering of the inscriptions suggests a date early in the second century, and Stavrianopoulou argues that the monument will have been erected ca. 190–180, probably by the family.[30] The statues do not survive, but three blocks – published by Stavrianopoulou as A, B, and C – carry inscriptions. Block A lines 1–33 is a decree honouring Eudamos, and A lines 34–62, less well preserved, a decree for Lydiadas. Block B has three badly preserved lines of a decree for Lydiadas (or possibly a continuation of the decree on Block A), and Block C has three badly preserved lines of a decree for Eudamos (and possibly also Lydiadas). Stavrianopoulou publishes the three texts with translation and commentary, a considerable achievement in view of the poor state of preservation of the surfaces.[31] Little can be learned from what remains of the texts on Blocks B and C, but the two inscriptions on Block A are very valuable.

After his death (Block A.29) Eudamos was honoured as a hero, and heroic cult was set up for him, in which his descendants (*ekgonoi*) were to play a significant role (Block A.12–20). Moreover, the *damiorgoi* in the *polis* were to announce the sacrifices conducted for Eudamos and all the other honours voted for Eudamos by the *polis* in "the contest which the Hellenes hold": Stravrianopoulou shows that the contest in question was the Eleutheria held at Plataiai as a celebration of Greek freedom.[32] It thus appears that Eudamos was honoured for bringing freedom or liberation to Megalopolis.

The decree for Lydiadas is less well preserved. For him, too, the honours were posthumous (Block A.36). The legible portions of text do not show whether he too received worship as a hero, but, since sacrifices are mentioned (Block A.54, in an unknown context), Stavrianopoulou thinks it likely that he did.[33] It is notable that, whereas in the second decree Lydiadas is consistently named with his patronymic ("son of Eudamos"), in the other decree the surviving mentions of Eudamos never include a patronymic.[34]

Until the texts on the *exedra* came to light Eudamos was known only from the Kaphyatan decree (*IG* V 2, 534) honouring Lydiadas, son of Eudamos. There is not a single reference to Eudamos in surviving Greek literature. Since the surviving texts on the *exedra* do not tell us what act of liberation he had performed to deserve worship as a hero, any explanation can only be deduced from what we know of Megalopolitan history in the third century. Stavrianopoulou (2002: 138–43) proceeds in that way, assuming that Eudamos' achievement must have occurred before his son Lydiadas became tyrant, and concludes that the act of liberation was the assassination of the tyrant Aristodamos, freeing Megalopolis from tyranny. She therefore identifies Eudamos with the man otherwise identified as Ekdemos or Ekdelos, one of the two who organized the assassination. She further assumes that Eudamos and his associate will have seized power in Megalopolis after the assassination, and that eventually Lydiadas will have benefited from his father's reputation and his friendship with Aratos. This reconstruction presents various difficulties. There is uncertainty about the name of Ekdelos/Ekdemos, but he never appears with a name beginning with Eu-. The suggestion that he and his associate took power after the assassination would have to be reconciled with the well-known events of the two men's careers, involving the liberation of Sikyon (which may admittedly have happened before the assassination of Aristodamos) and especially their major constitutional reform in Kyrene. Finally, the *exedra* would have been deeply ironic if it bore statues of Eudamos, liberator of the city from the tyrant Aristodamos, and beside him his son Lydiadas, the next tyrant.

A solution to these difficulties would be to suppose that Eudamos freed Megalopolis from the tyranny of his son Lydiadas by persuading Lydiadas to end his tyranny. Then Lydiadas' resignation from tyranny could be presented as an act of filial piety, yielding to the wisdom and love of freedom of his father. Polybios (2.44.5) says that Lydiadas gave up his tyranny of his own choice, and Pausanias (8.27.12) that he did so voluntarily, but both statements could be reconciled with a resignation urged upon Lydiadas by his father. It is striking that, as noted above, in Block A.1–33 Eudamos never appears with a patronymic, whereas in A.34–62, Lydiadas always has his patronymic: he is clearly presented as the son of his father. The fact that

Eudamos is not mentioned in any surviving literary account of the end of Lydiadas' tyranny is understandable if Eudamos' role in ending the tyranny was no more than a device used by Lydiadas to present his resignation as morally righteous. If Eudamos was indeed given such a role, then even after the end of his tyranny Lydiadas remained so powerful that, on his father's death, he could have him honoured as a hero who had liberated Megalopolis.[35]

The possible range of dates at which Eudamos could have been honoured by Megalopolis and these honours proclaimed at "the contest which the Hellenes hold" can be clarified by considering the political situation in Boiotia, including Plataiai, where the Eleutheria were held. Stavrianopulou (2002: 141) used this method to argue for the years 252–245, supposing that Eudamos was honoured before Lydiadas became tyrant. However, a later date is perfectly possible. Since Megalopolis seems, despite vicissitudes, to have been generally friendly to Macedon, a proclamation would have been possible from about 236, when Boiotia passed from attachment to Aitolia to Macedonian influence.[36] Good relations between Boiotia and the Achaian League continued in the 220s.[37] We do not know when Eudamos died, but any date between the end of Lydiadas' tyranny ca. 235 and his death in 227 could be reconciled with an announcement at the Eleutheria. The announcement would be valuable in giving widespread publicity among Greeks to a local event in Megalopolis,[38] but it would also strengthen the prestige of Lydiadas and his family in their local setting in Megalopolis.

Presumably the monument was erected by the family, perhaps by the tyrant's grandson Lydiadas,[39] but it would have required the permission of the *polis* for such a large structure to be erected in the agora. The texts on the monument will have been copies of decrees passed earlier,[40] and were thus evidence of a protracted effort over several decades to promote the family's local prestige by securing honours, including the major honour of heroic cult. It is also clear that after Lydiadas' death his family remained influential, and later set up a very public display of the family's status in the agora. Since there were at least six statues on the *exedra*, numerous members of the family must have been represented: Eudamos, Lydiadas himself, his son Aristopamon, and his grandson Lydiadas were no doubt shown, but there must have been other members of the family of whom we know nothing. In this effort to impress local opinion, the family could clearly call on local official cooperation, but it is does not follow that all Megalopolitans were convinced: Polybios for one will have known well the monument in the agora of his native city, but did not join in the chorus of praise.

It is interesting to compare the honours granted to Lydiadas with those for Philopoimen, Megalopolitan and Achaian statesman, on his death in 182.

Not only were the honours for Philopoimen at Megalopolis greater, "equal to the divine" (*isotheois*), but Philopoimen was also honoured in other Achaian cities and even beyond, at Delphi, whereas the honours for Lydiadas and his family – including the decree of Kaphyai posted at Lykosoura near Megalopolis – were simply local. Polybios, so reticent about Lydiadas, praised his fellow Megalopolitan Philopoimen to the Greek-speaking world in an encomium in three books (now lost), and more briefly in his history. Indeed in 146 BCE, after Rome had defeated the Achaian League, when some Romans proposed to remove statues and decrees honouring Philopoimen on the grounds that he had been anti-Roman, Polybios intervened personally, and successfully, to preserve these memorials.[41]

Local opinion about Lydiadas colours the varying reports of his death, as we can see from Polybios and from Pausanias. Plutarch, writing for a wider audience and with no particular local interest in Megalopolis, twice gives more or less the same account of the death.[42] In 227 Kleomenes led an army against Megalopolis but was prevented by an Achaian force commanded by Aratos from reaching the walls of the city and was forced to retreat. Aratos then halted his main force at a ditch or gully and gave an order not to pursue Kleomenes' men. Lydiadas was probably the Achaian cavalry commander (hipparch), the second most senior official of the Achaian League; in any case, despite Aratos' order, he led a significant number of cavalry against Kleomenes' right wing but took the cavalry on to unsuitable terrain, where some of Kleomenes' troops could counterattack successfully, killing Lydiadas and driving the Achaian cavalry back in confusion into the main Achaian force. Kleomenes seized the opportunity, attacked again, and won a victory (though he did not capture the city). Lydiadas died fighting bravely, and Kleomenes sent his body to Megalopolis dressed in purple and with a crown, though the purpose of this striking gesture, treating the dead Lydiadas as a king like Kleomenes himself, is not explained by Plutarch, and remains obscure.[43] Marasco (1981: 2.404–11) has argued convincingly that Plutarch's accounts of the death in the *Lives* of Aratos and Kleomenes are similar enough to be from the same source, namely the memoirs of Aratos. Aratos evidently acknowledged that Lydiadas had died bravely, but made it clear that Lydiadas was to blame for the Achaian defeat since he had ignored Aratos' order not to pursue and had moreover led the cavalry on to terrain so unsuitable that they were routed. (Though Plutarch does not say so, it is odd that Lydiadas was unaware of difficulties of terrain just outside his home city.) According to Plutarch (*Arat.* 37.3) Aratos was severely criticized by some Achaians for not supporting Lydiadas, and no doubt took the opportunity to defend himself in his memoirs.

Polybios (2.51.3) describes Lydiadas' death in this battle, but, as mentioned above, in the briefest possible terms. He writes of three defeats that the Achaians suffered at the hands of Kleomenes, saying of the second: "and the second time they were defeated in a pitched battle at the place called Ladokeia in the territory of Megalopolis, when Lydiadas also fell, and the third time ..." Such brevity is entirely consistent with Polybios' evident desire to say as little as possible about Lydiadas.

Pausanias (8.27.15), however, gives a quite different account. When Kleomenes attacked Megalopolis in 223, Philopoimen led the majority of the Megalopolitans to safety in Messenia, while some citizens fought to the death defending their city, among them Lydiadas who died nobly. This version shifts Lydiadas' death from the battle of 227 to the capture of Megalopolis in 223, when Lydiadas carried no responsibility for the defeat. The moral fault lay with Kleomenes, who attacked despite a truce. Remarkably, in his *Periēgēsis* Pausanias mentions the capture of Megalopolis by Kleomenes six times, and in five of these passages notes that Kleomenes breached a truce,[44] but, even though at 4.29.8 Pausanias records that some Megalopolitans were killed during the capture, it is only in his summary of the history of Megalopolis at 8.27.15 that Pausanias mentions Lydiadas' death. The obvious explanation is that it was at Megalopolis that Pausanias heard that Lydiadas died in 223 when Kleomenes captured the city. That means that by the second century CE local memory of Lydiadas' demise had shifted from a death in 227, certainly brave but not beyond criticism, to a purely heroic death opposing a treacherous attack in 223.

The available evidence thus allows us to see shifting and even conflicting attitudes at Megalopolis to the two local tyrants Aristodamos and Lydiadas. Plutarch reports on them from a distance, not being involved in local Megalopolitan disagreements. However, inscriptions set up in Megalopolis; the Megalopolitan historian Polybios; and Pausanias, who talked to the Megalopolitans of his day when he visited the city, show the interplay of different local attitudes. Both tyrants enjoyed strong local support in their own day, and were honoured locally even after death, Aristodamos by a prominent tomb and Lydiadas (and his family) by a large monument in the agora. Yet there was strong opposition. Under Aristodamos' tyranny some Megalopolitans fled into exile and two of them organized his assassination. Hostility to Lydiadas appears in the minimal references to him of the Megalopolitan historian Polybios. No personal connection between the two tyrants is recorded, but favourable memory of an earlier tyrant no doubt suited the family and supporters of Lydiadas. Polybios, however, always mindful of Megalopolis' reputation in the wider Greek world, says as little about Aristodamos as about Lydiadas. Yet when Pausanias visited Megalopolis four centuries later he heard a current local version of the tyrants' history that revered both men as honourable figures in the city's past. Aristodamos was remembered as "the Good," with no mention of assassination, and Lydiadas had died a hero.

## NOTES

1  On how Pausanias gathered information from local people, especially the elite, see Pretzler 2005a and 2007: 35–6 and 40–1. Pausanias was certainly interested in inscriptions (Zizza 2006), but even in his description of the agora at Megalopolis (8.30.2–31.8) never refers to the large *exedra* of Lydiadas' family (Stavrianopoulou 2002, discussed below) which stood in the agora or the important inscriptions on it along with statues of family members: if the *exedra* was still complete when Pausanias visited Megalopolis (cf. 8.30.5 on empty statue bases in the agora), the failure to mention it was presumably a matter of Pausanias' literary choice.

2  Berve 1967: 1.400–2 and 2.712–13 assembles the main evidence for the two men, apart from the very important epigraphic material that has been discovered more recently and is discussed below.

3  On Polybios' intense dislike of tyranny see Lévy 1996, and, e.g., Polyb. 2.59.6.

4  Berve 1967: 1.403–5 and 2.713, Gómez Espelosín 1991; Shipley 2018: 111–12.

5  Livy 34.33.1–2: *non tutam modo sed etiam honoratam inter cives senectutem egissent*. See Kralli 2017: 341 (and 316 on the date). Livy's source is Polybios (Briscoe 1981: 2), and Briscoe 1981: 104 notes that the examples of tyrants enjoying "safe and honourable old age" would include Lydiadas. It does not follow that Polybios himself shared the view that he attributed to Aristainos.

6  Mossé 2004: 152.

7  See also the illuminating analysis of "one-man rule" among Greeks by Luraghi 2013, and also Luraghi 2018 on the discourse of tyranny.

8  Piérart 1982, Charneux 1983: 256–62.; cf. Kritsas 2006: 427–9. See also Nielsen 2002: 497–9 on the end of the Arkadian federation.

9  Berve 1967: 1.400-1, 2.712; Shipley 2018: 112.

10  Polyb. 10.22.2. Polybios says that these Megalopolitans fled "the tyrants," which suggests that one or more others were associated with Aristodamos in the tyranny, the more so since a few words later in the same sentence Polybios refers to "Aristodemos the tyrant" in the singular. If there were other tyrants, the most likely explanation would be that one or more relatives, possibly a son or sons, were associated with Aristodamos in the tyranny. In that case the fact that we hear nothing more about them would suggest that they were subordinate to Aristodamos, and that they disappeared from the political scene at Megalopolis when he was assassinated. Berve 1967: 2.712 proposes, on the

basis of Polybios' "tyrants," that Aristodamos had a predecessor as tyrant, but there is no evidence that Aristodamos took over from a predecessor, and he did not inherit power from his adoptive father Tritaios if Pausanias' description (8.27.11) of Tritaios as an influential figure in Megalopolis, with no mention of tyranny, is reliable. Aristodamos certainly had no immediate successor as tyrant, since Polyb. 10.22.2 makes clear that Megalopolis was liberated by his assassination.

11 Fritzilas 2011: 112–15 suggests that the Aristodamos named on a third-century tombstone found in Megalopolitan territory might be a relative of the tyrant of that name, but, while that is possible, there is no evidence to suggest that it is likely.

12 The Temple of Artemis Agrotera stood on a hill in the southeastern part of the city, presumably visible to anyone arriving at Megalopolis on the road that led from Sparta up the Eurotas valley; the cult was emblematic of Megalopolitan victory over Sparta, since a Spartan king performed a sacrifice to Artemis Agrotera when, outside Lakonia, his army was in sight of the enemy: see Paradiso 2016. Pausanias evidently saw Aristodamos' buildings when he visited Megalopolis: if those within the city were destroyed in the sack of Megalopolis by Kleomenes III in 223, they must subsequently have been rebuilt, but not all public buildings were destroyed: see Lauter Bufe and Lauter 2011: 156.

13 On the date of the assassination of Aristodamos see Kralli 2017: 127. An old problem is whether the assassination came before or after the liberation of Sikyon: see recently Paschidis 2008: 278, n. 2 and Kralli 2017: 192–3, n. 39.

14 Their careers are summarized in, e.g., Stavrianopoulou 2002: 138, n. 67 (continued on 139).

15 On his tyranny see Berve 1967: 1.401–3 and 2.712–13; Kralli 2017: 127; Shipley 2018: 112–13. Pausanias (8.27.12) says that Lydiadas became tyrant roughly two generations after the death of Aristodamos, i.e., about 50 or 60 years later, which is clearly wrong, but "two generations" may be a misunderstanding, or a clumsy rephrasing, of a statement that Aristodamos and Lydiadas were two generations apart (i.e., that Aristodamos was of the same generation as Lydiadas' grandfather), since Lydiadas came to power at a young age (*neos*, Paus. 8.27.12). Suggestions have been made that individuals in his family were prominent at Megalopolis earlier: Taeuber 1986: 224–5 citing an Aristopamon in the fourth century, Habicht 1972: 113–14 citing Nikasippos, son of Eudamos, in the early third century, and Stavrianopoulou 2002: 124 suggesting that a *temenos* mentioned at A.9 in the text may have belonged to an earlier Lydiadas (but the reading of the name is uncertain). Family members may well have been prominent earlier, but there is no certain evidence.

16 The date is approximate, but generally accepted: see recently Kralli 2017: 177–8; Shipley 2018: 112.

17 See Kralli 2017; Shipley 2018.

18 See Pretzler 2005b: 21–2 and 32; Kralli 2017: 145, n. 93.

19 Conversely Pausanias' report (8.27.13–14 and 8.36.6, the only source) of an attack on Megalopolis by Agis IV, frustrated by the north wind (Boreas), does not mention Lydiadas even though the account at 8.27.13–14 follows immediately a reference to Lydiadas' reputation and glory.

20 On Philopoimen's date of birth see Errington 1969: 13 and 246–7. On his age when his two tutors took over his education see Polyb. 10.22.2, Plut. *Phil.* 1.2.

21 Ancestral *xenoi* of Aratos, Polyb. 2.48.4. On the Kerkidas contemporary with Philip II, Dem. *De cor.* 18.295. On the two men see Paschidis 2008: 236–8 (B.13.IV), 276–9 (B.33–4), and on the date of their embassy Paschidis 2008: 236, n. 7. See also Kralli 2017: 223–6.

22 López Cruces 1995: 3–37, Paschidis 2008: 276–9. The two men – if they were two – were contemporaries, since the poet was certainly writing during the reign of Kleomenes III of Sparta (López Cruces 1995: 16).

23 The passage comes in a discussion of how men, and tyrants in particular, can change their pattern of behaviour: on that theme in Plutarch see Swain 1989.

24 See Moreno Leoni 2015 on attitudes to ex-tyrants in the Achaian League.

25 On Alipheira see Maher 2017: 121–35.

26 This assessment of Polybios' view of Lydiadas is contrary to that of Kralli 2017: 293, "his all-too-good Lydiadas."

27 Shipley 2018: 67.

28 On the Spolienbau, considered to be probably Frankish or later, see Kreilinger 282–5 in Spyropoulos et al. 1996.

29 The *exedra* and its inscriptions are discussed in detail in Stavrianopoulou 2002: on the form and size of the *exedra* see Stavrianopoulou 2002: 117–18. Where in the agora it stood is unknown.

30 Stavrianopoulou 2002: 119–20 (lettering), 152–4 (date of erection), 123 and 150–1 (erection by family).

31 *SEG* 52.447–9 republishes the texts, correcting "obvious errors in spacing and stray punctuation," and supplying "subscript dots to match the text": the corrections do not affect the present argument.

32 Block A.20–2, Stavrianopoulou 2002: 134–8.

33 Stavrianopoulou 2002: 148, n. 99.

34 Stavrianopoulou 2002: 130, commenting on Block A.36.

35 It is likely that Eudamos died before Lydiadas, who became tyrant fairly young (Plut. *Arat.* 30.1, Paus. 8.27.12) but must have been at least in his forties when he died.

36 The exact date when Macedon ousted the Aitolians from Boiotia is not certain: see Scholten 2000: 272–3 "after about 236 ..."

37  See the survey of Plataian/Boiotian history in this period in Konecny and Marchese 2013: 40.

38  Note the comments in Kralli 2017: 2002.

39  Stavrianopoulou 2002: 152.

40  Stavrianopoulou 2002: 150, n. 105 (continued on 151).

41  See Errington 1969: 193–4; Kató 2006a and 2006b; Kralli 2017: 362–3 and 404, and especially Buraselis 2003: 194–5 on the honours for Philopoimen at Megalopolis. On Polybios' praise of Philopoimen see Polyb. 10.21.1–24.7; Errington 1969: 228–40; Olivera 2017. On Polybios' intervention to preserve memorials of Philopoimen see Plut. *Phil.* 21.5-6 and Errington 1969: 230.

42  Plut. *Cleom.* 6.2-4, *Arat.* 36.3–37.3. In a third account at *De sera numinis vindicta* 6 (= *Moralia* 552B) Plutarch's purpose is to contrast Lydiadas' behaviour as a tyrant with his greatly improved behaviour later, and he therefore says simply that Lydiadas died nobly fighting for his *patris* against the enemy.

43  See, e.g., Marasco 1980: 23–4 and 1981: 2.409–10; Kralli 2017: 222. The gesture is reported only at Plut. *Cleom.* 6.4.

44  Paus. 2.9.1–2, 4.29.7–8, 7.7.4, 8.27.15–16, 8.28.7, 8.49.4: only the last does not mention the breach of truce. See Moggi and Osanna 2000: 239; 2003: 423–4.

## REFERENCES

Berve, H. 1967. *Die Tyrannis bei den Griechen*. Munich.

Briscoe, J. 1981. *A Commentary on Livy*. Books XXXIV–XXXVII. Oxford.

Buraselis, K. 2003. "Political Gods and Heroes or the Hierarchization of Political Divinity in the Hellenistic World." In A. Barzanò et al. (eds.), *Modelli eroici dall'antichità alla cultura europea, Bergamo, 20–22 novembre 2001*. Rome: 185–97.

Charneux, P. 1983. "Sur quelques inscriptions d'Argos." *Bulletin de Correspondance Hellénique* 107: 251–67.

Errington, R.M. 1969. *Philopoemen*. Oxford.

Fritzilas, S. 2011. "Grave stelai and burials in Megalopolis." In H. Cavanagh, W.G. Cavanagh, and J. Roy (eds.), *Honouring the Dead in the Peloponnese: Proceedings of the Conference Held at Sparta, 23–25 April 2009*. https://www.nottingham.ac.uk/csps/documents/honoringthedead/fritzilas.pdf. Nottingham: 99–128.

Gómez Espelosín, E.J. 1991. "Plutarch and Justin on Aristotimus of Elis." *American Journal of Philology* 112: 103–9. https://doi.org/10.2307/295016.

Habicht, C. 1972. "Beiträge zur Prosopographie der altgriechischen Welt." *Chiron* 2: 103–34. https://doi.org/10.34780/n929-04hl.

Kató, P. 2006a. "The Funeral of Philopoimen in the Historiographical Tradition." In E. Stavrianopoulou (ed.), *Ritual and Communication in the Graeco-Roman World*. Liège: 239–50.

Kató, P. 2006b. "Rituale und Politik in Megalopolis am Ende der 180er Jahre." *Hungarian Polis Studies* 13: 43–51.

Konecny, A., and R. Marchese 2013. "The History of Plataiai: A Short Survey." In A. Konecny, V. Aravantinos, and R. Marchese (eds.), *Plataiai: Archäologie und Geschichte einer boiotischen Polis*. Vienna: 23–48.

Kralli, I. 2017. *The Hellenistic Peloponnese: Interstate Relations: A Narrative and Analytic History, from the Fourth Century to 146 BC*. Swansea.

Kritsas, C. 2006. "Nouvelles inscriptions d'Argos: Les archives des comptes du trésor sacré (IVe s. av. J.-C.)." In *Comptes rendus de l'Académie des Inscriptions et Belles-Lettres, Séances de l'année 2006, janvier–mars*: 397–434.

Lauter-Bufe, H., and H. Lauter. 2011. *Die politischen Bauten von Megalopolis*. Darmstadt and Mainz.

Lévy , E. 1996. "La tyrannie et son vocabulaire chez Polybe." *Ktèma* 21: 43–54.

López Cruces, J.L. 1995. *Les méliambes de Cercidas de Mégalopolis: Politique et tradition littéraire*. Amsterdam.

Luraghi, N. 2013. "One-Man Government." In H. Beck (ed.), *A Companion to Ancient Greek Government*. Malden, MA, Oxford, and Chichester: 131–45.

Luraghi, N. 2018. "The Discourse of Tyranny and the Greek Roots of the Bad King." In N. Panou and H. Schadee (eds.), *Evil Lords: Theories and Representations of Tyranny from Antiquity to the Renaissance*. Oxford: 11–26.

Maher, M. 2017. *The Fortification of Arkadian City-States in the Classical and Hellenistic Periods*. Oxford.

Marasco, G. 1980. "Storia e propaganda durante la guerra cleomenica. Un episodio del III. sec. a.C." *Rivista storica italiana* 92.1: 5–34.

Marasco, G. 1981. *Commento alle biografie plutarchee di Agide e di Cleomene*. 2 vols. Rome.

Moggi, M., and M. Osanna. 2000. *Pausania, Guida della Grecia, Libro VII: Acaia*. Milan.

Moggi, M., and M. Osanna. 2003. *Pausania, Guida della Grecia, Libro VIII: Arcadia*. Milan.

Moreno Leoni, A.M. 2015. "Memoria y tiranía en la Confederación Aquea helenística (s. III–II a.C.). Memory and Tyranny in the Hellenistic Achaean Confederacy (III–II Centuries BC)." *Emerita* 83: 133–56. https://doi.org/10.3989/emerita.2015.07.1335.

Mossé, C. 2004. *La tyrannie dans la Grèce antique*. Paris. [Republication, with new preface, of 1969 edition.]

Nielsen, T.H. 2002. *Arkadia and Its Poleis in the Archaic and Classical Periods*. Göttingen.

Olivera, D.A. 2017. "A Filopemén: Historia y retórica en Polibio." *Anales di Filología Clásica* 30.1: 33–42.

Paradiso, A. 2016. "Aristodemus 'the Good' and the Temple of Artemis Agrotera at Megalopolis." *Classical Quarterly* 66: 128–33. https://doi.org/10.1017/S0009838816000306.

Paschidis, P. 2008. *Between City and King: Prosopographical Studies on the Intermediaries between the Cities of the Greek Mainland and the Aegean and the Royal Courts in the Hellenistic Period (322–190 B.C.).* Meletemeta 59. Athens.

Piérart, M. 1982. "Argos, Cléonai, et le koinon des Arcadiens." *Bulletin de Correspondance Hellénique* 106: 119–38.

Pretzler, M. 2005a. "Pausanias and Oral Tradition." *Classical Quarterly* 55.1: 235–49. https://doi.org/10.1093/cq/bmi017.

Pretzler, M. 2005b. "Pausanias at Mantinea: Invention and Manipulation of Local History." *Cambridge Classical Journal* 51: 21–34. https://doi.org/10.1017/S1750270500000385.

Pretzler, M. 2007. *Pausanias. Travel Writing in Ancient Greece.* London.

Roy, J. 2010. "Roman Arkadia." In A.D. Rizakis and C.E. Lepenioti (eds.), *Roman Peloponnese III. Society, Economy and Culture under the Roman Empire: Continuity and Innovation.* Meletemata 63. Athens. 59–73.

Scholten, J.B. 2000. *The Politics of Plunder: Aitolians and Their Koinon in the Early Hellenistic Era, 279–217 B.C.* Berkeley.

Shipley, D.G.J. 2018. *The Early Hellenistic Peloponnese: Politics, Economies, and Networks, 338–197 BC.* Cambridge.

Spyropoulos, T., et al. 1996. "Megalopolis: 2. Vorbericht 1994–1995." *Archäologischer Anzeiger* 1996: 269–86.

Stavrianopoulou, E. 2002. "Die Familienexedra von Eudamos und Lydiadas in Megalopolis." *Tekmeria* 7: 117–56. https://doi.org/10.12681/tekmeria.183.

Swain, S. 1989. "Character Change in Plutarch." *Phoenix* 43: 62–8. https://doi.org/10.2307/1088541.

Taeuber, H. 1986. "Ehreninschrift aus Megalopolis für Aristopamon, Sohn des Lydiadas." *Tyche* 1: 221–6. https://doi.org/10.15661/tyche.1986.001.23.

Zizzi, C. 2006. *Le iscrizioni nella Periegesi di Pausania: Commento ai testi epigrafici.* Pisa.

*The fourth chapter in the lineup of Peloponnesian case studies takes readers to the most southern tip of the peninsula: the Mani region and its sanctuary site of Poseidon at Tainaron. Exploring how the local experience was subject to the environment, drawing both meaning and inspiration from it, Chelsea Gardner's chapter corresponds with the examination of environmental localism in the Kopais Basin at the beginning of the volume. Both places, however, could not have been more different in terms of their natural surroundings. The Mani was an environmental deathscape. A rugged and terrestrially inaccessible stretch of land, unfit for habitation due to the hot and dry climate, the lack of freshwater sources, and poor soil, the Mani evoked images of precarity. Gardner's chapter is divided into two case studies that flesh out the intense experience of place as well as its translation into a distinct discursive environment. In the first of these, she determines Tainaron's status and role in Peloponnesian affairs during the Hellenistic period. Notorious as a site for the gathering and recruitment of large numbers of mercenaries, Gardner relates this character trait to local particularities, subsumed under the rubrics of remoteness and political neutrality; discussion of the archaeological evidence of the Temple of Poseidon further enriches the interpretation. The second case study turns to the practice of local proxeny grants (see also chapter 4). Gardner discusses the epigraphical evidence for a tight-meshed net of exchanges that wove settlements together. Unlike the somewhat short-lived prominence the Mani gained as mercenary ground, the ties of guest-friendship attest to the longevity of localized interactions, bracketed by the shared experience of an extreme environment. In sum, Gardner's article illustrates a remarkable degree of adaptability to the challenges posed by the natural surroundings and, inspired by the ability to abide to a harsh place, resilience to cultural currents in the Hellenistic Mediterranean.*

*Keywords: Tainaron, Temple of Poseidon, League of the Free Lakonians, environmental localism, epigraphy*

# 12

# Global Activities in a Localized Context: Mercenaries, Proxeny, and the Small Local World of Hellenistic Mani

CHELSEA A.M. GARDNER

The Mani peninsula is the central of three peninsular projections off the southern Peloponnese; it is both bisected and disconnected from the rest of Lakonian territory and the entire Peloponnese by the imposing Taygetos mountain range, which dominates the landscape of Mani, rendering its territory arid, rocky, precipitous, and notoriously difficult on which to subsist, as well as to access by land (figure 12.1).[1] Geographically, the settlements of this peninsula are a part of Lakonia – the territory of Sparta in antiquity – as evidenced by our primary sources and reinforced by the anti-Spartan formation of the League of the Free Lakonians (Eleutherolakonian League) in the Roman period.[2] Scholarship on the ancient sites and settlements of this peninsula is often through a lens of Spartan history and politics, yet many of the parochial settlements within Mani were locally unique and largely independent places, primarily due to the terrestrial inaccessibility and perceived remoteness of the region – so remote and barren, in fact, that the site of Tainaron on the southernmost tip of Mani also served as the threshold between the world of the living and the dead, in its role as the physical entrance of Hades.[3] I have argued elsewhere that the settlements within the lower Mani peninsula, including Tainaron, were only geographically affiliated with Lakonia, and that there is no direct evidence that they were under the direct control of the Spartans, even in the Classical period during the

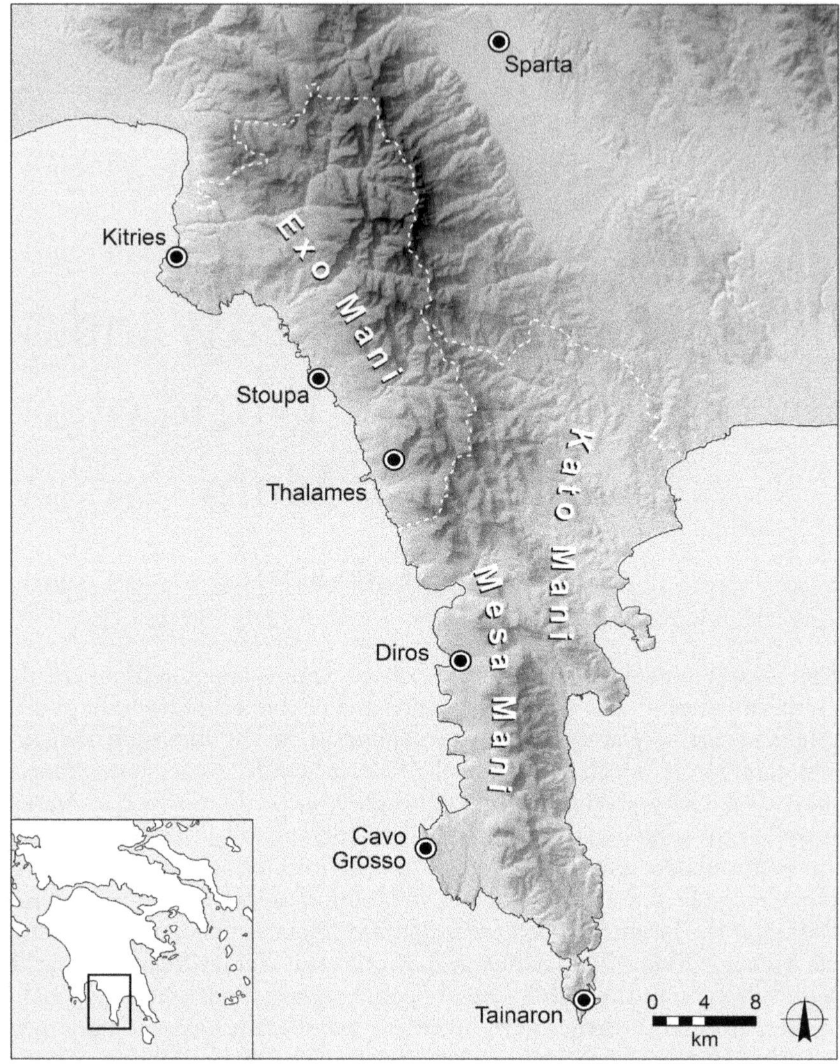


Figure 12.1.  Map showing the location and terrain of the Mani Peninsula, including regional divisions and relevant sites mentioned in this text. Elevation data courtesy CGIAR-CSI SRTM (Jarvis et al. 2008). Country boundary courtesy of GADM (http://www.gadm.org/). Map created by Rebecca M. Seifried; copyright Chelsea A.M. Gardner.

height of Spartan hegemony.[4] This argument for autonomy from Sparta becomes more evident in the extreme west and south of the peninsula (as one moves across the mountains and further from the plain of Sparta) in the region known as Mesa (Inner) Mani, and particularly at Tainaron, where there is also an important sanctuary of Poseidon, located atop the Matapan promontory. Tainaron itself is not only the southernmost point of Mani, but also the Peloponnese, mainland Greece, and, with the exception of Punta de Tarifa in Spain, of continental Europe.

In this chapter I present two case studies involving the site of Tainaron that demonstrate how local discourses in Hellenistic Mani were encouraged and perhaps even shaped by the physical environment. First, I highlight the autonomy of Tainaron during the Hellenistic period and its selection as a mercenary gathering place due to its local particularities: namely, geographic remoteness that afforded political neutrality. Second, I present the interconnectedness of the ancient settlements on the west and south of the Mani through the institution of proxeny and briefly present the recent discovery of a small Hellenistic "site" on the western coast of the peninsula. Together, these case studies showcase the local discourses that flourished within Hellenistic Mani, even when confronted with local-global exchanges on an expansive, Mediterranean-wide scale.

## Case Study #1: Tainaron and the Mercenary Phenomenon

During the final quarter of the fourth century BCE, Tainaron – which, up to that point, was best known as the mythical entrance to the Underworld and as the site of a sanctuary to Poseidon – took on the short-lived yet nonetheless impressive role of mercenary gathering place, on a scale unmatched by any other place in the Mediterranean at that time.[5] Much ink has been spilled as to why Tainaron was chosen as the place for this activity for such a brief period, but previous scholarship has always assumed that Tainaron was operating under the control of the Spartan state. Even Couvenhes' recent work, which successfully argued against the long-held notion that Tainaron served as a "mercenary-*market*" (italics added), did so through a lens of presumed Spartan control.[6] Yet, a further examination of the primary sources reveals no evidence for Spartan control of Tainaron or the activities of the mercenaries therein. In what follows, I discuss the literary evidence for the presence of mercenaries at Tainaron, then present the argument that Tainaron was chosen as the location for these global activities during the earliest years of the Hellenistic period precisely because of the "physical local" realities of this place:[7] namely, its geographic situation that rendered it centrally accessible via maritime routes yet still remotely located far away from the main centres of population.

*Literary Evidence*

A passage from Arrian's *Anabasis of Alexander*, written sometime around the middle of the second century, has been used as evidence that Tainaron functioned as a military base as early as 333 BCE:[8]

- 2.13.[6]: Ἄγις δὲ παρ' Αὐτοφραδάτου τάλαντα ἀργυρίου λαβὼν τριάκοντα καὶ τριήρεις δέκα, ταύτας μὲν Ἱππίαν ἄξοντα ἀποστέλλει παρὰ τὸν ἀδελφὸν τὸν αὑτοῦ Ἀγησίλαον ἐπὶ Ταίναρον …

- 2.13. [6]: And Agis, having received thirty talents of silver from Autophradates and ten triremes, dispatched Hippias to bring these things to his brother Agesilaus at Tainaron.

In the lines that follow, Agesilaus was then instructed to proceed to Crete with the crews of the ships. Jones has argued that this passage provides evidence not just for the presence of mercenaries on Tainaron, but for an actual mercenary market – even though this passage does not explicitly mention mercenaries whatsoever, let alone the hiring of mercenaries. Jones suggested that this possibility was "not unlikely" as the year of this event preceded the earliest mention of Tainaron as a mercenary gathering place (see below: Diod. Sic. 17.108.6) by a mere seven years.[9] In contrast, Badian, Griffith, and Launey have all argued that this passage provided evidence that Tainaron in this period "is clearly (as, indeed, was to be expected) a Spartan base, and there is no room for an international hiring-fair there."[10] While I agree with Badian and others that this passage provides no evidence for mercenaries – international, for hire, or otherwise (since, again, there is no actual mention of mercenaries in this account) – I must point out that the evidence for Tainaron's role as a Spartan base in this passage is as absent as the term "mercenary." Yet, and perhaps surprisingly, the common assumption that Tainaron functioned as a Spartan base is based almost entirely on this text. Agis is a Spartan, to be certain, but Sparta itself is not mentioned, nor is anything known about Agesilaus or Hippias beyond this passage.[11] Controlling exclusive access to a place such as Tainaron is quite different than simply using it, and there is no clear evidence for Spartan control of Tainaron at any period, let alone in this period of declining Spartan power.

In the previous century, Tainaron had been used as a muster area by Spartans and outsiders alike, owing to its geographically central maritime location and its recognition as a landmark. For example, a Herodotean narrative tells a story of the Korkyraians, who set sail from the island of Korkyra under the pretence of coming to the aid of the Greeks against the Persians in 481 BCE (7.168.2). However, they instead only went so far as the southern coast of the Peloponnese – to Pylos and Tainaron – where they waited to see which way the war would turn, while avoiding direct conflict and attempting to maintain neutrality.[12] The Korkyraian fleet waited in the bay near Tainaron because it provided a safe place to anchor while they purposefully delayed their advance in a convenient location, one that was as equally neutral as they themselves seemed to be. Likewise, Thucydides (7.19.4) briefly mentioned Tainaron in a passage that reveals its role as a muster area for the Lakedaimonian ships preparing to set out against the Athenians in 413/412 BCE.[13] These three authors (Arrian, Herodotus, and Thucydides) provide scant evidence for any contemporary operations on land at the site of Tainaron, revealing only that – in addition to its role as a sanctuary to Poseidon – Tainaron was recognized in antiquity as a known landmark near which to assemble, and that people, soldiers, and ships gathered there at least as early as the Persian wars.

So, in recognizing that Arrian's text does not provide evidence for mercenary activity, our earliest surviving evidence that explicitly records the presence of mercenaries on Tainaron comes from Plutarch's (or Pseudo-Plutarch's) *Lives of the Ten Orators*:

– 848e: συνεβούλευσε δὲ καὶ τὸ ἐπὶ Ταινάρῳ ξενικὸν μὴ διαλῦσαι, οὗ Χάρης ἡγεῖτο, εὐνόως πρὸς τὸν στρατηγὸν διακείμενος.

– 848e: And [Hypereides] even advised not to discharge the mercenaries on Tainaron, who were led by Chares, since he was well-minded towards that leader.

From this passage, scholars have derived the possible title of a speech in favour of Chares, written by the Athenian logographer Hypereides and typically dated to ca. 331 BCE.[14] Chares was a well-known Athenian general in the fourth century BCE, but his inclusion in this passage as a leader for mercenaries at Tainaron has been historically problematic for some, specifically due to his ties to Athens: "… the Athenians had no power either to disband or retain a garrison at Taenarum in 331 … [i]t is a mistake to imply that the garrison was an Athenian garrison."[15] As a consequence of this viewpoint, Griffith suggested that the author of this text intended to write "Leosthenes" rather than "Chares" (see below, Diod. Sic. 17.111); this name swap, however, has chronological implications that are not easily resolved, since a substitution of Leosthenes for Chares would place these events closer to the start of the Lamian War, rather than in the final years of the 330s. Moreover, Griffith's solution is "methodologically unsatisfactory,"[16] and it stems solely from a desire to divorce Tainaron from an Athenian connection due to the prevailing belief that Tainaron was controlled by Sparta. If one rightly takes the text at face value and accepts that the general is, in fact, Chares the Athenian, then we gain additional insight into the role and usage of Tainaron in the later fourth century BCE.

Our most comprehensive source for the evidence of mercenaries at Tainaron, despite being written over 250 years after the events in question, is Diodorus Siculus, whose work contains five separate passages that highlight the use of Tainaron as a gathering place for international mercenaries. The distribution of events recorded in these passages span a mere quarter-century, specifically the last quarter of the fourth century BCE – a particularly tumultuous time in the Greek world. The first of these five passages deals with events in 326/5 BCE and presents the actions of Harpalos, the satrap of Babylon, who fled from Asia to Attica after he found out that Alexander was sentencing to death those of his satraps who were accused of neglecting their duties:

- 17.108.[6]: … μισθοφόρους δ᾽ ἀθροίσας ἑξακισχιλίους ἀπῆρεν ἐκ τῆς Ἀσίας καὶ κατέπλευσεν εἰς τὴν Ἀττικήν. [7] οὐδενὸς δὲ αὐτῷπροσέχοντος τοὺς μὲν μισθοφόρους ἀπέλιπε περὶ Ταίναρον τῆς Λακωνικῆς, αὐτὸς δὲ μέρος τῶν χρημάτων ἀναλαβὼν ἱκέτης ἐγένετο τοῦ δήμου. ἐξαιτούμενος δὲ ὑπ᾽ Ἀντιπάτρου καὶ Ὀλυμπιάδος καὶ πολλὰ χρήματα διαδοὺς τοῖς ὑπὲρ αὐτοῦ δημηγοροῦσι ῥήτορσι διέδρα καὶ κατῆρεν εἰς Ταίναρον πρὸς τοὺς μισθοφόρους.

- 17.108.[6]: … having mustered 6,000 mercenaries [Harpalos] departed from Asia and sailed down to Attica. [7] Since no one devoted themselves to him, he left the mercenaries near Tainaron in Lakonikē, and taking his part of the money became a suppliant of the (Athenian) people. After his surrender was demanded by Antipater and Olympias, and after he handed over much money to those public speakers speaking on behalf of him, he escaped and put into port at Tainaron with the mercenaries.

This passage perhaps best illustrates the nature of Tainaron as a safe billeting place for mercenaries during this period. While he was away at Athens, Harpalos chose to send his 6,000 troops (and some of his money, it seems) to Tainaron specifically, suggesting that this was a place where Harpalos believed they would be safe upon his return.[17]

The next passage occurs in the same book, only a few chapters later, and presents events of the following year, 325/4 BCE, after Alexander ordered his satraps to dissolve their armies and lay off their mercenaries:

- 17.111.[1]: … μετὰ δὲ ταῦτα πανταχόθεν διῆραν ἐπὶ Ταίναρον τῆς Λακωνικῆς. [2] ὁμοίως δὲ καὶ τῶν Περσικῶν σατραπῶν καὶ τῶν ἄλλων ἡγεμόνων οἱ περιλειφθέντες χρήματά τε καὶ στρατιώτας ἀθροίζοντες ἔπλεον ἐπὶ Ταίναρον καὶ κοινὴν δύναμιν ἤθροιζον. [3] τὸ δὲ τελευταῖον Λεωσθένην τὸν Ἀθηναῖον, ἄνδρα ψυχῆς λαμπρότητι διάφορον καὶ μάλιστ’ ἀντικείμενον τοῖς Ἀλεξάνδρου πράγμασιν, εἵλοντο στρατηγὸν αὐτοκράτορα.

- 17.111.[1]: … After these events [the mercenaries] removed themselves from all places to Tainaron in Lakonikē. [2] Similarly, those surviving of the Persian satraps and the other leaders, having gathered both money and soldiers, sailed to Tainaron and assembled (their) collective forces. They finally elected Leosthenes the Athenian as commander, a distinguished man with brilliance of spirit who was especially opposed to the actions of Alexander.

Here we have the very Leosthenes mentioned above, and further details about this man and these disbanded mercenaries are revealed in the following book. After the death of Alexander in 323 BCE, Diodorus tells us that the Athenians quickly moved to assert their leadership using the funds given to them by (the now-deceased) Harpalos and the mercenaries who were waiting on Tainaron:[18]

- 18.9.[1]: ἀφορμὰς δὲ ἔσχον εἰς τὸν πόλεμον τό τε πλῆθος τῶν καταλειφθέντων ὑφ’ Ἀρπάλου χρημάτων … ὁμοίως δὲ καὶ τοὺς κατὰ τὴν Ἀσίαν ἀμίσθους γενομένους ὑπὸ τῶν σατραπῶν μισθοφόρους, ὄντας μὲν ὀκτακισχιλίους, διατρίβοντας δὲ περὶ Ταίναρον τῆς Πελοποννήσου. [2] διὸ καὶ τούτους προσέταξαν ἐν ἀπορρήτοις Λεωσθένει τῷ Ἀθηναίῳ τὸ μὲν πρῶτον ἀναλαβεῖν αὐτοὺς ὡς ἰδιοπραγοῦντα χωρὶς τῆς τοῦ δήμου γνώμης… [3] διὸ καὶ Λεωσθένης μετὰ πολλῆς ἡσυχίας μισθωσάμενος τοὺς προειρημένους παραδόξως …

- 18.9.[1]: And they had as a starting point for the war the great amount of money that was left behind by Harpalos … and likewise also the mercenaries down from Asia who became unemployed by the satraps, 8,000 (in number) and passing away their time near Tainaron in the Peloponnese. [2] So they commanded Leosthenes the Athenian in secrecy to first take them up as of his own judgment acting independently, separately from the city … [3] Whereby Leosthenes, with much silence, hired those [troops] mentioned above …

In these two passages (17.111 and 18.9), Diodorus relates that mercenaries, satraps, and other leaders alike removed themselves to Tainaron after being ordered to disband. In the second passage, we learn that there were 8,000 troops waiting at Tainaron – a truly astounding number considering the size of the area and its inhospitable terrain. Such an impressive number of people would surely put pressure on the arid landscape, and so there must have been a reason that these men chose Tainaron specifically; it is neither the closest nor the most convenient location to reach from coastal Asia Minor, nor does it boast the natural resources to support so many people.[19] While the site is located on the coast with easy maritime access, it was also, more importantly, an ideal place to convene to remain undetected – or at least undisturbed – by the Macedonian allies.

Several chapters later Diodorus mentions Tainaron again, during the events of 322 BCE when Thibron (former officer under Harpalos, who was also accused of killing Harpalos, see Diod. Sic 18.19.[2]) sent messengers to collect mercenaries from Tainaron to use as reinforcements in his campaigns in Libya:

- 18.21.[1]: ὁ δὲ Θίβρων … προχειρισάμενος δὲ τῶν φίλων τοὺς εὐθέτους ἔπεμψεν εἰς τὴν Πελοπόννησον ἀναληψομένους τῶν ξένων τοὺς ἐνδιατρίβοντας περὶ Ταίναρον. ἔτι γὰρ τῶν ἀμισθώτων γενομένων πολλοὶ διεπλανῶντο ζητοῦντες τοὺς μισθοδοτήσοντας καὶ τότε περὶ Ταίναρον ὑπῆρχον πλείους τῶν δισχιλίων καὶ πεντακοσίων.

- 18.21.[1]: And Thibron … having chosen those of his friends who were able, sent them to the Peloponnese so that they would take up those of the mercenaries spending time near Tainaron. For many of them were still not hired, wandering, seeking someone to pay wages, and at that time they were more than 2,500 ready near Tainaron.

The popularity of Tainaron as a place for mercenaries to gather persists in the following book of Diodorus, which is our fifth and last passage of relevance. Here Kleonymos, in the year 303 BCE, recruited mercenaries from Tainaron to help the Tarentines in their battle against the Lucanians and the Romans:

- 20.104.[1]: Κατὰ δὲ τὴν Ἰταλίαν Ταραντῖνοι πόλεμον ἔχοντες πρὸς Λευκανοὺς καὶ Ῥωμαίους ἐξέπεμψαν πρεσβευτὰς εἰς τὴν Σπάρτην, αἰτούμενοι βοήθειαν καὶ στρατηγὸν Κλεώνυμον. [2] τῶν δὲ Λακεδαιμονίων προθύμως ἡγεμόνα δόντων τὸν αἰτούμενον καὶ τῶν Ταραντίνων χρήματα καὶ ναῦς ἀποστειλάντων ὁ μὲν Κλεώνυμος ἐπὶ Ταινάρῳ τῆς Λακωνικῆς ξενολογήσας στρατιώτας πεντακισχιλίους συντόμως κατέπλευσεν εἰς Τάραντα.

- 20.104.[1]: But in Italy, the Tarentines were in a state of war against the Lucanians and the Romans, and they sent out ambassadors to

Sparta, asking for help, and for Kleonymos the general. [2] And after the Lakedaimonians eagerly gave them the requested leader and the Tarentines sent off money and ships, Kleonymos, having enlisted 5,000 mercenaries as soldiers at Tainaron in Lakonia, immediately sailed to Tarentum.

To summarize, in terms of the sheer number of mercenaries at Tainaron in the final decades of the fourth century BCE, the information from all the primary sources is as follows: in 331 there were an unspecified number of mercenaries with Chares on Tainaron; in 326/325 BCE there were 6,000 mercenaries who accompanied Harpalos to Tainaron; in 323 BCE that number increased to 8,000, gathered from all places in Asia, who elected Leosthenes as commander; in 322 BCE there were more than 2,500 who were hired for Thibron; and in 303 BCE there were still at least 5,000 mercenaries available for enlistment by Kleonymos. These numbers are impressive, but the phenomenon was relatively short-lived: we have no further evidence of Tainaron as a mercenary gathering place beyond these dates and little beyond the surviving words of Diodorus and Plutarch.

After examining the surviving literary evidence, there is no doubt that there were a significant number of mercenaries at Tainaron for a brief period of time in the latter half of the fourth century BCE. Although Couvenhes has successfully argued that this was not a free "market" for the purchasing of mercenaries, there are still many questions that remain unanswered regarding Tainaron's role as a mercenary gathering place during the early Hellenistic period, namely, 1) why was Tainaron chosen as the location for this activity, and 2) how was the organization of this operation maintained? I shall address the second question first, and then return to first question.

*Organization of the Mercenary Hiring*

Scholars often attribute the organization and administration of the Tainaron mercenaries (or the erroneous "market" therein) to the Spartan state: Jones, for example, proclaimed that the mercenary hirings "could not have happened without the co-operation of the Spartan government"[20] but did not substantiate this claim; Launey further argued that Tainaron was under the surveillance of Sparta and that government authorization was necessary for the enrolment of mercenaries.[21] As evidence for this stance, Launey cited another passage from Diodorus Siculus (19.60.[1]), wherein Aristodemos sailed to Lakonia in 316/315 and, "having received authority from the Spartans to enlist troops, gathered together eight thousand soldiers from the Peloponnesus" (καὶ λαβὼν παρὰ τῶν Σπαρτιατῶν ἐξουσίαν ξενολογεῖν, στρατιώτας ἤθροισεν ὀκτακισχιλίους ἐκ τῆς Πελοποννήσου). The obvious problem with surmising Spartan control of Tainaron based on this passage is that Tainaron was not actually mentioned within this passage. However, even if one were to interpret the meaning of this text as indicative of Spartan authority over the mercenary hiring at Tainaron (as Launey did), the translation of ἐξουσίαν can shift the meaning of the entire sentence. The noun ἡ ἐξουσία is related to the verb ἔξεστι, which can be roughly translated to "it is allowed/it is possible"; the relationship between these two terms allows for Launey's preferred translation of ἐξουσίαν as "permission," which certainly underscores his belief in the role of Sparta in Aristodemos' gathering of Peloponnesian troops. However, ἐξουσίαν can also be translated as "resources" in terms of wealth, arms, food, and so on (e.g., Thuc. 1.123; 4.39; 6.31; cf. Dem. 21.138; Pl. Leg. 828d), which would suggest an entirely different reading of Sparta's role in this event: "Aristodemos, having received *resources* from the Spartans to enlist troops, gathered together eight thousand soldiers from the Peloponnesus" (italics added). Note that this alternative reading still does not change the fact that the name Tainaron is not included in this passage, and there is no evidence as to where Aristodemos may have recruited his soldiers.

In contrast to Launey and Jones, Badian and, more recently, Couvenhes posit that Sparta lost control of Tainaron after the death of Agis III at the Battle of Megalopolis in 330 BCE.[22] While I disagree that Sparta controlled Tainaron even before the death of Agis, that is a topic beyond the scope of this chapter; suffice it to say that Badian and Couvenhes are correct in concluding that Sparta certainly was not in command of orchestrating the mercenaries who utilized Tainaron post-330 BCE, since there is no direct association between Tainaron and Sparta in any of the surviving passages that do explicitly mention Tainaron as a location for mercenaries. In Plutarch's passage (848e) as well as the first three Diodorus passages presented above (17.108, 17.111, and 18.9), only Athens and/or an Athenian are mentioned, and in the fifth passage (20.104), which is the only one to mention Spartans, we learn that the Lakedaimonians gave Kleonymos to the Tarentines and find nothing of direct Spartan association with Tainaron.[23] Moreover, in Diodorus' third passage (18.21), Leosthenes was commanded by the Athenians to hire mercenaries secretly, without revealing that he had permission/motivation to do so by "the city" – in this case, Athens.[24] This suggests that, under normal circumstances, Athens may have been able to grant some sort of permission to recruit mercenaries; this should not be interpreted as Athenian control of Tainaron, but rather that *stratēgoi* were expected to request state permission before recruiting mercenaries – this may well have been the situation at Sparta, too. Ultimately, however, within these five passages that described

Tainaron as a mercenary gathering place, there is no evidence to be found that suggests that these activities were carried out under the authority of the Spartan state.

### *Geographic Location and Archaeological Remains*

At this point, I return to the question of location, and why Tainaron was chosen as the site for the mercenary market. The answer to this is simple: the location of Tainaron was accessible by at least three harbours (Achilleios, Psamathous, and the small bays on the south of the Matapan promontory at Porto Sternes; figure 12.2) and was a known landmark that was centrally located within the Mediterranean, making it viable to bring mercenaries here from Asia (Diod. Sic. 17.108; 17.111), or to hire mercenaries and set off on campaigns in Italy (20.104) or Libya (18.21). Furthermore, it was precisely this rugged, terrestrially inaccessible location that provided a secure holding area of sorts for the mercenaries, and not, in fact, some form of outside control, the latter of which Badian argued: "If we do not hear of serious disturbances in Peloponnese, it must be because at Taenarum there were men willing and able to pay these mercenaries at least a retainer – enough for bare sustenance and the prospect of future employment. It is surely clear that otherwise the whole of Peloponnese (if not of Greece) must have been at the mercy of well-organised and desperate brigandage."[25] While Badian is right that something kept the mercenaries from plundering and sacking the towns of the Peloponnese out of boredom, this was not the existence of an organized force tasked with placating or even paying the troops, as he suggested; rather, the harshness of the topography, the apparent non-existence of navigable paths – let alone roads – to the north, and the the troops' unfamiliarity with the topography in this portion of (barely) mainland Greece provided reason enough for the mercenaries to remain in the isolated landscape of southern Mani, where they awaited prospective employers to sail in (the only means of access we hear of in these passages) and to hire the men by the thousands. In addition, this place may have even been desirable for the soldiers and generals themselves precisely because it was not under the jurisdiction of any one major political power, but nevertheless remained centrally accessible within the Mediterranean and was accessible by sea for potential employers. Ultimately, the geographic isolation of Tainaron provided the ideal location for a secure mercenary gathering place that was controlled by no one ruling power.

As mentioned above, the site of Tainaron was also the location of an active sanctuary to Poseidon, and because the harsh, mountainous terrain hindered overland communication and transportation, resources needed to be readily

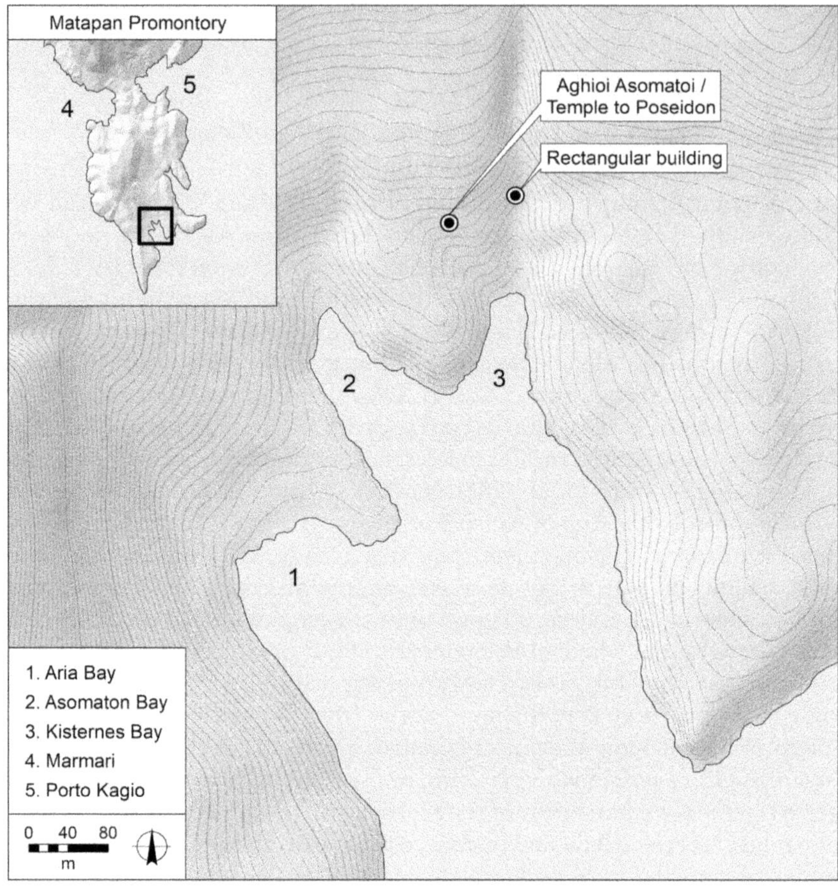


Figure 12.2.  Map showing the location of the harbours on the Matapan promontory and the archaeological remains at the site of Tainaron. Elevation data courtesy of the National Cadastre & Mapping Agency S.A. Map created by Rebecca M. Seifried; copyright Chelsea A.M. Gardner.

available or shipped in for visitors and officials at the sanctuary. The presence of thousands of mercenaries on the Matapan promontory would surely have put pressure on the availability of resources, which included, at a most basic level, food, fresh water, and shelter. There are no natural sources of fresh water anywhere near Tainaron, resulting in an abundance of cisterns used from antiquity until the premodern period.[26] Agricultural resources are also limited in this region, again owing to the dry climate, poor soil, and mountainous terrain.[27] It is thus important to consider the archaeological footprint of Tainaron in light of its role not only as a mercenary gathering-place, but also as a major ancient sanctuary, where people would regularly have required these basic resources for survival.

The location of the site of ancient Tainaron has never been in question, as the architectural remains at the bay of Porto Sternes have been long been identified with the religious structures of the Sanctuary of Poseidon and its auxiliary buildings. The only buildings at the site that have been dated (somewhat conclusively) date to the late Hellenistic period: specifically, the Hellenistic iteration of the Temple to Poseidon (the blocks of which comprise the north wall of the Byzantine church of Hagioi Asomatoi) and a domestic building with mosaic on the western portion of the site.[28] Architectural vestiges are scattered around the small bays of Aria, Asomaton, and Sternes, and upon the promontories that divide these bays. To the east and west of the central cultic space (comprising the Temple to Poseidon, a cavernous structure, and a rectangular building) are the remains of several unidentified auxiliary buildings.[29] In Cummer's description of the function of these buildings, he notes that "there was an extensive Hellenistic and Roman town at Tainaron, marked by rock-cut house foundations and cisterns around the large bay."[30] The interpretation of these buildings as belonging to a small settlement around the sanctuary is agreed upon by Mylonopoulos, Moschou, Bursian, Papachatzis, and Forster and Woodword, but perhaps because no superstructure survives on any of these foundations only Moschou has ventured a suggestion for specific interpretation for some of these buildings as multi-storey houses and as ship sheds.[31]

The architectural foundations throughout this region are often cut into the bedrock, and investigations into the area in 2007 revealed detachment grooves, indicating that these structures provided their own superstructures: the limestone mined during the quarrying of these foundations was then used as building material.[32] Unfortunately, there exists no map or plan of these foundations, or of the numerous rock-cut cisterns in the area (which give the region the toponym Kisternes). This lack of attention paid to the auxiliary buildings is perhaps surprising given the fact that those tasked with maintaining the day-to-day operations at the sanctuary at Tainaron would potentially utilize buildings for housing or storage, and the cisterns surely provided a solution for fresh water in the otherwise torrefied landscape. The fact that the superstructures of these buildings were quarried from the plots themselves suggests they could have been constructed relatively quickly, perhaps even upon demand, especially if bored throngs of mercenaries were stranded in this desolate place.

Beyond the remains at the three principal bays of the southern Matapan promontory, we find more clues about the occupation history. In 2017, informal field reconnaissance of the larger region revealed a ruined twentieth-century pastoral site just to the north of the sanctuary area, where there were visible scatters of Classical-Hellenistic pottery and a probable ancient rock-cut cistern. This site is unpublished and seemingly unknown, as is most of the promontory besides the area immediately around the bays.[33] One of the most common questions regarding the mercenary function of Tainaron concerns the logistics of housing so many men: simply put, where did they all go? The answer lies partially in the contemporary architectural remains presented briefly above, and specifically in the fact that many of the buildings were constructed in the Hellenistic period and their material was sourced locally. However, a complete picture of occupation remains obscured, and our understanding of the practical functioning of Tainaron will remain incomplete until more comprehensive archaeological investigations are undertaken, including the mapping of extensive archaeological remains around the site of Tainaron and the Matapan promontory in its entirety.

## Case Study #2: Proxeny and Proximity: The (Small) Local World of Tainaron and Western Mani

Despite the disproportionate attention that has been paid to the mercenary phenomenon at Tainaron, the use of this site as a mercenary gathering place was short-lived and limited to the early years of the Hellenistic period – specifically, the last quarter of the fourth century BCE. Surviving literary and epigraphic sources from the later Hellenistic period, however, provide further evidence for Tainaron's continued autonomy from Sparta and for the relationship between Tainaron and other settlements within Mani. Upon closer examination of the role of Tainaron in its capacity as a contemporary religious and political centre, the local discourse that is emphasized throughout southern and western Mani becomes more apparent. In this isolated region, the small local world of southern Mani becomes increasingly prioritized through shared institutions and material culture, while a simultaneous reinforcement of their distinction and separation from Sparta persists.

*Proxeny Decrees from Western and Southern Mani*

Two Hellenistic-period proxeny decrees discovered at Tainaron supply information about the contemporary relationship between Tainaron, individual Spartans, and the members of the Lakedaimonian League (*IG* V 1, 1226[34] and *IG* V 1, 1227).[35]

### *IG* V 1, 1226

1 [ἐπειδὴ Φίλων Λα]κεδαιμόνιος [εὔνους]
[ὑπάρχων τῶι κ]ρινῶι τῶν Λακε[δαιμο]-
[νίων πο]λ<λ>ὰς ϙαὶ μεγάλας χ[ρείας]
[παρέσ]χηται [καὶ] κατὰ κοινὸν καὶ [κατ᾽]
5 [ἰδ]<ί>ᾳν το<ῖ>[ς ἐν]τυ[γχά]νουσιν σ<π>[ουδῆς]
[καὶ φι]λο[τιμία]ς οὐθὲν ἐ<λ>λείπ<ω>[ν εἰς τὰ]
[π]ᾳρακ[αλούμ]ε{ι}να {παρακαλούμενα}, ἔδο<ξ>ε τῶι κο[ινῶι]
[τῶν Λακ]<ε>δ[αι]μονίων· Φίλωνα <Ἀ>ν<τι>[— —]
[… Λακεδ]αιμόνιον πρόξενον [εἶμεν]
10 [καὶ ε]ὐεργέτα[ν] τοῦ κοινοῦ [τῶν]
Λακεδ<α>ιμο{νο}νί<ω>[ν] {Λακεδαιμονίων} καὶ ἐγγόνυυ[ς αὐ]-
[τοῦ] ϙαὶ εἶμεν αὐτ[ῷ γᾶ]ς καὶ οἰκίας [ἔγ]-
[κτησ]<ι>ν <κ>αὶ ἐπινομίαν καὶ ἀτέλει[αν]
[καὶ ἀσ]υ<λ>ίαν καὶ πολέμου καὶ εἰ[ράνας]
15 [κ]αὶ τὰ λοιπὰ τίμια, ὅσ<α> καὶ το[ῖς ἄλλοις]
προξέν[ο]ι<ς> [κα]ὶ εὐεργέται[ς τοῦ κοι]-
ϝοῦ τῶν Λακεδαιμονίω[ν. τὰν]
[δ]ὲ [π]ρ[οξ]<ε>[ν]ί[αν] ταύταν ἀνα-
[γρ]α<ψάτω> ὁ ταμίας εἰς [στά]-
20 [λαν λιθίναν] καὶ ἀναθ<έ>τ<ω> εἰς τ[ὸ ἱερὸν]
[τοῦ Ποσ]ειδᾶνος τοῦ ἐπὶ Ταινά[ρωι].

Since Philo, a Lakedaimonian, being well-intentioned toward the League of the Lakedaimonians, performed many great services both for the League and for individuals, omitting no zeal nor generosity for the things that were required, it seemed good to the League of the Lakedaimonians that: Philo son of Anti-? should be a *proxenos* and benefactor of the League of the Lakedaimonians, both he and his descendants; and the right to purchase land and household, and the right of pasturage, and exemption from public burdens, and inviolability in both war and peace, and the rest of the honours that also (are granted) to other *proxenoi* and benefactors of the League of the Lakedaimonians. Let the steward inscribe this decree of proxeny on a stone *stēlē* and let him set it up at the temple of Poseidon at Tainaron.[36]

*IG* V **1, 1227**

```
   [— — — — — — — — —]
   [καὶ τὰ λοιπὰ τίμια, ὅσα]
   [καὶ τοῖς ἄλλοις προξένοις καὶ]
 1 [εὐ]ε[ργέ]ταις τοῦ [κοιν]οῦ τ[ῶν]
   Λακεδαμονίων. τὰν δὲ
   προξενίαν ταύταν ἀνα-
   γραψάτω ὁ ταμίας εἰς στά-
 5 λαν λιθίναν καὶ ἀναθέτω
   <ε>ὶς τὸ ἱερὸν τοῦ Ποσειδᾶ-
   νος τοῦ ἐπὶ Ταινάρωι.
```

and the rest of the honours that also (are granted) to other *proxenoi* and benefactors of the League of the Lakedaimonians. Let the steward inscribe this decree of proxeny on a stone *stēlē* and let him set it up at the temple of Poseidon at Tainaron.

Together, these decrees reveal information about the contemporary political context, since both include several references to the κοινόν τῶν Λακεδαιμονίων and are, as a result, often cited as the primary evidence for the existence of a Lakedaimonian League prior to the later (probably Augustan) League of the Free Lakonians (Eleutherolakōnes).[37] The earlier Lakedaimonian League was likely formed after Quinctus Titus Flamininus invaded Sparta in 195 BCE and released perioikic settlements from Spartan control, allowing these settlements to form a *koinon*. However, none of the settlements within the Inner Mani are explicitly called perioikic in the surviving literary sources and although Pausanias lists several settlements within the Mani peninsula as members of the later, Roman-period League of the Free Lakonians (3.21.7), there is no surviving evidence that any settlement within the Inner Mani was a member of this earlier, Hellenistic, Lakedaimonian League. The significance therein lies in the fact that the member cities of the Hellenistic Lakedaimonian League comprised settlements that were formerly under the direct control of Sparta and so the omission of any settlements from southern Mani in the surviving names of member cities or lists of perioikic settlements suggests that this previous Spartan control did not apply to them.[38]

So how does Tainaron factor in, if settlements in the southernmost portion of Mani were not members of this early Lakedaimonian League? Both decrees explicitly call for their erection at the sanctuary to Poseidon at Tainaron, which indicates that Tainaron functioned as the League's religious and administrative centre rather than a "member city" per se.[39] Whether the

Lakedaimonian League was itself primarily religious in function has been addressed elsewhere, but the fact that Tainaron was chosen as the main sanctuary for the Lakedaimonian League – as opposed to other important pan-Lakonian sanctuaries such as that of Apollo Hyperteleates at Asopus – is telling.[40] Tainaron was the obvious choice for the religious centre of the Lakedaimonian League for much the same reason that it was the ideal location for mercenary gatherings: namely, as a place that (had always) functioned outside of the control of the Spartan state.[41] By the time of the formation of the Lakedaimonian League in the second century BCE, Tainaron was well established as a safe place for those seeking refuge and had long served as a haven from Sparta and its political institutions, whether those individuals be helots, formerly enslaved persons, kings, mercenaries, or representative members of the newly formed Lakedaimonian League.[42]

The proxeny inscriptions discussed above were erected at Tainaron because the sanctuary was the official religious and administrative centre of the Lakedaimonian League, but also because these two decrees were issued by the league itself, rather than by an individual member city. The establishment of *proxenia* between Sparta and the Lakedaimonian League indicates a positive relationship between two political bodies that were firmly independent of each other. In total, 13 surviving proxeny decrees issued by the Lakedaimonian League and its member cities preserve the name of the city of the honorand, thus revealing information about local political relationships; approximately half (seven) of these honorands are Spartans. However, all those decrees granting proxeny to an individual Spartan issued by an individual member city (and not the league in its entirety) were issued by a settlement outside of Mesa (Inner) Mani (Kotyrta *IG* V 1, 961, 965, 966; Geronthrai *IG* V 1, 1112, 1113; Gytheion, *IG* V 1, 1145, 1533). That is to say, there is no surviving evidence that any settlement within Inner Mani was a member city of the Lakedaimonian League or that any of these same settlements held a relationship via proxeny with Sparta. Ultimately, the connection between Spartan proxeny and Inner Maniate settlements is solely that the decrees themselves were set up at Tainaron.

Instead, localized, inter-peninsular connections within Mani – specifically the settlements along the western coast of the peninsula – are much more discernible than indications of political relationships with Sparta. These localized interrelations can be elucidated in two late Hellenistic proxeny decrees from the west coast of Exo (Outer) Mani.[43] The first of these local decrees grants proxeny to judges (δικασταί) from the city of Hippola on behalf of the city of Gerenia, and the processes and benefits that accompany such an institution (*IG* V 1, 1336).[44] The city (Gerenia) ordered that this decree be set up at the Sanctuary of Machaon at Gerenia (modern Kitries), and that copies be sent to both Hippola (location unclear, but likely near Cavo Grosso on the west coast of Inner Mani) and the Sanctuary of Poseidon at Tainaron.

### *IG* V 1 1336

1    [ἐπ]ειδὴ παραγεν[όμε]νοι δικαστα[ὶ] παρ[ὰ τᾶς πό]-
[λι]ος τῶν Ἱππολ[α]ίων Νικάνδριππος [Νι]κα[ν....],
[Ξεν]οκλ[εί]δα[ς Νι]κοσθέ[νο]υ[ς, Φίλων] Δα[— — —]
[εἰς π]όλιν τ[ὰ]ν Γερην[ῶ]ν ἀνεστράφεν ἀξ[ίως]
5    [τᾶς τ]ε πόλ[ιο]ς [τᾶς ἀ]πος[τειλ]άσας καὶ αὐτῶ[ν]
[καὶ κατὰ π]ᾶν [ἀκο]λ[ο]ύθ[ω]ς τοῖς νόμοις, ὅσαι
[μὲν ἦσαν δ]ίκαι ὑπρτ[ίμ]η[τ]αι, τάσδε καὶ διέλ{ο}υσα[ν] {διέλυσαν},
[ὅσας] δ<ὲ> [βα]ρείας ἀνέλαβον, ἔκριναν καθὼς
[ἐνδ]εχόμενον ἦν [βέ]λτιστα, ἔδοξε τᾶι πό-
10    [λ]ει τῶν Γερηνῶν· προξένους εἶμεν καὶ εὐερ-
[γ]έτας τᾶς πόλεως τῶγ Γερηνῶν Νικάνδριπ-
[π]ον Ξενοκλείδαν Φίλωνα Ἱππολαίους καὶ
[ὑ]πάρχειν αὐτοῖς ἀτέλειαν καὶ εἰσαγόντοις
[κα]ὶ ἐξαγόντοις καὶ ἀσυλίαν καὶ ἐπινομίαν
15    [κ]αὶ γᾶς ἔνκτησιν καὶ οἰκίας καὶ τὰ λοιπὰ τίμια ὅσα καὶ τοῖς ἄλλοις προξένοις, αὐτοῖς τε
καὶ ἐκγόνοις· ἀναγράψαι δὲ τοὺς ἐφόρους τοὺς
περὶ Φιλωνίδαν τὰν προξενίαν εἰς τὸ ἱερὸν τοῦ
Μαχάονος· γράψαι δὲ καὶ ἀντίγραφον τᾶς προ-
20    [ξ]ενίας καὶ ἀποστεῖλαι γράμματα ποτὶ τὰ[ν]
[π]όλιν τῶν Ἱππολαίων καὶ τοὺς ἐφόρ<ο>υς, ὅπῳ[ς]
[ἀ]ναγραφῆι εἰς τὸ ἱερὸν τοῦ Ποσιδᾶνος τοῦ [ἐ]-
[π]ὶ ἄκρωι.

Since the judges being present from the city of the Hippolaians, Nikandrippos the son of Nikan-[?], Xenokleidas the son of Nikosthenes, Philon the son of Da-[?], returned to the city of the Gerenians in a manner worthy of the city that sent them and of themselves, and in a manner obedient to the laws in every way, and however many penalties (liabilities?) were assessed, these also they payed (dissolved?), and however many heavy (liabilities) they took up, they determined how it was best for the one receiving them – it seemed good to the city of the Gerenians: that Nikandrippos, Xenokleidas, and Philon, Hippolaians, should be *proxenoi* and benefactors of the city of the Gerenians, and that they should have exemption from public burdens both for imports and for exports, and inviolability, and the right of pasturage, and tenure of land and household, and the rest of the honours that also are granted to other *proxenoi*, they and their descendants; that the ephors around Philonidas should inscribe the decree of proxeny on the temple of Machaon; that they should also write a copy of the proxeny decree and send the letters to the city of the Hippolaians and to the ephors, so that it may be inscribed at the temple of Poseidon on the promontory.

There is a second, similar but shorter, decree from the city of Thalamai that also grants proxeny to individuals from Hippola (*IG* V 1 1312):[45]

### *IG* V 1 1312

```
1 — — — — —ΣΠΑ— — — — — —
[Ἱππολ]αίως προξένως ἦμε[ν]
[καὶ] εὐεργέτας τᾶς πόλεος τῶ[ν]
[Θ]αλαματᾶν αὐτώς τε καὶ ἐκγό-
5   [ν]ως, ἐπεὶ πολλὰς καὶ μεγάλας χ[ρεί]-
[α]ς εὐ[ερ]γετοῦντες ἥκοντι τὰμ πό-
λιν· ἦμεν δὲ αὐτοῖς ἰσοπολιτεία[ν],
γᾶς τε καὶ οἰκίας ἔνκτησιν καὶ ἐ-
πινομίαν καὶ ἀτέλειαν· ὑπά[ρ]χειν
10   δὲ αὐτοῖς καὶ τἆλλα τίμια, ὅσα κ[αὶ]
τοῖς ἄ[λ]λ[οις] ε[ὐερ]γέτ[α]ις.
                          vacat
12 ἔδοξε τῶι δάμωι· πρόξ[ενον]
[ἦμεν — — — — — ΚΤΛ.]
```

... that the Hippolaians be *proxenoi* and benefactors of the city of the Thalamitai, they and their descendants, since they performed many great services for the city voluntarily; that they have the enjoyment of citizen rights, tenure of land and household, the right of pasturage, and exemption from public burdens; that they have the rest of the honours that also are granted to other benefactors. [vacat] It seemed good to the people: that there be a *proxenos* ...

Together, these inscriptions yield crucial information about the political life of Hellenistic Mani outside of Tainaron proper. While the precise dates of these inscriptions are unknown, the content (i.e., proxeny decrees) suggests that these political actions were under the organization of the Lakedaimonian League, sometime after the early second century BCE. When comparing the information in these inscriptions with the only two proxeny decrees that survive from the Mesa (Inner) Mani peninsula (those just presented above from Tainaron – *IG* V 1 1226, 1227), these texts echo information about the privileges that such proxeny afforded, including exemption from duties on imports and exports (ἀτέλειαν καὶ εἰσαγόντοις καὶ ἐξαγόντοις), asylum (ἀσυλίαν), the right to graze flocks (ἐπινομίαν), the right to own land with a place to live (καὶ γᾶς ἔνκτησιν καὶ οἰκίας; γᾶς τε καὶ οἰκίας ἔνκτησιν), and "all of the rest of the privileges bestowed by proxeny" / "that are granted to other benefactors" (καὶ τὰ λοιπὰ τίμια ὅσα καὶ τοῖς ἄλλοις προξένοις/καὶ τᾶλλα τίμια, ὅσα καὶ τοῖς ἄλλοις εὐεργέταις).[46] As Kennell pointed out, such evidence reveals that member cities were very much independent of one another and that the member cities of the Lakedaimonian League did not enjoy full sympolity with each other.[47] Nevertheless, the granting of proxeny to Hippolaians by Gerenia and Thalames shows more localized connections in the region of the western coast of Mani.

The connection between the settlements along the western coast, as evidenced through the proxeny decrees, is supported by connectivity afforded through the seascape and a series of accessible bays; the west coast was either an actual or perceived localized micro-region for the ancient inhabitants, who were interconnected with one another on this side of the Taygetos range, which extended down to the Matapan promontory in the south. Further archaeological research is needed to test this hypothesis of interconnectivity, and specifically to determine whether there exists a marked footprint of shared material culture in this region, but the preliminary results of the ceramic analysis from a small survey at Diros Bay in the northwest coast of Mesa Mani sheds light on local activity here: namely, local pottery production and a complete absence of Spartan, Lakonian, or Messenian ceramic fabrics.[48] Moreover, the Diros Bay archaeological case study changes the known record of classical antiquity on the western coast of Mani – a region comprising a stretch of land between Hippola and Oitylos that is omitted completely from the ancient written sources – by revealing traces of human activity in a previously underinvestigated region. As Beck has demonstrated, localities can be inspired by physical infrastructure and chosen modes of communication.[49] As is the case with Tainaron, continued archaeological investigations along the western coast of Mani will likewise fill gaps in the material record of human occupation, and the localized interconnections between settlements along this coast will become increasingly apparent.

## Discussion and Conclusions

The Hellenistic Mani is poorly understood and often viewed through a lens of Spartan history and politics. This chapter is not meant to present an exhaustive record of the Hellenistic Mani in its entirety, but to focus on the localized phenomena and interconnections that existed far from Sparta, especially in the extreme south of the peninsula at the site of Tainaron, and along the western coast, where the distribution of archaeological and epigraphic evidence from the period indicates thriving local communities that were largely interconnected through political institutions. Tainaron was undoubtedly the most famous site on the peninsula in antiquity, yet upon closer investigation, it seems that even "global" activities such as the Hellenistic mercenary gatherings operated in a localized context because of the local geographic particularities of this place. The literary and epigraphic sources concerning Hellenistic Tainaron and the west coast of Mani are especially informative for what they lack: namely, any evidence whatsoever for the control of the sanctuary or the settlements by the Spartan state. Rather, the settlements within the western and southern Mani peninsula enjoyed new political relationships and communication with previously Spartan-controlled Lakonian and Messenian perioikic *poleis* due to the formation of the Lakedaimonian League in the face of a weakened Spartan state. This shows local resilience in the face of accelerated cultural change at the macro-level: the political activities and general turmoil of the Hellenistic Mediterranean do not seem to adversely affect the settlements in lower Mani so much as they seem to simply involve them, particularly Tainaron. The archaeological and epigraphic record along the western coast of the peninsula provides additional evidence for continued activity at Hellenistic settlements, including the civic institutions at Hippola (Cavo Grosso region), and the previously unknown site at Diros Bay. The material cultural evidence points to robust inhabitation in this small local world, suggesting population increases and perhaps more opportunities for identities of place to develop and thrive in these local settlements. Only further archaeological investigations – from famous sites like Tainaron to hitherto unknown places like Diros Bay – will shed additional light on the localism of the Mani peninsula in antiquity.

## NOTES

1  Allen 1997: 260; Rogan 1973: 34.
2  Cartledge 2002: 275; Richer 2008: 245; Shipley 2018: 27, 91.
3  Gardner 2021.
4  Gardner 2018.
5  Couvenhes 2008: 280; Griffith 1935: 260; Gardner 2018: 263–77.
6  See Couvenhes (2008: 284) for the principal argument against the market. Shipley (2018: 45) adheres to the idea of Spartan control.
7  For the idea of the "physical local," see Beck 2020: 29–40.
8  Brunt 1976: x, and 1983: 534–73. All translations are my own unless otherwise noted.
9  Jones 1967: 148.

10  Badian 1961: 25–6. Parke (1933: 201) and Launey (1949: 105) also used this passage as early evidence of a mercenary recruiting ground, largely based on a parallel passage by Diodorus (17.48.1–2) which noted that Agis had 8,000 mercenaries (after the Battle of Issos) but that did not explicitly mention Tainaron – or anywhere – as a place where the mercenaries were situated at any period. This brief example shows how ingrained into scholarship the notion of Tainaron as a "market" was, and Couvenhes (2008: 285) only recently dismantled this misconception. Others who argue that Tainaron was a Spartan naval base include Griffith (1935: 259) and Bosworth (1975: 29).

11  Couvenhes 2008: 285, n. 31.8.

12  Gardner 2018: 181. How and Wells 1912: vii 168.

13  Gardner 2018: 189.

14  "In defence of Chares on the mercenary force at Taenarum," Burtt 1954: 570–1. Nothing is known about this "speech," including historical context, date, whether it was published, and whether it even existed in the form of a public speech at all. Parke (1933: 201) situates Chares at Tainaron from 332 until his death in 325/324, at which point Leosthenes takes over.

15  Griffith 1935: 35.

16  Couvenhes 2008: 296.

17  Couvenhes 2008: 296; Laronde 1987: 83, n. 170.

18  Harpalos' 6,000 mercenaries were no longer on Tainaron, since they had been taken by Thibron when the latter murdered Harpalos – see Diod. Sic. 18.19. [2]; Geer 1947: 37. There are chronological issues regarding these two passages, since they seem to relate the overlapping events – see Couvenhes 2008 (289), Mitchel 1964 (13–17), Ashton 1983, and Worthington 1994.

19  Of course, the use of περὶ Ταίναρον to describe the location of the mercenaries could imply that the men were stationed in a much larger area, extending northwards from the promontory towards the harbours of Psamathous and Achilleion, and potentially even further north towards modern Kyparissos; the western coast is the only (nearby) possible place for sufficient agricultural production that could have provided a source of food for this many men. Nevertheless, it is impossible to say exactly where they were stationed, except that it must have been in close proximity to at least one harbour for the arrival and departure of the mercenaries.

20  Jones 1967: 148.

21  Launey 1950: 105 n. 1.

22  Badian 1961: 26.

23  Goukowsky (1981: 47–64), and most recently Couvenhes (2008: 288), believe that the narrative recorded in Diodorus 111.2 is out of place and actually records events of 332, wherein the Persians retreat to Tainaron, a "maritime Spartan base" following their defeat at Issos. This is a chronological leap of

almost a decade, and more importantly, there is no clear reason why – if the allied forces were truly returning to regroup in a Lakonian base – they wouldn't return to Gytheion, where access to reinforcements, medical aid, food, and resources would be much more readily available.

24 For Leosthenes' relationship to the mercenaries see also Paus. 1.25.5; and 8.52.5, who said there were 50,000 mercenaries but did not mention Tainaron specifically.

25 Badian 1961: 27.

26 Seifried 2019.

27 Horden and Purcell 2000: 175–80, 196, 225–8, 268.

28 Gardner 2021: 347–50; Mylonopoulos 2003: 234–5; Papachatzis 1976: 110; Panagiotopoulou 2001–4 [2012]: 290; Tsouli 2010: 548.

29 Gardner 2018: 299–307.

30 Cummer 1978: 36.

31 Mylonopoulos 2003: 235–6 and n. 152; Bursian 1853–5: 150; Papachatzis 1976: 442; Forster and Woodward 1906: 249. Moschou 1975a: 160, 167, figures 6–8: she reported that stairs were apparent in the building (2a) directly to the south of the chapel, and that the buildings on the west coast of the eastern bay were ship sheds.

32 Tsouli 2010: 547.

33 Moschos and Moschou (1981) indicate a possible ancient site in the vicinity on their map, but no information is provided.

34 *SEG* 11.938; this text was first published by Pouqueville in his *Voyage dans la Grèce*. In this volume, he recorded the find spot of this inscription as "à Asomatos," presumably the church of Aghioi Asomatoi. Pouqueville says the location is "À Asomato ou Liternes, à Magne" (1821: 170 (XIII)). Liternes may be an ancient name for Kisternes, one of the modern toponyms for the area. Shipley (2000: 368, n. 9) said that Cartledge (in Cartledge and Spawforth 2001: 77) dated this inscription to the 70s BCE, but there is no evidence of this claim in the work cited; Shipley incorrectly cited this inscription when *IG* V 1, 1174 was meant (thanks for N. Kennell for pointing this out); see Cartledge and Spawforth (1989: 183) for the correct inscription. The current location of this inscription is unknown.

35 *SEG* 11.938; Kolbe listed this as inventory number 74, but the current inventory number is unknown. It is inscribed on a fragmentary red marble stone (presumably *rosso antico*), was discovered in the chapel of Hagioi Asomatoi, and is currently located in the National Archaeological Museum in Athens.

36 Translation of *IG* IV 1226, 1336, and 1312 by Hilary Bouxsein.

37 Strabo 8.5.5; Kennell 1999: 198–9; Shipley 2000: 368; Mylonopoulos 2006: 145–6. This *koinon* was also called "League of the Lakedaimonians."

38 Shipley 2018: 91; Gitti 1939: 189–203; Kennell 2010: 180 suggests another possible foundation date for the league as 192 BCE, following the death of the tyrant/king Nabis, who attempted to retake the perioikic towns in the previous year.

39 Kennell 1999: 199; Accame 1946: 127.

40 Kennell 1999: 194–9.

41 Gengler (2010: 621) calls Tainaron the "federal sanctuary" of the league and places it outside of contemporary Spartan territory; this designation is more appropriate for the Roman-period Eleutherolakonian League. For federal sanctuaries in general see Funke and Haake 2013.

42 Helots: Thuc. 1.128.1; Eupolis' now-lost play *The Helots* (cf. scholia on Aristophanes' *Knights* 1226) and fragment 149 (Hdn. *On Singular Vocabulary* II p. 917.1). Enslaved persons: *IG* V 1, 1228, 1229, 1230, 1231, 1232, 1233. Kings: Plut. *Agis* 16.3 and 17.1–2; Plut. *Cleom.* 22.5.

43 The political division between Exo Mani and Mesa Mani is the ancient and modern boundary between the territory of Lakonia and the territory of Messenia, and occurs just north of modern Oitylo.

44 *SEG* 11.950; 13.268; 49.381; 59.2044; for discussions on various interpretations of the text, see Forster 1903/4: 175; Robert and Robert 1962: 138–9; and Wilhelm 1951: 75–7. This inscription is originally from Gerenia, despite its findspot in modern Leuktra. It was on a red marble *stēlē* in a private home and its current location is unknown.

45 *SEG* 11.945; this inscription was found in the ruins of a small church in Koutiphari, and at the time of the publication of *IG* V 1 it was built into a private building; its material, date, and current location are all unknown. If the restoration of the city-ethnic "[Ἱππολ]αίως" is correct, this inscription provides additional evidence for the granting of proxeny to citizens of Hippola.

46 Kennell 1999: 199; see also Cartledge and Spawforth 1989; 2002: 161 and n. 20.

47 Kennell 1999: 198–9.

48 Pullen et al. 2018; Gardner 2018: 551–601. For Messenian fabrics see Alcock et al. 2005: 151; for Lakonian fabrics see Catling 1996: 35. For local pottery production in the Hellenistic Peloponnese: Visscher 1996; Lawson 1996; *Corinth* VII.3; *Corinth* XVBl.l; Romano 1994; Bruneau 1970; Rudolph 1978; Bailey 1993.

49 Beck 2020: 33–4.

## REFERENCES

Accame, S. 1946. *Il Dominio Romano in Grecia dalla Guerra Acaica ad Augusto.* Rome.

Alcock, S.E., et al. 2005. "Pylo Regional Archaeological Project, Part VII: Historical Messenia, Geometric through Late Roman." *Hesperia* 74.2: 147–209.

Allen, P.S. 1997. "Finding Meaning in Modifications of the Environment: The Fields and Orchards of Mani." In P.N. Kardulias and M.T. Shutes (eds.), *Aegean Strategies: Studies of Culture and Environment on the European Fringe*. Lanham: 259–71.

Ashton, N.G. 1983. "The Lamian War – a False Start?" *Antichthon* 17: 47–63. https://doi.org/10.1017/S0066477400003063.

Badian, E. 1961. "Harpalus." *Journal of Hellenic Studies* 81: 16–43.

Bailey, D.M. 1993. "Excavations at Sparta: The Roman Stoa, 1988–91, Preliminary Report, Part 1(b): Hellenistic and Roman Pottery." *Annual of the British School at Athens* 88: 221–49.

Beck, H. 2020. *Localism and the Ancient Greek City-State*. Chicago.

Bosworth, A.B. 1975. "The Mission of Amphoterus and the Outbreak of Agis' War." *Phoenix* 29: 27–43. https://doi.org/10.2307/1087582.

Bruneau, P. 1970. "Tombes d'Argos." *Bulletin de Correspondance Hellénique* 94: 437–531.

Brunt, P.A. (ed.). 1976. *Arrian: Anabasis of Alexander*. Vol. 1, *Books 1–4*. Cambridge.

Brunt, P.A. 1983. *Arrian. Anabasis of Alexander*. Vol.2, *Books 5–7*. Cambridge.

Bursian, K. 1853–5. "Ueber das Vorgebirg Taenaron." In *Abhandlungen der königlich Bayerischen Akademie der Wissenschaften*. Vol. 1, band 7, *Abtheilung III*: 771–95.

Burtt, J.O. (ed.). 1954. *Minor Attic Orators*. Vol. 2, *Lycurgus. Dinarchus. Demades. Hyperides*. Cambridge.

Cartledge, P. 2002. *Sparta and Lakonia: A Regional History, 1300–362 B.C.* London.

Cartledge, P., and A. Spawforth. 1989. *Hellenistic and Roman Sparta: A Tale of Two Cities*. London.

Cartledge, P., and A. Spawforth. 2001. *Hellenistic and Roman Sparta: A Tale of Two Cities*. London.

Catling, R.W.V. 1996. "The Archaic and Classical Pottery." In W. Cavanagh et al. (eds.), *Continuity and Change in a Greek Rural Landscape: The Laconia Survey*. Vol. 2, *Archaeological Data*. London: 33–91.

Couvenhes, J.C. 2008. "Le Ténare, un grand marché de mercenaires?" In C. Grandjean (ed.), *Le Péloponnèse d'Epaminondas à Hadrien: Colloque de Tours, 6–7 octobre 2005*. Pessac: 279–317.

Cummer, W. 1978. "The Sanctuary of Poseidon at Tainaron, Lakonia." *Mittelungen des Deutschen Archäologischen Institutes, Athenische Abteilung* 93: 35–43.

Forster, E. S. 1903/4. "South-Western Laconia: Sites and Inscriptions." *Annual of the British School at Athens* 10: 158–89.

Forster, E.S., and A.M. Woodward. 1906/7. "Laconia: II. Topography." *Annual of the British School at Athens* 13: 219–67.

Funke, P., and M. Haake. 2013. *Greek Federal States and Their Sanctuaries: Identity and Integration*. Stuttgart.

Gardner, C.A.M. 2018. *The Mani Peninsula in Antiquity: An Archaeological, Historical, and Epigraphic Investigation into Regional Identity*. PhD diss., University of British Columbia. https://doi.org/10.14288/1.0365795.

Gardner, C.A.M. 2021. "The 'Oracle of the Dead' at Ancient Tainaron: Reconsidering the Literary and Archaeological Evidence." *Hesperia* 90: 339–58.

Geer, R.M. (ed.). 1947. *Diodorus Siculus: Library of History*. Vol. 9, *Books 18–19.65*. Cambridge.

Gengler, O. 2010. "Le paysage religieux de Sparte sous le Haut-Empire." *Revue de l'histoire des religions* 227.4: 609–37.

Gitti, A. 1939. "I perieci di Sparta e le origini del κοινόν τῶν Λακεδαιμονίων." *Rendiconti dell'Accademia dei Lincei* 715: 189–203.

Goukowsky, P. 1981. *Essai sur les origines du mythe d'Alexandre: 336–270 av. J.-C. 2: Alexandre et Dionysos*. Nancy.

Griffith, G.T. 1935. *The Mercenaries of the Hellenistic World*. Cambridge.

Horden, P., and N. Purcell. 2000. *The Corrupting Sea: A Study of Mediterranean History*. London.

How, WW., and J. Wells. 1912; 1928. *A Commentary on Herodotus*. Oxford.

Jones, A.H.M. 1967. *Sparta*. Cambridge.

Kennell, N. 1999. "From Perioikoi to Poleis: The Laconian Cities in the Late Hellenistic Period." In S. Hodkinson and A. Powell (eds.), *Sparta: New Perspectives*. London: 189–211.

Kennell, N. 2010. *Spartans: A New History*. Oxford.

Kolbe, W. 1913. *Inscriptiones Graecae*. Vol. 1, *Inscriptiones Laconiae et Messeniae*. Berlin.

Laronde A. 1987. *Cyrène et la Libye hellénistique – Libykai Historiai – de l'époque républicaine au principat d'Auguste*. Vol. 2, no. 1. Paris.

Launey, M. 1950. *Recherches sur les armées hellénistiques*. Vol. 1. Paris.

Lawson, J. 1996. "The Hellenistic Pottery." In W. Cavanagh et al. (eds.), *Continuity and Change in a Greek Rural Landscape: The Laconia Survey. Vol. 2: Archaeological Data*. London: 91–110.

Mitchel, F.W. 1964. "A Note on 'IG' II 2 370." *Phoenix*: 13–7. https://doi.org/10.2307/1086907.

Moschos, T., and L. Moschou. 1981. "Παλαιομανιάτικα: Οι Βυζαντινοί Αγροτικοί Οικισμοί Της Λακωνικής Μάνης." Αρχαιολογικά Ανάλεκτα εξ Αθηνών 14.1: 3–28.

Moschou, L. 1975a. "Τοπογραφικά Μάνης: Ἡ πόλις Ταίναρον." Ἀρχαιολογικά Ἀνάλεκτα εξ Ἀθηνῶν 8.2: 160–77.

Mylonopoulos, I. 2003. *Heiligtümer und Kulte des Poseidon auf der Peloponnes*. Liège.

Mylonopoulos, I. 2006. "Von Helike nach Tainaron und von Kalaureia nach Samikon: Amphiktyonische Heiligtümer des Poseidon auf der Peloponnes." *Historia: Einzelschriften* 189: 121–55.

Panagiotopoulou, A. 2001–4 [2012]. "Αρχαιολογικός χώρος Ταινάρου." *ArchDelt* 56–9, Meros B (Chronika): 290.

Papachatzis, N. 1976. "Ποσειδῶν Ταινάριος." *AEphem*: 102–25.

Parke, H. W. 1933. *Greek Mercenary Soldiers from the Earliest Times to the Battle of Ipsus*. Chicago.

Pouqueville, F.C.H.L. 1821. *Voyage dans la Grèce*. Paris.

Pullen, D.J., et al. 2018. "The Diros Project, 2011–2013: Surface Survey and Site Collection in Diros Bay." In A. Papathanasiou et al. (eds.), *Neolithic Alepotrypa Cave in the Mani, Greece: In Honor of George Papathanassopoulos*. Oxford: 407–26.

Richer, N. 2008. "The Religious System at Sparta." In D. Ogden (ed., *A Companion to Greek Religion*. Malden, MA: 236–52.

Robert, J., and L. Robert. 1962. "Bulletin épigraphique." *RÉG* 75: 130–226.

Rogan, D.E. 1973. *Mani: History and Monuments*. Athens.

Romano, I.B. 1994. "A Hellenistic Deposit from Corinth: Evidence for Interim Period Activity (146–44 B.C.)." *Hesperia* 63: 57–104. https://doi.org/10.2307/148242.

Rudolph, W. 1978. "Hellenistic Fine Ware Pottery and Lamps from above the House with the Idols at Mycenae." *Annual of the British School at Athens* 73: 213–34.

Seifried, R.M. 2019. "Seascapes and Fresh Water Management in Rural Greece: The Case of the Mani Peninsula, 1261–1821 CE." *Levant* 51.2: 131–50. https://doi.org/10.1080/00758914.2020.1789316.

Shipley, C. 2000. "The Extent of Spartan Territory in the Late Classical and Hellenistic Periods." *Annual of the British School at Athens* 95: 367–90. https://doi.org/10.1017/S0068245400004731.

Shipley, G. 2018. *The Early Hellenistic Peloponnese: Politics, Economies, and Networks 338–197 BC*. Cambridge.

Tsouli, M. 2010. "Αρχαιολογικός χώρος Ταινάρου." *ArchDelt* 65, Β′1 [2016]: 546–52.

Visscher, H. 1996. "The Roman Pottery." In W. Cavanagh et al. (eds.), *Continuity and Change in a Greek Rural Landscape: The Laconia Survey. Vol. 2: Archaeological Data*. London: 111–23.

Wilhelm, A. 1951. *Griechische Inschriften rechtlichen Inhalts*. Athens.

Worthington, I. 1994. "Alexander and Athens in 324/3 BC: On the Greek Attitude to the Macedonian Hegemony." *Mediterranean Archaeology*: 45–51.

*The following chapter extends, in exemplary fashion, the scope of the volume to examine how prioritizations of the local resonated beyond Hellenistic central Greece and the Peloponnese. Its geographical web is cast wide, projecting a Mediterranean canvas that connected Corinth and the Peloponnese to Alexandria in Egypt and Syracuse in the West. Studying the cultural entanglement of these places, Mark Thatcher explores what it meant to be Syracusan – fully recognizing the intricacies of the defining factors and corresponding expressions of such an ethnic self-identification. Syracuse, Thatcher alerts his readers, did not quite fit the notion of mainland Greek* poleis. *An Archaic Corinthian foundation on the eastern shores of Sicily, the city was both surrounded by and subject to power struggles between non-Greeks, which led its inhabitants to deliberate articulations of their own Greekness. Thatcher shows how Hieron II parlayed the denouncing of Syracuse's enemies as barbarians into a long-lasting rule. Strategies of othering complemented memories of the city's past grandeur in politics as well in poetry and more. In the third century BCE, Thatcher detects traces of these memories not only in Theokritos' poems, but in diverse bodies of evidence such as coinage, inscriptions, and, curiously enough, the modelling of the local topography; we encounter here the same nexus of local distinctiveness and attachment to place that we detected in Halikarnassos in chapter 1. In the final section of his chapter, Thatcher returns to a lively episode that marked the narrative point of departure at the beginning: an incident, described in Theokritos' fifteenth* Idyll, *in which the force of Hellenistic localism discharged into a crowded street in Ptolemaic Alexandria. The voice of the women involved in the scene suggests that the act of speaking – what is said and how it is said – might be a powerful tool of local self-assertion, allowing speakers to position themselves in the environs of cosmopolitan megacities.*

*Keywords: Alexandria, Corinth, Hieron II, Theokritos, Hellenicity,* polis *identity, local self-assertion, dialects*

# 13

# Being Syracusan in the Hellenistic World

MARK THATCHER

In Alexandria, sometime in the 270s BCE, two women – Syracusans who had settled there – set out across the city. They are bound for the royal palace, where Queen Arsinoe, wife of Ptolemy II, is holding a festival of Adonis. As these women, Gorgo and Praxinoa, make their way across town, a bustling urban metropolis is on display: the streets are crowded; the king's horses and chariots pass by; the women speak of petty crime committed by the native Egyptians – and how Ptolemy has put a stop to it. At the palace they hear a song sung by the daughter of a woman from Argos, as part of a ritual for Adonis that combines elements drawn from both Greek and Egyptian traditions. So far, this looks like a typical picture of the globalized Hellenistic world, full of the pageants of kings and cosmopolitan cities where diverse cultures meet.[1]

Then, an unexpected twist. A stranger in the crowd complains about the women chattering, and one of them responds vigorously: "Ah! Where's this fellow from? What's it to you if we chatter? Give your orders where you're master. We're Syracusan women that you're giving your orders to. And just so you know, we're Corinthians from way back, just like Bellerophon. We speak Peloponnesian, and Dorians are allowed to speak in Doric, I believe." In the midst of a wide-open world, Praxinoa expresses her local pride and insists on her right to adhere to her local customs and local identities. This scene is fictional, drawn from the fifteenth *Idyll* of the Syracusan poet Theokritos, and its poetics represent a methodological challenge, which I deal with below. While it has sometimes been read for what it can tell us about Alexandria under the Ptolemies,[2] it also represents a crucial piece of contemporary evidence for how Syracusans perceived themselves and their place in the world in the early Hellenistic period.

Sicily in the third century BCE faced a different set of challenges than the eastern kingdoms or the *poleis* of mainland Greece. In the middle of the century, the island became a battleground between Carthage – which had ruled western Sicily for 150 years – and the growing power of Rome. While parts of Sicily became a Roman province, the remainder consisted of an independent kingdom of Syracuse until the Second Punic War. Meanwhile, Syracuse maintained close relations with the Hellenistic kingdoms to the east, especially under its kings Agathokles (317–289) and Hieron II (ca. 276–215). Caught between Rome, Carthage, and the kingdoms to the east, Syracuse in the third century carved out a separate place for itself in the Hellenistic world. It had a long and glorious past (unlike many newly founded cities in the East), and yet unlike most of the older cities of mainland Greece it also served as an imperial centre. It was ruled by a *basileus*, who nonetheless governed carefully within a *polis* framework. Syracuse does not quite fit any model for a Hellenistic city, and its strong sense of local identity – both as a separate *polis* and as part of the larger region of Sicily – must be taken on its own terms. How did this unique situation shape Syracusan identity? What factors defined it? In short, what did it mean to be Syracusan in the third century? And what can this case study tell us about the role of localism and local identities in the wider Hellenistic world?

The kind of local identity I am concerned with here is *polis* identity: the subjective and internally defined self-perceptions by which the Syracusans collectively defined their community. Identities are typically complex, involving multiple elements that intersect in interesting ways, and they were created, negotiated, and articulated internally by the community members themselves. Studying this local identity therefore requires seeking to understand how Syracusans saw themselves, according to their own categories and value system.[3] Syracuse in the third century was by no means isolated from the larger Hellenistic world – in fact, it was closely connected to it, as we will see later. Nevertheless, Theokritos' story of Praxinoa suggests that its local concerns and interests took priority. Local history shaped Syracusans' outlook on the world, and Syracusans often prioritized local value systems over outside ideas. Rather than valuing a cosmopolitan Attic *koinē*, for instance, Syracusans instead drew meaning from their Dorian and Peloponnesian origins and from events in their city's past (such as the Deinomenid tyranny in the fifth century) that were irrelevant elsewhere. Taken together, these priorities and attitudes created a specific local discourse environment, or a set of common reference points, which were locally generated and shared among Syracusans, and which validated a local understanding of the world that might differ from what was understood elsewhere.[4] Thus, the question "what did it mean to be Syracusan?" can only be explored through close attention to local ways of thinking.

We can get a clear picture of how Syracusans constructed their identities in the third century from a variety of sources. Two poems of Theokritos, *Idylls* 15 and 16, loom large in this discussion, since as a Syracusan himself, Theokritos' articulations of Syracusan identity offer some of the best inside evidence we have. They must, however, be read sensitively and in conversation with other evidence. I will argue that three factors played particularly important roles in articulating Syracusan identity: first, its sense of Greekness, emphasizing its role as defender of the Sicilian Greeks against barbarian enemies; second, the memory of the city's past greatness, especially under the Deinomenid tyrants of the early fifth century; and third, pride in its Dorian, Corinthian, and Peloponnesian origins. None of these factors were entirely new in the third century, but some were reshaped to fit new circumstances, and each reflects the distinctive place of Sicily in the Hellenistic world.

## Defending Hellenism

Syracuse's long history of conflict with non-Greeks, who in Sicily were regularly labelled "barbarians," often led Syracusans to highlight their identities as Greeks. Carthage in particular had been a frequent enemy of Syracuse for centuries, as far back as the Battle of Himera in 480 BCE. Early in the fourth century, after years of alternating between success and disaster, the Syracusan tyrant Dionysios I agreed to divide the island between himself and the Carthaginians, who remained the major power in western Sicily for nearly 150 years. Yet during this time many Greeks, primarily under Syracusan leadership, renewed the struggle against the barbarian. In the 340s, the Syracusans invited the Corinthian Timoleon to Sicily to free them from the tyrant Dionysios II and to fight Carthage; his victory over Carthage at the Krimisos River temporarily won back much territory for Syracuse. Three decades later, Agathokles defended the city from another Carthaginian siege and even invaded Africa in 310. Pyrrhos continued the campaign in the 270s, and soon after his departure, one of his lieutenants, Hieron, embarked on yet another Carthaginian War – this one also involving the Romans. All of these rulers derived much of their legitimacy from fighting Carthage.[5]

Meanwhile, a second barbarian threat arose closer to home. In the 280s, a group of Campanian mercenaries – once in the service of Agathokles, but unemployed after his death – seized the city of Messina. Calling themselves the Mamertines (after the god Mamers, the Oscan equivalent of Mars), they quickly carved out a state for themselves in northeast Sicily.[6] Non-Greek mercenaries had been a growing presence on the island since the early days of Dionysios I, and their occupation of cities had a precedent: in 404,

Campanian mercenaries fresh from Dionysios' service had seized Entella, in western Sicily.[7] Messina became an Oscan-speaking city under the Mamertines,[8] who spent much of the next twenty years raiding other parts of Sicily. Their predatory behaviour, combined with long experience of the danger posed by Campanian mercenaries, led the Syracusans to perceive them as barbarians.

This historical experience, which unfolded over more than two centuries, deeply impacted how Sicilian Greeks, especially Syracusans, understood their own identities and their place in the world. In particular, they came to place great emphasis on their Greekness. To put it another way, Syracuse's local discourses, which had been shaped by this past history, drew attention to their Hellenic identity. While this kind of panhellenic thinking had long been available to all Greeks, it was not always prominent or important everywhere.[9] For Syracusans, though, identifying themselves as Greeks, and others as barbarians, developed an even deeper meaning, which was unique to this community: it became a key part of what it meant to be Syracusan, a sense of identity that was encouraged by a series of rulers.

The man who came to be called King Hieron II was able to parlay this component of Syracusan identity into a long-lasting kingship. Like many previous rulers of Syracuse, he found that the best way to unite the Sicilians under his rule was to focus their attention on a crusade against a barbarian enemy.[10] Hieron conducted a rapid and successful series of campaigns against the Mamertines, recovering substantial territory, and his victory at the Longanos River (on the north coast of Sicily, near Mylai, probably in 269) confined the Mamertines to the northeast corner of the island near Messina. Five years later, still under pressure from Syracuse, the Mamertines appealed to Rome for help. A consular army under Appius Claudius crossed the straits and occupied the citadel of Messina. After a brief stand-off, Appius defeated first the Syracusans and then the Carthaginians, and the First Punic War was under way.[11]

Two narratives of Hieron's campaigns, those of Polybios and Diodorus, highlight the barbarism of the Mamertines. Polybios (1.9.7–8) describes the Longanos campaign in this way:

θεωρῶν δὲ τοὺς βαρβάρους ἐκ τοῦ προτερήματος θρασέως καὶ προπετῶς ἀναστρεφομένους, καθοπλίσας καὶ γυμνάσας ἐνεργῶς τὰς πολιτικὰς δυνάμεις ἐξῆγεν καὶ συμβάλλει τοῖς πολεμίοις ἐν τῷ Μυλαίῳ πεδίῳ περὶ τὸν Λογγανὸν καλούμενον ποταμόν. τροπὴν δὲ ποιήσας αὐτῶν ἰσχυρὰν καὶ τῶν ἡγεμόνων ἐγκρατὴς γενόμενος ζωγρίᾳ τὴν μὲν τῶν βαρβάρων κατέπαυσε τόλμαν, αὐτὸς δὲ παραγενόμενος εἰς τὰς Συρακούσας βασιλεὺς ὑπὸ πάντων προσηγορεύθη τῶν συμμάχων.

Observing that the barbarians, due to their success, were behaving in a bold and reckless manner, he efficiently armed and trained the citizen troops and leading them out engaged the enemy in the plain of Mylai near the river Longanos. He inflicted a severe defeat on them, capturing their leaders, and put an end to the audacity of the barbarians. On his return to Syracuse he was proclaimed king by all the allies.

Polybios twice calls the Mamertines "barbarians," and their actions characteristically live up to this description: they are "bold and reckless," and they behave with "audacity." Elsewhere, he claims that they "broke truces" (*paraspondein*: 1.7.3), calls their actions "lawlessness" (*paranomias*: 1.7.4), and calls them *barbaroi* twice more (1.9.3, 4). Diodorus (23.1.4) takes this description even farther. During a brief negotiation with Appius Claudius, Hieron gives his reasons for refusing to withdraw:

ὁ δὲ Ἱέρων ἀπεκρίνατο διότι Μαμερτῖνοι Καμάριναν καὶ Γέλαν ἀναστάτους πεποιηκότες, Μεσσήνην δὲ ἀσεβέστατα κατειληφότες, δικαίως πολιορκοῦνται, Ῥωμαῖοι δέ, θρυλλοῦντες τὸ τῆς πίστεως ὄνομα, παντελῶς οὐκ ὀφείλουσι τοὺς μιαιφόνους, μάλιστα πίστεως καταφρονήσαντας, ὑπερασπίζειν.

Hieron responded (sc. to Appius) that the Mamertines, who had laid waste Kamarina and Gela and had seized Messina in so impious a manner, were besieged with just cause, and the Romans, harping as they did on the word *fides,* certainly ought not to protect assassins who had shown the greatest contempt for good faith.

Hieron ascribes further traits of barbarians to the Mamertines: they have done terrible deeds and committed great impieties, they are murderers, and they despise good faith.[12] Of course, these are later historiographical accounts, but Polybios, in particular, does not usually draw a sharp distinction between Greeks and barbarians.[13] It is therefore unlikely that this language originates with Polybios putting his own spin on events; more likely, this characterization of the Mamertines goes back ultimately to the contemporary situation of ca. 269 BCE. These characterizations strongly suggest that Hellenic identity was highly salient in Syracuse at this time, shaping Hieron's strategic thinking as well as popular responses.

The Syracusans were delighted at these successes. According to Polybios, the campaign was fought with citizen troops, not mercenaries. Sicilian tyrants had hired mercenaries regularly for more than two centuries, but in this case Hieron chose otherwise. His ability to mobilize the citizen manpower of Syracuse indicates that he had already built a strong relationship with them, and had proposed a rationale for the campaign – namely, defeating the barbarians – that they backed eagerly. Fighting the barbarians and safeguarding the Greeks of Sicily was a task they enthusiastically took on. What this shows is that Hieron's focus on Greekness was not merely his own idiosyncratic propaganda, but part of a much larger trend. Most Syracusans felt the same way. He had accomplished exactly what they, too, wanted to see happen – the defeat of the barbarians and the defence of Greekness – and this is what gained him their support.

Over the next several years, Hieron maintained his focus on Greekness through turbulent times. In 264, after the Mamertines summoned Roman assistance, four armies – those of Syracuse, Carthage, Rome, and the Mamertines – confronted each other at Messina. Polybios reports that Hieron thought that "present circumstances were favourable for expelling from Sicily entirely the barbarians who occupied Messina."[14] He therefore took a remarkable step: making an alliance with Carthage against the Mamertines. Hieron's goal of crushing the Mamertines forever thus overrode a centuries-long tradition of hostility towards Carthage, indicating the importance of the anti-Mamertine crusade in his articulation of Hellenic identity. Yet this alliance with Carthage was temporary. The Romans were victorious outside Messina, and the next year they swept through Sicily and began to besiege Syracuse. Hieron quickly saw that by switching sides and fighting with the Romans against Carthage, he could inscribe himself into that age-old identity predicated on hostility to Carthage. In terms of identity, this was actually a very small switch: Hieron was still basing his legitimacy on Hellenic identity, changing only from one barbarian enemy (the Mamertines) to another. Although the danger from the Mamertines had been more immediate, it was now overshadowed by the threat of Carthage, which had hung over Sicily far longer and was more deeply rooted in the consciousness of the Sicilian Greeks.[15]

A key piece of contemporary evidence, Theokritos' sixteenth *Idyll*, adds to this picture of the pervasive role of Hellenic identity – and of the Carthaginian enemy – at Syracuse in the third century. This poem, an encomium of Hieron II, probably comes out of this same context, early in the king's reign.[16] At lines 73–89, Theokritos focuses on Hieron's great deeds:

ἔσσεται οὗτος ἀνὴρ ὃς ἐμεῦ κεχρήσετ' ἀοιδοῦ,
ῥέξας ἢ Ἀχιλεὺς ὅσσον μέγας ἢ βαρὺς Αἴας
ἐν πεδίῳ Σιμόεντος, ὅθι Φρυγὸς ἠρίον Ἴλου.                    75
ἤδη νῦν Φοίνικες ὑπ' ἠελίῳ δύνοντι
οἰκεῦντες Λιβύας ἄκρον σφυρὸν ἐρρίγασιν·
ἤδη βαστάζουσι Συρακόσιοι μέσα δοῦρα,
ἀχθόμενοι σακέεσσι βραχίονας ἰτεΐνοισιν·
ἐν δ' αὐτοῖς Ἱέρων προτέροις ἴσος ἡρώεσσι                    80

ζώννυται, ἵππειαι δὲ κόρυν σκιάουσιν ἔθειραι.
αἲ γάρ, Ζεῦ κύδιστε πάτερ καὶ πότνι’ Ἀθάνα
κούρη θ’ ἣ σὺν μητρὶ πολυκλήρων Ἐφυραίων
εἴληχας μέγα ἄστυ παρ’ ὕδασι Λυσιμελείας,
ἐχθροὺς ἐκ νάσοιο κακαὶ πέμψειαν ἀνάγκαι                          85
Σαρδόνιον κατὰ κῦμα φίλων μόρον ἀγγέλλοντας
τέκνοις ἠδ’ ἀλόχοισιν, ἀριθμητοὺς ἀπὸ πολλῶν.
ἄστεα δὲ προτέροισι πάλιν ναίοιτο πολίταις,
δυσμενέων ὅσα χεῖρες ἐλωβήσαντο κατ’ ἄκρας.


There shall be a man who will have need of me as his poet,
when he has achieved as much as great Achilles or grim Ajax
on the plain of Simois where the tomb of Phrygian Ilos stands.          75
Already the Phoenicians beneath the setting sun, who inhabit
the farthest edge of Libya, tremble with fear;
already the Syracusans grasp their spears by the middle
and load their arms with their wicker shields;
and among them Hieron prepares himself like the warriors of old,          80
a horsehair crest shadowing his helmet.
Most honored father Zeus, and Lady Athena,
and you, maiden who together with your mother have as your lot
the great city of the wealthy Ephyraians by the waters of Lysimelea –
may stern necessity drive the enemy from this island          85
over the Sardinian Sea bearing news to wives and children of the deaths
of men dear to them, a small number of messengers from a great army.
May all those towns utterly ravaged by the hands of the enemy
be settled once more by their former citizens.


Theokritos emphasizes the struggle against the western barbarians and the
role of both the Syracusans and their king in fighting it. The poet names
Phoenicians – that is, Carthaginians – as the foe and highlights their fear
of Syracusan military might. While he does not use the word "barbarian,"
he does focus heavily on ethnic and cultural difference. The enemy lives
in the far west, "beneath the setting sun," and dwells on the edges of the
known world. They have arrived in Sicily from overseas, crossing a maritime
boundary that had long been a marker of identity in Sicily.[17] Their numbers
are given as "many," which might recall the massive size of the barbarian
armies that invaded both Greece and Sicily in 480. Yet, due to the prowess of
Hieron and the Syracusans, "few" will return. The Syracusans, by contrast,
are presented as traditional Greek hoplites, wielding shield and spear as they
march into battle.[18] This image, combined with their description as *"politai"*

in line 88, presents them as a citizen army defending their homeland – much as Polybios emphasized – and sets up a stark contrast between the Syracusans and their mercenary opponents. Among the latter can be counted not only the Mamertines but also the Carthaginians, who primarily employed mercenaries rather than their own citizens.

Meanwhile, their captain, Hieron, stands among them, leading his fellow citizens from the front while earning glory for himself. He is later described as a "spearman with his people" (103). He is compared to the Homeric heroes – not at all unusual for encomiastic poetry, but noteworthy in this context for its activation of a sense of shared panhellenic purpose in the Trojan War. Hieron's war against Carthage is made equivalent to past wars against barbarians. Moreover, Troy's namesake, Ilos, is described as "Phrygian." This activates a strand of thought in which Troy itself stands as an eastern barbarian, emphasizing even further the importance of Greek identity in the ideology of Hieronian Syracuse.[19] By placing himself in the role of protector of the Greeks of Sicily from the barbarians, Hieron succeeded in solidifying a legitimate position for himself.

The concept of Greekness in Hellenistic Syracuse thus faces in two directions. On the one hand, it is of course panhellenic, looking globally to other contemporary conflicts and back in time to both the Persian and Trojan Wars. Focusing on their Greekness links the Syracusans to a network of people who feel similarly, across the Mediterranean and beyond, and provides an important framework for understanding the local experience in Syracuse. Yet this same concept gains significant additional meaning in its local context, which is derived from Sicilian history and shaped by the political needs of Hieron himself. Hellenism means something different in Syracuse than it does elsewhere, showing how local concerns can redefine a global paradigm.

## Memory and Identity

Another aspect of Theokritos 16 brings into focus a different facet of Syracusan identity: the memory of the city's past greatness, especially under the two Deinomenid tyrants Gelon (485–478) and Hieron I (478–467). As a number of commentators have pointed out, the section of the poem quoted above draws heavily on Pindar's *Pythian* 1.[20] This earlier poem celebrates the victory of Hieron I over the Etruscans at Kyme in 474, as well as his brother Gelon's defeat of Carthage at Himera in 480. Beyond the shared focus on battles against a barbarian enemy, both poets place their honorand at the centre of the action (Theokritos' Hieron by name (80); Pindar's by the periphrasis "Syracusan leader" (73)), yet both also in different ways give the Syracusans an important role. Both refer to Phoenicians as the enemies (*Pyth.* 1.72; Theoc. 16.76). Both include a prayer to Zeus that, finally, expresses a wish about the barbarians: Pindar that their war cry would stay away (71–2); Theokritos that their defeat would be announced in their homeland (82–7).

This redeployment of Pindaric themes heightens the poem's focus on Greekness, which is a key element of *Pythian* 1, but it also gives Hieron's campaign a history, locating him within a centuries-long struggle that spans Syracusan history. By associating him with the most glorious earlier victories, those of the Deinomenids at Himera and Kyme, Theokritos places Hieron on a continuum with past rulers, with achievements to match theirs, and their memory encourages Hieron to imitate them.[21] By contrast, newer communities like Alexandria did not have this kind of shared history to draw on for self-definition, and while many cities in mainland Greece did have glorious pasts, their history of course differed from that of Syracuse. A form of identity rooted in the Syracusan past thus can only be valid within Syracuse's local discourse environment, where local history carries substantial local meaning. For Syracusans, remembering the Deinomenids in particular is a way of distinguishing themselves from others who do not share that history. Moreover, this is a history that impacts the present, since Hieron is looking back to the Deinomenids to see what a king ought to be. Thus, Syracusan identity in the age of Hieron II is also articulated by remembering the city's past greatness and striving to recreate it.

Patronage of poetry, the arts, and culture more broadly was another hallmark of the Deinomenids, especially Hieron I. Theokritos, too, urges his addressee to become a patron of poetry and make Syracuse once again a centre of Greek culture and poetry. The comparison to Hieron I and the poets who wrote for him is nowhere made explicit. Instead, Theokritos cites Simonides' praise for the Aleuad dynasty of Thessaly as a model for encomiastic poetry (especially 34–47). Yet Simonides also wrote for Hieron, along with Pindar and Bakchylides, and it is clear from the imitation of *Pythian* 1 that Theokritos intended this body of poetry to be very near the surface. For Syracusans the Deinomenid model would immediately spring to mind.[22] In fact, Hieron II was much less interested in literature than his predecessors. There is no evidence that Theokritos received the patronage he desired, and Syracuse did not become home to a thriving poetic community. Other arts and sciences flourished, however, including the most famous intellectual of Hieron's Syracuse, the scientist, mathematician, and engineer Archimedes.[23] But the king did rebuild Syracuse's large theatre in the Neapolis district, providing a popular venue for cultural performance that is still used today.[24] In this way he followed the example of his namesake, who sponsored performances of Aischylos.

The Deinomenids had also tied Syracusan identity to local topography, and Hellenistic Syracusans picked up on this. The island citadel of Ortygia and its freshwater spring, Arethusa, were felt to bear particular meaning, as part of what made Syracuse unique. Everyone who lived there, from Archaic times down to Hieron's day, shared in the experience of inhabiting its distinctive topography. Residents must have crossed regularly by bridge from the island to the mainland and back, and being surrounded by the sea would have affected their daily lives. While they were on the island, Arethusa would have been a key source of fresh water, as it was for the original settlers. Pindar placed these two sites at the heart of Syracusan identity, using their names in place of the city's by metonymy and linking them closely to his patron, Hieron I.[25] Recalling these earlier poems adds an extra layer of context to Theokritos' request that the Muses sing of Arethusa along with Hieron II (16.102). Moreover, Syracusan coins, from the Deinomenid period onwards, often showed a head of Arethusa surrounded by four dolphins, which depicts the watery site of the spring on its island.[26] Very similar types continued to be used throughout the fifth and fourth centuries, as late as the reign of Agathokles, showing the spring's continued significance.[27] Ortygia, meanwhile, was the site of Hieron's palace; in this he followed the model of Dionysios I, placing himself at the notional centre of the city and ensuring that the island maintained its prominence in the city's self-image. Thus, topography, reinforced by daily experience and building on long-standing Syracusan tradition, contributed to a local community's sense of distinctiveness, a perception that remained in place for centuries.

Hieron himself most explicitly laid claim to the memory of the Deinomenids through the names of his family members. Two of his children were named Gelon and Damarata, both extremely resonant names in Syracusan history (after the former tyrant and his wife). Together with the king's own name, these children's names suggest the Deinomenid dynasty reborn, and they link the entire ruling family to the memory of Syracusan history.[28] This link was designed to endure, moreover, since the younger Gelon was Hieron's designated successor until his death just a year before his father's, in 216.[29] Moreover, Gelon II dedicated a statue of his father at Olympia – one of six statues of Hieron II that stood there – and placed it next to a statue of Hieron I, which had been dedicated by *his* son Deinomenes two centuries earlier.[30] Not only are the two Hierons brought into conversation with each other, but so too are their sons: Gelon is following in the footsteps of Deinomenes, and the filial piety of the two sons demonstrates the continuity of virtuous Syracusan leadership over the centuries.

Meanwhile, the name and family of Hieron's wife Philistis, daughter of Leptines, evoke figures from the story of Dionysios I, the fourth-century tyrant: Leptines, brother of the tyrant, and Philistos the historian, one of his closest advisers. Hieron did not choose Philistis' name, of course, and according to Polybios (1.9.2) he contracted the marriage during his rise to power in order to take advantage of Leptines' wealth and political connections, not because she had a convenient name. Still, it is clear that he recognized the power of names and made use of them. While the age of Dionysios was remembered by many authors mainly for the excesses and cruelty of his rule, it was also a time of great Syracusan power, and clearly at home it could be remembered positively.[31]

The king ensured that the names of the royal family were well-known in third-century Syracuse. For example, they appear on an inscription in the *cavea* of the theatre, which names the various seating sections; some of the names can still be seen today. Along with at least two deities (Zeus and Herakles), four of the sections are named after members of the royal family: Gelon, his wife Nereis, Philistis, and Hieron.[32] The king may not have sponsored poets, but he carefully linked his name to theatrical productions: it would be seen by all the spectators, every time they entered the theatre. Moreover, for the first time in Syracusan history the city's coinage displayed portraits of the royal family: occasionally Hieron himself, sometimes Gelon, and – most commonly and most remarkably – Philistis, with the inscription *Basilissas Philistidos*. Her portrait is frequently combined with a quadriga, a traditionally Syracusan image which had appeared on coins since the beginning of the fifth century.[33] Hieron's coinage thus combined a reverence for Syracusan traditions with a radical innovation much in line with other contemporary Hellenistic monarchs: in fact, the closest parallel for the Philistis coins are those of Ptolemaic Egypt with portraits of Queen Arsinoe.[34]

In these ways the memory of past greatness was inscribed into the landscape of Syracuse and into the daily lives of its residents and even its visitors. Coins, inscriptions, and other media instilled in Syracusans a sense of pride in their city and its history, making it a part of what it meant to be Syracusan. Such an attitude was not unusual in the Hellenistic world. The so-called Pride of Halicarnassus inscription, for instance, as Hans Beck highlights in the opening chapter to this volume, constructs a local identity by celebrating the community's past achievements, ranging from mythical to historical to literary. The Lindian Chronicle similarly highlights, above all, Rhodes' long and glorious history.[35] While all of these cities used the same technique to construct their identities, the content naturally varied, since their histories differed, and the past of each city was valued only within each local discursive environment. Syracuse's past greatness mattered little to the people of Halicarnassus, but for Syracusans it was essential.

## We Speak Peloponnesian

Finally, we return to the palace at Alexandria, where we left Gorgo and Praxinoa. As we saw above, at Theoc. 15.89–93, Praxinoa expresses a third aspect of her Syracusan identity: pride in the Dorian, Peloponnesian, and Corinthian origins of the city.

> μᾶ, πόθεν ὤνθρωπος; τί δὲ τίν, εἰ κωτίλαι εἰμές;
> πασάμενος ἐπίτασσε· Συρακοσίαις ἐπιτάσσεις.                90
> ὡς εἰδῇς καὶ τοῦτο, Κορίνθιαι εἰμὲς ἄνωθεν,
> ὡς καὶ ὁ Βελλεροφῶν. Πελοποννασιστὶ λαλεῦμες,
> Δωρίσδειν δ' ἔξεστι, δοκῶ, τοῖς Δωριέεσσι.

> Ah! Where's this fellow from? What's it to you if we chatter?
> Give your orders where you're master. We're Syracusan women                90
> That you're giving your orders to. And just so you know, we're
> Corinthians from way back, just like Bellerophon. We speak
> Peloponnesian, and Dorians are allowed to speak in Doric, I believe.

With a strong defence of her Doric dialect and Corinthian origins, Praxinoa prioritizes a Syracusan interpretation of these facts – the discourse environment of her origins – over external frameworks that devalue such characteristics. In fact, Theokritos dramatizes the clash between these two sources of meaning, as the unnamed interlocutor takes a cosmopolitan attitude towards the Doric dialect while Praxinoa values it. The poem highlights the complexities that are typical of identity in an imperial centre: the Syracusan women embody the diversity of the capital and participate in the royal festival, but they also maintain their sense of local distinctiveness, without being subsumed into a larger Ptolemaic imperial identity.[36] Although scholars have recently begun to recognize Egyptian elements within Ptolemaic culture, showing that expressions of identity in Alexandria were far more complex than previously understood,[37] Praxinoa herself rejects all this in favour of defending her local identity. Much work on this passage has focused on the role of dialect,[38] but there is far more to it than that. Praxinoa is asserting a claim to Dorian, Peloponnesian, and Corinthian origins – all tightly interwoven but each worth considering. She claims continuity with past Syracusans who made similar claims, going all the way back to the foundation of the city, supposedly by Archias of Corinth in 733 BCE, and she maintains a unique local identity that contrasts with the sophisticated setting of Alexandria.

Of course, this scene, and the ideas about identity in it, cannot simply be taken at face value. It is a highly wrought piece of Hellenistic poetry, and I am drawing attention to only one out of many facets of a complex poem.[39] A number of scholars have drawn attention to a thick layer of irony in Theokritos' presentation of Praxinoa and Gorgo. Much of the poem showcases the cosmopolitan setting and cultural mixture of Alexandria, a far cry from Praxinoa's emphasis on pure Dorian Greekness. Should the Syracusan women be understood as so provincial and so foolish that they do not realize the cultural mixing and lack of ethnic purity that characterizes their world? Jay Reed argues that their "naive pride in being Greek points up their obliviousness to the larger ethnic view that enfolds theirs," especially the Egyptianizing elements that he sees in the poem. Simon Goldhill similarly asks, "Does the need to emphasize descent in this way highlight a fiction of Hellenization?"[40] Perhaps Theokritos does not intend readers to take seriously Praxinoa's statements of identity and is instead showing that they are both incorrect and irrelevant.

Still, while this external scholarly perspective is a valuable one, it neglects the experience of identity from the inside.[41] Despite – or perhaps even because of – the diversity and change happening in her world, Praxinoa deeply believes in her Dorian and Corinthian identity, and that, too, creates a certain kind of local reality. While she is a fictional character, she does, I suggest, represent something real. The irony that Theokritos is creating gains more emphasis from the contrast between the global and the local if the local identity she expresses is one that was deeply felt by many in Syracuse.

Moreover, each element in her claim can be traced in other sources, both in Hellenistic Syracuse and farther back. Theokritos may indeed be layering his picture with irony, but he is using building blocks with real meaning. Peloponnesian and Corinthian origins had been part of Syracusan *polis* identity for centuries. Thucydides' account of Hermokrates' speech at Kamarina, for instance, has him declare that "we are free Dorians from the autonomous Peloponnese, inhabiting Sicily."[42] That strong statement of identity brings together geographical origins and Dorian ethnicity. Syracusans also regularly remembered their origins in the Peloponnese in the myth of Arethusa, a nymph who was pursued by the river Alpheus as she fled to Sicily; the river followed her, flowing underwater until it emerged on the island of Ortygia, in Syracuse, to become the spring known as Arethusa. This story asserts a mythically justified relationship between Syracuse and the Peloponnese, and an ongoing one, since the spring still provides the water of Alpheus every day.[43]

The link to Corinth in particular gained further prominence in the fourth century, when the Syracusans summoned the Corinthian Timoleon to free them from their tyrants and from the Carthaginian enemy. His success brought tens of thousands of new settlers from the Peloponnese to repopulate Greek Sicily and resulted in a vast influx of Corinthian "Pegasus" coins, a type that Corinth had used for centuries and that was indelibly associated with that city.[44] In Sicily, these types were so popular that local mints, especially at Syracuse, began to include the iconic winged horse on their own coins. Throughout the reign of Agathokles and the turbulent periods that preceded and followed it, Pegasus types were prominent on Syracusan coinage; Hieron II occasionally used the type as well.[45] The combination of the name Syracuse with the Pegasus emblem powerfully asserts both the Corinthian origins of the colony and the contemporary relevance of that claim.

For Praxinoa, being Corinthian is a key element of being Syracusan. In an emphatic statement of identity, she says "We are Corinthians from way back" (*anōthen*). The last word highlights the lengthy history of her claim, which goes back almost half a millennium to the city's foundation by Corinthian colonists in the eighth century – and, in fact, even farther. Praxinoa does not seem interested in contemporary Corinth, which housed a Macedonian garrison in its citadel, the Acrocorinth, and would soon be described as one of the "fetters of Greece."[46] Rather, her point of reference is the mythical Bellerophon, a Corinthian hero who travelled to Lykia, defeated the Chimera with the help of Pegasus, and settled there. Praxinoa strongly identifies with Bellerophon as one of her countrymen; his story was highly relevant to her own sense of identity, perhaps in part because of their shared experience of travel and settling in a foreign land.[47]

Equally important, the linkage from Bellerophon to Corinth to Syracuse gives Praxinoa's city a glorious past, especially a mythical past, far beyond what many cities could boast. Similarly, Theokritos elsewhere describes the Syracusans as "wealthy Ephyraians," referring to Ephyra, an old name for Corinth (16.83–4). This is more than a mere poetic euphemism: it gives Corinth (and therefore Syracuse) an aura of antiquity, representing it as a place out of the dim mists of time. The same name was also used by Homer in the story told by Glaukos about his ancestry (*Il.* 6.152, 210), where the Lykian hero says that the hometown of his grandfather Bellerophon was Ephyra. These two names work together to give Syracuse a claim on the epic past. But Theokritos also bridges the gap between myth and history, since his phrase "wealthy Ephyraians" (*polyklērōn Ephyraiōn*) strongly suggests the *klēroi* allotted to the original settlers of Syracuse and thereby lays out a continuum between myth, early history, and the present.[48] Corinthian origins thus place Syracuse near the conceptual centre of the Greek world, and give it a prestige and a lineage that newer cities like Alexandria struggled to match.

Dorian ethnicity was equally central to Syracusan identity. The Dorians were one of the most prominent ethnic groups in the Peloponnese, and claiming Dorian ethnicity allows Praxinoa to link her city with such famous cities as Sparta, Argos, and of course Corinth. In earlier times, Pindar had praised Hieron I for giving his new colony of Aetna Dorian institutions, linking Syracuse and its ruler to a long tradition of Dorian *eunomia*.[49] Even as *koinē* Greek was developing in other parts of the Mediterranean, in Sicily Doric was still common.[50] In Theokritos, the reference to Dorians is usually understood as referring to the Doric dialect, and perhaps also to the literary genre(s) signalled by that dialect, and not to ethnicity.[51] Certainly, dialect is part of the issue. The stranger has complained that the Syracusans are πλατειάσδοισαι (88: speaking with broad vowels, an indication of Doric Greek), and Praxinoa responds with two verbs that describe how she speaks (κωτίλαι, λαλεῦμες).

Still, this is far more than an edict about proper pronunciation. For one thing, the stranger's dialect is the same literary Doric that the Syracusan women speak: clearly this is not meant to be an accurate mimesis of a real-life conversation.[52] For another, Praxinoa declares that "we speak Peloponnesian" – but Peloponnesian is not a dialect. Several dialects had always been spoken within its boundaries. Instead, this is a claim of identity: we speak like Peloponnesians, because we are Peloponnesians and Dorians. Moreover, her final line – "Dorians are allowed to speak in Doric" – refers not only to a dialect also to a people, the Dorians. Praxinoa's identity as a Dorian is what enables her to speak Doric, and clearly she is proud of belonging to this group. Her assertion of a pure Doric identity contrasts particularly strongly with Alexandria, whose population consisted of a mixture of Greeks from everywhere.[53]

Theokritos' scene at Alexandria, together with other evidence, strongly suggests the importance of Dorian, Peloponnesian, and Corinthian origins in Syracuse. This is despite the fact that Syracuse was not and never had been a purely Corinthian community. Recent work on colonial foundations has emphasized that most colonies were only nominally founded by a single mother city, attracting a mixed group of settlers from the beginning.[54] Moreover, Syracuse's population shifted over the next several centuries, as the city received influxes of new settlers throughout the fifth and fourth centuries.[55] Praxinoa's claims of ethnic purity are thus belied by the diversity of contemporary Syracuse, adding a further unnoticed layer to the irony observed by scholars such as Reed and Goldhill. Yet the constructed nature of identities often means that such realities are deemed irrelevant by insiders, who (in this case) prefer to believe in shared origins.

Theokritos' choice of Bellerophon as an emblematically Corinthian hero adds further complications. He was the grandson of Sisyphos, according to Homer (*Il.* 6.153–5), which makes him not a Dorian but a descendant of Aiolos. Since he lived two generations before the Trojan War, he also predates the Return of the Heraklids and so represents a pre-Dorian Corinth.[56] To a Hellenistic poet and his learned audience, recalling this genealogy might highlight the mutability of ethnic identity, by requiring a moment, sometime after Bellerophon, when Corinth *became* Dorian. At the same time, however, this genealogical datum may not have been prominent in the minds of everyday Syracusans: instead, they would think first of the Dorian ethnicity that had been claimed by Corinth for centuries. In this way, as Praxinoa does, they are likely to have combined different elements of their origins that – while not strictly aligned – overlapped sufficiently that they could be taken together as a key part of their identity. Dorian ethnicity and Peloponnesian origins were not unique to Syracuse, of course. Yet this mattered little to Syracusans like Praxinoa, who took special pride in this status, creating a local discourse environment that made these factors a key part of their identity.

Of course, *polis* identity in the forms I have discussed is only part of the story of Hellenistic Syracuse. While Syracusans often emphasized their distinctiveness and separateness, they were also eager to build ties with others.[57] Hieron's close alliance with Rome, during and after the First Punic War, is well known, but he also maintained close diplomatic and commercial ties with Ptolemaic Egypt, which can be traced through numismatic links.[58] Hieron even went so far as to build a gigantic warship, called the *Syrakosia*, which boasted 20 banks of oars and used enough timber for 60 triremes – and was too large to berth in any port in Sicily – and then gave it as a gift to one of the Ptolemies.[59] Elsewhere, his son Gelon made a dynastic marriage with Nereis, daughter of Pyrrhos II (king of Epirus 252–234). All of this built on the work of Agathokles, who married Theoxena, a daughter of Ptolemy I, and gave his own daughter Lanassa in marriage to Pyrrhos I.[60] Clearly these were long-term relationships, built and maintained over many decades, that helped secure Syracuse's place in the world. When Agathokles took the title of king in 305, he did so after the Successors had each assumed that title, and (in Diodorus' account) precisely because "he thought he was inferior to them neither in power nor in territory nor in deeds" (20.54.1). This motivation, if accurate, suggests that Syracuse perceived itself as the equal of the Hellenistic kingdoms, a self-perception that clearly exaggerates the city's real power. Nevertheless, even as much of the island became Rome's first overseas province, Hieron maintained a small empire in eastern Sicily, encompassing a number of other cities in the region most closely tied to Syracuse.[61] All of this enabled Syracuse to project to the rest of the world an image of their city as an imperial power, where the local and the global meet. Both elements are crucial to a full picture of Hellenistic Syracuse.[62]

Yet this case study has demonstrated that, alongside these globalist tendencies, local identities deeply mattered to people in the Hellenistic world. The individual histories of specific places and even local mythologies dramatically shaped self-perceptions and self-representations. Fully unpacking what it meant to be Syracusan in the age of Hieron II reveals a rich web of ideas, associations, and meanings that belie the "death of the *polis*" in the Hellenistic period. Even if Mediterranean connectivity and local pride are sometimes in tension, there is no real contradiction between them. The real story of the Hellenistic world is how these two impulses combine.


## NOTES

1 Many thanks are due to Hans Beck, Sheila Ager, and the participants in the Waterloo conference; audiences at Boston College and McMaster University also gave useful feedback. I thank Oxford University Press for allowing me to reuse material from Thatcher 2021.

2 E.g., Zanker 1987: 9–24; Burton 1995: 9–19; Hunter 1996: 131–8; Reed 2000. All translations, including this one of Theoc. 15.89–93, are from the respective Loeb volumes, lightly edited.

3 The bibliography on identity in the ancient world is enormous: see, e.g., Hall 1997; Hall 2002; Gruen 2011; Malkin 2011; Demetriou 2012. For the anthropological underpinnings of the concept, see Barth 1969; Jenkins 2014; Appiah 2018.

4 Beck 2018; Beck 2020, esp. 161–206. This is not to say, of course, that all Syracusans thought in lockstep; the local discourse environment was always shaped by "a polyphony of voices": Beck 2020: 34–5.

5 On this theme in Sicilian history, see esp. Prag 2010.

6 Tagliamonte 1994: 191–8; Herring 2000: 69–71; Orioles 2001; Prestianni Giallombardo 2006: 115–18; Zambon 2008: 33–53.

7 Diod. Sic. 14.9.8-9. The Oscan occupation of Entella (originally an Elymian community) is also attested via Oscan inscriptions found there and on its coins, while the appearance of Oscan magistracies such as the *meddix* side by side with Greek ones suggests a mixed culture; cf. Orioles 2001: 285; Prestianni Giallombardo 2006: 111–12.

8 Crawford 2006; Clackson 2012.

9 Similar phenomena were seen in Asia Minor and elsewhere, however, in response to the Celtic invasions of the early third century: see Nelson 2022. I thank Thomas Nelson for allowing me to see his work in advance of publication.

10 On Hieron's rise to power, see Berve 1959: 7–19; De Sensi Sestito 1977: 9–40; Hoyos 1985; Zambon 2008: 179–200.

11 Polyb. 1.8–12; for recent surveys of the outbreak of the First Punic War, with
further sources, see Lazenby 1996: 43–53; Hoyos 1998; Zambon 2008: 200–7;
Rosenstein 2012: 53–61; Vacanti 2012: 14–28.

12 Vacanti 2012: 42–3.

13 However, see Eckstein 1995: 119–25; Champion 2004. Walbank 1957–79: I.53–4,
ascribes the entire passage on Hieron's rise (1.8.3–9.8) to Timaios, which would
still place the words in a third-century Sicilian context.

14 Polyb. 1.11.7: Ἱέρων νομίσας εὐφυῶς ἔχειν τὰ παρόντα πρὸς τὸ τοὺς βαρβάρους
τοὺς τὴν Μεσσήνην κατέχοντας ὁλοσχερῶς ἐκβαλεῖν ἐκ τῆς Σικελίας.

15 On this move, see Prag 2010: 67–71; cf. Zambon 2008: 211–15.

16 For the date, see Gow 1950: 306–7; Hunter 1996: 83. Of course, the poem is also
several other things, including a "meditation on the relation between poet and
patron" (Hunter 1996: 77), a manifesto in defence of poetry, and a claim that
Theokritos is the equal of past poets: see Gow 1950: 305–24; Griffiths 1979:
9–50; Gutzwiller 1983; Dover 1985: 216–29; Hunter 1996: 77–109. Stephens
2018: 79–82, argues that the poem shows Hieron as a bad king, contrasted with
Ptolemy II in *Id.* 17.

17 See esp. the speech of Hermokrates at Gela in Thucydides (4.59–64).

18 These hoplites carry "wicker shields" (σακέεσσι ... ἰτεΐνοισιν, 79), which is a poetic
expression, used several times by Euripides (*Heraclid.* 376; *Troad.* 1193; *Suppl.* 695;
*Cycl.* 7; cf. Gow 1950: 320); applying it to hoplites underscores their heroism.

19 Erskine 2001: 61–92; cf. Hall 1989.

20 E.g., Griffiths 1979: 37–8; Gutzwiller 1983: 231–3; Hunter 1996: 82–90; Prag
2010: 66.

21 Cf. Hunter 1996: 86–7.

22 Gow 1950: 312–13; Hunter 1996: 83–7. The court of Dionysios I was also a
hotbed of literary (especially dramatic) production, although hardly any of this
work survives.

23 De Sensi Sestito 1977: 191–3; Wilson 2013: 83–98; Veit 2013. On Archimedes,
see Knorr 1978: 235–8; Netz 2013.

24 On the theatre, see Campagna 2004: 171–83; Marconi 2012: 179–80, 203–6.

25 *Ol.* 6.92-4; *Pyth.* 2.5–7; *Pyth.* 3.68–70; *Nem.* 1.1–6; Thatcher 2012.

26 Kraay 1976: 210; Thatcher 2012.

27 Kraay and Hirmer 1966: 293; Rutter 1997: 173.

28 De Sensi Sestito 1977: 183–4; see Haake 2013: 110–11, for sources. Hieron had
additional children, whose names are not recorded, except for one daughter, Herakleia.

29 De Sensi Sestito 1977: 125–35; Haake 2013.

30 Paus. 6.12.1–4; Portale 2004: 230–7.

31 A further example may be the mythicized stories of Hieron's birth and
upbringing, which mirror stories told about Gelon and Dionysios: Just. 23.1–6,
with Lewis 2000: 105–6.

32  *IG* XIV 3 = *I. Sic.* 824; cf. Bell 1999: 270–2; Campagna 2004: 173–83; Dimartino 2006: 704–5; Lehmler 2005: 122–7; Veit 2009: 368–9.

33  Head 1911: 183–5; Kraay and Hirmer 1966: 293; Rutter 1997: 177–9; Caccamo Caltabiano, Carroccio and Oteri 1997; Lehmler 2005: 89–95.

34  Head 1911: 184–5; Rutter 1997: 123, 178–9; cf. Kraay and Hirmer 1966: 382.

35  On these two inscriptions, see Higbie 2003; Isager and Pedersen 2004; Stevens 2016: 78–82.

36  Cf. Stevens 2016.

37  See esp. Reed 2000; Stephens 2003; Moyer 2011b; cf. Moyer 2011a.

38  See esp. Willi 2012; cf. Gow 1950: 290–1; Zanker 1987: 164–5; Hunter 1996: 119–23.

39  For other angles on the poem, see Gow 1950: 262–304; Dover 1985: 188–216; Zanker 1987: 9–24; Goldhill 1991; Burton 1995; Hunter 1996: 110–38; Reed 2000.

40  Reed 2000: 345–6; Goldhill 1991: 275–6; cf. Griffiths 1979: 84–6; Zanker 1987: 10, 164–5. On gendered aspects of this ironic presentation, see Burton 1995.

41  Cf. Zanker 1987: 19, who recognizes the "fierce pride" in their origins felt by immigrants to Alexandria.

42  6.77.1: Δωριῆς ἐλεύθεροι ἀπ' αὐτονόμου τῆς Πελοποννήσου τὴν Σικελίαν οἰκοῦντες.

43  Known as early as Ibykos (F 286 Page), and still relevant in the third century for Timaios (Γ 41 = Strabo 6.2.4); see Thatcher 2012.

44  Talbert 1974: 161–78; Rutter 1997: 167–74.

45  Head 1911: 179–80; Kraay and Hirmer 1966: 293; Rutter 1997: 167–74.

46  Polyb. 18.11.5, a description attributed to Philip V.

47  Cf. McInerney 2017, esp. 124.

48  Cf. *Id.* 28.17: Syracuse was founded by "Archias from Ephyra," similarly collapsing mythical and historical time.

49  Pyth. 1.60–6; Thatcher 2012: 77–83; Morgan 2015: 333–40.

50  Mimbrera 2012.

51  Gow 1950: 290–1; Zanker 1987: 164–5; Hunter 1996: 119–23; Willi 2012.

52  As noted by many commentators: e.g., Gow 1950: 290; Dover 1985: 207; Zanker 1987: 164–5; Hunter 1996: 119–23.

53  Bagnall 1984.

54  E.g., Malkin 2009.

55  Lomas 2006.

56  I thank Claudia Antonetti for this point.

57  De Sensi Sestito 1977: 165–78; De Sensi Sestito 1995; Portale 2004; Wilson 2013: 80–3.

58  Rutter 1997: 178–9.

59  Ath. 5.206d-9b = Moschion (*FGrH* 575) F 1; cf. Lehmler 2005: 210–32; Castagnino Berlinghieri 2010; Vacanti 2012: 96–102. The ship was also the subject of an epigram by Archimelos: Olson 2017.

60  Theoxena: Just. 23.2.6; Lanassa: Plut. *Pyrrh.* 9.1; cf. De Sensi Sestito 1977: 175–6; Lewis 2009: 106.
61  Berve 1959: 50–6; De Sensi Sestito 1977: 113–23; Bell 1999: 258–69.
62  On the intersection between the global and the local, see Stevens 2016; Beck 2020, esp. 5–7.

## REFERENCES


Appiah, K.A. 2018. *The Lies That Bind: Rethinking Identity, Creed, Country, Color, Class, Culture.* New York.

Bagnall, R. 1984. "The Origins of Ptolemaic Cleruchs." *Bulletin of the American Society of Papyrologists* 21: 7–20.

Barth, F. 1969. "Introduction." In F. Barth (ed.), *Ethnic Groups and Boundaries: The Social Organization of Cultural Difference.* Long Grove: 9–38.

Beck, H. 2018. "'If I Am from Megara': Introduction to the Local Discourse Environment of an Ancient Greek City-State." In H. Beck and P.J. Smith (eds.), *Megarian Moments: The Local World of an Ancient Greek City State.* Montreal: 15–45.

Beck, H. 2020. *Localism and the Ancient Greek City-State.* Chicago.

Bell, M. 1999. "Centro e periferia nel regno siracusano di Ierone II." In G. Vallet (ed.), *La colonisation grecque en Méditerranée occidentale.* Rome: 257–77.

Berve, H. 1959. *König Hieron II.* Munich.

Burton, J.B. 1995. *Theocritus's Urban Mimes: Mobility, Gender, and Patronage.* Berkeley.

Caccamo Caltabiano, M., B. Carroccio, and E. Oteri. 1997. *Siracusa ellenistica: Le monete regali di Ierone II, della sua famiglia e dei Siracusani.* Messina.

Campagna, L. 2004. "Architettura e ideologia della basileia a Siracusa nell'età di Ierone II." In M. Caccamo Caltabiano, L. Campagna, and A. Pinzone (eds.), *Nuove prospettive della ricerca sulla Sicilia del III Sec. a.C.: Archeologia, numisimatica, storia.* Messina: 151–89.

Castagnino Berlinghieri, E.F. 2010. "Archimede e Ierone II: Dall'idea al progetto della più grande nave del mondo antico, la Syrakosia." *Hesperìa: Studi sulla Grecità di Occidente* 26: 169–88.

Champion, C.B. 2004. *Cultural Politics in Polybius's Histories.* Berkeley.

Clackson, J. 2012. "Oscan in Sicily." In O. Tribulato (ed.), *Language and Linguistic Contact in Ancient Sicily.* Cambridge: 132–48.

Crawford, M. 2006. "The Oscan Inscriptions of Messana." In *Guerra e pace in Sicilia e nel Mediterraneo antico (VIII–III Sec. a.C.).* Pisa: 521–5.

Demetriou, D. 2012. *Negotiating Identity in the Ancient Mediterranean: The Archaic and Classical Greek Multiethnic Emporia.* Cambridge.

De Sensi Sestito, G. 1977. *Gerone II: Un monarca ellenistico in Sicilia.* Palermo.

De Sensi Sestito, G. 1995. "Rapporti tra la Sicilia, Roma e l'Egitto." In M. Caccamo Caltabiano (ed.), *La Sicilia tra l'Egitto e Roma: La monetazione siracusana dell'età di Ierone II*. Messina: 17–57.

Dimartino, A. 2006. "Per una revisione dei documenti epigrafici siracusani pertinenti al regno di Ierone II." In *Guerra e pace in Sicilia e nel Mediterraneo antico (VIII–III Sec. a.C.)*. Pisa: 703–17.

Dover, K.J. 1985. *Theocritus: Select Poems*. London.

Eckstein, A.M. 1995. *Moral Vision in the Histories of Polybius*. Berkeley.

Erskine, A. 2001. *Troy between Greece and Rome: Local Tradition and Imperial Power*. Oxford.

Goldhill, S. 1991. *The Poet's Voice: Essays on Poetics and Greek Literature*. Cambridge.

Gow, A.S.F. 1950. *Theocritus*. Cambridge.

Griffiths, F.T. 1979. *Theocritus at Court*. Leiden.

Gruen, E.S. 2011. *Rethinking the Other in Antiquity*. Princeton.

Gutzwiller, K. 1983. "Charites or Hiero: Theocritus' *Idyll* 16." *Rheinisches Museum für Philologie* 126: 212–38.

Haake, M. 2013. "Agathocles and Hiero II: Two Sole Rulers in the Hellenistic Age and the Question of Succession." In N. Luraghi (ed.), *The Splendors and Miseries of Ruling Alone: Encounters with Monarchy from Archaic Greece to the Hellenistic Mediterranean*. Stuttgart: 99–127.

Hall, E. 1989. *Inventing the Barbarian: Greek Self-Definition through Tragedy*. Oxford.

Hall, J.M. 1997. *Ethnic Identity in Greek Antiquity*. Cambridge.

Hall, J.M. 2002. *Hellenicity: Between Ethnicity and Culture*. Chicago.

Head, B.V. 1911. *Historia Numorum*. 2nd ed. Oxford.

Herring, E. 2000. "'To See Ourselves as Others See Us!' The Construction of Native Identities in Southern Italy." In E. Herring and K. Lomas (eds.), *The Emergence of State Identities in Italy in the First Millennium BC*. London: 45–77.

Higbie, C. 2003. *The Lindian Chronicle and the Greek Creation of Their Past*. Oxford.

Hoyos, B.D. 1985. "The Rise of Hiero II: Chronology and Campaigns." *Antichthon* 19: 32–56.

Hoyos, B.D. 1998. *Unplanned Wars: The Origins of the First and Second Punic Wars*. Berlin.

Hunter, R. 1996. *Theocritus and the Archaeology of Greek Poetry*. Cambridge.

Isager, S., and P. Pedersen (eds.). 2004. *The Salmakis Inscription and Hellenistic Halikarnassos*. Odense.

Jenkins, R. 2014. *Social Identity*. 4th ed. New York.

Knorr, W.R. 1978. "Archimedes and the Elements: Proposal for a Revised Chronological Ordering of the Archimedean Corpus." *Archive for History of Exact Sciences* 19: 211–90.

Kraay, C.M. 1976. *Archaic and Classical Greek Coins*. Berkeley.

Kraay, C.M., and M. Hirmer. 1966. *Greek Coins*. New York.

Lazenby, J.F. 1996. *The First Punic War: A Military History*. Stanford.

Lehmler, C. 2005. *Syrakus unter Agathokles und Hieron II: Die Verbindung von Kultur und Macht in einer Hellenistischen Metropole*. Frankfurt.

Lewis, S. 2000. "The Tyrant's Myth." In C. Smith and J. Serrati (eds.), *Sicily from Aeneas to Augustus: New Approaches in Archaeology and History*. Edinburgh: 97–106.

Lewis, S. 2009. *Greek Tyranny*. Exeter.

Lomas, K. 2006. "Tyrants and the Polis: Migration, Identity and Urban Development in Sicily." In S. Lewis (ed.), *Ancient Tyranny*. Edinburgh: 95–118.

Malkin, I. 2009. "Foundations." In K.A. Raaflaub and H. van Wees (eds.), *A Companion to Archaic Greece*. Malden, MA: 373–94.

Malkin, I. 2011. *A Small Greek World: Networks in the Ancient Mediterranean*. Oxford.

Marconi, C. 2012. "Between Performance and Identity: The Social Context of Stone Theaters in Late Classical and Hellenistic Sicily." In K. Bosher (ed.), *Theater Outside Athens: Drama in Greek Sicily and South Italy*. Cambridge: 175–207.

McInerney, J. 2017. "Callimachus and the Poetics of the Diaspora." In G. Hawes (ed.), *Myths on the Map: The Storied Landscapes of Ancient Greece*. Oxford: 122–40.

Mimbrera, S. 2012. "The Sicilian Doric Koina." In O. Tribulato (ed.), *Language and Linguistic Contact in Ancient Sicily*. Cambridge: 223–50.

Morgan, K.A. 2015.*Pindar and the Construction of Syracusan Monarchy in the Fifth Century B.C.* Oxford.

Moyer, I.S. 2011a. *Egypt and the Limits of Hellenism*. Cambridge.

Moyer, I.S. 2011b. "Finding a Middle Ground: Culture and Politics in the Ptolemaic Thebaid." In P.F. Dorman and B.M. Bryan (eds.), *Perspectives on Ptolemaic Thebes*. Chicago: 115–45.

Nelson, T.J. 2022. "Beating the Galatians: Ideologies, Analogies, and Allegories in Hellenistic Literature and Art." In A. Coskun (ed.), *Towards a "New History of Ancient Galatia."* Leuven, Paris, Bristol: 97–144.

Netz, R. 2013. "Science in Syracuse: Archimedes in Place." In C.L. Lyons, M.J. Bennett, and C. Marconi (eds.), *Sicily: Art and Invention between Greece and Rome*. Los Angeles: 124–33.

Olson, S.D. 2017. "Archimelus: On the Great Ship of Hieron II." In D. Sider (ed.), *Hellenistic Poetry: A Selection*. Ann Arbor: 149–52.

Orioles, V. 2001. "I Mamertini a Messana fra dominanza greca e identità italica." In C. Consani and L. Mucciante (eds.), *Norma e variazione nel diasistema greca*. Alexandria: 279–88.

Portale, E.C. 2004. "*Euergetikotatos … kai philodoxotatos eis tous Hellenas*: riflessioni sui rapporti fra Ierone II e il mondo greco." In M. Caccamo Caltabiano, L. Campagna, and A. Pinzone (eds.), *Nuove prospettive della ricerca sulla Sicilia del III Sec. a.C.: Archeologia, numisimatica, storia*. Messina: 229–64.

Prag, J.R.W. 2010. "Tyrannizing Sicily: The Despots Who Cried 'Carthage!'." In A.J. Turner, K.O. Chong-Gossard, and F.J. Vervaet (eds.), *Private and Public Lies: The Discourse of Despotism and Deceit in the Graeco-Roman World*. Leiden: 51–71.

Prestianni Giallombardo, A.M. 2006. "Il ruolo dei mercenari nelle dinamiche di guerra e di pace in Sicilia tra fine V e metà del III Sec. a.C." In *Guerra e pace in Sicilia e nel Mediterraneo antico (VIII–III Sec. a.C.)*. Pisa: 107–29.

Reed, J.D. 2000. "Arsinoe's Adonis and the Poetics of Ptolemaic Imperialism." *Transactions of the American Philological Association* 130: 319–51.

Rosenstein, N.S. 2012. *Rome and the Mediterranean 290 to 146 BC: The Imperial Republic*. Edinburgh.

Rutter, N.K. 1997. *The Greek Coinages of Southern Italy and Sicily*. London.

Stephens, S.A. 2003. *Seeing Double: Intercultural Poetics in Ptolemaic Alexandria*. Berkeley.

Stephens, S.A. 2018. *The Poets of Alexandria*. London.

Stevens, K. 2016. "Empire Begins at Home: Local Elites and Imperial Ideologies in Hellenistic Greece and Babylonia." In M. Lavan, R.E. Payne, and J. Weisweiler (eds.), *Cosmopolitanism and Empire: Universal Rulers, Local Elites, and Cultural Integration in the Ancient Near East and Mediterranean*. Oxford: 65–88.

Tagliamonte, G.L. 1994. *I figli di Marte: Mobilità, mercenari e mercenariato italici in Magna Grecia e Sicilia*. Rome.

Talbert, R.J.A. 1974. *Timoleon and the Revival of Greek Sicily, 344–317 B.C.* Cambridge.

Thatcher, M. 2012. "Syracusan Identity between Tyranny and Democracy." *Bulletin of the Institute of Classical Studies* 55: 73–90.

Thatcher, M. 2021. *The Politics of Identity in Greek Sicily and Southern Italy*. Oxford.

Vacanti, C. 2012. *Guerra per la Sicilia e guerra della Sicilia: Il ruolo delle città siciliane nel primo conflitto romano-punico*. Naples.

Veit, C. 2009. "Zur Kulturpolitik Hierons II in Syrakus." In A. Matthaei and M. Zimmermann (eds.), *Stadtbilder im Hellenismus*. Berlin: 365–79.

Veit, C. 2013. "Hellenistic Kingship in Sicily: Patronage and Politics under Agathocles and Hieron II." In C.L. Lyons, J. Bennett, and C. Marconi (eds.), *Sicily: Art and Invention between Greece and Rome*. Los Angeles: 27–36.

Walbank, F.W. 1957–79. *A Historical Commentary on Polybius*. Oxford.

Willi, A. 2012. "'We Speak Peloponnesian': Tradition and Linguistic Identity in Post-Classical Sicilian Literature." In O. Tribulato (ed.), *Language and Linguistic Contact in Ancient Sicily*. Cambridge: 265–88.

Wilson, R.J.A. 2013. "Hellenistic Sicily, c. 270–100 BC." In J.R.W. Prag and J.C. Quinn (eds.), *The Hellenistic West: Rethinking the Ancient Mediterranean*. Cambridge: 79–119.

Zambon, E. 2008. *Tradition and Innovation: Sicily between Hellenism and Rome*. Stuttgart.

Zanker, G. 1987. *Realism in Alexandrian Poetry: A Literature and Its Audience*. London.

*The concluding chapter to this collection traces the longevity of Hellenistic localism in the eastern Mediterranean under the Roman Empire. Timothy Howe unravels the ongoing story of local-global interventions in Antiochia in southern Asia Minor, located in a majestic spot on the folds of Mount Cragus from where its inhabitants overlooked the Mediterranean coast. From the end of the second century BCE, the settlement experienced a rollercoaster of political status changes: first an independent city, then part of the Seleukid domain, then royal capital of the expanding kingdom of Kommagene, subject to the warlords of the Roman Republic, only to become (once again) a capital city, this time of the Roman province Kilikia Tracheia. Each of these changes requested that the Antiochians adjusted to the ways and means of their new overlords; more generally, that they repositioned and oriented themselves in the Mediterranean world at large. Howe's article reveals a marked sense of resilience with which the people of Antiochia met these challenges. Negotiating notions of their Romanness, they blurred new imperial expressions of power with old local vignettes and symbols, for instance, Luwian names and the Cilician eagle. Hadrian and his entourage visited the city in ca. 131 CE; this was the prime opportunity for the provincial centre shine. Howe discloses the mechanics of reciprocal dedications such as coins, honorific statues, and inscriptions that communicated the imperial context before a local audience, while at the same time reassuring the people of Antiochia of the time-honoured ties they had to the local horizon. Septimius Severus' reign resonated similar responses in the city, which further hints at strategies of continuity rather than contingency. The chapter depicts, in conclusion, a local elite that not only successfully reconciled the ideas of foreign rule and rootedness in place but made active use of the intersectional opportunities that came with Roman domination.*

*Keywords: Hadrian, Septimius Severus, wine production, local elites, honorific decrees, acculturation, glocal intersectionality*

14

# Between the Local and the Global: Intersectional Elites at Antiochia ad Cragum in Roman Rough Cilicia

TIMOTHY HOWE

Taking its cue from studies such as those collected in Pitts and Versluys 2015, this chapter seeks to move the conversation about ruler/ruled beyond the current "Romanization binary" of acculturation or resistance.[1] By analysing some of the public spaces at Antiochia ad Cragum in Roman "Rough Cilicia" (Kilikia Tracheia), and the honorary inscriptions associated with them, I will explore the ways in which local and imperial public building and honorific decrees developed and nurtured shared practices between local and international elites. Over the course of 300 years, an intersectional identity developed, neither wholly local nor global, that articulated both engagement with imperial family and with local leadership and traditions. It is my hope that this exploration of material culture from the Roman period will underscore the spectrum of ways in which the glocalized behaviours of the eastern Mediterranean region that were nurtured in the Classical and Hellenistic periods persisted and evolved under Roman rule.[2]

Antiochia had a long history, as an independent *polis*, as a royal capital of the expanded Kommagenean kingdom, and as an administrative centre for the Roman province of Rough Cilicia. After the withdrawal of the Seleukid kingdom from Asia Minor, and the contraction of the powerful Seleukid navy around 100 BCE, the community later known as Antiochia, like many of the coastal population centres along the southern perimeter of Asia Minor, became a haven for piracy.[3] So successful were the Rough Cilicians as pirates that they orchestrated the famous capture of Julius Caesar in 75 BCE.[4] After

Pompey's pirate war of 66 BCE,[5] Antiochia, like much of Rough Cilicia, exchanged piracy for trade, becoming the primary producer of both Passum wine – a sweet rich wine much in demand around the eastern Mediterranean – and the locally produced amphorae that held it, which later came to bear the ANT-brand stamp denoting Antiochia as the city of origin.[6] Unfortunately, not much is known about individual elites during this early period in the city's history, for little of the Hellenistic community has been located and excavated, apart from the necropolis, yet what remains shows a persistent localism sustained by long-distance trade.[7] In the necropoleis, for example, we see a number of house- and temple-style tombs, which, although in a very ruined state and bereft of their dedicatory inscriptions, suggest a close cultural connection between the Antiochians and their Luwian relatives to the west in Lykia and Karia.[8] Indeed, better-preserved tombs from neighbouring Rough Cilician towns such as Lamos and Kestros show that local, Luwian names, local architectural styles, and local, traditional artistic imagery (such as the Cilician-style eagle) were significant characteristics of the region's elite.[9] Given the prevalence of house- and temple-style tombs at Antiochia, and the prevalence of eagle symbolism among its coins and later public monuments, I see no reason to suggest anything different transpired there during the Roman Republican period.

In the early first century CE, the city on the Kragos cliffs acquired the name Antiochia, when it became the capital of the expanded kingdom of Kommagene.[10] In 37 CE, the Emperor Caligula officially annexed the area and gave it to his friend Antiochos IV of Kommagene, who renamed the community after himself – hence, Antiochia. Two years later, the ever-fickle Caligula ejected Antiochos and returned the city to local rule, though the name persisted. Then, a few years later, in 41 CE, the new emperor Claudius restored Antiochos to his throne.[11] At this time, nothing seems to have changed on the ground, architecturally, epigraphically, or economically, though no inscriptions survive to document the rapid governmental shifts. And so, we see Passum wine and amphorae moving around the Mediterranean world in large quantities without any noticeable disruption.[12] But beginning in the reign of Vespasian, after Antiochos' death, the kingdom of Kommagene became officially Roman territory and Antiochia the capital of the new Roman province of Kilikia Tracheia.[13] Thus, in the space of 100 years the Antiochians had been invaded by Pompey and forced to give up piracy, shifted from raiding to trading and growing a specialty wine, experienced independence and the rule of a client king of Rome, were liberated from the same client king, and then quickly given back to him again, only to finally become an official part of the Roman Empire and have their city elevated to the status of provincial capital. Throughout these changes, Passum wine and amphorae still moved around the Mediterranean world and the Antiochians continued to bury their elites in traditional house-style tombs. Clearly, the Antiochian elite were survivors and like many peoples of the ancient Mediterranean world, remarkably resilient by modern standards. And just as clearly, the Antiochians were savvy enough to find a way to collaborate with global elites who could affect their lives, whether they be Hellenistic Seleukid, Republican Roman, Royal Kommagenean, or imperial Roman. The local leaders and their families were not eradicated, relocated, or otherwise purged or displaced. The Passum-export economy of Antiochia and local dedications seem blithely unaffected by any such shifts in global elites, and the Antiochian tombs show evidence for multiple burials in what seem to have been "family"-style interments.

It seems fair to say that even though we have little literary or epigraphic testimonia, the Antiochian elites had successfully weathered the social and political vagaries of Rome's eastern empire during the shift from republic to principate and, as their tombs, Luwian personal names, and local symbols attest, retained important elements of their distinctive local identity. And once Antiochia became an imperial Roman capital, we can see the Antiochians begin to map their new relationships with the imperial rulers of Rome onto the city's existing physical space. In this effort, the Antiochians had a well-paved path: the region and the city itself had a long tradition of locally valued prestige symbols and systems that helped signal and define rank and power, such as the Cilician eagle and the monumental house- and temple-style tombs.[14] Moreover, traditions of locally orientated euergetism distinguished the Rough Cilician elite from their less elite fellow citizens and assisted in local negotiations of status and positions of leadership, as elites competed to give, and thus be recognized as givers, through honorary statues and inscriptions on tombs and other public buildings.[15] Embracing their new imperial identities, the Antiochians adapted these local symbols not only to underscore their new status, but also to signal Antiochia's new relationships to powerful individuals beyond the city boundaries. As did many cities of the empire, the Antiochians integrated Roman emperors and their families into the local hierarchies and systems of honour, gift, and display.[16] And the imperial family seems to have eagerly encouraged such practices through financial gifts, visits, and public works of their own.

Unfortunately, much of the initial stages of these negotiations between local and imperial Roman elites at Antiochia are lost from the epigraphic and architectural record, though they are attested at neighbouring sites.[17] Not until the reign of Hadrian, in the first half of the second century CE, do we get a glimpse of the Antiochian reception of the intersection of the local and the global. At this time, we begin to see the *boulē* and the *dēmos* of Antiochia setting up honorific inscriptions for local elites that anchored (and highlighted) not only their leadership in local matters and their financial generosity, but also reference Hadrian and his father, Trajan – that is the Antiochians were conscious of the need to link the local with the global, the Antiochian and the imperial Roman. For example, a statue base found in the agora honours Hadrian for his generosity to the universe (and presumably the city of Antiochia).[18]

Αὐτοκράτορα Καίσαρ[α, θεοῦ]
[Τρα]ιαν[οῦ Παρθικοῦ υἱόν,]
[θεοῦ Νέρουα υἱωνόν,]
Τ[ραιανὸν Ἀδριανὸν]
5 [Σεβαστόν, τὸν κύριον καὶ] ?
[εὐεργέ]τ[ην τῆς οἰκουμένης,]
[ὁ δῆμος].


The Emperor Caesar, son
of the god Trajan the victor of Parthia,
who was son of the god Nerva
Trajan Hadrian
Augustus, the lord and
benefactor of the world,
the *dēmos* (honours).

Though no imperial cult centre has yet been found at Antiochia, and only this honorific statue base that attests to Hadrian's role at Antiochia survive, similar inscriptions and structures from public spaces in nearby Kestros and Lamos, and a dedication to Hadrian's wife Sabina (discussed below) from Antiochia, allow us to get some sense of the connections between Antiochia and the imperial visit by the emperor and his wife, Sabina, in the year 131 CE.[19]

Imperial visits to provincial cities were often the catalyst for various sorts of reciprocal dedications such as these, part of the infrastructure of euergetism throughout the Roman world.[20] With respect to Hadrian, the *Historia Augusta* (13.6–7) mentions that he dedicated temples and altars in his travels in the east; and Cassius Dio reports (69.5.2–3) that cities Hadrian visited likewise received imperial benefaction. It is well known that this peripatetic emperor toured most of the provinces of the empire and much has been written about his itineraries.[21] Although the literary sources are silent regarding a visit to Cilicia during his third itinerary, we know one must have occurred – or was expected to have occurred – as coins commemorating it (*Adventus*) were issued, probably in Tarsus, with Hadrian on the obverse and the personification of Cilicia on the reverse.[22] The date when Hadrian appeared in Cilicia has been open to question, but recent scholarship appears to have settled on 131, during his westward journey from Egypt.[23] If the date of the trip is generally accepted, the exact itinerary is not.[24] The only sure signposts are that Hadrian spent the winters of 130/131 in Alexandria and 131/132 in Athens. This time frame therefore gave him just over six months of optimum weather to make the journey. As for stops en route, dedications found in the cities of Cilicia and elsewhere provide evidence of the imperial entourage as it proceeded along the coastline, first in the Levant and then along southern Asia Minor to the Aegean.[25] All indications are that Sabina accompanied Hadrian. There is no doubt Sabina was in Egypt with her husband, as she left behind a graffito carved on one of the "statues of Memnon" in the necropolis of Thebes as testimony to her presence.[26] Scholars who claim Sabina's presence in the entourage point to dedications in Asia Minor, in both single or joint dedications along with Hadrian, including Kestros, Magydos in Pamphylia; Rhodiapolis, Patara and Tlos in Lykia; Tralles in Karia; Hierapolis in Phrygia; Pisidian Antioch; and Magnesia in Ionia.[27] At Antiochia the remains of a fine white marble monument sponsored by Sabina can be seen among the spolia of later Christian structures on the Antiochian acropolis.[28]

Accompanying the imperial couple was Julia Balbilla, an acclaimed poet and a member of the Roman elite and, most importantly for our purposes, the granddaughter of Antiochos IV, the eponymous founder of Antiochia.[29] We know Julia Balbilla was present along with Hadrian and Sabina in Egypt because she too left her mark on the Colossi of Memnon with verse graffiti that have long been known and studied.[30] Julia Balbilla had long been a friend of Hadrian and Sabina, along with her brother, C. Iulius Antiochus Epiphanes Philopappos,[31] and since the entourage was headed to Athens, it seems reasonable to assume that Balbilla, like her brother a resident of that city, would have accompanied Hadrian and Sabina. Moreover, Balbilla would have had a familial interest in visiting Antiochia and a special resonance for the local elites, given her blood relationship to the founder. There is no evidence that Balbilla had ever visited the region previously, and thus we can imagine the citizens of Antiochia as excited to greet Balbilla as they were to celebrate Hadrian and Sabina in the city. In a sense, Balbilla represents the high point that a local elite person could reach in imperial Rome, the epitome of intersectional glocal identity: scion of the city's royal family and close personal friend and confidante of the empress.

The effect Hadrian's visit in 131 had on the region, and the concomitant intersectionality of the local with the global, may be dramatically seen on Antiochia's coinage. Although the mechanism that provides the privilege of minting coins by provincial cities is not well understood, in the case of at least some of the cities of western Rough Cilicia, it may be that the emperor himself granted this right.[32] Prior to Hadrian, the only cities in the region who minted coins were Anemurion and Selinos. Beginning with Hadrian, however, the cities of Antiochia, Iotape, Kestros, and Lamos minted coins.[33] The use of a single coinage throughout the empire provided a sense of cohesion for its inhabitants and largely contributed to their conception of what it meant to be a part of the global Roman Empire. Although minting was not unique among the cities of Asia Minor, the fact that Antiochia was granted the right to mint by Hadrian legitimated the city's position as a provincial capital and its elites' personal connections with the emperor and his imperial authority. In producing coins with imperial obverses, that is, the head of the emperor,[34] the city of Antiochia ad Cragum signalled its position within, and commitment to, the Roman imperial system. By allowing Antiochia to mint, the emperor reinforced for Antiochia the nature of that position. And yet, the reverse images on Antiochian coins, featuring the eagle of Antiochia, served to legitimize and underscore the city's local identity. In other words, by producing a coinage with imperial obverses and local reverses, the Antiochian elite were positioning themselves within the hierarchy of the empire while also asserting the importance and continuity of local culture and leadership. In a tangible sense, these coins clearly and precisely proclaimed Antiochia's place in the Roman hierarchy.

Located nearby the Hadrian decree discussed above are several texts from a heroon that provide an opportunity to view the nuances of Antiochian glocal intersectionality. Three honorific inscriptions survive honouring a local notable, Toubon Komdios.[35] The longer and more complete inscription gives us some details:

[ἡ βουλὴ] καὶ ὁ δῆμος ἐτίμησ[αν]
    Τουβων Κομδιος, τὸν φιλόπατ[ριν],
    νεανίαν εὐσχήμονα καὶ ε[ὐγενῆ].

The *boulē* and the *dēmos* honour
Toubon Komdios for his love of his fatherland,
a respectable and well-born young man.

Notice that Toubon was praised by the *boulē* and *dēmos* for his love of the fatherland (φιλόπατρια) and for his elite status (νεανίαν εὐσχήμονα καὶ εὐγενῆ). The Toubon family was a respected (and long-standing) member of the local ruling elite – the εὐγενῆ listed here shows that. It is important to note, though, that Toubon has not been "Romanized" to any real degree.

He is using his Luwian name without any Greek or Roman additions. In a style not uncommon to the region, we see both his patro- and matronymics – Toubon Komdios, son of Nana and Toubon Komdios. This inscription is one of several connected to the heroon that Antiochia set up to Toubon in the agora, alongside a dedication to Hadrian.[36] Might Toubon's local fame come from his links to Hadrian and the emperor's patronage? This man did something pretty spectacular in the first half of the 100s CE to warrant a heroon. What better act than to facilitate Hadrian's visit and the rights of Antiochia to issue its own coinage?

In the 190s and early 200s CE, during the reign of Septimius Severus, the epigraphic record again shows us a moment of the local alongside the global. As with Hadrian in the 130s, an imperial visit seems to anchor the relationships. In 194 CE, much of Asia Minor had allied with Septimius Severus instead of his imperial rival Pescennius Niger.[37] In return for this support, and probably also for pragmatic reasons having nothing to do with it, Severus engaged in a massive road-building project, beginning in 195, when he campaigned against the Parthians and annexed Osroene, and again in 197, when he was audacious and successful enough to sack Ctesiphon and fix the Roman frontier at the Tigris River.[38] Mile markers at Antiochia[39] and a flurry of public works attest to his roadbuilding in the region and the new wealth and opportunity it brought. The most significant of the new structures was a locally sponsored monumental temple dedicated to the Divine Severus and his son Commodus.[40] Built of local marble on a grand scale, the Severan cult temple signalled Antiochia's support for the Severan family. And yet, like the coinage first produced under Hadrian, this impressive imperial cult temple also highlighted Antiochian identity, for Antiochian eagles were both placed on the pediment and located internally.[41] By funding a temple to the Severan cult, but then decorating it with local elite symbols such as the Antiochian crouching eagle, the Antiochians had negotiated a way to engage Roman culture that not only acknowledged the legitimacy and prestige of the imperial family, but also underscored (at least to a local audience) the leadership role taken by the Antiochians in creating and maintaining Severan legitimacy and power. To put it another way, the Antiochian elite devised an Antiochian way to honour Severus. In the past they had erected statues and a small-scale precinct to the imperial family of Hadrian and Sabina. They did not have to build a monumental temple to the Severans and place within it, and upon it, the Antiochian-style eagle. They chose to do so, most likely because Severus' road opened up economic opportunities that dwarfed the efforts of previous emperors and warranted special attention.

As with Toubon in the time of Hadrian, another local family appears in the epigraphic record under the Severans that allows us a glimpse of local elite conceptions of identity. In the early 200s CE, a certain Sourbis, a member of the local Asklepian priesthood, is allowed to put up a statue to the god in the remodelled Great Bath complex.[42] What is curious is that, unlike other inscriptions of the time, Sourbis is honoured under his full Roman name: M. Aurelius Sourbis. Although every provincial was enfranchised under Caracalla in 212 CE, it is possible that Sourbis, or his father, who was also named Sourbis, gained citizenship directly from Severus or Caracalla (in connection with the road construction of 195?). For our purposes, it is significant that the *boulē* and *dēmos* (which control public dedications) have chosen to include Sourbis' (new?) Roman name – Marcus Aurelius – alongside his Luwian name – Sourbis. Here, the Antiochians seem to be acknowledging and legitimizing his relationships with the imperial family – in this case Sourbis "adoption" as a Marcus Aurelius. And the family remaining prominent – in the next generation, Sourbis' daughter is honoured with a public statue.[43]

## Conclusions

The Antiochian elite devised a way to acknowledge and participate in the social, political, and economic world of Roman imperialism while at the same time preserving their local cultural integrity and power. Despite the fact that Rome came as a conqueror, and imposed its own global infrastructure, again and again at places like Antiochia we see a reassertion of the local, a piecemeal set of appropriations, adaptions, and modifications that allowed the ruling elites to maintain their local systems of power and thrive in an imperial marketplace of goods and ideas. This is most clearly seen in coinage and through honorific decrees and dedications. On both, the Antiochians simply added in the Roman emperor and members of his family, as and when necessary. Indeed, rather than showing a marked shift in the nature of the Cilician epigraphic landscape in the first century CE, when the city of Antiochia became a Roman possession, public monuments instead emphasized the continuation of sacred and political space within the new imperial Roman milieu. There is no Romanization or resistance but rather a continuation of practice that simply makes room for Roman elites and maps them into existing structures. The Roman imperial system seems to have functioned alongside (and on top of) local forms of leadership (and its negotiation) at Antiochia with those local elites manifesting a uniquely intersectional identity.

In the time-honoured manner, the Antiochians deployed inscribed dedications to stress the relationship between two (or more) parties in a fashion that served both to honour the donor – whether imperial Roman or Antiochian – and to assert the honouring body's right to determine leadership and honour within a given political context.[44] The fundamental act of setting up an inscription in the imperial period, then, should be understood much as it always has been: as a rhetorically charged moment in which the communicative act of writing is paramount to setting the dedication into its proper reciprocal context for the local audience.[45] By recording the recipient's name (and family connections) as well as the name of the granting body and the context of the relationship, the inscription publicly affirmed the local by stressing the important connections between the parties within the greater political landscape. Put into this context, the dedicatory inscriptions to members of the imperial family and local leaders at Antiochia can serve as windows on the intersectional socio-political relationships forged by the local elites. Indeed, dedicatory acts tell us much about local identity and values while at the same time offer little depth or insight into the rulers beyond the need to garner local support. And because of the local context (since inscriptions were placed on or near the gifts they commemorated) the emphasis is thus placed on the bottom-up direction of such honours.

I find it significant that Antiochian material and epigraphic culture was remarkably unchanged during the 500 years of Roman rule and my hope is that this survey of inscriptions and public space from a rather minor Roman provincial capital gives some sense of the rich vocabulary of the local Mediterranean elites as they found ways to legitimate their elite status and make use of global structures for their own purposes. As Woolf (2021: 27) has recently observed, "in each case the local re-asserted itself."

NOTES

1  Also useful for framing the discussion are Cecconi 2006; Van Oyen 2015; 2017; Wolf 2014; 2017; 2021; and Versluys 2021. As is the recent back-and-forth discussions in vol. 94 of *Antiquity* about the role of archaeology, material culture, and object agency in the Romanization and globalization-localization debates: Fernández-Götz, Maschek, and Roymans 2020; Versluys 2020; Garner 2020; and Jiménez 2020.

2  For a recent discussion of glocalization and periphery-metropole interaction as a dialectic between local and global in Classical and Hellenistic periods, with relevant bibliography, see, e.g., the essays in Hodos 2017; Beck 2020; and the Introduction in this volume. See Barrett et al. 2018 for a framing discussion on how glocalization theory can facilitate new approaches to archaeological evidence. See Woolf 2021: 26–7 for a recent plea to see the *longue durée* of local-global interactions when considering the Roman Imperial experience.

3 De Souza 2013; Rauh, Dillon, and Rothaus 2013. For a history of Antiochia see Hoff et al. 2015a: 201–5 and Hoff, Howe and Townsend 2021: 4–8.
4 Plut. *Caes*. 2; De Souza 2013.
5 Plut. *Pomp*. 24.7-8; App. *Mith*. 96.
6 Rauh and Will 2002; Rauh, Autret, Lund 2013; Dodd 2020: 27–30, 59–67.
7 Rauh et al. 2009: 293–8, 304.
8 Hoff et al. 2005. See Sofia and Nováková 2014 for a discussion of tomb styles among the elites of Asia Minor. See Cubas Díaz 2021 for the continuation of these traditions into the Byzantine period.
9 Rauh et al. 2009.
10 Cass. Dio 54.9.2; Tac. *Ann*. 6.41. See Hoff and Howe 2020 and Hoff, Howe, and Townsend 2021 for the historical development of the city name.
11 *OGI* 411; Cass. Dio 60.8.1; Joseph. *AJ* 19.276. Borgia 2013; Hoff et al. 2015.
12 Rauh and Will 2002; Dodd 2020: 67–70.
13 Suet. *Vesp*. 8; Joseph. *BJ* 7.219–43, esp. 238; Borgia 2013: 90.
14 Hoff et al. 2008a and 2008b; Hoff et al. 2015. See Cubas Díaz 2021 for the continuation of these traditions into the Byzantine period.
15 Wandsnider 2013; Argyriou-Casmeridis 2019.
16 For the dynamic connection between local elite and monuments of the imperial cult in Asia Minor see Kantirea 2019. Cf. Millett 2021.
17 E.g., at Kestros: Bean and Mitford 1970: 155–60, nos. 158–64. See Rauh et al. 2009: 290–4, for discussion of the region under the Flavians and Good Emperors.
18 *Antiochia Inscriptions* 18.06. For commentary see Hoff, Howe, and Townsend 2021: 11.
19 Kestros: Bean and Mitford 1970: 159, 163. Lamos: *AÉpigr* 2005 (2008) 1549; *SEG* 55.1518; Rauh et al. 2009: 288 (table 5) and 292.
20 Magie 1950: 620–1. Euergetism has long been studied; for a recent cogent analysis from an anthropological viewpoint relating to the region in question here, see Wandsnider 2013: 176–88.
21 E.g., Henderson 1923: 283–94; Magie 1950: 620–1; Halfmann 1986; Syme 1988: 159–70; Birley 1997; Boatwright 2000. For a contrary opinion regarding the dedication of bases as an indicator of imperial visits, see Højte 2000: 221–35.
22 Struck 1933, Pl. 3, 16; Toynbee 1934: 69; *BMCRE* III, 490; Birley 2003: 432 n. 57. On Hadrian's journeys see n. 53.
23 So argue Hoff, Howe, and Townsend 2021. For Hadrian's journeys and their dates, see Henderson 1923: 294; Magie 1950: 620–1; Halfmann 1986: 208; Syme 1988: 164–5; cf. Bean and Mitford 1970: 160; Brennan 2018: 138.
24 Brennan 2018: 131–41; H. Halfmann 1986; von Mosch and Klostermeyer 2015: 285–326.
25 For evidence regarding this itinerary see Halfmann 1986: 208 and Brennan 2018: 138–44.

26  Bernand and Bernand 1960, no. 32: [Σα]βεῖνα Σεβαστὴ/[Αὐτο]κράτορος Καίσαρος/[Ἀδρια]νοῦ, ἐντὸς ὥρας/[α΄(?) τοῦ Μέμνονο]ς δὶς ἤκουσε/ vacat. See also Cirio 2011; Brennan 2018: 125.

27  For a review of these dedications, see Brennan 2018: 139–41.

28  Antiochia Inscriptions 18.04; Hoff, Howe, and Townsend 2021: 12–13. In light of Baker and Thériault 2020: 68–70 the O and serif we had restored as the phrase ὁ δ[ῆμος] could also be Ὀλ[υμπεῖον] and refer to the title Hadrian acquired in 128/9, further strengthening the contemporaneity of the tour of 130/1 and the dedication.

29  Bernard and Bernard 1960: no. 29, ll. 15–16: εὐσέβεες γὰρ ἔμοι γένεται πάπποι τ᾽ ἐγένοντο, Βάλβιλλός τ᾽ ὁ σόφος κ᾽ Ἀντίοχος βασίλευς. Not much is known about Julia Balbilla, but her pedigree has been reconstructed; see Sullivan 1977: 796–7; Spawforth 1978: 252; Kleiner 1983: 17 and 95. See Hoff, Howe, and Townsend 2021: 17–19, for Balbilla's presence on this imperial journey.

30  See Rosenmeyer 2008; Cirio 2011; and Rosenmeyer 2018 for Balbilla and the Memnon inscription; cf. Brennan 2018: 127–37 for full references.

31  Kleiner 1983: 95 suggests that Balbilla may have been responsible for the construction of her brother's well-known tomb, the Philopappos Monument, and possibly is herself interred within.

32  There have been recent attempts to address this issue. e.g., Weiss 2005: 57–68.

33  See Levante 1991: 205–12, which discusses coinage of Antiochia, Kestros, and Iotape. Most recently see online *Roman Provincial Coinage (RPC)*: Antiochia: vol. III, nos. 3192–3 (https://rpc.ashmus.ox.ac.uk/search/browse?q=Antiochia+ad+cragum); Kestros: vol. III, nos. 3188–9 (https://rpc.ashmus.ox.ac.uk/search/browse?city_id=382); Lamos: vol. III, nos. 3189A, 3190–1 (https://rpc.ashmus.ox.ac.uk/search/browse?city_id=582); and Iotape: vol. III nos. 3181–2 (https://rpc.ashmus.ox.ac.uk/search/browse?city_id=552). Lamos' coinage apparently did not extend beyond Hadrian. Curiously, no coin of Hadrian survives from Kestros, but there is a single issue that features Sabina with the inscription ΣΑΒΕΙΝΑ ΣΕΒΑΣΤΗ, the same minimal titulature as on the statue base from the city. Kestros: *RPC* vol. III: 3188. For the mint at Antiochia see Hoff and Howe 2020: 166.

34  E.g., Alanya Museum inventory number AC 001. Full list in Levante 1991: 205–7.

35  Bean and Mitford 1970: 185, no. 204.

36  *Antiochia Inscriptions* 18.06. Hoff, Howe, and Townsend 2021: 11.

37  Hdn. 3.3.1–2, 6–8. Birley 1999: 108–20.

38  Gradoni 2013.

39  Hagel and Tomaschitz 1998: 37–8.

40  Hoff et al. 2008a; 2008b; 2009a; 2009b; 2010; 2012.

41  Hoff et al. 2008a; 2008b; 2009a; 2009b.

42  *Antiochia Inscriptions* 13.01 (unpublished). During the excavation season fragments from this statue were recovered.
43  *SEG* 20.97. See Destephen 2012 for further analysis of the role of women in civic euergetism in the Imperial period.
44  See Ma 2013 for a discussion of this dynamic across the Greek-speaking eastern Mediterranean.
45  So argues Culasso Gastaldi 2014.


# REFERENCES


Argyriou-Casmeridis, A. 2019. "*Aretē* in a Religious Context: Eusebeia and Other Virtues in Hellenistic Honorific Decrees." In E. Koulakiotis and C. Dunn (eds.), *Political Religions: Discourses, Practices, and Images in the Graeco-Roman World*. Newcastle upon Tyne: 272–305.

Baker, P., and G. Thériault. 2020. "Les empereurs romains à Xanthos nouvel apport épigraphique." *Epigraphica Anatolica* 53: 59–74.

Barrett, J.H. et al. 2018. "Discussion: Interdisciplinary Perspectives on Glocalization." *Archaeological Review from Cambridge* 33.1: 11–32.

Bean, G.E., and T. Mitford. 1970. *Journeys in Rough Cilicia, 1964–68*. Wien.

Beck, H. 2020. *Localism and the Ancient Greek City-State*. Chicago.

Bernand, A., and É. Bernand. 1960. *Les inscriptions grecques et latines du Colosse de Memnon*. Paris.

Birley, A.R. 1997. *Hadrian: The Restless Emperor*. London.

Birley, A.R. 1999. *Septimius Severus: The African Emperor*. London and New York.

Birley, A.R. 2003. "Hadrian's Travels." In P. Erdkamp et al. (eds.), *The Representation and Perception of Roman Imperial Power*. Leiden: 425–38.

Boatwright, M. 2000. *Hadrian and the Cities of the Roman Empire*. Princeton.

Borgia, E. 2013. "The Rule of Antiochus IV of Commagene in Cilicia: A Reassessment." In M. Hoff and R. Townsend (eds.), *Rough Cilicia: New Historical and Archaeological Approaches*. Oxford and Philadelphia: 87–94.

Brennan, T.C. 2018. *Sabina Augusta: An Imperial Journey*. Oxford.

Cecconi, G.A. 2006. "Romanizzazione, diversita culturale, politicamente corretto." In S. Janniard and G. Traina (eds.), *Sur le concept de 'romanisation': Paradigmes historiographiques et perspectives de recherche*, Mélanges de l'école française de Rome 118.1: 81–94.

Cirio, A.M. 2011. *Gli epigrammi di Giulia Balbilla: Ricordi di una dama di corte e altri testi al femminile sul Colosso di Memnone*. Lecce.

Cubas Díaz, J.C. 2021. *Das Sepulkralwesen im Rauen Kilikien am Ende der Antike: Funerärarchäologie und Grabepigraphik einer spätantiken Landschaft*. Asia Minor Studien 98. Bonn.

Culasso Gastaldi, E. 2014. "'To Destroy the Stele,' 'To Remain Faithful to the Stele':
Epigraphic Text as Guarantee of Political Decision." *Attic Inscriptions Online
Papers* no. 3: 1–11. https://www.atticinscriptions.com/papers/aio-papers-3/.

De Souza, P. 2013. "Who Are You Calling Pirates?" In M. Hoff and R. Townsend
(eds.), *Rough Cilicia: New Historical and Archaeological Approaches*. Oxford
and Philadelphia: 43–54.

Destephen, S. 2012. "L'Évergétisme aristocratique au féminin dans l'Empire romain
d'Orient." In B. Caseau (ed.), *Les Réseaux familiaux Antiquité tardive et Moyen
Âge in memoriam A. Laiou et É. Patlagean*. Paris: 183–206.

Dodd, E. 2020. *Roman and Late Antique Wine Production in the Eastern
Mediterranean: A Comparative Archaeological Study at Antiochia ad
Cragum (Turkey) and Delos (Greece)*. Oxford.

Fernández-Götz, D. Maschek, and N. Roymans. 2020. "Power, Asymmetries and
How to View the Roman World." *Antiquity* 94: 1653–6. https://doi.org
/10.15184/aqy.2020.210.

Garner, A. 2020. "Re-balancing the Romans." *Antiquity* 94: 1640–2. https://
doi.org/10.15184/aqy.2020.170.

Gradoni, M.K. 2013. "The Parthian Campaigns of Septimius Severus: Causes, and
Roles in Dynastic Legitimation." *American Journal of Ancient History* 6–8:
3–24. https://doi.org/10.31826/9781463214340-003.

Hagel, S., and K. Tomaschitz. 1998. *Repertorium der westkilikischen Inschriften:
Nach den Scheden der kleinasiatischen Kommision der Österreichischen
Akademie der Wissenschaften*. DenkschrWien 265. Vienna.

Halfmann, H. 1986. *Itinera principum. Geschichte und Typologie der Kaiserreisen
im römischen Reich*. Stuttgart.

Henderson, B.W. 1923. *The Life and Principate of the Emperor Hadrian*. London.

Hodos, T. (ed.). 2017. *The Routledge Handbook of Archaeology and Globalization*.
London.

Hoff, M., and T. Howe. 2020. "What's in a Name? New Inscriptions from Antiochia
ad Cragum in Western Rough Cilicia." *Epigraphica Anatolica* 53: 163–7.

Hoff, M., et al. 2006. "The Rough Cilicia Archaeological Project: 2005 Season."
*Anadolu Akdenizi Arkeoloji Haberleri* 4: 99–104.

Hoff, M., et al. 2008a. "The Antiochia ad Cragum Archaeological Research Project:
Northeast Temple 2007 Season." *Arastirma Sonuçlari Toplantisi* 25: 95–102.

Hoff, M., et al. 2008b "The Antiochia ad Cragum Archaeological Research Project:
Northeast Temple 2007 Season." *Anadolu Akdenizi Arkeoloji Haberleri* 6: 95–9.

Hoff, M., et al. 2009a. "The Antiochia ad Cragum Archaeological Research Project:
Northeast Temple 2008 Season." *Arastirma Sonuçlari Toplantisi* 27: 461–70.

Hoff, M., et al. 2009b. "The Antiochia ad Cragum Archaeological Research Project:
Northeast Temple 2008 Season." *Anadolu Akdenizi Arkeoloji Haberleri* 7: 6–11.

Hoff, M., et al. 2010. "The Antiochia ad Cragum Archaeological Research Project:
Northeast Temple 2009 Season." *Anadolu Akdenizi Arkeoloji Haberleri* 8: 9–13.

Hoff, M., et al. 2015. "Antiochia ad Cragum: Excavations at a Roman-Era City in Western Rough Cilicia." In S. Steadman and G. McMahon (eds.), *The Archaeology of Anatolia*. Newcastle upon Tyne: 201–27.

Hoff, M., et al. 2012. "Antiochia ad Cragum Archaeological Research Project: Northeast Temple 2011 Season." *Anadolu Akdenizi Arkeoloji Haberleri* 10: 9–14.

Hoff, M., T. Howe, and R. Townsend. 2021. "New Old Stones at Antiochia in Rough Cilicia: A Novel City Name and a Proposed Visit by Hadrian and Sabina." *Journal of Roman Archaeology* 34: 1–21. https://doi.org/10.1017/S1047759421000088.

Højte, J.M. 2000. "Imperial Visits as Occasion for the Erection of Portrait Statues." *Zeitschrift für Papyrologie und Epigraphik* 133: 221–35.

Jiménez, A. 2020. "Seeing in the Dark: Roman Imperialism and Material Culture." *Antiquity* 94: 1643–5. https://doi.org/10.15184/aqy.2020.177.

Kantirea, M. 2019. "The Topography of the Imperial Temples in the Greek East: A Political Answer to a Religious Question." In E. Koulakiotis and C. Dunn (eds.), *Political Religions: Discourses, Practices, and Images in the Graeco-Roman World*. Newcastle upon Tyne: 306–23.

Kleiner, D.E.E. 1983. *The Monument of Philopappos in Athens*. Rome.

Levante, E. 1991. "Cilician Coinage." *Numismatic Chronicle* 151: 205–12.

Ma, J. 2013. *Statues and Cities: Honorific Portraits and Civic Identity in the Hellenistic World*. Oxford.

Magie, D. 1950. *Roman Rule in Asia Minor*. Princeton.

Millett, M. 2021. "'Romanization,' Social Centralization and Structures of Imperial Power." In O. Belvedere and J. Bergemann (eds.), *Imperium Romanum: Romanization between Colonization and Globalization*. Studi Materiali 2. Palermo: 63–76.

Pitts, M., and M.J. Versluys (eds.). 2015. *Globalisation and the Roman World. World History, Connectivity and Material Culture*. Cambridge.

Rauh, N., and E.L. Will. 2002. "'My Blood of the Covenant' What Did the Apostles Drink at the Last Supper?" *Archaeology Odyssey* 5.5: 46–51, 62–3.

Rauh, N., et al. 2009. "Life in the Truck Lane: Urban Development in Western Rough Cilicia." *Jahreshefte des Österreichischen Archäologischen Institutes in Wien* 78: 253–312.

Rauh, N., C. Autret, and J. Lund. 2013. "Amphora Design and Marketing in Antiquity." In M. Frass (ed.), *Kauf, Konsum und Märkte, Wirtschaftswelten im Fokus Von der römischen Antike bis zur Gegenwart*. Wiesbaden: 145–82.

Rauh, N., M. Dillon, and R. Rothaus. 2013. "Anchors, Amphoras, and Ashlar Masonry: New Evidence for the Cilician Pirates." In M. Hoff and R. Townsend (eds.), *Rough Cilicia: New Historical and Archaeological Approaches*. Oxford and Philadelphia: 59–86.

Rosenmeyer, P. 2008. "Greek Verse Inscriptions in Roman Egypt: Julia Balbilla's Sapphic Voice." *Classical Antiquity* 27.2: 334–58. https://doi.org/10.1525/ca.2008.27.2.334.

Rosenmeyer, P. 2018.*The Language of Ruins: Greek and Latin Inscriptions on the Memnon Colossus*. Oxford.

Sofia, G., and Nováková, L. 2014. "From Western Anatolia to Eastern Sicily: Tombs of the Hellenistic Elite." *Anodos* 14: 171–92.

Spawforth, A.J.S. 1978. "Balbilla, the Euryclids and Memorials for a Greek Magnate." *Annual of the British School at Athens* 73: 249–60. https://doi.org/10.1017/S0068245400006262.

Struck, P.L. 1933. *Untersuchungen zur römischen Reichsprägung des zweiten Jahrhunderts. Vol. 2: Die Reichsprägung zur Zeit Hadrians*. Stuttgart.

Sullivan, R.D. 1977. "The Dynasty of Commagene." *Aufstieg und Niedergang der römischen Welt* 2.8: 732–98. https://doi.org/10.1515/9783110866940-018.

Syme, R. 1988. "Journeys of Hadrian." *Zeitschrift für Papyrologie und Epigraphik* 73: 159–70.

Toynbee, J.M.C. 1934. *The Hadrianic School: A Chapter in the History of Greek Art. Vol. 1*. Cambridge.

Van Oyen, A. 2015. "Deconstructing and Reassembling the Romanization Debate through the Lens of Postcolonial Theory: From Global to Local and Back?" *Terra Incognita* 6: 205–26.

Van Oyen, A. 2017. "Material Culture in the Romanization Debate." In A. Lichtenberger and S. Raja (eds.), *The Diversity of Classical Archaeology*. Turnhout: 287–300.

Versluys, M.J. 2020. "Nothing Else to Think?" *Antiquity* 94: 1646–8.

Versluys, M.J. 2021. "Romanization as a Theory of Friction." In O. Belvedere and J. Bergemann (eds.), *Imperium Romanum: Romanization between Colonization and Globalization*. Palermo: 19–32.

von Mosch, H.-C., and L.-A. Klostermeyer. 2015. "Ein Stempelschneider auf Reisen: Die Antinoosmedaillons des Hostilios Markellos und Hadrians Reise im Jahr 131/2 n. Chr." In U. Wartenberg and M. Amandry (eds.), ΚΑΙΡΟΣ: *Contributions to Numismatics in Honor of Basil Demetriad*. New York: 285–326.

Wandsnider, L. 2013. "Public Buildings and Civic Benefactions in Western Rough Cilicia: Insights from Signaling Theory." In M. Hoff and R. Townsend (eds.), *Rough Cilicia: New Historical and Archaeological Approaches*. Oxford and Philadelphia: 176–88.

Weiss, P. 2005. "The Cities and Their Money." In C. Howgego, V. Heuchert, and A. Burnett (eds.), *Coinage and Identity in the Roman Provinces*. Oxford: 57–68.

Woolf, G. 2014. "Romanization 2.0 and Its Alternatives." *Archaeological Dialogues* 21: 45–50. https://doi.org/10.1017/S1380203814000087.

Woolf, G. 2017. "Roman Things and Roman People." In A. van Oyen and M. Pitts (eds.), *Materialising Roman Histories*. Oxford and Philadelphia: 211–16.

Woolf, G. 2021. "Taking the Long View. Romanization and Globalization in Perspective." In O. Belvedere and J. Bergemann (eds.), *Imperium Romanum: Romanization between Colonization and Globalization*. Palermo: 19–31.

15

# Afterword: Reflections on Hellenistic Localism

SHEILA L. AGER

This afterword makes no claim to add new theoretical or evidentiary perspectives to the detailed discussions provided by the authors in this collection. Rather, it represents some perhaps random and no doubt idiosyncratic musings on meanings and implications of "localism" and of "Hellenistic." Hans Beck has aptly applied the term "kaleidoscope" to the complex variegation of the local and its interplay with the regional and the global; the papers in this volume explore the kaleidoscopic richness of the concept. Local history, local customs, local dialect, local cuisine, local ritual and belief: the articulation and description of local cultures was of great significance to the Greeks themselves, as evidenced by the plethora of parochial histories that appeared in the Hellenistic period. We have lost more than we have been able to preserve, but the pages of authors such as Pausanias and Athenaios are testament to this enduring ancient interest. The local is central to human experience, and one's local sphere is always at the centre of the human cosmos.

Taken on their own, however, descriptions of local habits and mores represent only static, if colourful, collections of often arcane information. Inherent in a more profound and dynamic contemplation of the meaning of localism is relationality. The concept of "the local" is by definition relational, and the papers collected here emphasize the reciprocal and complementary intertwining of local, regional, and global, whether through cultural exchange and influence, networks of trade and diplomacy, or the impact of regional and global conflict on local affairs. Several of our authors cite the important contributions of the Indian-American anthropologist Arjun Appadurai, and his characterization of globalization as a fluid process that is both bottom-up and top-down, where influence operates in multiple directions. In this respect, although we owe much of our knowledge of the Hellenistic Age to universal historians such as Polybios and Livy, it is the fifth-century historian Herodotus (whom we might call an anthropologist as much as an historian) who may be more representative of how the Greeks saw their world, with its interplay between small affairs and great, and its acknowledgment that "small affairs" often have far more dramatic consequences for those who experience them than do great.

The local may be experienced across a number of dimensions: political, cultural, economic, ethnic, geographic, religious, ecological, familial, and so on. This multiplicity of dimensions underpins the discussion of localism – or localisms – in the papers presented here. But as with the interaction between local and global, isolating individual dimensions without considering their connectedness to each other results in a partial and static portrait. A geographic dimension of localism might simply consider the concept of territory as a largely two-dimensional spatially curtailed delineation; but this would be to ignore the complex human relationship with territory, and the political, economic, and psychological meanings of "territoriality" (not to mention the differing concepts of "local territory" that different members of the same community might experience). If we employ the model of dimensions at all, it would be best to consider them as part of a fluid multi-dimensional matrix construct, one that should also embody the dimension of time.

One of the most significant aspects of localism, as Hans Beck points out, is that it embraces both the physical and the metaphorical. Of the two, if the physical local implies some kind of constraint, at least in terms of space and size (and perhaps time), the metaphorical is a place bounded only by the imagination. The metaphorical local, moreover, can travel with those who must depart from the physical local, whether temporarily or permanently. The metaphorical local is also a realm where local, regional, and global can intertwine most meaningfully and satisfactorily. A colourful example is that of the water nymphs referenced in some of the papers in this volume. Beck's introductory chapter takes for its core illustration the verse inscription from Halikarnassos, often known as the Salmakis inscription after the local nymph; Denver Graninger discusses Larisa, the eponymous nymph of the Thessalian *polis*; and Mark Thatcher references Arethousa, the Arkadian nymph who found a permanent home in Syracuse.

Nymphs are excellent mediators between the global (or perhaps cosmic) and the local. They make love with, or are pursued by, great universal gods such as Zeus or Apollo, or at the least with transient deities who are passing through a stage of a larger journey. But nymphs themselves are usually tied, literally "grounded," to a distinct physical locale; they thus represent perpetually that moment when global and local united. And ritual, as Beck points out, repeats, reframes, and refreshes that moment of "(g)local" entanglement. The moment lies at the core of community foundation, whether through the fruitful union of nymph and god, or the divine nurturance provided by the nymph, as in the case of Salmakis, or the nurturance to humans provided by the life-giving waters of their springs, in the case of Larisa and Arethousa.

In spite of their link to specific locales, nymphs are also, as Denver Graninger puts it, "genealogically pliable," a pliability which may also be geographic; in Thessalia Larisa is Thessalian, but she also has links to Argos and, through her association with Ino/Leukothea, a broader network of connections with places laying claim to some stage of Ino's tragic narrative. Arethousa may be an avatar of Syracuse – her head was displayed on Syracusan coinage down to the time of Agathokles – but her origins lie in the Peloponnese. As these chapters demonstrate, the flexibility of polytheism and the elaborate multiplicity of epichoric mythologies allowed for a kind of localism and a local-regional-global dynamic that may present a challenge to the modern Western imagination. Contemporary Western culture has been schooled by the experience of the nation-state, with its history of rigid religious dogma(s) and its conviction that the past is simply a collection of objective facts. Recent events in North America have highlighted the clash between the locally and tribally oriented beliefs and cultural systems of Indigenous peoples on the one hand and colonialist authorities on the other, authorities that sought to enforce statewide conformity of thought and behaviour by "taking the Indian out of the Indian," most tragically through the imposition of the residential schools. In Greek antiquity, conflicting religious beliefs could easily coexist, and communities cheerfully, if competitively, stole gods and heroes from one another.

Everyone wanted a stake in heroes such as Herakles, that most ubiquitous of local heroes; his mythic deeds and wanderings are a clear expression of that. Among the authors represented here, for example, Ruben Post points out that Herakles was intimately associated with the most distinctive structures of the Kopaic Basin, the *katavothres*, the drainage channels that enabled human utilization of this ecological resource. But this Boiotian claim in no way diminished the claims of Peloponnesian communities to a piece of the Heraklean action. And while disagreement over ownership of a border shrine might cause friction and even conflict between communities, clashes over actual dogma, in the sense of orthodoxy, were virtually non-existent in Greek antiquity: one returns to Herodotus and his famously non-partisan take on many of the conflicting local stories he recorded for posterity. Jerusalem today has been magnified and sanctified as the holiest of places, the central locale at the heart of three global religions. No other place can rival it; no other can legitimately claim to be the site of the Holy of Holies, of Christ's crucifixion, of Mohammed's ascent to paradise. But in antiquity, Herodotus' birthplace Halikarnassos could assert that it was also the birthplace – and the saviour – of Zeus, in spite of multiple such claims across the Greek world. Halikarnassos thereby declares not only the tremendous significance of its own locale, but also its exalted role on a global and cosmic scale.

The malleability of myth in particular made it a superb vehicle not only for expressions of localism, but also for connecting localism(s) to the global in a way that could be manipulated and controlled by the generators of the narrative. Dry history in Leopold von Ranke's sense of "wie es eigentlich gewesen," while impossible to achieve for reasons von Ranke would have dismissed, can be harder to manipulate (not that there have not been many successful attempts from antiquity through to the present day). We are actually most fortunate that the ancients, with the occasional exception of a Thucydides or a Polybios, were generally delighted to record local narratives that went beyond what could be established as "facts." James Roy's essay on the Hellenistic tyrants of Polybios' home city of Megalopolis demonstrates the challenge for us of gleaning information from a writer with global interests writing about his own city, given the reticence of Polybios' treatment of two important local figures from its recent past, Aristodamos and Lydiadas. From a perspective that is interested in uncovering local experience and local memory, a writer such as Pausanias can be immensely more valuable.

Nevertheless, that such narratological manipulation could extend to cultural expressions besides mythistory and genres of record other than the literary is evident from Timothy Howe's essay on Antiochia ad Cragum in the Roman period. Howe traces the behaviours of the elite(s) of Antiochia over time, and the ways in which they interacted with the regional or global powers that washed over their region. He points out that the dedications and public decrees for Roman emperors such as Hadrian and Septimius Severus not only pay accolades to the honouree, but also stake a powerful, if unstated, claim that the local honouring party, the issuer of the decree, is the one with the right to bestow this high status and legitimacy: "the honouring body's right to determine leadership and honour within a given political context," as Howe puts it. No matter how far removed such a claim might be from the historical reality of global power structures and hierarchies, such a claim could be of paramount importance to a local audience. These Roman-period decrees are the direct descendant of Hellenistic-era honorific decrees for Hellenistic rulers, and the relationship between the local Hellenistic city and the imperial ruler in whose orbit it was situated was likewise both top-down and bottom-up: the *polis* acquired status for itself by claiming the power and authority to grant it to others.

What, then, does "localism" mean in a "Hellenistic" setting? As several authors in this collection have pointed out, a consideration of localism in the centuries after Alexander inevitably draws our attention to the conventional characterization of the Hellenistic Age. Johann Droysen's nineteenth-century *Geschichte des Hellenismus* long dominated scholarly perceptions of the centuries after Alexander: a time defined by Hellenization, the rapid and dominant expansion of Greek culture, and its inevitable subjection and absorption of local and regional ethnicities throughout Asia and Egypt, nations unable to withstand the morally and intellectually superior civilization of the Greeks. The Hellenistic Age thus paved the way for the colonial expansion and "natural" dominance of Western civilization, heir to the legacy of the Greeks, and the self-acclaimed role of Western nations as the bringers of justice, truth, morals, prosperity, and clean drains.

This thumbnail description obviously encapsulates the most unsophisticated and the most Orientalist (in Saïd's terms) delineation of Droysen's concept of the Hellenistic; so simplistic, in fact, that it is perhaps unfair to ascribe it to Droysen himself without any further nuance. Nevertheless, it may serve as a point of departure for the observation that, fortunately, scholarship has moved some way in the past several decades, and the essays in this volume are in no way guilty of a hoary perspective that would equate global Hellenism with natural superiority and inevitable ethnic dominance. Yet, some of the qualities traditionally associated with the Hellenistic period, with "Hellenisticity" (a neologism which, despite its awkwardness, I prefer to the broader and less specific "Hellenism"), do present topics for reflection in the context of localism. For example, Alex McAuley remarks on the fact that one of the enduring markers of the Hellenistic Age was its cosmopolitanism; hence, localism has not typically been an item for consideration in our contemplation of this period. That the notion of cosmopolitanism is not simply a figment of the modern scholarly imagination may be suggested by Diogenes the Cynic's claim to be a *kosmopolitēs*, a citizen of the world, though Diogenes' own peculiar particularities should perhaps caution us against seeing him as a prophet of some kind of widespread subscription to a putative global world identity.

McAuley's chapter, like others in this volume, engages with what Peter Funke calls "the opportunities and possibilities of local self-assertion in a politically expanding world." Precisely because of the expansion of political and (even more) ideational horizons, individuals and communities may have clung ever closer to local meaning and local identity. I have previously posited the view that, in the shadow of omnipresent connectivity and exchange in the Hellenistic period, many communities and individuals may have experienced a crisis of identity and even a sense of "being adrift." The flip side of the Hellenistic *kosmopolitēs* – the citizen of the world – is the citizen whose sense of local identity is now under existential threat.

There may well have been a link between an expansion of perspectives in the Hellenistic period and an enhancement of local awareness for many, and this is certainly a fruitful avenue to pursue in terms of understanding how Hellenistic localism(s) might differ from earlier localism(s). And yet, I wonder now whether this binary representation of the Hellenistic experience may be more of a neat and tidy – and modern – scholarly construct than it is an accurate estimation of an ancient frame of mind. We certainly do have evidence of an intense interest in at least one dimension of local affairs – local histories – in the Hellenistic period, but the work of Herodotus, like that of his lost contemporary, the ethnographer and mythographer Hellanikos of Lesbos, demonstrates the long attachment to such history, well predating the Hellenistic period. The intervening centuries between the Classical Age writers and those of the Hellenistic Age simply added that much more material to the local records.

Moreover, are we perhaps injecting our own sense of "disappointment" into the Hellenistic world? More recent scholarship, and certainly the essays in this collection, eschew outmoded notions around the "decadence" of the period, the supposed degradation of traditional civic values and mores, and above all the decline of the *polis*, that institution so representative of Classical Greece. Nevertheless, do we as scholars still struggle, perhaps subconsciously, with a sense that somehow the post-Alexander centuries really do represent some kind of existential loss? Are we the ones who are compensating for this sense of loss by seeking signs of local vitality? It is certainly true that signs of local dynamism are indeed to be found everywhere in the Hellenistic era, as these essays have so amply demonstrated. Furthermore, the rapid and shattering political change wrought by Macedonian hegemony and its aftermath no doubt led to a more layered approach to local identity. But I wonder if a putative compulsion to discover and exploit the various dimensions of one's localism in the Hellenistic era, precisely as a response to a world that had become too large too quickly, is true to the actual experience of the ancients or if it is to some extent an imposition of the modern imagination. I do not question the degree of interest in local concerns; I only query the degree of change this represents.

Still, I do believe that localism is one among many lenses through which we may challenge or affirm conventional, and even less conventional, notions of Hellenisticity. And this clearly was a period of distinctly new opportunities and challenges, simply because the days of dominance of a single city or cities were past and there were new players on the stage, players with whom local communities negotiated new kinds of relationships. As we have seen, these interactions flowed in both directions, affecting both (or multiple) parties and contributing to the glocal systems of the Hellenistic world. But here it is necessary to emphasize the great variegation in what we mean by "localism" in the Hellenistic Age, a period where it would be more appropriate to speak of "localisms" (of course, this is arguably true in any period). The new players were not distributed evenly throughout the Greek world, nor, in spite of the fact that we speak of a Greek *oikoumenē* in both the Hellenistic and the Roman period, was there ever such a thing as a homogeneous "Hellenistic civilization."

Among the new players of course were the monarchs, chiefly kings, though queens also interacted with local communities. Although the Antigonid dynasty of Macedon, after the collapse of the Argeads and Kassander's dynasty, was a major player in Balkan affairs, it is from Asia Minor that we have the most evidence for the interplay between city and king: first Lysimachos, then the Seleukids and the Ptolemies, and ultimately the Attalids of Pergamon. In Balkan Greece, besides the Antigonid rulers, the big players were now the vastly expanded federal *koina*, especially the Achaians and the Aitolians. By their very nature, the federal leagues were intimately connected with the local, since they were constituted as a collection of local communities. And finally, there was Rome, from 200 BCE on more and more of a looming presence. Accustomed by now to building relationships with global powers, Greek *poleis* pivoted to establishing connections with Rome, though it was often a bumpy ride. A fulsome local history written by Memnon of Herakleia Pontike described how his *polis* initiated diplomatic relations with the Romans, even daring (if we believe Memnon on this point) to suggest that Rome reconcile with Antiochos III (*BNJ* 434 F 1 18.6–10). The passage in Memnon is a classic example of how the intrinsic worth and legitimacy of the local is enhanced, at least for a local audience, through its interaction with the global.

As explorations of localism in the Hellenistic world, the essays included here have much to say about the new political world orders and their impact on local experience and glocal engagement. Ruben Post explores Alexander the Great's efforts to ameliorate ecological functioning of the Kopaic Basin, as well as the intransigence of the locals that ultimately stymied those efforts; Joseph Scholten looks at the tension between local custom and global ambition in the Aitolian League; Alex McAuley examines the determination on the part of some communities to establish local connections that cut across the potentially restrictive barriers of federalism; Peter Funke notes the consolidation of micro-regions within the context of a much larger federation; and Chandra Giroux demonstrates how Sulla's battle with the forces of Mithridates at Chaironeia in 86 BCE was memorialized by the Chaironeians themselves as a glorious moment when their small community was (in part) responsible for the great Roman victory.

If there is one phenomenon that we may legitimately think of as magnified in the Hellenistic period, it is that of movement – to employ Hans Beck's words, a "quantum leap in connectivity and contact" – though here too we must be cautious about over-ascribing rigid categories of distinctiveness to different historical eras. Mythistory of course was already full of movement, especially when it came to foundation stories, such as the multiple accounts of Halikarnassian *ktiseis* included in the Salmakis inscription (which also manages to give a nod to autochthony, in the accommodating manner of myth). But there was undeniably an increase in the movement of individuals and groups across the Mediterranean and the Near East in the Hellenistic Age, movement that contributed to the expansion of horizons referenced earlier. Movement allows the larger world to impinge on the local, as crossroads communities such as Megara and Chaironeia well knew; it also allows the local to experience the global, both at home and abroad.

War, of course, gives rise to movement, whether in the case of local border skirmishes or in the clash of global powers engaged in hegemonic war. Wars define the orthodox temporal limits of the Hellenistic Age, even if modern scholarship rejects these narrow boundaries. War and wars were a persistent phenomenon in the Hellenistic period, from the constant struggle of Ptolemies and Seleukids over Syria to the micro-conflicts of Hellenistic *poleis* to the Roman wars, initially of chastisement and ultimately of conquest, with the Hellenistic kingdoms. Diplomacy too involved travel throughout the ancient world, whether it was a small group of judges dispatched from one *polis* to a neighbouring one with a mandate to resolve local disputes, an official delegation of *theōroi* sent to represent their community at one of the panhellenic festivals, an emissary bearing a letter informing a king that he had been awarded an honorary decree by a remote community, or a legation of ambassadors bent on persuading the Roman senate that a Roman military presence was urgently needed to settle local or regional conflict in the east.

Enduring warfare is in itself of no small importance in the consideration of Hellenistic localism, but so is the movement and dislocation brought on by strife, particularly for mercenaries and exiles. Chelsea Gardner's essay highlights the mercenary market at Tainaron, a locale isolated by land from the rest of the Peloponnese but accessible by sea. Rather than being solely dominated either by Sparta or by Athens, the mercenary community itself probably engaged in some level of local self-organizing, though it never seems to have reached the same level of actual state-building as did (for example) the "pirate" settlements of Cilicia in the first century BCE. As for the mercenaries who fought regularly in the armies of the Hellenistic kings, they adapted to a new local or created one for themselves, whether in Egypt or Asia.

With the opening up of new markets, new trade opportunities arose, with concomitant movement and development of networks. Trade implies the distribution of local goods – whether on a large scale or a small – to other locales. Some of those goods developed a cachet that had a global appeal, such as the clay figurines from Boiotian Tanagra, so popular that secondary workshops began to produce copies elsewhere in the Mediterranean. Boiotia also manufactured the best *auloi*, made from the reeds of Lake Kopais, though here, as Ruben Post informs us, it was the travel not of the goods themselves, but rather of their "consumers" – the famous Theban *aulētai* – that made the fame of the local instrument. And with trade went tourism, an increasingly popular pastime in the Hellenistic and Roman worlds, as evidenced by the popularity of Pausanias' guidebook. We still feel the pull of "being there," of actually travelling to a place where things have happened. In spite of the malleability of myth mentioned above, there were and are iconic locales that had singular claims unrivalled by any other place. Chandra Giroux talks about the dark tourism that brought visitors to the plain at Chaironeia where so many died, but it would have been no darker – and potentially just as reverential – as that which impels so many millions of people to visit Ground Zero in New York City.

The iconic locale thus pulls together the global audience. Perhaps the best example of this in the Hellenistic world were the panhellenic festivals, particularly at Olympia and Delphi. There, tourism, diplomacy, religion, and competitive culture combined to inspire journeys there and back again, delivering international success to feed local pride. The athletic, musical, and poetic performances associated with the festivals celebrated local achievement in a global arena, achievement that was also celebrated in the material record of commemoration through monument and inscription. The intensity of local pride in international competition is perhaps an eternal human characteristic, as we see in the modern Olympics (or for that matter, in a soccer hooligan brawl). Local dominance in a global venue could be celebrated through a victor's statue and a written record of achievements, and whether the monument was situated at the international sanctuary or in the home *polis* (or both), it memorialized that moment when local talent proved itself to be unrivalled in the global sphere. And the panhellenic sanctuaries provided an opportunity for advertising that pre-eminence not only in the sanctioned activities of the festivals but also in conflict and war. Pausanias' descriptions of the monuments of Delphi and Olympia are rich and significant repositories of subtle and not-so-subtle symbolic conflict and victory posturing, such as the Arkadian and Argive monuments celebrating victories over Sparta contraposed to Spartan monuments of their own victory over Athens, an assemblage that greeted the visitor immediately upon entering the precinct of Apollo (10.9.5–10.10.5). These monuments at Delphi represent the inverse of the intrusion of the international into the local: the Macedonian and Theban monuments at Chaironeia, discussed here by Chandra Giroux.

Most of the essays in this volume concentrate on Balkan Greece, in particular the Peloponnese and Boiotia. This geographic focus may be only partially coincidental. These regions were historically home to what might be considered by modern historians to be the archetypal *polis*, the independent local community par excellence. Athens does not play a large part here, but then Athens was hardly typical; neither was Sparta, though the peculiarity of Spartan life and customs is sufficiently marked that several of the authors here have chosen to delve into it. It is interesting to note that Sparta's leaders may have been trying to re-emphasize the *polis'* native culture precisely at a time when it was going through a prolonged period of upheaval: tyrannies, hostilities with its Peloponnesian neighbours and Antigonid Macedon, and coups or other changes of state authority that resulted in multiple layers of exiles, all demanding return to the homeland. Sebastian Scharff's contribution reflects on Spartan athletic prowess, both at home and abroad, suggesting that Sparta's pride in its athletes' victories strictly subordinated the athlete to the *polis* (as did other aspects of Spartan citizen life), and that agonistic competition functioned as a surrogate for *polis*-level political or even military competition (targeting Sparta's age-old enemies and neighbours Messene and Argos).

The *poleis* of old (Balkan) Greece, while theoretically constituted as autonomous, were no strangers to dominance by other powers in the Archaic and Classical periods. Sparta, Athens, and Thebes all at times exercised their authority regionally and even beyond. But perhaps the attraction of examining localism among the communities of old Greece in the Hellenistic era lies in the fact that, prior to the Macedonian hegemony, these regions had little to no experience of dominance by "the other," by a political and military power fundamentally different from themselves. Nor did they have much experience of membership in a federal organization not dominated by a single *polis*. In Asia Minor, on the other hand, the *poleis* had long been accustomed to the overarching supremacy of a non-Greek (or even Macedonian) superpower and a global political framework that exalted a single man, not a polity of citizens. Although the *poleis* of Asia Minor suffered materially in the decades of Macedonian conquest and subsequent rivalries between Hellenistic monarchs, they could look to their long-standing experience to guide them in how to relate to the global authority and engage that authority in their local interests.

There is therefore an intrinsic danger in emphasizing old Greece too much in our search for Hellenistic localism, or at least in drawing broad general conclusions from such a survey. Localism – like Hellenisticity – does not look the same everywhere, a truth that is inherent in the very concept. We are accustomed to the liberal employment of the term *oikoumenē*, whether in application to the Hellenistic or the Roman period. As I remarked above, however, even with respect to global phenomena, the term suggests too much homogeneity. It also may suggest that, even with a recognition of local and regional variation, there was a similarity in the entwining of the global, regional, and local across what is known as the Hellenistic world or the Roman empire. But localism – and glocal entanglement – would have looked and felt as different in Crimean Pantikapaion as it did in North African Kyrene, in Italian Taras, in Baktrian Demetrias, or in Phoenician Ptolemaïs.

So, for example, Mark Thatcher's essay speaks to the different challenges and frameworks experienced by a *polis* such as Syracuse in the west: "Hellenism means something different in Syracuse than it does elsewhere, showing how local concerns can redefine a global paradigm." Aside from the indigenous populations of Sicily and Italy with whom the Greek foundations of Magna Graecia would have interacted over the centuries, there was also the mega-power of Carthage to be considered, and Thatcher detects a particularly enhanced sense of "Greekness" in Syracuse's self-image. Syracuse, moreover, although it featured regular *polis*-type institutions for much of its history, was ruled by tyrants and *basileis* through the fourth and third centuries BCE. From the time of Agathokles on, the affectation of the local kings of Syracuse was that they enjoyed the same degree of international stature as the great monarchs of the Hellenistic east. And finally, Syracuse and its Sicilian and southern Italian neighbours were also the first of the Greek *poleis* to succumb to the dominance of the expanding regional hegemon, Rome.

As for Asia Minor, this was a place where the cities had a long experience of life lived under a highly exalted and non-Greek authority (even if at times the Persians had employed local Greek elites). Herodotus, as we have seen, is a rich repository of information that demonstrates the depth and tenacity of local memory among the Greek *poleis* in these regions. Should we expect to see any change in this pattern with the substitution of Macedonian for Persian rule? Perhaps not, though the level of interference in *polis*-life the communities of Asia Minor suffered under the Diadochoi and the warring kings of the third century BCE no doubt impacted the nature of local relationships with the dominant powers, no matter how transient they might have been. Antigonos I's enforced synoikism of Teos and Lebedos (Welles *RC* 3) in the late fourth century BCE provides an example; it is possible that the blending of the communities of Latmos (Herakleia Latmia) and Pidasa (*SEG* 47.1563), discussed here by Sara Saba, was also the work of Antigonos' heavy helping hand. As Saba points out, the new blended community also resulted in blended families, with (apparently and unusually) a new local self-definition and loyalty enforced via marriage regulations that required Latmians to marry Pidasans and vice versa. Nevertheless, traditional local identities remained strong: Teos and Lebedos did not remain synoikized, and the evidence suggests that neither did the sympolity between Latmos and Pidasa last.

The experience of the cities of Asia Minor, especially during the third century BCE, with Seleukid, Ptolemaic, Attalid, and even Antigonid rulers vying for dominance over these regions and fighting their battles through the medium of local communities and territories, whether through influence or force, brings up the question of localism and its link to conflict. It would be unfair to consider the Asia Minor *poleis* as nothing but passive local victims caught up in a global game of thrones: multiple wars were fought on the local or micro-regional scale throughout the Hellenistic period between *poleis* all across the Greek world. We may tend to think of localism as a unifying force, a recognition of shared experience and memory, tastes and styles, attitudes and predilections that binds a community together. But there are aspects of the local that lend themselves to conflict, both within the state, in the form of stasis, and beyond its borders. This is particularly the case if we allow that "the local" may embrace border zones, where boundaries are fuzzy, and things of value may lie in disputed territory. Contested borderlands are one of the most prominent issues in interstate conflict, in part because contiguity provides regular opportunities for friction, but even more so because land can have metaphorical significance, and intense emotional and historical attachments may be felt by both parties. The dispute between Sparta and Messene over the territory containing the sanctuary of Artemis Limnatis lasted for centuries through the Hellenistic and Roman period (Tac. *Ann.* 4.43). Previous conflict, moreover, is a significant predictor for subsequent conflict, and world history, not just ancient history, abounds with such enduring rivalries. Even conflicts with "mostly regional and global meaning," as Elena Franchi describes the campaigns of Kleomenes III of Sparta against Argos in the 220s BCE, could be given (g)local meaning through Sparta's local discourse environment: the historical enmity between Sparta and Argos, the deep-rooted Spartan *agōgē*, and the attachment to the hero Herakles.

As I stated at the beginning of this afterword, these reflections make no claim to add new revelations to the subject of Hellenistic localism; I believe it is the individual essays collected here that have made such contributions. I have tried to highlight some of the most salient aspects of localism in this era, such as relationality and networks, multi-dimensionality, mythical and metaphorical extension of local reality, all bound up with the workings of human experience and imagination. I would like to close with some (non-exhaustive) suggestions for future consideration that I hope might prove useful in pushing the field further. A few of these suggestions have been intimated in my previous remarks, such as the link between local attachment and conflict: I would suggest that there may be some value in pursuing questions of "dark" localism, the downside of what is often seen as a phenomenon emblematic of affinity and cohesion.

The Hellenistic Age is conventionally associated with expansion of horizons, whether or not all individuals or communities in this period experienced a concomitant shift in perspective. Even if we seek to modify – or reject altogether – our customary understanding of change in the world after Alexander, the expansion of our own scholarly horizons can only help us to fine-tune our sense of Hellenistic localism(s). More studies on the experience of the local in Greek *poleis* situated in the Hellenistic west, the Aegean, Asia Minor, or the Black Sea would help to flesh out what might turn out to be regional variations in the shape and flavour of localism. Expanding the geographical scope would also bring in the question of how localism played out in the new Hellenistic foundations. What did "the local" mean in a city like Alexandria, where Gorgo and Praxinoa loudly proclaim their right to speak the dialect of their Doric (Syracusan, Corinthian, and Peloponnesian, in that order) ancestors? Theokritos' portrait of the two women may also speak to the question of localism abroad: what do one's local experiences and affinities mean when one is out of place, whether temporarily or permanently? Gorgo and Praxinoa live in Alexandria (Praxinoa perhaps lives in a suburb), but they have "come from away." As for expanding our temporal limits, we have already seen that Hellenistic history does not end with the establishment of the Roman Empire, and that there is much scope for the exploration of continuity and change in local communities and organizations as Roman rule gradually extended itself across the Hellenistic world.

The work of Hans Beck and others in this volume has already demonstrated that local experience is not monolithic, any more than globalization is. Different members of the same community, even a very small community, have widely differing life experiences. Many of the papers in this volume that have discussed the heterogeneity of experience within the community have referenced occupational differences, the world of the farmer being quite distinct from the world of the perfumer in the agora. There has still been a tendency to privilege the world of the citizen, to the exclusion of exploring the localism of gender, or of status (especially free versus slave), or of ethnic origins. Throughout this afterword, I myself have tended to equate "the local" or "the community" (in general terms) with the *polis*. But gender, status, and ethnicity are all markers of identity that arguably went through displacement and change in the Hellenistic period. As Hans Beck points out in the introduction, "we ought to recall that there is no way of knowing whether this pursuit of Greek meaning-making resonated with the entire, ethnically heterogeneous population of the city, or was confined to the local elites." There is thus still vast scope for inquiry into the multivarious localisms of different layers in the population, even among those who shared the same household. Intersectionality is also an important point for consideration: not everyone in the same community has identical experiences of the local; but at the same time, single individuals may experience more than one brand of localism.

The recognition of ethnic origins and ethnic diversity – whether it be a matter of Doric versus Ionic, Peloponnesian versus Boiotian, or Greek versus non-Greek – raises the question of the mingling of populations, a phenomenon also associated with Hellenisticity (this also speaks to the matter of new foundations). What can we learn about indigenous localism, including how it may have interacted with Greek claims to indigeneity or even autochthony? How did the global rule of Greco-Macedonian monarchs affect the local experience of non-Greek populations? And do contemporary post-colonialist models and theories assist us, or do they obscure our vision with constructs that are better suited to a different era and a distinct world system?

As we expand those scholarly horizons, we need to maintain a close eye on methodology and continue to be watchful for how we may be imposing our own views of what localism and the Hellenistic are (or ought to be) on the experience of the ancients. It is a simple truism that everything we think we know about the past is really the result of the application of modern imagination and reasoning to a particular set of data: this is what keeps the past so alive and so relevant to the present and the future, as the past refuses to remain static. While it is the contention of this volume and this afterword that concepts such as "localism" and "Hellenistic" had real meaning in antiquity, it is also true that they have been defined by modern scholarship as a way for us to shape and frame our own insights. Many of our observations, while helpful to our own understanding, would not necessarily have formed part of the ancient consciousness.

As I write this, in the late summer of 2021, much of the world is hovering on the edge of a fourth wave of the COVID-19 pandemic, as the virus goes through a surge of new variants. These past 18 months or so have taught us first-hand about the varying strata of human experience, at the global, regional, and local levels. Local experiences of a truly global pandemic have been widely and wildly different around the world, and within the confines of the same community and the same family, individual experiences have varied greatly. At the same time, COVID binds us all, through our own deeply localized perspectives on an overwhelming and, for many, catastrophic global phenomenon. There is perhaps no more vivid contemporary example of what it means to be a participant in the vast kaleidoscope of human experience.

# CONTRIBUTORS

**Sheila L. Ager** is Professor of Ancient History and Dean of Arts in the University of Waterloo in Waterloo, Ontario.

**Hans Beck** is Professor and Chair of Greek History at Münster University and Adjunct Professor in the Department of History and Classical Studies at McGill University in Montreal.

**Elena Franchi** is Professor of Greek History at Trento University and Lead Investigator of the "Federalism and Border Management in Greek Antiquity" project of the European Research Council.

**Peter Funke** is Senior Professor of Ancient History in the Cluster of Excellence "Religion and Politics" program at Münster University.

**Chelsea A.M. Gardner** is Associate Professor of Ancient History in the Department of History and Classics at Acadia University in Wolfville, Nova Scotia.

**Chandra Giroux** is a contract instructor in the Department of Classics and Religious Studies at the University of Ottawa and a senior policy adviser in the Government of Canada.

**Denver Graninger** is Associate Professor of History at the University of California, Riverside.

**Timothy Howe** is Professor of History at St. Olaf College in Northfield, Minnesota.

**Alex McAuley** is Lecturer in Classics and Ancient History in the School of Humanities at the University of Auckland.

**Ruben Post** is Lecturer of Ancient History in the School of Classics at the University of St. Andrews.

**James Roy** is Emeritus Professor of Ancient History at the University of Nottingham.

**Sara Saba** is a member of the Research Group "Cultural Heritage" at the Fraunhofer Institute for Building Physics, Holzkirchen/Munich.

**Sebastian Scharff** is Research Fellow in the "Federalism and Border Management in Greek Antiquity" project of the European Research Council at Trento University.

**Joseph B. Scholten** is Associate Director in the Office of International Affairs at the University of Maryland, College Park, where he is also Affiliate Associate Professor of Classics.

**Mark Thatcher** is Assistant Professor of the Practice of Classics at Boston College.

# INDEX

# PHOENIX SUPPLEMENTARY VOLUMES